before the

MARKETING

Praise for *Marketing*

"This is an excellent marketing text, achieving the difficult trick of combining good theoretical content with strong practical emphasis. If marketing course tutors want their students to move into the world of marketing without the usual real world shock, then this is the book for them."

Professor Merlin Stone, Business Research Leader with IBM Consulting and IBM Professor of Relationship Marketing at Bristol Business School

"A salient aspect of this new text is the reader-friendly treatment of the historical origins and development of marketing, objectively presented from both the academic and practitioner perspectives. This picture is given greater depth by the inclusion of a range of topical and historical examples in mini-cases, vignettes and the more extensive 'Marketing Insights'. The clearly set out chapter-by-chapter objectives and the questions accompanying the cases serve to build up the student's knowledge of marketing principles and ability practically to apply those principles of marketing to contemporary scenarios. The clarity and the comprehensiveness of the book's approach make it an accurate reflection of, and well rounded introduction to, the study of such a diverse and evolving discipline."

Chris Blackburn, Principal Lecturer and Department Head – Marketing, The Business School, Oxford Brookes University

"Marketing is a thorough and thought provoking text for students and practitioners alike, destined to become a standard benchmark textbook on the subject. The learning outcomes are action oriented, bringing practical application to the fore. The use of contemporary and thought provoking "marketing insights" (mini cases), helps to put concepts into context, and should make students and practitioners, think more deeply about their application. The reader is taken quickly from introductory level of analysis to strategic thinking around concepts. Students will find the text stimulating, interesting and insightful, providing a clear and uncluttered account of contemporary issues in marketing."

Dr John W Lang, Judge Institute of Management, University of Cambridge

MARKETING

essential principles,

new realities

JONATHAN GROUCUTT   PETER LEADLEY   PATRICK FORSYTH

KOGAN PAGE

London and Sterling, VA

First published in Great Britain and the United States in 2004 by Kogan Page Limited

120 Pentonville Road	22883 Quicksilver Drive
London N1 9JN	Sterling VA 20166–2012
UK	USA
www.kogan-page.co.uk	

ISBN 0 7494 4114 3

British Library Cataloguing-in-Publication Data

A CIP record for this book is available from the British Library.

Library of Congress Cataloging-in-Publication Data

Groucutt, Jon.
  Marketing : essential principles, new realities / Jonathan Groucutt,
Peter Leadley, and Patrick Forsyth. – 1st ed.
      p. cm.
Includes bibliographical references and index.
  ISBN 0-7494-4114-3
  1. Marketing. I. Leadley, Peter, 1943- II. Forsyth, Patrick. III.
Title.
HF5415.G766 2004
658.8–dc22

                              2003024860

Typeset by Saxon Graphics Ltd, Derby
Printed and bound in Great Britain by Bell & Bain, Glasgow

This book is dedicated to:

Michael B Johnson (1944–2002)
Mentor and a very much-missed friend
Mike, thank you for everything

Jonathan

To Sheila, my wife, and colleagues at the University of Lincoln

Peter

Contents

List of figures

List of tables

The authors

Jonathan Groucutt is a Senior Lecturer at the Business School, Oxford Brookes University, England. Jonathan's personal research areas include complexity theory and its relationship to marketing, the history of marketing thought, and the strategic development of the global cruise-line industry. As well as co-authoring several books he has written over 40 business articles.

As well as academic experience, Jonathan has over 10 years' consultancy experience in marketing and management.

He holds Fellowships to the Royal Society of Arts, the Academy of Marketing Sciences and the Royal Geographical Society. He is also a Member of the Academy of Marketing, the Institute of Direct Marketing, the American Marketing Association, European Marketing Academy and the Strategic Planning Society.

Peter Leadley completed an indentured apprenticeship in general engineering and progressed in industry to become a product manager. A change in career led him into the world of academia, rising to the position of Senior Lecturer in Marketing at the University of Humberside. He took early retirement in 1997; however he has continued to teach at various universities as a visiting lecturer.

Peter has been an active member of the Chartered Institute of Marketing (CIM) since 1972. In 1996 he was presented with the President's Award from the Institute for services to the CIM and marketing in general. Peter was granted Chartered Marketer status in 1998. He is currently a visiting lecturer in marketing at Bishop Burton College, the University of Lincoln and the University of Hull. In his free time he pursues his hobby of railway modelling.

Patrick Forsyth runs Touchstone Training and Consultancy, which specializes in training in various personal skills necessary to marketing, communications and management. He has worked in consultancy for more than 20 years in the UK, continental Europe, Singapore and Malaysia. He conducts training in all its forms: public seminars, in-company programmes and one-to-one tutorials. He has written extensively on marketing matters and has many successful books in print. These range from titles focusing on marketing overall, *Marketing Stripped Bare* (a guide for non-marketing management), and particular skills, *Powerful Reports and Proposals*, to more general topics, *Successful Time Management*, and a book on careers: *Getting a Top Job in Marketing*. (All these titles are published by Kogan Page.)

Acknowledgments

No textbook can be written without the support of both individuals and organizations alike. We wish to acknowledge the copyright works of the following organizations that are cited in the text: American Marketing Association, Barrington Marketing Services, British Broadcasting Corporation, CACI Limited, Chartered Institute of Marketing, English, Welsh and Scottish Railways, the Institute of Direct Marketing, *Direct Response* magazine, Johnson and Johnson Inc.

We have attempted to credit and acknowledge all reference sources. However, if we have inadvertently missed any individual or organization we apologize. We will fulfil any obligations in the following edition of this text.

A special thank you to the following for their advice, unstinting support and encouragement: Shereen Baig (a very special thank you), Ian Bathgate, Chris Berry, Michael Brown, Beth Brown, Professor George Corfield, Susan Daly, Christine Ewers, Dr Paul Griseri, Colin Horner, Michael B Johnson, Peter Boynton, Dr John Lang, Dr Beverley Lee, Gareth Owen, Peter A Taylor, Adrian Sims and Simon Williams.

Finally but never least, to our students who over numerous years have questioned theories, challenged ideas and provided alternative scenarios. They have made marketing probably the most pleasurable subject to teach. Thank you.

Jonathan Groucutt
Peter Leadley
Patrick Forsyth

London 2003

Introduction

Marketing is so basic that it cannot be considered a separate skill or work within the business. Marketing requires separate work, and a distinct group of activities. But it is a central dimension of the entire business. It is the whole business seen from the point of view of its final result, that is from the customer's point of view. Concern and responsibility for marketing must permeate all areas of the enterprise.

(Drucker, 1994)

Management thinker Peter Drucker wrote these words originally in 1954. Already by then companies and organizations, of all dimensions, were developing a marketing approach to business. Much has evolved since then. We are now in the 21st century, and it will most likely be a period of great change – though not always for the betterment of society.

So why should we study marketing?

Probably all lecturers and tutors would argue, to a greater or lesser extent, that their particular subject is 'special'. We believe that marketing, as an academic subject, has specific added values. It is a stimulating, complex and challenging subject. Furthermore, it is 'alive':

it is visible to every one of you, every waking moment of your lives.

There are clear links to strategy, economics, psychology, management, history, sociology, political science, mathematics, communications, law, ecology, geography, anthropology and the creative arts. As Wilkie and More (1999) state, 'Marketing can be studied from several intriguing perspectives. It is these qualities that make marketing such a rewarding subject to study.'

What is more, marketing is evolutionary and dynamic. Additionally, lecturers and tutors can learn from their students. Who better to tell you what brands are in or out of favour (and why?), or what brands are recognized in China or Africa than students from China and Africa? Marketing as a subject can be a mutual learning experience – that has significant value in itself.

The objectives of this book

We have set out to research and write a textbook aimed primarily, though not exclusively, at the undergraduate market. Our aims have been to:

■ Write a book that is student-oriented in its use of language. Hopefully it is relaxed and free flowing as a one-to-one conversation. At the same time, it provides to you material of a high academic standard.

■ Provide numerous international examples, rather than focusing purely on American and/or British examples.

■ Draw together a range of thinking on the subject of marketing and its role in contemporary society.

■ Consider the link between marketing and strategy (including strategic tools).

■ Develop a synthesis between the theory and the application of marketing.

Structure of the book

There are 15 chapters which span a diverse range of material from early developments in marketing thought and activity to the impact of e-marketing. Each chapter is subdivided into the following sections:

■ Introduction.

■ Learning objectives. These should be the outcomes of reading the chapter.

■ Main issues of the chapter.

■ Chapter summary. This provides a brief summary of the key points.

■ Exercises and questions for review and critical thinking. These are designed to provide you with the opportunity to expand your knowledge by research and reflection of the key issues.

References to works cited and notes are given at the end of the book. They also provide useful sources of further reading.

Reflective and questioning

Throughout the text we have raised issues for you to consider and research further. This book does not purport to be the final word on the subject of marketing. It does not have all the answers or contain all the views on the subject. However, it is written to provide you with the basis for thought and the critical evaluation of marketing.

Target audience

This book is primarily aimed at undergraduates and general diploma-level students. In addition, the authors believe that it will benefit anyone studying marketing for the first time. This includes those new to management and/or embarking on a general management/business/marketing postgraduate qualification.

Tutor material

Tutors who adopt this text can request additional teaching material. The tutor CD contains MS PowerPoint™ slides for all 15 chapters. The slides outline:

■ Chapter introduction.

■ Chapter learning outcomes.

■ The key issues addressed by the chapter.

■ Summary.

■ A key reflective question.

Student and lecturer feedback

Our objective is to update this book on a regular basis, so that it forms the basis for analysing and understanding contemporary marketing issues. Therefore we welcome constructive feedback, no matter how small, from students and lecturers alike. Please address your comments to:

Jonathan Groucutt
c/o Kogan Page Publishing Limited
120 Pentonville Road
London N1 9JN
United Kingdom

1

What is marketing?

Introduction

> Marketing today is not a function; it is a way of doing business. Marketing is not a new advertising campaign or this month's promotion. Marketing has to be all-pervasive, part of everyone's job description, from the receptionist to the board of directors. Its job is not to fool the customer nor to falsify the company's image. It is to integrate the customer into the design of the product and to design a systematic process for interaction that will create substance in the relationship.
>
> (McKenna, 1991)

Although written in the early 1990s, McKenna's quotation above still illustrates the importance of marketing to both profit-oriented companies and not-for-profit organizations. To a greater or lesser extent everyone is involved within the 'marketing' process. The objective of this chapter is to define marketing within a contemporary environment and to illustrate some of the key concepts that have been the backbone of marketing thought during the 20th century.

To absorb the material in this and other chapters you will need to start thinking outside the 'box'. Try not to compartmen-talize material. This is important in two aspects. First, many of the key concepts stated in this chapter pervade this textbook, and thus you should not consider them in isolation. What is important is to think of the linkage between the chapters, and how individual elements, such as price and promotion, are used to sell a product or service. Second, consider your wider business studies. Think of how the various modules within a business course fit together. Think of how marketing interrelates with these other modules. You will start to get a flavour of this as you read through this chapter.

Learning objectives

On the completion of this chapter you should be able to:

▌ outline how marketing impacts upon everyone's lives, no matter where they live, what they do, their age or income;

▌ discuss the basic principles and concepts of marketing within a contemporary business environment;

- debate the different perspectives surrounding the development of the marketing mix framework;
- discuss the development of relationship marketing.

How to define marketing

Marketing touches every aspect of our waking lives, from our very birth to our death. What is important to remember is that marketing is dynamic and not static. Organizations, whether for profit or not-for-profit, must adapt their marketing to changing internal and external environmental factors (see Chapter 2). Organizations that remain 'static' in their marketing thinking are prone to failure, most especially within hypercompetitive environments (consider, for example, global markets and e-business).

From whatever angle we look, the action of marketing takes place. It is all around us, whether we see it or comprehend it. Just consider all the following areas, where 'marketing' in one form, or another, occurs:

- **Business:** raw materials and components for manufacturers, plant and equipment, capital projects such as buildings, hydroelectric generating facilities and transportation/logistical facilities. Companies market their products and/or service expertise to other companies, and indeed governments.

- **The arts:** exhibitions of paintings and sculptures, rock and classical music concerts, pop and rock groups, discos, various music venues, symphony orchestras, artists, film and television production companies, movies, television series and radio programmes. All these have to be promoted or marketed, often in both a business-to-business and a business-to-consumer environment. For example, a production company makes a drama series, then markets it to television companies (the business-to-business element), which then market it to their viewers, who then may buy it on DVD (the business-to-consumer element).

- **Sporting events:** the Olympic Games, the World Cup, the World Series baseball championships, international cricket tournaments and athletic championships. Consider the amount of sponsorship that was linked to the Sydney 2000 Olympics – that's marketing impact on a global and dynamic scale.

- **Fashion designers:** fashion, like marketing, is continually evolving, continually in a state of flux. Consider the marketing of the latest fashions and reflect on how long this fashion lasts. Is it purely for one season (for example, summer) or for several years? Consider also the differences between marketing fashions for men and women.

- **Retailers:** clothes, CDs, DVDs, furniture, books, magazines, electrical goods, perfumes/cosmetics, food and drinks. The retailer is marketing the products on behalf of intermediaries and/or the manufacturer. Equally, the retailer is marketing the store, and the service provided, to the customer.

- **Publishers:** newspapers, magazines, books and music. This covers everything from the latest 'airport' fiction to this marketing textbook. Consider how newspapers compete for readership, how they are different in their focus – the type of audience they target, the price they charge and the promotional techniques they adopt to persuade you to buy. (Consider, for example, the marketing campaigns that helped J K Rowling's *Harry Potter* books become a global phenomena.)

- **People:** whether they are movie stars in Hollywood, London or Bombay, television celebrities, politicians, or someone who has won a fortune on a national lottery – all are marketed or promoted in one form or another. So when the home of a famous movie star appears in a glossy magazine, that person is being marketed to us as readers of that magazine. We may not consider it as 'marketing', we may be purely interested in knowing more about our favourite movie star – but nevertheless it is marketing.

▌ **Internet providers:** Web sites, e-mail addresses and support merchandise.

▌ **Political parties:** especially near the time of local and national elections. They are marketing to us their respective policies, and attempting to influence us to vote for them, rather than the other parties.

▌ **Non-profit organizations:** for example charities seeking additional or ongoing donations for particular events/causes. For instance, think of the work of the Red Cross, the Red Crescent and UNICEF. They are funded by ordinary people, and they must communicate messages of both need and hope to those who can best support their good works.

▌ **Education centres:** higher education, for example, is a highly competitive environment. Colleges and universities need to fill their undergraduate and postgraduate courses. They compete on the range of courses available, location, facilities, structure of courses, quality of teaching and modes of delivery (increasingly via the Internet). Competition is no longer confined to national boundaries, it is increasingly transnational and global. You may want to reflect upon why you chose the particular degree course you are now undertaking. How did your college market it to you? What influenced your choice of degree course?

▌ **Tourist attractions/locations:** whether it is the Tower of London, the Empire State Building in New York, the Taj Mahal in New Delhi or the Sydney Opera House in Australia. They are all marketed to tourists and visitors in one form or another.

▌ **Travel companies:** flights and holidays to global destinations designed to generally suit every price range and holiday requirement. These range from beach holidays to luxury cruises.

▌ **The government:** promoting better health care, whether that is around the home in terms of hygiene, informing children of the dangers of smoking or taking precautions against sexually transmitted diseases such as AIDS. Prior to legislation, both the American and British governments ran marketing campaigns on the importance of wearing a car seatbelt. Other campaigns may include alerting drivers to the dangers of drinking alcohol and subsequently driving.

▌ **Medicine:** the marketing of prescription only and over the counter (OTC) medicines to doctors, hospitals, pharmacies and potential consumers.

▌ **Banks and financial companies:** different forms of savings and loan schemes, mortgages, pension plans and varying types of insurance. They will market to both consumers (like university students) and other businesses (new as well as established organizations).

The list is virtually endless.

Marketing, as we shall see, is above all dependent upon people – whether that is the person who designs and creates the product, those involved in the manufacture of the product, the marketer, the sales person, the wholesaler, the distributor, the retailer or the customer. All influence the marketing of the product or service, and ultimately its success or failure.

In the 20th century marketing played an increasingly significant role in determining corporate strategy and policy, influencing product development, pricing, methods of distribution and promotional techniques. Most importantly, perhaps, it started to build a relationship with the customer. Its role in the 21st century is bound to be increasingly significant and diverse. The one thing that is clear is that marketing is evolutionary, in constant change. Marketing, as stated earlier, is a dynamic force.

In the 1950s the management thinker and visionary Peter Drucker (1994) wrote:

> There is only one valid definition of business purpose: to create a *customer* (his italics).

> Because of its purpose to create a customer, any business enterprise has two – and only these two – basic functions: marketing and innovation. They are the entrepreneurial functions.

> Marketing is the distinguishing, the unique function of the business.... Marketing is not only much broader than selling, it is not a specialized activity at all. It encompasses the entire business. It is the whole business seen from the point of view of its final result, that is from the customer's point of view. Concern and responsibility for marketing must therefore permeate all areas of the enterprise.

In 1999 Raoul Pinnell, Global Head of Brands and Communication at Shell International, wrote:

> Marketing is an extremely potent force for competition. We have just seen the crumbling of totalitarian states (the fall of Communism in Eastern Europe), the dismantling of inefficient nationalized industries, and marketing has played its part and the customer has gained. There have been benefits, it has been a force for good. It has been part of the process.
>
> (Wheeler, 1999)

Defining marketing

In Pinnell's view marketing is clearly an 'overwhelming' force. However, how do we define marketing? This is not as clear cut as we may think! Wind (1997) has defined marketing as follows:

> Marketing, as a management function, appears to be in decline. Marketing as a management philosophy and orientation, espoused and practiced throughout the corporation, is however seen increasingly as critical to the success of any organization.

Drucker, Pinnell and Wind's quotes not only place marketing at the centre of 'business', they make it all-encompassing. Assuming this perspective means that organizations that pay lip service to marketing are, in essence, risking their future existence.

Guptara (1990) identifies six activities that come under the umbrella title of marketing. They are:

1. Identifying the needs of existing and potential customers (an emphasis on satisfying customer requirements is central to any definition of marketing).

2. Determining the best product strategy.

3. Ensuring the effective distribution of products.

4. Informing customers of the existence of products and persuading them to buy those products.

5. Determining the prices at which products should be sold.

6. Ensuring that after sales service is of the right quality.

While Guptara (1990) uses the word 'product' throughout, we should consider this to cover service provision as well. Such a provision must also include charitable donations, for the work of not-for-profit organizations is generally under-represented when marketing is discussed. It is, however, clear that such organizations can be heavily reliant on marketing, especially as a means of communicating the purpose of good causes and generating revenues.

There are various definitions of marketing. The UK's Chartered Institute of Marketing defines it thus:

The presence of marketing is everywhere. Moreover we engage and interact with it every waking moment of our lives. This montage of images illustrates how marketing imagery and exchanges are very much part of our normal lives, wherever we live. Above: The historic Plaza de España in Seville, now a mixture of government offices and tourist centre. Below: The crowded Souk in Marrakech, a mixture of small workshops and shops, a true marketplace.

Above: Even a small petrol station bristles with marketing imagery. Below: A busy street in Paris illustrates the diversity of marketing images that the average Parisian faces on a daily basis.

Marketing is the management process responsible for identifying, anticipating and satisfying customer requirements profitably.

(CIM, 2003)[1]

The American Marketing Association states:

Marketing is the process of planning and executing the conception, pricing, promotion and distribution of ideas, goods and services to create exchanges that satisfy individual and organizational objectives.

(AMA, 1985)[2]

(This tends to focus on the 4Ps of marketing – product, price, promotion and placement (distribution) – rather than consider a wider range of issues. We will discuss the origins and development of the marketing mix later in this chapter.)

Chee and Harris (1993) believe that there are certain points worth stating regarding this definition:

1. It identifies the market variables of product, price, place (distribution) and promotion that are used to provide customer satisfaction.

2. It assumes that the customer segments to be satisfied through the organization's production and marketing activities have been selected and analyzed prior to production, so that the customer, client or public determines the marketing programme.

3. It recognizes that marketing concepts and techniques pertain to non-profit organizations, as well as to profit-orientated business.

What is key to these definitions is the customer, as stated by Drucker and others earlier. Thus we can consider marketing as the 'management of exchange relationships'. The organization (for profit and not-for-profit) will be judged by customers, suppliers, intermediaries and competitors according to their own personal experiences. Thus people are central to the future development, indeed evolution, of marketing as a subject and a practice.

Marketing's relationship to other functional units

It is important, at this early stage, to consider the relationship that marketing, as a subject, has to other areas of business and, indeed, to your curriculum as a whole. While the focus of this book is obviously marketing, it is very easy to forget the direct and indirect influences of other functional units, or areas of study.

Marketing, human resource management, finance and information management, for example, should not be confined to 'functional' boxes. They all interrelate within the real world, and thus it is important to consider how finance, for example, impacts upon marketing activities, and how human resources management practices (for example, training and reward systems) contribute to the success or failure of the marketing effort. Marketing may be classified as a function, concept or process. However, without the right people and the appropriate level of support resources it is merely a figment of the imagination. Thus it is imperative that as you read through this text you consider the impact of the other functional elements of a business. Do not consider any of them in pure isolation.

The 20th century and the development of marketing thought

While marketing as a function has existed for centuries, it was the dawn of the 20th century that saw a change in the perception of marketing. It was between 1906 and 1911 that the word 'marketing' was first used as a noun rather than as a verb (Petrof, 1997). Until then 'marketing' tended to be referred to as trade, distribution or commerce, and it was the work of Art W Shaw and Ralph Stan Butler that developed this new discipline (Petrof, 1997).

Sheth and Gross (1988) suggest that the period 1900–50 can be classed as the classical period of marketing thought. They identified four different schools of thought during this period (Jeremy, 1998):

▋ The **commodity school** (led by Melvin T Copeland at Harvard University in the early part of the century) emphasized production. (Refer to the development of the Ford Motor Company below.)

▋ The **functional school** (started by Art Shaw, also at Harvard University) focused on marketing functions from transportation to selling.

▋ The **institutional school** (associated with the University of Minnesota, again in the early part of the century) was concerned with marketing structures.

▋ The **regional school** studied spatial gaps between sellers and buyers.

These various schools of thought reflected the changing patterns of business and society during that period. From the 1950s to present two other schools of thought have developed – concept and societal.

The following section illustrates several of the key events that have shaped marketing thought and approaches. They are predomi-nately US-based events. However, for one reason or another, they have influenced, indeed shaped, marketing activities in many other countries – and they still do!

At this point it is perhaps worth adding a note of caution. Some students may think that there are clear demarcation lines between one philosophy and another: that, for instance, a production orientation occurred prior to the Second World War and was then superseded by a functional or selling orien-tation. This is not the case; there are always situations where orientations overlap. Indeed, there are companies operating today that have very much a production orientation, rather than being focused on tailoring their product to the needs of their market. They may be the only company (a monopoly) oper-ating within that market. Thus the customer has no choice but to buy that product.

It is clear that the development of mass production techniques had, and continues to have, a major impact upon the development of economies and thus societies. Perhaps the chief protagonist was the industrialist Henry Ford (1863–1947). On 13 June 1903 he founded the Ford Motor Company with a nominal capitalization of $100,000, with help primarily from James Couzens and Alexander Malcolmson, as well as others (Ford, 1922). His industrial philosophy was simple – reduce the price of the product, increase the volume of sales, improve production efficiency, increase output to sell at still lower prices and then repeat the cycle.

In 1908 he developed a mass production technique based upon a stationary assembly line, on which he had built the Model T, nick-named the 'Tin Lizzy'. Over the year he sold 10,000 cars at approximately $850 each (Ford, 1922). In 1913 he unveiled a 250 foot (76.2 metres) moving assembly line, or conveyor belt, at his Highland Plant in Michigan. The design of the production lines was highly analytical and sought the optimum organi-zation of work tasks among work stations, optimum production line speed and the careful synchronization of simultaneous working operations. (Many of the 'operational' procedures were based upon the work of Frederick Taylor and his scientific management approach. Henry Ford took this approach further, resulting in the term Fordism – a highly controlled and regimented system.)

Henry Ford's overall objective was to cut the labour required to assemble a car chassis from 14 hours to under two labour-hours. This was the first example of mass production using a moving assembly line. It later became the model and benchmark by which other companies increased production and revenues. The savings obtained in time and finance realized by mass production techniques enabled Ford to sell the vehicle at a price the public could afford. The Model T, available in black only, retailed for approximately $500 (Ford, 2001).

From its initial capitalization of $100,000 the Ford Motor Company grew into an industrial giant with a surplus balance of nearly $700 million by 1927. Between 1908 and 1927, when the last Model T rolled off the assembly line, over 15 million were built (Ford, 2001).

The success of Ford's operations led to the adoption of mass production principles by industry throughout North America. Soon these techniques were being deployed throughout mainstream Europe. These methods made a significant contribution to the expansion of manufacturing industry that was the focal point of much of the 20th century. The result has been a phenomenal increase in wealth and development within the industrialized world.

On Tuesday 29 October 1929 – later known as Black Tuesday – Wall Street, the financial heart of the United States, collapsed. Subsequently millions of dollars were wiped off the value of shares in literally a matter of hours. Once successful and wealthy business people faced both financial and personal ruin. The collapse of Wall Street forced the closure of many US banks involved in stock market

speculation, leading to a recall of US overseas investments. This loss of credit had serious repercussions on European economies – most especially Germany's, a country attempting to rebuild itself after the defeat of the First World War. This led to a recession followed by a severe depression in Germany.

The collapse of Wall Street resulted in a steep fall in the levels of international trade as countries attempted to protect their domestic economies. Perhaps for the first time there was a realization that economies were becoming increasingly linked. (Economic convergence was one of the factors that led to an increasing globalization of business activity in the 1980s and 1990s. It is also one of the main risk factors of globalization. A collapse in one or more major economies can lead to a global recession.) The resultant world economic crisis led to a period of low output, low investment and mass unemployment. For both the United States and Europe the recovery was slow and painful, most especially for the unemployed and poor. True recovery was not achieved in the United States, for example, until the mid-1930s following the introduction of President F D Roosevelt's New Deal programme. Various public works projects were developed, and special farm loans to rebuild the agricultural heartlands were introduced. As well as providing a much needed stimulus to a flagging economy, this also revitalized cultural life and community spirit, bringing political stability.

The Great Depression had changed people's perceptions and buying behaviours, not just in the United States but in Europe as well. Business people began to realize they had to sell their products and services within an environment where the customers now had increasing choice. In addition to choice, the customer had, in many cases, the opportunity to substitute one similar product for another (later to be described as brand switching). For example, they might swap one particular brand of soap for another with a similar shape and fragrance, but possibly slightly lower price. However, there was a growing awareness that products had to be supported by substantial promotional campaigns.

From the early 1930s the salesperson gained importance within the organizational structure and framework of the business. This unfortunately led to unscrupulous and aggressive pressure tactics to secure the sale. For many customers and business people alike this 'hard sell' approach was unacceptable and unethical. Equally, it was damaging to the reputation of salespeople generally who were doing an 'honest day's work for an honest day's pay' (Griseri and Groucutt, 1997).

It is an unfortunate fact of life that some of these 'hard sell' tactics are still prevalent today, even though they have been outlawed in many countries. These practices can only be a short-term approach to increasing sales performance, rather than a longer-term relationship-building one.

The aftermath of the Second World War bore witness to a devastated Europe and Japan. While the US mainland had not been physically damaged, the country still had made sacrifices. Throughout Europe there was a period of austerity and food rationing while countries and their peoples reconstructed their lives out of the devastation. While Europe and Japan rebuilt, the situation in the United States was generally different. Manufacturing plants that had supported the US war machine now geared up to produce large quantities of consumer goods. Within the United States, Europe and the Far East, as a result of the war various social, economic and political changes started to occur. The following is based upon Kotler's (2000) analysis:

▌ The servicemen and women (throughout the world) returning from war were now more aware of the world, as a result of their often terrifying experiences. Thus they were more likely to challenge salespeople and make rational choices over products and services.

▌ A significant proportion of women had left their home life to work in factories, and other normally male-related occupations. This further helped the emancipation of women, thus leading to greater choices in terms of careers and purchasing power. (However, it can be argued that women until the 1990s were often still stereotyped as the person who 'looked after the home'. Increasingly both men and women have worked to dispel this and other stereotypes.)

▌ Technology that was developed prior to and during the war provided many benefits in peacetime. These include communications and transportation. The jet engine had not only military but commercial potential: for example, the development of the Boeing 707 (and subsequent variants) and the ill-fated DeHavilland Comet (the world's first commercial passenger aircraft).

▌ The reconstruction and rebuilding of war-torn Europe and Japan led to the modernization of their industry. This was a critical factor in their emergence as significant business forces from the 1960s onwards. With such extensive damage new industrial complexes were built housing the latest technologies. This was a transformational step change for their industry.

▌ The later formation of powerful trading blocs, such as the European Economic Community (now the European Union), expanded the range of products and services available. As will be seen in Chapter 14 there are now a significant number of regional trading blocs, each bringing together powerful marketing forces.

▌ The period of austerity of the war years eventually gave way to the prosperity of the 'swinging' 1960s. This period heralded an enhanced interest in marketing and how it could be used to promote an increasing array of products and services to a booming population. Equally, there were now more competitors within the market-place. Thus companies needed to seek the means of gaining a legitimate advantage over competitors. (See Chapter 7.)

As Jeremy (1998) states, after the Second World War managerial marketing and parallel consumer behaviour, emphasizing the control of the individual rather than aggregated behaviour within the marketplace, displaced the classical school. Customers were now overall more knowledgeable, and they had more choices. During this stage companies/organizations began to identify what customers really wanted. The result was an attempt to tailor their activities to satisfy those needs as efficiently and effectively as possible, although this action would not necessarily affect a monopolist, such as a state-controlled utility company (water and power suppliers).

In 1951 Robert Keith, the Vice President of Marketing at the food manufacturer and distributor Pillsbury, introduced a seminal principle to the business community – the marketing concept (Keith, 1960; Stokes, 1994). However Ralph Cordiner, then Chairman of General Electric, is apparently often credited with introducing the marketing concept to the US business community. In describing General Electric's philosophy, the 1952 Annual Report stated: 'an advanced form of marketing, formulated by the Marketing Services Division. This, in simple terms, would introduce the marketing man at the beginning rather than at the end of the production cycle and would integrate marketing into each phase of the business' (Petrof, 1997). Grönroos (1997) also states that it is attributed to McKitterick (1957). Grönroos (1997) goes on to state that:

This customer-oriented approach to doing business is, of course, nothing new. For example, in a book on advertising and marketing communications published in 1916 in Norway, the author, Romilla (Robert Milars), gives the following piece of advice: 'Fersek at se paa tingen fra kundens saide av disken' (try to look at the situation from the customer's side

of the counter). And according to an old Chinese saying' 'customers are precious things; goods are only grass'.

The marketing concept has the customer as the nucleus or focus of all marketing mix decisions. (Reflect back on the definitions of marketing discussed earlier.) Therefore the marketing concept is very appealing as it focuses on the customer. Lazo and Corbin (1961) wrote that the marketing function evolved into a basic attitude and understanding that must pervade the entire business by interpreting the concept of client relationship to all functions.

However, as pointed out by Pelton, Strutton and Lumpkin (1997), this creates a very one-sided approach to reconciling a company's or organization's mission with the markets it serves. This is because it may position marketers as reactive (rather than proactive) exchange partners, by adapting channels of distribution to meet the needs of the market.

In consumer research, as in marketing studies, there was a shift in focus from aggregated to individual behaviour. Ideas such as opinion leadership, the diffusion of innovations, brand loyalty, industry and product life cycles and market segmentation based upon demographics were developed and became integral components of marketing vocabulary (Pelton et al, 1997).

During the mid-1960s there was the increasing study of behaviour through economic psychology (considering customer expectations), behavioural psychology (considering individuals' subconscious motivators), organizational behaviour (aspects of power and conflict) and social psychology. All these contributed to the development of marketing thought and subsequent actions.

Sheth and Gross (1988) suggest that from the mid-1970s there was an adaptive marketing phase. Their contention is that there was a shift back to aggregated marketing behaviour. The driving forces were the new opportunities and threats being posed by

changing regulation (for example, deregulation of utility services, rapidly developing
technology and the onslaught of global
competition (Jeremy, 1998)). Two schools of
thought emanated from these driving forces.
The first was the macro-marketing school that
considered marketing as a social function or
institution. The second was the strategic
planning school, which is concerned with
environmental dynamics and proactively
adapting the company or organization to the
environment. Associated with this approach
is consumer market research that looked
towards international marketing, consumer
satisfaction and behavioural modification
issues.

As Palmer and Hartley (1999) suggest, the
idea that the overriding purpose of marketing
is to satisfy individuals' needs profitably is
increasingly being challenged. During the
1990s, partially as a rejection of the 'greed is
good' orientation, consumers began to seek
out products that would provide a benefit way
beyond their own needs (*Wall Street*, 1987).[3]
Here individuals were looking at products
from an ethical and social responsibility
standpoint. This can be considered as societal
marketing, a concept where the company or
organization's tasks are to determine the
needs, wants and interests of the target
markets, and provide the desired satisfaction
more effectively and efficiently than
competitors in a way that preserves or
enhances the consumer's and society's well-
being (Kotler, 2000).

Several factors were at work here. Since the
late 1980s, technology has provided instanta-
neous media coverage from virtually everywhere in the world. An event happens, and it is
beamed globally. Such media opportunities also
mean the actions of companies far removed
from their domestic market cannot escape
scrutiny. The revelations in the 1990s of the
environmentally unfriendly actions of major oil
companies in Nigeria promoted a public outcry
in Europe. A hostile media savaged companies,
while consumers actively (and vocally)
boycotted the companies' products. The
companies' reputations were damaged – some
irrevocably. Only significant investments in
environmental clean-up operations of the Niger
Delta, and the introduction of ethical and social
responsibility programmes, have restored (or
rehabilitated) some of these companies in the
minds of the consumers.

The media has also alerted the public to the
following issues, to name but a few:

▌ Western companies off-loading cheap
products (for example, tobacco) to less
developed nations, while employing people
from the same countries at extremely low
rates of pay.

▌ The use of child labour often in hazardous
jobs such as the manufacture of matches,
fireworks and carpets.

▌ The mis-selling of personal pensions and
assurance policies in the UK.

▌ Cartels operating to fix the prices of
products ranging from cars to washing
machines.

▌ The manufacture, marketing and distribution of products that companies knew
were harmful to the buyers of those
products: for example, cigarettes.

▌ The destruction of Brazilian rainforests by
timber companies.

▌ The testing of cosmetics and tobacco
products on animals.

▌ The selling of weapons systems to
oppressive political regimes.

▌ The pollution of the atmosphere, rivers and
oceans with dangerous chemicals. These
may be used to manufacture products and/
or be contained within the products
purchased by the consumer.

▌ The poor financial returns to farmers who
grow crops for consumption in developed
nations.

■ Oil spills from supertankers and the resultant impact upon the natural environment. A major example is the 1998 disaster in Alaskan waters when the tanker *Exxon Valdez* ran aground, spilling thousands of litres of crude oil.

Consumers have moved towards products that are considered more environmentally and ecologically friendly and where people have not been exploited in their manufacture. Hence we now see a greater range of products labelled, for example:

■ Not tested on animals.

■ This product does not contain CFCs.

■ This paper is from recycled sources.

■ This paper is from sustainable sources.

■ This wood is from sustainable forests.

■ The chemicals contained in this product are biodegradable.

As Jeremy (1998) underscores:

> Marketing, once little more than a sole proprietor's self-advertisement, is now a function of giant corporations and large consulting firms. Marketing, once no more than a public announcement in newspapers and magazines, has come to span a whole range of functions and sub-functions.

The marketing mix framework

Today much debate and controversy surrounds the development and ongoing use of the marketing mix concept. As Baker (2000) contends, marketers have experimented with different combinations of product, pricing, promotion and distribution.

During the late 1940s Culliton (of the Harvard Business School), in his study of manufacturers' marketing costs, described the business executive as a '"decider," and "artist"

– a "mixer of ingredients," who sometimes follows a recipe as he goes along, sometimes adapts a recipe to the ingredients immediately available, and sometimes experiments with or invents ingredients no one else has tried' (Culliton, 1948).

Culliton's phrase appealed directly to Neil H Borden, also of Harvard Business School, who rephrased the 'mixer of ingredients' into the 'marketing mix' (Borden, 1964). For him it consisted of important elements or ingredients that comprised a marketing programme. Indeed, Borden's original 'marketing mix of manufacturers' contained the 12 components listed in Table 1.1.

Borden did not believe that his list was definitive, and thus suggested that others may have different perspectives. Frey (1961) suggested that marketing variables should be divided into two parts, as depicted in Table 1.2.

However, it was E Jerome McCarthy who in the 1950s developed the mnemonic, the 'four Ps' which has become the most enduring of the marketing mix frameworks (Rafiq and Ahmed, 1995). McCarthy regrouped Borden's 12 elements into **product**, **price**, **promotion** and **placement** (also known as **place**, for distribution). This is perhaps the most widely recognized concept in marketing, providing a central organized structure or foundation for marketing activity. Each of these elements can, in turn, be considered as a 'mix; for example product mix, promotion mix and so on' (ibid). Originally McCarthy defined the marketing mix as 'a combination of all the factors at a marketing manager's command to satisfy the target market' (ibid) – see Table 1.3. With Perreault, McCarthy later revised this as 'the controllable variables that an organization can co-ordinate to satisfy the target market' (ibid).

As Baker (2000) contends, it is the manipulation of the elements within the marketing mix that provides a strategic framework for marketing.

Table 1.1 Borden's original marketing mix

Action	Description
Product planning	Policies and procedures relating to: ▌ product lines to be offered – qualities and design; ▌ markets to sell – whom, where, when and in what quantity; ▌ new product policy – research and development programmes.
Pricing	Policies and procedures relating to: ▌ price level to adopt; ▌ specific prices to adopt; ▌ pricing policy – one price or varying price or maintaining a constant price; ▌ margins to adopt – for company, for trade.
Branding	Policies and procedures relating to: ▌ selection of trade marks and copyrights; ▌ brand policy – individualized or family brand; ▌ sale as a private label or unbranded.
Channels of distribution	Policies and procedures relating to: ▌ channels to use between plant and consumer; ▌ degree and selectivity among wholesalers and retailers; ▌ efforts to gain cooperation of the industry.
Personal selling	Policies and procedures relating to: ▌ burden to be placed on personal selling and the methods to be employed in manufacturer's organization, wholesale segment of the trade and retail segment of the trade.
Advertising	Policies and procedures relating to: ▌ amount to spend – that is, the burden to be placed on advertising; ▌ copy platform to adopt – product image desired and corporate image to be desired; ▌ mix of advertising – to the related industry, through the industry, to consumers.
Promotions	Policies and procedures relating to: ▌ burden to place on special selling plans or devices directed at or through the industry; ▌ form of these devices for consumer promotions, for industry (B2B) promotions.
Packaging	Policies and procedures relating to: ▌ formulation of packaging and labelling.
Display	Policies and procedures relating to: ▌ burden to be placed on display to help create sales; ▌ methods to adopt to secure display within point of sale locations: for example, a department store or bookshop.
Servicing	Policies and procedures relating to: ▌ providing services needed.
Physical handling	Policies and procedures relating to: ▌ warehousing; ▌ transportation; ▌ inventories.
Fact finding and analysis	Policies and procedures relating to: ▌ securing, analysis, and the use of facts in marketing operations.

Table 1.2   Frey's analysis

Descriptors	Marketing variables
The offering	Product, packaging, brand, price and service
Methods/tools	Distribution channels, personal selling, advertising, sales promotion and publicity

Table 1.3   McCarthy's 4Ps

Mix variable or element	Description
Product	Traditionally this has been called a 'good', a concept that has its origins in economics. It can be considered as a collection of features and benefits that provide customer satisfaction.
Price	This is considered the only element of the mix to be revenue generating, in the pure sense. Price reflects more than the economic cost of producing the product. There is also the value perceived by the customer.
Promotion	Here the full range of marketing communication activities are considered, including: advertising, direct marketing, face-to-face selling, public relations, sales promotions, e-marketing and word of mouth.
Place (placement or distribution)	This covers location, distribution channels and logistics.

Yudelson (1999) suggests that there have been six major challenges to McCarthy's four Ps:

▪ A focus on the customer via the marketing concept or orientation.

▪ The broadening of marketing to include not-for-profit, services, good causes (charities) and even politics.

▪ Identification of exchange transactions as the core of marketing.

▪ The introduction of total quality management (TQM) with an emphasis on customer satisfaction.

▪ The extension from transaction marketing to relationship marketing.

▪ Identification of the company or organization as a member of a complete value chain (an issue we return to when we examine Porter's theories in Chapter 7).

As Yudelson (1999) suggests, McCarthy's four Ps provided a suitable and effective nomenclature for the study and analysis of marketing. However with the greater expansion of marketing beyond business-to-consumer (B2C) and business-to-business (B2B) into services, there was concern that the four Ps did not relate to services. Magrath (1986) was one of the first to postulate that the four Ps should be expanded to encompass **personnel**, **physical facilities** and **process management**. Additionally others sought to either add to or redefine the nomenclature, for example:

▪ Borden and Marshall (1959), Traynor (1985) – **probing** (to cover marketing research).

▪ Nickels and Jolson (1976), Patty (1997) – **packaging**.

▪ Mindak and Fine (1981) – **public relations**.

▪ Judd (1987), Baker (1997) – **people**.

▌ Payne and Ballantyne (1991) – **people, processes** and customer service for relationship marketing.

▌ Kotler (1986) – **public relations** and **power**.

▌ Kotler (2000) – **probe** (researching the market), **partition** (segmenting the market), **prioritize** (specifying markets to target) and **position** (deciding a role with respect to the target market).

▌ Booms and Bitner (1981) – **process, physical evidence** and **participants**.

▌ Yudelson (1999) – **performance, penalty, perception** and **process**.

▌ LeDoux (1991) – **preservation** (this was in response to environmental concerns that came to the forefront in the late 1980s and early 1990s).

As you can see from the above sample, there is a diversity of views on how the marketing mix framework can be enlarged. This list only scratches the surface of the views relating to the relevance or not of the marketing mix framework. As Rafiq and Ahmed (1995) contend, the proliferation of numerous ad hoc conceptualizations has undermined the concept of the marketing mix, and what is required is a more coherent approach.

As stated earlier, there has been concern that the classic 4Ps do not incorporate the characteristics of services – namely inherent intangibility, perishability, heterogeneity (variability), inseparability and ownership. See Table 1.4.

However, as demonstrated from the above list, the 4Ps can be extended to incorporate factors that can bind the 4Ps for a service orientation. As Rafiq and Ahmed (1995) suggest, the most influential to date of the

Table 1.4 The characteristics of service orientation

Service element	Description and implications
Inherent intangibility	This refers to the lack of 'physical' substance. In contrast to a product there is no substantial material or physical aspect to the service – for instance, no taste, visible presence or even 'feel' to it. For consumers this can present clear difficulties, as they may not be too sure what they have purchased.
	Example: A person who has difficulties in their lives, for instance severe stress, may visit a psychotherapist for help. Until the course of treatment is over, the individual cannot judge the quality of the final outcome.
	Marketing implications: This lack of 'feel' needs to be overcome. Therefore, salespeople can use physical or conceptual illustrations to help customers be more confident in their purchase, and to show what the service is actually delivering. Equally, the salespeople can focus on the benefits the consumer will derive by purchasing the service. This can be helped by appropriate promotional materials.
Perishability	This is where the service cannot be stored for later consumption, thus it has to be consumed at the designated time.
	Example: A seat on the 12:15 train from London King's Cross Station to Inverness in Scotland. The service – provision of the seat and journey – has to be consumed by the customer at the desired time.
	Marketing implications: Operational systems must be devised to deliver the service at the designated time. This will include the provision of suitably trained employees to carry out duties associated with the train journey. Additionally, in order to prevent an impossible demand for consumption of the service (too many people wanting to travel on this specific train) the supply–demand relationship must be considered. A railway company may, for example, have price variants to encourage people to 'consume' train services at different times of the day. Thus, trains to Inverness may have a variety of fares.

Table 1.4 *continued*

Service element	Description and implications
Heterogeneity or variability	It is difficult to maintain consistency of standards in terms of service. It is much easier with a product where there may be exacting processes, for example, in the production of a chocolate bar. With services it may be difficult or impossible to create a precise standardization, for service tends to mean an interaction with people. The approach taken by one person may be different, if only slightly, from another although they are in the same organization. *Example*: The next time you go into a restaurant watch how people are served. You may find that one member of staff acts different from another. For instance, one may genuinely smile, another may not. However, it may be the smile (as well as the food – the product) that turns a first-time customer into a repeat customer. *Marketing implications*: Taking the example above, heterogeneity of service can assist an organization in terms of customer retention, revenue generation and competitive advantage. Much of this is dependent upon the culture of the organization, and this is often driven by senior management. The issues organizations must thus consider are quality control, effective employee selection, training and motivation.
Inseparability	This is where the actual service cannot be separated from the service provider. The creation or performance of a service may occur at the same time as full or partial consumption of it occurs. *Example*: The service provided on a British Airways' first class flight from London to New York is inseparable from the actual flight itself. The service does not exist until it is actually consumed or experienced by the person who is on the flight. *Marketing implications*: As the service is inseparable from the experience there is the need for high-quality and reliable customer care. This can only be achieved by well trained and caring employees who seek to create standards of excellence and real customer orientation and satisfaction. This is exactly what a customer would expect and receives on a British Airways' first class flight.
Ownership	A fundamental difference between a product and service is that of ownership. The purchasing of a service only allows 'access' to that service – not ownership. The buying of a product, however, confers ownership of that product to the buyer. (However there may be restrictions on what you can do with the product. For example, you may have bought this textbook or been given it as a gift. Thus you own it, and thus can read it as often as you want and store it on your bookshelf. However, you cannot reproduce the words in the book for sale to someone else. That would be a breach of copyright, a breach of the terms of ownership.)

alternative frameworks has been Booms and Bitner's seven Ps marketing mix. They have extended the four Ps to include participants (often now referred to as people), physical evidence and process (see Table 1.5).

In their original article, Booms and Bitner (1981) intended their additional three Ps to be limited to service marketing. However, there are academics and writers, for example Levitt (1972), who suggest that 'there are only industries whose service components are greater or lesser than those of other industries. Everybody is in service.' Enis and Roering (1981) suggest that the product is defined as a bundle of benefits (with tangible and intangible benefits), therefore the often cited call for a unique service marketing strategy is inconsistent with such a definition of a product. Hence in explanations of the term 'product', it is often considered interchangeable with service.

Raqif and Ahmed (1995) contended that a marketing mix was needed that cut across the boundaries of goods, services and industrial

Table 1.5 Extended marketing mix

Mix variable or element	Description
People (participants)	This includes, customers, employees and suppliers, the 'communities' involved in the marketing relationship.
Physical evidence	This is the tangible aspects of the 'delivery' of the product or service: for example, the layout of a supermarket.
Process	This is the assembly or flow activities that support the fulfillment of the marketing mix: for example, credit card transactions.

marketing – a generic marketing mix. Increasingly the Booms and Bitner marketing mix framework has been adopted, although certainly debate will continue.

We have adopted the generic marketing mix of seven Ps. It may well be, in time, that further Ps are added to the mix, for example a case could be made for performance being separated from product in order to consider performance across a wide range of variables. Performance is not only associated with the total quality management of a product, it also relates to people, processes and physical evidence.

Relationship marketing – relationship building and management

As stated in the opening paragraph to the above section, there has been significant controversy over the relevance and future of the marketing mix. As we examined earlier, there is a body of researchers who suggests that the marketing mix does not cross product/service boundaries. However, there is also a group who believe that by extending the marketing mix concept it can encompass the mutual needs of both products and services, while others believe that in today's business environment, product and service are so intertwined that they can only be defined through the marketing mix concept.

Equally, there are writers who suggest that the marketing mix be replaced by the 'new'

concept of relationship marketing. This has led to much fierce debate within the academic world. In this section we consider some of the issues, and suggest that students seek out the original articles to continue the debate.

It was in the early 1980s that Berry (1983) introduced the term 'relationship marketing' within a services marketing context. As we have outlined earlier, relationships were significant, in fact key, to business success until the 18th and 19th centuries. It was only with the development of mass manufacturing techniques – production orientation – that relationships (in some cases) became secondary to the business/financial transaction. However, as Webster (1994) states, even during the production orientation phase some industrialists, such as Henry Ford, were conscious of the role of relationship building to business success. (This is also borne out by Ford's own writings – see Ford, 1922.) Following Webster's view, we must be careful not to assume that people's actions during a period of history change because of manufacturing or selling techniques. It is clear that not all companies display a marketing or societal concept today. Many are still (especially when you look internationally) production and sales oriented.

Berry (1983) views relationship marketing as a strategy to attract, maintain and enhance customer relationships. Rapp and Collins (1990) go further by stating that the goals of relationship marketing are to create and maintain *lasting relationships* (our emphasis) between the company or organization and its customers that are rewarding for both groups. Blomqvist, Dahl and Haeger (1993) provide an outline of the key characteristics of relationship marketing:

▌ Every customer is considered an individual person or unit.

▌ Activities of the company or organization are predominately directed towards existing customers.

▌ It is based on interactions and dialogues.

▌ The company or organization is trying to achieve profitability through the decrease of customer turnover and the strengthening of customer relationships.

Here we should consider 'profitability' not only in the strictest sense of a commercial enterprise, but also as the 'profit' or benefits gained by not-for-profit organizations. In this case it may be an individual who donates a fixed amount (say via direct debit facilities) to a charity each month.

Grönroos (1997) suggests that many of the definitions or descriptions attributed to relationship marketing are too narrow, in that only the relationship between the supplier and its customer is included. It is clear that if the value chain approach is taken, there are additional points where value added can significantly improve the overall marketing relationship. This is where a 'value' is added to the product, at any point from the manufacturing stage to after sales care. It is this 'added value' that may create a competitive advantage for the organization, through building a better relationship with the customer. (We revisit the concept of value added when we examine Porter's work in Chapter 7.)

However, Grönroos (1997) suggested that in the late 1990s relationship marketing was still in 'its infancy as a mainstream marketing concept'. Kotler (2000) suggests that

'companies must move from a short-term transaction-oriented goal to a long-term relationship-building goal'. As Grönroos (1997) contends, 'thus for a firm pursuing a relationship marketing strategy the internal interface between marketing, operations, personnel and other functions is of strategic importance to success'. (Here you may want to reflect back to the earlier section on marketing relationships with other functional areas.)

The view might be taken that relationship marketing is a totally new concept or approach. This is where such views can be challenged. As Petrof (1997) states, authors have for decades underscored the concept of synergy with the importance of integrating all company efforts. He quotes Stanton, Sommers and Barnes who suggested in 1964 that 'All company activities in production, finance as well as in marketing must be devoted first to determining what the customer's wants are and then to satisfy those wants while still making a reasonable profit'. True, this quote from 1964 still emphasizes the profit motive; however it can easily be applied to not-for-profit transactions, as stated earlier. Polanyi, writing in 1957, stated that marketing cannot limit itself solely to consumption and trade. As a social institution it must take into consideration the satisfaction of the psychological and social needs of people (consumers and business partners).

There is no disputing the importance of relationships within the marketing process; however it is not new. Relationships were critical to the success, indeed survival, of the ancient merchants of Rome and Greece, for instance. In the world that predated the super and hypermarket world we now live in, local retailers often knew their customers by name, and what they liked and disliked. If they had not built strong effective relationships with their customers, they would have failed. Even today, in some cities and countries the local store displays high customer retention values due directly to the fact of the relationship. Such shops may be more expensive than the supermarket; however, it is their approach to customers that contributes to their overall success.

We feel that it is crucial that students do not grasp relationship marketing as something new – a new way of marketing. It has always been there; however, the tools and approaches that can be used to enhance the relationship may be new or revised. For example, the techniques used in marketing communications (promotion) can greatly (if used wisely) enhance the 'relationship'.

Grönroos (1997) and Rapp and Collins (1990) suggest that marketing communications is central to reaching customers, and the focus on relationship building leads to an interest in emphasizing dialogues and creating, for example, advertising campaigns that facilitate various types of dialogues with identified and targeted customers. Reichheld (1993) states that 'building a highly loyal customer base cannot be done as an add-on. It must be integral to a company's basic business strategy.'

Hunt and Morgan (1994) contend that the process of relationship marketing lies in the development and growth of trust and commitment among partners. They define trust as a 'willingness to rely on an exchange partner in whom one has confidence and commitment' 'as... an enduring desire to maintain a valued partnership'. They suggest that trust receives positive support from communication and shared values. Relationship commitment is sustained through the same shared values together with relationship benefits and relationship termination costs (ending the relationship has a cost to be borne). Morris, Barnes and Lynch (1999) suggest that these variables collectively act positively upon commitment.

Here we need to be reflective. The marketing concept of the 1950s placed the customer at the centre of marketing activity. All elements needed to be effectively and efficiently combined to bring customer satisfaction. The societal marketing concept (1980s/1990s) was an active move away from the 'greed is good' scenario (not that it has disappeared), where companies and organizations had to regain people's trust. We only have to reconsider the ethical and social responsibility issues of the past 30 years to realize that 'trust' often has a fundamental impact upon the success of a business or organization (here we include charitable organizations). We refer students to the chapter on ethics and social responsibility and the level of trust that Johnson and Johnson were able to build by their handling of the Tylenol capsule sabotage (See Chapter 3).

Of course technology has had, and continues to have, an impact upon society. This is especially so with the development of sophisticated databases (data warehousing and data mining linked to direct marketing – see Chapter 10) and the use of the Internet and World Wide Web. The use of these systems provides the marketer with the ability to react more efficiently and effectively to the customer, adapt to market changes and encourage repeat purchasing behaviour. Linked to relationship marketing is the concept of permission marketing. Postulated by Godin (1999), permission marketing is where a company regularly communicates with customers because the customers have given their 'permission' for the company to do so. For example, a customer might request regular updates via e-mail on new product developments or sales promotions. Increasingly academic publishers are using this technique to build relationships with academics. This alerts the tutor to the latest range of texts and supplementary materials available, and is a good source of customer feedback. We will return to this topic in a later chapter.

While there may be debate on the development of relationship marketing, it is clear that it is vital for marketers to develop and build upon successful relationships. As you read through this text, always bear in mind that a person (it may be you) is at the heart of the transactions that take place.

Future evolutions

In this chapter we have considered various schools of thought (from commodity to societal) and approaches to the subject of marketing. As we stated earlier, marketing is evolutionary. Thus how it functions, and what comprises 'marketing' in the future may be very different from how we perceive it today. It could be argued that even the subject, the very term 'marketing', may evolve into something else.

Perhaps this is a radical thought? Not really. The name or term is not the issue. The real issue is whether 'marketing' actually works (both effectively and efficiently) for the companies and organizations that deploy it. In order to determine this, marketing must be measurable and marketing departments must be accountable. As we intimate throughout this text, it is not a question of haphazardly throwing large amounts of finance at marketing a product or service to an audience. On the contrary, effective and efficient marketing is about strategically deploying an array of resources to assist the company or organization to gain and critically sustain a competitive advantage within defined targeted markets.

Chapter summary

In this chapter we have considered the various definitions of marketing, and to some extent found them lacking in terms of development. We have also examined the evolution and development of the marketing mix. This concept remains core to the studying of marketing; however it is not without its detractors. Those detractors tend to focus on the development of relationship marketing as a possible replacement for the marketing mix. Both concepts have value to marketers, and these values should be developed in harmony with each other.

In this book we examine how both the seven Ps of the marketing mix and relationship marketing operate within both B2C and B2B environments. While both concepts have their detractors and their inherent flaws, for the moment they remain essential to the studying of marketing.

As we progress through this book you will see how the various elements that we call 'marketing' fit together – very much like an enormous jigsaw puzzle. It is important to recognize that marketing is not a static environment, but constantly changing and developing. That is what makes marketing a truly exciting and dynamic subject to study.

Exercises and questions for review and critical thinking

1. The marketing mix has been criticized by various authors. Using this and other texts, detail the different perspectives and draw a conclusion. Once you have read through this textbook reflect back upon your conclusion. Do you have any additional thoughts/views on this topic?

2. Critically evaluate the views expressed regarding the marketing concept and relationship marketing. What do you consider to be the similarities and differences between these two approaches? What do you think can be learnt from studying these two areas?

2

The business and marketing environment

Introduction

In this chapter we consider the environment in which business and marketing operates. In this context Palmer (2000) sees marketing as 'a system which must respond to environmental change. Just as the human body may die if it fails to adjust to environmental change (for example by not compensating for very low temperatures), businesses may fail if they do not adapt to external changes such as new sources of competition or changes in consumers' preferences.' While we agree with Palmer's perspective, companies must look far beyond the environment in which they operate. For example, major external forces such as politics can (to a greater or lesser degree) support or hinder an organization's marketing and strategic ambitions.

While it can be argued that many of the micro environmental factors are 'controllable' (although the level of control is variable), the external factors tend to be uncontrollable. That is, the organization cannot normally change the parameters to meet its expectations. It may have to change or adapt to the external environmental conditions in order to survive.

In this chapter we explore some of the micro and macro issues that companies and their marketing teams need to consider.

Learning objectives

On completion of this chapter you should be able to:

▌ outline the micro and macro factors that influence marketing decision making in organizations;

▌ evaluate the potential impact of the micro environment on the marketing of a product or service;

▌ analyse the potential impact macro factors may have within a local, regional, national and international context;

▌ debate future micro and macro environmental issues, and consider what actions organizations may need to adopt to survive within turbulent environments.

The business and marketing environment

Business and marketing operate together within environments. These are usually divided into micro and macro environments, and are usually illustrated as two concentric circles. We have taken a slightly different approach; however the outcomes are fundamentally the same. The shapes relate to the FORCES that interact or engage (to a greater or lesser extent) with the organization and its markets (Figure 2.1). We have incorporated levels of engagement on both the horizontal and vertical axis, as these forces engage the breadth and depth of both the organization and its markets.

In the sections that follow we elaborate upon the forces that comprise both the micro and macro environments.

Micro environmental forces

The micro environment can be described as the organizational environment. This comprises very loosely the internalities of the organization: that is, the forces over which the organization has some control, or perhaps 'influence' is a better way of describing the level of power the organization possesses. However, there must be some caution here. While the organization has some control (within legal frameworks) over its employees and to some extent suppliers, the level of 'control' over customers is debatable. True organizations can and do influence their customers, but this is not control in the absolute meaning of the word. The constituents of the micro environment should be considered to be the stakeholders both of the organization and the industry sector in which it operates.

Figure 2.2 shows the micro environmental forces that engage with the organization.

The point here is that they tend to be local issues. These may be related to suppliers, the employees' local community, the local regulators/local government and the direct customer. To an extent these issues can be 'controlled' (to a greater or lesser degree) by the company's management. Often in marketing texts these are considered as the 'controllables'; however they are only controllable to a limited degree depending, for example, on geographical location, local regulations and political intent.

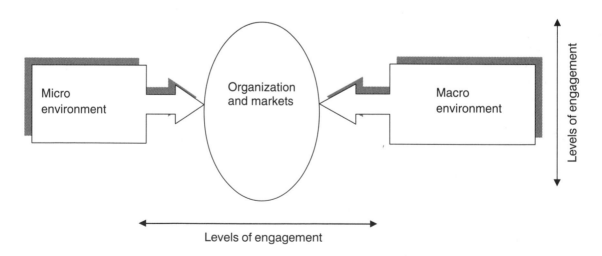

Figure 2.1   The micro and macro environments

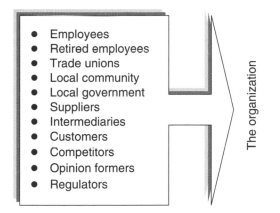

Figure 2.2   The micro environmental forces that engage with the organization

Thus external factors can influence or determine the micro factors. For example, a company can influence customers to buy a product or service. The element of 'control' is governed by what is acceptable within a particular area or region. For instance, on the one hand there will be consumer protection laws; on the other the organization will have legal redress in order to obtain payment from customers (Business-to-consumer and Business-to-business, B2C and B2B) if they renege on payment.

Employees

The employees (at whatever level) are critical to the success of any organization. Consider, for instance, a manufacturing company and a service company. The manufacturing company may win orders not on price, but on the quality of product manufacture and the ability to meet the customer's deadline. The ability to deliver to such specification is a combination of people and other resources, such as equipment.

The people employed by a service provider are the front-line interface between the customer and the service. For example, the employees of a hotel can make or break the customer's perception of the hotel.

Retired employees

Those who retire from an organization can remain a value asset to that organization. They may be consumers of the company's product or services, and/or word-of-mouth spokespersons (see viral marketing in Chapter 11).

In Chicago during September 1982 several people who had purchased the painkiller Tylenol died of cyanide poisoning. It is believed that someone tampered with the containers while they were on the store shelves, depositing sufficient quantities of cyanide to be fatal to anyone who ingested it. Tylenol was manufactured by McNeil Consumer Products, a subsidiary of Johnson & Johnson, and was the leading analgesic in the marketplace. The board of Johnson & Johnson decided to withdraw Tylenol from the market, a move that effectively wiped US $2 billion off the company's share value (Green, 1999). As part of a coordinated campaign letters were sent to both domestic employees and retired staff keeping them updated and thanking them for their continued support during the crisis. Eventually Tylenol was reintroduced, this time in tamper-proof containers, and it recovered market share.

Trade unions

Trade unions have an important role in protecting the rights of employees. When there is a good working relationship between management and the trade unions, the outcomes tend be focused within the organization. However, when there is a poor working relationship between management and the trade unions it often impacts upon the organization's customers. Thus their perception of the organization, its products and services may become negative. Thus they may seek substitutes.

For example, persistent industrial action on say a railway network may drive passengers to seek alternative forms of transport on a regular basis. Indeed, the local or regional bus companies may actively target the disgruntled train passengers with reduced fares and new routes.

During the 1970s industrial disputes in Britain's car and shipbuilding industries did much to destroy their reputations. This was especially the case in the shipbuilding industry. As both management and trade unions engaged in vilifying each other, customers sought suppliers in other countries. Thus Britain's shipbuilding industry, once market leader, collapsed.

The local community

The members of the local community are important stakeholders in many businesses. They could be affected in several ways: see Table 2.1.

Local government

Here we refer to local government, but that can include regional governments as well. Local governments devise their own laws, which often are in conflict with the national or federal laws. Companies need to be aware of the local laws and how they may impact upon the marketing of their products or services. For instance, in 1920 the US federal authorities imposed nationwide prohibition, which prevented the commercial manufacture, transportation and sale of alcohol in the United States. This became an unworkable piece of legislation and in 1933 this Act was repealed. While in the vast majority of the United States you can purchase and consume alcohol, there remain (as of the time of writing this textbook, 2003) many US states that continue to allow counties and principalities (the local communities) to ban the sale and consumption of alcohol within their borders.

Therefore local governments may act differently from their national governments on major issues. Equally, local governments are responsible for planning and environmental issues, so the location of manufacturing plants, distribution facilities, retail outlets and even billboards comes under local jurisdictions.

Local governments can also benefit from companies in the form of local taxation.

Suppliers

Palmer (2000) categorizes suppliers as 'those that provide an organization with goods and services which are transformed by the organization into value added products for the customers. Very often, suppliers are crucial to an organization's marketing success'. Palmer focuses here on the value added and the responsibility suppliers have to their customers. In Table 2.2 we have summarized the key relationships between suppliers and their customers. Several of the factors will reappear in later chapters, for instance the development of the value chain, adding value to each process of manufacture, marketing and distribution.

Intermediaries

This group often provides an important link between the manufacturer, for example, and its retail outlet. For example, food manufacturers such as Cadbury Schweppes and Premier Foods in the UK distribute their products through retailers. There can be many types of intermediaries, some operating only within a B2B environment, whilst others have

Table 2.1   The stakeholder role of the local community

Stakeholder role	Comment
Consumers	They may consume the product or service provided by the business. For example, they purchase products from the local supermarket.
Employees	They may be employed directly by the company or indirectly by a supplier to that company.
Impacting factors	The local community can be affected by the actions of the company. This can manifest itself in several forms: for instance pollution and its consequences, redundancies that will impact upon the amount of income families have available to purchase other products or services within the local community, and finally closure. The closure of a business, most especially if it is the main employer within the area, can have a devastating impact upon that community. It is not only the employees of the company who are affected. In turn local suppliers to that company must either seek new markets or equally face closure. Other businesses such as supermarkets, restaurants and other product and service providers will be affected. These businesses may need to reappraise the type of products stocked and the subsequent prices charged.
Local pressure groups	There may be local pressure groups who campaign against the levels of pollution being emitted by the company (see the point above). They may also campaign against the location of distribution facilities (risk of road congestion, pollution and potential dangers to young children crossing busy roads), the erection of billboards (visual pollution) and the location of retail outlets (for instance a new petrol station). If the pressure groups are successful it may prove difficult to meet identified customer demand.
	Since the late 1990s there has been much debate regarding the expansion of airport facilities in the UK. Both the airport authorities and the low-cost airlines, especially, want additional runway capabilities to meet predicted demand. However, local communities are objecting to further expansion due to the potential impact upon their community: various forms of pollution that will lead to a reduced quality of life and a lowering of property values.
Benefits from the company relationship	The local community can derive benefits from the company beyond those of employment. Businesses and organizations can interact with local communities through such activities as sponsorship (see Chapter 11). For instance, they may help to raise funds for a local charity, hospice or hospital. A supermarket may work with both the local community and local government in the recycling of used products such as glass, newspapers and tin cans.

connections throughout the supply chain network encompassing both B2B and B2C groups. Intermediaries are examined in more detail in Chapter 13.

Customers

It does not take 'rocket science' to realize that customers (whatever form they take) are crucial to the very survival of an organization. It does matter whether that organization is a for-profit-company (such as Cadbury Schweppes, Nike or Diesel Jeans), a not-for-profit organization such as a charity (for example, Save the Children Fund, the Red Cross/Red Crescent or UNICEF), or a government (any democratically elected political party needs voters to support it). All these groups have one thing in common: they

Table 2.2 The key relationships between suppliers and their customers

Key relationships	Comment
Reliability of delivery	This can be crucial where there is a highly competitive industry and the raw materials or components are in short supply. For example, in the early 1990s there was a shortage of computer chips. This was for two main reasons. First, there was enormous demand, and second, a large fire destroyed a major manufacturing plant in the Far East. Other manufacturers struggled to maintain component flow, and this had a direct impact upon computer manufacturers and their revenue generation. With the adoption of just in time (JIT) systems, manufacturers and retailers need suppliers who can provide on-time, on-schedule deliveries wherever they are required in the world. We need to consider this in the global context.
Pricing	Companies operating in highly dynamic markets where there is minimal product or service differentiation may have to focus on price. In order for a retailer, for instance, to sell its own-label brand of washing powder, it may need to target price-sensitive customers. In order to achieve target market penetration it will have to obtain the best possible price from its washing powder supplier. The combination of lower supplier price and reduced margins may allow the retailer to sell in volume the low-cost own-label brand to price-sensitive customers.
Product development	Suppliers can work closely with manufacturers in the development of new end-user products. This may require re-tooling of machinery to meet the new specifications demanded by the customer and the product end user. Consider, for example, the companies supplying the components for the new Airbus A380. In order for this aircraft to carry 500+ passengers, new components have to be designed and tested (to new exacting standards), and then manufactured to meet the increasing level of orders.
Marketing support	Suppliers also become involved in the marketing of the end-user product or service. This may be in the form of piggybacking (see Chapter 14). An example of such marketing support is Intel and its link to computer hardware suppliers. This is often reflected in the advertising for computer hardware, where the Intel logo appears accompanied by its specific theme tune within UK advertisements for computer hardware suppliers.

have customers. They may be in various forms, with various powers of influence, but they have customers. Thus within their various 'micro environments' the organizations have to both influence and work with their customers.

This can also be viewed as a macro environmental factor, through the relationship between society as a whole and businesses.

Competitors

Unless an organization operates within a monopolistic economic environment it will have competition with the market. Porter (1980) defines competitors as 'a group of firms producing products that are close substitutes for each other'. (It should be noted that Porter included acts of service within products. Therefore you need to think of the competitive environment as including both product manufacturers and service providers.) Thus the different chocolate bars produced by Cadbury and Nestlé are competitive products. Three levels of competition can be identified, which are considered in Table 2.3.

As you can see, a competitor may not be a

Table 2.3   Types of competitor

Type of competitor	Comment
Direct	This is where a customer has to make the choice between two companies that provide virtually the same product or service. There may be minimal differential between the two products. For example, two four-star hotels in central London will have very similar types of facilities. The only differentiator may be price. If customers are slightly price-sensitive they may opt for the slightly cheaper hotel.
Indirect	A couple decide to take a week's vacation in Inverness in the Highlands of Scotland, and they need to examine how they will travel from London to Inverness. They could drive, take the daytime train, take the overnight sleeper or fly by various local airlines. Their final decision is likely to be made on the basis of time, flexibility, price, restrictions (for example, when they can return to London or the cost of an airline ticket in relation to the time they actually want to fly, peak time or off-peak) and availability.
Substitute or need	The couple who were examining the potential options of travelling to Inverness in Scotland might decide not to spend their week's vacation in the Highlands of Scotland. Instead they might decide to spend this time at home undertaking necessary improvements to their home. Thus their week is spent on DIY. Therefore they will spend their vacation budget (or at least part of it) on buying paint, wallpaper, tools and other essentials for their DIY activities.

direct rival to a particular product or service provider. The real issue is on what customers will spend their available funds. Will they buy the latest CD by their favourite band or will they have a hamburger instead? That is the nature of a competitive environment (see Chapter 7).

Opinion formers

These are the individuals or groups who help us decide on what we will either purchase or ignore. These influencers can range from street-wise kids to the media, all saying what is good or bad, no matter what your age range or income level. Companies aiming at the youth market need to know what is cool and wicked now, and what could be in the future. These companies need to be able to tailor their products and services to an ever-changeable and thus difficult market. Equally, companies that market to the 50+ segment of society need to realize that people of this age are more

active than older people were in the past, and prepared to invest in enjoyment.

The difficulty for companies is twofold. First, they *must* truly understand the needs of the target market. Second, they need to react to the unpredictability and dynamics of a volatile global marketplace. As we shall see in the next major section of this chapter, that unpredictability is often totally beyond the control of the company and the business sector in which it operates.

We cover the role of opinion formers in more detail in Chapters 10 and 11 when we discuss various aspects of marketing communications.

Regulators

Depending on the type of industry in which they operate, businesses may be subject to an element of intervention from a regulator. The regulator may be semi-governmental or totally independent. This might depend upon the type of industry being regulated and the culture of the government in power at the time. The government may have either a very centralized and controlled view or a decentralized 'hands off' approach, leaving the decision making to the regulatory body.

The regulator's power may cover a range of issues, from safety through to whether the consumer is receiving a quality product at a fair price within a competitive environment. Regulatory bodies often operate in the nuclear, telecommunications, financial services and utility industries.

Macro environmental forces

These are environmental issues that directly affect industries as well as individual companies and organizations. These can be highly dynamic and volatile forces, and should never be underestimated by a company or organization.

We will concentrate on these macro forces here, because of their sheer volatility: they can have a severe influence on the marketing operations of an industry or company. Indeed, they can influence the success or failure of a company, or even under extreme circumstances that of a whole industry. As is implied by the previous statement, the organization has little or no control over these factors.

These factors are often referred to under the mnemonic PESTEL. Two other mnemonics exist, PEST and SLEPT. In these latter cases the (physical) environment or ecology is omitted.

Politics

Within the UK, for instance, legislation is influenced and determined by both the government of the day and the policy makers within the European Union. This legislation affects how companies operate within the UK market, the European market and overseas marketplaces.

Both UK and European Union legislation cover:

- competition policy: for example UK Monopolies and Mergers Commission (MMC) rulings, and European Union rulings on fair competition;

- transport and distribution;

- economic and fiscal policy;

- employment legislation;

- environmental issues and protection;

- consumer rights: these broadly cover the health and safety of consumers, protecting consumers' economic interests, and consumer information and education.

Of course, if the company operates outside the UK and EU, the laws pertaining to the host

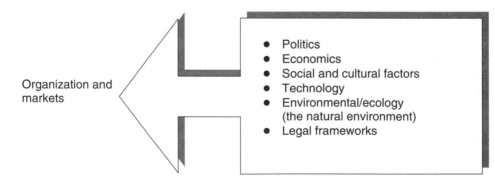

Figure 2.3   Macro environmental factors

country (that is, the country where it manufactures, locates international offices and/or sells products or services) will bind it, thus controlling how it operates and markets its products and services. See Chapter 14.

Many of these issues will be discussed in more detail in Chapter 4, 'Buyer behaviour'.

On the question of politics we should consider the issue of political power, for it is those who hold power who influence both political decisions and consumer issues.

Pressure groups

We have placed pressure groups under 'politics' as they have gained increasing political influence. Once they may have been considered a 'fad' or 'cranks' by some politicians, but it has however become clear that they can often have a significant influence on public opinion. Few governments can ignore such increasing influence.

During the 1980s there was the rise of various pressure groups, especially in relation to the environment. Organizations such as Greenpeace and Friends of the Earth highlighted numerous green issues to a wider global public and political community through the deft use of public relations. The attempt, for example, by Shell Petroleum to sink an old North Sea drilling platform in the Atlantic led to extensive media coverage and

political debate. Eventually, under mounting public and political pressure, including an increasing public boycott of Shell products, the company had to rethink its means of disposal.

Terrorism

While terrorism has been, sadly, a part of human existence for several centuries, it appears that few marketing texts have directly referred to it as an issue for review. Czinkota and Ronkainen (1995) are perhaps two of the few who have considered it as a component of political risk. No doubt as a result of the events of 2001 and 2002 more texts will cover this subject area. However, terrorism goes much further than a 'political' risk for companies operating within a particular country or region.

What is clear is that terrorism, especially in the early years of the 21st century, has had a marked effect upon the lives of virtually everyone. The long-term impact of such tragedies as the 11 September 2001 attacks on New York and Washington, and the car bomb explosion in Bali on Saturday 12 October 2002 are unknown. What is evident is that, in addition to the appalling human tragedy in relation to death and injury, many more lives have suffered through resulting business failures. In Table 2.4 we have summarized

---

Marketing insight: McDonald's and Bermuda

Let us take the case of McDonald's. For several years McDonald's operated on a US military base on the island of Bermuda. When the US troops moved out in September 1995 McDonald's wanted to open a more general operation on the island. However, local residents and the island's government decided to contest McDonald's right to set up a restaurant. As a result there was a long drawn-out battle. Finally in 1996, the island's government passed an Act of Parliament (the Prohibited Restaurants Act) preventing McDonald's and any other fast-food restaurant from establishing itself on the island. McDonald's appealed to the British Privy Council in London. However the appeal was rejected in July 1999 (Jefferson News Tribune, 1999).

Table 2.4 The impact of terrorism on marketing activities

Issues	Comment
Airline travel (traditional markets)	Prior to 11 September 2001 several airline companies were financially struggling within a highly competitive environment. This was especially the case for US domestic and transatlantic services. The hijacking of the aircraft used in the attacks on New York and Washington led many people to reconsider air travel. Subsequently, the major carriers saw a rapid decline in passenger numbers. Although airlines implemented drastic strategic actions (massive cost reductions), for some it was too late to save the business. Thus the closure of, for example, Belgium's Sabena, Australia's Ansett and Switzerland's Swissair (later reborn as Swiss).
	The terrorist attack on the island of Bali further increased the pain for European, American and Australian airlines, as most travellers to Indonesia, Thailand and Malaysia use scheduled flights rather than charter airlines.
	In March 2003 US and British military forces invaded Iraq. The fear of terrorist reprisals as a result of this action had a marked effect on the major international carriers. The further downturn within the market resulted in United Airlines, the US's second largest carrier, filing for Chapter 11 bankruptcy protection in order to stabilize its financial situation. By early April 2003 American, the world's largest airline, was in negotiation with its staff to reduce salary costs (and other costs) to stave off either Chapter 11 or full-scale bankruptcy. At the time of writing (April 2003) American may have just survived.
	The major airlines were both reducing routes and significantly reducing fares in order to both maintain customers and win over new ones.
Airline travel (new markets and growth areas)	However other airlines, both domestic and specialist charter, were to see significant improvements in their businesses after 11 September. In the UK low-cost operators such as easyJet saw a significant rise in passenger numbers. This desertion from the major carriers was perhaps in the belief that terrorists would not hijack a low-cost carrier but focus on national carriers. If so that belief was challenged in August 2002 when a man was arrested after attempting to take a loaded gun onto a London-bound Ryanair flight at Stockholm's Vasteras Airport.
	The second growth area after 11 September was in chartered private jets. Many corporations sought to fly their executives in private jets rather than 'risk' them on major national carriers.
Vacation destinations	The terrorist attacks in New York and Washington in 2001 led to reduced popularity of US and Middle Eastern destinations. Tourism economists believed that it would take the tourist industry some three years to recover the losses incurred since 11 September 2001. That was, however, before the car bomb attack in Bali in October 2002. While major cities such as London had witnessed a downturn in the tourist market after 11 September, locations such as the island paradise of Bali (known as the Island of the Gods) had remained relatively buoyant. In 2001 some 1.5 million visitors visited the island, which the Indonesian government always insisted was a safe destination to visit.
	As well as major tour operators and airlines, local companies suffered as a result of this terrorist attack. Within hours of the explosion there was an exodus of tourists, governments issued warnings not to go to Bali, and as a result thousands cancelled their vacations.
	It will take several years for Bali to recover its image of a paradise island with green forests and unspoilt kilometres of white sandy beaches. Both the Indonesian government and the tour operators face a difficult task in restoring visitor confidence.

Table 2.4   *continued*

Issues	Comment
Local economy	Terrorist attacks such as those in the United States and Indonesia have a severe impact upon the local economy. As visitors seek alternative destinations B2C providers, such as hotels and restaurants, are affected by a dramatic downturn in revenue. In turn the B2B providers who supply them also see a downturn in demand. Indeed, they may be forced to review their cost and pricing strategies to maintain viable positions. The medium and long-term fallout from such terrorism is often greater than first contemplated.
New market development	Chapter 4, 'Buyer behaviour', refers to security issues in terms of influencing the purchasing of particular products or services. Political risks (including the threat of terrorism) create or further develop B2B and B2C markets. National agencies such as the police will purchase specialist anti-terrorist equipment to help protect citizens. Equally, the ordinary consumer may seek reassurance through the purchase of personal survival packs. To meet this demand stores opened in America to sell a range of products to ordinary civilians. These products ranged from biohazard suits (protection against chemical and biological warfare attacks) to anti-radiation pills. At the time of writing (April 2003) it is difficult to examine whether new destinations will replace, for example, Bali. There is a view that increasingly no destination can be deemed safe, and that terrorism can strike at any time in any place. This may remain the case, or hopefully the situation may change so that once more ordinary people can travel to a variety of locations to enjoy their splendours, whatever form they may take.

some of the business and marketing issues that result from acts of terrorism.

A potential anomaly – how powerful is business?

While we have emphasized the influence and impact of politics and governments, we must acknowledge that there are potential anomalies. As companies and individuals become increasingly powerful and wealthy within a global business environment, they too could influence political decision making. There are global corporations and individuals with sufficient financial resources to eliminate the debts of less developed nations (LDNs).

Table 2.5 illustrates the wealth comparisons between several global companies and poor nations. Although they are not like-for-like comparisons in that the method of statistical compilation is different, in the final analysis there remains a marked difference in wealth. As you can see from the table, these corpora-

tions individually generate significantly more wealth than the combined GDPs of several nations.

While there is no evidence that corporations or individuals exert an unethical influence or power over particular nations, this nonetheless poses an interesting academic debate for the 21st century. What is clear is that these global corporations and individuals will significantly increase their wealth and power bases over the coming decades. The question is whether this will pose a threat to democracy and the power of nations (not corporations) to determine their future. Some writers on globalization have (rightly or wrongly) expressed such fears.

Hertz's (2001a) basic thesis is that global corporations are slowly taking over the role of the state, that business people are becoming more powerful than politicians, and finally that commercial interests are paramount. However, some of these issues may have a positive value. For instance, Hertz (2001a)

Table 2.5   Comparison between company and country wealth generation

Company	Revenue (US $M)	Country	GDP (US $M)
Daimler Chrysler	159,985	Chad	1,546
Ford Motor Company	162,558	Nicaragua	2,110
Exxon Mobil	163,881	Namibia	3,211
Wal-Mart	166,809	Kenya	10,601
General Motors	176,558	Sri Lanka	15,661
		Uruguay	19,544
		New Zealand	52,684
		Chile	71,145
		Ireland	71,405
		Singapore	95,429
		Norway	146,430
Total value	829,791		489,766

Source: Adapted from Hertz (2001b).

describes the charity work of Microsoft co-founder Bill Gates. He has created a US $21 billion foundation to develop health and education in developing nations. This is significantly more than many wealthy and powerful Western nations have devoted to such vital work. Thus benefits can be derived.

However, it is clear from her research that free market capitalism has been disseminated internationally, if not globally. This is, in part, through the governments of Western nations (mainly the United States and the UK) advocating a free-market approach to business, where intervention from the state is minimal. This was very much the philosophy of both the Reagan and Thatcher governments. Indeed, the British Government under Thatcher undertook a massive sale of public assets to the private sector (including utilities, railways and defence facilities). Between 1979 and 1997 this raised some £67 billion for the UK Treasury. However, it placed these industries in private ownership (albeit, often via public limited companies and shares on the stock market) (Hertz, 2001b).

Hertz (2001b) considers the differing aspects of the relationship between corporations, government and consumers. It can be extrapolated that on the one hand corpora-tions can 'influence' government action. On the other consumers (vital to the survival of corporations) can in turn influence the actions of corporations. To quote Hertz (2001b):

In the US, the quid pro quo being exacted by George W's [Bush] corporate backers is becoming all too clear. Since being elected, the President has opened up the Arctic National Wildlife Refuge to oil drillers, retreated from his promises of protecting forests, made moves to weaken the requirements on mining companies to clean after themselves and in recent weeks both reversed a campaign pledge to regulate CO_2 emissions from power plants and trashed the Kyoto treaty on global warming. The interests of the US people suborned to those of the major US energy giants that bankrolled him: $47 million was all it cost.

In a world in which power increasingly lies in the hands of corporations rather than governments, the most effective way to be political is not to cast one's vote at the ballot box but to do so at the supermarket or at the shareholder's meeting.

Because, when provoked, corporations respond. While governments dithered about the health of GM foods, supermarkets [in the UK – our emphasis] faced with consumer unrest pulled the products off the shelves overnight. While nations spoke about ethical foreign policy, corporations pulled out of Burma rather than risk censure by customers.

George W. [Bush] may have backed down on his campaign pledges to limit CO_2 emissions, but BP, a corporation, continues to spearhead their reduction. And when stories broke over the world of children sewing footballs for Reebok for a pittance, what did governments do? Nothing. But the corporation, fearing a consumer boycott, stepped in with innovative plans for dealing with the child labour problem [See Chapter 4, 'Buyer behaviour'.]

Delivering a quality product at a reasonable cost is not all that is now demanded of corporations. The key to consumer satisfaction is not only how well a company treats its customers, but increasingly whether it is perceived as taking its responsibilities to society seriously. People are demanding that corporations deliver in a way that governments can't or won't.

Hertz's treatise suggests that corporations have succeeded governments as the real political force within the global economy. As we can see from the above quotes and the example of new philanthropy (the Bill Gates example), corporations can both be influenced by, and be beneficial to society. However, as Hertz (2001a) suggests, it is society and the people within that society who have to make judgments as to what is acceptable and what is not. But that in turn poses dilemmas in as much as both sides of the argument will defend their case through opinion formers – often the media. All groups therefore will use marketing communication strategies and tactics to convince society of the benefits of one action over another, for example the globalization versus anti-globalization perspective. This perhaps means that marketing (in the widest sense) has a greater role to play in the future development of societies as a whole.

Trade activities

In Chapter 14 on international marketing we consider the various forms of tariff and non-tariff barriers that governments can impose on foreign companies marketing within their country. However, it is important that we briefly consider a country's possible trade activities here, as it will illustrate another often political externality that can affect companies and their markets.

In early 2002 the US government announced tariffs on steel imports in order to protect the home-based industry from cheaper imports from Japan, Europe and Korea. It was partly seen as a means of stemming the flow of bankruptcies in the US steel industry (some 30 over a three-year period) and safeguarding jobs. In March of 2002 the US government imposed tariffs of up to 30 per cent on certain steel imported products. However, this resulted in threats from Japan of taking retaliatory action by imposing tariffs on US imports (BBC, 2002a).

What this exemplifies is that although there is a move towards global trade liberalization, countries will continue for the time being to use tariffs in one form or another to regulate imports. The difficulty for companies engaged in marketing across borders is that they become caught between governments and their trade policies.

Home trade union disputes – wider implications

A trade union dispute in one country can have far-reaching implications for companies within other countries. This can be exemplified by the 2002 US port dispute. The trade union and management of US West Coast ports began negotiations on a range of issues, from pensions to new technology and its impact upon employment. However, negotiations reached a stalemate and the employees were effectively locked out of the docks. This brought all port operations to a standstill (BBC, 2002b).

This lockout had a significant impact on Asian importers, among others. Car manufacturers in the United States who are reliant on parts and materials from Asia had to airfreight parts into the country. This is an expensive means of transportation for the car manufacturers, and thus adds to production costs. However, it provided valuable revenue for airlines such as China Airlines and Korean Air who increased the number of cargo flights into California (BBC, 2002b).

The lockout lasted 10 days until at the instruction of George W Bush the Federal courts ordered the reopening of the ports. It is estimated that the dispute cost the US economy in the region of US $1 billion to US $2 billion per day. Thus the United States lost in the region of US $10 to 12 billion in goods and services overall (BBC, 2002b).

This provides a good example of externalities that have both a negative and positive impact for certain sectors of the market. On the negative side there are the shipping lines and the car manufacturers, while on the positive side the air cargo carriers saw additional revenue generation, although only for the short term.

Economics

Both industries and individual companies are affected by a diverse range of economic measures or instruments. These may be defined by the economic conditions, globally or regional, and/or by the influence of a government or central bank. For example, as we shall see interest rates are an economic condition that affects both industry and customers. In some countries the decision to raise or lower interest rates is within the domain of government. For others, such as the UK, it is the role of the Bank of England, effectively acting as a central bank.

It is important to recognize that global economies are becoming increasingly interlinked. If there is a serve downturn in the economic fortunes of one region it may impact upon other regions on a global scale. An example of this is the economic meltdown of the Far East in early 1998. The political and economic crises in Indonesia, combined with the economic crises within Malaysia, South Korea and Japan, led to concern among many economists that there would be a global recession. As economies and stock markets fell, this scenario appeared to be a real possibility. However, the strength of the US economy reduced the risk of a recession within the United States and subsequently within Europe. This does not mean, however, that there has not been an impact upon the business environments of the United States and Europe. Indeed, many companies lost significant levels of orders, and saw retrenchment within Far East markets. However, it could have been much more drastic.

Table 2.6 details the various economic cycles that are a part of business life. However, the consequences of such economic 'events' can have far-reaching implications for both B2C and B2B customers.

Linked to economic cycles is the rate of inflation. Governments and central banks carefully watch inflation rates and will intervene in the market with fiscal policies to control the level of inflation. Table 2.7 illustrates the various levels of inflation and the economic risks (and marketing fallout) associated with them.

Inflation

This can be described as the continuing annual increase in the general level of prices, such that it costs more to purchase a typical bundle of products and services chosen by consumers. Of course, even when the general level of prices is stable, some prices will be rising. During periods of inflation, however, the impact of the rising prices will outweigh that of the falling prices (Gwartney and Stroup, 1987). Therefore when inflation increases, the purchasing power of the national currency tends to decline. In essence,

Table 2.6   Business or economic cycles

Economic event	Comment
Recovery	This is the point where the economy moves out of either a recession or a depression. It displays the first signs of growth. There is often a 'feel good' factor associated with recovery as the population and the government look forward to an improved economic future. Retail sales, often severely depressed under recessions and depressions, may begin to show the first signs (albeit slow) of an upward trend. Manufacturing output increases and the population begins to spend again. At first the consumer and business spend may be cautious as the passing recession or depression will still be relatively 'fresh' in people's memories.
Boom	This generally follows a period of recovery. The economy is now working at full capacity. Overall product and service demand are high, as are wages, while unemployment is low. However, there is always a risk of the economy overheating as consumers increase both their spending and debt levels. In such cases the central bank or government may attempt to regulate the economy by increasing interest rates.
Steady growth	This is probably the aim of most governments. The economy is growing steadily, manufacturing and service industries are successful and the population is both investing and purchasing. The government and/or central bank monitors growth rates and may take marginal actions through interest rates to either increase growth potential or reduce consumer spending if it believes that the economy will either slow or grow too rapidly (often called 'overheating').
Recession	This is a sharp and prolonged slowdown in the rate of growth of General Domestic Product (GDP). A recession can be associated with falling levels of investment, low manufacturing output, depressed business confidence, rising unemployment and an increasing number of business failures. With increasing levels of unemployment there is a reduction in the level of individual spending power. As a result competition increases as companies battle to hold on to market share. This may result in the strategy of price cutting to maintain price-sensitive customers. The critical point to consider is that all social classes, to a greater or lesser degree, are affected by economic recessions. However, recession can also provide marketing opportunities. During the global recession of the early 1980s, Levi Strauss, the world's largest apparel company, realized that US customers were moving away from the higher priced US $60 jeans. However, there was a significant upturn in business for Levi's Classic 501™ which retailed at the significantly lower price of US $25.
Stagnation	This is where the economy is for all intents and purposes stationary: it is neither growing nor declining. During the late 1990s the Japanese economy went through a period of stagnation. The Japanese government through various fiscal policies attempted to persuade the population to increase their personal expenditure in order to revitalize the retail and thus manufacturing sections of the economy.
Depression or slump	This is a severe or prolonged downturn in the economy. The outcomes of a recession are replicated; however the impact is both harsh and sustained. The depression following the Wall Street Crash of 1929 lasted some four years. It resulted in massive unemployment, poverty and countless company failures.

buyers receive less for the value of their individual pound, dollar, yen, euro, baht, rouble and so on.

When prices decline, or the rate of inflation is negative, there is a deflationary situation.

Economists generally tend to categorize inflation into five levels or states and these are defined in Table 2.7.

Gwartney and Stroup (1987) outline three key negative aspects to inflation. These are developed in Table 2.8.

Income levels

In Chapter 4, 'Buyer behaviour', we consider the role of income levels in relation to an individual's ability or desire to purchase a product or service. The ability to purchase is dependent upon several factors including an individual's earning potential (the level of his or her skill abilities), the accepted pay rate for the job he or she undertakes, the organization's ability to pay that rate and any government pay policy. For instance, a government may impose strict pay controls on public sector employees. This is usually for two key reasons. The first is the government's ability to deliver such pay scales, and the second is to prevent inflationary tendencies within the economy. Inflationary pressures have in the past been attributed to 'wage inflation' due to rapid increases in wages and salaries and their domino effect resulting in higher prices to meet the higher wage costs. This has created an inflationary spiral, resulting in an increase in interest rates to release the inflationary pressures.

An individual's ability to buy is obviously key to the pricing of products or services to meet certain demand. In many developed,

Table 2.7   Levels of inflation

Level of inflation	Comment
Zero	There is a view held amongst some economists that there can be a zero inflation state. In their view governments should devise fiscal policies to achieve such a zero state. Alternatively, other economists argue that zero inflation would lead to stagnation within the economy, that there must be some level of inflation in order for the economy to grow and thus prosper.
Normal or moderate	This may be considered as a low rate of between 2 and 3 per cent per annum. Here prices are rising relatively slowly.
Stratum or strata	This is where inflation reaches double figures. In addition to the initial pressure on the economy, there is a risk that inflation levels could rise even further, thus developing into hyperinflation.
Stagflation	This is a combination of rapid inflation and sluggish economic growth. The key for governments is to implement policies that reduce the rate of inflation while developing more efficient utilization of resources and increasing production.
Hyperinflation	This is a very rapid and sustained growth in the rate of inflation where money dramatically loses its value to the point where other mediums of exchange may be used. During the 1920s, Germany suffered from hyperinflation where the annual rate, at its highest, climbed to 1 billion per cent. In order to survive many people bartered goods for subsistence levels of food. During the 1970s several South American countries recorded inflation rates in the order of 700 per cent and 1,000 per cent.

Table 2.8   Overall negative impact of inflationary trends

Negative aspect	Comment
Price changes can affect long-term contracts	When long-term contracts are arranged, for example a family organizing a mortgage, it is impossible to predict the future rates of inflation. If the underlying rate of inflation increases dramatically it can change the results or outcomes of the contracts. As well as mortgages, life insurance and pension arrangements can be affected.
Price changes cause uncertainty	If individuals (whether buyers or sellers) are uncertain whether prices will increase, remain static or even decrease, they may be undecided on what to charge or pay for a product or service. This is especially so when there is a time dimension to the contract.
Scarce resources can be wasted	This states that decision makers will spend more *valuable* time trying to forecast prices rather than organizing production. In addition, speculative practices will be used to hedge against the future direction of prices. So funds may be invested in gold, silver and paintings rather than into productive investments, such as buildings, plant and technical developments. Such investments act to reduce the range of production capabilities and product improvements.

and increasingly in developing nations, the ability to pay is supported by the use of credit card facilities. At a time of low interest rates (for example, in the UK during the late 1990s and early 21st century) there is a greater tendency to use credit facilities, especially when the economy is displaying sustained growth and individuals are becoming more affluent.

Fiscal policies

Governments and/or central banks will attempt to 'manage' the economy through fiscal policies. These include raising revenues through various forms of taxation, and influencing levels of investment and expenditure via the interest rate mechanism. Below we consider the key elements of a country's fiscal policy.

Interest rates

Increases in interest rates are used by governments and central banks as a mechanism to reduce consumer spending, thus hopefully controlling the rate of inflation. If a government stipulates that it wants to keep the rate of inflation pegged at, say, 2 per cent, then it or the central bank will use increases in interest rates to stabilize the inflation rate. The increases are usually in the order of 0.25 per cent, although some countries, in order to control spiralling inflation rates, have doubled the rate of interest in one swift move.

While bringing inflation towards the government's stated targets, interest rate increases can have an effect on consumer spending. As consumers see an increase in their mortgages, bank loans and credit card payments, and thus a reduction in their levels of liquidity, there will be the tendency to reduce overall spending. This is precisely what the government seeks by increasing interest rates. By reducing the level of spending and borrowing, so inflationary pressures generated by an overheating of the economy are reduced.

However, in the process retailers and manufacturers face increased business pressures as they compete for the consumer's reduced spending power. If interest rates are not carefully managed by the government, the economy can stagnate, resulting in further reductions in consumer spending, with subsequent impact on manufacturing and retailing.

Taxation systems

Although taxation is an economic measure, its rates and limits are decided by the Treasury departments of governments. Taxation can generally be divided into two forms, direct and indirect. Direct taxation is the amount withdrawn from an individual's salary on either a monthly or annual basis. The rates of taxation vary from country to country, and can also be determined by the scale of salary or payment received.

Indirect taxation is a tax placed on certain products or services. For example, in the UK indirect taxes cover beer, wines, spirits and tobacco. Effectively, consumers have a choice whether to buy these products or not. If they purchase these products they pay the tax as part of the purchase price. For the Treasury, a one penny increase on the price of a packet of 20 cigarettes can accumulate several hundred million pounds in revenue over a 12-month period. That, of course, assumes an inelastic product: that is, the number of people buying the product before budget day will continue to buy the product after budget day once the price has increased. In other words, the product is not price sensitive. Needless to say a product does not remain price inelastic no matter how many increases take place. It stands to reason that there comes a point when consumers will stop or reduce expenditure on a particular product or service as it becomes increasingly expensive. Therefore treasuries have to finely balance increases in tax against expected losses in sales in order to ensure revenue generation.

How does taxation impact the consumer? In very general terms, if there is a decrease in the rate of direct taxation, there is the likelihood that consumers will have increased levels of liquidity, or spending power. The net result might be that they spend more in retail stores, and this could boost the economy. An increase in the rate of taxation may have the opposite effect.

Increases in the rate of indirect taxes could limit the number of purchases an individual makes of a particular product. For example, if an individual smokes 40 cigarettes per day, he or she might cut down to 30 or even 20 per day. This reduces his or her expenditure, and thus revenues to both the tobacco manufacturer and the Treasury. Alternatively, the individual concerned might continue smoking 40 cigarettes per day, and reduce his or her expenditure on other items.

Value of currency and exchange rates

Foreign exchange rates represent the price of a nation's currency in terms of the currencies of other nations. When a nation's exchange rate rises, its exports (both visible and invisible) become more expensive and therefore less competitive within regional or global markets. Imports, however, will become cheaper. As a result there is the risk that cheaper-priced imports will 'flood' the market to the detriment of home-produced goods. Equally, when a nation's exchange rate falls, import prices tend to rise, with the potential risk of increasing inflationary pressures.

The effects of exchange rates are clearly experienced when you travel abroad on holiday. When and where you change your currencies often determine the amount of currency you receive in exchange.

Of course countries operating within Europe's eurozone are trading in one currency. Thus, for example, a company that manufactures a product in Germany and sells it in France faces no exchange rate issues.

Devaluation of the currency

The financial crisis that struck beleaguered Russia in July/August 1998 is an example of how currency weakness and devaluation affect the buying power of the individual. The

devaluation of the rouble in August significantly increased the cost of products and
services for the average Russian family. This
affected the purchasing power of consumers,
thus impacting upon domestic as well as
foreign-imported goods.

The global economy

As Perrcault *et al* (2000) underscore, marketers
have often focused their attention purely on
their home economies. Since the mid-1990s
the world's economies have converged. Thus
there is greater interconnectivity between
economies. As a result severe economic fluctuations within one country or region will have
a domino effect upon other economies. The
economic meltdown of the Tiger economies
of South East Asia in the late 1990s affected
every other economy to a greater or lesser
extent. Economic change affects levels of
employment, individual prosperity (thus
spending power), national productivity and
competition.

The Internet is changing the face of global
economics and business. A company need no
longer be the other side of town, it will
increasingly be on the other side of the world
and selling its products via the Internet.

As economies converge and become linked,
so each country becomes dependent upon
others for global economic stability. Therefore
marketers need to be aware of the possible
outcomes of economic movements, not just
within their markets but in other markets as
well.

Societal and cultural factors

We can describe these as life styles, values,
norms and beliefs that individuals or groups
within a society possess. Cultural values vary
from country to country and region to region.
These will also impact upon such issues as
international marketing, which we discuss in
Chapter 14.

Cultural factors may also be governed by
religious beliefs, which themselves drive the
law making within a country. For instance,
the deep Islamic religious beliefs of many
Arabs drive the law making in Saudi Arabia
and elsewhere. This affects how people from
that society undertake business relations,
what types of products and services can be
marketed, and how they are marketed.

Our attitudes within society have changed
significantly, and they continue to change.
We must, as marketers, consider society as
'fluid'.

Here we outline some of the changing
patterns and roles within society. These
changes do not apply to every individual or
society. However, the comments provide us
with a general impression of how societies
change. As marketers we need to be sensitive
to these changes. We should consider these
factors not in isolation but, like many other
things in marketing, very much as integrated.

Demographics

Demographics is the study of the characteristics of society, and is vital in the understanding of how societies change and
develop, and what motivates people to
purchase products and services. As with so
many aspects of marketing, demographics are
evolutionary, in a state of flux. Generations
change, and thus it is important that
marketers understand (and can effectively
react to) the resulting changing trends.

Here are a few key factors that currently
influence marketers.

▌ Although often still portrayed as such in
television commercials, women have
generally moved away from the stereotype
of purely looking after the home and
children. More women work in a much
greater range of jobs and careers than they
did in the 1960s–90s. This will no doubt
increase. Many women are now on the
boards of major international companies;

indeed some lead the company or organization. Leading examples include Clara Furse (the London Stock Exchange: the first woman to be appointed to such a position in its 228 year history), Pamela Convor (President and Chief Operating Officer at Cunard shipping line), Carly Fiorina (Hewlett Packard), Victoria Barnsley (HarperCollins, UK), Marjorie Scardino (Pearson), Nicola Horlick (SG Asset Management) and Dame Stella Rimmington (Former Director General of MI5, the British Security Service, the first woman to hold such a position in any intelligence organization). While it can be argued that the 'glass ceiling' has not been shattered – that is to come – more women are now the decision makers. Equally, more women are increasingly involved in do it yourself (DIY). This is evident from not only purchases at DIY stores but also the plethora of DIY programmes on television hosted by, and including, women. This is no longer the sole province of men.

▌ An increasingly large proportion of men take greater responsibility around the home. They buy the food, do the cooking and look after the children. Men tend to share the responsibilities for home making. There are an increasing number of men within the United States and Europe who are the home makers. This is especially so where their partners have highly paid careers.

▌ Working couples who lead extremely busy lives demand quality convenience foods and other services. Research conducted in the UK in 2002 indicated that the convenience food sector had increased by 68 per cent from 2000 to 2002. On average the British work 44 hours per week, the highest hours in Europe, and this is a trend that is set to continue into the future. According to the research the growth areas within the UK (2002–07) as a result of busy working lives should be house purchasing 28 per cent, life assurance 50 per cent, accident and health cover 47 per cent, personal pensions 37 per cent, private medical insurance 32 per cent, health and fitness 59 per cent, fast food 30 per cent, dry cleaning and laundry 16 per cent and domestic and garden help 16 per cent (BBC, 2003a).

▌ Generally, within the developed nations there is increasing affluence. Many couples decide to remain childless so that they can continue pursuing a range of activities and lifestyles.

▌ Children now have a greater influence on family purchases than they did previously. These influences can range from the type of groceries to even a new car or a holiday. Advertisers have developed television commercials, especially in the United States and Europe, for car manufacturers that appeal to the whole family, rather than the principal driver alone.

▌ Within many countries there is increasing acceptance and respect for the gay and lesbian community. The 'pink' pound, dollar and euro have influence, power and style. In many areas, for instance the West Coast of the United States, this is an important opinion-forming group.

▌ Population dynamics are changing in many developed nations. As a result of medical technology, higher living standards, better nutrition and health care, people are living longer. The UK population, for instance, is now living longer than ever before. The average life expectancy in 1999 was 75 years for men and 78–80 years for women. This compared with 70 years for men and 76 years for women in 1979 (ONS, 2002). By 2014 it is expected that the proportion of the population over 65 years old in the UK will exceed that under 16 years old (ONS, 2002). Therefore companies need to consider how such a shift will affect their particular business enterprise.

▌ Not only are they living longer but they are becoming more adventurous. In many cases gone are the stereotypes of the elderly who while away their hours sitting in a chair. For many retirement is not the beginning of stagnation, it is a period of freedom. This is a trend that is most likely to continue.

▌ According to research conducted by IDG (in the UK), future retirees will have a greater demand for convenience than is evident in today's older generation. This links into the point made earlier regarding hectic lifestyles and the need for convenience products and services. As the Institute of Grocery Distribution suggests, this has significant implications for the future direction of the grocery market, for instance (IGD, 2002a).

▌ The average size of the UK household is becoming smaller. This may be for many reasons – increasing number of single people, people living together but with no children (both may work and believe in a no children lifestyle), smaller family units – but the outcome is that the norm is no longer the larger family with several children. As family units become smaller, there is a likely demand, for instance, for smaller pack sizes for grocery items (IGD, 2002b).

▌ Taking a cruise through the Mediterranean, the Aegean, or within the Caribbean used to be considered suitable only for the retired or the extremely rich. Not so any more. Since the 1980s there has been an increasing trend to cruise-ship vacations. The industry has reacted to this demand with a greater number of megaships that are able to carry over 3,000 passengers. The major cruise companies continue to place significant orders for new ships to cater for a range of segments within this expanding market.[1]

▌ There has been an increase in multiracial/ multicultural societies. Cities like London have a diverse range of ethnicity. This displays itself through a range of cultural experiences such as festivals and restaurants. It is clear that since the 1970s the British public has developed a wider appreciation for international cuisine, from African through to Thai. This is not only evident in the varied restaurants, but also in the range of international food products available in general (rather than specialist) supermarkets. The most popular takeaway meal in the UK used to be fish and chips; now it is curry. Further diversity can open up a greater range of possibilities of sharing cultural ideas.

Education and experiences

The mixture of improved education levels and experience has resulted in consumers seeking (indeed demanding) more information prior to purchase. Through this information they can question and seek out rival products to make comparisons. Today, consumers are not necessarily loyal to one product or service. They are prepared, for numerous reasons, to substitute one product for another. This substitution may be not on the grounds of price or packaging, but on the ethical and social responsibility stance of the company or organization concerned. In an earlier section we considered the work of Hertz and how companies react to consumers' concerns. An increasingly educated population will ask questions and seek answers, and will not be prepared to accept an inadequate response. The educated society of the future will be more investigative and questioning of products, services and organizations.

Attitudes

During the 1960s there was rarely public discussion about contraception. Society as a whole is not so reticent today, and condoms are advertised on television, in the cinema, on billboards/posters and in family magazines.

Dress codes have changed significantly within a more relaxed society. Within Victorian society, the middle classes as well as the wealthy would 'dress' for dinner. Not so today. Even within the 1970s it was considered *de rigueur* to wear evening dress – a long gown or black tie/dinner suit – when attending a classical concert at, for example, London's prestigious Royal Albert Hall. Except on very special occasions, formality has given way to a more casual dress sense. Maybe this move, along with education, has made classical music – a multi-billion-pound business in its own right – more accessible to a greater range of people.

Health concerns

There is an increasing interest in health and fitness. Since the 1980s there has been a burgeoning trend towards exercise and healthy eating. This has developed partially as a response to health scares concerning heart conditions, cancers and the possible risks of eating, or not eating, certain types of foods and vitamins/minerals.

Ethics and social responsibility issues

In Chapter 3 we consider the buyer's response to ethical and social responsibility issues. For example, in the 1980s there were international campaigns against the fur trade, and in the 1990s there were equally successful campaigns against testing on animals for the production of cosmetics. An increasingly educated society has questioned the ethical stance of various companies and organizations. Many companies have flourished as a result of their ethical and social responsibility issues. Others who, for one reason or another, have ignored such ethical calls have suffered financially.

The unethical actions of the (once) corporate giants Enron and WorldCom in 2001/2002 caused outrage amongst consumers who began challenging other companies and their accounting records. As a result, several companies issued public statements that they would review both their current accounts and their future accounting procedures.

Since the 1980s powerful groups have formed who use effective media communications to publicize unethical practices. The use of the media in this way has led to boycotts of products and services. In Chapter 3 we consider how the Benetton brand was damaged in the United States by an advertising campaign that many Americans felt was socially irresponsible and unacceptable.

Environmental issues

There is also increasing concern for the world's natural environment. No longer is the protection of the earth the domain of naturalists, geographers and a few so-called 'revolutionaries and eco warriors'. Today, there is a much greater awareness, especially via television and educated magazine articles, of the potential and actual damage that civilization has caused to this planet.

This increasing concern has expressed itself through the types of products that are purchased, and indeed boycotted. Additionally, the concern is a global one rather then purely what may happen within one's home country. Incidents such as the devastating nuclear disaster at Chernobyl in Northern Ukraine have illustrated graphically that environmental disasters are not confined to a country's borders.

Various companies have reacted to the move towards natural environmental issues. These include the UK-based retail companies the Body Shop, Boots the Chemist, Sainsbury's and Tesco.

Personal rights and freedoms

For example, shopping hours have radically changed to meet the needs of consumers. Within the UK the major supermarkets are open seven days per week. The larger stores may be open for 24 hours over Friday and Saturday. As Christmas approaches stores may remain open continuously for several days in the week before Christmas. While this also benefits the consumer, there are indeed substantial financial benefits for the retailer.

As we can see from this brief outline, societies have changed and adapted, and continue to change and adapt. Marketers need to consider not only today's societal issues, but tomorrow's. For instance, the demographics in Europe are dramatically changing. Should marketers focus on a shrinking youth market, or an expanding and relatively prosperous and active over-50s market? Of course, it partly depends on the product or service on offer. However, products can be tailored to meet market needs. It depends if the focus is on the market or not.

Technology (and science)

Medicine, food processing, communications, new materials/processes, computers and transportation are perhaps the key technological breakthroughs that have revolutionized our lives. Indeed, there is no end to the impact that technology has now, and will continue to have on our existence. Technology does not stand still, change is continuous, and as marketers we need to consider how technological development both impacts upon and supports our marketing objectives, now and in the future.

Here we consider some aspects of technology that have had profound effects upon society, and in turn created or influenced markets.

Medicine

Developments in medicine have radically altered society's view of longevity and quality of life. Life expectancy depends upon many factors: nutrition, disease control, environmental contaminants, war, stress and living standards. However, through developments in medicine the populations of developed and developing countries have a greater opportunity to live into their 80s and beyond. Disease prevention and early diagnoses of potentially life-threatening illnesses have significantly improved the quality of life for several generations.

In terms of medicine, there is the marketing by major pharmaceutical companies of new drugs, treatments and specialist equipment to doctors' surgeries/medical centres and hospitals. We also need to consider another area: as people grow into old age they have their own sets of needs and requirements. In order to significantly improve their quality of life in old age, retirees will seek activities complementary to their lifestyle. For example holidays can be aimed exclusively at people aged 55 and above, and designed to cater for their needs. In the UK the Saga Group has cut a very successful niche within the marketplace by providing a range of services to the 55 and over age groups.

Materials

The search for new materials is never-ending. During the 20th century a wide variety of new materials were discovered and later developed. For instance, synthetics such as nylon have a range of uses from stockings to parachutes. Equally, the development of new types of biodegradable lightweight plastics has benefited not only consumers but the environment as well.

Processes and new production techniques

Research and development units seek to develop not only new materials but also new ways to process and manufacture components. For instance, the development of unleaded petrol had significant benefits for both industry and society as a whole. The development of robotics has created not only the potential for efficiency gains in manufacture, but safer working environments. Once people spray-painted cars on production lines, with limited protection; not any more. Today, people control the computer systems that guide the robotic arms that spray-paint the cars in their myriad colours.

In 2000 at the Farnborough Air Show in England Airbus launched its A380 super-jumbo concept, a plane capable of carrying 500 passengers. With a delivery date of 2006 Airbus and its suppliers have to push the boundaries of technology. For example, the A380's wing will be significantly larger than on any other passenger aircraft. However, until recently it was impossible to fabricate one piece of metal of the right size, able to withstand the pressures and turbulence of flight, so a new production technique was devised by British Aerospace to link two sections together. It is not a weld in the conventional form: that would present a potential weakness in the wing and could lead to a catastrophic failure of the aircraft. Instead, the edges to two pieces of wing section are melted at a specific temperature so that their molecular structures fuse. So sophisticated and complex is this technology that it is deemed top secret, and the specifics remain classified. Clearly, it may have defence capabilities in the future. However, such technologies as will be developed for the A380 will have benefits not only within the aerospace industries but potentially for other products as well.

Companies will continue to develop, and then adapt, processes and production methods to initiate the development of new markets. Some of these markets will be niche-focused, others will have a much wider appeal. Just think of the microwave. The Raytheon Company developed a prototype microwave oven in 1946 in the United States. In 1967 it marketed the first domestic microwave oven. By 1976 over 60 per cent of

US homes had a microwave and they outsold conventional gas ovens. Today, microwaves are a feature of most US households.

Food processing, storage and packaging

Innovations in food processing, storage and packaging have had a significant impact upon our daily lives. In 1810 the French confectioner Nicolas Appert invented the preservation of pre-cooked food by canning, and in 1812 he had opened the world's first commercial preserved food factory. Since then there have been various modifications in the preservation and packaging of food-stuffs. Table 2.9 illustrates some of the inventions, and you may want to reflect upon how they both changed society and created new market opportunities for manufacturers and retailers. What are the opportunities for the future?

Communications

Printing and the printing press

In China, the art of printing using a single wooden block dates from AD 868. From the 10th century the Chinese used separate pieces of type so that each page could be printed from an arrangement of standard characters. Movable type (letterpress printing) was developed in Europe during the 15th century by Johannes Gutenberg (c 1400–1468) in Germany and William Caxton (c 1422–c 1491) in England. Caxton reputedly printed the first book in English (when he was in Cologne) and the first book in England.

There was no further substantial development until the 19th century. By then steam power had replaced the hand operation of printing presses. This made it possible for printers to undertake long print runs, thus achieving economies of scale. Additionally, hand composition of type (small metal letters taken from a box and placed individually to

Table 2.9 The development of innovations

Date	Development
1812	The British engineer and inventor Bryan Donkin improves on the work of Nicolas Appert by combining heat sterilization with sealed tins. He subsequently builds a factory to supply the Royal Navy with canned meat and vegetables.
1856	The US food technologist Gail Borden and the German-born Swiss Henri Nestlé independently develop condensed milk.
1858	The American Ezra Warner develops the can opener. Previously cans were opened by using a chisel. The can opener becomes one of the first labour-saving devices for the domestic kitchen.
1863	The French chemist Louis Pasteur discovers pasteurization. Consider the range of food products that are either wholly pasteurized or have pasteurized ingredients.
1863	US engineer William Davis develops refrigerated railway freight wagons for the transportation of perishable goods.
1906	French biophysicists Jacque d'Arsonval and Georges Bordas develop freeze-drying to preserve food.
1917	US food technologist Clarence Birdseye invents uncooked quick-frozen foods, the beginning of the Birds Eye Food Company.
1953	US scientist Robert Boyer patents edible synthetic protein made from soya beans.
1959	Ermal Fraze invents tab-opening (ring pull) aluminum cans (patented 1963).
1993	The US Calgene company create a genetically modified tomato, the beginning of genetically modified or GM foods. Since then a variety of GM products have been launched into the market. These foods are readily available in the United States. However, in Europe both legislators and consumers are reticent about such modified products.

create a line of text) was replaced by keyboard-operated machines.

Throughout the 19th and 20th centuries there was a range of technical introductions that aided the speed and quality of printing: Linotype, Monotype, offset printing and gravure. Since the 1960s and the development of phototypesetting, printing has been very much computer controlled. Now many publications are produced using computers to enter text, while desktop publishing packages allow images of text and pictures to be arranged on the screen. The combination of computer systems and sophisticated copying machines has provided some publishers with print on demand facilities. Rather than printing numerous copies of a book, and then waiting to sell them (with funds tied up in the stock), the publisher can print a limited number and then gauge demand. As demand increases it can print to meet that demand. For smaller publishers, this can be a more cost-effective means of operating.

Over the centuries, the introduction of new printing techniques has enabled the development of marketing communication techniques: for example, the creation of advertising and direct mail campaigns. The economies of scale now achieved make it highly cost-effective for companies to print large volumes of direct mail leaflets, which are distributed to targeted individuals within a determined catchment area (see Chapters 10 and 11).

The telephone

The Scots-born US inventor Alexander Graham Bell (1847–1922) developed and patented the analogue telephone in 1876. By

1879 telephone exchanges had opened in London, Liverpool and Manchester. Today we can dial direct, via national and global digital networks, to any country in the world. We can communicate via standard telephone, videophone, satellite phone, mobile phones, fax, voice mail, texting and e-mail. Communication is now a truly global 24-hour event.

Once the telephone became the mainstay of everyday communication, it became a marketing tool. Originally this was described as telesales, however now it is a combination of telemarketing (inbound and outbound) and mobile marketing. The development of the mobile phone not only increased the opportunities for telemarketing but also provide the opportunity to use texting as a means of marketing communication. With the introduction of picture messaging and video, companies will be able to link directly to current, as well as potential, customers. M-commerce, linked to wireless technologies, may provide significant opportunities for marketers in the future.

Television

On 2 November 1936 the BBC opened the world's first regular television service from studios and transmitters at Alexandra Palace in North London. These first tentative transmissions were in black and white and very limited in scope. Today, with digital technology and global links, the story is very different. We can watch world events unfold before our very eyes, whether it is civil war ravishing a country, the rescue of passengers from a stricken yacht, or astronauts attempting a dangerous manoeuvre of a billion dollar satellite from the cargo bay of the space shuttle thousands of miles above the earth.

As well as the potential diversity and immediacy, there is the opportunity through advertising to promote an ever-increasing range of products and services.

Computers and computerization

Since 1946 when the world's first general purpose, fully electronic digital computer, ENIAC (an acronym for electronic numerator, integrator, analyser and computer), was completed at the University of Pennsylvania, the role of the computer has impacted dramatically upon our lives. Today, it would be inconceivable not to have some daily contact with a computer of some sort or another. This can range from drawing cash from a bank's ATM, to buying groceries at a supermarket which uses a barcode reader to record the purchase price, to boarding a jet to a holiday destination. In one way or another computer technology will directly or indirectly affect our daily lives.

The development of the information superhighway, the Internet and e-mail has revolutionized how many companies do business. Business people and marketers now talk of e-commerce as a strategic element of their business. As we shall examine in later chapters, Web sites can be an effective promotional vehicle for both products and services. E-mail has made it significantly easier for both individuals and companies to communicate globally. Thus this has the potential to increase competitive pressures on companies.

Transportation

Since the 13th century ships and shipping have aided the development of international trade. The use of new technologies and materials has enabled companies to build faster, larger and more specialist ships to transport a range of products internationally, and now globally. The introduction of the first steel freight containers in the 1950s revolutionized cargo handling, making it more cost-effective and time-efficient.

The first passenger flight (London to Johannesburg) using a jet aircraft was made in 1952 by a de Havilland DH106 Comet. However the Comet had a chequered history, and so the first great success of the passenger jet age was the four-engined Boeing 707, introduced in 1958.

The 707 intercontinental version flew at over 950 kph with an average range of 7,000 km. This revolutionized air transport in terms of both passenger and cargo movements. The 707, which had been the workhorse of many airlines, was superseded by the wide-bodied 747 which made its first commercial flight in 1970.

As a result of the development of long-haul, wide-bodied and more fuel-efficient aircraft, companies were able to move an increasingly wider range of products. Add to this improvements and developments in specialist technologies, and that range has increased still further. For example, the global freight forwarder Emery Worldwide has harnessed technology that allows it to provide customers with a 'Priority Fresh' service for perishable goods. Under its Perishable Goods Specialty Marketing Group, more than 3 million pounds of seasonal raspberries, blueberries and blackberries from South America are delivered fresh throughout the United States within 48 hours of orders, hermetically sealed in styrofoam and aluminum e-containers each weighing over 200 pounds (Emery Worldwide, 1995).

In another example Emery Worldwide provides services for the US Red Lobster chain of restaurants. Known as 'pier to plate', Emery collects fresh fish and seafood from Red Lobster's wholesalers at five US inland and coastal ports, and delivers overnight to the US $1.5 billion restaurant chain's 600 locations in North America. The programme handles 22 different species of fresh fish, as well as imported frozen fish and seafood. Red Lobster sells freshness as a marketing advantage – from pier to customer in less than 36 hours (Emery Worldwide, 1995).

Stanton, Etzel and Walker (1994) believe that technological breakthroughs happen in three significant ways:

▌ Start entirely new industries, as computers, robotics, mobile (wireless) communication facilities have done.

▌ Radically alter, or virtually destroy, existing industries. A good example of this is the introduction of television in the United States. When television developed in the 1950s, the various film studios witnessed declining audiences for their movies. In an attempt to win back audiences they marketed a range of technical innovations which ranged from the outright gimmicky, such as 3D images, to the more impressive techniques of stereo sound, improved colour stock, wide-screen processes (including CinemaScope™, VistaVision™ and later Panavision™), and the development of thrilling visual effects. The cinematic result of these could not be duplicated on small monochrome home television screens. Needless to say some of the smaller studios, who could not afford the development of such technical standards, eventually did lose out to television. In addition, some of the studios saw the opportunities of television and began making movies and serials for the television market. Warner Bros is an example of a studio who actively sought out this new distribution channel for their product. Today many of the movie studios own (directly or through parent companies) television networks or television production companies (for example, News Corporation–20th Century Fox movie studios and 20th Century Fox News Channel). Equally, they are actively involved in video and DVD distribution (Universal Studios).

▌ Stimulate markets and industries not related to the new technology. Various examples within the home environment can be provided. The first is new easy-to-use home appliances, such as the microwave cooker, dishwasher and highly improved washing machines. Second is the increasing availability of frozen foods and high-quality pre-prepared microwave meals. These factors have provided some householders with additional free time which can be used for other activities.

The environment/ecology

Surprisingly this is not normally included as an external factor. However, the natural environment has a potential marketing impact in several ways. Table 2.10 illustrates the impact natural disasters have on regions and nations.

Legal frameworks

Legal frameworks are usually, although not exclusively, driven by political decisions. Thus it is important to link legal frameworks with the political environment on a local, national and regional level. The following is an expansion of the categories outlined by Stanton *et al* (1994).

Fiscal policies

As stated earlier, taxation systems and interest rates affect the level of disposable income

Table 2.10 The relationship between events and the natural environment

Event	Comment
Climatic	Extreme weather conditions severely impact on societies and organizations. These can manifest themselves in the form of heavy rain storms, hurricanes and cyclones. In early 2002 heavy rain storms over Europe led to severe flooding in Germany and the Czech Republic. This led to billions of euros in damage and lost revenue as business and industrial operations and society were disrupted. In October 1998 a hurricane swept across Central America. Over 12,000 people were reported dead and some 6.5 million affected by the storm. While some markets will be disrupted (even destroyed), others will prosper: for example, companies who supply medical and rescue equipment and building contractors involved in reconstruction of damaged areas. If the earth is suffering from global warming, as suggested by several climatologists, changing weather patterns will change agricultural patterns, favouring the higher latitudes. However, we will not know, of course, what the impact of technology will be. Will weather be a determining factor in agriculture in the future? Will there be genetically modified products that can be grown under a variety of conditions? What will be the consumer demand for these products? How will they be marketed?
Geological	This includes everything from minor tremors and landslides to major earthquakes and volcanic eruptions. Various parts of the world are prone to deep and extreme underground movements that result in earthquakes. Currently there is no way we can either prevent or reduce these earth movements. Therefore we need to respond to these external forces by using materials and techniques that hopefully reduce their impact. As a direct result of the external forces, new building techniques and materials are developed and marketed. In addition, special services are promoted to the governments of countries that are especially prone to the more violent earthquakes. These services include potential life-saving lifting equipment, medical supplies and specially trained rescue teams. The human tragedy when a devastating earthquake strikes can be untold. In addition to the direct human cost virtually everything can be lost: homes, offices, factories, farms, shops, distributors, wholesalers, schools, libraries, churches, leisure centres and hotels. For those left behind there is the agony of rebuilding every fabric of their lives. If farms and industry are affected there could be impact beyond the immediate area. For example, if the industry was producing components for overseas companies, its reduced output could affect the availability of the finished product, and possibly the price.

Table 2.10   *continued*

Event	Comment
Human influence or impact	The focus here is on the human influence upon the natural environment and how, in turn, that can have an external impact on other industries, societies and markets. During the 20th century there were numerous examples of devastating environmental incidents. For example, the US tanker *Exxon Valdez* ran aground on Bligh Reef in Prince William Sound in Alaska. Over 10 million gallons of oil were released into the water. At the point of impact and subsequently local marine and wildlife were destroyed, despite valiant rescue attempts. Apart from the loss of a beautifully diverse natural wilderness, the local fishing industry was destroyed. Generations of families lost their heritage and their livelihood. However, the impact was not just upon the fishing families: all the communities within Prince William Sound suffered. It will take years for these communities to recover, if they ever do.
Disease	The spread of both human and animal diseases can have a devastating impact upon individual societies and trade between societies. For example, bovine spongiform encephalopathy (BSE), an incurable brain disease in cattle, was first identified in the UK in 1986. This disease quickly spread throughout UK herds and resulted in thousands of cattle being culled and their carcasses being burnt to destroy the infection. Links were made between BSE and a human form, Creutzfeldt–Jakob disease (CJD). As a result, the British Government reappraised what parts of cattle could be consumed, by both humans and animals. Concern among health officials in various countries led to bans on the importation and sale of British beef. Several UK fast-food outlets sought supplies of beef from Ireland and other European countries rather than use British beef. The British beef industry was devastated as a result of the spread of the infection. It will take several years for it to regain its market share.
	In March 2003 there was an outbreak of SARS (severe acute respiratory syndrome). By mid-April 2003 this flu-like virus, which can be spread by travellers, had killed over 200 people and infected some 4,000 worldwide (BBC, 2003b). Whilst this was not (at the time of writing, April 2003) considered in any way to be a pandemic, concerned individuals cancelled trips to the Far East (China was considered the original source of the outbreak). This in turn had an early impact upon the airlines already struggling with falling revenues, massive debts and travellers' fears of increased terrorism.
Pests	Pests can devastate crops, often in vulnerable regions of the world. Farmers have used both organic and inorganic means to reduce the impact of these pests. However, inorganic measures such as the use of pesticides and insecticides can create their own ecological problems if overused, for example, polluted rivers that in turn affect the local population and wildlife. Chemical companies are continually seeking improved formulas that will have reduced environmental effects while also reducing pest damage.

available. These are usually controlled by the Treasury departments within government.

Social legislation

Governments may impose legislation that regulates the use of certain raw materials or finished products. For example, the concern over pollution levels and global warming has led several governments to decrease the level of permitted emissions from factories, products and vehicles.

Chlorofluorocarbon (CFC), a synthetic chemical, was used as a propellant in aerosol cans, as a refrigerant in refrigerators and air conditioners, and in the manufacture of foam boxes for takeaway food cartons. Scientific research indicated that when released into the atmosphere CFCs break down into chlorine atoms under the influence of ultraviolet radiation from the sun. These in turn destroy the ozone layer, allowing harmful radiation to reach the Earth's surface. On this scientific advice, on 1 June 1990 93 nations agreed to phase out the production of CFC. Refrigerators and freezers made after 2000 contain no CFCs in their insulation foam. While such action is clearly beneficial to the environment in terms of preventing ozone damage, as the marketing insight box indicates, such legislation can cause other problems.

Consumer legislation

Governments may seek legislation to protect consumers from a variety of unfair business practices. This legislation varies from country to country, although there is some harmonization within the EU. The legislation usually covers health and safety (including, for instance, food ingredients and the testing of pharmaceuticals), misleading advertising (and associated promotions such as door-to-door selling), the labelling of products (especially in relation to toxic substances such as solvents and garden pesticides) and consumer credit (the clarity of documentation so that consumers are not misled and are clearly aware of the interest/repayment costs/liabilities). Perhaps over-arching this legislation is a general EU intention to extend consumer choice. The objective is that products legally manufactured within one member state should be allowed into all member states. Thus EU consumers have a choice of products on offer. (See Chapter 4 and the section on consumerism.)

Government relationships with industry

Governments may bring in legislation that affects the regulation of certain industries. For example, there is extensive legislation in the UK that regulates financial institutions. These regulations dictate how companies can market financial products such as insurance policies and pension plans. The laws are devised to create fair business practices, and protect the consumer from mis-selling.

Governments may seek an element of fair competition within the marketplace. In Europe both national and regional governments have sought legal frameworks to curb

---

Marketing insight: stockpiling of UK refrigerators

In January 2002 the European Union (EU) introduced a new law that prevents the export of used refrigerators and freezers outside the EU without their first being stripped of harmful chemicals. Previously some 2 million refrigerators a year had been exported for reuse, but the removal of the insulation foam (which contains the CFCs) renders the refrigerators useless, so as a result of the new legislation they had to be disposed of within the EU. The 3.5 million refrigerators that are discarded within the UK each year further exacerbate the problem, and soon stockpiles grew of used refrigerators that could not be disposed of. The end result is a backlog of slowly rusting refrigerators that pose their own environmental problems (Cooper, 2002).

These laws will ultimately place a financial burden on industries as they strive to meet the demands of the regulators. There could also be a resultant cost borne by the consumer in the longer term.

anti-competitive actions by companies. This includes the creation of monopolies through the acquisition of one company by another. Governments may see this as detrimental to both the development of business within an industry sector, and consumer choice.

Governments may seek to impose tariff barriers by law. As will be discussed later, countries use tariff barriers to protect indigenous companies from external competition. Equally, they may decide to subsidize industries to meet the competitive challenges from foreign or multinational corporations.

Government relations with other nations

Marketers can often be at the political whims of governments. Political disputes, whether minor or major, can lead to legislation that reduces or prevents the marketing of products/services. This is discussed in detail in Chapter 14, 'International perspectives', but it is important to signpost some issues here.

The geopolitical map of the world illustrates the tensions between nations. The classic example is Cuba. In 1960 the United States broke off diplomatic relations after all US businesses in Cuba were nationalized without compensation. Since then it has been illegal for US companies to undertake business relationships with Cuba. However, in the late 1990s relations appeared to improve, at least on the surface. The UK does have diplomatic and business agreements with the Cuban government, and holidays in Cuba are actively marketed by travel companies in the UK.

National versus local legislation

It is important to stress that while there may be national laws, these may be modified, or indeed, reversed by local legislators. Here are a few historical and current examples.

In 1979 the Monty Python film *The Life of Brian* received a British Board of Film Classification certificate: in essence a legal permission for the film to be screened throughout the UK. However, some local authorities took exception to the tone of the movie and banned it from local cinemas. As a result local cinemas lost out financially as cinemagoers literally travelled to the next county to see the movie.

From the 1980s to the 1990s the pressure to provide consumers with information often created tension between the European Parliament (EU) and the national governments of member states. The confusion over British beef in late 1999 highlights the problem. While the European Parliament stated that British beef was safe and lifted the ban on imports to the EU, France and Germany stood fast in maintaining a ban. The governments of both Germany and France stated that their scientific advice suggested there was still a threat from CJD, the human form of BSE.

Product legislation

Various countries have introduced safety codes for a range of products. In the UK there is the British Standards Institute (BSI), which is government funded but independent. Its role is to interpret international technical standards for the UK and set its own standards. For consumer goods it sets standards to which products should conform (BS Standards), as well as testing products to see that they do conform to the appropriate standard.

Marketing legislation

There is also legislation that specially relates to marketing and marketing activities. Table 2.11 outlines some of the key features of this type of legislation and how it impacts on both customer and the organization.

Marketing insight: labelling in Russian

In May 1997, the Russian government introduced a law requiring all imported food products to be labelled in Russian. Laydia Tarashkova of the Russian State Sanitary Supervision Committee commented, 'There were many incidents where people got sick because they ate bad food or food which was outdated.' The government resolution required all foreign food products coming into the country to feature Russian-language labels or packaging for nutritional information, manufacturing date and ingredients.

Timothy Lamb, General Director of Heinz, stated that he welcomed the law, pointing out that products labelled in Russian sold better than those in foreign languages. However, three years earlier Russian consumers had preferred foreign-labelled products because they were synonymous with quality. By January 1997 Heinz was marketing some 130 products in Russia, from ketchup to Uncle Ben's sauces to baby food (Wendlandt, 1997).

Table 2.11   Areas for key marketing legislation

Marketing legislation	Comment
Advertising or promotion	This is the implementation of advertising standards, in essence what images/words can and cannot be depicted within the media. In the UK advertising must be deemed truthful, legal and decent. In the UK complaints from the public are investigated by the Advertising Standards Association. If the complaints are upheld, the organization or company responsible for the advertisement is requested to either withdraw it from circulation or modify it to not cause offence.
Selling practices	In many countries salespeople are bound by strict legal controls. These regulate the type and range of information they can communicate to customers. This covers both written information and face-to-face discussions. Additionally there has been a move, especially in the UK, for agreements to be stated in clear concise terms in order to remove ambiguity that may confuse the consumer. Individuals or organizations who deliberately seek to mislead customers can face prosecution, resulting in heavy fines and/or imprisonment. There can also be immense reputational damage to the organization concerned.
Pricing	In some countries there are active measures to make sure companies are engaged in fair price competition. These measures may include restriction on cartels (an agreement among national or international companies to set mutually acceptable prices for their products). A cartel may restrict supply or output, or raise prices to increase the profits of the member organizations. Many governments believe that this form of oligopoly does not benefit the consumer.
Pricing: data protection and freedom of information	There is an increasing move by governments to, first, protect the privacy of the individual (for example, through the registration of databases by the users), and second, provide individuals with access to publicly held information (this may or may not be personal information). The United States has for years operated a Freedom of Information Act. The UK's Freedom of Information Act (2000) will be fully enforced by 2005.

Analysing the environment

Marketing teams must continually analyse and forecast the potential 'turbulence' that may occur in both the micro and macro environments. From such analysis companies may be able to develop viable strategies and tactics to ensure a sustainable competitive advantage. Table 2.12 outlines some of the issues marketing teams will need to consider. This is an area we revisit in Chapter 7 when we consider marketing and strategy in greater depth.

Chapter summary

In this chapter we have considered the micro and macro environments and their relationship to the organization. It is clear from this introductory review that companies and organizations must continually analyse and appraise the activities within these environments. Recent history has demonstrated how volatile and turbulent these environments can be, so in order for companies to sustain any form of competitive advantage they must be vigilant.

Table 2.12   Analysing the environment

Areas for analysis	Comment
Competitors	What new products have they launched? What products have they modified? What products have they repackaged? What brands have they extended? What new markets have they penetrated? What prices do they charge across the brand range? What promotions are they using and where? Have they retrenched from any markets? What is their market share by product/brand/region? Has there been a change of management, and if so what impact has it made? Where are their products within the product life cycle?
Government	Is the government considering new legislation that could affect the company or organization? The legislation may relate to employment conditions and controls, product safety, corporation taxation, export trade and tariff controls.
Employment	Is there a sufficient supply of skilled labour within the locations the company operates in? Should the company source its products from another country? Should it engage in foreign direct investment (FDI)?
Economics	The economic situation, nationally, regionally and globally. Can the changing economic situations in another part of the world impact on the organization? An example of this is the changing fortunes of the Far East economies in early 1998, and how they have impacted on international businesses in other regions.
Business and industry trends	What are the developing business and industry trends? How will they impact on the organization in the short, medium and longer term? Companies that fail to watch and interpret trends may discover that they are operating within a rapidly decreasing market. Those companies that are able to spot changing trends may be able to diversify their business and/or product ranges and thus maintain a viable business. For example, companies that manufactured horse-drawn carriages and were not able, or willing, to become suppliers to the automotive industry saw their businesses evaporate as the motor car replaced horse-drawn carriages.
Societal trends	A company must also respond to fundamental changes in society. Over time people's tastes change, their discretionary purchasing power rises, falls and rises again, luxuries can become necessities and previously popular goods and services can become unfashionable.

Areas that were once described as 'controllable' can no longer be thought of in such a rigid mindset. Equally, corporations have gained significant power over the past 20 years or so. In many ways they have subsumed the responsibilities of local and national governments. While this can be used for the good of society it can also be used to influence governments to take actions that may, in the longer term, be detrimental to certain sectors of the population and the natural environment. However, it is also clear that the power of the individual consumer is also growing, and that can in turn have an influence on companies and organizations, and also on governments.

It would be naïve for any marketing team or organization to believe that what has gone before in terms of marketing activity will be applicable in the future. The micro and macro environmental landscapes will be in a constant state of flux, and thus organizations must find methods and techniques for the continual monitoring and analysis of possible future trends. Otherwise they will face possible extinction.

Exercises and questions for review and critical thinking

1. Critically examine how the political environment can impact on the consumer's ability to purchase a product imported from another country.

2. Select an industry and examine how changes in technology have affected that industry and the customers' perception of its products or services.

3. By using the Internet, and other library resources, research the regulations that affect the marketing of products and services within your local or regional area. Do you believe that they are necessary, relevant and effective? Justify your statements.

4. There has been significant media coverage on the convergence of the world's economies to form what has been called a 'global economy'. Choose two companies, one local to you and one multinational. Examine how this global economy affects the operations of both companies. Do you see differences and similarities in the two operations?

5. Several writers suggest that there have been significant societal changes over the past 20 or so years. What have been these changes and how have they affected both businesses and industries? From your reading around the subject, what future societal changes do you think will take place, and why?

6. Critically evaluate how terrorism has affected both business and marketing operations.

7. 'Companies that take an ethical and socially responsible stance will gain a sustained competitive advantage over companies that do not take such a stance.' Evaluate this statement. You may want to research additional information from your university library and the Internet to fully appraise this issue.

8. Many textbooks have suggested that micro environmental factors are controllable whilst macro environmental factors are uncontrollable. What is your opinion of this perspective and why?

9. Using your national government as an example, examine how its current fiscal policies influence the consumer's purchasing of products and services.

10. What do you consider to be the key environmental issues for the future and why?

3

Ethical marketing and social responsibility

Introduction

Incorporating virtues of truth, trust and justice is not only the best strategy to run a company, but the cheapest. It's the only way forward for businesses of the future. The conscious 90s consumer won't stand for greedy executives from the 80s. The public is tired of hearing about scandals...

(Handy, 1995)

Although Charles Handy wrote this quote in 1995, ethical scandals continue to blight business and industries worldwide. The Enron and WorldCom scandals of 2002 were two extremely high profile and disturbing cases. However, they were not the only ones – just the biggest financially, at least till now!

According to surveys in the 1990s, only 2 per cent of UK consumers had faith in the senior management of companies, while some 75 per cent of American consumers would actively boycott certain products because of serious ethical concerns (Handy, 1995). Unfortunately there are numerous examples of poor judgment, or complete lack of an ethical stance, peppered throughout the history of civilization.

The problem for today, and tomorrow, is that ethical dilemmas and conflicts of interest are growing in both complexity and frequency. Therefore marketers, at all levels, need to be cognizant of the potential issues facing both them and their organizations. This chapter focuses upon some of the key ethical issues that marketing teams have faced, and continue to face today.

Learning objectives

On the completion of this chapter you should be able to:

▌ outline the potential ethical implications of a marketing activity;

▌ demonstrate an understanding of consumers' perception of social responsibility and how this perception may impact on future marketing decisions;

▌ debate the potential impact consumer boycotts can have on the financial stability of a business;

- debate the potential consequences of voluntary and legislative measures to curb unethical marketing activities;

- demonstrate an understanding of codes of conduct used within the marketing environment;

- link the views/issues raised within this chapter (for example branding, international environments and marketing communications) and augment them with other chapters.

How we define ethics

The idea of ethics has received many different interpretations over the centuries. The Greek philosopher Aristotle (384–322 BC) talked about living the good life, while the English philosopher and economist John Stuart Mill (1806–1873) talked instead of the rightness and wrongness of individual actions. Definitions of this kind conceal far-reaching perspectives on what ethics is really about, which often leads to conflicting recommendations for managers. This issue is further complicated by the ambiguity in the term 'ethics' when applied to business. At times it can be taken to refer to the morals of the business, and at other times it may refer more narrowly to professional codes of conduct (Griseri and Groucutt, 1997).

Griseri and Groucutt (1997) suggest that ethics within the business context can be interpreted as 'the study and practice, within organizations, of the moral aspects of corporate and individual behaviour, the justifications of these, and the methods organizations use to secure and maintain morally sound behaviour'. It can be questioned whether business and ethics can go together at all. However, there are numerous examples of good ethical practice. The idea that business is intrinsically unethical ignores two key aspects: first, consumer reactions to morally unethical behaviour, and second, the individual behaviour of those who run businesses.

If consumers considered business to be incompatible with moral values, every outrageous action within an organizational context would be explained as 'just business'. 'Business is business' would justify all and any actions. But instinctively most consumers recognize that it does not. The very fact that people disapprove indicates that consumers feel that 'business is not just business'. Moral values are relevant: they apply to business just as much as to personal behaviour.

Equally, the original statement assumes that the very people who run businesses are intrinsically unethical. This is clearly not the case: there may be degrees of ethical commitment, but to imply that everyone in business is just 'out for the fast buck at the expense of all others' is quite wrong.

Generally in the ancient world it was felt that there was a link between business and ethics; the Roman poet and satirist Horace (Quintus Horatius Flaccus, 65–8 BC), somewhat ambiguously advised people to make money 'by right means if possible'. The satirist Juvenal (Decimus Junius Juvenalis, c 55–c 130) bemoaned that 'In Rome, all things can be had at a price', stating indirectly that perhaps everyone can be 'bought' – thus behave unethically, and possibly illegally too. Again, this has been reflected in contemporary business life.

In medieval Britain, although many feudal practices were barbaric and cruel, there was still a direct recognition of moral elements in trading practice. Tradespeople who sold short measure (less than was promised to the customer), for example, could often expect a time in the stocks as punishment – to be pelted with rotting fruit and vegetables by irate customers. While this was unlikely to be physically very painful, the level of embarrassment was perhaps much greater.

The first major attempt to separate organizational activity and ethics was made by the Italian writer Niccolo Macchiavelli

(1469–1527), who claimed that rulers of states should not be trammelled by moral values. Perhaps more pertinent to company practices were the views of the Scottish economist and philosopher Adam Smith (1723–1790) who argued that trade is not carried on for benevolent reasons: butchers do not sell meat because they have a concern for the customer's diet, but because they want to make a profit (Smith, 1776).[1] By realizing that they serve their own best interest by taking their business elsewhere, consumers impose their own punishment on unfair and unjust practitioners. This forms the basis of contemporary approaches to marketing theory: the consumers' right to choose from whom they buy.

Marketing ethics can therefore be described as the principles, values and standards of conduct considered appropriate for marketers (Churchill and Peter, 1998). However, as Churchill and Peter illustrate, marketers often struggle to find solutions to (often complex) ethical problems, for the difficulty they face is that ethical standards vary from one person to another, from one region to another, and from one culture to another. What are considered acceptable practices in one country (small-scale bribes, for instance, to get the mail delivered) are considered both illegal and unethical in another (see comments on the US Foreign Corrupt Practices Act later in this chapter). Then, of course, there are the internal corporate culture issues and pressures, along with the ensuing financial pressures. The collapse of the energy giant Enron is a classic case where the company and its employees perceived themselves 'untouchable' by the realities that affected other companies. The company seemed 'awash with cash' where deals 'brokered on the edge' could reap fortunes for the players involved. Who could lose from such deal making? Well, those who invested in the marketing hype could. They lost everything.

The risks of unethical behaviour are compounded as business becomes more dynamic and global. A Harris Poll conducted for *Business Week* magazine reflected the public's perception of companies at the end of the 'boom or bust' period of the 1980s (Laczniak and Murphy, 1991). Those interviewed were asked, 'If you had to say, which of the following things do you think business would do in order to obtain greater profits?' The results were:

Deliberately charge inflated prices	62%
Harm the environment	47%
Knowingly sell inferior products	44%
Put its workers' health at risk	42%
Endanger public health	38%
Sell unsafe products	37%
None	8%
Not sure	4%
(Sample: 1,247)	

Compare this survey (in very general terms) with those highlighted in the introduction to this chapter. We could argue that perhaps very little has changed. However, that would be unfair. There have been numerous transformational steps taken since the boom and bust periods of the 1980s. For example, companies have signed up to ethical charters and there is greater transparency in accounting and marketing practices. Additionally, the consumer has gained a very active voice (as we will see later in this chapter). Today and tomorrow, companies and indeed governments that behave unethically will face the wrath of the ordinary citizen. However, it would be naïve to think that all companies, organizations and indeed governments will suddenly change their colours overnight. You just have to look at such companies as Enron and WorldCom to realize that will not happen.

Boycotts: the power of the consumer

Consumers do have a personal power that they can exact, if they so wish, on organizations they perceive as unethical or socially irresponsible. They can boycott the products and services marketed by that organization. A boycott can be described as an organized activity in which consumers avoid purchasing products or services from a company whose policies or practices are seen to be unfair or unjust (Hoyer and MacInnes, 1997). However, it goes beyond just an individual deciding not to purchase a particular product or service. As we will see from the 'Marketing insight' on Benetton (page 74), individuals can galvanize action via word of mouth or (perceived as) negative viral marketing (see Chapter 11).

The term 'boycott' emanates from the name of Charles Cunningham Boycott (1832–1897). He was a British army captain and the estate manager for Lord Erne in County Mayo in Ireland. When poor harvests struck in 1879, making famine likely, the Irish politician Charles Parnell (1846–1891), President of the Irish National Land League, requested that Boycott and Lord Erne lower rents in order to ease the tenants' burden. Instead Boycott attempted to evict tenants who could not pay their rents. Parnell then urged the tenants to avoid any form of contact or communication with Boycott. Thus his name became the source of the verb 'to boycott'. It is, however, most likely that forms of 'boycott' took place prior to the latter half of the 19th century.

In the 1990s environmental groups highlighted the plight of dolphins that were caught in long drift nets set to catch tuna. These enormous drift nets caught not only tuna, but dolphins, turtles and other marine creatures who subsequently drowned. Consumers boycotted tinned tuna, which in turn affected sales. Eventually the result was a change of policy. Now tuna is caught with rod and line, or special nets to protect dolphins and other marine wildlife. Here is one example where direct boycott action had a desired effect. Companies realized a policy change was vital for the survivability of the product, if not the business, even if they only considered it from a profit perspective. Let's not forget that the boycott could have spread to other products made by the same companies. That would have had a much more devastating effect on revenue generation, and most likely profits.

In a 1999 MORI (www.mori.co.uk) survey, some 28 per cent of the British population (10 million) stated that they had either boycotted a company's product on ethical grounds, or chosen a product or service from a company because of its ethical reputation (Worcester, 1999). That is just in the UK! However, companies involved in export may be faced with the same reaction in many European countries, and to a large extent in the United States where product boycotts are on the increase.

Are boycotts successful?

Of course it depends on whom you ask. Companies may not want to state that a boycott against their products or services was successful. Those participating in the boycott will want to support their corner and clearly state that they are 'having an effect'. Independent verification may not always be possible. However, we can assume that some (for instance, the boycott in the tuna fish/dolphin debate outlined earlier) are successful. Again, we will see this with Benetton in the United States later in this chapter. Equally, some boycotts for a variety of reasons will not be successful. Additionally, we cannot assume that because a company or organization is being boycotted by one group of people, everyone is boycotting them, or indeed the boycott is justified in the first place.

However, as we illustrate later there are numerous areas that give rise to potential ethical concerns. Obviously not all individuals and companies are ethical in their behaviour. You only have to view the individuals and companies who have been found guilty of breaching legal statutes, to realize that the

Marketing insight: United Students Against Sweatshops

The American Collegiate licensed merchandise business is estimated to be worth US $2.5 billion. An increasingly large proportion of this merchandise was being produced outside North America, and thus under different working conditions. In 1998 a group of students, concerned over workers' rights and conditions within these countries, started a protest movement. Within a year United Students Against Sweatshops (USAS) had been formed, and published a Worker Rights Consortium which demanded better wages for workers, independent human rights verification, and the public disclosure of factories that produced university clothing and footwear.

This created one of the biggest waves of student activism in the United States in years. Through peaceful demonstrations and sit-ins students demanded that universities drop suppliers who did not comply to these standards. This ongoing campaign, as well as official and media reports on workers' conditions and profits, has placed increased pressures on manufacturers to be more open. In October 1999 Nike, under mounting pressure, released the names of 41 non-US factories engaged in manufacturing athletic apparel for US universities. Previously such companies considered this information competitor sensitive.

Indications show that many academics and university administrators support USAS's actions. You need also to consider this as a domino effect. Already over 100 US universities have members belonging to USAS.

By 2003 this movement had become an international organization of student and community members at over 200 campuses. While it is not the policy of the organization to advocate the boycotting of companies (it prefers to increase the pressure for change), it is most likely that individuals will boycott key garment manufacturers. You need to consider the following:

1. Do such individual boycotts truly impact upon the company?
2. Can groups bring to bear collective pressure for change?
3. Should groups advocate both boycotting and increasing the political pressure on companies to create change?
4. Are there other alternatives?

Sources: Griffin, 1999; www.usasnet.org

world is far from a perfect ethical environment. That is the nature of humankind, and it would be naïve to think otherwise.

What is clear is that marketing and ethics are much higher on people's agendas. The ethics of marketing practices are now open to greater scrutiny. For another example of boycotts see the 'Marketing insight' on Benetton, Toscani and the Death Row advertisements (page 74).

Why ethics is important to marketing

As we stated in Chapter 1 we are targeted by marketing activities virtually every moment of our waking life. From an early age till our very deaths, products, services and concepts to 'enrich' our lives are placed before us. We also concluded that societal marketing had gained credence because the media had alerted the public to a range of ethical issues, from the mis-selling of pensions in the UK through to the poor financial returns to farmers who grow crops, which when processed are sold at a premium in developed nations. As a result a growing number of consumers have moved towards purchasing ethically sound products and services. Many companies and organizations have gained competitive stature based upon their ethical stance within the marketplace, for example Body Shop International and the UK's Co-operative Stores.

Customers are a strategic asset, the virtual lifeblood of any organization, no matter how large or small. Equally, if the current thinking is to develop relationships, and indeed permission, marketing, in order to build any relationship there must be trust. This trust is equally important whether it is the local corner grocery store or a supermarket chain, whether it is business-to-business or business-to-consumer. If this trust is lost, the buyer may be lost to a rival, especially in a highly competitive marketplace.

Potential ethical problems associated with marketing

Various authors have highlighted some of the ethical problems that can arise in marketing situations. The following notes adapt and expand their individual and collective research/points of view. These issues can be considered both individually and collectively.

Traditional small-scale bribery/ questionable payments

This involves payment of small sums, usually to speed up routine government action. For example, it is purported that in Mexico the postal officials used to charge a small 'surcharge' for delivering the mail to the offices of international companies. While this was

illegal under Mexican law, such payments were ignored and often considered as a local tax.

Large-scale bribery

This is a relatively large payment intended to allow a violation of the law or designed to influence policy directly or indirectly: for instance, the awarding of a contract. Although the story in the 'Marketing insight' (page 67) dates from the 1970s, it has become a benchmark case. From this one example came a raft of legislation to curb (successfully or otherwise) such excesses.

Gifts

These may include gifts received after the completion of a transaction, or lavish entertainment to secure a marketing venture. Some organizations set a ceiling on the value of a gift an individual can receive. Gifts beyond this limit may be auctioned within the company (proceeds to charity) or the gift might be donated to a charity. The key difficulty here is a cultural one. In many countries (for instance, India and the Far East) it is common practice for people to give gifts to their visitors or those who have helped them (ethically and legally). It is a sign of good faith and thanks. Thus it would be dishonourable for the recipient to refuse the gift. The giver would 'lose face' in the eyes of their colleagues and tradition itself. Thus both individuals and companies must be culturally sensitive to such actions without being ethically compromised.

Pricing

This may include unfair differential pricing, tactical pricing with the objective of eliminating local competition, dumping products at prices well below that in the home country and pricing practices that are illegal in the home country but legal in the host country (for example, price fixing agreements). Price fixing is where competitors reach an

Marketing insight: Lockheed

In the 1970s intermediary agents of Nippon Air (the official Japanese airline) approached aircraft manufacturer Lockheed regarding a potential order. To secure a large order for its TriStar (L1011) passenger aircraft it would have to pay US $12.5 million to intermediaries and government officials (De George, 1993). As De George states, 'Nippon Air should have bought it without it requiring any secret payments; on the other hand, if the asking price was US $12.5 million too high, Nippon Air should have negotiated the price down. As it was, Nippon Air paid the full asking price, but Lockheed netted US $12.5 million less.'

Another question here is, if Lockheed had refused to pay the bribe would the intermediaries have still recommended the TriStar? If not, the intermediaries would have perhaps entered such negotiations with other aircraft manufacturers until someone agreed to the under-the-table payments. However, that does not mean Nippon Air would have purchased the right aircraft for their needs, or the safest aircraft. Such a deal can rule out the best product and best value for a company and its own customers (De George, 1993).

When the Lockheed payments were eventually made public, the US government charged it with falsification of its financial records and tax violations. The practice was, however, an accepted (though secret) way of conducting business in Japan. Nevertheless, the reactions in both the United States and Japan were severe. The Lockheed executives and the company's reputation was now tarnished, and its future was in jeopardy. (It would later be acquired by the Boeing Corporation.) In Japan the public's reaction clearly indicated that it did not approve of such practices, especially as it brought the country and thus its people into disrepute. The government ministers involved in the scandal were charged with criminal activity (one subsequently committed suicide) and the government eventually fell (De George, 1993).

In the mid-1970s the US Stock Exchange Commission (SEC) investigated various allegations and discovered that over 400 US companies had made questionable or illegal payments in excess of US $300 million to foreign governments, officials, politicians and political parties (Dept of Justice, 1999). The Lockheed incident precipitated the investigations and was the cornerstone of the US government introduction of the Foreign Corrupt Practices Act in 1977. In essence, this Act 'prohibited corrupt payments to foreign officials for the purpose of obtaining or keeping business' (this includes subsidiaries of US parent companies). Congress believed that it would bring a 'halt to the bribery of foreign officials and to restore public confidence in the integrity of the American business system' (Dept of Justice, 1999).[2]

In 1997, the United States and 33 other countries signed the OECD Convention on Combating Bribery of Foreign Public Officials in International Business Transactions.

agreement on what price to charge within the marketplace.

Products

This can focus on several areas:

- Products that have been banned for use in the home country but are sold in another country. Some pharmaceutical products refused licences by the US government's Federal Drugs Administration (FDA) (www.fda.gov) among other international agencies have been exported to developing countries. Consumers in developing nations are taking these products in the belief that they will benefit them. They may well benefit, with little or no side-effects. Alternatively, the damage from the side-effects may outweigh the benefits.

▌ A company may omit to provide vital information about the side-effects associated with using the product (Palmer and Hartley, 1999). In certain countries companies must, by law, state any known side-effects associated with using the products. UK, European Union and US laws regarding pharmaceuticals are particularly good examples. However, other countries may not be so prudent in their law making. As a result, companies may produce and sell products that they know may (or indeed do) have side-effects associated with usage, which may range from the mild to the outright lethal.

▌ Unsafe products. This can be related to the point above. Unsafe products can fall into two categories: one, products launched onto the market where the manufacturer knows that under certain conditions the product is unsafe/dangerous, and two, when the manufacturer discovers a flaw in the product once it has been launched, or has been in the market for some time. In such cases the company will usually issue a product recall notice (associated with marketing communication activity within a range of media). (See the 'Marketing insight' on Tylenol, page 80.)

▌ Products that appear unsuitable or are inappropriate for use by people in the host country. The 'Marketing insight' on Nestlé illustrates the problems that can arise when a company seeks to sell a product within another country environment very different from its own. It also illustrates how companies can seek to remedy a situation (which was probably preventable in the first place), yet remain a focal point of boycott activity.

Creating an unwholesome demand

It could be argued that some products are marketed that have potentially detrimental effects. Some observers may cite tobacco and alcohol. Stanton, Etzel and Walker (1994) use the case of handguns in the United States.

While legal under US law, some handguns are marketed at low prices, and it is believed that these low-cost guns are mostly used in committing crimes. Some say the marketing of these inexpensive handguns is socially unacceptable. Others argue that it is the responsibility of the US government to take the necessary legislative action (perhaps unlikely with a powerful gun lobby in place). Others still argue that it is the collective responsibility of both groups. This is a complex issue beyond the confines of this textbook. However, there is, as Stanton *et al* indicate, a clear moral and ethical issue here. Yet, it seems far from being reconciled.

Style obsolescence

Stanton *et al* (1994) refer to the criticism by observers levied against products that have 'built-in' obsolescence. Perhaps the classic in this category is fashion, most especially women's fashion. Fashion, it could be argued, encourages consumers to discard clothes before they are worn out. The same perhaps could be argued against any product that has the aura of style attached to it, be it music CDs, computer games, mobile phones or computer software, including operating platforms.

Packaging

Here there are several areas for consideration.

Wasteful and unnecessary

According to research conducted in the early 1990s, US consumers perceived that plastic represented a high level of packaging waste

Marketing insight: Nestlé and baby milk formula

There continues to be much written about Nestlé's introduction of its infant powdered milk formula into developing nations during the late 1970s and early 1980s. Criticism was levelled at Nestlé on a number of accounts, including the accusation that many mothers in developing nations could not afford to purchase the formula in the quantities required for proper nourishment of their children. As a result they diluted the formula, and the babies received insufficient amounts and suffered from malnutrition. Under normal circumstances the formula needed to be mixed with boiled sanitized water. However there were examples of the formula being mixed with unsanitized, even polluted water. The overall result was an increase in malnutrition, incidence of disease and even death amongst infants (Dobbing, 1988).

Such was the public concern at the time that it led to an international boycott of all Nestlé products. The company instigated a range of new practices and guidelines including a Nestlé's Infant Formula Charter. This Charter sets out its policy towards the marketing and distribution of infant formula within developing countries. For instance in developing nations, to quote, 'Nestlé leaves the recommendation of appropriate breast milk substitutes to health professionals and for almost 20 years has stopped all promotion of infant formula to the public. This commitment to a ban on promotional activities means: no advertising, no store promotion, no price incentives, no "milk nurses" and no educational material mentioning infant formula' (Nestlé, 2003). It also emphasizes that it 'compl[ies]with both the letter and the spirit of the World Health Organization's Code of Marketing of Breast Milk Substitutes'.[3]

There are several points that make this case particularly interesting.

- A company the size of Nestlé and with immensely talented people made a number of critical errors of judgment in launching the infant formula into the developing nations.
- The company instigated new procedures and operational guidelines.
- The company has stated that it will 'take disciplinary measures against any Nestlé personnel who deliberately violate this policy'. Equally, it 'invites government officials, health professionals and consumers, to draw to its attention any Nestlé infant formula marketing practices in developing countries which they consider are not in conformity with [its] commitment'.[3]
- However, as of 2003 the Nestlé boycott remains active in approximately 18 countries, and in the UK supporters include religious, health and consumer groups, student unions, businesses, celebrities and politicians (*Ethical Consumer*, 2003).

This provides an interesting case of a global brand that, although it has taken remedial action, still faces an international communications challenge.

(Ottman, 1994). This, according to the research, is not the case. As Ottman suggests:

Consumers do not understand the role that packaging plays in the overall marketing process, or why specific packaging materials are chosen over others. The presence of some packaging materials, such as outer cartons required for safe product transport and impactful in-store display, is perceived by many consumers as excessive and wasteful.

In the future, what is perceived as excess packaging could well become a significant negative brand attribute and cast an unfavourable halo on its manufacturer. Smart marketers will incorporate consumers' perceptions into package design and educate consumers on packaging's many benefits.

Size and real value of content

In highly competitive environments some companies may be driven to distort the real value of the contents. Large packages take up more shelf space, thus commanding more attention from the consumer who may perceive that the package contains more (Churchill and Peter, 1998). That is unfortunately not always the case.

Images

Pictures on the packaging may be enticing; however the contents may belie the image portrayed. Images of fruit on a carton do not necessarily mean that there is any real fruit juice inside. In some countries, like the UK, there are strict enforceable laws aimed at preventing such misrepresentation.

Product testing

Here there are two areas for discussion.

Inaccurate or incomplete testing

This may be the result either of the need to launch the product by a particular deadline, and/or the cost implications of testing/ delayed launch. The result could be a product that is unsafe to use. This relates to the earlier issue of unsafe products.

Testing on animals

Since the 1980s much has been written on animal testing for the cosmetic, pharmaceutical and tobacco industries. Companies such as the Body Shop International have done much to focus consumer, media and industry attention on animal testing. Some companies now actively market the fact that neither the ingredients nor their final product are tested on animals.

Deceptive selling tactics

These can be divided into two main areas, bait and switch, and pressure or hard selling techniques.

Bait and switch

Hoyer and MacInnes (1997) describe this as a technique that draws a customer into a store by advertising a product or service at a very attractive low price. Then the salesperson attempts to persuade the customer to trade up to a higher-priced product. To support the deception, the salesperson might state that the original item is out of stock, or make some disparaging remark about the product. This is an attempt to make the customer not want it, and thus consider buying the higher-priced (perceived better quality) product.

Pressure or hard selling techniques

Although for the most part customers trust salespeople, that trust can be exploited, and even betrayed. Customers are a strategic asset, the virtual lifeblood of any organization, no matter how large or small. However, it is quite incredible how many companies and managers have looked upon customers as only short-term, rather than long-term assets.

With increasing pressures on sales executives to meet targets and overall margins, there will always be a temptation to take short cuts, especially if the sales teams of the main competitors are implementing virtually the same aggressive strategies. Malpractices in both the UK and the United States over the selling of investments, insurance, pensions and other financial products have led to new regulations and significant fines for the companies concerned. Of course, the major detriment to such organizations has been the highly visible negative publicity that such exposure has created.

Competitor intelligence gathering

In today's turbulent business environment, the need for knowledge is paramount. As companies compete on both a regional and global basis, they must analyse their competitors as much as their target markets.

It should be the goal of every company to understand its direct, and indirect, competitors by gathering continuous information, and thus seek a competitive edge. An organization must constantly compare its brands, pricing, advertising, promotion, levels of service and distribution with those of the competitors. A company can shape its marketing strategy by understanding its competitors':

▌ strategies (research and development, manufacturing, marketing, operational and financial);

▌ objectives, strengths and weaknesses (these will often include sales, market share, profit margin, return on investment, cash flow, levels of new investment and capacity utilization);

▌ reaction patterns (analysing how they would react to price cutting or the introduction of new products).

Gathering marketing and competitor intelligence is a vital part of business operations. Dynamic global competition and deregulation of industries are making competitive intelligence gathering more widely practised.

However, the issue is to what lengths a marketer or company should go in order to obtain such information. The problem is that it is not always clear what is legal and ethical. Obviously, using electronic surveillance equipment to spy on competitors is both illegal (in most countries) and unethical. However, increasingly there are 'grey areas' where companies, in order to gather marketing information, may behave unethically, but legally.

On the other hand, illegal activities in the United States have become so widespread that the government introduced the Economic Espionage Act in 1996. This covers the stealing of trade secrets, which include customer information, marketing plans and product blueprints (Bartram, 1998).

Some marketers and, indeed, companies, may take the view that, to quote an old cliché, 'all's fair in love and war'. They take the view that intelligence gathering, by whatever means, is necessary and legitimate in order to gain competitive advantage. Getting caught, though, can mean a high price in terms of potential criminal prosecution (in the United States there are severe fines and possible prison sentences), litigation, ruined personal reputations, damaged staff morale, share price falls and the public's perception of the organization. Customers may adopt an ethical stance and withdraw their business, for if we think about it they would be well in their rights to ask the question, 'How can we trust you?'

Illegal/immoral activities in the host country

These practices may include knowingly polluting the environment, maintaining unsafe working conditions, and product/ technology copying of patents, trademarks or trade names.

Marketing to children/young people

According to research the average US child watches more than 20 hours of television per week, and sees more than 20,000 commercials per year (Churchill and Peter, 1998). During the mid to late 1990s there was increasing concern at the level and intensity of marketing to children. Research indicates that children can be vulnerable to certain marketing activities (Ferrell and Ferrell, 2000). The view taken is that children are often too impressionable to make value judgments regarding sophisticated television and Internet advertising. Critics view this type of advertising as irresponsible as it 'manipulates' children's desires (Ferrell and Ferrell, 2000).

This, however, is not new. During the early 1960s advertisers were targeting both children and their parents during the commercial breaks in children's television shows. Then there was a wide range of promotions from Action Man™ and Barbie™ to Lego™ and Meccano™ metal building kits. What are arguably different today are the possible scale and intensity of the message, supported by dramatic computer-driven visual effects.

Various countries are considering legislation that will protect the privacy of children using the Internet. According to research, approximately 89 per cent of the Internet Web sites aimed at children collect personal information. However only 54 per cent disclose the intended use of the information, while less than 10 per cent of the sites attempt to gain parental consent (FTC, 1998).

In general, such messages may result in one-time sales only. They are less likely to build long-term relationships (FTC, 1998).

Marketing to the elderly

As with the young, the elderly too can become vulnerable to aggressive selling techniques, and the delivery of unwanted goods.

Marketing communications

Advertising deception

In the United States both the Food and Drugs Administration (FDA) and the Federal Trade Commission (FTC) have definitions for deceptive advertising (Churchill and Peter, 1998). The FDA defines a deceptive advertisement as one that: 'either through (1) its verbal content, (2) its design structure, and/or visual artwork, or (3) the context in which it appears causes n per cent of a representative group of consumers to have a common incorrect impression or belief' (Hoyer and MacInnes, 1997). (The n per cent – that is, the percentage affected by the advertising – will vary and is determined by the nature of the situation and how severe the consequences of this incorrect belief really are. The FDA determines the n per cent.)

The FTC defines deceptive advertising as: '(1) a misrepresentation, omission, or practice that is likely to mislead the consumer, (2) consumers acting as they normally would in relation to a product or service or in a consumption situation, and (3) a material misrepresentation (one that will affect their choice)' (Hoyer and MacInnes, 1997).

There needs to be a word of caution, though. It is vital to remember that because consumers may hold an incorrect belief regarding a product or service it does not mean that deception has necessarily taken place. There may be some degree of miscomprehension involved. Normally, for example, the FTC would consider deception had possibly occurred when between 20 and 25 per cent of consumers held an incorrect belief (Hoyer and MacInnes, 1997).

Stereotyping in advertising – how we portray people

Advertising in various countries often stereotypes people. Whether they are women, ethnic and minority groups, young, mature or elderly people, advertising can alienate consumers who feel that they are not being represented accurately. Both advertisers and companies have now realized the bottom-line impact of offending such groups. Advertising is changing to portray a better image of these groups. However, there is still some way to go to redress the balance. Marketers need to reflect on their previous ethical behaviour in creating such potentially negative advertising.

Advertising that offends

This can be very subjective indeed, and varies from country to country. What offends one person is a source of amusement or pleasure for another – just ask any comedian. However, it is clear that some advertisements do distress and offend people. In the UK the Advertising Standards Authority monitors complaints from the public, and subsequently has the power to enforce the removal of offending advertisements – those that breach statutory codes. The 'Marketing insight' on Benetton and its Death Row advertising illustrates that advertising that offends a particular group can have a detrimental effect upon the company's business, if only in the short term.

Questionable commissions to channel members

This could include unreasonably large commissions or fees paid to channel members, such as sales agents and importers. This may lead to an unfair competitive advantage, as one company's products are aggressively marketed over those of another.

Involvement in unlawful political activities

This relates to a combination of marketing and political activities. This may include exertion of the political influence of multinationals, or engaging in marketing activities whilst there are sanctions or embargoes imposed by the home country (country of origin) on the host country (country of sale). A related issue arises when the United Nations imposes sanctions on a country, and a company actively seeks to market to that embargoed country.

In Chapter 2 we discussed the issues surrounding the increasing wealth, and thus political influence, that several large multinational corporations can exert. Reflect back to Chapter 2 and consider the future potential ethical issues that could be the outcome of such influence.

Impact of marketing

Here we need to consider the ethical fallout of marketing certain products into less developed and developing nations. US and British tobacco companies have been criticized for their often aggressive marketing campaigns in Asia (Churchill and Peter, 1998). In Asia cigarettes are much cheaper than in the United States or Europe. There is little or no regulation over who buys them, so they are easily accessible to children. There is an argument that young children may become addicted, thus becoming lifelong consumers. There is less awareness of the potential health risks than in the United States and Europe, even though there are government health campaigns. (Asian governments are slowly increasing the pressure on tobacco companies by demanding more health warnings, and by introducing health-oriented campaigns.)

Another example is the changing food habits of people in developing nations. Churchill and Peter (1998) cite an example of the low-fat diets of Asians and how US-based fast-food companies are introducing them to potentially higher-fat cheeseburger and chicken dishes. Will the problems of high-fat diets and high cholesterol levels, now so prevalent in developed nations, soon impact on developing nations?

Counterfeit goods/brand piracy

While most countries have signed up to various international agreements to protect copyright and trade marks, counterfeiting remains

Marketing insight: Benetton, Toscani and the Death Row advertisements

In the early 1980s Benetton launched the United Colors of Benetton advertising campaign. The images, created by Italian photographer Oliviero Toscani, had young children and teenagers from different countries and ethnic groups, laughing and smiling together, all wearing colourful Benetton clothes. It was a striking campaign of racial harmony within a global setting. It stood out through the clutter of so much clothing advertising at the time. It was a winner for both Toscani and Benetton.

Over time, though, Toscani's work for Benetton became increasingly controversial, from images of a young man dying from AIDS to the blood-soaked uniform of a dead Bosnian Croat soldier. Slowly the imagery created by Toscani was moving further away from the Benetton brand. Earlier images of a newborn baby, while creating some controversy, significantly helped to project the Benetton brand high in the consciousness of the consumer audience. However, there was to be one controversial campaign that was to damage (if only for a short while) the Benetton image: Toscani's Death Row campaign.

In late 1999 Benetton, which was building a global brand awareness, aimed to increase its presence in the US market. It embarked upon a deal with the Sears Store group whereby Benetton would have 800 instore outlets. This would create a major positioning for Benetton in the US marketplace within a relatively short time frame. Meanwhile Toscani was developing a new advertising campaign for the US market. He had obtained permission to photograph 26 prisoners on Death Row awaiting execution. Through his pictures he wanted to convey 'misery and suffering'. For him it had become a moral crusade, and the campaign was launched in January 2000.

However, for one family in particular this was a Benetton campaign too far, for in the images they saw a photograph of the man who had kidnapped, tortured and then brutally murdered their son. They then embarked upon their own campaign to halt the advertising campaign. They called their friends, who in turn called their friends and so on. This word-of-mouth campaign became state news, then US-wide. Sears storecard holders outraged by the Benetton campaign cut up their store cards and sent them back to Sears. The adverse publicity was beginning to prove too much for the Sears' board, and it decided to take immediate action and terminate the agreement with Benetton. In one day 400 of the in-store outlets were closed. The pressure of the ever-growing criticism and boycotts from Sears' customers had proved too much for the retailer. Benetton had hoped to generate some US $100 million in the first year. Now its avant-garde marketing was impacting on their revenue stream.

The 18-year relationship between Toscani and Benetton ended, and a new approach to advertising was employed. By 2002 Benetton was once more seeking to develop a high-profile presence in the US marketplace.

Source: BBC (2001a).[4]

prevalent. Counterfeiting affects virtually all major branded products, from computer software through to cosmetics, jeans and videos.

One of the problems is that if a country has signed up to an international agreement it does not necessarily mean it puts a high priority on copyright and trade mark enforcement. Already over-stretched law enforcement agencies and governments will tend to focus on crimes they, and perhaps the public, consider more serious.

For the company whose products are being pirated, there is not only the loss of revenue, but the real risk of damage to its brand image and identity. This will occur if the consumer buying the low-cost counterfeit product considers it a genuine product, but of poor quality.

Labour practices

In 1996 the United Nations Children Fund and the International Labour Organization (ILO) estimated that there were some 250 million child workers in the world (ILO, 1996). This in itself had an enormous impact upon world opinion, from the ordinary citizen through to the leaders of nation states. Subsequent research, however, indicates that the 1996 figures were conservative. According to the ILO (2002):

there were some 352 million children aged 5 to 17 engaged in some form of economic activity in the world in 2000, including 211 million in the age group 5 to 14 years. The Asia-Pacific region has the largest number of child workers in the 5 to 14 age category, 127.3 million. It is followed by Sub-Saharan Africa and Latin America and the Caribbean with 48 million and 17.4 million, respectively.[5]

'Economic Activity' is a broad concept that encompasses most productive activities of children: it includes both work that is permissible under ILO child labour conventions and that which is not. It also covers categories such as unpaid work, illegal work and work in the informal sector. 'Child labour', however, is a narrower concept: it excludes the activities of children 12 years and older who are working only a few hours a week in permitted light work and those of children 15 years and above whose work is not classified as 'hazardous'.

Of the approximately 246 million children in child labour, nearly 171 million were in hazardous situations or conditions. In other words, children in hazardous work constituted about half the number of economically active children and more than two-thirds of those in child labour. Of these children, a stunning 111 million children were below 15 years of age.

During the latter half of the 20th century and the early part of the 21st century, companies faced an increasingly diverse range of pressures. Some of these we highlighted in Chapter 2, while others are considered in Chapters 4 and 7. For the purpose of this section we can condense them into the following categories:

▌ **Customer demands** – reduced prices and high quality.

▌ **Cost reduction** – to meet customer expectations, thus companies must seek suppliers (both component and finished products) that can deliver at low cost. That has usually, although not always, meant sourcing internationally.

▌ **Increased international and global competition** – competition is no longer within a defined locality, it can now be literally anywhere in the world.

To meet these 'demands', companies have increasingly outsourced. As we saw in the 'Marketing insight: United Students Against Sweatshops' (page 65), this raises concerns over who are engaged in the manufacture of products and the conditions within which they work. The figures presented by the ILO are indeed shocking, regardless of whether the children are making products for their local market or the international one.

Some companies have, from an early stage, attempted to take an ethical standpoint on the issue of child workers. In the next 'Marketing insight' there is an examination of Levi Strauss's early work in this field.

Marketing insight: Levi Strauss

Today, many designer-labelled and well-established home brands of clothing are not made in the UK, France, Italy or North America. This is despite the fact that these countries may be where the designer label and brand originated. The outsourcing of clothing manufacture to companies in North Africa, the Indian subcontinent and the Pacific Rim can bring substantial savings of labour and product costs. However, such outsourcing can also raise ethical issues concerning labour conditions (Griseri and Groucutt, 1997).

In 1992, in order to bring its international sourcing practices in line with its own ethical code, the world's largest apparel manufacturer, Levi Strauss, began enforcing International Labour Organization (ILO) standards. These standards bar the employment of children under the age of 14. Two Bangladeshi contractors had admitted to Levis that they hired children under 14; however they were prepared to dismiss them (Mitchell and O'Neal, 1994). The contractors, however, pointed out to Levi Strauss officials that the boys and girls employed by them, and other local apparel suppliers, provided their families' sole economic support. In most cases they were the eldest children in large single-parent families (Mitchell and O'Neal, 1994).

Levi Strauss Bangladesh staff faced an ethical dilemma. They could ignore the ethical code formulated thousands of miles away in the comfort of an office in San Francisco, or they could dismiss the children, with the subsequent financial repercussions upon their families. The latter decision could lead the children to work for more unscrupulous manufacturers, enter prostitution or fall into abject poverty.

Levi Strauss considered the options and negotiated a compromise with the contractors. If the contractors continued to pay the children's wages, and agreed to hire the children back when they had reached the age of 14, Levi would send the children to school, paying for their uniform, books and tuition (Mitchell and O'Neal, 1994).

Although the deal may sound expensive, the level of investment in financial terms was relatively small. The greater benefits came from the corporate reputation of Levi Strauss with the local community, and in terms of the brand image throughout the rest of the world. Whether the factory was in San Francisco or a small town in Bangladesh, Levi Strauss had to remain committed throughout to an ethical policy.

As Robert Haas, Levi Strauss Chairman and CEO, commented on this particular issue in 1994, 'In today's world a TV exposé on working conditions can undo years of effort to build brand loyalty. Why squander your investment when, with commitment, reputational problems can be prevented?' (Mitchell and O'Neal, 1994).

Over the years there has been much debate over attempts by various international bodies to eliminate the use of child labour in the Bangladeshi garment industry. A rejection of a Memorandum of Understanding by the Bangladeshi Garment Manufacturers and Exporters Association (BGMEA) prompted the Child Labor Coalition, a US-based child rights group, to announce a general boycott threat against Bangladeshi garments within the American marketplace. Such action would have had a severe impact upon the Bangladeshi garment industry, which in 1994 alone earned an estimated US $900 million from exports to the United States (*Bangladesh Observer*, 1995).

In early July 1995, the Memorandum of Understanding was finally signed. The signatories were the BGMEA, UNICEF and the ILO, while members of the Bangladeshi government and the US Ambassador were witnesses. Under the accord, all workers under the age of 14 left the garment industry by 31 October 1995. They were sent to schools to be jointly run and funded by UNICEF, the ILO, BGMEA and the Bangladeshi government. In addition, the children received payments to replace their previous earnings. In many ways these issues were pre-empted by Levi Strauss's own ethical beliefs and actions (*Bangladesh Observer*, 1995).

Levi Strauss had direct access to its suppliers, and thus was in a position to influence them. We have to recognize that not all outsourcing from a brand's headquarters may be totally within the company's control. Company X, a major brand based in New York, for example, may outsource from one supplier in the Far East. That supplier may well, in turn, subcontract to several other suppliers to meet inventory and time scheduling requirements. As long as the product meets the required manufacturing standards and delivery dates, managers at Company X's New York offices probably will not consider the individuals who have actually made their products.

Business is global: outsourcing and subcontracting are now the norm. The difficulty for some companies is tracking the various stages of subcontracting. If they have subcontracted to one major supplier, as long as quality targets are obtained, they may not be aware of the working conditions within the companies to whom their main supplier subcontracts. However, companies do have a responsibility to track right through their outsourcing and subcontracting procedures in order to check the working environments.

As Robert Haas stated, the global media can have a negative, as well as a positive, effect on a brand. By tackling the issues head-on, Levi Strauss gained particular advantages (Griseri and Groucutt, 1997):

- It had remained true to its ethical code, having clearly stated that it was not confined only to the US border or its own factories.
- By taking a moral stance, so to speak, it accommodated a diverse range of consumer views and opinions, not least those who would have boycotted its products.
- It generated positive media coverage.

In 1991 Levi Strauss became the first multinational company to develop a comprehensive code of conduct to 'ensure that individuals making our products anywhere in the world would do so in safe and healthy working conditions and be treated with dignity and respect'.[6] Levi's code, known as the Global Sourcing and Operating Guidelines, is in two parts. First, country assessment guidelines cover health and safety conditions, the human rights environment, legal system and political, economic and social environment. Second, the business partner terms of engagement cover ethical standards, legal requirements, environmental requirements, community involvement and employment standards (child labour, prison labour/forced labour, disciplinary practices, working hours, wages and benefits, freedom of association, discrimination, health and safety). If companies breach these guidelines they risk the termination of the business partnership.

However, Levi Strauss is not without its critics. As of 2003 it remained on a boycott list in relation to the payment of compensation to workers who had been made redundant when a San Antonio, Texas, factory was relocated to Costa Rica (*Ethical Consumer*, 2003).

Questions/activities

1. Search the Internet and update this case study to determine how the situation has developed since this published information.
2. Search the Internet to discover cases where companies have been accused of exploiting child labour. Consider both the ethical and public relations implications for the companies.
3. There is an argument that there are degrees of child employment, some minor, some harsh and thus unacceptable. Some argue that in some countries, if children are not employed to produce goods for developed countries, they and their families will starve and the economy of that country will sink even further. Critically evaluate this perspective. What is your perspective and why?

Ethical codes of practice

Earlier in this chapter we stated that trust is a fundamental element in the relationship between companies and their customers. In this section we consider codes of ethics or codes of practice (this relates to the Levi Strauss example above), and how they can influence a company or organization to behave in a particular way. At the end of this chapter we state in detail the American Marketing Association's Code of Ethics. This is a comprehensive statement; however other marketing associations have their own codes, and we urge students to study a range of ethical codes.

Like the Levi's example quoted above, the pharmaceutical giant Johnson & Johnson knew that if it breached the trust of its customers, not only would it lose customers, it would lose the public relations, and thus the marketing, battle as well. The 'Marketing insight' on Johnson & Johnson illustrates several key issues:

- It is a classic example of how, in the face of disaster, honesty and directness can engender trust in the mind of the consumer.

- It was most likely the first case of consumer terrorism and fatal product tampering.

- It is considered a classic in terms of crisis management and crisis communication strategies.

The Johnson & Johnson credo

We believe our first responsibility is to the doctors, nurses and patients, to mothers and fathers and all others who use our products and services.
In meeting their needs everything we do must be of high quality. We must constantly strive to reduce our costs in order to maintain reasonable prices.
Customers' orders must be serviced promptly and accurately.
Our suppliers and distributors must have an opportunity to make a fair profit.
We are responsible to our employees, the men and women who work with us throughout the world.
Everyone must be considered an individual.
We must respect their dignity and recognize their merits. They must have a sense of security in their jobs. Compensation must be fair and adequate, and working conditions clean, orderly and safe. Employees must feel free to make suggestions and complaints. There must be equal opportunity for employment, development and advancement for those qualified. We must provide competent management, and their actions must be just and ethical.
We are responsible to the communities in which we live and work and to the world community as well. We must be good citizens – support good works and charities and bear our fair share of taxes. We must encourage civic improvements and better health and education. We must maintain in good order the property we are privileged to use, protecting the environment and natural resources.
Our final responsibility is to our stockholders. Business must make a sound profit. We must experiment with new ideas. Research must be carried on, innovative programs developed and mistakes paid for. New equipment must be purchased, new facilities provided and

new products launched. Reserves must be created to provide for adverse times. When we operate according to these principles, the stockholders should realize a fair return.

The credo

Johnson & Johnson is a well-established manufacturing brand that produces everything from Baby Oil and Reach™ toothbrushes to artificial corneal lenses, blood testing equipment and prescription drugs. In 1935 'General' Robert Wood Johnson – Chairman from 1938 until 1963 and son of the founder – spelled out the company's moral stance and obligations to employees and local communities during the Depression. In a pamphlet entitled *Try Reality*, he urged his fellow industrialists to embrace what he termed 'a new industrial philosophy'. Robert Johnson defined this as the corporation's responsibility to customers, employees, the community and stockholders (Johnson & Johnson, 1992).

Some eight years later, in 1943, this philosophy was formalized into a four paragraph, 308 word 'credo' of good behaviour that is reproduced here. As Lawrence G Foster, former Corporate Vice President of Public Relations stated in 1994, 'Robert Wood Johnson felt very strongly that the credo was not just a flag waving, do-good document, but rather a very intelligent, albeit demanding, way to manage a business. The first responsibility is to the customer, and this triggers many decisions, many of them difficult and sometimes costly' (Trevino and Nelson, 1995).

As you can see from the Johnson & Johnson credo the company places its customers first, even beyond its return on investment for shareholders. The case study (see 'Marketing insight: Tylenol® and the actions of Johnson & Johnson') very much tested the resolve of the board of directors to follow the credo.

The consumer's role in ethical marketing

Davidson (1998) believes that 'buyers also have moral obligations and responsibilities – to be informed about the seller's ethical behaviour and to consider that behaviour specially when deciding whether to make the purchase.' We have seen that some consumers boycott both products and services if they believe that companies have acted in an unreasonable manner. The list of potential ethical marketing issues also illustrates that marketing can be subject to intense criticism. However, consumers continue to buy products and services that may be ethically dubious.

There are, of course, reasoned arguments for this continued purchasing behaviour. For example, the consumer does not have access to the information. Environmentally aware consumers may themselves actively seek out information – but does the mass consumer? While governments create legislation to compel manufacturers/retailers to supply information to consumers (labelling, for example), they may not communicate ethical issues, such as testing on animals or the working conditions under which the product was manufactured.

Do consumers really care about ethics? Obviously some do or there would not be the proliferation of ethical products (for example, cosmetics) or services (ethical investments), or the increasing level of boycotts. However, some people are more interested in the price and the convenience of the product/service, rather than the ethical considerations. For example, are people willing to pay more for an ethically manufactured product? If consumers are on low incomes, they will tend to be price

Marketing insight: Tylenol® and the actions of Johnson & Johnson

McNeil Consumer Products, a subsidiary of Johnson & Johnson since its acquisition in 1958, produced Tylenol®. During the 1960s Tylenol®, an acetaminophen-based analgesic, was introduced to the market as an over-the-counter (OTC) product, and was considered a safe substitute for aspirin, which is known often to irritate the stomach. Thus Tylenol® was heavily promoted to doctors, pharmacists and the public alike as an alternative to aspirin. By the early 1980s it was the leading analgesic on the market with a 35 per cent share and annual sales of US $400 million (Green, 1992).

Tylenol® became McNeil's best-selling product, and in all its forms and strengths attained a 35 per cent share of the OTC analgesic market, with annual sales in the region of US $400 million. The aim was to achieve a 50 per cent share of the market by 1986. Tylenol® alone represented 8 per cent of Johnson & Johnson's total revenue, and 17 per cent of corporate revenue. This was more than the three rivals – Anacin, Bayer and Bufferin – combined.

In late September 1982, a Chicago journalist telephoned Johnson & Johnson's headquarters in Brunswick, New Jersey. His call was to gain their reaction to a report that the extra-strength capsules in the Tylenol® product range had been contaminated. Over a matter of days seven people were to die within the Chicago area. The cause of death was linked to cyanide in Extra-Strength Tylenol® capsules. Medical tests showed that there was as much as 65 milligrams of cyanide in some of the victims' capsules (50 milligrams is a lethal dose).

When the Chicago authorities confirmed on Thursday 30 September that Extra-Strength Tylenol® had been contaminated, executives at both McNeil and Johnson & Johnson announced an immediate recall of 93,400 bottles that bore a particular batch number. These had been manufactured at McNeil's Washington Plant in Pennsylvania.

When the crisis broke there was a 20 per cent fall in the company's share value on Wall Street, effectively 'wiping off' US $2 billion (Green, 1992). At the time perhaps no management could have anticipated a disturbed individual lacing capsules with cyanide poison, and placing the containers back on the supermarket and drug store shelves. Commenting in 1984, the then President and Chief Operating Officer of Johnson & Johnson, David Clare, stated:

> The climate was one of sheer unbelieving that this had happened. Shock, absolute unhappiness associated with the fact that people were dying. They were dying potentially through the use of one of our products.
>
> We just didn't know what had happened. We did not know how extensive it was. What the cause was. What the problem was in any dimension. It appeared to be localized, but we weren't sure.
>
> We were in an ethical dilemma. There were those who were arguing that we should not withdraw [the product]. Because all you're going to do is demonstrate to some sick individual that they can have a major nationwide impact upon a major product through their individual action at some locality.
>
> … We argued what was the right thing to do, and finally came down to there was no choice, from our standpoint. We had to protect the public.… So first and foremost we had to protect the public. (Freudberg, 1984)

Public fears ran high after the poisoning scares, although the public had stopped purchasing Tylenol®. In the words of David Clare, Johnson & Johnson wanted to show 'that we wanted the product out of their homes and off the shelves, just in the off chance that they might have some contaminated product' (Freudberg, 1984). The decision was taken to remove all Tylenol® from supermarkets and drug stores, first in Chicago and then nationwide. This decision was initially to cost the company over US $100 million, the retail value of removing some 31 million containers. However, in some 8 million samples tested, two containers were found to be contaminated. Thus the withdrawal probably prevented further deaths.

Public faith deeply affected both the company and the brand. According to Reputation Risk Management expert Peter Sheldon Green (1992) 'The uniqueness of Tylenol®, which enabled it to capture more than a third of the total US painkiller market, was in the marketing of the product. The value of the Tylenol® brand was a function of public perception and public perception only – not the uniqueness of the product itself.' In addition, Johnson & Johnson despatched more than 500,000 mailgrams to doctors, pharmacists, hospitals and wholesalers alerting them to the potential dangers.

Within days further deaths were linked to another batch coding, this time from the Round Rock Plant in Texas. Initially, there was speculation that a disgruntled employee had tampered with the capsules at the point of manufacture; however as two plants hundreds of miles apart were involved it seemed an unlikely proposition. As a result of its subsequent investigation the US Food and Drug Administration (FDA) publicly exonerated McNeil of any failure. Both batch numbers were from shipments that had been to the Chicago and surrounding districts, and investigators suspected that the tampering had taken place after the shipment reached Illinois. Thus, the only source of contamination was via the point of distribution – the shelves at the drug stores.

While it was an act of external sabotage and consumer terrorism, the company and its executives had to be seen to act responsibly to the customer. The company's reputation was enhanced because executives, including the then President and Chairman of the Board (1973–89), James E Burke, were readily available to meet the press. Helplines were quickly established to take calls from concerned customers. Johnson & Johnson's management of the crisis was highly visible, demonstrating its commitment to its customers.

Reactions

Within two days of the Tylenol®-related deaths occurring within the Chicago districts there was nationwide media coverage. In essence a wave of panic set in. Poison control centres through North America were receiving calls from worried consumers who had taken Tylenol® and feared for their lives. In reality, if they had taken Tylenol® laced with cyanide, in the quantities that had already been discovered by the authorities, the chances were that the caller would already have died. The key is that in these types of circumstance individuals do not always think clearly – they were genuinely frightened.

Consumers also discarded other drugs in fear that they too might be contaminated. The FDA received over 270 reports of suspected tampering with other products including foodstuffs. Of these 36 proved to be genuine 'copycat' product tamperings.

Media coverage

▪ Press enquiries exceeded 2,500.
▪ In excess of 125,000 news clippings were generated (possibly the widest domestic coverage since the assassination of President John F Kennedy on 22 November 1963).

- There were hundreds of hours of television and radio news coverage.
- According to a survey undertaken by Johnson & Johnson, more than 90 per cent of the US public knew about the Tylenol®-related deaths within the first week of the crisis.

What Johnson & Johnson did

- In the early stages of the crisis Johnson & Johnson's CEO James E Burke formed an emergency strategy group which met twice a day to make decisions on the rapidly developing situation. This strategy group included David Clare, President; Wayne Nelson, Company Group Chairman; Arthur Quilty, Executive Committee Member; David E Collins, Chairman of McNeil and Lawrence G Foster, Corporate Vice President of Public Relations.
- A special team was set up at Johnson & Johnson's Brunswick headquarters. This included McNeil Chairman David E Collins, a legal expert, a PR specialist and a security expert.
- An immediate, responsive and open public relations policy was undertaken at all levels. The objective was to minimize the potential spread of rumour and disinformation by providing valuable information and guidance for the media, and thus the consumers.
- The company made consumer safety its prime concern.
- The company's reputation was enhanced because executives, including Burke, were readily available to meet the press. Johnson & Johnson's management of the crisis was highly visible, demonstrating its commitment to its customers.
- Burke appeared on the *Donahue* and *60 Minutes* network television shows to answer questions on the crisis. These networked chat shows had high viewer ratings.
- Senior executives were interviewed for newspaper and magazine articles including *Fortune International* and the *Wall Street Journal*.
- A charge-free consumer helpline was established within the first few days of the crisis to respond to enquiries. Within the first 11 days, more than 136,000 calls had been made to the company. A total of 88 telephone lines were eventually made available, such were the demands. There were 33 at McNeil and 55 at other locations.
- Consumers were offered the opportunity to replace the Tylenol® capsules with tablets. Those customers who had thrown away the bottles of the extra-strength capsules could obtain the tablets by calling a charge-free telephone number.
- In the weeks following the incidents, Johnson & Johnson Worldwide Video Network produced five one-hour video programmes (approximately one per week) to keep their employees fully informed of developments.
- Letters were sent to domestic employees and retired staff keeping them updated and thanking them for their continued support during the crisis.
- A US $100,000 reward was offered for information leading to the arrest and conviction of the person or persons responsible for lacing the Tylenol® capsules.
- Members of Johnson & Johnson's Corporate Relations Department visited over 160 Congressional offices in Washington supporting proposed legislation making product tampering a federal crime.
- Johnson & Johnson supported moves by the FDA for the introduction of tamper-resistant packaging.

The reintroduction of Tylenol®

- Although it was advised by marketing experts to rebrand Tylenol®, the company decided that it would be reintroduced. At the time, James E Burke stated in a company PR briefing document that 'It will take time, it will take money, and it will be very difficult; but we consider it a moral imperative, as well as good business, to restore Tylenol® to its pre-eminent position' (Nash, 1998).

▊ The Emergency Strategy Group decided to reintroduce Tylenol® capsules in tamper-resistant containers. Less than six weeks after the first announcement to the nation of the Tylenol®-related deaths, there was a sales conference to plan the reintroduction of the drug.

▊ On 11 November 1982 a teleconference of the announcement was beamed to 29 cities via satellite, and received extensive coverage on the television news broadcasts.

▊ The triple-sealed packages had glued box ends, a plastic band around the cap and an aluminum seal across the bottle opening. They preempted the proposed FDA regulations.

▊ Within 10 weeks of the recall the capsules were back on the shelves.

▊ A new television commercial was broadcast. McNeil's Medical Director outlined the changes.

▊ The McNeil sales force was reinforced by teams from Johnson & Johnson's other subsidiaries. More than 2,000 salespeople made presentations to the medical community. It has been estimated that more than a million presentations were made by the end of the year.

▊ The company offered coupons to the value of $2.50 towards the purchase of Tylenol®. The consumer had to telephone a charge-free number to be placed on a list to receive the free coupon. By the first week of December, the coupon offer had generated over 200,000 calls from US consumers.

▊ The general belief is the re-emergence of Tylenol® would not have been possible had the company failed in its responsibility to act quickly and decisively in the public interest as news of the crisis was breaking.

▊ The decisive action of recalling the product before the US government intervened showed courage on the part of the executives who made that decision. The executives' courage was strengthened by the knowledge that the company would support their decision, and by the company's credo that they all respected (O'Reilly, 1994).

The nightmare returns

▊ On 10 February 1986 the company was informed that a woman had died in New York after taking two Extra-Strength Tylenol® capsules contaminated with cyanide. (This now made eight poisoning victims in all.)

▊ The company immediately informed all retailers in the area to remove all Tylenol® capsules.

▊ The Press Office handled calls throughout the night.

▊ A charge-free telephone number was made available, and again thousands of calls from worried consumers were handled.

▊ All Tylenol® advertising was suspended.

▊ Several more contaminated bottles were discovered in surrounding areas. New York and several other states immediately banned the sale of Tylenol® capsules.

▊ Johnson & Johnson issued a national alert, supported by the FDA, to advise consumers not to use Tylenol® capsules.

▊ The decision to recall its capsules and scrap their further production cost Johnson & Johnson an estimated US $150 million.

▌ On Monday 17 February 1986 the company announced that it would no longer sell OTC drugs in capsule form as it was impossible to prevent outside tampering. In addition to Tylenol®, Johnson & Johnson had sold two other OTC drugs in capsule form. Tylenol® would now be produced in caplet form. Although the company was not directly responsible for the actions that led to the deaths, it nonetheless instigated the design for new tamper-resistant packaging. Such packaging is now standard on virtually all health and food products.

▌ The company introduced the caplet to replace the capsule, and Tylenol® was again re-introduced into the market.

Final thoughts

In James E Burke's view the company's response to the Tylenol® crisis provided the strongest evidence in support of an ethical code, in their case the credo:

> I do not think that we could have done what we did with Tylenol® if we hadn't all gone through the process of challenging ourselves and committing ourselves to the Credo. We had dozens of people making hundreds of decisions and all on the fly. And they had to make them as wisely as they knew how. The reason they made them as well as they did is they knew what the set of beliefs that the institution they worked for were, so they made them based on that set of beliefs. We made very, very few mistakes. I think that the Tylenol® story is the most powerful thing that has occurred in American business to underline the value of a moral statement.
> (Freudberg, 1984)

▌ For a relatively short period Tylenol® was withdrawn from the marketplace completely, thus allowing other brands to capture its market share. However, on reintroduction Tylenol® once again became a leading household brand name. Just over 10 years from this tragic incident, the highly competitive US painkilling medicine market was worth US $2.2 billion per year. Of that Tylenol® was by far the strongest selling brand with more than US $1 billion in sales. It was Johnson & Johnson's biggest consumer brand (O'Reilly, 1994).

▌ This has probably been the largest product recall in business history to date. It remains an example to other companies.

▌ As of May 2003 no one has been charged with the Tylenol® product tampering and the subsequent deaths. It remains an 'open' file at the FBI.

Questions/activities

1. Search the Internet to obtain the latest financial report for Johnson & Johnson. This will illustrate its financial strength and global reach. Compare the market share of Tylenol® today with its position in the 1980s.

2. During the 1980s Johnson & Johnson was able to sustain a short-term economic loss when it withdrew Tylenol® from the market. However, critically evaluate the following scenario. A company with a product defect, knowing that a product recall could lead to bankruptcy, does not recall the product. The product defect is non-life-threatening and the directors believe that by not recalling the product they will save the business, and hence jobs. Some people would call this unethical, and in some countries this would be deemed illegal if discovered and the directors would face prosecution.

sensitive. Will they place ethics over price and convenience? Some will, some will not.

This goes to the crux of Davidson's (1998) argument: that there are two combined areas of ethical judgement. This judgment stems from, first, that the manufacturer's/seller's ethical behaviour is an attribute of the product or service. Second, consumers, weigh up the various ethical considerations along with the other attributes. It is this combination that eventually drives our buying habits.

It is clear that in the 21st century consumers will have access to more information. How they interpret and use that information will be the issue. Not all consumers are ethical, some through lack of awareness, others through choice.

An ethical framework

In Table 3.1 we present a simplified framework for ethical decision making (based on Sternberg, 1994).

Limitations

As with all frameworks this has its limitations. We briefly explore them below.

Table 3.1   An ethical framework

Step	Action	Questions and comments
1	The need to clarify the question for ethical decision making	How many issues does the question raise? What are the solutions implicit within the question? (These must be issues that a business, as opposed to say a government regulator, can handle.) Who is asking the question? Why are they asking the question? Which individuals or groups will be affected by any decision taken? Whose responsibility will it be to make the decision? And why?
2	Determining the relevance for this particular business	Is it relevant to business and industry generally? Is it a case of business ethics or government policy? Is it relevant to this particular company or organization? Can the issue or issues be resolved by normal business criteria? (For example, the use of recycled material may be cheaper, or at least, comparable to non-recycled material (and of the same quality). Thus recycled material could be used – this would be a normal business decision.
3	Identify circumstantial constraints. These constraints limit the variety of possible solutions to a problem.	This is the focus on honouring contracts already in place. For instance, suddenly changing to a 'greener' or more 'environmentally friendly' component has its merits. However, immediate severance of contracts impact upon 'trust', 'loyalty' and the workforce in the contractual company. It could be argued that such 'immediate' severance is an unethical act. The culture of the company or organization may inhibit certain actions from being taken. The expectations of society as a whole, or the power exerted by the key stakeholders, may become an issue. Business is bound by its 'classical' concerns regarding costs, product availability, market share and debt burdens.
4	Assess available options	What is the long-term effect on shareholder values? Are the actions in accordance with justice? Do the actions follow ordinary decency? Clearly any decision that includes stealing, coercion or lying is an unethical decision. Such unethical action could have major ramifications for the company or organization.

People

The basic premise of ethics is based upon how people think and react to issues. As we have already seen, and is evidenced by the endless press reports on corruption highlighted in the media, not everyone is ethical. It would be clearly naïve to think so. However, as we have seen, ethical decision making is not a clear-cut issue. There are 'grey' areas, and thus degrees of ethical behaviour. Thus in considering such a framework, you need to consider the personal qualities and motives of the individual(s) involved. These factors will (to a greater or lesser extent) drive their actions.

Shareholder power

This can operate in a myriad of ways. However, for simplicity we will take two perspectives.

(1) Pro-ethical stance. As we discuss in Chapter 4, consumers have become a powerful force in their own right. Many have become shareholders directly or indirectly through investment funds. Increasingly the small investors have grouped together to become a potentially powerful lobby. Thus if they believe that the company's board is acting, or considering acting, in a perceived unethical manner, they can voice their opposition at the annual general meeting or extraordinary meetings. If the group commands significant votes it can vote off or remove members of the board. However, we must return to the issue of what constitutes unethical behaviour. It can be a matter of perception. In the United States various lobby groups have become shareholders of major companies in order to press their particular cases. While this should be welcomed and encouraged, there is a caveat. Such groups must take a balanced view of what is possible and realistic at a point in time. Unfortunately, not all do, and that does not benefit the progress of ethical decision making.

(2) The dividend and share values. We must not lose sight of the fact that a function of a commercial enterprise is to generate returns for its shareholders – its investors. However shareholders can, and do, exert pressure on a company to maximize both dividend and shareholder values. This pressure may push the boards or directors of some companies to act irresponsibly and unethically to achieve such goals.

External factors

Factors beyond the control of the company and its directors may influence or drive actions that may be deemed unethical. An example could be political influence or force, especially where the country is governed by a dictatorship.

These limitations, however, should not detract from the overall benefit of employing such frameworks.

Chapter summary

What we see in terms of social responsibility is a change in perception. It is no longer only the view of groups of environmental activists, it is the general public at large. Business, large or small, can no longer use the excuse that it's just a 'handful of cranks'. Concern for the environment, ethics, society and social responsibility is now the preserve of everyone.

Being socially responsible, however, does not just mean producing a series of written statements. Producing a series of corporate ethical and environment policies is a relatively easy process. It is the continued implementation and refinement that is most challenging for the company. Once the process has started, it cannot be reversed. Social responsibility must be directed from the top and permeate the organization, from individual and management actions to where raw materials and finished articles are sourced, and what price is paid for those materials.

Investing in such ongoing actions creates costs; however we need to strive for the longer-term benefits for both society and the company. When we consider the marketing mix (product, price, promotion, placement/ distribution – people, process and physical evidence), perhaps we also need to consider *performance*: not just in terms of product quality, or financial returns, but in ethical/ environmental performance. In essence, this is what the company has achieved, for as the surveys illustrate, customers are becoming more socially and ethically aware. Therefore, social responsibility now has a marketing imperative. However, it must be supported by real substance.

If the growing body of research is to be believed, a company's attitude to social responsibility in the 21st century could be critical to its overall success.

Code of Ethics: American Marketing Association (www.ama.org)

As this is a marketing textbook, we felt that the codes of practice from a professional marketing organization should be included. Founded in 1937 as a professional non-profit organization for marketers, the AMA purpose is to promote education; to assist in personal and professional career development among marketing professionals; and to advance the science and ethical practice of marketing disciplines. The AMA is now the world's largest professional society for marketers, consisting of more than 45,000 worldwide members in 92 countries.

Responsibility of the marketer

Marketers must accept responsibility for the consequences of their activities and make every effort to ensure that their decisions, recommendations, and actions function to identify, serve and satisfy all relevant publics: consumers, organizations and society.

Marketers' professional conduct must be guided by:

1. The basic rule of professional ethics: not knowingly to do harm.
2. The adherence to applicable laws and regulations.
3. The accurate representation of their education, training and experience.
4. The active support, practice and promotion of this Code of Ethics.

Honesty and fairness

Marketers shall uphold and advance the integrity, honor and dignity of the marketing profession by:

1. Being honest in serving consumers, clients, employees, suppliers, distributors and the public.
2. Not knowingly participating in conflicts of interest without prior notice to all parties involved.
3. Establishing equitable fee schedules including the payment or receipt of usual, customary and/or legal compensation for marketing exchanges.

Rights and duties of parties

Participants in the marketing exchange process should be able to expect that:

1. Products and services offered are safe and fit for their intended uses.
2. Communications about offered products and services are not deceptive.
3. All parties intend to discharge their obligations, financial and otherwise, in good faith.
4. Appropriate internal methods exist for equitable adjustments and/or redress of grievances concerning purchases.

It is understood that the above would include, but is not limited to, the following responsibilities of the marketer.

In the area of product development management:

1. Disclosure of all substantial risks associated with product or service usage.
2. Identification of any product component substitution that might materially change the product or impact upon the buyer's purchasing decision.
3. Identification of extra-cost features.

In the area of promotions:

1. Avoidance of false and misleading advertising.
2. Rejection of high pressure manipulations, or misleading sales tactics.
3. Avoidance of sales promotions that use deception or manipulation.

In the area of distribution:

1. Not manipulating the availability of a product for the purpose of exploitation.
2. Not using coercion in the marketing channel.
3. Not exerting undue influence over the reseller's choice to handle the product.

In the area of pricing:

1. Not engaging in price fixing.
2. Not practicing predatory pricing.
3. Disclosing the full price associated with any purchase.

In the area of marketing research:

1. Prohibiting selling or fund raising under the guise of conducting research.
2. Maintaining research integrity by avoiding misrepresentation and omission of pertinent research data.
3. Treating outside clients and suppliers fairly.

Organizational relationships

Marketers should be aware of how their behavior may influence or impact on the behavior of others in organizational relationships. They should not encourage or apply coercion to obtain unethical behavior in their relationship with others, such as employees, suppliers or customers.

1. Apply confidentiality and anonymity in professional relationships with regard to privileged information.
2. Meet their obligations and responsibilities in contracts and mutual agreements, in a timely manner.
3. Avoid taking the work of others, in whole, or in part, and representing this work as their own or directly benefit from it without compensation or consent of the originator or owner.
4. Avoid manipulation to take advantage of situations to maximize personal welfare in a way that unfairly deprives or damages the organization or others.

Any AMA member found to be in violation of any of this Code of Ethics may have his or her Association membership suspended or revoked.

Code of Ethics for Marketing on the Internet

The Internet, including on-line computer communications, has become increasingly important to marketers' activities, as they provide exchanges and access to markets worldwide. The ability to interact with stakeholders has created new marketing opportunities and risks that are not currently specially addressed in the American Marketing Association code of ethics. The American Marketing Association Code of Ethics for Internet Marketing provides additional guidance and direction for ethical responsibility in this dynamic area of marketing.

The American Marketing Association is committed to ethical professional conduct and has adopted these principles for using the Internet, including on-line marketing activities utilizing network computers.

General responsibilities

Internet marketers must assess the risks and take responsibility for the consequences of their activities. Internet marketers' professional conduct must be guided by:

1. Support of professional ethics to avoid harm by protecting the rights of privacy, ownership and access.
2. Adherence to all applicable laws and regulations with no use of Internet marketing that would be illegal, if conducted by mail, telephone, fax or other media.
3. Awareness of changes in regulations related to Internet marketing.
4. Effective communications to organizational members on risks and policies related to Internet marketing, where appropriate.
5. Organizational commitment to ethical Internet practices communicated to employees, customers and relevant stakeholders.

Privacy

Information collected from customers should be confidential and used only for expressed purposes. All data, especially confidential customer data, should be safeguarded against unauthorized access. The expressed wishes of others should be respected with regard to the receipt of unsolicited e-mail messages.

Ownership

Information obtained from the Internet sources should be properly authorized and documented. Information ownership should be safeguarded and respected. Marketers should respect the integrity and ownership of computer and network systems.

Access

Marketers should treat access to accounts, passwords, and other information as confidential, and only examine or disclose content when authorized by a responsible party. The integrity of others' information systems should be respected with regard to placement of information, advertising or messages.

Copyright: The American Marketing Association

Exercises and questions for review and critical thinking

1. 'Marketing departments and companies should act ethically.' Critically evaluate the merits of this statement. What are the possible advantages of ethical behaviour, and the disadvantages of non-ethical behaviour?

2. Study the ethical codes of two companies of your choice. Consider within the codes what percentage of the codes can be directly linked to marketing activity. On examining this do you believe that a suffi- cient percentage has been assigned to marketing, or do you think there is a need for more? It is important to provide evidence to support your view.

3. Do you think there is a need for more ethical codes of practice that are enforceable in law? Why?

4. Do you believe that marketers should receive training in ethical behaviour? Why?

5. 'Boycotts of products and services don't work.' Consider this statement and construct arguments for and against.

4

Buyer behaviour

Introduction

In this chapter we consider the role of the customer within the marketing operation. Various authors have suggested that customers are now more powerful than they have ever been before, and that this power (or influence) is bound to increase with time. Some however are more sceptical, believing that there will always be 'manipulation' of customers by companies and governments alike.

However, we need to understand what drives, influences or determines an individual's buying behaviour. Why do customers buy one product or brand rather than another? Why do some customers remain loyal to one brand, even though another (with the same ingredients) may be cheaper? Why do some customers easily switch from one brand to another? What effect do family, friends and even the media have on people's buying decisions? Are the factors that influence corporate buying the same as for consumer buying? This chapter explores some of these decision-making issues.

Learning objectives

On completion of this chapter you will be able to:

▌ analyse the factors influencing consumer and organizational buyer behaviour;

▌ outline the differing customer types, and consider how marketers attempt to influence them;

▌ demonstrate an understanding of the development of regulations to protect consumer interests, and consider how these impact upon business environments;

▌ explain the relationship between consumers and marketing ethics.

Who or what is a customer?

In 1912 Leon Leonwood Bean starts the beginnings of the LL Bean mail order business based upon the philosophy of looking after the customer.[1] This is a view that was encapsulated in LL's Golden Rule:

LL's Golden Rule
Sell good merchandise at a reasonable profit, treat your customers like human beings, and they will always come back for more.
Leon Leonwood Bean
© LL Bean, Inc.

Today LL Bean is both a retail and mail order business specializing in outdoor-oriented clothing and activities. A private family-owned business, it generates annual revenues of over US $1 billion. The operational statistics (listed below, taken from LL Bean's Web site) illustrate the scale of the business.

In 2002:

▪ over 16,000 different items were available;

▪ 13 million customer calls;

▪ 11.3 million items shipped;

▪ 3 million visitors to the Flagship Store (built on the site of the original store of 1917);

▪ over 7,000 customers participated in more than 800 Outdoor Discovery School classes;

▪ peak holiday season: 115,000 customer calls and over 105,000 packages shipped on busiest day.

The company has focused on customer service and the following statements (displayed on posters at LL Bean) demonstrate the value that they award to customers (Kotler, 2000):

A customer is the most important person ever in this office, in person, by mail or on the telephone.

A customer is not dependent upon us... we are dependent upon them.

A customer is not an interruption to our work... they are the purpose of it. We are not doing a favour by serving them, they are doing us a favour by giving us the opportunity to do so.

A customer is a person who brings us their wants. It is our job to handle them profitably, both to them and to ourselves.

Without customers or buyers a company or an organization (either for profit or not-for-profit) does not have a 'business' or operational purpose. This is the argument used to support a customer orientation. (You may want to reflect back on the relationship issues discussed in Chapter 1.)

The marketing concept suggests that both companies and organizations should focus their operations on their customers' needs, rather than, say, being driven solely by the organization's technical competence to produce a particular range of products or services, or a belief in the power of the sales force to sell anything.

We must be mindful that there are different types of 'buyers', and thus we must categorize them for efficiency. See Table 4.1.

Business to government (B2G) is often underrated in terms of discussion. However, just consider for a moment how much governments spend on buying materials and resources (including knowhow) from other countries. The most prominent example is military equipment and support.

Types of buyer

Figure 4.1 illustrates the different types of buyer (this also links to Chapter 5, 'Segmenting, targeting and positioning'). As can be seen, the marketer commences with a

Table 4.1 Buyer categories

Buying group	Description
Consumer buying	▪ business to consumer (B2C) ▪ charity to consumer (C2C)
Organizational or business buying	▪ business to business (B2B) ▪ business to government (B2G)

Figure 4.1 Types of buyer

mass audience, then progresses upwards with a decreasing – but all-important – number of customers. Many factors will influence whether a prospect converts to a customer and remains a loyal customer. These issues must be considered in relation to the factors that influence buyer decision making, which are illustrated later in this chapter.

Suspects

A suspect is a person, or group of people, the marketer has reason to believe could be interested in the product or service on offer. Suspects have not previously enquired or bought the product/service. For the marketer they are an unidentified audience. One way a marketer could target this group is to place an advertisement in a newspaper this target group tends to read.

Prospects: identifying target audiences

Prospects are individuals who have not bought the marketer's product or service; however they have indicated a possible interest. At this stage it is only 'tentative'. For example, the marketer places an adver-tisement, say for a holiday resort, in a national newspaper and an individual responds by requesting further information. The prospect may be gathering information from several sources to help him or her in a personal decision-making process. The prospect may be currently in a position to buy or may be considering a purchase some time in the future. Either way, how the marketing team reacts may make the difference between a purchase (and the possi-bility of a long-term customer) and no purchase.

First-time buyer/customer: converting enquiries to sales

Here the customer has made their first purchase. This may be his or her only purchase of a particular product or service, or he or she may become a loyal long-term customer. It may depend upon how the organ-ization develops the relationship with the customer. That may be dependent upon a mixture of the customer's experience of the product and service, and whether the organi-zation takes a short-term or long-term view.

Repeat buyer/customer: winning repeat orders

Here the customer has made more than one purchase, and might show every indication that he or she will become a long-term buyer. There is an opportunity for a relationship to develop between the customer and the organization. Several factors will influence whether customers make repeat purchases in the future. These include the following:

▮ Some products are one-off purchases: for example, the purchase of a new house. In some cases the customer never buys another house, and the existing one may be handed down through several generations of the family.

▮ There may be a long time span between purchases, as for example with buying a new car. An individual may be loyal to a particular brand, but not choose to trade in the old model for a new one for several years. Some car buyers keep their car for five years before replacing it with a new model.

▮ The relationship between the customer and the organization. If a positive relationship is developing, the customer may, depending upon his or her personal circumstances, increase his or her purchasing. For example, he or she might visit a particular restaurant on an increasingly regular basis because the food (product) and staff attitude (service) are to his or her personal taste/liking.

▮ FMCGs (Fast Moving Consumer Goods) such as toothpaste, soap and shampoos create the opportunity for constant repeat purchases. However, other factors impact here. These include:

   ... quality of the product/delivery of the service;

   ... pricing;

   ... packaging.

Advocates: helping to build brand loyalty over a longer time period

These are customers who are loyal to the product or service and purchase on a regular basis (bearing in mind the points raised above in relation to frequency of purchase). Additionally, they tend to strongly recommend the product/service to their friends and colleagues. Examples include the following products or services:

▮ a restaurant;

▮ an Internet discussion group;

▮ an airline;

▮ a brand of coffee;

▮ a particular shop – anything from clothing to a food store;

▮ a university or college course;

▮ an insurance company.

The buying decision process

Customers engage in a buying decision process, in which buyers undergo a series of steps in order to formulate their final decision. Engel, Blackwell and Miniard (1990) define a series of steps a consumer might undertake in order to choose a particular product or service. These steps are illustrated in Figure 4.2.

Now for a more detailed analysis of each stage of the process:

The recognition of an unsatisfied need/want/desire

Although an individual may be aware of his or her needs, wants and desires, that alone will not generate a buying decision. In our lives we have many needs, wants and desires; however we are limited by the amount of time and finance we have available. These needs, wants

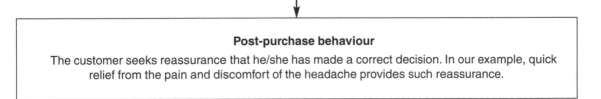

The recognition of an unsatisfied need/want/desire

The customer recognizes a need and subsequently takes action. For example, a woman may develop a headache while out shopping and seek to remedy the resulting discomfort as soon as possible by purchasing a painkiller.

The level of involvement

The customer determines how much time and effort she will invest into satisfying a need. In the example, she will probably want to find a quick remedy for two possible reasons: (1) to effectively reduce the pain and discomfort; (2) so she can continue shopping, out of either need or desire. Therefore she will limit the level of involvement.

Identification of the alternatives

The customer considers the various alternatives available to him or her. In our example, she will probably identify that there are several types of analgesics available: aspirin, paracetamol and ibupofren. These are available as either well-known branded drugs or own-label drugs. (The differences in brand types is examined in a later chapter.)

Evaluation of the alternatives

The customer analyses the potential advantages and disadvantages of the various alternatives identified. In our example, the customer may consider the strengths available, whether she is allergic to any of the ingredients, any possible side-effects, whether the painkiller is in tablet or capsule form, the number of tablets/capsules contained in a pack and the price.

Purchasing decision

The customer decides whether or not to make a purchase. In our example, the customer might decide to buy the own-branded paracetamol capsules because of 'the strength, they are easy to swallow and the overall value for money'.

Post-purchase behaviour

The customer seeks reassurance that he/she has made a correct decision. In our example, quick relief from the pain and discomfort of the headache provides such reassurance.

Figure 4.2 The buying decision process

and desires compete for both our time and money, thus choices have to be made. With the limitations placed on us, we realize that needs tend to have greater importance than desires. For example, if we have a limited amount of money, buying groceries to satisfy our basic need for food will have a priority over buying a newly released CD or DVD that we desire. True, owning the CD or DVD would bring us some personal pleasure and comfort; however the basic need normally holds a greater priority.

The level of involvement

Once the need, want or desire has been recognized, the customer decides how much time and effort (involvement) will be undertaken. The level of involvement undertaken must be considered from the perspective of the individual rather than from that of the product or service.

High involvement

Here the individual actively seeks out and evaluates information before making the final purchasing decision. An example is the purchase of a new car. Here the potential buyer seeks information on various models in order to consider such factors as performance, comfort, safety features, reliability, after sales service, price and payment options. He or she might then discuss the possible alternatives with the whole family prior to making the actual purchase.

Low involvement

If individuals already have the information they need available, they will probably not seek out any further information. Let's take the painkiller example. If a woman with a headache knows exactly what brand she wants, she can go directly to the pharmacist and request that brand by name. Since she knows which brand will cure her headache, there is no need for her to consider or analyse any further information.

Impulse buying can also be considered as a form of low involvement. With impulse buying there is no advanced planning on the part of the individual. A classic example is a shopper standing at the checkout counter at the supermarket. While standing in line he sees an array of confectionery and the store magazine displayed. The list of articles on the cover of the magazine, along with value for money offer vouchers highlighted on a corner flash, may entice him to purchase the magazine. The purchase takes place even though he had no intention of buying magazines when he entered the supermarket.

A note of caution: we must realize that consumers are individuals, and what constitutes a high level of involvement for one person may not for another.

Laurent and Kapferer (1985) identified four factors that influence the overall level of involvement (see Table 4.2).

Identification of the alternatives

Here the customer seeks out and identifies a range of products and brands which may satisfy his or her particular needs. In our example the shopper with the headache identified that there were several types of analgesic available – aspirin, paracetamol and ibuprofen – that could reduce the severity of the pain. In addition, they could be provided in various forms – tablet or capsule – and by different manufacturers, including well-known brands and own-label branded labels.

Stanton et al (1998) suggest that the search for alternatives is influenced by several factors:

▌ How much information the customer already has from previous experiences and other sources (for example, family and friends as well as literature).

Table 4.2 Factors that influence the level of involvement

Factors	Description
Self-image	The level of involvement will tend to be high when the decision impacts upon the individual's self-image: for example in the purchase of fashion items or particular makes of cars, such as a sleek stylish £150,000 Aston Martin.
Perceived risk	The level of involvement will tend to be high when there is an element of risk associated with the purchase. The level of perceived risk can obviously vary from one individual to another. An individual may be particularly sensitive to certain types of medicines, thus will have a high level of involvement in choosing, for example, the right painkillers. He or she may want to purchase one that while removing the pain of the headache is gentle on the stomach, which may not be the case for all types of painkiller. At another level an example is the purchase of a new house. If the wrong decision is taken (for example, location, type of house, structure) it could be an extremely costly error of judgment. The level of perceived risk may increase in relation to the price of the purchase and location.
Social factors	The level of involvement will tend to be high when there is a direct link to social acceptance: for example the joining of a particular sports club or society, or the type of wines purchased for a dinner party.
Hedonistic influences	The level of involvement will tend to be high when linked to a high level of pleasure as a result of the purchase. This could range from buying a particular brand of luxury Belgian chocolates, through to choosing fine wines, a particular restaurant for a special occasion (St Valentine's Day or an anniversary/birthday) or a luxury holiday. A poor choice could severely impact on the level of overall pleasure gained from the experience.

■ The consumer's level of confidence in that information.

■ The expected value of additional information. This can be defined as the amount of time and money necessary to seek out and analyse further information, and the expected return on that investment.

Evaluation of the alternatives

Once the alternatives have been identified, the consumer will evaluate them in relation to each other, prior to making a decision to purchase or not. At this stage the consumer may decide not to purchase any of the alternatives, perhaps because he or she believes all the elements of his or her need are not fulfilled at this stage. He or she could decide to wait until more alternatives become available in the future.

An example of this is a couple seeking to purchase a new sofa for their home. Having considered the various designs, sizes, fabrics and colour schemes available, they decide to wait a further year until the new ranges are available in the furniture stores.

The consumer will use a set of criteria in order to compare and contrast the different alternatives. The criteria may be determined or influenced by various factors. Table 4.3 lists some of those factors, and relates them to the example of the shopper with the headache.

Purchasing decisions

Once evaluation of the alternatives is complete the consumer has to take the

Table 4.3 Possible buying criteria

Criteria	Influencing factors
Past experience of using a particular brand(s)	The consumer may have used particular brands in the past and believe that one is more effective than another. (In reality they may have been composed of exactly the same ingredients; however she perceives that one brand was more effective than another.)
Past experience of using a particular product	In our example the shopper had a choice between aspirin, paracetamol and ibuprofen. She may have discovered that, for example, aspirin irritates her stomach so she tries to avoid taking it.
The experience of friends and family	In a previous discussion a family member or friend may have recommended a particular brand of analgesic for its effective action. Therefore this information may influence the evaluation. Equally, the advice might be not to buy a particular brand because it had little or no effect. With this information the consumer may immediately discount this branded item without any further evaluation.
The influence of advertising/marketing	The consumer may have seen a television advertisement for a new brand of analgesic. Therefore she seeks out this brand at the pharmacy, reads the packaging and evaluates it alongside the other brands.
Specialist advice	The consumer may seek some form of guidance within the store. In our example she might ask the pharmacist for advice, even though the final decision rests with her. Equally, she might be taking other medicines, and her doctor has advised that taking aspirin as well could cause mild, but unpleasant side-effects. Therefore she will seek to avoid such additional discomfort.

decision whether to purchase or not. As we discussed above, the decision not to purchase may only be a relatively temporary one until other alternatives become available.

In many situations once the decision to purchase is taken, the time span between the decision and acquisition is relatively small. In our example of the shopper with the headache, she hands over the packet and the money to the salesperson at the checkout counter. It is a simple and fast transaction.

However, in other situations the decision to purchase will lead to a series of additional interrelated purchase-related decisions. Here we will use the example of a couple purchasing a new washing machine.

The couple may be loyal to a particular electrical retailer, and have decided to place their purchase with them. On the other hand, they may have no loyalty to any one store. There is also the factor of experience within particular

purchasing environments. For example, the couple in our example would go to their local high street or shopping mall electrical retailers rather than a store like Harrods in London or Macy's in New York, even though both perhaps sell the brand and model of machine they seek to purchase. Among other factors, such as price, they might have no experience or feel uncomfortable purchasing in such exclusive stores.

Their decision to place the order at a particular store could be based on the criteria listed in Table 4.4.

Post-purchase behaviour

Prior to purchasing the product/service, customers use a set of criteria to evaluate or analyse the range of alternatives available. Once they have 'experienced' that product

Table 4.4   Criteria in purchasing decisions (an example)

Criteria	Description
The level of helpfulness of the sales staff	In the pre-decision phase, if the staff of a particular store show that they are knowledgeable, have spent time with the couple answering their questions, have been courteous and nothing has been too much trouble, the couple may be influenced to purchase from that particular store. This is the role of people within the marketing mix. See Chapter 12.
The layout of the store	The display and range of products on show may be influencing factors. See Chapter 12.
Discounts/ sale offers	If there is strong local competition, some stores may seek to discount the product on a regular basis, or have frequent special offers. See Chapter 9.
Additional charges	Some retailers may charge for a local delivery and fitting, whilst others do not. This could be a deciding factor, especially if the couple are price-sensitive. See Chapter 9.
Methods of payment	In addition to cheques and credit cards, the store may offer an interest-free monthly direct debit payment system. This would allow the couple to spread their payments, say over a 6 or 12-month period, at no extra cost. Again, this may be beneficial to the couple if they are particularly price-sensitive.
After sales service	In addition to the standard guarantee/warranty, the retailer may offer a special after sales service including a telephone helpline/support service, and the ability to extend the guarantee/warranty beyond the statutory period.

they may revise their criteria and evaluation in the light of new information. The product/service they have purchased may exceed their expectations; on the other hand it might not.

For example, a couple decide to take a two-week vacation in the Mediterranean. They seek sun, sand, quiet and a full-board hotel at a reasonable price. They consult travel brochures and discuss the options with their local travel agent. They subsequently make a decision and purchase a holiday package.

On arrival at the hotel (the point of consumption of the product) they find that it is located in a noisy resort full of discos, the beach is too small to cope with the influx of tourists, the dining room in the hotel is overflowing with guests, and the staff are unable to cater for the number of diners. Additionally, a new hotel is being built next to their hotel. In order to meet construction deadlines, the building work continues from morning till dusk every day.

Clearly, as a result of these accumulative problems, the couple do not enjoy their

holiday. What they have experienced is a difference between the expectation of the product and the product's actual performance. This dissatisfaction is known as cognitive dissonance, and is quite a common occurrence.

This holiday example is based on a real case, and may sound extreme. However, during the 1990s many UK tour operators faced complaints from disgruntled holiday-makers over the differences between what the companies marketed and the reality of the situation. To reduce the level of cognitive dissonance tour operators have revised the information available to travel agents, and contained within their brochures. In addition, they have sought to improve communication with their customers, and have sought to reassure them with money-back guarantees if the holiday does not meet their expectations.

Let us consider another example. A customer buys a red pullover from a leading department store. The label states his size and he believes the colour suits him. However, when he returns home and wears it his partner suggests that the colour does not suit his complexion, it is too bulky and not a good fit. Now the consumer suffers anxiety over the purchase of the pullover, with the unattractive features (as stated by his partner) gaining in importance and magnitude. Thus he begins to doubt the wisdom of his choice. The level of cognitive dissonance can be reduced if the consumer knows that, as long as he has a receipt, he can take it back to the store to either exchange it for something more suitable, or gain a refund.

Although, a refund – whole or in part – is useful, it would not undo the discomfort experienced by the couple in the holiday example. They might not have the opportunity to take another vacation for 12 months. Their anger at the holiday company could remain forever, and they might seek further compensation/publicity through the courts, and/or inform all their friends and family. (We consider the power of word-of-mouth publicity in Chapter 11.)

The problems potentially associated with making purchasing decisions for ourselves also apply if we are buying a present for someone else. The UK book retailing chain Books *etc* (acquired by the US-based Borders Group in 1998) introduced a book return policy. Anyone who bought a book at one of their stores and was dissatisfied with it – for example, did not like the storyline – could receive a refund or another purchase, as long as the original book was returned with its receipt within 14 days. We consider here a couple of examples of the value to the customer.

(1) A friend has recommended a particular fiction title. A customer goes into the store, and buys the title priced at £14.95. On reading the first few chapters she finds it excessively violent, and decides not to carry on reading it. Obviously, for her it was an ill-chosen title, and a poor recommendation from her friend. Her cognitive dissonance will be high because she has paid £14.95 (perhaps a high price for

her) for a book from which she has derived very little, if any, pleasure.

(2) It is Christmas and a man decides to buy a friend the latest cookbook by a renowned chef. It costs £25.00, and on presenting it to his friend he sees a sparkling new copy already on her bookshelf. He could keep it for himself; however he might already have bookshelves full of such titles. In both cases, the opportunity to return the book reduces the cognitive dissonance, the customer's level of anxiety that he or she could be wasting both time and money.

Can such a system be abused? Of course. When Books *etc* first introduced this system there were suggestions that customers would use it purely as a type of library: purchase one book, read it then bring it back to exchange for another, then repeat the process. A minority might attempt this; however the majority will most likely use it as it was intended.

Business to consumer (B2C)

In July 1962 a local entrepreneur, Sam Walton, opened a new variety merchandise store in Rogers, Arkansas. Across the front of the store was a sign that stated WAL-MART. On one side of the sign was written 'We sell for less', whilst on the other 'Satisfaction guaranteed'. These have remained the philosophies of the company (Walton and Huey, 1992). In his autobiography, Walton underpinned these philosophies by stating:

The secret of successful retailing is to give your customers what they want... if you think about it from your point of view as a customer, you want everything: a wide assortment of good quality merchandise; the lowest possible prices; guaranteed satisfaction with what you buy; friendly, knowledgeable service; convenient hours; free parking; a pleasant shopping experience. You love it when you visit a store that somehow exceeds your expectations, and you hate it when a store inconveniences you, or gives you a hard time, or just pretends you're invisible.

(Walton and Huey, 1992)

Many of the issues raised by the late Sam Walton are now core elements in the operations of UK-based supermarket chains. Since the late 1980s there have been radical changes in the operations, indeed look of many supermarkets. In a highly competitive environment UK supermarkets have sought to enhance their relationship with customers. The following are a selection of actions implemented by supermarkets in the battle for customers and subsequently increased revenues.

▌ Diversity and range of products – especially in relation to fresh fish, vegetables and fruit. More exotic ranges are now imported.

▌ Increased range of organically produced foods. These may range from free-range eggs to fruits and vegetables that have not been treated with inorganic fertilizers and pesticides.

▌ Longer opening hours. Until the early 1990s supermarket opening hours were generally limited to 9 am to 6 pm, Monday to Saturday. The UK Sunday Trading Laws prevented opening on Sundays. Indeed, these laws severely restricted what could actually be sold on a Sunday. In many ways it was the smaller corner shops, especially in urban areas such as London, that began to break the mould. They would open earlier and close later in order to maximize customer opportunities. Indeed, some risked prosecution and financial penalties to open, at least for a limited period, on Sundays.

With flexible work patterns, greater levels of shift work, the dynamics of society, consumer demand and the need to increase revenues and profitability, the supermarket chains extended their opening hours. Indeed, they fought for the opportunity to open seven days a week. Once this was achieved supermarkets experimented with the concept of 24-hour shopping. In the build up to Christmas 1996 a couple of supermarket chains opened key stores for a straight 48-hour period. The result was less congestion of customers, and more time to shop, thus a greater opportunity for the customers to purchase more, which in turn increased revenues. Today it is standard for key stores in urban areas to be open 24 hours straddling the Friday morning to Saturday evening period.

▌ Increased range of in-store facilities. Today, in many stores there are toilets, baby-changing facilities and cafés.

▌ Free car parking – both at out-of-town sites and within some urban areas.

▌ Petrol stations – the larger sites now sell petroleum products at competitive prices, often linking additional savings via loyalty card schemes.

▌ Wide range of payment systems – today a variety of credit cards can be used for payment, in addition to cash and cheques. Also, many stores operate a 'cash-back' scheme whereby cash can be obtained on a customer's credit card at the point of purchase.

▌ Automatic teller machines (ATMs) – many of the larger stores have a range of ATMs in order for customers to obtain cash readily.

If new products and services are developed with an inadequate regard for customers' needs, an expensive sales effort will be needed to persuade customers they should purchase something from the company that does not exactly match their needs.

Consumerism

Consumers today are more powerful than at perhaps any other time, and that power is increasing. If a company wants to succeed it must win the hearts and minds of its customers, and it appears the odds are often stacked against the company. One survey revealed the following customer trait: a typical business hears from only 4 per cent of its dissatisfied customers. The other 96 per cent just quietly go away and 91 per cent will never return.

However, there is perhaps worse to come. Dissatisfied customers tell 11 to 15 people about their experience, who in turn tell another 11 to 15 people, and so on. On the other hand, satisfied customers only tell 5 to 7 people about their experience, who in turn tell another 5 to 7 people, and so on.

In addition, the media are often quick to highlight consumer issues. There are specialist programmes on both radio and television, and usually a journalist on major newspapers dedicated to such issues. An item showcased on prime-time television has a potential viewing audience of millions. If a company has failed to take the consumer into consideration, or rectify the situation, and this fact is publicized, it could suffer a slump in sales, and thus revenue.

As the primary consumer products have always been food items, early consumer protection centred on the preparation and selling of food. The ancient Egyptians established laws to control the handling of meat and oils. The Greeks and Romans had laws to determine the quality of bread, and to prevent the dilution of wine with water. For those who dared to tamper with food and break the law, punishment was often most severe. The death penalty for consumer fraud was apparently not uncommon (Felton, 1991).

Prior to the current deluge of legislation to protect consumers, it was the buyer's responsibility to decide on the 'suitability' of the product. Unless there was a stated and specific guarantee, buyers purchased goods at their own risk. In law this was known as *caveat emptor*, a Latin phrase that means 'let the buyer beware'. In essence it meant that the seller was providing no warranty or any other contractual support to the customer. Buyers therefore had to undertake their own investigations and bear any ensuing risk of any flaws or defects within the product.

Let us take the example of the man buying a sweater he subsequently regrets. It used to be unlikely that the store would exchange it, even if the customer provided a valid receipt. Today it is a very different picture. In the UK, Europe and North America, for example, the consumer has a statutory right to return the product and obtain a refund if the goods are unsatisfactory. Indeed, companies now actively promote the option to return goods if the customer is not totally satisfied with them. For many companies this has become a means of gaining competitor advantage as we will examine later.

Steiner and Steiner (1994) describe consumerism as 'a movement designed to improve the rights and powers of consumers in relation to sellers of products and services. It is a protest movement of consumers against what they or their advocates see as unfair, discriminatory, and arbitrary treatment.'

Although consumerism has been around since the dawn of business itself, it is only in recent history that it has gained momentum. Here we must return to the United States in the early to mid-1960s. During this period several factors combined to establish the consumer movement as we know it today. On 15 March 1962 President John F Kennedy delivered a special message to Congress in which he stated the need for a Consumers' Bill of Rights. In this he outlined four basic principles or consumer rights (Felton, 1991):

- the right to product safety;
- the right to be informed and protected;

▌ the right to choose from a variety of products;

▌ the right to be heard by government.

Later, Gerald Ford during his Presidency (1974–76), added a fifth (Felton, 1991):

▌ the right to consumer education.

Although the Bill never became law, it nonetheless influenced consumers, government and managers.

In April 1975 the European Union's Council of Ministers adopted its first consumer information and protection programme. Five basic consumer rights were stated (Leonard, 1998):

▌ the right to safeguards for health and safety;

▌ the right to economic justice;

▌ the right to redress for damages;

▌ the right to information and education;

▌ the right to consultation.

In many ways this legislation is similar to that espoused by US Presidents Kennedy and Ford. However, it was the publication in 1965 of Ralph Nader's book *Unsafe At Any Speed* that perhaps was the turning point in consumerism. A bestseller, *Unsafe At Any Speed* was an analysis of the US car industry and the potential dangers associated with particular makes of cars.

Nader subsequently became one of the leading advocates of consumerism. A graduate of both Princeton University and Harvard Law School, he was called to the Connecticut Bar in 1959. In *Unsafe At Any Speed*, he was critical of welding on General Motors' Chevrolet Corvair automobile, accusing the manufacturer of a lack of concern about automobile safety. Such was the public outcry as a result of the issues raised in the book, the US government intro-

duced improved car safety regulations in 1966. Since then Nader continues to battle through various organizations for the rights of the ordinary consumer. Such has been the power of the consumer movement that it led one anonymous writer to state 'Keep in mind that Ralph Nader could be the first customer for your new product.'

Today in the United States there are over 50 federal government agencies that directly influence consumer rights and protection. In addition, there are hundreds of state and local agencies concerned with consumer affairs. The seven major federal agencies engaged in US consumer protection are:

▌ The Consumer Product Safety Commission. Formed in 1972, this sets safety standards for consumer products. These safety standards cover design, construction, contents, performance and labelling. In addition, it has the statutory power to enforce standards on companies and organizations.

▌ The Environmental Protection Agency. The EPA establishes standards including air quality and pollution levels, water quality, pesticide levels, noise levels for construction equipment, transportation (excluding aircraft) and engines.

▌ The Federal Aviation Authority. Responsible for airline safety throughout the United States, and also involved in investigations of crashes overseas of aircraft belonging to US-based airlines.

▌ The Federal Trade Commission. Established in 1914, the FTC promotes fair competition in interstate commerce. It aims to protect consumers from false and deceptive advertising and unfair trade practices, regulates packaging and labelling of consumer products, and ensures appropriate credit rating disclosure and reporting.

▌ The Food And Drugs Administration. The FDA regulates the safety, effectiveness and labelling of food, drugs, cosmetics and medical products.

▊ The Food Safety and Quality Service. The FSQS regulates the meat, poultry and egg industries for safety and purity by inspecting interstate-shipped produce. It is also responsible for the labelling regulations affecting these particular products.

▊ The National Highways Traffic Safety Administration. This agency establishes motor vehicle safety standards, determines car fuel economy standards and enforces the laws relating to speed limits.

In Europe the rights mentioned above are intended to be implemented with concrete measures, and also take into account other Community policies, including agriculture, the economy, social affairs and the environment.

Policy measures that have been adopted cover the following categories (Leonard, 1998).

Food products

Lists of permitted substances and purity standards have been established for foodstuff additives, such as colourings, antioxidants, preservatives, emulsifiers, stabilizers and gelifiers. Pesticide residues in fruit and vegetables and erucic acid in oils and fats for human consumption have been limited to specific levels. Directives are also in force relating to the labelling of foodstuffs, specifying ingredients, quantity, nutritional values and the date by which they should be consumed.

Pharmaceuticals

EU Directives control the testing, patenting, labelling and marketing of these products.

Misleading advertising

Consumers can complain to the courts which are empowered to require advertisers to prove the accuracy of their advertised claims.

Consumer credit

All credit agreements must be in writing, be clear and understandable, and indicate the actual interest rate being charged.

Personal (face-to-face) selling

This directive aims to protect consumers against hard sales techniques. In addition, there is a 'cooling off' period which allows consumers time to reflect on their purchase and change their minds, if they so wish. This is especially the case in purchase of insurance policies and pension plans.

Product liability

This imposes strict liability on producers for damage caused by defects in their products.

Consumer information and education

In addition to the directives regulating the labelling of food products, others require electrical household equipment to be marked with its estimated energy consumption, and food to be marked with unit prices (by the kilogram or litre).

Further ongoing measures will cover:

▊ commercial transactions involving consumers;

▊ consumer information and education;

▊ consumer representation;

▊ the health and safety of consumers.

Consumers and ethics

Although Chapter 3 discusses the role of ethics in marketing in detail, it is perhaps appropriate at this juncture to have a brief discussion of ethics in relation to the customer. Textbooks, journal and newspaper articles often now consider the 'customer as king', or as 'dictator'; in essence, that the 'customer is always right'.[2] True, as we have seen above the customer now has more power, indeed more legal support, than at any other time. It is likely that this power and support will expand. However, we should add a word of caution. While we wholeheartedly support the rights of the customer, the customer is not always right.

Sorrell (1994), in an article for the *Journal of Business Ethics*, poses an example where the actions of the customer could be questionable. This is drawn from real life and relates to a chef and restaurateur who caters for gourmet tastes, and who is considered by most of his customers and other leading chefs and restaurant critics to be a master cook.

One day a customer who comes to the restaurant because of the chef's reputation sends back a dish that is cooked by the chef and asks that it be altered to his (the customer's) specification. The chef refuses and the meal ends in some acrimony, though the customer is not charged. Who is in the right? It might be thought that the customer is. After all, his meal was very expensive, and it was he who had to eat it. Surely he should have had the dish prepared to please him. In a more run-of-the-mill restaurant with a different chef, this way of reading the case would plainly be correct. What makes the reading controversial here is that the chef is out of the ordinary and that the customer came partly because of the chef's reputation. This fact makes the customer's situation comparable to that of someone who commissions an artist to paint a portrait. The one who commissions the painter may also be paying a great deal of money, and he may dislike the portrait, but it is not obvious that the artist is obliged to repaint the portrait to please him, even if the one who commissions it is the only one who will ever see it. In the case of the portrait commission one buys the artist's ability, but one has to allow the artist freedom to exercise it in a way that he judges appropriate. It may be the same with the master chef. Of course, even the painter and the chef can be careless and unscrupulous in painting and cooking, not bothering to exercise their ability: in that case the customer is wronged: he is not getting what he pays for. Nevertheless, it is possible for the customer to get what he pays for and still not be pleased.

This example illustrates some of the potentially 'grey' areas in ethical debate. Equally, there are customers who blatantly seek benefits to which they are not entitled. There is one story, which may be apocryphal. A young man goes into a well-known American department store. He wants to return four sports car tyres, because they are unsuitable. The sales assistant checks the price of the tyres and asks for the sales receipt in order to credit the customer's account. However, the customer does not have the receipt. Nevertheless the account is credited. You may think that this is how customer service should operate. You are right. However, the twist to the story is that this particular department store does not sell this type of sports car tyres!

It is said that when asked why this 'customer' had received an apparently undue payment, one of the store's directors replied that '99 per cent of their customers are honest, the remainder are not'. The belief was that if some of that 99 per cent had seen the store dealing unfavourably with that particular customer, it could have created a poor image. They would probably have seen a commotion, obviously not aware of the real issues behind the case.

Marketing insight: University students as customers

In some colleges and universities students are called 'customers' or 'clients' rather than students or undergrads/postgrads/freshers. The idea behind this is that they often pay fees (this is now the case in most countries) and that they are entitled to excellent customer service. There is no doubt that they should be entitled to respect, dignity and related customer service. However, the payment of fees does not guarantee an award at the end of the course, nor should it mean a certain flexibility on how many examination resit or assignment resubmission opportunities a student has, or any other flexibility in the regulations.

The student is entitled to received a detailed student handbook that must clearly state the regulations, which must be administered fairly across the student population. Students' rights as citizens of the college or university must be clearly stated. However, anything that breaches good conduct should be classed as unethical – that covers students, staff and the institution. Of course, any unethical practices that denigrate a university qualification affect everyone in the longer term.

What this tells us is that there are both clear-cut and more complex issues in consumer ethics that need to be taken into consideration.

Why do consumers buy?

In this section we consider the reasons that motivate consumers to buy particular products or services. Marketers need to understand why individuals or specific social/societal groups purchase particular goods or services. Attempting to understand such behavourial characteristics assists marketers in targeting the most appropriate groups for their products or services.

Although we as individuals make the final purchasing decision, our approach or influences will differ depending upon whether we are buying for ourselves, a member of the family, friends, or for an organization.

Table 4.5 lists a series of factors that influence purchasing decisions to a greater or lesser extent. We should never consider these purely in isolation. It is most likely that several factors will converge to influence a purchase, in both the short and longer terms. For ease of identification we have attempted to place the many and varied reasons for buyer behaviour into categories. As with any attempt to 'catalogue', there will be behaviours that fall outside the categories or overlap several. However, we hope that this structure provides an efficient way of understanding buyer behaviour.

People

The family

For simplicity of presentation we are dividing family influences into five categories. However, in many families these points will overlap.

Immediate family/gender issues

The dynamics of family life have changed significantly since the 1960s. Today more of the decisions that affect the family as a whole are taken by the entire family. Women, once purely seen as homemakers, have become career minded and independent. Issues often left solely to the husband in the past (for example, the purchase of a new car) are now joint decisions, at least in some countries. Children have also increased their influence

Table 4.5 Categories of buyer behaviour

Step	Category or group	Description or comments
1	People	We are influenced to a lesser or greater degree by people. They may be our friends, our family, our heroes (for example football players or pop stars), our teachers and our co-workers.
2	Culture	Cultures vary throughout the world. To a greater or lesser degree they influence our lives. The cultural perspective may stem from a belief in one's own country or from religious teachings.
3	Lifestyle	Lifestyles can be both real and aspirational. We may be contented with our lifestyle and purchase products and services to fulfil our lifestyle. This may include fashion items from clothes to furniture. Equally, we can be aspirational, slowly developing our lifestyle to meet our aspiration of how we want to live. This can include buying into a degree programme.
4	Economic/ financial	Our economic and financial circumstances can dictate our buying behaviour. Someone who is unemployed and living on state benefits will be extremely price-sensitive and will focus on purchasing basic products. On the other hand, a highly successful stock broker in the City of London is likely to be much less price-sensitive, and able to purchase a wider range of products or services. These purchases may include luxury items, such as a sports car or yacht.
5	Media	The media can have tremendous influence on what we buy. This can range from reviews of films, plays and books (which may be either positive or negative) through to healthy eating campaigns. The influence of the media can be both a negative and positive. It can reveal injustices or unethical behaviours that may influence us to boycott a particular product or service. The media is a potent force.
6	Necessities	This covers the items – often basic items – that we need to continue living. This includes food, heat and shelter.
7	General/ miscellaneous	These cover the influencers that fall outside the above categories: for example, the influences of the government and the weather.

within the immediate family circle, and may be consulted on such things as what make of car the family should purchase. The influence of women and children will not happen in all families and across all ethnic groups; however in many countries they have attained significant levels of influence.

Relatives

The level of influence may depend upon the closeness of the family in emotional terms, and its ethnicity. Families of Indian or West Indian origin, for example, tend to be more close-knit. Here various members of the family – grandparents, uncles, aunts, cousins and so on – can have an impact on the decisions of others.

Family experiences

We are, to a greater or lesser extent, influenced by family experiences. As children we may experience certain situations that have a long-lasting influence on our purchasing decisions. For example, if we grew up eating a range of Heinz products, liked the taste and looked forward to eating them, we would probably be influenced to buy that brand as we became older. In turn because we felt comfortable with that brand we might subsequently introduce it to our own children.

Family connections

In communities or societies where there are close-linked families, for example within the UK's Indian community, extended family connections may be particularly important. Individuals might buy from extended family members because it is expected that they do so. This may mean travelling a distance to shop at a particular store (for example, a small supermarket) rather than visiting somewhere more local. These 'connections' are still important within most integrated communities. However, as communities become more fragmented and new generations become more independent in their actions, the connections may weaken, and eventually break down.

Pressure

We should not forget that within families pressure can be brought to bear on individual members to purchase certain products or services. This is especially true within certain cultures where the father, as leader of the household, may dictate what family members can and cannot do. Many of these issues are beyond the realms of marketing; however they will impact on potential purchases. For example, the type and style of clothes a young woman wears may be her father's choice and not hers.

While this may not be applicable within your own cultural frame of reference, you must bear in mind what happens within others.

Friends

Friends may influence in two major ways. First, they may make a recommendation. This could be anything from a particularly good book to a restaurant that is ideal for a relaxed dinner. As they are friends we are more likely to trust their judgment than that of an acquaintance, or indeed a total stranger. If we derive some benefit from the recommendation, for example the pleasure of reading a particular book, we are more likely to seek out other books written by that author. In the case of the restaurant we may become a frequent visitor, and recommend it to other friends and members of our family.

Second, friends may buy us a gift. This will have a similar effect to the above examples. Again, if we use the book example, if we derive pleasure from reading it we might seek further titles by that author.

For the affection and love of others

People buy gifts (everything from cards and flowers to expensive jewellery and holidays) for the people they love, whether they be partners, family or friends.

Special occasions

This can be linked to the last heading. We might buy a gift for a special occasion such as a silver or golden wedding anniversary. The person buying the gift might be one of those celebrating the anniversary (giving the gift to his or her partner), another member of the family or a friend. The same applies to weddings. The level of involvement in the purchase of the gift will depend, among other factors, on the closeness of the buyer to the recipient.

Longing and belonging: social acceptance, peer or group pressure

In order to achieve social acceptance we may buy products or services that help us relate to a particular social group. For example, teenagers may seek to buy particular fashion brands of clothes in order to become a member of a specific group. Failure to buy a brand could lead to the individual being ostracized from the group. The teenager's peers pressurize them to conform to a particular dress code. In turn the teenagers

The trust engendered in friendship means that friends can influence purchasing behaviour through their views on various products and services. This may come in the form of recommendations or equally comment as to the failings of a particular product or service. This links into the value of 'word of mouth' as discussed in a later chapter.

may pressurize their parents for the money to make the necessary purchase.

Such peer pressure can affect very young children. In some UK schools the head teachers have banned certain fashion brands from school premises to reduce the impact of such peer pressure on the pupils.

Gender issues

Although under the United Nations Charter we are all considered equal, whatever our gender, there are regional variations. In Western nations the rights of women have been asserted, and placed in law. What is accepted within a Western cultural environment may not be within another cultural environment.

We must also remember that the links between culture and religion also vary. For example, in some Islamic states such as Pakistan it is possible for a woman to gain significant power. This is shown by the rise of Benazir Bhutto (1953–) who was Prime Minister for two terms of office, 1988–90 and 1993–96. However in more fundamentalist Islamic states, such as Afghanistan under the former Taliban regime, that was not the case. The Taliban came to power in September 1996 following a civil war, and imposed strict Sharia law. Under these restrictions women, who had formed 70 per cent of the workforce, were banned from working, including as teachers and doctors. They were also prohibited from studying or attending university. The Taliban regime was overthrown in 2002 with the help of US, European, Canadian and Australian forces. Subsequently a democratic government was elected, and slowly women were able to return to their education and former careers. This example may be an extreme, but it helps illustrate the gulf between different societies in terms of the purchasing power of women.

Culture

The national culture of a country can be described as the 'specific learned norms based on attitudes, values and beliefs which exist in every society' (Daniels and Radebaugh, 1998).

The cultural identity of a nation may influence the level of nationalism and patriotism, which may be reflected in the purchasing of home-country products rather than imported ones. The governments of both the United States and the UK have in the past appealed to their citizens to buy only products 'made at home'. Often the levels of unemployment and balance of payments have influenced this appeal to an individual's sense of patriotism. However, as major global economies become increasingly interdependent, and ownership of companies becomes multinational (for example, some formerly British car companies are owned by

US and German-based parent companies), this may have less effect.

We should not consider culture purely in a national sense. Within nations there are regional and local variations that must be taken into consideration. There are, for example, marked differences in the behaviour of people in the highly liberalized communities of California and those in the generally conservative southern US states. A product may be successful in one area, whereas it may be shunned in another. It may be one nation, but attitudes, values and beliefs may vary significantly, and we must consider that in terms of buyer behaviour.

Religion plays an extremely important role in the lives of many people throughout the world. Table 4.6 gives just a few examples of how people's religious beliefs will ultimately affect their purchasing decisions.

Lifestyles

Health concerns

Since the 1980s there has been growing concern about individual health and fitness. This has resulted in a plethora of fitness videos, health foods, health clubs, health-oriented

Table 4.6 Religion and its influence on purchasing decisions

Religion	Influence
Islam	Islam has strict dietary laws that prevent the consumption of alcohol, certain meats and meat/blood-related products such as gelatin.
Judaism	Among orthodox Jews there is strict observance of dietary laws. Food must be Kosher, therefore only animals that chew the cud and have cloven hoofs, such as cows and sheep, can be eaten. Thus pigs are excluded. Only fish with scales and fins can be eaten, thus all shellfish are excluded. There are also rules for the slaughter of animals and the preparation of food.
Jehovah's Witnesses	The orthodoxy states that they should not become involved in the affairs of the world. Therefore Witnesses do not have televisions and do not exchange gifts at Christmas.
Roman Catholicism	The Roman Catholic church's doctrine prevents the use of artificial contraception, such as condoms or the pill. There are approximately 100 million Roman Catholics.

magazines, alternative medicines and vitamin and mineral capsules. Additionally, there has been a growing body of evidence of how damaging the sun's rays and pollutants can be to our skin and internal organs. There is an increasing danger of contracting skin cancer, for instance, from spending time in the sun even in temperate climates such as the UK's. Thus sun creams and sun blocks are being sold for the international vacation market but also for those who remain in the UK.

The growing concern arising out of the international AIDS crisis has led to the increased use of condoms in several countries. Among some younger groups it is 'cool' to use a condom.

The increasing stresses and strains associated with everyday life, combined with toxic air pollutants, influence many to purchase food supplements such as antioxidants. Since the late 20th century the health food and supplement industry has grown significantly because of our fears, and our desire to live longer and more healthily.

The late 1990s witnessed growing concern about the quality of food being produced. This was not confined to one country, but became of global concern. Such issues as the BSE scare in the UK, factory farming methods, the types of food supplement fed to animals, methods of transportation of live animals (veal crates in Europe), increasing risk of food poisoning (especially by *E.coli* and salmonella) and the development of genetically modified foods all focused consumers' attention on the type of food they ate. The result was an increase in the purchasing of free-range and organically grown foods. Although initially these food products were sold at premium prices, it became clear to supermarket chains, especially in the UK, that consumers were seeking a healthier option, so in many but not all cases prices have fallen to increase overall demand.

Since the late 1980s magazines covering health issues have dramatically increased their circulation.

Safety features

This is a sphere of influence overlooked in many textbooks; however it is an important one. Some manufacturers claim it has become paramount in the minds of many consumers, especially when purchasing cars and toys.

Although governments have introduced laws governing basic standards of product safety, it can be argued that consumers often seek higher levels of benefit. Some companies have been able to build their reputation on their very high safety standards, for instance Volvo cars.

A new area of consumer concern is deep vein thrombosis (DVT), associated with being seated in relatively cramped conditions for a long period, as tends to happen on long-haul flights. Increased awareness through widespread media coverage means that consumers are now better informed of additional risks when flying. By mid-2001 some airlines were advertising that they were working to increase leg-room on aircraft (although in some cases this appeared to benefit business class passengers, rather than those passengers travelling economy class). For many travellers their choice of airline depends on a range of safety standards, including the amount of leg-room available to economy class passengers. With air travel set to expand rapidly over the next 10 years or so, the amount of space available to passengers may actually become a key marketing issue.

Distress purchasing

This is where there is some immediate urgency attached to the purchase. For example, imagine it is the middle of a particularly cold winter and the gas central heating system fails. There is no heating and no hot water. This will cause distress to the family who will most likely call for assistance. A gas company may be able to send one of its emergency teams. Similarly if pipes freeze or burst we need a 24-hour plumbing service. There is often a premium charge for this type of quick-response service, covering call-out and repairs.

Here we can start considering the work of the psychologist Abraham Maslow. He developed a hierarchy of needs (which we examine in detail later in this chapter) where certain purchases are emotional and basic to the fulfillment of personal needs. In this particular case there was an emotional response to the freezing and bursting pipes. There was a critical need for emergency plumbing services.

Ethically driven purchasing

Environmental concerns

As with health concerns, in recent years there has been a growing consciousness of our natural environment. Companies such as the Body Shop International have led the way in providing cosmetics and toiletries that have not been tested on animals. Growing consumer awareness has led to a radical change of thinking about animal testing. Likewise many consumers now seek out products that:

▌ are recyclable, or their packaging is recyclable;

▌ do not contain environmentally damaging chemicals: for example, the vast majority of batteries produced for general consumer use are now mercury and cadmium free;

▌ contain only paper or wood from sustainable forest resources.

Impact upon other people/nations

To some extent this ties in with environmental factors. Through the media we are made increasingly aware of the plight of others. Child labour, for instance, is still rife in many parts of the world (see Chapter 3). Many consumers within developed nations seek products that are guaranteed not to be made

by children. Significantly, there was an active boycott of carpets from India when it was learnt that a large quantity were made by young children working long hours in hazardous conditions (Sidhva, 1995).

In the UK there has been the introduction of products (coffee for example) labelled 'fair trade'. While they are generally more expensive than comparable products, the manufacturers stress that a fair price has been paid to the original producers. Additionally, some goods (for example, pewter items from South Africa) are sold with the promise that a proportion of the price goes to help provide education/medical facilities in that country.

Individual personality

Our own personality or psychological make-up influences what and how we buy. For example, an extrovert might buy very bright, lively-looking clothing. The clothes could be in fashion, or very different from the norm.

Pleasure and personal satisfaction, physical and aesthetic

Certain foods (for example chocolate) have to many a highly pleasurable flavour. Certain furnishings (for example sofas, carpets, paintings and ornaments) may bring aesthetic satisfaction.

Ownership

This may be the need or desire to own certain products: for example, a particular model of sports cars, or a collection of CDs by a particular pop group or performer.

Collecting

This partly links into ownership above; however there is a distinction. A collector could be described as someone who wants to have everything associated with a particular hobby or fashion. For example, he or she might collect the memorabilia associated with the James Bond movies, the *Star Wars* saga, pop stars or a football team. Another example is stamp collecting, where many collectors want copies of all the stamps issued for a particular region or era.

The objective is often to have a set of everything, for example all the publicity material associated with the James Bond movies from *Dr No* (1962) to the present, whatever the language it is printed in. Collecting can become an obsession in some personalities.

Fashion

What do we mean by fashion? The *Oxford English Reference Dictionary* describes it as 'a current popular custom or style especially in dress or social conduct'. Associated with this definition is the term 'fashion victim' who can be described as a person who slavishly follows trends in fashion. There are several additional points we need to consider here:

▍ This encompasses the desire to have the latest fashion items and accessories, which range from jewellery though to mobile phones.

▍ Of course, it is not just designer fashion we need to consider. What happens in the department or shopping mall is equally relevant. Leading retailers have seasonal collections covering spring, summer, autumn and winter. This is particularly applicable to women's fashion which tends to have a relatively short life cycle compared with men's fashion. (Product life cycles are covered in Chapters 7 and 15.) Some women change aspects of their wardrobe every year to be in fashion with that particular season's colours and styling.

▍ Fashion can tie in with social acceptance and peer pressure, though this is not always so. This is particularly the case where the fashion items, for example sports wear, are associated with a particular age group, local movement/group or gang.

Trust and beliefs

We tend to buy many products or services because we trust the product and the manufacturer. People buy products from the Body Shop International, for example, because they trust not only the quality of the ingredients but also the ethical stance the company takes on various issues, such as testing on animals.

Of course, if that trust is damaged the public may quickly desert the product in favour of a substitute (See 'Marketing insight: Ratner jewellers'). Consumers might be supportive of a small or medium-sized business but feel betrayed if the management sold all or part of the business to a larger company, especially if the larger company has a controversial reputation. Customers could be lost as a result, and never return.

Marketing insight: Ratner jewellers

By the late 1980s the Ratner Group was the world's largest jewellery chain, employing 25,000 staff with 1,300 stores in the UK and 1,000 in the United States. The company, floated on the UK Stock Exchange, was worth some £680 million and in 1991 announced group profits of £120 million – the seventh year in succession that profits had doubled.

One of the keys to Ratner's success was marketing real jewellery to a mass audience through high street stores. However, the marketing success of Ratners was to be compromised on 23 April 1991 when the Chairman and CEO of the Group, Gerald Ratner, addressed the annual lunch of the Institute of Directors at the Royal Albert Hall in London. Ratner, a high-profile and successful businessman, was buoyed by the company's continued extraordinary profile growth. In his speech he attempted to be lighthearted; however that was to be his downfall:

> We sell things like a teapot for two quid or an imitation open book to lay on your coffee table. The pages don't turn – but they have beautiful curled corners and genuine antique dust. I know it is in the worst possible taste, but we sold a quarter of a million last year. We also do cut glass sherry decanters complete with six glasses on a silver-plated tray – that your butler can serve your drinks on – all for £9.99. People say, how can you sell them for such a low price? I say, because they are total crap!

He received a round of applause and decided to carry on in search of more applause and laughter.

> Some people say they cannot even see the jewellery for all the posters and banners smothering the shop windows. It is interesting, isn't it, that these shops, that everyone has a good laugh at, take more money per square foot than any other retailer in Europe. Why? Because we give the customers what they want. We even sell a pair of earrings for under £1.00 which is cheaper than a prawn sandwich from Marks & Spencer. But I have to say that the earrings probably won't last as long!

Ratner had used these jokes before (even to the press), and so within the confines of a business lunch did not think they would have any impact on his business. However, his jokes were widely reported, with banner headlines, by the tabloid media. A £500,000 PR campaign was mounted to limit the damage and at the company's July annual general meeting he apologized to shareholders: 'My comment was made in a light-hearted manner…. My mistake was not in realizing that a tongue-in-cheek joke would be so widely misquoted.'

By that October sales had fallen dramatically, as had the shares – now the company was worth £237 million. The name Ratner had become something of a joke. Customers perceived that they could not possibly buy goods which carried that name on the box. They felt it would be an insult to the person they were giving the present to.

The company tried several measures to rebuild sales, everything from repositioning the different store brands and new discounts to the introduction of new product ranges. In August 1992 the company announced 2,000 redundancies in the UK and United States and the closure of 326 stores. On 25 November Gerald Ratner left the company which he had built from virtually nothing. At the time of his departure the value of the group had fallen to £49 million.

On 10 September 1993 Ratner transformed itself into the Signet Group plc. By 2001 it was once again the world's largest jewellery retailer with some 1,436 stores and the United States accounting for 70 per cent of sales. In the UK the Signet Group operates under the brand names H. Samuel, Ernest Jones and Leslie Davies. In the United States it operates under the brands Kay Jewellers, Jared – The Galleria of Jewellery and several other regional brands.

In 2002 Gerald Ratner returned to the jewellery business with an online jewellery store.

Questions/activities

1. Obtain a copy of the latest Signet Group annual report, either as a hard copy or via a Web search. Consider whether the company could have survived without the departure of Gerald Ratner and the rebranding of the group. In your view what would have been the public perception of the company, and why?
2. View the Web sites of the subsidiary companies and consider the range of products and services on offer. How do you rate them? Would you buy these products, if not why not?

Sources: Tibballs (1999) and the company's annual reports.

Occupation

Our experience and knowledge gained through our occupation might influence our purchasing decisions, though it does not always do so. For example, members of the medical profession who are aware of the potential side-effects of certain food products or stimulants (such as coffee and alcohol) might consume less or none of them. In addition, they might completely avoid all forms of tobacco. Equally, being aware of the potential health benefits of eating vegetables and fruit, they might eat more than average of these.

Social class/social level

This is a combination of demographic features. It can be defined as a grouping of social stratification based primarily on economic and occupational factors. However, it also refers to people's style of living, sense of group identity, education and type of residential neighbourhood.

Table 4.7 depicts the UK's socioeconomic groups as defined by the 2001 census. As you can see there has been an attempt to move away from the earlier standard classifications of upper class, upper middle class, middle class, lower middle class and lower class.

These types of categories have been criticized as stereotyping people. However as Stanton *et al* (1998) conclude:

- A social class system exists in virtually all societies.

- There are substantial differences among classes with respect to overall buying behaviour.

- Due to diversity, it is most likely that social classes will respond differently to marketing programmes. Therefore it is necessary to target programmes specifically to the relevant social groups. This also makes for good business practice. Efficiently targeting the right group provides the opportunity to maximize the return on marketing investment. For example, if we were to manufacture and market an exclusive watch retailing at £5,000 it is unlikely that we would advertise it in a tabloid newspaper. Our preference would be exclusive retail outlets, for example in London's Bond Street or Mayfair. Advertising would be directed towards magazines whose readers tended to be affluent.

Table 4.7 UK socioeconomic groups

Social class	Occupations	Examples
1	Higher managerial and professional occupations	Chief executive officers
1.1	Employers and managers in large organizations	Company directors and senior managers
1.2	Higher professional	Surgeons, lawyers
2	Lower managerial and professional occupations	Company managers and police officers
3	Intermediate occupations	Administrators, personal assistants
4	Micro and small company employers, freelance workers	Small business owners and self-employed
5	Lower supervisory, craft and related occupations	Foreman/woman
6	Semi-routine occupations	Drivers, hairdressers
7	Routine occupations	Car park attendants, cleaners

Source: Office of National Statistics (www.statistics.gov.uk).

Economic and financial issues

Economic circumstances

An individual's economic circumstances will directly affect the level of his or her purchasing power. Here we need to consider an individual's level of both disposable and discretionary income.

Disposable income

This is the income left to consumers after they have paid all compulsory levies from the state such as income and property taxes.

Discretionary income

This is the amount of income that the individual consumer decides to spend. While a consumer may have a large disposable income, he or she might decide to save a high proportion and spend the remainder on basic items.

These issues will be affected by:

- **The level of income growth over the period of an individual's working life.** Some people enjoy significant salary increases as their personal experiences and job knowledge develop over time. This is often seen in the professions, as the status/experience of the individual develops. Of course, for the majority income decreases as they approach retirement and their pension becomes their sole form of income.

- **Changing status.** An individual's economic status may be affected by redundancy, career move, a substantial inheritance or a multi-million pound lottery win.

- **Level of taxation.** If tax rates are increased this will reduce the level of disposable income. Conversely, if rates are reduced it may increase levels, depending upon the amount of personal debt.

- **Levels of debt.** If personal levels of debt increase, for example, the purchase of a new house with a larger mortgage, so will the repayment levels. This will impact upon the amount of income available for other purchases.

- **Interest rates.** Governments and central banks regulate interest rate levels. If there are inflationary pressures, they may increase interest rates to reduce the overall level of consumer expenditure, thus maintaining agreed inflation targets.

Pricing structures

Customers may be sensitive to price levels for several reasons.

Past family/life experience

No matter how much wealth they accumulate, some people's experience tells them always to seek out value for money. Thus they may be extremely cautious about what they buy and where they buy it.

This can be a generational experience. For example, those who were children in Europe during and just after the Second World War experienced food rationing. The harshness of the experience varied greatly depending upon whether the child was in the UK or in war-torn Europe. For all those children, though, growing up in conditions of severe food shortages will have affected their personal value systems. For many this experience taught them not to be extravagant, seeking the maximum value at the lowest price.

Low incomes

Individuals or families on low incomes will generally aim to maximize their range of purchases by seeking the lowest prices. They may shop at a food discounter, for example, rather than a major supermarket chain in order to make extra savings.

Economic and financial experiences

The deep recession that affected the UK economy during the early 1990s impacted on all social strata. However, one group that suffered significantly was the professional middle class. Many had invested in house purchases during the period of substantial growth of the late 1980s. When the economic recession struck property values collapsed. This left many home owners with high mortgages but with negative equity; effectively their home was now valued at less than the original purchase price. If they sold it they would still have a debt, often substantial, to the mortgage lender.

In addition, there was instability within the employment market as the level of redundancies and company failures increased. Many who had had relatively successful careers found themselves unemployed and struggling to meet their debts, including mortgages on properties with negative equity. At that time their ability to make purchases beyond basic needs was strictly limited. This experience has remained with many people. While their financial situation may well have improved significantly since that recession, the experience alone will have made them cautious. They will seek out products at the right price, even though they may compromise slightly on quality.

Tariff barriers

Punitive tariff barriers imposed by the government may reduce the number of local consumers purchasing imported goods. As well as a means of raising extra 'taxes' it is also a method of persuading home consumers to buy locally.

Financial investment – financial security

This could include, for example:

- A 20-year-old who decides to invest in a pension plan to provide financial protection in later life.

- A husband who invests in life insurance policies so that his family is financially protected in case of his premature death.

- An individual who invests in a work of art in the belief that it will gain in value, thus providing a sound financial investment. The individual might or might not appreciate the aesthetic value of the work of art; it could be merely a financial investment.

Media

Editorial

An individual may be influenced by a review he or she reads in a magazine, newspaper, on the Internet, or hears on the radio or television. The review could cover anything from a movie, play, opera or concert through to a book or CD. Virtually every major newspaper has a review or lifestyle section where specialists discuss their subject areas. Magazines or Web sites devoted to a specific area, for example classical music, may well feature numerous reviews on the latest CDs available, analysing them on performance, recording quality and overall value for money.

The influence may be greater on an individual if he or she has a particularly high regard or respect for the reviewer. If the critic writes a rave review, say about a particular classical music CD, then the reader might be tempted to make it a forthcoming purchase. However, if the critic considers it to be the worst recording of a particular work, and so not value for money, the reader might well be tempted to seek another recording.

Advertising

Advertising can be described as a paid-for communication overtly intended to inform and/or influence people. While some advertising is designed to keep the company's profile high in the mind of the customer, others are intended to influence a purchase directly. For example, a major multinational might run a series of corporate advertisements in the media to highlight the diversity of the business. Here it would be informing people of its range of experience, and of things about the company they might not already know. The global energy company BP ran such a corporate campaign in the UK in the 1980s, in which it highlighted its work beyond the petrol station forecourt.

An example of an advertisement that could influence an individual to make a purchase is a special offer in a magazine. An advertisement for vitamin supplements stating that specific supplements were heavily reduced for a limited period would be likely to influence purchasing decisions. This could be especially important for those people who regularly used food supplements.

Necessities

Basic human needs

As stated earlier the humanistic psychologist Abraham Maslow (1908–1970) proposed a theoretical hierarchy of human needs. He postulated that within every human being there is a hierarchy of five needs, arranged in the order in which the individual seeks to fulfill them. Although Maslow's hierarchy was developed as part of a theory of motivation, especially concerning issues within the workplace, it also has a bearing on customer behaviour.

Figure 4.3 details Maslow's hierarchy. Beneath each of Maslow's classifications we have given a description for that particular classification, then the possible impact or influence on buyer behaviour.

General

Problem solving

Often we purchase a product or service to resolve a problem, which may be of minor or major consequence. On one level this could be a chemically based cleaner that removes a stain – for example, a wine stain – from a carpet. On another level this could be helping to choose the most appropriate school or college for our children's abilities, to help them develop for the future and be successful. As you can see from these two examples, the range of problems to be resolved may be many and varied.

The government

The government can influence consumers in many ways, for example through economic and legislative actions. As stated earlier in this chapter, governments can urge people to be loyal to local brands, rather than imported ones. In the 1970s the then British Government urged consumers to buy British manufactured goods rather than cheaper imports; this included cars. However, the British car manufacturing industry was in turmoil and could not compete against more competitively priced Japanese and European models.

Another example is from the late 1990s when the Malaysian Government urged people to 'buy local'. Of course the population might still end up buying a popular global brand simply because it is manufactured locally. For example, Unilever (Malaysia) Holdings Sdn Bhd is one of the largest producers of consumer products in Malaysia.

Ease of purchasing

This ties in with process, physical evidence, direct marketing and e-marketing which are discussed in later chapters. Underhill (1999) states that retailers can actually make it difficult for us to buy! He cites as an example a bookshop which placed its shopping baskets

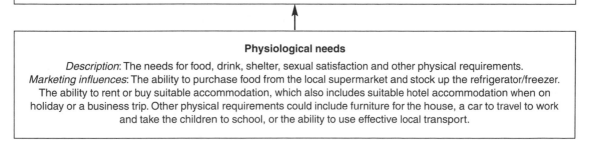

Self-actualization
Description: The need for self-fulfilment, growth and achieving personal potential.
Marketing influence: In marketing terms this may have similar attributes to self-esteem. For example, an individual seeks to improve his or her educational or professional qualifications. He or she successfully completes a Masters degree programme, then decides to take a specialist professional qualification. His or her goal might be fulfilled on successful completion of the course, as it not only gains him or her an award but increases his or her job prospects. Today we see more universities and professional institutions marketing a range of training programmes. The underlying theme in the marketing material is about helping individuals to achieve their long-term ambitions and goals.

Self-esteem
Description: The need for self-respect, reputation, achievement, autonomy and status.
Marketing influence: Undertaking part-time courses which would potentially increase job rewards, for example an MBA programme. Other courses include multiple skill development: computers, languages and self-expression. In addition, there are a range of self-development courses that are designed to develop both skills and personal awareness/effectiveness.

Social needs
Description: The need for affection, belonging, acceptance and friendship.
Marketing influences: Joining various activity/sporting groups, regular visits to clubs, pubs/bars, wine bars – here the owners may market the venue as a friendly place to meet with other regular visitors.

Safety needs
Description: The need for order, security and protection from physical and emotional harm, as well as assurance that physical needs will continue to be met.
Marketing influence: The purchase of burglar alarm/smoke detector systems for the home. Buying suitable clothes for extreme weather conditions, for example, winter in the Highlands of Scotland or travelling across the Sahara Desert. For a general family holiday abroad the purchase of medicines to relieve travel sickness or upset stomachs. The belief in the quality and reliability of a particular branded product, for example a make of car may be purchased because it is renowned for its advanced safety features and engineering. The mobile telephone may have safety implications. For example, many parents buy them for their children, so that the children can keep their parents informed of their whereabouts. In addition, if the car breaks down it is a safe and convenient means of contacting a breakdown service, especially when the driver is stranded in an unfamiliar area on a winter's night.

Physiological needs
Description: The needs for food, drink, shelter, sexual satisfaction and other physical requirements.
Marketing influences: The ability to purchase food from the local supermarket and stock up the refrigerator/freezer. The ability to rent or buy suitable accommodation, which also includes suitable hotel accommodation when on holiday or a business trip. Other physical requirements could include furniture for the house, a car to travel to work and take the children to school, or the ability to use effective local transport.

Figure 4.3   Maslow's hierarchy of needs

just in the corner by the entranceway. The point he makes is that people who enter the bookshop may be thinking of purchasing only one book, no more. Therefore they are unlikely to collect a basket on the way into the store. Most people will walk around the store in order to find the particular book they want to purchase. It is this walking around that is key. As they walk around, consumers may come across other items of interest: books, cards or CDs. Increasingly, bookshops are being converted into more relaxed places to shop, with seating throughout the stores (this allows the consumer to browse at leisure), cafés and easy to carry baskets scattered throughout the store.

The development of call centres and the Internet has provided consumers with the opportunity to purchase a range of products and services from the comfort of their home. As Internet facilities improve more consumers are likely to take the opportunity to purchase over the Web.

Marketing insight: easyJet

Launched in November 1995, easyJet is now one of Europe's major low-cost airlines. By November 2002 it was offering 89 routes from 36 different European locations, and carrying over 9 million passengers per year. On 1 August 2002 easyJet and Go (another low-cost carrier) merged. This merger reinforced easyJet's position within the marketplace and will dramatically increase its passenger carrying capacity.

The Internet has been a key element in the development of easyJet, and is critical to its ongoing success. The company started selling seats via the Internet in April 1998. By October 1999 over a million seats had been sold via the Internet. However this was dramatically superseded five months later when in March 2000 2 million seats were reached, only for sales to reach 3 million a mere three months later. By February 2003 approximately 90 per cent of sales per week were made online.

EasyJet operates a ticketless travel system. Passengers receive an e-mail containing their travel details and confirmation number when they book online. For the airline this reduces significantly the cost of issuing, distributing, processing and reconciling millions of tickets per year. This helps to reduce costs to the individual traveller. Additionally, it reduces the amount of paperwork for the passenger. All passengers need is their passport and confirmation number.

EasyJet also operates a system whereby it sells one-way fares rather than return tickets. This allows passengers to return when they wish, rather than be tied to specific return fares or minimum stays at a location. Again customers may consider this a benefit to their ease of purchase, a convenience. Of course for others it may not be; they might prefer an inclusive return ticket package.

Questions/activities

1. Check out the easyJet Web site and analyse the differences that have occurred since the writing of the text above. Consider how they have further developed the consumer's ease of purchase. What further incentives could be introduced for customers?
2. Compare and contrast easyJet with other low-cost airlines, not only in Europe but elsewhere. Focus especially on the convenience of purchasing the tickets.

We will return to easyJet in later chapters. You may want to cross-reference these examples to build an overall picture of easyJet as a company operating within a highly dynamic and competitive marketplace.

Source: easyJet.com.

The weather

Changes in the weather may influence consumer purchasing behaviour. Here are a few examples:

▨ A sudden and prolonged downpour of rain may send people into department stores to buy umbrellas.

▨ Prolonged periods of cold weather may increase people's purchasing of specific clothing items such as hats, gloves and scarves.

▨ A long spell of hot weather may increase the purchase of various products ranging from ice cream to suntan lotion and sun blocks. Equally, it may see a decrease in the purchase of certain products, for example chocolate. (As the UK has basked in longer and hotter summers, chocolate manufacturers have sought to combine their branded chocolate with ice cream. Hence, the introduction of Mars Ice cream, for instance.)

Unusual circumstances

We have included the following example, although it is perhaps unusual, because it illustrates how price-sensitive individuals can be. In the mid-1990s there was extreme public concern in both the UK and Europe over BSE (bovine spongiform encephalopathy), colloquially known as 'mad cow disease', and its possible link to the human equivalent variant CJD (Creutzfeld-Jakob disease). The European Union took steps to ban the importation of British beef. Many supermarkets witnessed a significant drop in the purchase of British beef. Either consumers were turning away from meat products or they were seeking alternative sources, such as beef imported from the Netherlands. Indeed, when concern was originally raised of a possible link between the two diseases several fast-food outlets issued statements within days stating that they would import Dutch beef.

With the decline in sales of British beef, supermarkets found themselves overstocked with a product that has a very limited shelf life. In Kensington, West London, a major supermarket chain decided to sell its British beef at significantly reduced prices, even up to 50 per cent off the standard price. The aim was to see if it could possibly move some of the stock rather than having it wasted.

The response was so overwhelming that television and radio news crews arrived on the scene. In one Saturday morning virtually all the stock of British beef within that single store had been sold. A television news reporter asked one customer who had purchased a large amount of British beef if she had purchased British beef over the previous weeks (at precisely the time the BSE crisis flared in the media). She replied 'No'. In reply to the reporter's question why she was buying such large quantities of British beef today, she replied, 'It's cheaper than normal.'

Of course we need to place this in context. Some of the customers who bought British beef on that particular Saturday would have probably purchased some anyway. Others, though, had stopped buying British beef because they thought they could become ill from eating it. However, in this case the cheap price won over their individual fears.

Customer loyalty

An individual may feel loyal to a particular brand or store, and this will influence his or her purchasing decisions. For example, a child of the 1960s might have been raised on Heinz foods (as a baby, child and teenager). Such experiences can influence people to remain loyal to that particular brand.

Organizational buying

Here we consider business-to-business (B2B) and business-to-government (B2G) buying. Companies and governments basically purchase two types of product.

Identical products

By this we mean products manufactured by one company that can be purchased in both consumer and business markets. An example is ballpoint pens. You as a student might purchase one or two; a company or government department might place an order for hundreds, if not thousands. Also consider the operation of utility suppliers, such as gas and electricity. They supply both domestic and industrial markets. The scale and method of charging are significantly different, but it is exactly the same product.

Land Rover, owned by Ford, have for decades manufactured 4×4 vehicles for both the organizational and consumer markets. Their reputation for ruggedness, durability and reliability have made them ideal vehicles for the military and emergency services. Here they are depicted in the style of Italy's elite police force, the Carabinieri.

Specialist products

Specialist products can range from fertilizers sold to farmers, oil-based products and earth moving equipment to the latest in passenger aircraft.

Eckles (1990) has outlined how business marketing differs from consumer marketing. We have developed his comments further, adding current examples.

- **Types of customer.** The customer and his or her level of expertise in purchasing is different, and often much more sophisticated in B2B, with complex decision making involved. Large business organizations often employ teams of professional buyers and procurement managers.

- **The size of the order.** This can range from a few items of relatively insignificant value (for example, several boxes of pens or pencils) to many items of high value (for example, the purchase of cars for senior executives and the sales force). Companies such as Unilever create strategic business units (SBUs) and brands purely aimed at the commercial/industrial marketplace.

- **Technical expertise.** The products and services may involve much detailed engineering data and product specifications. For example, consider the computer hardware and software facilities within your college or university. It is most likely that your computer facilities department worked closely with suppliers to determine the student and faculty needs, both now and in the near future. On another level, a government wanting to purchase military equipment will work closely with the manufacturers so that their specific needs are met.

- **Time horizons.** The time horizon of an order's completion may range from a few hours to many weeks, months or even years.

For example, a stationery supplier might be able to deliver locally a company's requirements within a matter of a few hours from receipt of a telephone or Internet order. However, the delivery of an aircraft or a new passenger train may take many months from order confirmation to actual delivery.

- **Prices and pricing flexibility.** Price flexibility may exist in business markets since prices can be customized in a bid situation, or the sales representative may offer either a larger trade-in allowance or a quantity discount, which can affect the final price. Again, as an example consider the purchase of a ballpoint pen. You as a student might spend say 40 pence for one. However, on bulk orders that cost can be reduced to 10 pence. Even that could be negotiable depending upon the company's long-term relationship with its supplier.

  The cost of purchasing a passenger aircraft will vary depending upon the configuration and special feature options that an airline requires. These options – such as flight capabilities, interior design and range of avionics – will affect the price. For example, the price of a Boeing 777–300 ranges from US $178.5 million to US $2035 million (at 2002 prices).[3]

- **Product type.** In the business market product type can range from a small item, such as an industrial washer, to a very large item, such as a hydroelectric generating plant, a commercial aircraft or an oil-drilling platform.

- **Participant sophistication.** In business marketing this is high at almost all levels because of the participant's professional training and/or experience. There may be several people involved in the purchasing decision, ranging from the procurement management team through to the board of directors.

The building of an extension to this marina will require the construction company, the local authorities and financiers to consider time horizons, costs and the technical expertise required. In addition, detailed planning will decide the type of equipment and raw materials required for a safe and efficient build.

Chapter summary

In this chapter we have considered the role of the customer within the overall marketing operation. As we also see in other chapters, during the 20th century the customer has become increasingly powerful. This trend will no doubt continue long into the 21st century. Through legislation customers now have legal support for their basic rights, as first postulated by President John F Kennedy. Since his day customers have become more vocal, and it has been shown that it is a naïve company that fails to listen to its customers. With competition so dynamic, the battle is on to win the hearts and minds of customers.

Also in this chapter we considered the multifarious factors that influence, motivate and drive customers to purchase products and services. These range from family influences, through basic needs to cultural influences and the individual's emerging lifestyle. In some instances customers spend time considering whether to purchase or not, in other cases it is purely an impulse buy. Retailers and other distributors need to understand and appreciate the complexities of buyer behaviour, in order to position their products and services effectively.

Exercises and questions for review and critical thinking

1. If you are a non-UK student study the consumer protection laws in your own country. Compare and contrast them with the legislation that has been introduced in the United States, UK and Europe.

2. Some texts or articles state that the 'Customer is King'. Do you believe that the customer is always right? Support your case with evidence.

3. Take a product or brand of your choice. Briefly outline the factors that influence you to purchase that particular product. If any one of those influencers changed, would it affect your decision to purchase that particular product?

4. 'The media is an extremely powerful influencer when it comes to people's buying decisions.' Dissect and analyse this statement, considering the arguments for and against. What is your own personal view and why?

5

Segmenting, positioning and targeting

Introduction

Segmentation was first discussed in the 1950s at a time when product differentiation was the key marketing strategy. During the 1970s and 1980s segmentation increased in popularity, especially as a means of increasing sales volumes. This was a means of increasing the competitive edge. Since the early 1990s segmentation has been a key component in direct marketing and increasingly now in Internet marketing.

As Dibb (1998) states, the segmentation of markets can provide:

a better understanding of customers' needs and wants. Thus allowing greater responsiveness in terms of the product(s) or service on offer. The enhanced appreciation of the competitive situation also allows the business to better understand the appropriate segments to target and the nature of the competitive advantage to seek. Furthermore, a segmentation approach can add clarity to the process of marketing planning, by highlighting the marketing programme requirements of particular customer groups.

In this chapter we:

▌ examine the way a market or markets can be subdivided into smaller sub-markets or segments;

▌ consider how a company can use these segments to improve its marketing effort to ensure it delivers the required benefits to its potential customers;

▌ discuss some of the methods available to organizations to identify the types of segments that exist in their markets;

▌ see how organizations can actually use the techniques to ensure that their marketing efforts are effective.

This chapter links into Chapter 7 on strategy and marketing, so it is important that you consider the relationship between the two chapters.

Kotler (2000) and Dibb (1998) among others have developed and enhanced an STP schematic which illustrates the relationship between segmentation, targeting and positioning. This is illustrated in Figure 5.1.

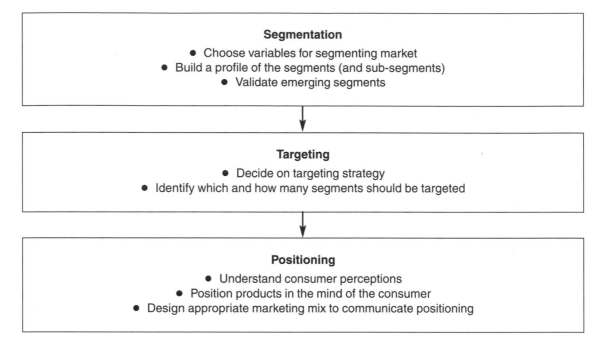

Figure 5.1   The STP schematic

Source: Dibb (1998).

Learning objectives

On completion of this chapter you should be able to:

▌ outline the concept of segmentation;

▌ critically evaluate the various methods of segmenting markets;

▌ identify appropriate methods for targeting potential customers;

▌ determine how a product or brand is positioned within the market;

▌ debate how positioning can be used to gain a competitive advantage.

What is a market?

So far we have considered what marketing is and what shapes it. We also now understand the environment within which companies are organized and operate, and the importance of customers and competition within dynamic environments.

We have, however, tended to consider the market as a large collection of people somewhere in the world beyond the boundaries of our immediate environment, the very people that companies have to inform about what they can offer. This may be in the way of benefits and satisfactions to resolve their problems and needs. However, we must consider that a proportion, and possibly a large proportion, will have no interest in the product or service being marketed. In fact they are not really part of the company's target market. Therefore what the company must do is clearly identify those people, or organizations, that are actually interested in the products/services. Only once a company has done this can it really use the concept of marketing in such a way that it can influence the potential market(s).

If a company concentrates on the benefits or satisfactions customers seek from what it offers, it can start to identify its target customers. The company first needs to define the products or services it offers in terms of benefits or customer requirements, rather than by the features they contain. If this is done, the potential market, or the people the company is trying to find, become much easier to define.

For example, many people go swimming. However, ask yourself who would really readily jump into a large hole filled with chlorinated water. It does not sound appealing, but that is not exactly what the providers of the swimming pool are really offering. The large hole is the physical product (its shape and structure) and may even contain additional (PR added value) features such diving boards and slides. The benefit or satisfaction is based around healthy exercise, relaxation and the chance to meet friends and acquaintances in an enjoyable social atmosphere.

Thus an organization must identify what business it is in before it can really consider any of the functions of marketing. This business must be considered from the customer's or user's view point, not that of the supplier.

Perreault et al (2000) suggest that ideal market segments meet the following four criteria:

▌ **Homogenous (similar) within.** Customers within the segment should be as similar as possible with respect to their likely responses to the marketing mix variables (product, price, promotion, place, people, process and physical evidence) and their segmenting dimensions.

▌ **Heterogeneous (different) between.** Here, the customers within different segments should be as different as possible with respect to their likely responses to the marketing mix variables and their segmenting dimensions.

▌ **Substantial.** The segment should be large enough to sustain costs and thus be profitable.

▌ **Operational.** The segmenting dimensions should be useful for identifying customers (geodemographics and lifestyle analysis, for example) and the appropriate marketing mix variables.

There are many examples of incorrectly defined businesses. If we consider the vast leisure industry, Leadley (1992) makes the point that 'Sports shops selling running shoes, track suits and associated athletic wear have been known to define their business in terms of providing athletic apparel and try to aim their business at athletes. Yet much of the apparel sold by this type of shop is worn by people who wish to be fashionable.'

As we all know, tracksuits and trainers are not just worn by athletes. They are now worn by all sectors of the population as general leisurewear (whether they were intended for that or not). The benefits that can be obtained from these types of product have been extended beyond their original functional use to one of casual clothing. However, not all the population have, or will, take to wearing tracksuits and trainers, only particular identifiable segments of the population. These segments must, of course, be identified correctly if the manufacturers of the leisurewear are to exploit this broader potential market.

We can see therefore that it is important for organizations to identify correctly the business they are in, and therefore correctly identify their potential customers. This will ensure that all their marketing efforts can be directed at potential customers, so that resources such as time, money and effort are used both efficiently and effectively. If it carefully considers the composition and characteristics of the potential markets there is a greater opportunity for the organization to be successful.

Segmenting markets

We have considered the concept that people only buy products or services that offer some benefit or satisfaction to them. Even fast food is not eaten by the whole of the UK population. It is therefore important that organizations only offer their products or services to people who may actually want them. There is no point in offering the products or services to people who have no need or desire to own or use them. In fact, it can be counterproductive as it shows that the organization does not really consider the needs of the market.

A company must consider a potential market very carefully and try to identify groups of people who will benefit from what it offers. This is achieved by segmenting the market into much smaller sub-markets (sub-segments or sub-sets), whose characteristics, in the form of benefits sought, can be identified more easily.

Kotler (2000) defines segmentation as follows: 'Market segmentation is the subdividing of a market into homogenous subsets of customers, where any subset may conceivably be selected as a market target to be reached with a distinct marketing mix.'

While this was first postulated in the early 1970s and Kotler has since broadened his approach, other writers, such as McDonald and Dunbar (1995) still use a very similar definition. This tends to suggest that the basis of the definition is as sound today as it was some 35 years ago. Kotler (2000) has taken the concept of segmentation further by considering that markets can be divided and identified in five different ways:

- **Mass market.** Here all buyers are considered as the same. This has the advantage of economies of scale and reducing costs, so it is a method that is generally liked by accountants. However the concept of 'one size fit all', as Kotler (2000) considers it, is difficult to sustain in today's drive for mass customization and differentiation. Many organizations have now moved away from the mass market approach.

Even Coca-Cola, which was originally only available in one size of bottle, is now available in a number of types and sizes of container as well as a number of different formulations. Otherwise, offering only one product would not have been in keeping with the changing requirements of the marketplace.

- **Segmented market.** Kotler (2000) considers this to be a *large* (our italics) identifiable group within a market, that has some attribute that makes it different from the mass market. The actual differences may not be that great. However, they are discernible and therefore consumers can have a product or service that more closely matches their needs.

- **Niche market.** Kotler (2000) also considers 'niche markets', which are seen as a more narrowly defined group, typically a small market whose needs are not being well served. Often these groups will pay a premium price for the benefit received. An example of a niche market is UK pizzas produced using organic produce. While slowly expanding, as of late 2001, it was relatively small within the larger UK market as a whole (Mintel, 2001).

- **Local markets.** Here the benefits being offered reflect the character of the region or small location being served. This could be a small country town or village where there is only one grocery store.

- **Individual markets** (also known as one-to-one marketing and micro marketing). This offers customized products or services to meet potential customers' exact needs. This type of marketing approach is not uncommon in the automotive industry, for example. Certainly Volvo can customize a car from its range with the choice of about 4,000 options of colour, engine, trim and so on. The 'Marketing insight' below briefly illustrates how the Internet company Amazon.com focuses on an individual's needs by understanding their buying habits.

Marketing insight: Amazon.com and customization

Although Amazon.com has a large international market it aims to build a one-to-one relationship with its customers. This it attempts by linking pre- and post-purchasing with personalized recommendations it believes individual customers will appreciate, because they meet their needs or interests. This is only possible through linking large databases of information on similar customers and their purchasing habits.

None of these methods can be considered as unique. It is possible to consider a number of niche markets within a segment, for instance, and possible individual markets within a niche, like the example of Volvo. This is especially true in business-to-business markets, although the concept has been extended to a number of consumer markets.

Wilson and Gilligan (1997) also provide a very explicit definition of segmentation: 'The process of dividing up a varied and differing group of buyers into smaller groups, within which broadly similar patterns of buyers' needs exist.' In the next 'Marketing insight' (English, Welsh and Scottish Railways) we highlight how potential users of freight carrying services can be divided into a number of specific groups, enabling user needs to be identified and satisfied more easily.

Marketing insight: English, Welsh and Scottish Railways

If we consider an organization like the English, Welsh and Scottish Railways (EWS) in the UK, we can readily see how the concept of identifying the market can be used. We do not all directly require the services of a freight carrying railway company. In a sense, no organization really wants rail transport. The benefit, or satisfaction, the manufacture or supplier seeks is to move its products or goods to its customers in the most effective way possible. Potential customers, as suppliers, are not really interested in the physical way the products are moved, provided they arrive at the destination safely and on time. We consider distribution in more detail in a later chapter.

By examining EWS we can see how organizations find it useful to consider their potential markets, not as a single market but a series of smaller sub-divisions or segments. EWS is the UK's largest rail freight operator, and is owned by an international consortium led by Wisconsin Central Transport Corporation of the United States.

The company organizes its marketing on commodity lines, such as coal and steel, which are probably the largest current markets available. Much of this business involves the movement of coal from mines or special shipping terminals to electricity generating plants, using specially designed coal wagons in long train formations. These are often referred to as 'merry-go-round' trains as the distance covered may not be that long, but the trains run almost continually to ensure there is adequate coal available at the generating plant. However, the company has expanded its range of operations to embrace a wider market in the movement of goods or freight.

EWS is currently involved in:

- bulk freight;
- distribution;
- mail and parcels;
- infrastructure maintenance;
- special passenger trains;
- train maintenance and driver hire.

The company also runs over 1,000 special passenger trains each year, including steam loco-motive-hauled trains and locomotives for prestige services such as the *Venice–Simplon Orient Express*. Further market segments have also been identified which include:

■ food and drink for major retail chains;
■ white goods and other manufactured products;
■ forest and agricultural products;
■ automotive components and finished vehicles;
■ defence industries.

These markets have not yet been developed but are seen as natural extensions to the segments that EWS currently serves. To ensure that the needs of the markets it serves are met, EWS has established customer delivery centres in various parts of the country and a range of business development departments covering:

■ forest products;
■ consumer goods;
■ international carriage;
■ automotive;
■ government contracts.

These are in addition to the established segments being served:

■ construction;
■ infrastructure services;
■ intermodal;
■ metals;
■ minerals;
■ petroleum and chemicals;
■ rail express services.

EWS realize that to develop into new market sectors will require different skills and products to offer to the potential customers. While the company must not alienate its core business and the customers served through this business, it was made clear at the 1999 Rail Freight Conference that 'the main scope for further rail growth lies in finished product, calling for a different approach from EWS's other flows. It therefore requires new terminals, stock management, data sharing and delivery services.'

The company has stated that 'the growth strategy is based upon exploiting rail's environ-mental and congestion-busting advantages and by offering the quality of service customers require at prices they are able to pay'.

EWS has identified clearly the business it is in and have developed a policy of identifying potential markets it is able to serve. This has only been possible by realizing that not all rail freight is the same. It is a diverse business that needs to be segmented into definable groups of potential customers.

Questions/activities

1. What criteria could you use to segment (1) a local passenger train service and (2) a long-distance passenger train service? You may want to focus on services within your own region and country.

Source: Information courtesy of EWS London, reproduced with kind permission.

The advantages of segmentation

Obviously segmenting markets requires thought and analysis. Equally, it is not a one-off project. Markets and the buyers within those markets change, thus companies must continually monitor any changes that take place within the market segments. Failure to do so can lead to new entrants into the market gaining a competitive advantage because they have been better market watchers. Such ongoing analysis requires organizational resources, so the work must be justified financially. The benefits of undertaking such work must therefore be identifiable and shown to be of value.

Ability to compare marketing opportunities

The major benefits can be considered as being able to see and compare marketing opportunities that exist within the marketplace. These could be in the form of gaps within the market where a particular benefit is not readily available from other suppliers. Therefore the attributes required could be offered to that particular segment to fill the perceived gap. Care must be taken to ensure that the segment is sufficiently substantial to allow an adequate return on the investment.

Effective allocation of marketing budget

The use of segmentation can also help guide the effective allocation of the marketing budget. The aim is to concentrate expenditure on markets that will provide the highest return, and hence be the most profitable. It helps to ensure that the marketing effort is not wasted on products and services that cannot be effectively, or competitively, offered by the organization.

Ability to make adjustments

Segmentation also allows an organization to make fine adjustments to the marketing mix specifically to suit the market. It may only be necessary to modify one aspect of the mix to change the effect or perception of the offering, and therefore make it more appealing to a chosen segment.

The concept of segmenting markets should ensure that marketing can achieve the specified objectives of the organization. This can only be done if:

- the characteristics of the individual market are known;
- the influence of specific buying groups upon those markets is understood;
- sales promotion is directed to the specific market segments;
- these segments are exploited to achieve the defined marketing objectives.

Methods of segmenting consumer markets

However for a market segment to be of any real value a company must consider the characteristics that are going to identify the market segments. The most common ones in use are:

- geographical/cultural;
- demographics;
- buyer behaviour;
- geodemographics;
- lifestyle analysis.

Geographical/cultural

This can be seen as two separate characteristics. However, they are usually very closely linked because sub-cultures tend to form within similar geographical areas. Also the smaller the geographical area, the more likely the culture (lifestyles) in that area will be similar.

If you consider the campus of your university to be a geographical location, you will find that the culture on that campus generally reflects the interests of the students studying there. Obviously this method of segmentation is very broad. That said, it is a useful starting point for dividing the market into homogenous sub-sets of customers, for example first-year undergraduates studying a BA or BSc in Business. These then can be used to help define the variables of the appropriate marketing mix.

Demographics

Here details of age, sex, ethnicity and religion, for example, are used as a basis to define the market the company is trying to reach. The first characteristic, sex, can neatly halve the population for some products, and much reduce the number of potential customers.

Very few men wear lipstick, so from this fact alone lipstick manufacturers only really have to consider women as the potential market. If we then couple this with age, we can further split, or segment, the market as differing age groups usually require different colours and styles of lipstick, and so on. Again, we find that the various age groups tend to have definable lifestyles and hence similar needs and wants. This helps the company to ensure that the benefit(s) the product or service offers match closely the needs of the potential market.

Buyer behaviour

By using, or understanding, the way potential buyers behave, companies can focus their attention on particular segments. For example, some customers may be 'brand loyal', always buying the same brand of washing powder, coffee, breakfast cereal and so on. It is possible to identify these people and their shopping habits, as they may also be loyal to one retail outlet. This allows producers to target these segments to keep the brand name and image visible in the mind of the customer (through advertising and other forms of promotion – see Chapters 10 and 11). Such promotions (for instance, special offers) can potentially increase or reinforce brand loyalty.

Geodemographics

This is a combination of geographic and demographic information to help build profiles of individuals or groups of people. It is a consumer targeting system based upon the concept that where someone lives indicates something about his or her lifestyle, and perhaps the products he or she buys. Since the 1970s several companies have developed sophisticated geodeomographic models, for example CACI with ACORN™ and Experian with MOSAIC™. To illustrate geodemographics we have included the US ACORN™ system.

Originally introduced in 1977, ACORN (A Classification Of Residential Neighbourhoods) identifies key clusters of the population with a region or country. The objective is to discover geographic areas where people are likely to have similar lifestyles and purchasing habits. ACORN™ comprises six categories, 17 groups and 54 types.

Here we illustrate both the US and UK ACORN™ systems. As you will see they are detailed in their descriptions of neighbourhoods, thus showing the level of specificity geodemographics can attain. When you look at these categories, consider the grouping to which you, your friends and family could be allocated.

In the US, the ACORN™ neighbourhood segments are subdivided into 43 clusters, which are collected into nine groups. These are reproduced below:

Group 1: Affluent families
Group 2: Upscale households
Group 3: Up and coming singles
Group 4: Retirement styles
Group 5: Young mobile adults
Group 6: City dwellers
Group 7: Factory and farm communities
Group 8: Downtown residents
Group 9: Non-residential neighbourhoods

In the UK CACI has developed the following ACORN™ families:

▮ Scottish*ACORN™, identifying the inherent differences within the Scottish marketplace.

▮ UK*ACORN™, highlighting consumer types.

▮ Financial*ACORN™, targeting people according to the financial products that they are likely to purchase.

▮ Investor*ACORN™, developed using census information and share ownership to identify areas of high disposable income, and people most likely to purchase high-value products.

▮ Workforce*ACORN™, comparing the difference in the profile of the population at a given location during working hours and at weekends.

▮ Custom*ACORN™, developed using a company's customer purchasing data to construct company-specific targeting classifications.

(We direct students who are interested in discovering more on the above geodemographic classifications to log onto the CACI Web site, www.caci.co.uk or www.caci.com).

Several further refinements have been made to the concept. In addition to developing a lifestyle concept, ACORN™ also has a system of targeting classifications. This breaks down the population of an area into six categories known as UK ACORN™ Consumer Types. These are reproduced below:

Category A: Thriving

These are people who have achieved wealth and are financially independent.

Group 1

Type 1:   Wealthy suburbs, large detached houses
Type 2:   Villages with wealthy commuters
Type 3:   Mature affluent home owning areas
Type 4:   Affluent suburbs
Type 5:   Mature, well-off suburbs

Group 2

Type 6:   Agricultural villages, home based workers
Type 7:   Holiday retreats, older people, home based workers

Group 3

Type 8:   Home owning areas, well-off older residents
Type 9:   Private flats, elderly people

Category B: Expanding

These are people who are successful in their chosen careers.

Group 4

Type 10: Affluent working families with mortgages
Type 11: Affluent working couples with mortgages, new homes
Type 12: Transient workforces, living at their place of work

Group 5

Type 13: Home owning family areas
Type 14: Home owning family areas, older children
Type 15: Families with mortgages, younger children

Category C: Rising

Developing and affluent sectors of the community.

Group 6

Type 16: Well-off town and city areas
Type 17: Flats and mortgages, singles and young working couples
Type 18: Furnished flats and bedsits, younger single people

Group 7

Type 19: Apartments, young professional singles and couples
Type 20: Gentrified multi-ethnic areas

Group 8

Type 21: Prosperous enclaves, highly qualified executives
Type 22: Academic centres, students and young professionals
Type 23: Affluent city centre areas, tenements and flats
Type 24: Partially gentrified multi-ethnic areas
Type 25: Converted flats and bedsits, single people

Category D: Settling

These are mainly those who are home owners, and usually more mature people.

Group 9

Type 26: Mature established home owning areas
Type 27: Rural areas, mixed occupations
Type 28: Established home owning areas
Type 29: Home owning areas, council tenants, retired people

Group 10

Type 30: Established home owning areas, skilled workers

Type 31: Home owners in older properties
Type 32: Home owning areas with skilled workers

Category E: Aspiring

These can be classified as younger skilled workers and new home owners.

Group 11

Type 33: Council areas, some new home owners
Type 34: Mature home owning areas, skilled workers
Type 35: Low rise estates, older workers, new home owners

Group 12

Type 36: Home owning multi-ethnic areas, young families
Type 37: Multi-occupied town centres, mixed occupations
Type 38: Multi-ethnic areas, white collar workers

Category F: Striving

Older, less prosperous areas.

Group 13

Type 39: Home owners, small council flats, single pensioners
Type 40: Council areas, older people, health problems

Group 14

Type 41: Better-off council areas, new home owners
Type 42: Council areas, young families, some new home owners
Type 43: Council areas, young families, many lone parents
Type 44: Multi-occupied terraces, multi-ethnic areas

Type 45: Low rise council estates, less well-off families
Type 46: Council areas, residents with health problems

Group 15

Type 47: Estates with high unemployment
Type 48: Council flats, elderly people, health problems
Type 49: Council flats, very high unemployment, singles

Group 16

Type 50: Council areas, high unemployment, lone parents
Type 51: Council flats, greatest hardship, many lone parents

Group 17

Type 52: Multi-ethnic, large families, overcrowding
Type 53: Multi-ethnic, severe unemployment, lone parents
Type 54: Multi-ethnic, high unemployment, overcrowding

©CACI

As well as ACORN™ there are other means of customer profiling. They include targeting by age and the value of the individual's home or street value. What these geodemographic tools illustrate is that the analysis is becoming ever more sophisticated.

The information to define the various groupings is extracted from a number of sources. The main ones are (information from CACI):

▍ **Census statistics:** socioeconomic data, housing, household and age.

▍ **Demographic data:** age, household composition, population movement.

▍ **Financial data:** County Court judgments, CCN Consumer Searches.

▍ **Housing data:** address type.

▍ **Retail data:** accessibility.

While these systems are based on types and location of dwelling occupied by the particular market segment, they can trace their roots back to the original socio-economic groupings. These have been used for many years, especially by the media. Various published media, such as newspapers and magazines, tend to be bought by different types of people who can usually be divided into these socioeconomic groups. This is particularly so with newspapers. The media use this information when selling advertising space to ensure that the potential advertisers can target their prospective customers with some degree of certainty.

The socioeconomic category groups for the United Kingdom, as defined for the 2001 Census, are listed in Table 5.1.

It is also possible to segment groups by the stage in the family life cycle. Nine stages are usually identified, and much of the basis of this work can be attributed to research undertaken by Wells and Barr in the early 1960s. Again this type of classification is very useful in segmenting consumer markets, and is used by the leisure and tourist industry, among others, to target leisure and holiday details to parts of the population most likely to use what is offered. This ensures that what is offered reflects the lifestyles and therefore the needs of that part of the population. The stages that were identified are:

▍ bachelor stage;

▍ newly married;

▍ full nest 1 (<6) with children under 6 years old;

▍ full nest 2 (>6) with children over 6 years old;

▍ full nest 3 (dep.): children 18+ at home, perhaps in higher education;

Table 5.1 Social economic category groups in the UK

Social class	Occupations	Examples
1	Higher managerial and professional occupations	Chief executive officers
1.1	Employers and managers in large organizations	Company directors and senior managers
1.2	Higher professional	Surgeons, lawyers
2	Lower managerial and professional occupations	Company managers and police officers
3	Intermediate occupations	Administrators, personal assistants
4	Micro and small company employers, freelance workers	Small business owners and self-employed
5	Lower supervisory, craft and related occupations	Foreman/woman
6	Semi-routine occupations	Drivers, hairdressers
7	Routine occupations	Car park attendants, cleaners

Source: Office of National Statistics.

▌ empty nest 1 (head at work): children now left home;

▌ empty nest 2: both parents now retired;

▌ solitary survivor in work;

▌ solitary retired.

This has been further refined to form the SAGACITY lifecycle groups that are again built around the lifestyle of the various components of the population. Four stages are identified:

▌ dependant;

▌ pre-family;

▌ family;

▌ late.

Against each stage the income and occupation is plotted to identify the various groups and their potential purchasing power. This needs to be correlated with other factors, but is again a useful method of segmenting markets. This method also allows organizations to ensure that the products and services they offer will meet the needs of a definable set of potential customers. This group must be clearly identified before any form of communication to them is undertaken.

All the methods discussed equate purchase behaviour with specific criteria, but in practice they give a very close correlation so they are very useful for segmenting markets. Often a number of methods are used together to cross-check the results and refine the target audience even further.

Lifestyle analysis

This is the analysis of the way people choose to live their lives. People's feelings, beliefs, needs and desires influence their buying behaviour (see Chapter 4). We must realize that the factors that determine an individual's lifestyle are often immensely complicated. Marketers attempt to gain a greater understanding of potential and actual customers by analysing different types of lifestyle.

Through detailed surveys it is possible to collect and collate a wealth of information. Companies often sponsor research companies to undertake such data collection. In the UK, for instance, surveys are regularly conducted to discover people's purchasing habits, likes and dislikes. The collection of such information assists companies in targeting their potential customers more successfully, thus, for instance, increasing the return on investment from direct mail. The questionnaires are detailed, with sections relevant to specific industry categories. The areas covered include:

- grocery shopping, from which supermarkets are visited, and the frequency of those visits through to the types of brands purchased;

- holidays;

- home life: type of home and mortgage;

- occupation;

- potential future purchases;

- leisure activities;

- charities supported;

- purchases made by mail order;

- health: any specific illnesses, and type of health insurance cover;

- motoring: type of car, breakdown service membership and the type of petrol station used;

- home computing facilities;

- which newspapers and magazines are read;

- home finance: types of banking accounts, investments and credit cards;

- pets, ranging from number, size and age through to which brand of pet food is purchased, how frequently and where it is purchased;

- television/radio: how many hours a day each station is watched or listened to, and which types of programme are enjoyed.

- home improvements, from which DIY stores are visited through to planned improvements.

From such data researchers can build an individual profile. For example: 'Enjoys reading fiction, listens to jazz and classical music, prefers tailored holidays to packaged holidays, has investment and insurance policies and has a platinum credit card. Lives in his own house with a small mortgage, partner and two Welsh Border collie dogs.' This is only a snapshot; however it should provide an essence of the information collected. Such information, overlaid on geodemographic data, helps to create a powerful selection profile for both current and potential customers.

By knowing what people buy, how they buy, where they buy and what they hope to buy, a company has a greater opportunity to create offers targeted directly at the known preferences of individuals.

Generally, within Western societies, people are more inclined to cooperate in an action that will make shopping easier and more enjoyable, hence people's willingness to complete detailed questionnaires on their shopping and lifestyle habits. Additionally, there are usually incentives that accompany such questionnaires, such as prize draws of £5,000.

However we must consider other societies in which individuals may not be so willing to reveal so much detail about their purchasing and lifestyle habits. For example consumers in Eastern European countries, who for a significant part of the 20th century lived in police states, may be hesitant to reveal such information. This will probably change as those societies are modified under the influence of new generations of consumers.

Lifestyle Plus™

In October 1997 CACI launched a new lifestyle database, Lifestyle UK™. This featured information on over 44 million individuals, each one selected by over 300 lifestyle attributes. The database contains lifestyle information on individuals and not households, with over 90 per cent of the data being less than two years old.

Each of the 44 million consumers on the database is scored from 0–99 on the propensity he or she displays for each of the 300 lifestyle variables. This allows companies to rank their entire database on any given set of characteristics, based upon how well they match their requirements.

Each section of the system is completely tailored, recognizing that a company's database is unique. For example, a company or organization may want to select individuals using a combination of income, leisure interests and known purchasing power or behaviour, or a company may want to target suspects who most closely match their existing client base.

CACI have also developed the technology to enable a company to enhance its own customer data. A company's customers are matched with CACI's Lifestyle UK™ database and are tagged with any of the 300 lifestyle selections. As a result this means that a company's database can be improved by adding items such as income and types of newspaper read, which may not otherwise be held on the database.

People UK™

In October 1998, CACI launched another new product into the UK market. People UK™ is an individual-level, geodemographic-lifestyle segmentation system that is not specific to any market sector. Unlike previous systems that have worked at post code level, People UK™ was designed to assign different people within the same household to different types, the objective being to bring a new level of precision to individual consumer targeting.

This targeting tool focuses on life stages, or age/family status along with key lifestyle characteristics. It summarizes individual lifestyle characteristics into 46 discrete types. The characteristics are taken from CACI's Lifestyle UK™ database which includes 300 pieces of lifestyle information for each individual. See Table 5.2, where the '£' sign indicates the level of financial security/wealth.

B2B segmentation

We have tended so far to concentrate mainly on business-to-consumer (B2C) markets.

However business-to-business (B2B), or industrial markets, can be and are successfully segmented. The main characteristics used include:

- **Benefits sought:** what exactly is the user looking for from the product and/or service?

- **Type of application:** where and how will the product be used?

- **Type of customer:** industrial, local authority and so on. Here the segmentation can be based upon Standard Industry Codes or Classification (SICs). This can be described as a standardized method of classifying businesses. Originally developed by the US government in the 1930s and introduced in the late 1940s, it has undergone several revisions since. The UK system follows the same principles as the International Standard Industrial Classification (ISIC) as issued by the United Nations and the NACE (Nomenclature des Activitiés Etablies dans les Communautés Eurpéennes) system as used by the European Union.

  In 1997 the US government announced that a new system, NAICS (North American Industrial Classification), would be introduced to improve compatibility with Canada and Mexico. NAICS includes new and emerging industries and services, and will be revised to accommodate new industries.

  [Note: The SIC codes can vary from country to country. Further details can normally be obtained from your own government's Web site.]

- **Customer size:** large-scale customers may be more directly involved with the development of new products.

- **Usage rate:** light or heavy users, often relate to the size of the customer company.

Table 5.2   People UK™'s database

Lifestage 1: Starting out		
££££	Silver spoons	Young people with affluent parents
££	Popcorn and pop music	Singles in low value housing
££	Friends in flats	Young flat sharers
££	Urban multi-cultural mixed	Metropolitan singles

Lifestage 2: Young with toddlers		
££££	Legoland families	Prosperous marrieds with pre-school children
££	Caravans and fun fairs	Young families in mid-value homes
£	Struggling singles	Single parents on low incomes

Lifestage 3: Young families		
£££££	On the right track	Up-market executive families
££££	PC parents	Affluent, liberal young families
£££	School fetes	Aspiring couples with young children
£££	Car boot sales	Traditional families with average incomes
£££	Camping and cottages	Moderate incomes, outdoor pursuits
££	Loan-loaded lifestyles	Low incomes and high loans
£	Satellites and scratchcards	Poorer families without bank accounts

Lifestage 4: Singles/couples no kids		
££££	Telebanking townies	City flat sharers with affluent, active lifestyles
£££	Solvent sets	Financially aware middle-aged singles/couples
££	On the terraces	Blue collar singles
£	Pools and pubs	Poorer singles in deprived areas

Lifestage 5: Middle-aged families		
£££££	Serious money	Wealthy families in exclusive areas
££££	Affluent intelligentsia	Cultured well-off couples
££££	Two-car suburbia	Prosperous people with teenage children
££££	Conventional families	Comfortable households with traditional values
£££	Cross-channel weekenders	Moderately well-off settled families
£££	Garden and pets	Established families in country areas
£££	Neighbourhood watch	Average incomes, suburban housing
££	Staid at home	Families with teenage children in lower value suburban housing
££	Tabloids and TV	Lower income families with older children

Lifestage 6: Empty nesters		
££££	Prosperous empty nesters	Older couples living in expensive housing
£££	Young at heart	Older couples with active interests
££	Cautious couples	Modest lifestyles and moderate means
££	Radio 2 fans	Average incomes and traditional attitudes
£	Urban elderly	Poorer couples in council housing
£	Beer and bookies	Low income families with teenage children

Table 5.2 *continued*

Lifestage 7: Retired couples		
££££	The golden years	Affluent couples
£££	Cultured living	Retired couples with up-market leisure interests
££	Keeping up appearances	Retirees in bungalows
£	Put the kettle on	Inactive retirees
£	Counting the pennies	Elderly couples in low-value housing
£	Just coping	Impoverished elderly couples
Lifestage 8: Older singles		
£££	Older affluent urbanites	Older metropolitans in expensive housing
££	Active pensioners	Older people with active lifestyles
££	Theatre and travel	Elderly city dwellers with up-market interests
££	Songs of praise	Charitable elderly singles
£	Grey blues	Pensioners living in very poor areas
£	Church and bingo	Very old and poor singles
£	Meals on wheels	Poorest elderly in council flats

© CACI Limited

- **Loyalty of customer:** loyal customers may receive special treatment, for example, through special product offers or financing terms.

- **Geographic location:** often certain industries locate in particular parts of a country because of the supply of raw materials and so on.

- **Situational factors:** what are the tactical requirements of any particular purchase situation?

This list is not exhaustive but provides an indication of the factors that a company may wish to consider when seeking ways to segment B2B markets. Often more is known about the particular purchasers in these types of markets. These details need to be considered in association with others to ensure that prospective customers are targeted correctly with the right products or services. It is necessary for the B2B service provider to be very familiar with the purchasing routines of its potential markets. Knowing the way any potential customer operates will allow a much more accurate segmenting of the market.

In many cases B2B involves working with individual segmented markets. It is from this concept that relationship marketing has been further developed. The identification of the very small segments allows suppliers to develop a special relationship with their customers.

We have considered the more standard approaches to segmentation. However, an organization has to develop its own particular segmentation characteristics, based on the particular requirements of the product/market it is working in. Leadley and Hutchings (1994) present a model that could be used for market segmentation in the tourism industry (see Table 5.3).

Conditions for segmentation

Whichever method a company uses to segment the market, there are six conditions that must be met before the method can really be of value. If any of these conditions cannot be met then it is advisable to seek an alternative method of segmenting the particular market (Dibb, 1998).

Table 5.3   Leadley and Hutchings' segmentation model

Main segment	Main sub-segments
1 Holiday tourist	A Package fully inclusive B Package partly inclusive C Independent travel agent D Independent private
2 Business traveller	A Travel agent B Employer's travel dept C Individual business D Individual including short holiday
3 Special or common interest traveller	A Hobby B Culture C Religious D Archaeological/historical E Ethnic/anthropological F Flora and fauna G Sport H Family visits I Shopping J Prestige trips K Competitions

Accessibility

The segment chosen must be *accessible*. It must be possible to communicate with people in the chosen segment so that the company can advise them of the benefits that are being offered. Without this condition it will not be possible to make any sales and the segment will be of no commercial value.

Appropriateness

The segment defined must be *appropriate*. There is little point in trying to break a market into defined segments if there is little or no call or use for what the company offers to that segment. However, it is necessary to consider the longer term at this stage, so while the benefit offered might not be required now, if it is likely to be required in the foreseeable future, it may be worth considering the segment.

Measurability

The segment that is to be used must be *measurable*. Often this will only be in broad terms. However, a reasonable indication of the size of the market is crucial before any attempt is made to enter that market. The potential market must be large enough to obtain an adequate return on any investment that the company has placed into developing the product and the market.

Stability

The segment defined must be *stable*. This is a relative relationship, but any movement or trends in that segment of the market need to be predictable (where possible) so that future planning can be undertaken. If the trend is downwards, care must be taken to ensure that the market segment will last long enough to make it worthwhile.

Sustainability

The defined segment must be *substantial*. Again this is a relative term. Care must be taken when considering the segmenting relationship to the total size of the market. A supplier of specialist models may have a market segment that consists of approximately 1,000 potential customers. While this would be of no value to a manufacturer of baked beans, it can be considered substantial in the particular product/market that is being served by the model maker.

Uniqueness

The segment that is being considered must be *unique*. This implies that it can be viewed as being different in some measurable way from other segments that may be under consideration as part of the marketing effort.

Marketing strategies available

Undifferentiated marketing

This means that one marketing mix is used for the whole market. The major features of this strategy are that the whole of the market is aimed for, rather than specific segments, which are not considered as being sufficiently different to warrant special consideration. The same marketing mix is used to present the offering to everyone, and the resources and objectives used are limited to the extent that they are sufficiently general to meet the overall requirements of the marketplace.

Concentrated marketing

As a strategy this means that the marketing is aimed at only one segment, with one specific marketing mix. The objective usually is to maximize market share by using resources to focus on excellence within the limited market. The strategy is about being the market leader in the specialist field or market chosen.

Differentiated or multi-segment marketing

This is where a number of market segments are identified and a different marketing mix is developed for each of the segments. The resources and objectives are focused on growth, and this can be achieved by careful development of each of the unique marketing mixes in the selected markets.

Real-time segmentation

As we discussed in the 'Marketing insight' on Amazon.com (page 131), Amazon's objective is to build a one-to-one relationship with its customers. Through the use of sophisticated data mines and analytical tools it can channel recommendations and other supportive information to its customers. Lerer (2002) suggests that the Internet provides the platform for 'real-time segmentation'. He states:

> Through questionnaires, click stream analysis and simple screening questions, it is possible to customize a web page for an individual. While online segmentation and the resulting attempts at segmentation may be crude.... Once individuals and their information needs are better identified, web application servers are powerful tools in delivering the appropriate content and customizing the user experience.

Although it is in its early days there are tremendous future opportunities for real-time segmentation. However, it is one thing to have the technology to drive such developments, and it is very much another to apply them effectively. This has perhaps been one of the greatest problems in marketing: the effective and efficient application of segmenting tools.

Targeting

Having considered the process of segmenting it is necessary to ensure that the best use is made of the segments by specifically targeting them with a product or service. A company may not wish to try to exploit all the segments it has identified. The most likely reason is that it cannot effectively serve all the segments in any market. Therefore it is necessary to prioritize the segments carefully against a chosen set of criteria.

However, having segmented the market a company can look specifically at those segments that will offer the most effective return on investment (ROI), and specifically target those with its product or service. Consideration can be given to the strength of competition within the various segments and the loyalty levels of their customers. Perhaps the competition is not meeting the requirements of the marketplace, therefore an opportunity may exist for the company to exploit by offering exactly what that segment actually desires. This may provide the company with the advantage of being the first to serve that segment, and so enable it to build up a solid, loyal customer base.

Consideration must also be given to the long-term objectives of the organization. Some segments may not be pursued because they do not meet with the overall objectives of the stakeholders. The organization must also consider whether it has the skills and knowledge to move a product into the segment, or if these might become available in the future. Also to target any segment the organization must develop a significant advantage over its competitors. It should only enter segments when it can offer something that is desired by the market and is not offered by the existing suppliers. This approach can help build a sustainable competitive advantage, perhaps over the longer term.

A company may also have a share of the market in the chosen segment, and the size and potential of this should be considered when looking at which segments to target. When in competition, it is often desirable to go for a market leader strategy to ensure an adequate return on investment.

Like all markets, segments are dynamic. The needs and wants of the population making up the segment are likely to change over time, and if possible the effect of these changes on the potential of the segment must be considered. This usually requires the use of forecasting techniques, but a good marketing information system (linking data warehousing and data mining techniques) should provide the necessary data.

The organization will have other factors to consider when analysing which segments to target, and again they must not be considered as mutually exclusive. Many smaller organizations choose to concentrate on a single segment. While this involves an element of risk (if perhaps additional competition enters the market or potential customers' wants and values change), it means that it is possible to become extremely proficient at serving the requirements of that market. A market leader should find it possible to retain customers in the face of newer entrants into the market segment.

Larger organizations may select segment specialization. This may be by market, perhaps aerospace, or by product, such as semiconductors. Whatever specialism is chosen it must be a viable one for the organization. It must be looking to becoming the leader, or at least one of the major players, in that specialized market.

Very large companies may opt for full-market coverage by offering all the groups with the product or service that they need. As we have seen, Undifferentiated Marketing or Differentiated Marketing can cover the spectrum of the market. However, it must be remembered that each of the segments must be researched and will no doubt need totally different promotion and communication strategies. The development of the marketing mix variables must form the basis of the chosen marketing communications strategy.

Consideration of the ethical issues when selecting targets is important. Kotler (2000) suggests that care must be taken to ensure that unfair advantage is not taken of any groups, in particular children and the elderly.

With the advent of improved communication, more sophisticated customers and an oversupply of goods and services in most markets, it is becoming necessary for organizations to look to satisfying customers who can choose from a very wide range of offerings from global markets. Organizations need to focus on markets that they understand, so that they can offer differentiated products that meet the requirements of the discerning customer. This can only be done by carefully thought-through segmentation and targeting policies.

Positioning

There are a number of definitions for positioning. However, in simple terms it is the arranging for a product or service to occupy a clear, distinctive and desirable place in the minds of the target customers relative to any competing products.

This really emanates from the concept of product differentiation. The offering must have a distinct image and thus a position when compared with other similar or substitute products. The position of a product or service is set by the potential customers and not by the manufacturers. Therefore the supplying organization has only limited control over the position occupied in the marketplace by what it has to offer. However it is able to influence the position by careful and consistent use of the marketing mix. An existing brand will usually have a position in the minds of consumers, so the use of the existing brand name can help in the positioning of a new product (see Chapter 8 on products and brands). Care must be taken,

however, to ensure that any new products (brand extensions) launched into the market under the brand name will not damage the reputation or position the brand currently has.

The position that a product holds is dependent on several variables. These variables can only be established by effective and efficient market research (see Chapter 6). Not all products are positioned using the same variables. While price and quality are perhaps the two most common, many others can be used. Availability and colour may be more important in some markets than price or even quality. Even if a company thinks it understands the market in which it operates, it is very easy to get too close to the product and lose sight of what benefits are being sought by the customers. (Reflect upon the various aspects of the marketing mix, and how elements beyond price, for instance, can influence purchasing behaviour. See Chapters 9, 10, 11, 12 and 13.)

Perceptual mapping

A tool commonly used by marketers to show perceptions and positioning of brands visually is perceptual mapping, sometimes called 'positioning maps'. An example from the UK car industry is shown in Figure 5.2. This particular map was developed in 1986 to give an understanding to one of the marques (brands) shown of what the car buying public thought was important and where that particular marque was positioned in relation to its competitors. While the marques have no doubt tried to reposition themselves since 1986, and other marques would now be included, it is interesting that the relative position of the various marques have not changed that much since this map was first postulated.

Care must be taken when deciding which variables should form the axis of the perceptual map. It is the variables that existing or potential customers use that are

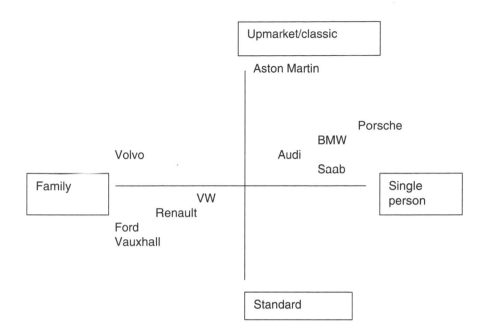

Figure 5.2   Position map for UK car brands

important, as these are the ones they will use to position the product. While it may be convenient for the supplier to use ones it finds easy, these will not allow useful analysis of the perception of the product in the marketplace.

While an organization cannot dictate the exact position of a product in its customers' minds, it can go some way to exerting a strong influence by matching its positioning strategies to the knowledge it has of the target market. The position of the product can be decided by considering the following variables:

▌ attribute(s);

▌ price/quality;

▌ competitor(s) within the market;

▌ application(s);

▌ product user;

▌ product class.

Which particular strategy should be adopted will always depend on the particular market

being served. The particular strategy chosen must come from the analysis of the market. Dibb *et al* (1997) propose a commonsense and step-by-step approach as follows:

▌ Define the segments in a particular market.

▌ Decide which segment(s) to target.

▌ Understand what the target consumers expect.

▌ Develop a product that caters for the needs of the segment.

▌ Evaluate the positioning and images, as perceived by the target customers of competing products.

▌ Select an image that sets the product apart from the competition.

▌ Inform the target consumers about the product.

If such a sequence is followed, it should help ensure that the product or service occupies the right space in the minds of target customers. This position should provide the supplier with a competitive edge, allowing it to gain higher market share within the chosen segment. This is because it should be able to better match the product/service to customers' requirements. However, if its competitors are already strong in the market, the company must be sure that it can better match the requirements of that chosen segment. What it is offering must be seen as not only being different, but desirably different by the customers.

Why segmentation fails

You might think it is curious to have a section near the end of this chapter on failure. The point is that most marketing texts discuss segmentation, targeting and positioning as if they were the salvation of marketing, the panacea for all marketing ills. The same could be said of other marketing tools; however as with virtually any theory or concept, segmentation is flawed. Thus it is important to understand some of these flaws in order to use some of these tools more effectively.

Various authors, such as Dibb (1998) and Wright (1996), have highlighted the difficulties associated with segmentation. As Dibb (1998) crucially states, 'in some cases, marketers become too entrenched in the detail of segmentation because they lack expertise in linking the process into the business' strategic planning.' Here she focuses on companies' failure to view segmentation from a strategic perspective with longer time horizons than a mere few weeks. However, this is not the only perceived weakness of the segmentation process. Here briefly we consider the other difficulties (Dibb, 1998):

▌ Some marketers fail to understand that segments must be meaningful to the prospective and current customers, as well as the company. Piercy (1992) provides the example of a corporate bank that divided

up its customers by turnover and size. However, such groupings may fail to differentiate between customers' product requirements and actual buying behaviour.

▌ A tendency to over-emphasize the segmentation detail rather than consider the underlying objectives. Here the over-emphasis is on the collection and ordering of data. While data collection is important, as we have seen, there still needs to be a critical evaluation of the segment. For example, is it valuable now, and what is its likely value in the future? Segments, like markets, may not always remain valuable contributors to the balance sheet.

▌ A failure to understand that market segments can change, cease or develop. For example, since the 1970s there has been a dramatic change in the UK holiday market. Generally, a more affluent UK society has sought vacations outside the UK, to a variety of international destinations and of varying standards. Companies that have not reacted or adapted to these changes have often lost the competitive battle.

▌ Segments are dynamic. Companies must realize that they cannot look at a segment as a 'snapshot in time'. They are fluid, and thus companies must be able (through real-time database analysis, for instance) to track the changing pattern of segments.

▌ Linked with the above is reaction time. It is one thing spotting a change within the segment, it is quite another being able to react to that change within a significant time frame. By 'significant' we mean an effective time frame in order to maintain a competitive position. If a market leader is unable, for whatever reason, to adapt rapidly to changing or modifying segments, it will most likely lose its competitive position.

Although there are potential difficulties in using segmentation, there are clear benefits as well. Active debate among academics, researchers and practitioners suggests that segmentation leads to an improved understanding of customers, the ability to counter competitive actions and use resources effectively and efficiently.

Chapter summary

In today's dynamic and uncertain world, companies need to analyse carefully and decide on the segment(s) that are attractive to them, not only now, but those that could be profitable in the future. To coincide with this, companies must target the appropriate segment(s). They need to consider the benefits actually sought from the target audience and how these can be best delivered. Finally, companies need to position the offering making sure what they have to offer meets the total requirements of the segment and emphasizes the specific attributes sought.

In order for these criteria to be delivered, the company needs to manipulate the marketing mix to match the segment. This may range from mass customization through to the communication mix reinforcing the brand image/identity to the target audience.

Marketing insight: the BBC

The British Broadcasting Corporation has developed a very sophisticated segmentation base whereby its radio and television audiences are segmented into 'tribes'. While these are referred to as the 100 tribes, there are in fact over 100 possibilities in the UK. The BBC states the reasons for this process as follows:

- More than any other broadcaster, the BBC needs to understand its audiences. The unique way in which the BBC is funded means that it needs to make sure the needs of the individual and specific communities are served. It must make sure it reflects and enriches life and culture in the UK and is truly accountable to its audiences.
- In the new digital age, with the possibility of hundreds of new television and radio stations, as well as online media, it will be more important than ever that the BBC understands its audiences' changing needs in order to maximize the value delivered and build brand loyalty to the BBC brand.
- For new and existing commercial activities, a full understanding of consumers provides the foundations for maximizing value.

The BBC needs to understand its audiences in increasingly sophisticated ways, and this meant:

- that the traditional descriptions of audiences (for example, 16–34 ABC1s) had limitations;
- that the descriptions were expressed in a jargon that most people could not interpret – what does ABC1 actually mean in terms of the BBC's audience?
- when used at the macro level, they do not represent homogenous groups of individuals: all C2DEs are not the same, nor are all 16–34-year-olds;
- the BBC felt it needed to go beyond technical definitions to find more effective ways of describing what audience groups are really like.

The aim for the BBC was clear. It needed to understand its audiences through the method of segmentation it used. The criteria for the segmentation were based on:

- The possibility of breaking down the BBC's target audience into smaller groups that shared common characteristics and needs, which could be matched more closely to the BBC's output (programming, publications, merchandise, trails and other communications).
- Each group should share as many characteristics as possible, but each group should also be as different as possible from the next.
- The segmentation also had to be:
  - **relevant**: it needed to display a real difference between groups' consumption of BBC services, and attitudes to the BBC licence fee;
  - **actionable**: it needed to be based on real data, to be able to be tracked over time and to enable the BBC to prioritize target groups;
  - **meaningful** to non-researchers: it needed to bring the individuals in the segment to life;
  - **simple**, both conceptually and linguistically.

The BBC realized that no segmentation method will ever be perfect, but that it needed a practical solution that it could use and that could be refined over time. The concept that supports segmentation is that it can be used to aid decision making. The BBC therefore considered that meaningful segmentation would allow it to understand:

- how different audience groups consume BBC services, to allow identification of audiences it needed to develop;
- the value each audience group gets from the BBC, to facilitate the allocation of resources against each audience group;
- how different audience groups feel about the BBC, to allow it to prioritize key communication tasks;
- the lifestyles, motivations and media preference of audience groups to facilitate commissioning, production and scheduling of programming.

The BBC therefore segmented its audience into approximately 100 groups, which it described as the 100 tribes of the UK. Each tribe has certain characteristics:

- Its characteristics are measurable, meaningful and actionable for the BBC.
- The tribe is relatively enduring.
- Its members recognize that they share a common culture or experiences.
- It is large enough for the BBC to serve in a consistent way.
- It is important enough to people's lives for them to expect the BBC to serve them.

It defined three segment prisms within which each segmentation groups individuals in different ways, and each has a different role.

Lifestages

These are based on demographics that explain the greatest variance in media consumption. Everyone in the UK is included once and once only. This is useful for managing a portfolio of brands and services. This prism contains 41 groups ranging from children to the retired.

Social communities

These segment people on the basis of the communities they belong to. People can belong to more than one community (for example, Muslim in north-west England). These are the groups that the BBC has to serve and understand as part of the public service broadcasting remit. This prism contains 25 groups based on regional, ethnic, religious and other communities.

Communities of interest/passions

These are the groups of people who share a common drive or enthusiasm. These individuals can belong to many tribes. These create specific programming opportunities, creating cultural reference.

Any individual can be in all three prisms, for example, young mothers, Muslim, passionate about gardening.

The BBC has collected in-depth information on each tribe and this information is updated on a regular basis. The biggest problem is ensuring that the data are comparable across tribes, although indications are that this is so. All the data is available to all the local radio and television stations and is used by both the station and the BBC centrally to monitor performance and develop programmes in response to the requirements of the various segments that have been identified.

Questions/activities

1. Contact a major broadcaster within your own country. Determine how it segments its audiences, then compare this to the BBC's approach. (If you are a UK student contact a cable, satellite or commercial terrestrial station.) This question can be tackled either individually or as a group exercise.
2. Could the BBC's approach to segmentation be used for another business sector? If so, what sector, and how could it be implemented?
3. We have already seen that lifestyle and geodemographic data can change (this is also something we refer to later in this textbook). How would changes in lifestyles affect the BBC's approach to segmentation? You may want to test this out with the findings you have established from Question 1 above.

Source: Details provided by BBC London and reproduced with permission.

Exercises and questions for review and critical thinking

1. Why is it important for marketers to segment markets? Do you think there are any cases/examples where a market would not be segmented?

2. Describe, in detail, the methods that can be applied to segment a market.

3. Consider critically why positioning is important to the marketing of a product or service.

4. Draw positioning maps for the following product groups: soft drinks, perfumes, watches and clothes. Then list the factors that you believe differentiate the products from each other.

5. How would you segment the market for toothpaste?

6

Marketing research

Introduction

This chapter explores the process of marketing research and its role in the achievement of strategic marketing and organizational objectives. Additionally, it will help you understand the academic concepts underlying business research and develop practical research skills.

Clearly, it is necessary to have valid information to make any rational decision. Making effective marketing decisions requires accurate marketing information. The type of decision(s) to be made will vary from organization to organization and from time to time. However, they all have the same basic requirement for accurate information as the basis for effective decision making. It is therefore essential that organizations collect and analyse data on both the micro and macro environments within which they operate.

We have seen that environments are dynamic and hence continually changing, therefore data must be collected on an ongoing basis and be made available to all those that may need to use it to help them make decisions that will improve the (current and future) prospects of the organization. Obviously vast amounts of data and information are available, so it is necessary to be very selective about what is collected, how it is analysed, how long it is kept (like many other items, data loses value with age), and how it is used.

Learning objectives

On completion of this chapter you should be able to:

▌ demonstrate an understanding of the role played by marketing research in the development and implementation of marketing strategy;

▌ outline the benefits marketing research can bring to the business environment;

▌ define a management information system and its role in the decision-making process;

▌ demonstrate an understanding of the marketing research process;

- identify the most appropriate research methods to resolve a marketing problem;

- evaluate the contributions of both qualitative and quantitative research methods.

Marketing information

Most companies and organizations create some form of marketing information system (MkIS), also sometimes called a marketing intelligence system (MIntS). This is usually a sub-set of the organization's overall management information system (MIS). How complex or sophisticated this system is will depend on the size of the organization, and the markets being served. The system can be anything from a very simple handwritten one using index cards through to a purpose-designed computer system of great complexity. The most important thing is that the data is contemporary and relevant to the needs of the organization. Old data is usually of no value and can be counterproductive as it may lead to the wrong conclusions being drawn.

All organizations, from the simple sole trader through to large multinational corporations/enterprises (MNC/MNEs), need to collect and analyse marketing data. However, the data being collected must be considered carefully to ensure that what is collected will help the organization more closely meet the needs of its target markets.

Careful consideration must also be given as to how the information will be collected and the most appropriate way to analyse and distribute the analysis to the relevant people within the organization. The information produced must, of course, actually be used in the decision-making process, otherwise the exercise will have been futile and the chances of an inappropriate decision being made greatly increased.

What marketing research is

The American Marketing Association defines marketing research as:

the function that links the consumer, customer and public to the marketer through information. Information is used to:

- identify and define marketing opportunities and problems;
- generate, refine and evaluate marketing actions;
- monitor marketing performance

and

- improve the understanding of marketing as a process.

Marketing research

- designs the methods for collecting information;
- manages and implements the data collection process;
- analyzes the results

and

- communicates the findings and their implications.

(Bennett, 1988)

Burns and Bush (2000) simplify this statement by defining marketing research as 'the process of designing, gathering, analyzing and reporting of information that may be used to solve a specific marketing problem'.

Marketing is about meeting the needs of potential and actual customers. Therefore it is necessary to understand fully what their needs are now and might be at some time in the future (in the short, medium and longer term). This should allow the organization to ensure that the product or service being offered will provide to the customer the benefits being sought. To do this it is necessary to research the potential market in some detail in order to obtain the necessary information.

Before any research can be carried out it is necessary to have considered the likely target market (see Chapter 5 on 'Segmenting, positioning and targeting') and have a clear objective of what the company is trying to establish about it. This will ensure that the basic function of marketing research is obtained: to help organizations meet the needs of their customers, and to ensure that their products or services are sufficiently different from those of their competitors.

A major point that should be noted, at this stage, is that it is necessary to ensure that the cost of undertaking the research is not greater than the value of the benefits it will provide. We look at methods of establishing this later in the chapter.

Marketing research tends to mean different things to different people. As a result, it is important that a clear understanding of the process exists before its use can be appreciated. As stated earlier, marketing research must form an integrated part of a marketing information system to ensure that the organization is kept fully up to date with any changes or developments within the marketplace. This is why it is necessary to undertake marketing research that directly involves the collection and analysis of data about the marketplace.

However, just collecting and analysing data from the marketplace is not necessarily going to be that useful if it is collected in an *ad hoc* manner. The collection and analysis must have a clear purpose in mind and be undertaken in a clear, systematic way. Only if objective and systematic parameters are considered and used will the data collected and subsequently analysed be of any *realistic* value to the organization. Otherwise, it will be a waste of resources.

Marketing research is not a decision-making system. The research and analysis cannot provide the company with the answer to any problem, or dictate the strategy to be used to meet the needs of the marketplace. It is purely an aid to decision making that should offer several possible answers to a stated marketing problem. The most appropriate way forward is still down to the marketing directors and managers concerned.

What the research should do is highlight the potential problems and indicate ways forward that are of *least risk* for the organization.

Marketing research is used to reduce the risk, or turn uncertainty into a measurable risk. This should lead to the most effective marketing action being implemented. It can also be used to monitor plans and strategies that have already been implemented. Feedback from such monitoring can assist companies in reviewing their strategies, and pre-empting or reacting to problem situations. This is perhaps most especially the case in volatile or dynamic markets (although it could be argued that most markets today have become volatile and dynamic).

Here we should highlight the difference between marketing research and market research. Marketing research is really about considering the more general aspects of what is happening within the marketplace and how effective particular marketing strategies are performing within that broader market. Market research is concerned with an in-depth investigation into the potential of a specific market sector. In reality, the boundaries are not that clear. Most people refer to the whole process as marketing research, as we have done here, as one is inevitably linked to the other.

The market for research

The value of the research market is often underestimated. With the following tables we attempt to demonstrate that commercial enterprises are increasingly taking the use of marketing research seriously. In Table 6.1 we have listed the world value for marketing research data, while Table 6.2 shows the 10 largest countries in terms of their investment in marketing research.

It is interesting in Table 6.2 to note the significant difference between the United States and the individual European countries, with the UK leading the way. Equally, by comparing Tables 6.1 and 6.2, you can see that

Table 6.1   World value for marketing research data (2000)

Region	Value US $ million*
Europe (total)	5,944
15 EU members	5,492
Asia Pacific (total)	2,130
North America (total)	6,356
Central & South America	697
All other nations	136
World total	**15,263**

Source: ESOMAR, *Marketing News* (8 July, 2002)

Table 6.2   Ten largest markets by country in value of marketing research data (2000)

Country	Value US $ million*
United States	5,922
United Kingdom	1,623
Germany	1,290
Japan	1,206
France	958
Canada	434
Italy	415
Spain	273
Australia	273
Netherlands	228
Total	**12,622**

Source: ESOMAR, *Marketing News* (8 July, 2002)

* The values include total expenditure on marketing research in that country by domestic and international clients. However, it does not include spending on work undertaken by non-commercial institutions such as governments and universities, or that by advertising agencies and management consulting firms using their own resources to conduct research.

the United States invests more in marketing research than the current 15 member states of the European Union (as of 2002). This underlines two points: first, the US's predominance in marketing research, and second, the fact that it has been a key component of many US companies' marketing activities for some considerable time. For other countries marketing research is a relatively new phenomenon.

The potential benefits of marketing research

We can consider that the principal benefit of marketing research is to reduce the level of risk or uncertainty within the decision making process. Quee (1999) however suggests that there are other benefits that should also be considered. These include:

▌ It provides a means of more accurately defining problems and thus research objectives.

▌ It provides a more reliable method of predicting possible outcomes of a marketing or business decision.

▌ It can provide a company or organization with a competitive advantage, for as the English lawyer, philosopher and essayist Francis Bacon (1561–1626) wrote, 'For also knowledge itself is power'. If a company has information on market trends and customer preferences, it will be better equipped to meet the demands of that market.

▌ It can provide a more effective return on investment. If a company has a good understanding of customer preferences and the market, it can direct funds more efficiently to projects, such as new product developments (NPD) or promotions.

▌ Efficient and effective marketing research can lead to the creation of new marketing opportunities for a company or organization. Marketing research might alert a company to a specific gap within the marketplace, for example, which it is able to fill, thus increasing its revenue generation potential.

▌ Marketing research can help reduce overall business risk. As we will see in Chapter 8, new product development can be an extremely high-risk scenario. Effective marketing research can help companies avoid the costly embarrassment of launching inherently flawed products.

▌ Marketing research can assist in monitoring the overall effectiveness of the company's marketing plan.

Who uses marketing research?

While the uses for marketing research can be many and varied, there are key business sectors that can benefit from marketing research. Quee (1999) divided these business users into five broad groups. However, we have further subdivided one of the groups and added a new group.

▌ **Consumer product manufacturers.** These companies, especially the producers of FMCGs, are the largest investors in marketing research.

▌ **Industrial/commercial product manufacturers.** While they tend to be less dependent upon marketing research than FMCG manufacturers, it is still important for them to evaluate product performance and customer needs.

▌ **Retailers and wholesalers.** Retailers need to understand consumers' expectations of the shopping experience. This is also important in terms of which items should be available in-store.

▌ **Media groups.** The editorial teams at television news companies (for example, the BBC and CNN), radio stations (for example, the BBC), newspapers (for example, the *Financial Times*) and magazines (for example, the *Economist* or *Business Week International*) are continually searching for information on consumer profiles, attitudes and opinions. Examples include the countless surveys on how a population intends to vote at a particular election, and whether the UK should join the European Monetary Union and adopt the euro, and when.

▌ **Business services.** Advertising companies, business consultants (including general marketing research companies), public relations companies, banks and consumer financial institutions all seek information on customer attitudes, brand awareness, leisure activities and purchasing intentions. These companies are also very heavy users of marketing research techniques.

▌ **Clubs and societies.** Whether small or large, clubs and societies usually undertake some form of research to seek out views of their membership (see the 'Marketing insight : Model Railway Society Survey' on page 179).

▌ **Not-for-profit organizations.** Government departments, universities, charities and voluntary organizations all require information. In terms of government activities, these may range from a national census through to the attitudes of business people to new export services/regulations. Charities also need to know how people will donate in the future, and to what good causes.

In many cases this research is undertaken on behalf of the company/organization by international research companies such as Gallup (www.gallup.co.uk), AC Nielsen (www.nielsen.com) and MORI (www.mori.co.uk).

The drivers for the development of marketing research

Quee (1999) has considered several drivers that have influenced the development of marketing research. Here we consider and adapt some of his key points.

Changing neighbourhoods

Prior to the growth and expansion of supermarkets, residents would use their local neighbourhood shops. Generally, the store owner would know his or her customers by name and their individual preferences. Instinctively the store owner was conducting his or her own marketing research by considering overall what his or her customers liked and disliked.

Obviously local stores have not completely disappeared; indeed in some countries they remain the main business force. However, it is probably true that in many places contemporary store owners are not as close to their customers as were traditional store owners. With the emergence of supermarkets and out-of-town hypermarkets there is a need for more information on customer buying habits and preferences. Indeed the need for marketing information is now not just local, but international and global, so the organization's spread of research needs is often much greater.

What is now interesting is the use of technology, especially the Internet. By building, in essence, one-to-one communications with customers through Web purchasing and loyalty cards it is possible for large retailing organizations once more to act like the local store owner, even though the conversation is not face to face but remote (in reality, or virtual). Future generations will use voice-activated e-mails and shopping functions to converse in real time with the online supermarkets. Therefore there is a significant opportunity to gather relevant market research and build data warehouses to improve overall targeting efficiency.

The move from needs to choice

In many countries the level of disposable income has significantly increased since the 1960s. Today companies know that, in highly developed economies, certain items (for example, television sets and washing machines) are taken as standard purchases. With this in mind, their focus is in marketing the brand name, not the need for such items. Therefore, marketing researchers are interested to understand the customers' preferences in terms of product features/benefits and after sales service.

Changing attributes of the marketing mix

While price still plays an important role in the marketing mix, it may not now be the sole determinant of purchase (a point made in Chapter 5). Again with increasing affluence, within developed and developing economies, other factors may influence the purchase of a particular product or service. These include brand image, brand identity, quality and efficiency of the packaging, and after sales service. As with the point about needs and choice, marketing research is important in gauging customer preferences.

Customer focus

Today, the focus is on customers. They have greater influence than they have ever had before, as was stated in Chapter 4. They can make or break a product or a brand, no matter how much money has been invested in the launch of that product. Indeed, they can make or break a company. Therefore once again, marketing research, if used effectively and efficiently, can help discover what customers want today and probably tomorrow. As a result, marketing research has significantly widened in scope since its introduction at the beginning of the 20th century.

What marketing research can do

Marketing research can identify as much about the markets as an organization wishes to consider. For instance:

▮ It can indicate the total market potential, which is the first step in deciding whether it is worth pursuing the identified market.

▮ It can indicate market trends and how it is changing in size and/or structure.

▮ It can identify the factors that are causing the change and thus allow forecasts to be made of future potential.

▮ It can indicate what market shares are possible for the players in the market along with details of current and possible competitors.

▮ It can provide the answers to how, where, why and when they compete.

▮ It can indicate how it might be possible to counter the competition by highlighting

the strengths and weaknesses of each of the major competitors.

▮ It can detail the current methods of distribution of the product or service to customers.

▮ It can illustrate potential gaps in the current distribution methods.

▮ It can provide a basis for considering what the market actually requires. This can be especially useful when considering what products should be available in the marketplace.

▮ It can identify what types of products and services potential customers may be seeking. It is important to identify benefits sought rather than the features of the product, so the research must be directed towards identifying needs and wants. This will also allow any unsatisfied needs to be identified, thus revealing gaps in the market that may need filling.

▮ It can illustrate how the organization's products compare with those offered by competitors in terms of quality, performance, reliability, maintenance and so on. The customers may perceive much of this, rather than be certain what is the case. However, without this type of data it may not be possible to ensure that the product or service has a positive differential advantage over competitors.

The marketing research process

If we believe that market research is a systematic, objective collection and analysis of data, with regard to the marketing of products and services, then obviously it must be carried out in a systematic and objective way. There are several basic steps in undertaking market research, and these can be outlined under the headings shown in Figure 6.1.

Establishing the need for marketing research

↓

Problem definition

↓

The research objective

↓

The research brief: determining research design

↓

Identifying information types and sources:
primary and secondary data

↓

Question design

↓

Data collection

↓

Data analysis and interpretation

↓

The final research report

Figure 6.1   The marketing research process

Establishing the need for marketing research

First, it is important that a company accurately determines the need for such research. In some cases the company may decide not to undertake marketing research. The following factors may influence such a decision.

▌ **The information is already available.** The information that the company requires may already be available within the company, through external agencies or both. In many cases the company can purchase current secondary research data that is sufficient for its analytical and planning needs.

▌ **There is insufficient time to conduct research.** Decisions may have to be made within a very short time frame that prevents any research being undertaken. The company may either decide to press ahead with say, a product development, or to abandon the development as too risky. This action may be due to severe turbulence within the micro and macro environments. Of course, pressing ahead with a new development can be a high-risk scenario. It may result in a tremendous success. On the other hand it could be an unmitigated disaster leading to the collapse of the company.

▌ **Resources are not available.** The company may not have sufficient people and financial resources to undertake such research. After all marketing research can be a costly process, and thus beyond the reach of many micro businesses and small and medium-sized enterprises (SMEs).

▌ **The costs outweigh the value of the research.** In some instances the costs of providing the research will be greater than the value or quality of the research itself. Companies, no matter how large, must consider the costs of undertaking various business exercises including marketing research.

Problem definition

This is always the first step in any form of market investigation, and should outline the problem in the context of the organization's operations and plans (current and future). It is normally made in the form of a marketing problem to which an answer is required. It needs to consider, if the problem were solved, what would be the advantage to the organization? Can this advantage be quantified in terms of increased market share, revenue and thus profits, for example?

Defining the problem is always very difficult (this should never be underestimated). A poorly defined problem will result in work being undertaken that will not provide the necessary information for the correct decisions to be made. Indeed, it may lead the organization in the wrong direction with possible dire consequences.

Zikmund (1994) considers that there are six steps in the process of defining a problem:

1. It is necessary to ascertain the objectives of the decision maker involved, including the type of decision that has to be made.

2. A clear understanding of the background to the perceived problem is required.

3. The symptoms must be clearly isolated before the problem can be identified.

4. It is important that the *real* problem is resolved not the symptoms.

5. The unit of analysis must be determined.

6. Finally, as a result of the above it is possible to state the research question and the research objectives.

Much time is spent considering problems that are familiar. This can often lead to a form of myopia that tends only to give very narrow answers to the problem. It is necessary to consider the wider implications of the problem, and perhaps consider the whole problem in a different and new (often radical) way. This will usually allow for much more creative and better solutions to emerge.

The research objective

It is necessary to develop a marketing hypothesis before it is possible to progress to deciding what type of research is required. The hypothesis should be developed as a range of scenarios for the marketplace that are plausible, rational and in reality quite probable. Any of the scenarios, if proven, could lead to different marketing actions being required. It is therefore necessary to consider each of the possible scenarios as part of the research process.

The actual design of the research is affected by the different hypotheses, and the task of the marketing researcher is to confirm or deny each of the hypotheses. Only when this is done conclusively can the information be passed onto the decision maker(s) for consideration.

The research objectives can clearly be seen as being fundamental to obtaining the right data to answer any marketing problem. It is therefore necessary to ensure that:

▌ there is absolutely no ambiguity (or confusion) in the phrasing of the research question;

▌ the objective is always quantified;

▌ the objectives set are actually achievable (there can be a tendency to aim for impossible goals);

▌ any answers received will make a contribution to the solution of the marketing problem;

▌ the objectives are simple and understandable.

The research brief: determining research design

Once the objectives of the research have been established it becomes possible to implement the process. A number of steps are involved, the first of which is to develop the research brief itself. This will contain:

▌ the relevant background information;

▌ the objectives of the research;

▌ how these will assist the marketing process.

Details of the methodology that will be used to collect the data need to be set out, along with the timing involved and the cost associated with collecting and analysing the data.

From the research brief it may be necessary to conduct some exploratory research to confirm that the research methodology is sound (or valid). This research may subsequently lead to changes in the brief. This will help to develop the formal research proposal that will detail the methodology used to undertake the research. This will then be followed by the main data collection stage using both desk (secondary) and field (primary) forms of research. Once all the data is collected and verified it will need to be analysed and interpreted, and finally the results presented to the necessary parties in the form of a comprehensive report.

Exploratory research

The exploratory research is intended to verify the scenarios that have been developed. It is used for:

▌ gaining background information;

▌ defining terms of the research;

▌ clarifying the research problem or hypothesis;

▌ establishing research practice.

Two techniques are often used. The first is the use of experience surveys, where people within the organization are encouraged to state their ideas based on their experience of the identified problem. The second is a careful analysis and interrogation of the organization's marketing information system to see what data already exist within the organization. It may be possible to consider similar problems in other organizations by analysing readily available case study material. (This may be obtained through industry sources such as trade associations or other professional bodies: see Table 6.3.)

Often, at this stage, pilot studies are conducted using a range of techniques which include focus group interviews and projective techniques. While some of these can be time-consuming they do often help ensure that the final research programme will meet its major stated objectives. However, there are costs involved, and these may be beyond the budgetary resources of smaller organizations.

Identifying information types and sources: secondary and primary data

In this section we consider two main types of data, secondary and primary. Secondary data (also known as desk research) is data/information that has previously been gathered/analysed by someone else for another purpose rather than the current research project. This data/information can be either internal or external.

Primary research (also known as field research) is data/information that is gathered, analysed and presented specifically for the current research project.

Secondary research

In many cases a company will seek out secondary data prior to undertaking primary research. Such data/information may provide valuable insight for the research team preparing for the primary research. However, it is important that secondary data is evaluated effectively because not all information will be reliable, relevant and/or valid for the current research project.

Burns and Bush (2000) suggest five criteria for such an evaluation:

▌ **What is the purpose of the study?** One of the problems sometimes associated with secondary research is that studies are undertaken to prove a particular point of view. This is especially so where a favourable outcome would benefit a particular side of a debate (for example, a particular manager or department). Of course not all research falls into this category; however researchers using the secondary data sources need to discover and understand the nature of the original research. Was it truly independent or was it to support a particular point of view? If the latter, is it flawed biased research? Indeed, the basis for it may have been unethical.

▌ **Who collected and analysed the data?** This refers to the credibility of the organization that undertook the original research. Assuming there was no bias (see the above point) and the marketing research company is competent, there is an excellent chance that the data will be valid. Generally, well established marketing research companies are very protective of their reputations. Therefore it is unlikely that they would engage in any unethical

actions. Normally they are open with regard to the methods and procedures they used to gather the data.

▌ **What data was collected?** The title of the piece of research may not accurately reflect what was actually measured, and how it was measured. Thus it is important for a company to obtain an accurate picture of what type of data was collected.

▌ **How was the data collected?** Understanding how the original data was obtained is important to realizing whether it is useful or not. There are many different means of collecting data, and these can have an impact, to a greater or lesser extent, on the quality of the information/results obtained.

▌ **How consistent is the data/information with other forms of information?** Again, this links back to the reliability and validity of the data collected and analysed. If several independent companies report similar findings then the findings are probably reliable. However if large differences (using the same variables) are reported, there will be uncertainty as to the reliability of the data and subsequent analysis. For example, if company A said that eating a particular product was very good for you, yet 10 others said that it was harmful, the reliability of company A's data would have to be examined. It might turn out that company A had been funded by the industry that makes that particular product. Again, we can see a potential ethical issue.

Internal and external secondary data

As stated earlier, secondary data can be subdivided into internal and external. Table 6.3 illustrates the different types of data sources that can be used by a company or organization.

Table 6.3   Internal and external data sources

Category	Source of information	Description
Internal	Sales records	Provides details of an individual's purchasing history.
	Payment records	Provides details of an individual's payment history. For example, does the person pay on time?
	Inventories	Details of which products are selling and which are not.
	Research reports	Various departments may have already conducted previous research. Pooling such information can be of value across the organization.
External	Company directories and indexes	These directories provide information on companies and organizations operating within various sectors. Publishers of such directories include Dun & Bradstreet (www.dnb.com).
	Competitor information	Includes marketing literature, annual report and accounts. Information can also be obtained through public relations material in newspapers and magazines.
	Government reports	Various forms of economic and market statistics. Includes census information. Increasingly available via the Internet.
	Commercial information sources	Research reports on countries and business sectors. For example, Mintel (www.mintel.co.uk) provide a range of reports on consumer products and markets.
	Industry sources	Reports from professional and trade associations. These could include developments within the industry sector, including possible new entrants to the market.
	Other sources	Can include research undertaken by universities and specialist institutes or think tanks such as Demos in the UK (www.demos.co.uk).

Internal sources

This is information or data that is stored within the company or organization itself. This may be in the form of sales records, inventories or specific research reports. This is generally the most cost-effective and easiest form of information gathering. Data can be sourced from many areas; however it is always best to start with the internal sources. All companies and organizations collect and analyse internal information on a day-to-day basis. However, often this information is not readily available outside the accounting or finance functions, for example. Yet this information provides general data about the state of the markets being served by the organization.

The marketing information system needs to collect and analyse data on sales volumes by product, the value of the sales made on either a weekly or monthly basis, and to develop moving averages to plot the trends over time. Details of the products or services' costs along with the margins generated and the overheads attributed allow the marketing department to analyse the most profitable products and therefore decide which to concentrate on. It also allows comparison with competitors' products, as their costs are likely to be similar. This way competitors' pricing strategies can be monitored and countered, if necessary.

Details of stock levels and stock turnover rates will allow the sales department to push slow-moving items through the distribution chain. However this can only be achieved if the details are known and monitored through the marketing information system.

Details of enquiries from new or potential customers need to be recorded and their performance monitored. This will allow contact via the sales force, and ensure that any sales publicity is correctly targeted to them.

Another crucial source of data is from sales call reports (relevant to both B2B and B2C environments). This allows the ratio of sales to calls to be monitored and also whether any geographical area is performing better than the norm. The reports should contain details of potential customers' objections to purchasing the product, and these can be used to monitor the design and features of the product range. The reports should also contain details of the needs and benefits sought by potential customers, as this can form the basis for new product development.

Much, if not all, of the vast quantities of information a typical organization stores will probably be stored on databases. Companies are increasingly employing analytical tools to extract the right information at the right time. While a data warehouse can be extremely valuable, companies need to consider more than the data mining techniques of drill down and drill through. They need to be clear what sort of information they are trying to obtain.

External sources

External secondary data is a variety of information held externally to the company or organization. This includes industry/sector marketing reports from independent research companies, newspapers, magazines, full-text databases, government reports, membership organizations (such as the American Marketing Association or the UK's Institute of Direct Marketing) and Internet sources (although there is much biased information on the Internet, there are an increasing number of reliable sources).

This information may be available through specialist libraries, such as City Business Library which is situated in London's business district. This can be highly cost-effective, depending upon the source of information required. If it is from a specialist reference library it may be either free or at a minimal charge. However, research reports needed to be purchased from independent research consultants can be very expensive, ranging from £250 to over £1,000 Sterling. This can be prohibitively expensive for micro businesses, SMEs and voluntary organizations.

The research tends to rely upon information that is published by many sources. It can be used as an end in itself as it is quite possible that all the data or information required to answer the research question has been obtained by others. It may be necessary for the organization to analyse and interpret the data in a different way, but this does not reduce the value of the data. The data may, however, only be suitable for background and a basic support to primary research activities.

Uses of secondary data

The secondary data collected has many uses:

- It can provide a very useful backdrop to the subsequent primary research by identifying which companies are operating within the market.

- It can provide an indication of the type of data that is likely to be collected, and help set the sample size and type of sampling techniques to be used.

- The data acquired can be used instead of that obtained by primary research. This will probably be the case if the cost of the primary research is likely to be prohibitive.

- It is a source of data obtained over longer time frames, showing trends that can be used for forecasting. This is the idea of 'looking back to look forward'. In other words can historical trends help the company plan for the future?

▌ Many organizations use it as a technique when they are considering the acquisition of another company. Such information can allow them to construct a profile without alerting the marketplace to their intentions. (If they were known, the target company could mount a defence and/or other companies might also consider a takeover challenge. Such a challenge might manifest itself as a 'dawn raid' on the shares of the target company.)

However, just collecting secondary data is of no value in itself. The secondary data must be relevant to the research objectives. Secondary data is not always cheap. Some of the published reports, as stated earlier, can cost well over £1,000, therefore it might be more cost-effective to undertake primary research. Additionally, not all the data that may be required will necessarily have been published, so primary research may be the only means of obtaining the necessary data.

Checks must be made that the secondary data published does not contain any bias. The data must be up to date to be of any value. The accuracy must also be checked, thus the following questions should be considered:

▌ Was the sample used to collect the base data representative?

▌ Were the questions used properly constructed and executed?

▌ How was the data analysed?

▌ Was the sample used large enough to verify the findings?

▌ Is the raw data available as well as the interpreted results?

▌ How well was the research supervised?

Finally, it is necessary to establish if the data is sufficient for the company's particular needs:

▌ Does the data published meet all the required criteria as set out in the research brief?

Primary research

Once the secondary research has been completed, any gaps in the available data should normally become obvious. These gaps will need to be filled before the data collected can be analysed properly and used in the decision making process. This can, at this stage, only be achieved by the undertaking of primary research. This may require data to be collected of a qualitative, quantitative or pluralistic nature.

▌ **Qualitative research** is the collecting, analysis and interpreting of data by observing what people say and do.

▌ **Quantitative research** involves the use of structured questions where response options have been predetermined (for example, a scale of 1 to 5 where 5 is the highest and 1 the lowest), and a large number of respondents (a large sample) is involved.

▌ **Pluralistic research** is a combination of both qualitative and quantitative research, where the advantages of both can benefit the research project.

It is useful to consider the use of qualitative research first as it is often the most useful to the marketing decision-maker. This type of research is used to produce diagnostic information to answer the questions:

▌ What?

▌ Why?

▌ When?

▌ Where?

▌ How?

It is intended to provide understanding of behaviours within the marketplace, rather than measurement. This knowledge is usually obtained from small samples of potential consumers, either individually or in groups. The researcher may interview these potential consumers for anything up to an hour to obtain an in-depth understanding of what the consumers are interested in, why they have that interest, and how their required satisfactions may be or are met.

This type of study can be used for basic market exploratory studies to:

▌ obtain a general feel of the marketplace;

▌ consider possible new product development;

▌ help in the design and development of advertising themes and storyboards, as well as diagnostic studies into the behaviour of segments of the potential market.

Interviewing is not the only method used to obtain the required data. A number of methods are available, all of which can be used to support the findings of each other.

Observation techniques

Perhaps one of the easiest primary research methods is observation. Zikmund (1994) has defined this as 'The systematic process of recording the behavioural patterns of people, objects and occurrences without questioning or communicating with them.' As Quee (1999) states, there are three implications of observations:

▌ The activity and behaviour of the respondent should be observable.

▌ The observer should note the observations either simultaneously with the action or immediately after.

▌ The respondent (or the person under observation) should not be aware of him or her being observed.

It is possible to observe human behaviour and the physical actions that emerge from that behaviour. This can be linked to evidence of the stimuli that may have created the behaviour. For example:

▌ The verbal and expressive behaviour of the individual in response to stimuli can be recorded and compared with other individuals to look for specific response patterns.

▌ Spatial relations and locations between individuals and groups can examine group pressure and positions of dominance and response. For example, do people buy because of peer pressure from their friend(s) when they are out shopping? (See Chapter 4 and the discussion on peer pressure.)

▌ Temporal patterns can establish the effects of time on the response of individuals and groups. For example, does the shopper make an instant decision or does he or she wait and consider the purchase? Indeed, a customer may continue his or her shopping (perhaps at other stores within a mall) and then return to make a purchase. This return could be several hours later.

▌ The reaction to physical objects can be recorded and compared with reactions to other objects and the overall effect on the individual's behaviour. This can be very useful, for example, in determining the type of store layout or display for the product. For instance, is the display eye-catching? Do people stop and stare at it? Does it attract not only browsers and lookers but purchasers as well?

There are various types of observation technique:

▌ Direct/indirect

▌ Disguised/undisguised

▌ Structured/unstructured

▌ Human/mechanical

Direct observation

This is where behaviour is observed in real time, as it happens. Perhaps the most often quoted example of direct observation is watching supermarket shoppers at the fruit and vegetable counters carefully examining the produce for freshness. Shoppers can be observed picking up and gently squeezing avocados to see if they are ripe or not. Equally, in a car showroom the behaviour of potential customers can be observed. For example:

▌ Do they appear comfortable within the showroom environment? For instance, do they physically appear comfortable, perhaps walking straight to the car?

▌ Do they carefully examine the car models, or is it just a cursory glance?

▌ Do they open the doors of a car and examine the interior or not?

▌ Do they approach any salespeople or not?

▌ Do they take any brochures, or do they just leave?

These and other factors can help determine the overall behaviour of the shopper. This can lead a company to consider various issues, for example:

▌ Is the environment conducive for the shopper?

▌ Is the produce fresh enough, and does it look fresh?

▌ When should shoppers be approached to see if they need assistance?

Indirect observation

This is where the researcher observes the effects of past behaviour rather than the real-time behaviour itself (Burns and Bush, 2000). This analysis includes Archive and Physical Traces.

Archive

While this is secondary data it is nonetheless observable. For example, electronic scanner information collected over time can provide a researcher with data on behavioural reactions in relation to price changes. For instance there may be price insensitivity to minor changes, say one or two pence, however any more and there may be an increase in price sensitivity.

By drilling down through databases a company can analyse the purchasing history or archive of an individual. For instance, Internet retailers such as Amazon.com will be able to observe an individual's purchasing history. What do they like? What have they bought? When did they buy? What did they pay (including whether in the case of a book it was new or secondhand – this could indicate price sensitivity)? How did they order (one book at a time or several to obtain free delivery status)? As you can see, an archive can provide a wealth of information on individuals and their behaviour. The test for the company is analysing that information effectively to understand the customer better.

Physical traces

This is the observation of a past or current event. Burns and Bush (2000) refer to studies which used 'garbology', which is the examination of rubbish bins to determine the level of recycling of particular types of containers.

Disguised observation

As Proctor (2000) states, activities need to be observed under 'normal' conditions. When people are observed directly there is a tendency for them to behave differently. In some cases this awareness (of being observed) may have a marginal effect upon their behaviour. However, many people do both consciously and subconsciously change their behaviour. For example, if a sales team within a department store know that they are being observed by the sales manager they may be more attentive to customers than normal. Also consider your own behaviour when you are being watched. Is it natural or slightly defensive? (Think of when your tutor walks past you in the lecture theatre. How do you feel?)

To overcome such behavourial changes companies often employ disguised observation techniques. One technique is the mystery or secret shopper. The mystery shopper has two key functions. The first is to observe competitor companies. Here researchers shop on behalf of the retail client at a competitor's store. Their objective is to:

▌ Observe the environment, that is the physical layout of the store (see Chapter 12), the use of shop window and internal displays, and the level of store traffic (the volume of people moving through the store at different times of the day, and how it is guided). (When you next visit your local supermarket observe the physical layout of the store, and consider why it is set out that way. Then visit a rival supermarket and see if it is different. If so, why?)

▌ Customer service: how the staff interacts with their customers. For example, are they friendly and supportive or not?

▌ Pricing policy and special promotions. The focus is on the difference between the two retailers. One retailer in London's Oxford Street regularly checks its competitors' prices on a range or basket of household products. Its objective is to either match competitor's prices or charge slightly lower prices.

As you can see this type of observation goes beyond just determining pricing policy differences. By observing and analysing a range of issues, such as store layout, it is possible to determine the advantages one store may have over another. This, for example, could be the positioning of sales promotions within a certain section of the store (for instance the first floor). This could increase impulse buying as customers move through the store to reach the first floor.

The second mystery shopper function is to observe their own company's activities. Retailers may employ mystery shoppers to observe how their own staff behave under certain conditions or situations. This can range from normal shopping habits through to the difficult or complaining customer. How staff handle a variety of situations could be the key to the company's success or failure within the marketplace. Such observations are also a good indicator as to the range and level of training that needs to be implemented.

Other methods

Companies can also use other methods, for example the use of one-way mirrors or hidden cameras.

Structured observation

This is the process where the specific behaviours to be observed are identified. A checklist is prepared and this helps the researcher to focus on specific behaviours, and thus ignore all others. For example, he or she might observe whether shoppers in the fruit and vegetable section of a supermarket squeeze the produce to check for freshness, and how they do it.

Unstructured observation

This is where the researcher notes all behaviour patterns. As Burns and Bush (2000) suggest, this type of 'open' observation may be used for initial exploratory research.

Human observation

As the word 'human' suggests, a trained individual undertakes the research. This can range from the types of direct and indirect observation described above, through to a researcher with a hand-counter checking the number of people entering a shop over a given time period. Of course, the latter example could be particularly tedious for the researcher. Such boredom will probably increase the range of error.

Mechanical observation

To overcome both the boredom and thus possible errors, mechanical devices can be used. Various techniques are employed:

Electronic counters

These can count the number of people who enter the store or the metro station, logging also the time of day. These can be useful in determining the busiest times of the day or week. For example, a metro or railway company can determine the required platform staffing levels during the day depending upon customer numbers. Thus the company can provide sufficient staff to assist customers in providing both information and a safe environment.

Electronic point of sale (EPOS)

This is the scanning of barcodes as the shopper pays for the products at the checkout counter. This provides both the store's warehouse and head office with immediate data of sales by product and product range (units and value), and a real-time stock control system. Additionally, researchers can analyse any changes in customer buying behaviour. Here are a few examples:

- **Loyalty cards.** A supermarket customer who has a loyalty card has it scanned before his or her groceries are scanned. The purpose of scanning the loyalty card initially provides two sets of information. First, it registers the card for the allocation of the points that will be accrued from the shopping experience, and second, it

provides information on the shopper's buying habits. Over time (for instance one year) an analysis could be conducted of the individual's purchases. This would indicate his or her regular purchases, and any significant changes in buying patterns that may indicate a change in his or her lifestyle. For instance, purchasing nappies and other items on a regular basis would indicate the arrival of a baby in the family. With this information the customer can be targeted with special promotions directed purely at loyalty cardholders. However, they would be relevant to the customer in question. This reinforces the relationship within the marketing experience.

- **Reaction to price changes/sales promotions.** A researcher can see how customers have reacted to a particular price change: for example, a major reduction in particular brands of canned foods due to adverse competition, or conversely, a significant price rise due to shortages of produce. This is particularly useful in gauging the success of a sales promotion over a set time frame.

- **Reaction to adverse environmental conditions.** In Chapter 4 we used the example of BSE in the UK and how consumers were reducing their beef consumption. Instead they were purchasing other meats as well as fish. When one supermarket in London dramatically cut the price of beef to clear it off its shelves, it sold out within hours. In this case price was the issue. However, the foot-and-mouth disease crisis in the UK during 2001 showed that consumers opted for other meats/fish, or increased purchases of vegetables. Electronic scanning can assist in providing researchers with information on buyer changes as a result of, for instance, a health scare, or an ethical issue that has led to a product boycott.

- **Reaction to television programmes.** Since the mid-1990s there have been a plethora of cookery programmes on British television, the highest ranking being the BBC's programmes featuring Delia Smith. During her programmes she raved about certain ingredients and kitchen implements. This usually resulted in a surge in the purchase of those very ingredients and implements.

▌ **Changes in local economic conditions.** For example, a major local employer might either drastically reduce its workforce, or go bankrupt. This would impact on the local community, with an increase in price sensitivity being recorded. This could be reflected in lower priced (often poorer quality) goods being purchased.

▌ **Changes in demographics.** Equally, the area may become more affluent due to both economic and demographic changes. This may be reflected in the type of produce being purchased from the supermarket.

Monitoring clicks on a Web site

This is of increasing importance as companies attempt to forge a closer relationship with the customer. Currently we can monitor how many people access a site, but that only provides a basic statistic. However, as more transactions are conducted via the Internet, just like with the loyalty card, companies will be able to build profiles of customer buying behaviour.

Audimeter

This was developed by the marketing research company Nielsen to record when a television set is on and which channel is being viewed (Burns and Bush, 2000). Television company sales teams, advertisers and advertising agencies need to know audience sizes and demographics at different times of the day and week. The data from an audimeter can be transmitted digitally to the research centre for compilation. However, while it may record when the television is on and which channel is selected it cannot determine if anyone is watching the programme. Thus this information needs to be supplemented with survey techniques.

Discussion or focus groups

For a more detailed level of qualitative data the use of discussion groups (focus groups) can be used. These usually comprise six to eight people who are encouraged to share their views on a particular topic of interest with the researcher. The members of the group are only recruited if they are:

▌ relevant to the topic of the study;

▌ users, or buyers of a particular product type or service;

▌ potential users or buyers;

▌ of a relevant demographic profile, or job type.

It is normal for up to six groups to be recruited for each respondent type. This is to ensure that the results obtained from the groups are typical (that is, normal). The discussion will normally last about an hour and it is normal to record it for future detailed analysis. Video recording is now a more popular method of keeping a record of the proceedings. This allows for a deeper understanding of the interactions within the group and what, if any, influence the moderator had on the discussions.

A moderator, who will ensure that the discussions do not stray too far from the major topic that the researchers are interested in, controls the groups. However he or she allows sufficient room for the group to feel at ease and not feel that they are being pressurized into a particular line of thinking. The moderator will also provide stimuli to the group when necessary, which may take the form of illustrations, product samples, draft advertisements or product descriptions.

The results will never give quantitative answers, mainly because most of the discussion will centre on opinions, and will therefore be subjective. However, by very careful analysis of the recordings it is possible to gain insight into the potential customers' reactions to the company's ideas and concepts.

The group moderator obviously plays a very important role in the way the discussions develop. Therefore, it is important for organizations to use properly trained researchers to carry out this type of exercise.

In-depth individual interviews

Another very popular method of qualitative research is the in-depth interview. The interviews tend to be long, upwards of an hour, and are semi-structured or unstructured in nature. Because of the nature of the interview it has to be face-to-face and respondents are encouraged to consider their answers, and talk freely about the topic. This should allow for better understanding of the perceptions and motivations of the respondents. Provided the respondents have been chosen with care, and accurately represent the population or market under review, then the data recorded will be valuable.

The interviews are usually video recorded so that full analysis can be undertaken after the session. These types of interview are undertaken when it is important that views of individuals are not affected by the views of others, as may occur in focus groups. This will allow deeper penetration into sensitive subjects by the researcher. It is obviously important to obtain the views of more than one respondent, so this data collection method can be quite expensive to execute.

The important aspect of this type of interview is the need to listen. By showing an active interest in what the respondent is saying, the interviewer encourages him or her to say more and therefore provide more useful information. This active listening approach also allows the questions to develop in order to obtain an even deeper understanding of the subject.

It is important to ensure that the researcher maintains confidentiality, so that the respondents cannot be identified, and thus influenced by external groups. (You may want to consider later the various ethical issues that may impact upon marketing research.) The choice of the respondents will be dictated by the research objectives. However, they are likely to be chosen on the basis of their demographic profile, or because of their purchase or use of the product or service in question.

The in-depth interview is mainly used in B2B markets for the following reasons:

▌ With the geographical spread of potential respondents, it would not be possible to have a focus group discussion.

▌ There is a risk of competitive information being accidentally leaked during a focus group discussion.

▌ There can be reticence in discussing issues in front of competitors.

Overcoming barriers: projective techniques

It is possible that barriers to communication will need to be overcome when using either focus groups or in-depth interviews. The reasons for these barriers are many; however, they are often due to the respondent's difficulty in articulating or phrasing an answer. The use of projective techniques can often help to overcome these problems, and this is a common method of relaxing the respondent.

Zikmund (1994) and Hague and Jackson (1996) describe a number of possible techniques to overcome barriers.

▌ **Indirect questions.** This is the easiest and most common form that can be used to further the discussion once an initial response has been elicited. The technique is often linked to a third-person test, where the respondent is asked what other people (the third person) might do in the particular circumstances.

- **Word association.** An equally simple technique is word association. This can range from simply asking respondents to say what comes into their mind when a particular word is mentioned, to asking respondents to complete a sentence from a prompt given by the researcher. The questions can be either of the open format or specifically focused to reduce the number of options available for the answer.

- **Other projective techniques** used to move the respondent to think in a broader context include the use of role playing, fantasy or imagining, and future scenario thinking. All these techniques are designed to see if there are any perspectives on the topic that may not have been discovered before. Equally, it is useful for discovering attitudes towards certain products or the associated service or promotion issues.

Projective techniques can use pictures as well as words. With the Thematic Appreciation Test (TAT), for example, the researcher shows the respondents a series of pictures and asks them to try to explain what is occurring or what the people portrayed might do next. Often these pictures take the form of cartoons with a speech bubble that the respondent has to fill in, indicating the reply or thought that might be given in response to the situation. This allows respondents to interpret the situation in their own way, and in the process uncovers their thoughts and prejudices. Again the use of these techniques is limited in marketing research.

While qualitative research gives some understanding of what might be happening, it is usually necessary to further the investigation to obtain quantifiable data to try to overcome some of the ambiguities that may emerge from the qualitative findings. This allows for rational decisions to be made

regarding the marketplace. Qualitative research is very useful in an exploratory sense as it provides a broad understanding of the topic. It often indicates areas that warrant further in-depth research to establish usable hard data. The major benefit of this type of research is that it generates insight and can clarify business problems to allow proper hypothesis design and testing.

Sampling

To ensure that a measure can be determined of market potential, it is necessary to undertake some form of quantitative research. In order to do this a sample or samples of the overall population have to be selected. Then the samples can be tested via questionnaires.

This type of research is designed to measure consumer opinions, attitudes and behaviour to the various brands, products or services that are available. It can also be used to measure market size, brand share, frequency of purchase and general trends in the marketplace. While it would be possible to measure the opinions and attitudes of the whole market it would be very expensive and time-consuming. It is therefore the practice to use a representative sample of the market, and use this to determine the measure for the whole. While the type of data that can be collected by using sampling techniques is vast, it is probably easier to condense the data into three classifications (Hague and Jackson, 1996):

- market measures;

- customer profile or segmentation;

- attitudinal data.

Market measures

These are used to quantify and describe the dynamics of a particular market. They are especially useful in:

- calculating the total size of the market;

- finding out how the market is changing over time;

- discovering who has what share of that market;

- indicating who is buying what.

Table 6.4 gives an example.

Customer profile or segmentation

It is possible to make the measure at various points along the distribution chain, depending upon the type of data required. Usually the data is required to gain knowledge and understanding about the potential customer base, and particularly to discover if the needs and wants of potential customers are being met and if there are any gaps in what is being supplied to the market.

Attitudinal data

A major use of quantitative research is to measure attitudes. It is normally considered that attitudes play a major role in the purchase decision process, thus the requirement for data on the perceptions, awareness, beliefs and preferences of the potential market. This can inform the company on how the market may react to any

new product, or even a change in the marketing mix, especially a potential change in price.

While it may be considered that attitudes are really the area for qualitative research, the data obtained will only provide evidence that there may be a problem. Quantitative research will allow the company or organization to obtain a measure of that potential problem, and the links to such measures as the potential purchase or frequency of purchase.

It is not normally possible to obtain the views of everybody who may be part of the potential market. The potential market is normally referred to as the 'population', and while it may be possible to contact all of this population as is done every 10 years in the UK (and many other countries) in the form of a census, it is very costly and time-consuming. It is normal to consider only a sample of the population, that is a selection of the members of that defined population in which a company has a particular interest.

Sampling is based on the theory that there is a relationship between the population and the sample drawn from it. This is based on the probability that if members are selected at random they will provide a miniature representation of the whole population. The estimates drawn from that sample will differ from the true population values only by a defined measurable amount. Any differences are referred to as 'sampling errors'. The validity of

Table 6.4   Sample market measures

Buying of men's products by women	Per cent by value
Pyjamas	60.3
Socks	42.3
Underwear	43.8
Knitwear	33.0
Shirts	29.8
Ties	27.3
Trousers and jeans	22.5
Total men's wear	26.7

Source: Taylor Nelson Sofres (1999).

the chosen sample will depend on the sample size relative to the variability of the population, and the method of determining the sample used.

A number of steps are required in selecting a suitable sample, all of which need to be considered carefully.

Defining the population

This is probably the easiest part provided the market has been correctly described. This is, of course, the potential market for the company's product or service.

Specify the sampling frame

This is a list of elements from which the sample will be drawn. A simple example could be all the students studying marketing in the business school of a particular university. Even with a sample frame like this it is possible to exclude some members from the list (for example, those students taking joint degrees such as business studies and history), and this is where the first potential source of error may occur.

Specify the sampling unit

This is a single element or a group of elements subject to selection in the sample. This is to ensure that the same criteria are used for the selection of the respondents in the sample.

Specify the sampling method

Which type of sampling method is the most suitable for the research in question? This will depend on a number of factors including the accuracy required, the time available and the likely cost of collecting the data. The sampling available is usually considered to be of two types, non-probability sampling and probability sampling. In non-probability sampling the chances of any member of the population being chosen is unknown. In probability

sampling every element in the population has a known probability of being chosen.

Determining the sample size

This is the number of respondents or observations that are to be made. To estimate the sample size it is necessary to estimate the standard deviation of the population, decide on the margin of error acceptable and determine the confidence level. To do this requires a knowledge of statistics. In simple terms the size of the sample will equal the confidence level multiplied by the standard deviation then divided by the desired magnitude of error with the result squared.

Selecting the sample

Once the sample is selected it must be adhered to. Under no circumstances must any changes be made to the sample design during the research, otherwise the results will be invalid.

Data collection

Once the sample of respondents has been selected it is necessary to obtain the data. A number of methods are available for the collection of what is essentially quantitative data. These are discussed below.

Personal interview

This is perhaps still the most popular form of data collection method. It has the advantage of giving a high level of completed returns, and the results tend to be more accurate as the interviewer has control. However it is expensive, and poor interviewing techniques can induce bias and unethical practices. These interviews can take place in the home, the office or in a high-traffic environment such as a railway station or a shopping centre.

Telephone interviews

This is the quickest of all the interviewing methods and the cost per interview can be relatively low. Also the interviewers are easier to train, so there is generally less chance of interviewer bias. The major problem is that telephone subscribers may not be actually a true representation of the population at large, and the numbers of questions that can be asked is strictly limited. It is also difficult to check the data obtained, even using callback systems.

Mailed questionnaires

In many countries mailing costs are low compared with other methods and a wide geographic coverage is possible. The questions can be standardized, and there is no chance of interviewer bias. However very low response rates can make for an imbalance of samples, and it is not possible to check easily if the respondent has been honest or not.

Computer-assisted techniques

Questionnaires can either be sent via e-mail or completed online through a Web page. With the wider availability of Internet facilities, companies are increasingly seeking to use online questionnaires. This links into Permission Marketing (see Chapter 1) where, once permission has been granted, customers can be asked their views regularly on a range of issues, from customer service to product ranges. As technology develops the computer interface may employ voice activation and video interaction. The latter will allow an interviewer to conduct a one-to-one interview without leaving his or her office. This may be particularly useful to online banks which want to know their customer's views.

Panel techniques

This is particularly useful for the study of trends over specific time frames. Causal rela-tionships can be studied better. The panel needs to be updated regularly, otherwise the panel can develop into a mode of providing the answers that seem to be wanted, rather than the truth. The panels used are similar to those used for in-depth interviewing; however the questions used are more structured, although the panel should be encouraged to develop ideas. The panel will meet on regular occasions so that the trends in the market can be explored.

The method actually used will always depend upon the reason for the research. The actual sample size and accuracy of the data will indicate which data collection method is most suitable. However, the costs involved must be considered. Whichever method is used, the design of the questions used will ultimately define the accuracy of the data obtained.

Questionnaire design

Questionnaire design is not as easy as it may at first seem. Any mistakes or ambiguity in the questions can lead to the whole research programme being of little or no value. Zikmund (1994) lists five major decisions that are required for effective questionnaire design:

1. What should be asked?

2. How should each question be phrased?

3. In what sequence should the questions be arranged?

4. What questionnaire layout will best serve the research objectives?

5. How should the questionnaire be pre-tested and how will it be revised?

Before a questionnaire is developed, thought must be given as to the purpose of the proposed survey. Questionnaires are about gaining information that can be used for making marketing decisions. Therefore a clear understanding of what decisions have to be made and why is crucial. The type of information is likely to contain:

- facts and figures that can be used to support expenditure and plan production/operations

- opinions that can be used to develop new ideas for products, promotions and/or improve service

- motives that lead to the purchase, or otherwise of a particular product or service

- past behaviour and what stimuli may have caused this behaviour

- possible future behaviour (and changing stimuli) including intent to purchase.

However, to be sure that a true answer will be obtained there are several criteria that must be considered:

- Respondents must be able to *understand* the question.

- They *must be able* to provide the information requested.

- They *must be willing* to provide the information.

It is important that when the sample is being chosen from the sample frame these basic requirements are remembered. Zikmund (1994) is at pains to list a number of 'avoiding' phrases in the art of asking questions. These are:

- Avoid complexity, only use simple conversational language.

- Avoid leading and/or loaded questions.

- Avoid ambiguity by being as specific as possible.

- Avoid double-barrelled items, and make sure only one question is asked at a time.

Double-barrelled items are where two different questions are posed as one question.

- Avoid making assumptions; the aim of the research is to find usable data. The assumptions can come later during the analysis.

- Avoid burdensome questions.

The sequence of asking questions is very important and needs very careful planning. The respondent needs to be relaxed, therefore the first questions should be of a general nature to build the confidence of the respondent – but not so simple as to belittle his or her knowledge. Once the opening questions have been asked, the remaining questions should naturally funnel towards the specific data that is required. The use of filter questions and skips is important to the flow of the interview. A skip is where if the respondent answers 'yes' to a particular question, say Question 5, he or she is directed to another question, for example Question 10. The intermediate questions are of no relevance to this respondent. Such techniques ensure that respondents are not asked questions that they cannot answer, or are of no value.

Questions can be of three types:

- **Open ended.** This is where the answer can be quite long and respondents are free to state ideas/views in their own words. These require careful recording and analysis, if they are to be of value.

- **Closed.** This is where a predetermined set of answers is available for the respondent to choose from. This can be in two forms: multiple choice/multi-choice or dichotomous (a choice from two answers).

  - *Multiple choice*: as this suggests the respondent may have a choice of answers. Perhaps the most common is related to customer service levels, where a respondent can tick one of a series of boxes.

For example:

	Poor	Good	Very good	Excellent
How do you rate the cleanliness of this store?	[ ]	[ ]	[ ]	[ ]

Another method is to ask respondents to rate something on a scale, for instance 1 to 5 where 5 is the highest standard.

– *Dichotomous*: This is where a simple 'yes' or 'no' response can be used.

▌ **Control questions.** These are also required to ensure that respondents are answering truthfully, and not just trying to give answers they think might be required.

Marketing insight: Module evaluation form

This is an example of a module evaluation form that includes both open and closed questions.

Table 6.5   Module evaluation form

	1 = lowest 5 = highest				
The module	1	2	3	4	5
Followed closely the previously published workbook scheme					
As a whole, was relevant to my current job					
As a whole, was useful context to any job					
As a whole, was interesting					
The assignment set was appropriate					
The lecturer					
Set and followed a clear outline and objective					
Stimulated my interest in the subject					
Demonstrated mastery of the subject					
Effectively explained difficult concepts/ideas					
Encouraged questions and discussions					
Encouraged experiential learning					
Was adequately available for consultation					
Demanded high standards					
Used readings/texts relevant to the course					
Explained the assessment system clearly					

What did you like most about the module? What did you like least about the module? How do you think the module can be further developed?

Questions/activities

1. Compare and contrast this survey with one that you may have completed at your own college/university. Are there any other questions that you believe should be included in either survey? If so, state the purpose of the question (what is it that you want to discover?), and whether there should be open or closed questions.
2. The above evaluation form is for an individual module or unit of a course. Devise a question-naire that would encompass a student's overall experiences within a college or university.

Question bias/errors

While it is better to avoid bias in the questions this is not always possible. Provided it is recognized and considered at the analysis stage, some unavoidable bias can be acceptable. However too much bias, especially if amplified by the interviewer, can lead to the data being of no value. There are a number of common mistakes made in the design of questionnaires, and these should be avoided at all costs:

▌ asking two or more questions in one;

▌ not defining the terms used, such as what is meant by 'frequently';

▌ using leading questions so that the respondent thinks a particular answer is required;

▌ asking questions that lead to an inaccurate answer.

When designing a questionnaire there are a number of guidance points that are worth considering.

▌ What is the purpose of the survey? Has this been agreed with the relevant managers in the organization? Are the terms of reference clear?

▌ What variables are to be measured? Are these clear and in fact measurable? Is a questionnaire the most appropriate way to measure these variables? How is the sample

to be drawn? What sampling frame is to be used and what does the total population look like?

▌ Details of the size of sample that is to be used, bearing in mind the time it will take to complete each questionnaire. Also the make-up of the sample, especially if quota sampling is to be used rather than a pure random sample. The make-up of the respondents may be vital in some surveys to ensure an accurate set of data is obtained. It is also necessary to consider the frequency of the interviews. It may be necessary to carry out the research over a period of time to establish trends in the information being prepared.

▌ The type of enquiry will have an effect on the design of the questionnaire. Is it a short factual type of survey or an in-depth diagnostic piece of research that is looking for deeper understanding and supporting facts? The method of carrying out the research needs to be considered, as the design of a questionnaire for face-to-face surveys will be different from one for a telephone or self-completion type of approach. It will also be necessary to give very careful consideration as to how the collected data will be analysed, and therefore the coding systems that will be used. Methods of actual measurement of the responses will also have to be considered at the design stage.

Marketing insight: Model Railway Society survey

A simple questionnaire that was used by a small society to collect data is shown below. While a range of data was collected, its specific purpose was to discover the number of visitors who had only found out about the show from the local newspaper. This was required to see if the expenditure on the display advertisement had been justified. Most advertising research relates to finding out if people can actually remember or recall the advertisement. However, this does not measure the effectiveness of the actual reason for advertising, which is usually to increase sales.

The questionnaire was completed by a convenience sample of show visitors, and two incentives were included on the questionnaire to persuade people to complete them. One was to ask for them to vote for the best layout at the show. Most visitors like to feel they are appreciated when they visit model railway shows. The other offered them the chance to win a model railway of their own. The data collected proved to be very useful, and allowed the society to establish whether the expenditure on the advertisement had been recouped from an increase in attendance.

We have illustrated the questionnaire section with a survey from a model railway club in north-east England. This example has been used to show that any organization, large or small, can use a questionnaire to improve their overall knowledge of customers.

HULL MODEL RAILWAY SHOW 1999

To enter the draw for the Hornby CORNISH RIVIERA EXPRESS train set please complete the details below. Prize sponsored by Hornby Railways and 53A Models

How did you find out about the show? Please tick all that apply.

[ ] *Railway Modeller* magazine   [ ] *British Railway Modelling*
[ ] *Continental Modeller*   [ ] *Model Railway Enthusiast*
[ ] Other modelling magazine _____
   (please specify)
[ ] *Hull Advertiser Series*   [ ] *Hull Daily Mail*
[ ] Poster (in window)   [ ] Poster (at another exhibition)
[ ] Word of Mouth   [ ] Local radio
[ ] Other (please specify) _____

Morrill Cup for best layout

Each year the visitors to the Hull Model Railway Show are asked to vote for which in their opinion is the best layout at the show. The layout with the most number of votes is then awarded our Morrill Cup for that year. **Please indicate which layout you think is best.**

Stand Number_____ Layout Name_____

Please **print** your name and address below.

Name _____

Address _____

_____Post code _____

Analysis of questionnaires from the 1999 show

The adult equivalent of visitors to the show was 1,586. A total of 165 completed questionnaires were received. Due to lack of evidence to the contrary it has been assumed that the 10.4 per cent who completed the questionnaire are a representative sample of the visitors to the show.

The major concern of the committee was whether the expenditure on the advertisement in the *Hull Daily Mail* newspaper (HDM) and the *Advertiser* series had been worthwhile, so these figures have been given special attention.

23 per cent of the respondents only saw details of the show in the *HDM* or the *Advertiser* series. This would equate with 365 of the visitors only finding out about the show from this source. If we use an average income per visitor of £1.97 then this equates to a total income of £719.05 that may be attributed to the advertisement.

A further **4 per cent** saw the advert in the *HDM* and elsewhere and **5 per cent** saw the advert in the *Advertiser* series and elsewhere.

The other sources of finding details of the show were (in percentages):

Railway Modeller	17.5
British Railway Modelling	7.2
Continental Modeller	1.0
Model Railway Enthusiast	5.0
Other model magazines	2.0

It would appear that the free notices coupled with editorial do have some effect. A number of the respondents indicated that they had seen the details in more than one magazine. It is interesting to note that the *Continental Modeller* does not have an exhibition diary but 1 per cent of the respondents saw the details there.

Posters in local windows were seen by 14.5 per cent. Posters at other exhibitions were seen by 8.5 per cent. Again many of the respondents indicated that they had seen the details in other places and not just on the posters. Word of mouth was given by 25 per cent of the respondents, although again often as one of a number of ways they had heard about the show. The term 'other' accounted for 13 per cent, with respondents indicating that they always came, saw the flyer at school, and again often gave this as one of a number of ways they heard about the show.

Source: Hull Model Railway Society.

Data analysis

Once a researcher has collected both the qualitative and quantitative data it must be analysed. Raw data from any study is of little value until it is converted into a suitable form for analysis, interpretation and presentation. As Burns and Bush (2000) indicate, there are five different types of statistical analysis commonly used by marketing researchers. These are detailed in Table 6.6.

The development of software packages such as SPSS® (www.spss.com) provides marketing researchers with the data analysis tools. Such packages, combined with the rapid development in computing power, most especially in desk and laptop computers, enable the marketing team to undertake complex analysis. It is no longer the domain of specialist marketing research companies.

The final research report

Once the research data has been analysed it must be compiled into a clear and logical format. This must convey the research results, key indicators, recommendations with supporting evidence and conclusions. There are two issues to bear in mind here. First, the quality of the report projects the dedication and professionalism (or otherwise) of the individual/team who compiled it. Consider for a moment a client's reaction if the

Table 6.6 Types of statistical analysis

Type	Description	Example	Statistical concepts
Descriptive	Data reduction	Describe the typical respondent, describe how similar respondents are to the typical respondent distribution	Mean, mode, median range, frequency, standard deviation
Inferential	Determine population parameters, test hypothesis	Estimate population values	Standard error, null hypothesis
Differences	Determine if differences exist between groups	Evaluate statistical significance of difference in the mean of two groups in the sample	T-test of differences, analysis of variance
Associative	Determine associations	Determine if two variables are related in a systematic way	Correlation, cross-tabulation
Predictive	Forecast, based on statistical model	Estimate the level of Y, given the amount of X	Time series analysis, regression.

Source: adapted from Burns and Bush (2000).

research company they hired presented a disjointed, illogically presented report. The information contained within it might be relevant and accurate; however the client's perception could be the direct opposite.

Second, the client company may use this report as a basis for making significant decisions on the future of a product, the business or indeed the company. Therefore the information must be presented in such a form as to aid effective decision making.

The following is an outline structure. As you read around the subject area, you will see that authors may include additional sections. These additions are often dependent upon the nature of the report and the research company's style guide (report structures, layout, font/typeface and so on).

Content of a marketing research report

▌ **Title page.** This often includes the research title, the client's name, the name of the researcher/research company and the date of submission.

▌ **Table of contents.** This will include section titles and any relevant subheadings with accompanying page numbers, list of tables (titles and page numbers), list of figures (titles and page numbers) and list of appendices (titles and page numbers).

▌ **Executive summary.** This is often called a Management Summary or an Abstract. As it suggests this is a summary or 'skeleton' of the report that allows executives to understand quickly the key issues behind the research findings/recommendations. The summary usually includes a statement of research objectives, a statement of the methodology used, a statement of the key findings, a statement of the conclusions and recommendations for action. Additionally, it may include other materials that the researcher may consider relevant at this stage: for example, if there were any major limitations to the research study that needed to be drawn to the attention of the reader.

▌ **Introduction.** This provides the background to the report and will include a statement of the research problem, the research objectives, details of the research team and acknowledgments.

▌ **Methodology.** This should outline how the research was conducted and will usually include the type of study undertaken (for example, qualitative/quantitative), the population studied, sample design, size and method, and which data collection methods were used and why. There may also be a case here for a brief explanation why certain data collection methods were not used.

- **Analysis and findings.** This is where the results of the research are stated. This section should provide information on the analytical frameworks adopted and the results of the analysis. Often the results are illustrated using tables, charts and figures rather than purely text. Such illustrations not only diagrammatically represent information, they also add value to the overall look and feel of the report. As we stated earlier the 'look' of the report is important, and thus all diagrams need to be well structured and labelled for ease of reference by the reader.

- **Limitations.** There is no such thing as perfection. All marketing research reports have their limitations, some more than others. As such reports may be the basis for an executive taking a particular decision it is vital that limitations of the research are clearly indicated. Limitations can cover many areas, for example:

  - Budget: for instance this may have been insufficient to employ a range of research techniques, thus only one was used.
  - People: there may have been difficulty in recruiting sufficient or the right calibre of staff to undertake the questionnaire interviewing. Additionally, there may have been interviewer bias.
  - Time: this may be linked to budget but there may have been time limitations due to the urgency of the report.
  - Sample selection and size: there may have been problems in achieving or selecting the right sample size.

- **Conclusions and recommendations.** As Quee (1999) states, the researchers' role is not just to present a series of facts, they have to draw conclusions on the basis of the findings. There is a critical perspective to remember here. In many cases the researcher will be external to the company or organization. While he or she may have a general knowledge of the company and its operations, he or she is unlikely to have the kind of specific knowledge that comes from being an insider. However, this should not – based upon the facts of the study – prevent the researcher from making recommendations. The manager, director or board can assimilate these recommendations with additional internal information. The researcher, though, must be clear that the recommendations are based on exacting research criteria (both collection and analysis).

- **Appendices.** This is where a copy of the questionnaire and other details are presented. It is important that anything placed in the appendices is referenced within the main body of the text.

General points

In presenting a written report there are a few general points that should be considered:

- Who is the audience? Any report needs to focus upon who is actually going to read it. This may determine the level of detail necessary within the different sections, for example methodology. If the audience is not marketing research knowledgeable it may be necessary to explain terminology within an additional glossary.

- Sentence structure/grammar and spelling need to be checked prior to submission. There is nothing more irritating to a manager than to read a report full of typographical and grammatical errors, especially if the report has been an expensive commission. Companies often employ professional proofreaders to check for such errors prior to submission to the client.

- As stated earlier, visuals can make an important contribution in explaining research findings. However there must be an explanatory link between the main body of text and the diagrams.

Using a research agency

Many organizations use a research agency to carry out their work for them. While this may seem an expensive option it can be cheaper in the long term than the organization under-taking the work themselves. The reasons for this are:

- **Objectivity.** The agency is independent so the research becomes an independent piece of work, rather than a company study. There will be no preconceived ideas of the likely outcome and less chance of bias entering the results.

- **Anonymity.** There will be non-disclosure of the client's identity, which will protect not only the client but also the respon-dents. The respondents can be sure that any information given will be kept in confidence and will not be used for anything not directly connected with the research.

- **Timing.** A good agency will start and finish a project on time. This cannot always be guaranteed with in-company research.

- **Skill base.** The agency will have industry knowledge and easy access to secondary data that may not be readily available to the company requiring the data. They will also be highly skilled and proficient in marketing research techniques.

However using a research agency does not mean that a company can totally abdicate responsibility for marketing research. They must brief the agency very specifically on what they require.

Ethical issues in marketing research

As with any marketing activity there are ethical implications that need to be considered. There are various groups involved when it comes to marketing research and ethics (Quee, 1999).

Society

Society as a whole should be informed of critical marketing research results. Additionally, the results should be objective, unbiased and available for scrutiny.

The client

Again the client should expect certain ethical standards. These would include unbiased reporting of data, confidentiality (as agreed with the researchers in advance) and appli-cable quality standards during the period of research.

The researcher

Here the researcher must expect ethical stan-dards from both their client and their respon-dents. From the client there would, for example, be agreements on confidentiality of research techniques and no pressure to amend or bias research results. From the respondent, a researcher would expect confidentiality (where stipulated) and no attempt to distort information intentionally.

The respondent

The respondent should expect to have a choice whether to participate or not, and whether that is in full or not. For example, there may be questions on the survey/questionnaire that the respondent feels are too personal. It should be made clear to respondents that they are not being forced to answer these questions. The ethos must be one of volunteering information without any fear of duress.

Chapter summary

The aim of this chapter has been to introduce the concepts of marketing research. Details of the various statistical techniques have not been included: however, they are available in detail in any of the marketing research texts specified in the references. Much of the statistical analysis can now be carried out using standard computer programs that only require the user to have a passing knowledge of the basic mathematical techniques involved. Careful selection of the package to be used is required, however.

In the future the development of analytical tools will be significant. There are significant amounts of information stored in data warehouses. Companies need to consider how analytical tools can be applied to marketing research to data mine information on customers. There will inevitably be links to the development of e-marketing, e-business and e-commerce.

Exercises and questions for review and critical thinking

1. You are the marketing manager of a major soft drinks company. You are planning to develop a new brand of fruit drink aimed at the teenage market. What marketing information would you need to determine whether there is a market for this new soft drink? How will you obtain this information? Why have you chosen these methods of data collection? What are the potential marketing research problems that you might encounter? How will you overcome these problems?

2. Consider in detail the ethical considerations that a company should take into account when planning a marketing research project. In your answer suggest how you would reduce/eliminate unethical practices.

3. Critically evaluate the Internet as a marketing research tool.

4. Critically evaluate why there has been a dramatic rise in the use of marketing research by companies and organizations over the past 20 years. What do you think will be the impact of marketing research during the next five years and why?

5. Explain in detail how observation techniques can be used to gather marketing research information. Outline the possible limitations of these techniques.

7

Marketing and strategy

Strategy is the great Work of the organization.
In Situations of life or death, it is the Tao of survival or extinction.
Its study cannot be neglected.
Sun Tzu, Chinese strategist and scholar (c 500–320 BC)
(quoted in Wing, 1989)

Introduction

This chapter considers the relationship between marketing and strategy. The development of a marketing strategy depends heavily upon:

▌ analysing and adapting the marketing mix;

▌ analysing the marketplace;

▌ linking marketing to the overall strategic direction of the organization;

▌ applying the appropriate strategic tools and techniques.

A joint paper produced by the Chartered Institute of Marketing and Cranfield University published in 1998 concluded that 'Organizations fail to understand their customers, provide them with an unsatisfactory product or service and then expect a

marketing department to sprinkle a bit of "magic marketing dust" at the end of the process' (CIM, 1998).

A strategic approach to marketing is crucial to the long-term success of any organization. Marketing strategy must be developed from the overall strategic plan. It is therefore necessary to ensure that the strategic plan is clear before developing the generic marketing strategy.

Learning objectives

On completion of this chapter you should be able to:

▌ debate the concept of marketing management and its role in developing a marketing strategy;

▌ evaluate a given marketing strategy by using appropriate tools of analysis;

▌ critically evaluate the use of portfolio and other models;

▌ develop a marketing plan from a given marketing strategy;

■ discuss the problems associated with the implementation of strategies and plans.

Defining strategy

In order to understand the relationship between strategy and marketing we must define 'strategy'. The term 'strategy' and its usage are far from new. The Greek, Roman and Chinese empires all employed strategy. The Chinese scholar and strategist Sun Tzu (Wing, 1989) employed strategy and tactics as the mainstay of his text *The Art of War* (which is still referred to today). He believed that winning requires good strategy and that those who are well skilled in battle can overcome their enemy's army without fighting. He concluded that 'The ultimate strategy is to subdue the enemy's army without engaging it. To take cities without laying siege to them. To overthrow his forces without bloodying swords' (Wing, 1989).

Although this has direct military connotations there is a parallel to marketing and business strategy that we will develop throughout this chapter. Anderson and Vincze (2000) interpreted this strategic perspective as doing the right thing. This can be equated to *marketing strategy*. Anderson and Vincze (2000) refer to the Prussian military strategist Carl von Clausewitz (1780–1831). In his seminal text *Vom Kriege* (*On War*, published posthumously in 1833), von Clausewitz suggested that winning was based on fighting the large-scale battle. Anderson and Vincze interpret this as doing things right: in other words, in the marketing context, developing action-oriented *marketing tactics*.

So what do we really mean by strategy and tactics? It is only by understanding the meaning of strategy that we can consider how tactics and techniques can be used to achieve the overall objectives of the organization. As you will see from the examples cited below, there are many definitions and views associated with the word 'strategy'. Each one has a relevance to how both marketing and business are conducted. Perhaps this is more so in the turbulent 21st century.

Johnson and Scholes (1999) defined strategy as:

> the direction and scope of an organization over the long term which achieves advantage for the organization through its configuration of resources within a changing environment, to meet the needs of markets and to fulfill stakeholder expectations.

Let us examine this further by deconstructing the basic components of this definition (see Table 7.1).

Quinn (in Mintzberg *et al*, 2003) offers a related definition:

> A strategy is the pattern or plan that integrates an organization's major goals, policies and action sequences into a cohesive whole. A well-formulated strategy helps to marshal and allocate an organization's resources into a unique and viable posture based on its relative internal competencies and shortcomings, anticipated changes in the environment, and contingent moves by intelligent opponents.

On the other hand Grant (2002) states:

> Strategy is about winning.... Strategy is not a detailed plan or programme of instruction; it is a unifying theme that gives coherence and direction to the actions and decisions of an individual organization.

As you can see, Grant's perspective starts with the view that strategy is about winning. This may be the case under certain circumstances, but not in all. A charity, for example, may take the view that stability within the marketplace (charities do operate within a competitive marketplace) is more important than taking risks to be the number one charity. Some companies, as we will see later in this chapter, prefer to be followers rather than market leaders. Their goals of a 'sustained' position are achieved and they are not in direct battle or conflict with the market leader. Such conflicts can have a long-term damaging effect on the loser.

Table 7.1 Analysis of the definition of strategy

Issue	Comment
Direction and scope	Strategy gives form to the breadth and depth of the objectives the organization wants to achieve. It 'points the company' towards its objectives – the direction it needs to follow. Of course, the 'micro and macro environments' in which the organization operates cannot be ignored. These will ultimately impact upon the organization's direction. It is how the organization handles such 'turbulence' that may define success or failure of its strategic direction.
Long term	This is the time span of the strategy to be implemented. However, there is much debate over what 'long term' really means in today's turbulent environments. Long-term planning used to refer to anything from 5+ years to 10+ years. While the life of a Western company could be defined as 40+ years, a long-term plan has been significantly scaled down. Many organizations view the long term as no more than 18 months, simply because so much can change within that period. (Reflect back, for instance, to Chapter 2 and how political issues such as terrorism can impact upon a business. Another example is the environmental/ecological issue of the outbreak of SARS in March 2003.)
Achieves advantage	The objective is to achieve an advantage. That may be a minor advantage or a major one that places the company far out of the reach of its competitors. However, that large-scale advantage may be short-lived if competitors can replicate it in some form. For example, it may be a revolutionary new technical innovation, for example, the mobile phone. However that technical advantage was relatively short-lived as new players entered the market and developed similar technologies. The real key for companies and organizations is to achieve a *sustainable* advantage.
Configuration of resources	Both resources and core competences need to be used efficiently and effectively to develop and implement a successful strategy.
Changing environment	The micro and macro environments in which an organization operates are changeable and complex. A strategy should be defined to help an organization to predict (scenario plan) and react to the variant degrees of turbulence it will experience within these environments. Companies must be flexible in order to react to the dynamics of the marketplace.
Needs of the market	An organization must focus upon its market(s), and thus the strategy must reflect market needs. If the organization loses sight of who its customers are and their changing/developing needs, it will most likely fail. Business history texts are full of examples of organizations that failed to understand the dynamics of market need, and in turn failed.
Stakeholder expectations	The stakeholders are many and varied, from the employees and the local community to shareholders and financial institutions (banks and fund managers). Equally their expectations from an organization will be varied. For example, the local community's expectations may be a safe environment free from pollution. The organization's strategy may be to revise its production processes or diversify into the development of a safer new product. An example would be lead-free petrol. A shareholder's expectation may be improved dividends and share performance. The two may not be incompatible, as one may lead to another.

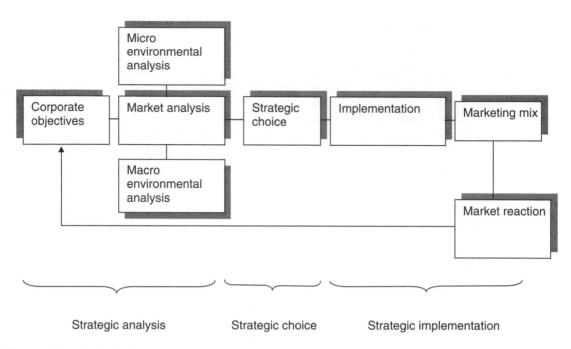

Figure 7.1   A strategic process

In Figure 7.1 we provide a flow chart or process that illustrates (in a basic structure) the relationship between different critical areas of strategy. First there is the strategic analysis. This covers the organization's corporate objectives and an analysis of the market(s), the micro and macro environmental factors that impact upon the organization. Second there is strategic choice. Here the organization chooses the strategies that it will implement. Finally, there is strategic implementation. As the title infers it is the implementation of the various strategies. You will see from the diagram that we have linked implementation to the marketing mix. It will be through the marketing mix that these strategies will be delivered. Their success or failure will cause a market reaction.

We have placed a feedback loop from market reaction to corporate objectives to illustrate that the organization must take account of such reactions. For instance, if the customers start brand switching (changing to another brand), the organization needs to be aware of

the reasons for switching. By processing such information it may be able to prevent a decline in the market share for that product.

Of course, the world does not operate as a static model. This strategic process must be considered as an illustration of events. In reality there would be dynamic information flows moving around and across the various elements.

The relationship between marketing strategy and corporate strategy

There is clearly a relationship between marketing strategy and corporate strategy. In Figure 7.2 we illustrate the various strategy levels within an organization: Corporate, Business and Functional. Each one plays a vital role in developing and implementing strategies. As we will see in this and other chapters, the interrelationship between these levels is often crucial to the survival of the organization.

Levels of Strategy

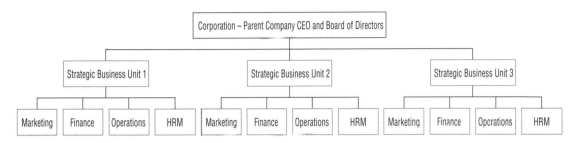

Figure 7.2 Strategy levels

Corporate strategy

The focus of corporate strategy is on the overall purpose of the organization, and the scope or range of activities it must undertake to fulfil its business objectives. In order to fulfil these business objectives, the organization must consider:

▪ the markets in which it should compete;

▪ the present resources that should be used, and those that should be acquired;

▪ the allocation of resources among its chosen market;

▪ the micro and macro environments in which it decides to operate.

The stakeholders associated with the organization will have a set of expectations that they wish the organization to meet. However, these expectations may not always be in concert with each other. The local community suffering from pollution will have different stakeholder expectations than say a shareholder who is seeking a return on investment from an increased share price and dividends.

Corporate strategy usually seeks to answer the following questions. What business are we in? And what business or businesses should the company be in? These are critical questions for any organization, for all organizations need to understand the dynamics of both the market (the customers) and the environments in which they operate. Levitt (1986) argued that a market orientation should determine the strategic direction of an organization, otherwise it risks suffering from what he called 'marketing myopia': that is, being focused upon one business capability and ignoring the world around it.

In the 1960s several US railway companies were asked, 'What business are you in?' The reply was, 'the railroad business'. This was at the time when there were various changes taking place in the United States, for instance:

▪ A growth in transcontinental and regional airlines. This was in part due to the development of more efficient passenger and cargo aircraft, such as the Boeing 707 and 727 fleets.

▪ An improved road network, both regionally and transcontinental.

▪ The development of more efficient and larger trucks, including refrigerated vehicles.

▪ The demand for more efficient distribution methods to meet rising customer expectations.

As the fledgling airline companies proved they could carry both goods and people faster and cheaper over similar distances, so several US railway companies saw a decline in their business. However, not all railway companies saw themselves purely as railway companies. Canadian Pacific, for instance, took much more the line of 'we are in the transport business', and invested in aircraft, ships and tracking. It outperformed and outlasted many of its US rivals.

Another example is British Petroleum. During the 1990s it rebranded and repositioned itself, dropping 'British Petroleum' in favour of BP. It was no longer purely in the petroleum business but in the energy business. Today, while it is still involved in drilling, refining and selling petrol, it is also heavily involved in the development of alternative fuel sources including windpower generation.

These brief examples illustrate the importance of understanding the business in which the company or organization should operate.

Business level strategy: strategic business units

Johnson and Scholes (1999) define strategic business units (SBUs) as separate 'units' for strategy-making purposes. Eckles (1990) suggests that an SBU is 'a self-contained operation within a corporation that is responsible for the manufacture and/or marketing of a service, product, or related product line'.

However, these distinctions are not reflected in the underlying organizational structure. For example an SBU can be a division or subsidiary or a major company. Equally, it can be a large profit-centred department within an organization. The critical definer is that an SBU is part of an organization for which there is distinct demand for products or services. Therefore the needs of the SBU's customers are clearly defined.

Care is needed here, since writers including Levitt (1986) point out that developing SBUs must be done carefully. Falling into the trap of defining them solely in terms of the products

or services provided will not create stable strategic units. They need to be defined in terms of customer satisfaction sought, as the way of meeting what the customer actually seeks from the organization. Abell (1980) highlights the three major elements that should be considered when trying to define the SBU:

▌ the customer who will be served;

▌ the customer need that will be satisfied;

▌ the technology that will be used to meet these needs.

While technology has significantly developed since Abell (1980) defined the elements, the basic concept is still relevant today.

Once the SBUs have been established, Wilson and Gilligan (1997) consider the next area of planning to be based around evaluating the existing business portfolio. Many tools are available to do this, and these will be considered as this chapter progresses. It is necessary to establish a balanced portfolio of goods and services that offer revenues and profits, and others that promise to offer profits in the future. This means that a way of evaluating both the current portfolio and the future portfolio must be established. All portfolios will contain products that provide profit now, those that have provided profit in the past, and those it is hoped will provide profit in the future. The marketing strategy should be designed to ensure that the changes in the portfolio are timed to meet the changing needs of the marketplace.

Once the SBUs have been developed it is also necessary to project their future role in both the organization and the marketplace. The basis for these projections will be related to any expected change in the markets being served. Markets develop and change over time, and it is necessary to evaluate these changes in order to predict the likely definition of the market in the future. Likewise, customers change. This is mainly due to the changes in the demographic profile of the markets being served. In general the demographic profile of Europe is gaining a larger population of people who are near to or have reached retirement age. These people tend to develop different needs and wants as they progress through the later stages of their lives. Organizations should not assume that they will remain loyal to a particular type or brand of good or service, or that they will necessarily be replaced as customers by the following generation (see Chapters 4, 5 and 8).

There may be changes in the level of competition in the market, and any likely changes must be predicted and strategies developed to cope with them. New competitors may enter the market and existing ones may leave. By careful analysis of the market it is possible to predict these changes. Often these changes are brought about by changes in the broader environment, and these changes will often indicate the likely changes that will occur in the micro environment of the organization. The SBUs must also be aware of any likely changes in corporate support. As organizations develop they are likely to identify new objectives. SBUs must have alternative strategies in place to cope with these likely changes.

The business level strategy seeks to answer the following questions:

▌ How should we compete in each of our businesses, thus creating a sustained competitive advantage?

▌ Can we identify new opportunities or possibly new markets?

▌ Can we identify new products or services that meet the customer's needs?

▌ Can we deliver new products or services that meet the customer's expectations in terms of quality and price?

However, for a small company with only one product line, or a large organization that has diversified into a range of different products or markets, a separate business level strategy is not necessary. In these cases the business level strategy merges into the overall corporate strategy.

Functional units and strategy

Functional units are often considered as the operational units within an SBU or an organization as a whole. They cover such areas as marketing, research and development (R&D), and finance. The functional level strategy seeks to answer the question 'How do we support the business level and corporate strategy?'

A critical factor here is often overlooked. While these functional areas are often represented as isolated boxes (see Figure 7.2), they need to have an integrated functionality. Marketing does not work in isolation from either finance or operations. There must be a sharing of knowledge in order for the organization to be both efficient and effective within the market. Later in this chapter we examine Porter's value chain, and it becomes clear from that model that there has to be some form of relationship between these functional units.

All this may seem common sense, yet surprisingly there is a growing body of evidence that suggests that functional units do not always coexist and share crucial information. Many of the factors relate to human resource management issues which are beyond the scope of this text. However it is the functional units that will be implementing the strategies and tactics. Confusion or a lack of information at this level can severely damage an organization's ability to gain, and fundamentally sustain, competitive advantage.

Situational analysis: the marketing audit

We have stressed elsewhere that for an organization to be successful it must have a competitive advantage within the marketplace. A starting point for this is a full understanding of the organization's marketing assets. These are the basic strengths of the organization, but it is also necessary to have an understanding of competitors' marketing assets. These will form the basis of the threats to the competitive advantage that any organization may have. Only once the assets are understood is it really possible to consider a generic marketing strategy for any organization.

Kotler (2000) defines a marketing audit as:

> an independent examination of the entire marketing effort of a company, or some specific marketing activity, covering objectives, programme, implementation, and organization, for the triple purpose of determining what is being done, appraising what is being done, and recommending what should be done in the future.

Baker (2000) contends that marketing audits are necessary to monitor changes within both micro and macro environments. He suggests that in addition to evaluating both past performances and present practices, the marketing audit should identify future threats and opportunities and so provide a basis for policy formulation and planning. As we will see later in this chapter both the balanced scorecard model and scenario planning assist in determining possible future actions.

Kotler, Gregor and Rogers (1977) devised a tabular overview of the marketing audit. Below we illustrate the key headings and subheadings from this overview. We have extended the marketing function audit section to include the full generic 7Ps of the marketing mix. In the original only the 4Ps (product, promotion, price and place) were highlighted.

Marketing environment audit

1. Macro environment.
2. Micro environment.

Marketing strategy audit

1. Marketing objectives.
2. Strategy.

Marketing organization audit

1. Formal structure.
2. Functional efficiency.
3. Interface efficiency.

Marketing audit system

1. Marketing information system.
2. Marketing planning system.
3. Marketing control system.
4. New product development system.

Marketing productivity audit

1. Profitability analysis.
2. Cost-effectiveness analysis.

Marketing function audit

1. Products.
2. Price.
3. Promotion.
4. Placement (distribution).
5. People.
6. Processes.
7. Physical evidence (physicality).

Adapted from Kotler, Gregor and Rogers (1977)

It is necessary to consider the level of detail required to produce an objective marketing audit. It is not something that can be concocted in a matter of an hour or so by one executive. It requires planning, thought and combined input.

Cannon (1968) suggests that there are five phases or steps in defining a marketing audit. These are:

1. Define the market.
2. Determine the performance differentials.

3. Determine the differences in competitive programmes.

4. Profile the strategies of competitors.

5. Determine strategic planning structure.

One of the weaknesses in many organizations is the lack of frequency of conducting marketing or business audits. Organizations that consider that, within today's turbulent world, annual marketing audits are sufficient are perhaps deluding themselves. Dynamic changes both internally and externally mean that organizations must be able to judge how these changes will affect marketing and thus ultimately business performance.

Product–service positioning

We have already considered positioning within Chapter 5, where we also examined segmentation and targeting. However, it is useful to revisit positioning here because it helps place the product or service within a clear strategic and competitive context.

Porter (1985) suggests that effective strategic management is the positioning of a company or organization, relative to its competitors, in such a way as to outperform them. Lynch (2000) uses the term 'competitive positioning' as a means of describing 'the choice of differential advantage that the product or service possesses against its competitors'. However, Kotler (2000) defines positioning as 'the act of designing the company's offer so that it occupies a distinct and valued place in the target customers' mind', while Ries and Trout (1986) define positioning as 'Positioning starts with a product. A piece of merchandise, a service, a company, an institution, or even a person.... But positioning is not what you do to a product. Positioning is what you do to the mind of the prospect. That is, you position the product in the mind of the prospect.'

As the above demonstrates, there are different (to a greater or lesser degree) defini-tions of positioning. However, what is clear is that positioning is the location of the product, service or company within the competitive environment. That may be in the mind of the consumer, the physical world consumers inhabit, or both.

Positioning is based upon relevant criteria suitable for comparison:

▌ product features;

▌ quality;

▌ price;

▌ image;

▌ established reputation.

A marketing department can, for example, consider whether its brands and those of its competitors differ in terms of quality of performance, quality of conformance (consistency), service, delivery, reputation, prestige and so on. These are tools by which companies can create strong differentiation of a brand, and a strong marketing position.

The technique for trying to understand how various competitive brands are positioned relative to one another is the positioning map. These can be drawn for any market and can be constructed based on either judgement or market research. In either case, they are helpful in visualizing where products are currently positioned, and in identifying opportunities to change the position of a current brand.

In Figure 7.3, Brand X is a consumer computer company. It needs to study carefully the positions taken by its major competitors in the same target market. In this example we are assuming that the companies will position themselves in relation to product quality and price.

The issues become:

▌ Where should Company X position itself?

▌ What factors need to be taken into account to achieve this position?

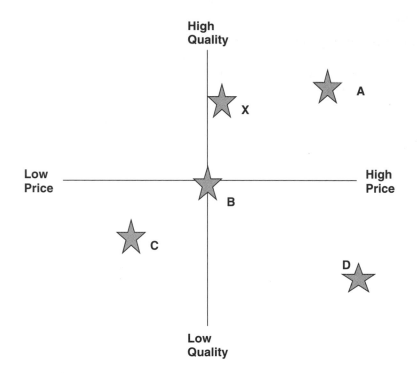

Figure 7.3   Product positioning map

Table 7.2   Product positioning

Competitor	Position
Competitor A	This competitor occupies the high quality/high price position within the marketplace.
Competitor B	This competitor occupies the average quality/average price section within the marketplace.
Competitor C	This competitor markets a slightly below average quality product for a low price.
Competitor D	This competitor markets a low quality product for a high price. A company may be able to achieve this if the market has a limited supply of the product (or the company holds a monopolistic position within the market) and there is a real demand for the product. Of course if the monopolistic position changes and other entrants are allowed into the market, this producer may have to rethink the relationship between quality and price.

What factors must be considered to secure this position? It is one thing positioning a product within a market; it is quite another retaining that position.

The main point is that companies today must carefully choose not only their customer targets but also their competitor targets.

According to Ries and Trout (1986), products generally have a position within the mind of the consumer. For example, Hertz holds the position of the world's largest car rental company. Ries and Trout (1986) believe a competitor has only three strategy options; such options are reflected in Table 7.3.

The marketing mix essentially involves calculating and developing the tactical details of the positioning strategy. Therefore a company that decides upon a high-quality position must realize that it has to develop and produce high quality products, charge a high price, distribute through high-class retailers, and advertise in high quality media. Crucially, it must be able to sustain this position, something that is more easily taken for granted then actually becomes a reality.

Not all buyers will notice or indeed be interested in the various ways one brand differs from another. Nor is it useful for a company to describe to each prospect every detail of difference. Each company will want to

Table 7.3 Possible strategic options

Strategic option	Comment
Strengthen its current position in the mind of the consumer	During the 1970s Avis Car Rentals made a strong point about its second position within the car rental market. In its promotion it stated, 'We're number two. We try harder.' This was believable to the consumer at that time. However, companies must be aware that customers may change their mind about the product or service. Thus the company must approach this from a basis of fluidity rather than rigidity.
Search for a new unoccupied position	This involves finding a gap or unfulfilled position within the market. For example, the Milky Way chocolate bar was positioned as the one that 'lasts longer'. No other product held that position in consumers' minds.
Deposition or reposition the competition	This, in essence, is an attack on the competitor to destabilize the consumer's confidence in a competitor and its product(s) and/or service(s). For example, vodka brand X might state in its advertising that it actually comes from Russia, whereas its rival brand Y comes from somewhere else, but definitely not Russia, thus raising in the consumer's mind the suspicion that because brand Y is not original Russian vodka it must be an inferior product. This, of course, may not be the case. However, planting that doubt in the mind of the consumer may initiate brand switching and destabilize the competitor brand within the marketplace. However, there needs to be a word of warning here. Planting doubts in the mind of consumers about a rival's products or services can: be illegal, depending upon local laws – issues of defamation could arise; be unethical; result in the company under attack retaliating, perhaps leading to a battle where both parties take their eye off their businesses, with mutually negative consequences. In the longer term the company may succeed with such a proposition. Equally it may collapse.

promote those few differences that appeal most strongly to its specific target audience. In developing a positioning strategy a company or organization must decide how many differences, and importantly which differences, to promote to the target market. Table 7.4 highlights the different types of positioning strategy a company could adopt.

However, as Kotler (2000) indicates, there are potential risks in increasing the number of claims for either a brand or company. The company's customers may become sceptical about the number of benefits the product or service can realistically offer. Such healthy scepticism is good for the company because it assists them in being realistic about the deliverability of benefits. Also, companies and brands need to display a clear position in relation to their competitors. If they offer too many benefits their position in the market, from the customer's perspective their image may become blurred.

Positioning a company, product or service is not as straightforward as is often suggested. It can be fraught with difficulties and risks, and a company could discover that it has undertaken the wrong positioning strategy. Table 7.5 illustrates the four potential positioning risks that a company must seek to avoid.

Kotler (2000) suggests that a company should promote its major strengths provided that the target market actually values these strengths. The company should also recognize that differentiation is a continuous process.

The company must not only develop a clear positioning strategy; it must also communicate it effectively. Quality is communicated through other marketing mix elements: for example, a high price usually signals premium quality products to consumers. Quality images are also reflected in packaging, distribution, advertising and other forms of promotion.

SWOT analysis

As we have seen earlier in this book, customers and consumers do not buy goods and services, so much as the benefit or want

Table 7.4 Types of positioning strategy

Positioning strategy	Comment
Single benefit	This is where the company or organization focuses on communicating one particular benefit to its target audience. This benefit may be in the form of lowest price, best quality or best service. Some supermarkets have developed a particular position by using 'guaranteed lowest prices' as their single proposition to the marketplace. These supermarkets are aiming at customers who are particularly price-sensitive, where every cent or penny counts. One such target audience can be students. A car brand could be positioned, for example, on the basis of either its safety proposition or performance capability.
Double benefit	This is where the company focuses on two attributes. For example, the company may offer a combination of low prices and good quality products. An example of double benefit positioning of a brand was Arm & Hammer© PM toothpaste, which states 'a combination of ingredients proven to fight plaque' and 'a combination of ingredients proven to help fight odour-causing germs'.
Triple benefit	Here the company focuses on three benefits which could be, for example, low prices, good quality products and efficient service. A toothpaste brand might focus on fighting decay, protecting against bad breath and producing whiter teeth. With three propositions it will appeal to more segments of the market.

Table 7.5 Risky positions

Potential risk	Comment
Under-positioning	Some companies discover that buyers have only a vague idea of the brand and the features/benefits of that brand. Customers may not be aware of anything particularly special about the brand.
Over-positioning	Customers may have too narrow a view of the brand. Therefore a consumer might think that a particular glass company, for example, only produces luxury items that retail at high prices. However, it may produce a range of standard glassware at much lower prices. Another example could be a classical music CD company that is known for high-priced CDs, but might have a budget range that sells for significantly less.
Confused positioning	Customers could be confused about the position of the brand within the marketplace. This confusion may result from the company making too many claims about the brand, or changing the brand's positioning too frequently.
Doubtful positioning	Customers may find it hard to believe the claims made by the company about its brand in view of the individual product's features and promoted benefits, the price and/or the name of the manufacturer.

satisfactions that they provide. Few of us really want a metallic disc with a hole punched in the centre, and yet many of us buy CDs in their various forms. Understanding and being able to clearly describe the benefit being offered by the product or service is the major key to developing a viable marketing strategy and marketing plan. To do this a company must undertake an objective SWOT analysis of its environment.

A SWOT analysis is an examination of a company's strengths, weaknesses, opportunities and threats. While it can be applied to many areas of the business, in marketing it has relevance to brands, markets, promotions and channels of distribution. During this process, management will also begin to re-evaluate the company's current mission and objectives. If changes are required in the overall direction of the business, this is where those changes are most likely to originate.

Davidson (1997) suggests that a SWOT analysis has three main functions. These are highlighted in Table 7.6.

A SWOT analysis can be illustrated as a matrix structure (Figure 7.4) where the internal analysis relates to strengths and

weaknesses, whereas an external analysis relates to opportunities and threats.

Internal analysis

Strengths

Strengths focus on the activities where a company or brand is successful and which can be fully exploited. For example, a company might have a strong management team and/or large cash reserves. In the latter case the company may use such resources to acquire competitive brands, thus increasing its market share and defensive position (see the later section on competitive market positioning strategies).

Weaknesses

Weaknesses focus on the activities where the company or brand has not been successful and/or does not have the resources it really needs to be successful. One area of weakness may be the degree to which the company takes risks, exploits innovation and rewards performance. In a risk-aversive company, management is probably more likely to develop strategies that minimize financial

Table 7.6   The functions of an SWOT analysis

Function	Result and value
Strategic planning	This is the connecting link between business analysis and strategy development.
Offensive actions	A company can use its strengths to attack a competitor's weaknesses. For instance, one company may have internal logistics problems, resulting in a poor distribution network and thus late deliveries. Another company may have internal logistics strengths, resulting in an efficient and wide distribution network with on-time delivery. Equally, a company can identify and exploit opportunities within the marketplace.
Defensive actions	The company highlights the potential threats against it over the short, medium and longer term. It develops strategies and tactics to protect itself from attack. This may include the preparation of a counterattack. For example, in the 1980s the photocopier giant Xerox decided to enter the mainframe computer market in direct competition to IBM. While Xerox's computer department was engaged in an all-out frontal assault on IBM in the marketplace, IBM counterattacked by entering the photocopier market with a competitive product. This bold and risky strategy shook Xerox as it was now battling IBM on two business fronts. After several years Xerox withdrew, at cost, from the computer market, selling its technology to Honeywell. IBM remained in the photocopier market for a while, perhaps as a protective move before itself withdrawing from that market.

Adapted from Davidson (1997) and James (1985)

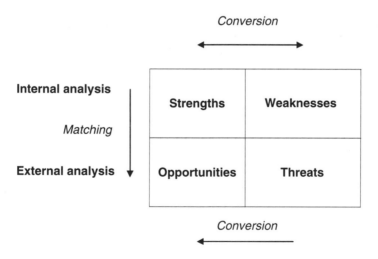

Figure 7.4   SWOT matrix

As stated above, a SWOT analysis must be an objective identification of the internal and external factors affecting the company, market or brand.

exposure, and react to changes within the external environment rather than attempt to anticipate them (Lynch, 2000). This may lead to the company being overwhelmed by events and competitive forces. Thus the weaknesses potentially increase the level and ferocity of external threat against the company or brand.

Weaknesses can be displayed in relation to the marketing mix: see Table 7.7.

External analysis

Opportunities

Opportunities are positive external factors that can aid the company to, for example,

develop new international or niche markets, launch new products or extend a brand range. However, an opportunity to one company may actually pose a threat to another. A company might see an opportunity within a specific overseas market for a product it already successfully manufactures and distributes within its domestic market. They have already determined that there is only one competitor within the new overseas market, and that competitor is indigenous to that market. However the product manufactured and distributed by the indigenous company is of poor quality. Thus the indigenous company

Table 7.7   Relationship between weaknesses and the marketing mix

Mix element	Potential internal weakness
Product	There are potentially several product weaknesses. For instance, production may be inefficient leading to high costs (this impacts upon prices). The product might be of poor quality and unsuitable for the market. The product could be in need of revitalizing and repositioning. It might have been superseded by other products, and thus should be withdrawn. If this is the only product that the company produces, the company's very existence will be in jeopardy.
Price	The company may not be competitive with its current pricing structure. Of course, if production is inefficient leading to high costs, the company may not be able to reduce its prices to match competitors.
Promotion	For example, a lack of investment in marketing communications would lead to a poor awareness of the brand within the marketplace. Equally, poorly targeted promotions can exhaust budgets with little or no return on investment.
Placement	Inbound and outbound logistics: poor internal logistics and inefficient distribution networks lead to late deliveries and disgruntled customers. If these customers are manufacturers operating on a just in time (JIT) basis, as do many car manufacturers, their production line might be halted. The stopping of a production line can result in significantly high daily losses for the company. Customers could thus seek alternative suppliers.
People	Inexperienced staff and poor morale can lead to inefficient customer service. This in turn leads to customers brand switching.
Physical evidence	An ineffective layout within a supermarket chain can lead to customer confusion and irritation. The customer may choose to shop at another supermarket on the basis that the layout is easier to navigate and products are easier to find.
Process	Complex and inefficient processes can impede delivery of a product or service. For example, if an online ordering process is complex (in terms of data required), difficult to navigate to find relevant information (cost of postage and packaging) and slow in its activation, a customer could seek an alternative product source.

is facing a potential threat from the overseas company.

Threats

Threats are negative external factors. A company has to consider what the likely impact will be on its business from such a threat within the market. Taking the example above, the indigenous company will have to evaluate the level of threat posed. It will also need to analyse its internal environment to consider how it can eliminate inherent weaknesses, in this case the factors that lead to the manufacture of a poor quality product. It may have strengths, such as a new intake of high-quality management who may be able to turn around the business and produce a much improved product. Equally, in analysing the external factors, a company might see opportunities as a result of a competitive threat. For instance, it could seek protection from its government through the implementation of tariff and non-tariff barriers, or seek some form of alliance with the overseas company. The indigenous company, for example, could have particular strengths in local distribution and promotion. Thus some form of alliance or merger could prove an opportunity for both companies.

A guide to strategy formulation

A SWOT analysis can be used as a guide to strategy formulation through matching, conversion and the resources availability. These three factors should be considered as interrelated.

Matching

This is the linking of appropriate organizational strengths to market opportunities.

Conversion

This is the conversion of weaknesses into strengths in order to exploit a particular market opportunity. Equally, a company may seek to convert a threat into an opportunity that can be matched by existing strengths.

Resources

The amount and quality of resources available internally will impact on the type of strategic plan developed and how it is ultimately implemented. The key areas for consideration are:

- The skill levels of the employees, technical and managerial.

- The morale of the employees: strong morale aids efficiency.

- The company's resources in terms of the quality of marketing, production, operations, research and development, human resource management and financial management.

- The financial strength of the company: reserves, cash flow and relationship with its banks and other financial institutions.

- The level and success of product innovation.

- Customers' perception of the company's products.

- Customers' perception of the company's service provision.

All companies and organizations are constrained in some way by the resources and employee skills available.

Figure 7.5 illustrates how the SWOT analysis feeds into the formulation and implementation of strategy. As with all techniques or tools, a SWOT should not be considered in isolation. In this diagram Robbins and Coulter (1996) show how a SWOT analysis filters into the formulation of business/organizational strategies. These in turn will guide or preset the structure of the company's marketing strategies.

Figure 7.6 shows a SWOT analysis of a US fast-moving consumer goods (FMCG) company in 1999. Therefore it presents purely a snapshot in time. It is clear from the SWOT that the company faced several internal and external challenges.

So what could a company do with a SWOT like this?

The company could take various actions incorporating matching and conversion. In Table 7.8 we illustrate the possible action that the company could undertake over some of these issues. Of course, as with any type of analysis it should be reviewed continually in the light of changing environmental factors.

As you can see from the table the company had an opportunity to both match and convert issues based upon the original SWOT analysis. Thus a SWOT does not become an endless list of thoughts with no real outcomes. By considering the issues objectively, a business can develop potentially effective action-oriented strategies.

Industry life cycle

Porter describes the industry life cycle as the 'grandfather of concepts for predicting industry evolution' (Lynch, 2000). An industry usually comprises many different companies producing similar or related types of product. For example, shipbuilders produce cargo vessels, and the music industry produces vinyl records, cassettes, CDs and mini disks. Lynch (2000) suggests that the nature of corporate strategy will change as industries move along the life cycle (see Table 7.9).

The industry life cycle is not without criticism. Table 7.10 briefly outlines the key arguments against the industry life cycle.

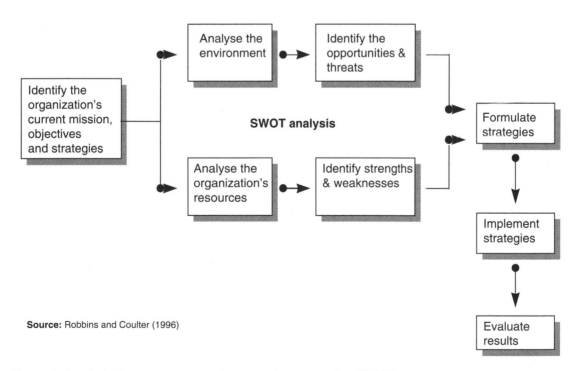

Source: Robbins and Coulter (1996)

Figure 7.5   A strategy management process incorporating SWOT

Internal analysis

Strengths	Weaknesses
• Strong financial background. • Strong brand name. • Global reputation. • High brand valuation. • International distribution network.	• Aggressive management style – both at home and overseas. Very much an ethnocentric culture. • Concern regarding the abilities of the CEO to build the brand further and to negotiate with government regulators. • Worldwide unit sales falling, yet marketing expenditure dramatically increasing. • Profits down on previous year. • Slow to introduce new products (the competition are faster movers in the market). • Slow to react to health scares in certain key countries regarding the company's product.

External analysis

Opportunities	Threats
• Potential new regional markets. • Companies could be acquired thus expanding share in current and future markets. • Markets for new products within this FMCG sector.	• EU and other countries could block expansion through acquisition under competition rules. • Established and new competitors within the market. Have already taken some market share within key territories. • Risk of economic downturn in several markets. • Anti US feeling in several countries, especially China (due to US attack on Chinese Embassy in Belgrade during Kosovo conflict).

Figure 7.6 SWOT analysis of a US FMCG company, 1999

Lynch (2000) suggests the industry life cycle is a useful tool in identifying the dynamic factors shaping an industry's evolution. Perhaps a case in point is the changing fortunes of the Hollywood movie industry. In Figure 7.7 we sketch the key rises and falls of the industry, and in Table 7.11 we show the key environmental changes that impacted upon that industry and how it responded, or in some cases did not respond, to these forces.

When reviewing Table 7.11 consider some of the issues discussed in Chapter 2 regarding the marketing environment, and the relationship between companies, their customers, suppliers, competitors and government. Additionally, later in this chapter we consider Porter's five forces model. Again, when reviewing that model consider how that model could have affected the Hollywood movie industry. As you can see from Table 7.11, the Hollywood movie industry has

Table 7.8 Analysis of possible matching and conversion of FMCG company 1999

	Strength to opportunity	Weakness to strength	Threat to opportunity
Matching	Use strong brand name and reputation to develop new market opportunities. Seek to acquire companies or participate in alliances to build share in new regional markets. Consider the development of new products that will not weaken core brand.		
Conversion		Reconsider the role of the CEO and ethnocentric view of the corporate culture. This may mean replacing the CEO and other members of the board. Decentralize management so that local/regional managers can be better placed to exploit the market. Restructure the company to maximize longer term revenues. This may result in the reduction of staff levels.	Discuss issues openly with competition regulators. Seek to work together. Hedge against economic downturn in risk countries. Attempt to establish better cultural and governmental relationship where the brand is under attack because of its US link.

undergone various changes within its life cycle. It remains alive but has had to deal with numerous changes within its 100-year (to date) existence.

Product life cycle

As the industry life cycle highlights an industry, so the product life cycle highlights the stages in the life or history of a product. (See Figure 7.8.) We can draw a parallel between a product life cycle and the human life cycle. With humans there is birth, growth, maturity, decline and eventually death. Our life span may be short or long. Through this period we may undergo life-threatening illnesses that we survive. The same can be applicable to a product, although a product life span may be significantly longer than that

of a human being! Just consider for a moment the age of products such as Coca Cola or Kellogg's cornflakes: they are both over 100 years old.

It is important to realize that the product life cycle can be modified. Think of product modification itself: changes in design, ingredients, size, packaging, rebranding and positioning, for instance. All these factors can contribute to extending the life cycle of a product. However, we must remember that a product or service will only survive if it meets a real need or desire on behalf of the customer (and over an applicable time frame).

Understanding which stage the product has entered will have significant impact upon the effectiveness of the marketing strategy undertaken. Astute marketing managers use the life cycle concept to make sure that the introduction, alteration and termination of a

Table 7.9 Industry life cycle

Strategy	Introduction phase	Growth phase	Maturity phase	Decline phase
Customer strategy	Innovative product. There may be some experimentation with the product and the realization that there may be some unreliability.	Increasing number of early adopters. Quality and reliability increasingly important.	A mass market developed.	Selection on the basis of price.
R&D strategy	High input.	Some input for minor modifications.	Low input.	No R&D.
Company strategy	Seeks dominance in the market. R&D particularly important in winning position.	Reacts to competitor moves with marketing initiatives and technical improvements.	Highly competitive environment. Difficult to increase market share if not market leader. Can be an expensive move. May need to seek cost reductions.	Cost control particularly important. The company may seek to exit the industry/market. However, that too could have significant cost implications.
Impact upon profitability	High priced products. However heavy investment in R&D and entry into new market/category could result in loss.	Prices may start to decline as more competitors enter the market. However, growth potential for profits.	Potentially high level of competitive pressure. Need for continued investment. Profits may be high, but under pressure – stable rather than growth.	Competition based upon price. Low growth phase. This may lead to losses. Company may need to cut costs dramatically in order to maintain profitability, if not survive.
Competitor strategy	There will be a few competitors. However, interest in this sector may lead to companies attempting to replicate the new product.	Increased level of competition. Competitors may attempt to innovate based upon the company's product or develop the sector further.	Competitive pressure based upon marketing communication through various types of promotion. At this stage there will be lower product differentiation (for example VCRs). There may be fewer larger competitors left within the market.	Competition based mainly on price. There will be fewer competitors as others collapse financially or seek an exit from the sector.

Adapted from Lynch (2000)

Table 7.10 Criticisms of the industry life cycle

Criticism	Comment
Measuring the duration of the life span.	It has been suggested that it is difficult to measure the duration of the whole life cycle, and that there is no specific formula. If you think about it, it is currently difficult to predict the life span of a human being. We can guess; however, unforeseen factors may intervene to shorten or indeed lengthen the life span.
Identifying a particular stage within the life cycle.	Difficult to identify a precise stage an industry has reached within the life cycle.
Changing shape of the life cycle curve.	Companies may be able to alter the shape of the curve. For instance, the camera market has been rejuvenated through the introduction of smaller lightweight digital cameras. Chips have replaced film as a means of storage and the images can be downloaded onto the computer and CDs.
The type of competition can vary.	The type of competition may vary regardless of where the company is within the life cycle. Competitive activity is not static, it changes, develops and modifies over time.

Adapted from Lynch (2000)

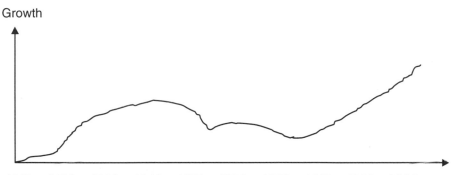

Figure 7.7 The rises and falls of the Hollywood movie industry

product are timed and executed properly. By understanding the typical life cycle pattern, marketers are better able to maintain profitable products and terminate unprofitable ones (Baker, 2000).

A product life cycle is generally described as a side-on S-shaped curve, or perhaps more accurately the mathematical sine wave curve (~). This cycle is then generally divided into several differing stages or lives. While some authors suggest four stages – introduction, growth, maturity and death – we suggest, like others, that there can be several additional stages. This allows marketers to increase the level of precision when analysing product life cycles:

- research and development;

- introduction;

Table 7.11 The Hollywood movie industry and key environmental changes

Period	Threats	Reactions and developments
1900s		Pioneering work. A niche market. Very few competitors.
1920s	Technology	The silent movie industry grows. Hollywood begins to take shape as a film centre. Increasing number of new entrants. Competition increases but not all newcomers survive. First experiments with talking pictures.
1930s	Technology political/legal	Technological developments in sound and colour. Companies unable to convert to producing talking pictures collapse. New entrepreneurs from Europe influence the development of larger studios. The industry is dominated by a few large players. The federal government consider the studios' ownership of the cinemas anti-competitive, and the studios are forced to sell their cinema chains to independent companies which can choose which movies to show. Thus the market becomes more competitive.
1940s	Technology. Further developments in sound and colour processing	Industry remains buoyant during the Second World War. A mixture of escapist and propaganda movies keeps US cinema attendance high. Many of the major studios reach their high point.
1950s	Technology – television and wide-screen formats	The introduction of television threatens the existence of the movie companies and the industry. Some companies react by introducing technological gimmicks and improvements. The gimmicks include 3-D movies which did not work successfully. Improvements included wide-screen formats, some of which were more successful than others. For the cinema owners the levels of investment were too high. Some companies, such as MGM and 20th Century Fox, revised their product output, opting for large-scale epics and musicals which could not be replicated by the television companies. Many of the small companies could not survive – they had neither the product nor the financial resources to develop their position. By the end of the decade some of the major studios had already started to downsize, preferring to hire staff when required rather than having them as permanent employees.
1960s	Television and international movies	The television industry becomes a major threat. Several studios decide to produce dramas for television as well as the cinemas. Loose partnerships are formed. Increase in foreign movies being shown in the United States, especially British and French. The US companies, through distributors, increase global marketing.
1970s		Television dominates. Several international markets shrink, including the UK.

Table 7.11 *continued*

Period	Threats	Reactions and developments
1980s	Video, satellite and cable companies	The broadcasting market opens up with subsequent growth in satellite and cable television companies. A plethora of channels operating 24 hours a day. Major studios begin to merge or seek to exploit technologies. Companies such as Warner Bros and 20th Century Fox set up video arms to market their movies to a video rental audience. Companies are acquired to form part of global media interests, such as News Corporation's acquisition of 20th Century Fox. They are no longer only in the movie business, but the media and entertainment business. The video sell-through market rivals the rental market, and companies reduce their costs and subsequently prices. Economies of scale make the sell-through market advantageous.
1990s	Technology, DVD and multiplexes	The movie companies exploit digital technologies in partnership with cinema chains. While multiplexes were not a new concept, new technologies and design helped revolutionize the cinema as a place of entertainment. Large-scale productions revitalize the industry. International markets are regenerated.
2000s	Technology, flat/wide-screen televisions and surround sound	The cinema remains a family experience. Large-scale productions such as the Harry Potter and *Lord of the Rings* movies dominate. Several major companies still dominate, however there are several new entrants such as Steven Spielberg's Dreamworks which increase their market share. New threats come from technologies associated with television. Digital broadcasting has dramatically increased the number of TV stations available. Equally, technology companies develop a new generation of televisions that can provide a 'home entertainment experience'. Although the Hollywood movie industry shows signs of growth, there are possibly more threats to the industry on the horizon.
Beyond 2000	Technology and mergers	Technology will help increase the all-round entertainment experience within cinemas. Equally, cinema owners will improve internal conditions providing a range of added-value services from catering to shopping. In terms of companies there may be further mergers as larger conglomerates consider demergers or disposals to focus on their original core businesses. It was clear at the end of 2002 that large-scale movies, such as Harry Potter, *Lord of the Rings* and James Bond dominate the cinema screens. This places increased pressure on the small-scale, small-budget movies to gain screen time. The smaller studios and film makers may come under increasing competitive pressures.

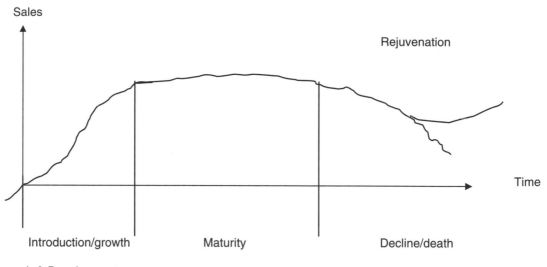

Figure 7.8 Stereotypical product life cycle curve

- growth;
- maturity;
- decline;
- re-staging/rejuvenation/revitalization;
- death/extinction/termination.

The point at which these stages begin and end tends to be arbitrary, but an indicator can be the percentage changes in real sales year on year.

Although the S-shaped curve is generally considered typical, researchers have defined a range of patterns. Tellis and Crawford (1981) identified 17, whilst Swann and Rink (1982) considered 10 variations.

In Figure 7.9 and the matching Table 7.12 we have created some variants on the classic life cycle model. The table describes the possible scenarios under which each life cycle may exist. As you can see some life cycles are particularly short and do not adopt a classic sine curve, whilst others are more 'in-keeping' with the classic model.

Product life cycles: the 'for' and 'against' arguments

Urban and Starr (1991) state that the concept of the product life cycles is widely accepted because 'it is easily understood, it is intuitively appealing and because examples have been published for many industries where some life cycle pattern has been evident'. Another supporter of product life cycles is McDonald (1996) who states, 'The important point to remember... is that the concept of the product Life Cycle is not an academic figment of the imagination, but a hard reality which is ignored at great risk.' However, not all academics consider the product life cycle of practical value to marketers. They tend to think of it as more a theoretical conscript with little empirical support.

Bennett (1999) summarizes the objections to the product life cycle, as follows:

- Many products cannot be characterized in generalistic life cycle terms (basic food produce or certain industrial materials).

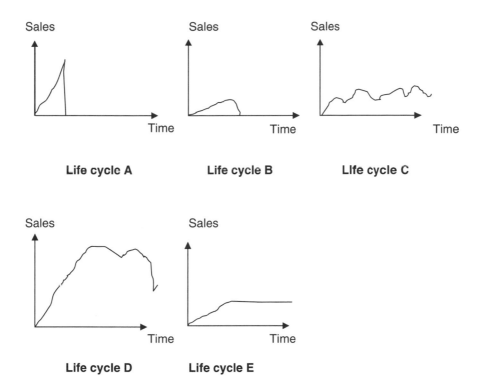

Figure 7.9 Life cycle variants

Table 7.12 Possible life cycle variants

Life cycle	Comment
A	This life cycle is particularly short; however the product achieves high sales over this short period. This is generally reflective of high-fashion designer clothes brands, especially women's wear that also tends to be seasonal. It could also be the life cycle of a blockbuster movie which achieves large revenues but has a relatively limited run because of other movies coming into the marketplace.
B	Like life cycle A above, this is a relatively short life cycle; however unlike life cycle A it does not generate high sales revenue. This may be a product that has been introduced into a market for which there is little or no demand.
C	This life cycle goes through periods of decline before being rejuvenated and achieving new growth within the market. The rejuvenation in this case may be due to an improved product formulation or modification (for example, detergents) and/or new packaging.
D	This highlights quite rapid growth but a short maturity stage before decline and then resurgence within the market.
E	This curve demonstrates a relatively short growth stage before maturity is reached. This may identify a specialist product or service that has established itself within the market.

- The length of life of a new product cannot be predicted reliably in advance. The life of some new products can be quite long; for others it is not. (Refer to the section on new product development in Chapter 8.)

- Variations in the marketing effort will affect the duration of life cycle phases, and determine the timing of transitions from one stage to another. This refers to the skill of the marketing department to anticipate changing environmental conditions and react effectively to those changes.

- Competitor's behaviour may be the primary determinant of the company's sales, regardless of the age of the product.

- Numerous random factors can influence the duration of phases, turning points and level of sales: for example, the impact of external or macro factors on the business environment.

- Products do not face inevitable death within predetermined periods. Termination of a product's life is a management decision. Highly skilful marketing may extend a product's life span.

- Management can never be sure of the phase in its life cycle in which a product happens to be at a particular time. How, for instance, could management know that a product is near the start and not at the end of its growth phase, or that a fall in sales is a temporary event, rather than 'the start of a product's decline?' (Bennett, 1999).

Supporters of the product life cycle concept can suggest means of overcoming some of these objections. However, perhaps the product life cycle needs to be considered as an aid to determining the position of a product within a market, not the sole determinant. We revisit the product life cycle in Chapter 15, where we assemble possible strategic and tactical reactions to positions on the life cycle.

Portfolio analysis

In this section we consider various portfolio models that have been designed to evaluate different aspects of the marketplace. They can be considered as an aid to strategic thinking and a way of guiding marketers to exploit market opportunities effectively and efficiently. However, as Dibb (1995) suggests, any organization managing a portfolio of products or brands needs regularly to review its portfolio so that there is a balance between the introduction of new products, resourcing of mature offerings and divesting of the outdated.

Ansoff growth matrix: product portfolio

Ansoff (1987) developed the product portfolio as a means of analysing the combination of an organization's activities within existing markets and potential markets with current and new products. Figure 7.10 illustrates the growth matrix structure while Table 7.13 details the activities within the four quadrants.

The concept raised by Ansoff (1987) is that the review of the product portfolio is only one part of the equation for a successful marketing strategy. It is also necessary to review the markets that are being served. Wilson and Gilligan (1997) suggest that new areas for the business to enter need to be identified carefully. It is important to ensure that any new area can be exploited by the use of the organization's current marketing and operational assets and capabilities. While the assets and organization's capabilities should be developed over time, entering totally new markets with new products is considered to be a very high-risk strategy for any organization. This is equally applicable to well established organizations and new entrants.

There is another perspective to accommodate. Ansoff's matrix was developed at a time when companies actively sought

Product

	Present/existing	New
Present/existing **Markets**	Market Penetration	Product Development
New	Market Development	Diversification

Figure 7.10   Ansoff's growth matrix: Ansoff (1987)

Table 7.13   Individual matrix strategies

Strategy	Tactics
Market penetration. The organization seeks to sell more products within its existing market.	The organization can increase usage from existing customers and gain new customers through competitive pricing, special promotions (for example loyalty cards) and expanding the range of uses for the product or service (breakfast cereal as an all-day snack food).
Market development. The organization seeks new markets for its existing products or services.	The organization could develop new regional and international markets, repackage its products for new market segments (hair care products sold into beauty salons repackaged for the consumer market), use new distribution channels to attract new customers (airlines using the Internet for online purchasing), or introduce differential pricing structures to attract new customers (credit card companies with fixed interest rates for a specific time frame).
Product development. This is the launch of new products within existing markets.	Product development can include improvements to existing products as well as the development of totally new products. An example is the enhancements to mobile phones, ranging from texting through to real-time video. In addition to meeting customer needs, product development often forces competitors to innovate in order to remain within the market. Competitors may seek an exit strategy, although there are costs incurred with such strategies. As well as potentially forcing competitors out of the market, product innovation may also create (at least in the short term) a barrier to entry.
Diversification. This is where a company develops a new product for a new market(s).	An organization may seek to use either horizontal or vertical integration to achieve its strategic objectives. Horizontal integration is where the company develops activities that are directly complementary to its current activities. There are two components to vertical integration. Backwards vertical integration is where the company becomes its own supplier of raw materials or components. Forward vertical integration is where the company becomes a distributor and/or retailer of its own products.

expansion and diversification. However growth and diversification may not be the ideal strategic option, especially during times of extreme turbulence or changing market trends. Companies may decide to retrench as the best strategic option to defend their long-term position. Retrenchment can take several forms, which can be implemented individually or in combinations:

Reduce product range

A company may decide to divest itself of unprofitable products or services to focus on key revenue and profit generators.

Withdrawal from markets

The organization may seek to withdraw from unprofitable or difficult markets or territories. In 2002, as part of a major strategic review, British Airways decided to either scale down or cease its flights on certain unprofitable routes to focus on more profitable services. Since then many other airlines have followed British Airways' approach in order to survive within an extremely volatile market.

Divest non-core businesses

Companies that have diversified can become inefficient and thus suffer from high costs, lower margins and reduced profits. Thus they may retrench by divesting themselves of non-core businesses. Between 1995 and 1996 the international conglomerate Hanson plc divested itself of most of its chemical, insurance, energy and retailing interests to focus on building materials and equipment (Naylor, 1999).

As you can see there are various approaches to retrenchment that companies may take to remain competitive, indeed to survive. Such actions may be necessary in the short term. However, companies such as Hanson plc viewed retrenchment as a long-term aim in order to be highly focused. By being so focused a company can aim to develop a strong position within one or two key market sectors. Needless to say, while being focused a company must develop an effective marketing mix to sustain competitiveness within the market.

Profit impact of marketing strategy (PIMS)

Originated in 1972, this was later implemented as a strategic planning model for the General Electric Corporation to examine the viability of SBUs. The early research demonstrated a strong correlation between market share and profitability by using a database of GE businesses. Subsequent work resulted in empirical research and a database of over 7,000 businesses (Shaw, 1998). From this research two empirical findings stand out:

1. the association between market share and profitability;
2. the association between perceived quality and return on investment. Figure 7.11 illustrates the key factors measured by PIMS: market inputs, customers and outputs.

Buzzell and Gale (1987) list six of the most important linkages between strategy and performance as defined by the PIMS model:

▪ In the long run, the most important single factor affecting a business unit's performance is the quality of its products and services, relative to those of its competitors.

▪ Market share and profitability are strongly related.

▪ High investment intensity acts as a powerful drag on profitability.

▪ Many so called 'dogs' and 'question marks' businesses generate cash, while many 'cash cows' are dry. (See the Boston Matrix, Figure 7.12.)

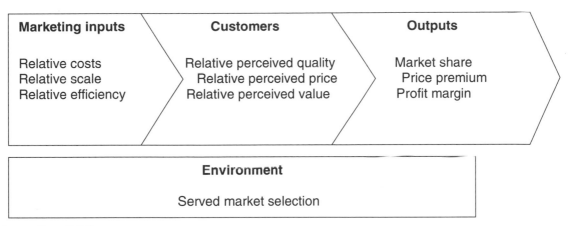

Source: Shaw (1998)

Figure 7.11 Key factors measured by PIMS

▌ Vertical integration Is a profitable strategy for some kinds of business, but not for others.

▌ Most of the strategic factors that boost return on investment also contribute to long-term (shareholder) value.

As you can see from this list an organization needs to be able to fine-tune the relationship between the marketing inputs and stakeholder values (including customers) to maintain longer-term market share and profitability. Moreover this must happen within a constantly dynamic environment.

Boston Consulting matrix: the growth-share matrix

Bruce Henderson and his colleagues at the Boston Consulting Group developed the growth-share matrix, often known as the Boston Box. (See Figure 7.12.) It was developed to assist managers in determining how they should use funds from successful products to fund growth in other businesses. The matrix has been described as 'a technique for a season rather than one for all seasons' (Moore, 2001). Even Henderson tended to see

it as 'a milestone on the search for insight into business system dynamics, but certainly not the end of the road'. (Moore, 2001).

Mathematicians will realize that to portray 'relative' shares the scale used must be logarithmic and not linear. So while the vertical axis, product/market growth, is divided in a linear fashion, the horizontal axis, relative market share, must be divided using a logarithmic scale. By dividing both of the axes into two equal parts it is possible to form a simple 2 by 2 matrix, with the horizontal axis using x 1 at the mid point with x 10 and x 0.1 forming the outer limits. The vertical axis is also split into two at the centre point of the growth rate for the product/market. The Boston Consulting Group, because of the use for which the model was developed, set 20 per cent as the maximum, 0 per cent as the minimum and 10 per cent for the centre point, this being the rate at which they considered saturation or maturity started to set in, as the growth rate would be slowing at that point on the product life cycle.

Each quadrant in the matrix was then given a name to identify its potential cash flow and its position within the portfolio. The original names were 'question mark', 'star', 'cash cow' and 'pet' which was later changed to 'dog'. The strategy for each quadrant in the matrix

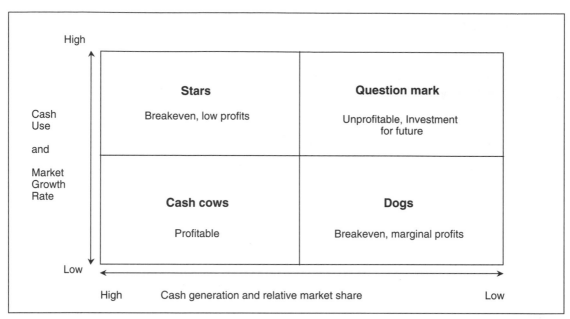

© Boston Consulting Group

Figure 7.12   Boston growth matrix

can be developed from an understanding of the present performance, in cash flow terms, of the products or SBUs within each quadrant.

Question marks (high market growth, low relative market share)

Starting with the 'question marks', these can be seen to be in a high growth area of the marketplace but with a low relative market share within that market. This shows that the organization's nearest competitor(s) have a larger share of the available market. The products within this quadrant need careful consideration as a number of strategies are available for them. Often 'build' strategies are employed to try to gain market share from the competition, with the objective of turning the products into 'stars'. However this strategy can be extremely expensive, as competitors will be keen to keep their larger share of the market and will have developed defensive and offensive strategies to ensure they do so.

A market strategy of 'hold' is a possible option for these products, depending on the market, but 'question marks' tend to be net users of cash, producing a negative cash flow that the organization may not wish to accept. However, it is possible to obtain positive cash flows with this type of product given time and the appropriate marketing strategies.

Stars (high market growth, high relative market share)

The 'stars' are products in a high market growth area, still probably in the growth stage of the product life cycle, and with a large relative market share. However, they will be under attack from competitors which also want the potential cash flow obtainable from holding a large market share.

A defensive marketing strategy is normally required here so that the position within the market can be maintained in the face of any competition. This type of strategy can be expensive, usually in terms of promotional support for the products, and therefore these products tend to provide only modest cash flows. While these cash flows are ideally positive in some circumstances, the cash flow generated by stars can be negative. Therefore the amount of resources invested to defend their position must be analysed carefully.

Cash cows (low market growth, high relative market share)

'Cash cows' occur when the market growth rate has slowed but the products on offer have obtained and are maintaining a relatively high market share within the chosen market. A hold or defensive strategy is still required here; however the cash required to maintain the market share position should not be as great as that required to maintain stars. Products in the cash cow quadrant are usually generators of large positive cash flows, this cash being used to maintain stars and develop question marks. However it should be remembered that these products are likely to be in a mature or even declining area of the product life cycle, and they will need investment to ensure they remain viable.

Pets or dogs (low market growth, low relative market share)

'Pets' or 'dogs' are usually negative generators of cash flow and should be considered for disposal if at all possible. However care must be taken when considering the most suitable marketing strategy for products or SBUs in this quadrant. Not all 'dogs' are net users of cash, and they may support the rest of the product range in the mind of the customer. In fact many companies can survive, and even thrive, with a product portfolio of mainly dogs if they are managed properly. The view of the Boston Consulting Group is that dogs should be avoided at all costs, but this is purely because of the perceived problems of cash flow rather than any other marketing reason.

Strategies

Consideration must always be given as to the best way to handle difficult question marks, weak cash cows and dogs. A strategy of harvesting, that is, maximizing the short-term cash flow, will provide a possible solution to obtain a reasonable return on the investment already made by the product.

The next stage, once the positions of the various products in the portfolio have been established, is to develop marketing strategies to:

1. provide the best overall cash flow for each of the products;

2. plot the desired position that the product will occupy in an agreed time frame, using forecasting techniques.

The positions are correctly shown not as small dots or crosses but as circles that represent, to scale, the actual sales value generated currently by each of the products and what this will be at the end of the forecast period. Ideally question marks should be moved to become stars. The stars should be moved to become cash cows, as the market matures and cash cows perhaps move back to become question marks, so that the cycle is repeated. Note that under no circumstances does the organization want any part of the portfolio to become dogs!

Two further categories have been proposed by Barksdale and Harris (1982): 'war horses' and 'dodos'.

War horses

These are currently market leaders; however their ability to maintain appropriate levels of cash generation is under threat because of negative market growth. This decline can either be temporary or terminal. If it is temporary, the company may seek to support the product or service through, for example, investment in marketing communications until there is a turnaround. The company will be looking longer term at the return of positive cash generation. However, if the decline is viewed as terminal, the company will normally adopt a harvesting strategy to maximize revenue from repeat purchases by loyal customers, and provide only minimal marketing support.

Dodos

Like its namesake the product or service is destined for extinction. The product or service will display a low share within a declining market. Companies may decide to terminate the product before its financial contribution turns negative, thus consuming precious and costly resources. An example of a product with low share within a declining market is the typewriter. It has been superseded by the introduction of the computer.

Like all strategy models the BCG matrix must not be used as a panacea for all marketing problems. It can cause problems if used incorrectly. It was designed to help solve a particular problem at a particular time, and may not be suitable for the requirements of any other market or organization.

There is also the problem of carefully defining the market and the competition. As Levitt (1986) has pointed out, it is necessary to think carefully about the market in which the organization actually operates. Identifying and defining the markets being served are prerequisites of any marketing strategy. The term 'relative' would tend to suggest that the competitors are of a similar size and specifically trying to sell into the same market segments. So while it might be possible to consider, for example, the product ranges of Ford and General Motors using the BCG matrix, to try to compare either with niche British sports car manufacturer Morgan Cars would be rather pointless.

GE variant: the General Electric business screen

The General Electric Corporation with the management consulting company McKinsey & Co has developed another portfolio type planning model. Davidson (1997), for example, suggests that the GE matrices overcome some of the disadvantages of the BCG model by incorporating a broader range of measures. The GE business screens can be used to classify SBUs or major products based upon two key factors: market attractiveness and business position.

Market attractiveness

This includes market share (as with the BCG model), market size, the degree of difficulty in entering the market (consider barriers to entry in the Porter model, discussed later in this chapter), the competitors (number, type, size, current and potential future ones), technological requirements (and speed of technological change), external environmental factors, and profit margins.

Business position

This includes market share (as with the BCG model), the size of the SBU, the strength of differential advantage, research and development capabilities, production and operational capacity, quality of financial management (cost control), core competencies and expertise within the organization.

Weighting of the criteria

Management assigns different weightings to market attractiveness and business position. This provides an element of flexibility, as some criteria will be considered more important than others. For example, in assessing market attractiveness management might rate political factors (within the macro environment) higher than the strength of competition. The company could for example have business interests within a country that is displaying political unrest, thus creating a threat to the stability of the business within that region.

Once weightings have been attributed to all the market attractiveness and business position elements, each SBU is weighted in relation to all criteria. Finally, overall ratings (usually numerical scores) are calculated for each SBU. On the basis of these scores each SBU is designated as high, medium or low, in relation to market attractiveness and business position. As a result of these ratings the organization's SBUs can be plotted on a grid, as depicted in Figure 7.13.

The ideal location for an SBU is the upper left cell because it presents the most attractive market opportunities, and this is the optimum business position for the organization to seize those opportunities. The worst location for an SBU is the lower right cell because it presents the least attractive market opportunities, and this is a very poor business position because there is no opportunity to develop the SBU. It is a critical position for the SBU.

Various strategies can emerge from the GE matrix depending on where the SBU is positioned. We consider each in turn below and indicate the equivalent BCG position.

Invest strategy (equivalent to stars)

The SBUs located in the three cells in the upper left portion of the matrix require investment in resources including marketing. Such investment will further build and strengthen the position of the SBU.

Protect strategy (equivalent to cash cows)

These are the SBUs located diagonally from the lower left cell through to the upper right cell. Resources need to be allocated selectively to defend the SBU's position within the marketplace. These SBUs require protection because they usually generate cash for new SBUs or less successful ones.

Harvest strategy (equivalent to question marks)

Here there is a lack of market attractiveness coinciding with a poor business position. As with any harvest strategy the focus is on maximizing remaining profit potential with minimal investment in resources. The organization may at some stage seek to either sell these SBUs to another company or close them.

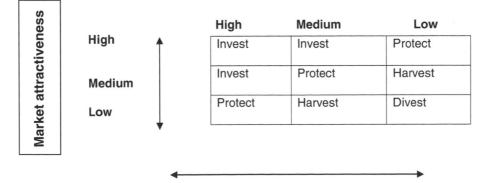

Figure 7.13 The GE business screen

Divest strategy (equivalent to dogs)

SBUs located in the lower right cell face a difficult situation with low market attractiveness and low business position. Clearly this is a weak SBU and one that should receive no further investment in resources. The organization is faced with either selling it to another company or closing it down. The longer the organization takes to implement such action, the greater the drain on resources in order to maintain some operational functionality.

As Stanton, Etzel and Walker (1994) suggest, an organization can employ all four strategies. For instance it can harvest profits from SBUs before divesting them, then use the resources derived from the sale or closure to invest in and protect other SBUs within the organization.

Porter's five forces model

Marketing, operations, human resource management, production, supply chain management/logistics and finance are all capable of providing the organization with a competitive edge, and thus potential success within the marketplace. We say only 'potential' because the advantages may only be short-lived. What an organization needs to seek is sustainable advantage.

Porter (1980) believes that competitive forces shape strategy. He created a model (Figure 7.14) that states there are five key or

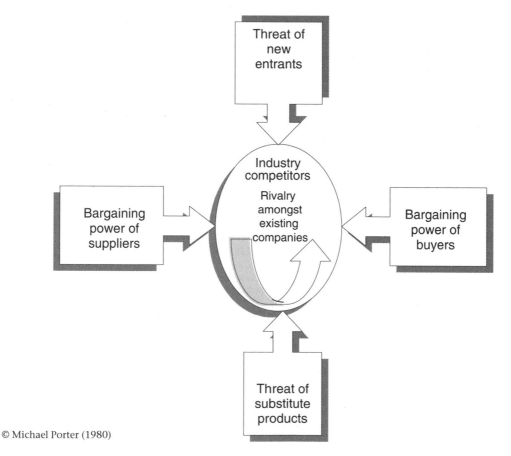

© Michael Porter (1980)

Figure 7.14   Porter's five forces model

distinguishing forces that govern the role of competition within the marketplace. These can be described as the threat of new entrants, the threat of substitution, the bargaining power of suppliers, the bargaining power of customers and the rivalry between current competitors.

The threat of new entrants

As Porter and others suggest, the freedom of entry into an industry is generally regarded as an indicator of the level of competitiveness (Lynch, 2000). Of course some industries have been, or remain, commercial or state-owned monopolies, for example the utilities industries (water, gas and electricity, especially nuclear power) in some countries.

As Porter (1980) suggests, the greater the barriers to entry, the less the threat of new entrants moving into the marketplace. Many factors can reduce the threat of new entrants, and thus the threat against the established organizations within the market. Porter (1980) proposes that there are seven major barriers. In Table 7.14 we have in parentheses suggested possible changes to these scenarios where appropriate.

The threat of substitution

Porter (1980) describes the threat of substitution as 'identifying substitute products is a matter of searching for other products that can perform the same function as the product of the industry'. As Baker (2000) suggests, companies aim to differentiate their products, because if they do so significantly enough to be 'perceived as unique by a sufficient number of users to comprise an economically viable market then the threat of competition is latent rather than active'.

However, as Baker (2000) reports, companies may become complacent, thus exposing themselves to attack from new entrants into the marketplace. The UK clothing and food retailer Marks & Spencer

was for a very long time a powerful force within the marketplace with its own-label brand, St Michael, but it became relatively complacent within the marketplace. As a result it found itself under attack from a range of multiple and own-label retailers (for example, Gap) and required drastic measures to remain viable within the marketplace. In March 2001 Marks & Spencer announced that it was closing its European mainland stores, including a major store on the fashionable Boulevard Haussmann in Paris. By September 2002 it had managed to regain a relatively strong market position; however it had done so at some cost.

The bargaining power of suppliers

According to Porter (1980), a supplier group can hold significant power if the company operates within a concentrated market and there is a degree of substitutability.

Concentration

This is where the supply is dominated by a few suppliers, and thus it is more concentrated than the industry it sells to. An example of this is tyre manufacture, which is dominated by a few major manufacturers: Bridgestone, Goodyear, Michelin and Pirelli. Compare these with the number of large-scale automotive manufacturers. This is particularly so in Formula 1 motor racing where the competition is between two major companies, Bridgestone and Michelin.

Degree of substitutability

A buyer may be tied to a specific supplier simply because its particular requirements can only be met by that supplier. Of course, there may be new entrants into the market (especially in markets where there is rapid technological change), thus offering the buyer a possible alternative and competitive source of available supply. Notwithstanding that, the

Table 7.14 Potential barriers to entry

Major barriers	Comment
Economies of scale	An established company may have been able to obtain significant economies of scale through judicious use of resources, cost control management and increased sales. A potential new entrant that does not have high levels of investment and/or is not able to achieve equal economies within a relatively short time frame will be at a cost disadvantage. Its alternative may be to differentiate its product; however this may be equally difficult for it. (Of course economies of scale can change through technological changes, thus allowing new competitors into the marketplace. An example is the wider availability of microcomputer chips and assembly practices, which allowed for the cloning of IBM standard machines in the 1980s. This dramatically changed the shape of the personal and business computer market, and reduced IBM's dominance within the marketplace.)
Product differentiation	In order to establish their product, possible new entrants will have to significantly differentiate their product from established rivals. They may also need to invest heavily in marketing communications to establish their product within the marketplace. On both counts significant levels of investment may be necessary, without any guarantees of success and return on investment. The risk may be too great. (As we have already seen differentiation can create a unique character for a product that prevents or delays the entry of rivals into the marketplace. We must not be so naïve as to think that companies cannot develop improved differentiated characteristics to outperform market leaders. We just have to look at the development of the immense rivalry amongst passenger plane makers to witness the significant changes that have taken place over the past 50 years to gain market share.)
Capital requirements	As noted later in discussing differentiation strategies, substantial investment may be required to introduce a new product within the marketplace. This may deter potential new entrants. (It is clear that some industries, such as heavy engineering, computing software and pharmaceuticals, require significant levels of investment to develop new products and enhance existing ones. It is very clear that not all established companies, let alone totally new entrants, can match these significant levels of investment. However, companies with a portfolio of successful brands may use some or all of them to finance a move into a new product sector. Large companies, such as the pharmaceutical giants, can allocate financial resources to new developments from the operating profits garnered from long-established successful products. The same can be said of major Hollywood film studios. They can plough the financial resources from their portfolio of box-office smash hit movies such as *Titanic* (1997) and *Gladiator* (2000) into other productions. Smaller studios or new entrants into the market will not have this financial power, at least to start with. However, if they are successful say with a first hit then they may be able to build such a portfolio. However, the risks in such a volatile industry can be enormous.)

Table 7.14   *continued*

Major barriers	Comment
Switching costs	These are the costs incurred by existing companies if they decide to switch from existing suppliers to new entrants. A change of supplier may mean costs incurred in retaining staff and the installation of new equipment. Thus the buyers often remain with their suppliers, which in turn prevents new entrants gaining ground within the supplier marketplace. (An example of switching costs is the photocopier lease/rental industry in the UK. Because of the complexity of both the photocopiers and the lease agreements (tying companies into complex and expensive agreements), it was difficult for new and innovative lease/rental companies to enter the marketplace. With innovations in technology, photocopiers are generally easier to use. Additionally, UK government regulation (combined with adverse publicity towards the photocopier retailers) resulted in less restrictive and punitive agreements. This allowed for more companies to enter the marketplace.)
Access to distribution channels	A well-established company with a powerful reputation within the marketplace will have access to strong distribution channels. In the movie industry we can clearly see that a company with the history, industry and financial reputation of Universal Pictures will command a strong distribution outlet for a blockbuster movie. Millions of dollars will have been invested in pre-production, production and post-production, to say nothing of the marketing of the picture. However, a small budgeted picture made by an equally small production company may not receive distribution at all, regardless of its quality. It may be a minor masterpiece, however it still may not receive theatrical distribution; it may receive a television airing, or indeed no showing at all. Some manufacturers are vertically or forward integrated, owning or controlling their distributors. This creates a further barrier to entry. However note that in some countries this is illegal. The argument is that it is anti-competitive and prevents other companies from entering the marketplace and creating competition. In the 1930s the Hollywood studios owned the cinemas, and showed their own films to the exclusion of others (small independents). This was deemed illegal and the production companies had to sell off a large proportion of the cinemas, thus opening up some additional competition within the market. (Companies planning to enter the market may seek a form of unique distribution, for example via direct mail or the Internet (for example, easyJet did this with airline tickets). Such an approach can provide virtually immediate differentiation of a product or service.)
Cost disadvantages independent of scale	These can be described as specific factors that a potential new entrant may find it difficult or impossible to replicate. (These can be considered as follows. Technology: a key example is the protection of a technological/chemical process through a patent. Infringement of patents, as some major companies have found to their cost, can be expensive not just financially but in terms of reputation. Location: a company might be sited near high-quality raw materials or a key market, and thus be in a position of advantage over possible new entrants.)

Table 7.14 *continued*

Major barriers	Comment
Government policy	Government protectionism of local industry: although there are free trade agreements and pressure to open up international markets further, governments can still be protective of indigenous industry. This can be in the form of tariff and/or non-tariff barriers. (See Chapter 14 on international marketing.) (Some industries are clearly protected by government policy, most especially utility industries. In some countries, the UK for example, the utility industries have been taken out of state ownership and privatized. This has slowly allowed other private or public limited companies to enter the marketplace (it has to be stated mainly other utility companies) to compete for business among the customer base. Thus the UK electricity companies can now compete against British Gas for the supply of domestic gas. What this demonstrates is that the supply of a product service can be dictated by government action.)
Retaliation	A possible new entrant will have to consider whether the key players within the market will take retaliatory action. (In 1977 Laker Airways launched a low-cost scheduled service named Skytrain™ between London Gatwick and New York. Utilizing two new DC-10 aircraft, having no reservation system and charging for the meals on board, it achieved the necessary cost reductions. These were passed on to the passengers in the form of lower fares. The major competing scheduled airlines attempted to stop the Skytrain™ service through legal action. When such actions failed they reduced their fares to those of Skytrain™. The difference, though, was that they maintained their free on-board services. By the early 1980s Skytrain™ had been forced to close. This was a clear warning to other companies who were considering such direct route competition.)

new entrant will have to match the existing supplier, or indeed gain an advantage through some form of differentiation (for example, price, design or other forms of value added).

The supplier's products are very important to the overall success of the buyer's business. This can mean that the suppliers dictate conditions to the buyers if the market is concentrated (see above). Alternatively, as Thompson (1990) suggests, if a buyer is regarded as a key customer it may receive preferential treatment, and assistance.

The supplier group's products are usually either differentiated, or it will have built up switching costs. As we stated earlier, pharmaceutical companies can use their vast resources from the success of one product to develop another. This may create one or two key products within the marketplace, thus medical practitioners may have little choice in prescribing certain medicines for particular illnesses. This is particularly the case where there are only one or two treatments, which is the case currently (2003) for HIV and AIDS. Of course, this will change in the future as patents lapse and new products are introduced onto the market.

The supplier group poses a credible threat of forward integration. Forward integration can be described as a situation where an individual supplier, or groups of suppliers, acquire the buyers of their products, thus controlling more of the overall supply chain. (Governments may introduce legislation to prevent such integration on the basis that it is anti-competitive.)

The bargaining power of buyers

Porter (1980) proposes eight conditions where buyers will exercise power, which are grouped below under the headings of concentration, customers facing fewer switching costs, and rivalry between competitors.

Concentration

First, under this condition, the buyer group is concentrated or purchases large volumes relative to sales. Here we can consider the volume and range of brands a supermarket purchases to maintain normal stock levels. Thus a supermarket chain such as the UK retailer Sainsbury's has significant bargaining power over suppliers, especially if they are producing own or private-label brands for the supermarket. However, the reverse may be true if the supermarket chain is dealing with major international brands such as Heinz, Coca-Cola and Kellogg's which hold bargaining power.

Second, the product it purchases represents a significant fraction of the buyer's costs or purchases. This means that the buyer is a major customer of the supplier, and if dissatisfied can move its purchasing power to the supplier's rivals. We need to bear in mind that all things are relative. For example, a marketing consultancy company may dedicate a large proportion of its costs to printing financial annual reports for its customers. However, this provides a relatively small fraction of the total revenue of the printing company it uses. While it may be a loss if the marketing consultancy moved its business to another printing company, it would not result in financial collapse or bankruptcy.

Third, the products it purchases from the industry are standard, undifferentiated products. Examples of these are basic chemicals and other raw materials.

Customers face few switching costs

Fourth, the company earns low profits, thus it will be active in seeking cost reductions from suppliers. This may be particularly the case when industries experience recessions or slow-downs within the economy. In order to survive in such environments, companies may actively seek cost reductions from their suppliers. This is a double-edged sword in that the supplier may also be operating at the edge of its margins, thus any further reductions could have a severe impact on the survivability of the business. Equally, the maintenance of a cash flow may gain support from the bank and stave off the creditors. This is often a difficult decision for companies to make, and can mean the life or death of the business, with an impact upon employees and suppliers alike.

Fifth, buyers pose a credible threat to backward integration (also known as vertical integration). Backward integration is where customers obtain control of their suppliers.

Sixth, the industry's products are unimportant to the quality of the buyer's products or services.

Rivalry between current competitors (also known as industry competitors)

Originally Porter called the seventh condition 'jockeying for position'; however we have adopted Baker's (2000) phrase as it clarifies Porter's meaning. Ever since more than one company produced similar, substitutable products there has been competition. Historical records often describe the level of rivalry or competition at a particular period as intense. As international and global markets open up and expand (especially powerhouse countries like China), the competitive environment will become increasingly dynamic and diverse.

Finally, Porter (1980) suggests that the intensity of this competition (and companies seeking critical advantage) is the function of several factors. These are illustrated in Table 7.15. It is important that you understand the impact this model has upon marketing activity. Thus you need to consider how companies and organizations could use Porter's five forces model as you read through this text.

Table 7.15 Intensity of competition

Intensity of competition	Comment
Structure of competition	Numerous and/or equally balanced competitors increase competitive pressures. Interestingly we have seen several high profile mergers and acquisitions in recent years, thus changing the dynamics in certain industries and increasing competitive forces. Equally, the rise of major companies/conglomerates from the developing nations (especially in the computer hardware and software industries) will create more competitiveness within those sectors. However, in many countries mergers and acquisitions require government approval before they can be completed. Governments tend to have two major concerns: the concentrated (almost monopolistic) power of a few extremely large companies, and the impact upon employment and regional investment.
Rate of growth of a particular industry	For example, slow growth tends to increase the pressure on competitors and their fight for market share. This is usually apparent during recessions where there is a downturn in the economy and customers (companies or individuals) are seeking alternatives or lower costs. (Customers may become particularly price-sensitive.)
Degree of differentiation	A lack of differentiation or switching costs tends to increase competition, especially price competition.
Capacity augmented in large increments	For example in the shipbuilding and steel industries in the UK, smaller and medium-sized companies merged or augmented their facilities. The merger of two or more companies can increase the competitive strength of the new business both domestically and internationally. The UK shipbuilding and steel industries found themselves in the midst of a highly competitive global marketplace. Thus merging or augmentation of resources was necessary (among other activities) in order to compete on a global stage. In many ways the UK companies failed to grasp the increased competitiveness of their global market early enough. This partly explains the dramatic shrinkage of these industries.
Strategic objectives	Companies may face increased competition as they attempt to build their product portfolios rather than purely maintain their existing portfolios.
High exit barriers	Competition tends to be high when the cost of exiting an industry is also high. The high cost may be due to lack of diversification opportunities within other industries/sectors or the high cost of closing down plants (for example, high staff redundancy and relocation costs, and reduction in revenues over the short to medium term).

Criticisms of Porter's five forces model

Porter's model is often viewed as a useful early step in analysing the environment. However, it is not without its critics. Lynch (2000) suggests that there are six main criticisms of the five forces model. These are detailed in Table 7.16.

Competitive advantage: generic strategies

Marketing departments must understand the nature of competition within their industry and the strategies that can be employed to gain an advantage over rivals. Once again, we must reflect upon the issue of gaining competitive advantage. It is one thing gaining that advantage, it is very much another holding on

Table 7.16 Criticisms of the five forces model

Criticism	Comment
Static	It suggests that this analytical framework is static whereas the actual competitive environment is dynamic and turbulent.
The organization's interests come first	It assumes that the organization's own interests come first. This is unlikely to be the case with respect to non-government organizations, charities and government departments, for instance.
Buyers are the same as any other aspect of the micro environment	Lynch (2000) quotes Aaker, Baker and Harvey-Jones as disagreeing fundamentally with this point. They argue that the customer or buyer is more important than any other aspect of the micro environment. While the customer is a focal point, all aspects of the micro environment must be considered. However, what counts is the degree to which all these factors are considered. Moreover, the degree of consideration will vary from business to business and industry to industry.
The environment is a threat to the organization	The model seems to suggest that the starting point is that the environment is a threat to the organization, leading to the conclusion that both buyers and suppliers are threats that need to be handled judiciously. However, increasingly companies seek closer cooperation with their suppliers. This action cannot be successful if the supplier is considered as a threat. Equally, organizations are increasingly seeking a partnership with their customers in order to develop loyalty and advocacy (consider viral marketing, for example). This cannot be successful if the customer is considered a threat.
Human resources and strategy	Lynch (2000) suggests that the strategic analysis ignores the human resource aspect of strategy. For example, it does not consider the country's culture, nor management skills. For a marketing strategy to be successful it must carefully consider, analyse and integrate the people element (see Chapter 12).
Predictive rather than emergent	Once the analysis is complete, it is suggested that the organization can formulate a strategy. This is a predictive approach rather than an emergent approach. An emergent approach suggests that elements are developed as the strategy proceeds, so they can be both proactive and reactive as the environment changes.

to it. Thus it must be remembered that the aim is to achieve sustained competitive advantage.

Porter (1985) suggests that there are three fundamental ways in which a company or organization can achieve sustainable competitive advantage. These are depicted in Table 7.17.

Cost leadership strategy

Cost leadership should not be confused with 'price leadership': because the organization has the lowest cost does not mean that it should necessarily charge the lowest price. As Porter (1985) states:

> a firm sets out to become the low-cost producer in the industry... a low-cost producer must find and exploit all sources at cost advantage. Low-cost producers typically sell a standard, or no-frills, product and place considerable emphasis on reaping scale or absolute cost advantages from all sources.... If a firm can achieve and sustain overall cost leadership, then it will be above an average performer in its industry provided it can command prices at or near the industry average.

Table 7.17   Competitive scope and advantage

Competitive scope	Competitive advantage	
	Lower cost	Differentiation
Broad target	1. Cost leadership	2. Differentiation
Narrow target	3A. Cost focus	3B. Differentiation focus

Source: Porter (1985) © Michael Porter (1985)

Cost leadership strategies should be used to improve profitability and enhance the offering by building such things as brand equity. The cost advantage will allow the organization greater flexibility in its pricing strategies. However, as the cost leadership advantage will usually have been obtained through investment and experience, the extra revenues should be used to develop both of these further and develop new products. This contributes to building the marketing assets of the organization.

Cost leadership can provide a suitable defence against each of Porter's five competitive forces (Moore, 2001):

▪ **Competitors:** by enabling the organization to remain profitable when its rivals have eliminated their margins through price competition.

▪ **Buyers:** here buyers seek to reduce prices to match the level of their most efficient supplier.

▪ **Suppliers:** providing more flexibility to cope with input cost increases from suppliers.

▪ **New entrants:** raising entry barriers of an economy of scale or cost advantage nature.

▪ **Substitutes:** placing the organization in a favourable position relative to its competitors with regard to substitution.

However Moore (2001) suggests that a cost leadership strategy has inherent risks. These include:

▪ Changes in technology that render past investment or experience obsolete. (This is also a criticism of the PIMS model.)

▪ Experience inexpensively gained by industry entrants or 'me-too' competitors through imitation or investment in state of the art facilities. They may be able to gain a competitive edge, or at least disturb the market leader's position.

▪ Emphasizing cost reduction to the point where product or marketing changes are not undertaken can result in slippage within the market. Once a competitor gains ground, it may be difficult to maintain either a leadership or a competitive position.

▪ Cost increases which reduce price advantages necessary to combat a competitor's differential advantage. Thus the organization no longer holds a cost advantage over its competitors.

Differentiation strategy

Here Porter (1985) suggests that a company seeks:

> to be unique in its industry along some dimensions that are widely valued by buyers.... It is rewarded for its uniqueness with a premium price.... A firm that can achieve and sustain differentiation will be an above average performer in its industry if its price premium exceeds the extra costs incurred in being unique.... The logic of the differentiation strategy requires that a firm chooses attributes in which to differentiate itself that are different from its rivals.

Differentiation should be used to *add value* to the products and services being offered by making them desirably different to those offered by the competitors. The differentiation can be real or perceived, but it must be stated clearly.

Branding is often used to establish differentiation within the market, and brand image can form a strong distinguishing feature for a product which will make it more desirable to potential customers. Additional features, provided they can be shown to give additional benefits, are also a good way to differentiate a product or service. However a competitor may create its own version of the product, especially if it sees the pioneering company increasing sales or market share.

Moore (2001) suggests that differentiation provides a mechanism for the organization to use Porter's five forces model, however in a different means to cost leadership:

▊ **Competitors:** it insulates the organization from rivalry by using brand loyalty to lower the customer's price sensitivity.

▊ **Barriers:** the existence of brand loyalty and the need for competitors to overcome uniqueness provide entry barriers.

▊ **Suppliers:** it yields higher margins with which to offset supplier power.

▊ **Buyers:** they are less price-sensitive because they have no comparable alternatives.

▊ **Substitutes:** having achieved customer loyalty, an organization is often better positioned than its competitors within the market.

Focus strategy

As Porter (1985) states, this type of strategy is based upon 'the choice of a narrow competitive scope within an industry'. In other words it is unlike cost leadership and differentiation in that it is not an industry-wide strategy. Porter continues, 'The focuser selects a segment or groups of segments in the industry and tailors its strategy to serving them to the exclusion of others.' There are two sub-sets

here: first, cost focus, 'where a company seeks a cost advantage within the target segment', and second, differentiation focus, 'where a company seeks differentiation in its target segment'.

Again this involves adding value to the product or service, but accomplishing this by targeting the product or service carefully at a specific segment or market type. It is important that the chosen segment can clearly identify with the product benefits being promoted. The focus may be because the product is only applicable to one market. This strategy can be very useful for smaller businesses, allowing them to make the most of their marketing-based assets. However a very close watch on the marketplace is needed to ensure that the organization adapts to any changes in the benefits sought by the chosen market segment(s).

However, as Moore (2001) concludes there are inherent risks with a focus strategy:

▊ The cost differential between the broad-range competitors and the focused organizations widens to eliminate the cost advantages of serving a narrow target (possible niche) market, or to offset the differentiation achieved by focus.

▊ The difference in desired products or services between the strategic target and the market as a whole.

▊ Competitors develop sub-markets within the strategic market, and then out-focus the focuser.

'Stuck in the middle'

Porter (1985) maintains that in order to obtain long-term success a company must be clear about its generic strategy. It is suggested that if a company does not make a choice between the three strategies above, it will be caught somewhere in the middle. As a result its overall performance may be affected.

Marketing insight: Generic competitive strategies

Here we outline under the three strategies examples of products and companies we believe have chosen a particular strategy.

Cost leadership

Throughout the text we refer to easyJet, a highly successful, UK-based low-cost airline (see, for example, Chapter 4). Several low-cost airlines entered the UK market in the 1990s, with the view of first, increasing overall airline passenger numbers, and second, taking market share from the leading airline groups. It proved to be a highly competitive marketplace, and there have been failures en route. easyJet has aggressively marketed itself as a low-cost no-frills airline, and to date this has proved a successful strategy.

Differentiated strategy

Again from the travel industry we can consider two very different products and companies. Royal Caribbean's *Voyager of the Seas* is currently one of the world's largest passenger ships with the capacity for 3,800 passengers. Launched in 1999, it displays several unique features for a cruise ship, including a four-storey shopping mall that is virtually the length of the backbone of the ship, and the largest slot-machine in the world.

The differentiation here is the sheer size and range of unique features. Of course, it may not remain the largest passenger ship afloat. Other companies are seeking to gain this crown. However, *Voyager of the Seas* should still remain a differentiated product because of its unique onboard facilities.

Staying with the travel business, consider the UK-based company Saga Holidays. This company's *raison d'être* is to cater for the needs of people aged over 50. Its scope has broadened beyond holidays to encompass insurance (home, vehicle and health), a magazine and gardening products. It realized early on that people over 50 increasingly have high spending levels and enjoy their forthcoming or current retirement.

Yet another example of differentiation strategy is food. For many years tinned tuna has been available within supermarkets. Originally it was contained in brine, then vegetable oil, then soya oil (as this was considered the most healthy in terms of preventing or reducing heart disease). Heinz then developed Heinz tuna with additional ingredients such as mayonnaise and garlic. These by their very nature became ready meals, thus differentiating themselves from the normal tins of plain tuna.

Focus strategy

Now consider other cruise lines that have developed other forms of focus differentiation. Several cruise lines focus on the luxury end of the cruise market, for example SilverSeas, which tends to have a maximum of 300 passengers per ship. Compare that with Hebridean Island Cruises, a UK-based company that focuses on small and luxurious cruises. Its Italian-built British flagged and maintained *Hebridean Spirit* is like no other international cruise ship: with just 50 cabins there are only between 50 and 70 passengers. The style of the ship is very much 'traditional country house style of furnishings'. The overall aim is the luxury of a private yacht. As the company states, 'service to the customer is our *raison d'être*'. Again the company is seeking to differentiate itself from the rest of the cruise ship industry. Equally we can compare luxury country hotels that have a limited number of guests with the luxury city hotels that have high numbers of rooms and suites at equally high prices.

Porter's value chain model

Value has often been underestimated as an important contributor to gaining competitive advantage. The value chain can be described as a sequence where value is added to the product and/or service at each step of the chain. The basic principle underlying the value chain is that the organization should examine its cost and performance (in the widest sense) at each stage in order to seek improvements that benefit the customer. By effectively analysing the value added at each stage of activity, an organization can be better informed as to its potential/current competitive advantage (or not, as the case may be).

Competitive advantage is an advantage that a company has gained over a key competitor(s). This advantage may be gained by offering the customer higher value through lower costs, improved product features or service benefits, or better servicing and distribution. However, as Thompson (1990) states, Ohmae argues that it is vital to remember that competitive advantage must be sought for one purpose: to serve the customer's real needs. Although a company or organization will be seeking to be highly competitive against its rivals, again we see a customer focus. Here you may want to reflect back on the marketing concept/relationship marketing.

A company can gain such advantage by analysing the value that can be added through skills, core competences and resources.

Skills

As Day and Wensley (1983) state, 'superior' skills are the distinctive capabilities of the organization's key employees that separate them from the competitor's employees. Superior skills mean that organizational functions are performed more effectively to the benefit of the employees, the organization and crucially the customer. Everyone within the organization has a 'marketing' role. Indeed, everyone has a 'value added' role that can be communicated through his or her individual and group skill sets. Of course, this highlights the importance of effective, efficient and relevant training of employees.

Quality of resources

Here we can define the quality of resources as those resources that enable skills to be demonstrated within the marketplace, thus potentially gaining a sustained competitive advantage. These resources can include the following:

- research and development;
- scale and type of production facilities;
- financial resources;
- brand equity (the value of the individual brands);
- distribution coverage (the number of retailers who stock and sell the product);
- investment in marketing communications, for the advertising, sales promotion and size of sales force within the marketplace.

Core competencies

This is the proficiency of an organization in a critical functional activity or a particular business specialization. It is a combination of both the skills component and quality of resources that leads, for example, to a technical innovation and development. This then provides the organization with a product and/or service which in turn provides it with a competitive advantage.

Consider, for example, the British Aerospace (BAe) development team at Filton in England. They have designed new technology to construct the special extra-long wing that will form the superjumbo Airbus A380 aircraft. This technology 'welds' two sections together by melting the materials so that the molecular structures intertwine, thus providing strength beyond the normal welding of materials.

Porter (1985) suggests that an examination of the value chain provides an ideal framework for analysing the activities of a business. As Thompson (1990) suggests, it is useful for assessing the ability of the various functions (for example, marketing) to contribute towards competitive advantages, and enables the allocation or distribution of costs incurred in operating the business to be evaluated.

Porter (1985) argues that in order to achieve (or attempt to achieve) a competitive edge, the company or organization must be considered as part of a wider system or environment. He suggests the following framework:

suppliers → the company → distributors → customers

Porter's value chain is illustrated in Figure 7.15.

Porter (1985) suggests that there are five primary activities which represent the activities of physically creating the product or service, then transferring it to the customer with the support of appropriate after sales service. These primary activities are:

- **Inbound logistics.** These activities involve receiving, storing and distributing inputs (for example, raw materials and packaged goods, such as tinned food) internally. They include warehousing, materials handling, stock control and internal transportation systems from, for example, the warehouse to the production/assembly floor.

- **Operations.** These activities transform the raw materials or other inputs into a finished product or service. This will include machining, assembly and manufacturing systems.

- **Outbound logistics.** These activities relate to the physical collection and distribution of the finished products or services to customers. For tangible products this also involves warehousing, material handling and transport. In the case of intangibles (services) it may mean making arrangements for bringing the customers to the services (Johnson and Scholes, 1999). An example is a bus hired by a supporter's club to take its members to a football or cricket match.

- **Marketing and sales.** These are the various activities by which potential or actual buyers are made aware of the product or service, and how to obtain it. This covers

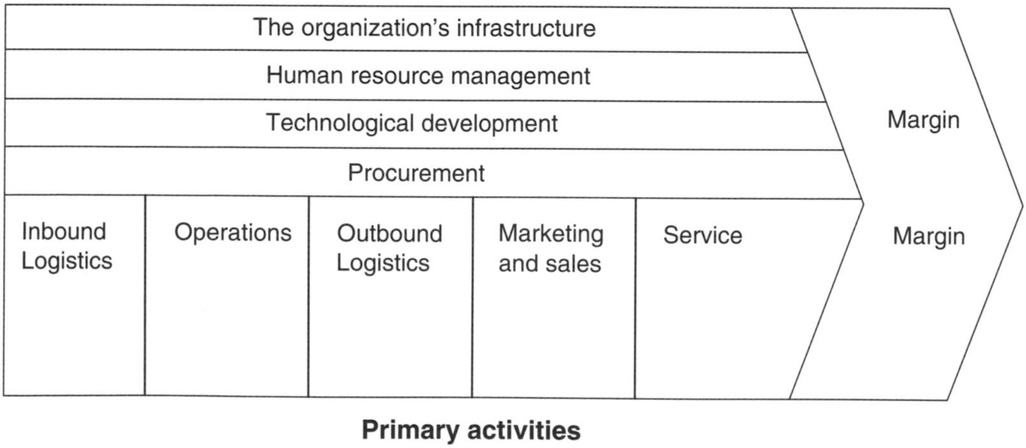

Primary activities

Source: Porter (1985) © Michael Porter (1985)

Figure 7.15   Porter's generic value chain

the full range of the marketing mix: product/service, pricing, promotions, placement (distribution channels), physical evidence, processes and people (for instance, customer service or sales staff).

■ **Service.** This activity provides the necessary service assistance to support the product or service. This includes installation, repair, training the customer on how to use the product (for example, computer software packages or new machinery on a manufacturing line), warranties/guarantees and after sales customer care.

These five primary activities are linked to four support activities which, as you can see, are drawn laterally across the top of the primary activities. This is because they can impact upon one or more of the primary activities at any given time. The four support activities are:

■ **The organization's infrastructure.** This includes the overall structure of the organization, corporate planning, financial controls, management abilities and the quality control mechanisms. These and other activities are crucially important to an organization's strategic capabilities across the full range of primary activities.

■ **Human resource management.** This relates to all activities relating to recruitment, training, developing and rewarding people throughout the organization. It is vital to remember that people are vital to the success of any business enterprise, no matter how small or large. As with the organization's infrastructure this impacts on all primary activities.

■ **Technology development.** Technology, especially in today's rapidly changing global environment, encapsulates a multitude of areas and thus must be considered in the broadest terms. Technology development may relate to:

– Product: research and development to create or enhance a product. This may include improved packaging, for example the Tetrapack™ which allows for the easy opening of containers, thus preventing spillage.
– Processes: this is technology that enhances a particular process. This can cover a wide range of processes: improved methods of smelting steel to remove damaging impurities, the spray painting of vehicles on an assembly line by computer-controlled robotic arms rather than by people, barcode readers to improve the process flow of components or finished products (for example, in a supermarket or department store), logistics movements: the satellite tracking of products being shipped globally and the ordering of products via the Internet (in both business-to-consumer and business-to-business environments).

■ **Procurement.** This is the acquisition or purchasing of any components that will be used within the primary activities. In many companies and organizations there are managers or even large departments responsible for the procurement of components. This is not only to obtain the right components at the right time and in the right quantity, but also to ensure quality and financial control.

The point of the value chain is for organizations to consider where they can add value to the product or service that they are delivering. This is an important concept not only in corporate strategy, but also in marketing strategy.

The balanced scorecard

In 1992 Kaplan and Norton introduced the balanced scorecard model, which is a set of measures that complement financial information with operational measures on customer satisfaction, internal processes and the organization's innovation and improvement activities. It is these operational measures that are the drivers of future financial performance. Kaplan and Norton (1992, 1996a, 1996b) believe that as companies transform themselves for international and global competition that is based upon information, the company's ability to exploit intangible assets will become more decisive than its ability to invest in and manage physical assets. An example of this is Internet-based companies selling comparable online products and services.

The balanced scorecard provides the answers to four key questions (Kaplan and Norton, 1992):

▊ How do customers view the company? (Customer perspective)

▊ What must the company excel at? (Internal perspective)

▊ Can the company continue to improve and create value? (Innovation and learning perspective)

▊ How do the shareholders perceive the company? (Financial perspective)

Figure 7.16 illustrates the link between these four question areas, and positioned in the centre is strategy and vision.

Kaplan and Norton (1992) suggest that the balanced scorecard forces companies to focus upon a core of critical issues and measures. These are:

▊ A single management report bringing together disparate elements of a company's competitive agenda: customer orientation, reducing response times, improving quality, reducing new product launch periods and managing long time frames.

▊ Guards against sub-optimization. There is always a risk that improvements within one operational area are achieved at the expense of another. As Kaplan and Norton (1992) state, companies can reduce the

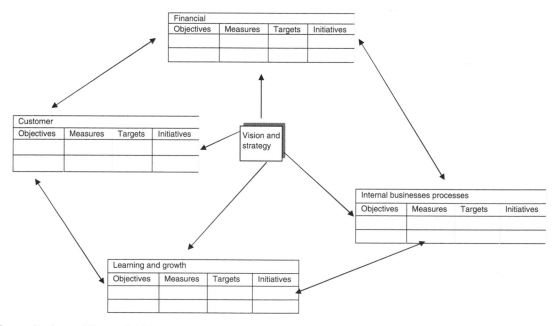

Source: Kaplan and Norton (1992)

Figure 7.16   The balanced scorecard

time frame between product development and launch in two different ways:

1. by improving the management of new product introductions. Expenditure on setup can be reduced either by cutting setup times, or by increasing batch sizes.

2. by releasing to market only products that are incrementally different from existing products. Production output and yields can rise here but the increases may be due to shifts in the product mix. The shift is to more standard easy-to-produce lower margin products.

Kaplan and Norton (1992) suggest that the four perspectives (see below) of the scorecard permit a balance between:

▌ short and long-term objectives;

▌ desired outcomes and the performance drivers of these outcomes;

▌ hard objective measures and softer more subjective measures.

Customer perspectives

The focus here is to identify the customer and market segments in which the organization will compete. It also measures the organization's performance within these targeted segments. The organization seeks to measure the outcomes from the analysis of customer satisfaction, customer retention, new customer acquisition, customer profitability and market share.

Financial perspectives

Kaplan and Norton (1992) identify three stages:

Rapid growth

These are companies in the early stages of their life cycle. They have to make considerable investment to develop products/services and business infrastructure. Financial objectives focus on sales growth, and this can be achieved through:

▌ increased sales to existing customers (for example, more usage);

▌ sales in new market segments or territories;

▌ sales to new customers;

▌ sales from the introduction of new products or services into the market;

▌ establishing or reorganizing marketing, sales and/or distribution channels (growth through improving efficiencies).

Sustain

The majority of companies probably occupy this position. They obtain investment and reinvest in the business. Generally these companies are expected to:

▌ earn returns on invested capital;

▌ maintain or develop their market share year on year;

▌ increase the wealth of the business.

Financial objectives usually focus on a mixture of traditional and new financial instruments, such as:

▌ return on capital employed;

▌ operating income and gross margins;

▌ economic value added;

▌ shareholder value.

Harvest

Here the company has achieved maturity within the life cycle. There is no longer a need for significant investment, only that necessary to manage and maintain facilities and capabilities. The financial objectives here focus on cash flow as there will be little or no investment.

In their research Kaplan and Norton (1992) concluded that companies tended to use three financial 'themes' to achieve their business strategies:

▌ **Revenue growth and mix:** developing products and services, reaching new customers and markets, modifying the marketing mix to provide higher value-added capabilities.

▌ **Cost reduction/productivity improvements:** reducing direct and indirect costs, and the sharing of resources to gain overall improvements.

▌ **Asset utilization/investment strategy:** the most effective use of assets through reducing working and physical capital levels.

Internal business processes

The company must identify the critical internal business processes that enable it to deliver on the value propositions of customers within the targeted market segments, and satisfy shareholder expectations of solid financial returns on their investment. It is within the internal business processes that Kaplan and Norton (1992) suggest there are two fundamental differences between the traditional and scorecard approaches to performance measurement. In traditional approaches the emphasis is on monitoring and improving existing business processes. In contrast the Scorecard approach usually identifies new processes in which the company must excel to meet both customer and financial objectives (Kaplan and Norton, 1992). Thus the issues most critical to the company's strategic success are highlighted.

The second difference is that the scorecard incorporates innovation processes into the internal business process perspective. By using traditional performance measures companies tend to focus on improving and controlling existing operations (products and services).

However, companies may need to create entirely new products and services to meet the emerging needs of both current and future customers. As Kaplan and Norton (1992) suggest, the innovation process may be a more powerful driver of financial performance in the longer term than the current short-term operating cycle. However, companies need to analyse both the current and future potential. The scorecard provides measures that allow both the short and longer-term perspectives to be analysed.

Learning and growth perspective

This concentrates on identifying the infrastructure and capabilities that the company must have to compete and develop long-term growth. The focus here is on people and their skill levels, management and marketing information systems, and organizational procedures.

Figure 7.17 illustrates how an entire chain of cause and effect relationships can be established as a vertical vector through the four scorecard perspectives (Kaplan and Norton, 1992).

Competitive market positioning strategies

Organizations seek to adopt certain market positions. Kotler (2000) identified four key descriptors to position organizations within competitive marketplaces. In Table 7.18 we have identified the key descriptors. As we shall see later, each of these strategies can be used to secure and defend a market position, or to make a challenge in an attempt to gain market share and thus potential leadership. Kotler's key descriptors are:

▌ market leadership;

▌ market challengers;

▌ market followers;

▌ market niches.

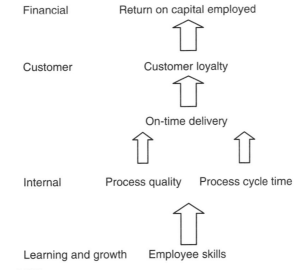

Source: Kaplan and Norton (1992)

Figure 7.17 Cause and effect relationships

These are diagrammatically represented in Figure 7.18 and described in Table 7.18.

Of course Kotler's (2000) descriptors are not the only method of identifying competitive market positions. Miles and Snow (1978) suggest that organizations can adopt positions based upon their planned product–market development. They called these positions Defenders, Prospectors, Analysers or Reactors. Although this model was developed in the late 1970s, Adcock (2000) and others believe the categories are still valid because they are useful when considering the most appropriate activities an organization can adopt,

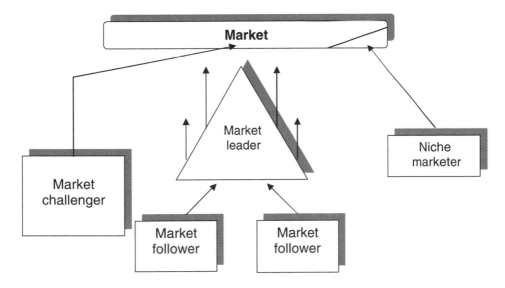

Figure 7.18 Potential market positions

Table 7.18 Potential market positions

Market position	Description
Leaders	These are organizations that are the leaders within all or some of their markets. They maintain their positions by taking decisive action within viable markets, exiting markets that are no longer suitable and pursing opportunities that will enhance their position.
Challengers	These are organizations that engage battle with the market leaders to increase their own market share. They may deploy a range of tactics including introducing new innovations, superior customer service, lower prices, better distribution networks, payment schemes and effective branding/promotions. An example is easyJet, the low-cost European airline. Since its formation in the early 1990s easyJet has gained market share from other low-cost carriers as well as the major airlines (the market leaders). If a challenger successfully increases its market share at the expense of the market leader, it could eventually become the new leader. It in turn will face competitive pressures from new, as well as existing, challengers.
Followers	These are organizations that seek to maintain their profitable market share. They will not attack either the market leaders or challengers. However they will usually be able to develop new products and innovative pricing, promotions and distribution without facing retaliation from the market leaders and challengers.
Niche	These are organizations that dominate a smaller market segment or niche. Market leaders and challengers may have overlooked the potential within this market segment, or consider it too specialist a market for them to enter. The market nichers focus on being the best within that specific market segment.

depending upon both its and environmental circumstances. Of course these positions should not be considered static. Companies can and do move from one position to another. In Table 7.19 we have detailed Miles and Snow's topologies.

Prospectors can be considered as pioneering organizations that actively seek out new opportunities within a diversified market. These can be new products or services, or new marketplaces. However, once they have developed a position they tend to move on to the next opportunity. The potential weakness here is that they may not have had the opportunity to build a very strong brand presence and position. While they may be profitable and successful, their position can come under attack from competitors.

Compare prospectors with defenders. Defenders aim to create and maintain a secure market position. They develop strategies that will protect their business and market position by focusing on building very strong brands and developing value-added relationships with their customers. While they may not be innovators in the sense of prospectors, they will concentrate on operational efficiency and marketing as a means of raising barriers to entry for potential new players within the market.

Analysers tend to span both prospector and defender positions. Such organizations develop strong brand positions (the defenders) while also seeking out new opportunities (prospectors). However, they tend to develop product–market opportunities within sectors they are already involved in, or areas with which they have some familiarity. As they are not pioneers they will seek to minimize the overall risk. Analysers often

Table 7.19 Miles and Snow's topologies

Descriptor	Comment
Defenders	These are organizations that have a narrow product–market domain. These organizations tend to be expert in particular fields and do not seek opportunities outside this domain. As a result such organizations tend not to make radical changes to their technologies, structures or operations. Instead they focus their energies on continually improving efficiencies within their existing operations.
Prospectors	These are organizations that continually search for new market opportunities. They can also be considered as first movers within the market. As part of this search they will experiment with responses to emerging environmental trends. Miles and Snow suggest that these organizations are often the creators or drivers of change. They often create uncertainty within the marketplace, forcing their competitors to respond. However, as these organizations have a strong focus on product and market innovation there is a tendency for them to be inefficient.
Analysers	These are organizations that operate within two types of product–market domain. One is stable (to a greater or lesser degree), the other changing or volatile. In the stable domain, the organization operates within a routine structured format. In the more volatile domain, the organization closely observes its competitors. If it sees a competitor developing or launching a new product or service that would suit its needs it will seek to create a version of it rapidly.
Reactors	These are organizations that perceive changes within their often turbulent environments. However, they are unable to respond to the turbulence effectively. This is usually because the organization lacks a consistent strategy–structure relationship that allows it to adjust prior to being forced to do so.

Adapted from Miles and Snow (1978) and Adcock (2000)

succeed by providing improvements to products or services in the form of higher value (including features and benefits), or lower costs than the pioneers (prospectors).

Many Japanese companies, such as Sony and Panasonic, can be considered early analysers. During the 1970s and 1980s they were able to improve household electronic products significantly and develop a market position. Today they are more prospectors, as they are pioneers in several fields of electronics and have established a relatively strong international position.

The problem for organizations that are reactors is that they often (though not always) witness changes within the market, but they only react when forced to. Then it may be too late to save the organization. Reactors are companies that have lost the competitive edge and are, for whatever reason, unable to develop and pursue effective and efficient competitive strategies. During the 1970s and 1980s many UK car companies became reactors: they lost the ability to be competitive. The result was shrinking market share, acquisition and closure.

As we have already seen, organizations need to analyse how they will manoeuvre within the marketplace to gain or defend a position. Here strategy returns to its origin within warfare. Organizations can adopt several positions to defend or outposition their competitors. As often on the battlefield these positions are mobile, not static. Below we consider the different strategies and tactics that organizations can implement.

Market leader strategies

Kotler (2000) suggests that market leaders must practise three different overall strategies to retain leadership:

Increase total market demand

This can be achieved by:

▌ **Introducing new users to the product or service.** These can be categorized into three groups. First there are people who have chosen to use one product (brand A) rather than another (brand B). Their choice may be based on price or the range of features and benefits available. Here the organization adopts a market penetration approach to persuade buyers to switch brands (from A to B). Second, there are buyers who have never used the product and may not be aware of its features and benefits. Here the organization will seek to develop a new market segment. Finally, there may be markets in other regions or indeed countries. Here the organization is seeking a geographic expansion approach.

▌ **Increasing overall usage.** This means persuading the customer to use the product or service more often. In the consumer market, for instance, hair shampoo manufacturers may suggest to 'apply generously to wet hair, lather, rinse and repeat'. Equally, they may suggest that users 'shampoo two to three times per week for the best results'. Additionally, they usually suggest using conditioner after shampooing. This also increases the usage of the conditioner as it links it to each time the consumer uses that brand of shampoo. Within the B2B environment organizations such as marketing and management consultancies may develop additional projects with their clients, thus increasing their overall usage.

▌ **Developing new uses for the product.** Here organizations use marketing communications to promote increased usage of the product. For example, in the UK Kellogg's promoted several of its cereal brands as snack foods that can be eaten at any time of the day or night. No longer were they purely breakfast foods. Developed at Du Pont in 1937, Nylon® was the world's first synthetic material. First it was used for bristles in toothbrushes, then famously for women's stockings, then in parachutes. It has subsequently been used for a range of products including shirts, carpeting and car tyres.

Protect its current market share from competitive attack

The organization seeks to defend its position actively from any competitive attack. It can adopt a mix of six strategies to achieve this strategic objective.

Position defence

The organization seeks to reinforce its position though 'fortification'. For example, it could expand into a related sector to increase its overall strength within the market. Equally an organization could introduce new products that render the existing ones obsolete. This can leave competitors struggling to maintain their position, let alone attack the market leader. For instance, Gillette introduced a new range of innovations including the bonded blade, the optimum shaving angle, the double-sided razor and the disposable razor. These, and others, have helped Gillette over the years to defend its overall market position successfully.

The idea is to present a defence that will intimidate a potential challenger. (See Figure 7.19.)

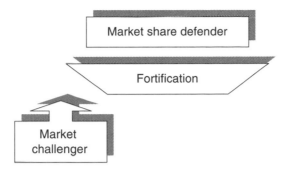

Figure 7.19 Position defence

Pre-emptive defence

The organization creates a market awareness or 'threat' which informs any potential challenger seeking to attack a market sector that it will face a pre-emptive strike. For example, powerful companies such as Procter & Gamble can launch major marketing communications campaigns to 'defend' a brand's market position if it comes under threat (even though not attacked) from a competitor. (See Figure 7.20).

Flanking attacks

The organization establishes subsidiaries or 'outposts' that can protect the main market from attack. A competitor may challenge the subsidiary, allowing the organization to use marketing resources to protect the subsidiary and the organization's overall market position. (See Figure 7.21.)

Counteroffensive defence

This is an organization's response to a real attack rather than a perceived threat. As we saw earlier Xerox launched an attack on IBM's mid-range computer market. IBM retaliated by entering the photocopier market. This meant that Xerox had to battle on two market fronts. Eventually Xerox withdrew, selling its computer business to Honeywell. IBM had successfully defended its market position.

James (1985) cites the example of the pen company BIC and wet-shave company Gillette within the US market. BIC sought to create a volume market for disposable razors. Gillette already had a well-developed distribution system, so it counterattacked by focusing its resources on marketing communications to out-promote BIC. However, BIC was relatively new to the market, so it had to both promote the product and develop efficient

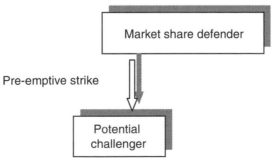

Figure 7.20 Pre-emptive defence

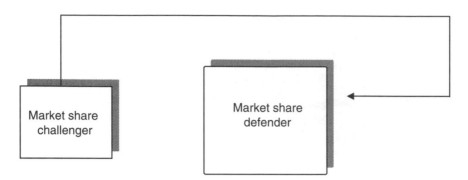

Figure 7.21   Flanking attacks

and effective distribution channels. Thus BIC was fighting on two fronts, and this demanded a level of resourcing it could not supply (James, 1985). The result was Gillette maintained its market position. (See Figure 7.22.)

Mobile defence

The market leader seeks to expand into new territories that not only increase its business opportunities but also serve as new centres for both defence and offensive strategies. Since the 1980s numerous companies have expanded to develop a strong international and global presence. While such expansion can reap enormous financial benefits, it can also be an inherent weakness to the business. If the organization faces dynamic international or regional competition it may have to defend itself across several territories simultaneously.

Even for cash-rich companies the risks may be too great, and they may have to contract to maintain their position within the market. It can be argued that British Airways used mobile defence strategies by increasing the number of European and International routes it flew. In the late 1990s and early 21st century the low-cost European airline easyJet significantly increased the number of routes it flew. Its acquisition of rival Go aided its route expansion and thus its market position. Once acquired, the Go brand was phased out and easyJet became Europe's largest low-cost airline. Here the market share defender can use either defensive or offensive strategies to protect its market share. (See Figure 7.23.)

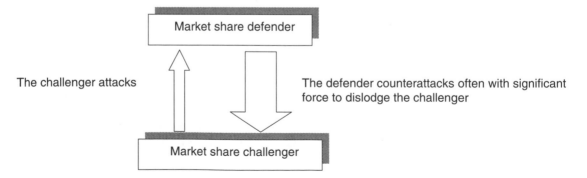

Figure 7.22   Counteroffensive defence

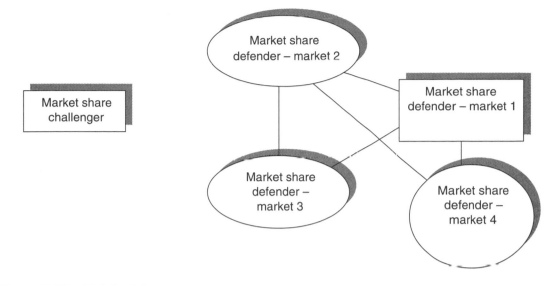

Figure 7.23   Mobile defence

Contraction defence (strategic withdrawal)

Organizations that overextend themselves, spreading their products and businesses too thin, may face a competitive onslaught. As Eckles (1990) suggests, 'strategically, the leader has to regroup and concentrate its forces at decisive points to maintain victory, otherwise the leader becomes vulnerable and could fall of its own weight, high costs and mismanagement'. An example of contraction defence is British Airways, which has had to rethink its activities radically prior to and since 11 September 2001. The resulting actions have been either the closure or reduced frequency of some routes, staff redundancies, closure of unprofitable operations, fare reductions on certain sectors and a renewed marketing communications effort. Many other airlines have since followed this approach in order to survive within the marketplace. (See Figure 7.24.)

Expand market share

The organization seeks to increase its overall market share, which can in turn lead to increased profitability, though not always.

Market challenger strategies

Market challengers can use the following strategies to attack the market leader or a market segment.

Frontal attack

This is a direct attack on the market leader's position. The winner from such a battle will be the company that has the resources, tenacity and marketing skill to overwhelm the entrenched market leader.

For many years Boeing, Lockheed and McDonnell-Douglas dominated the aircraft industry. Then in 1970 Airbus (then a European consortium) was formed, and four years later its first aircraft, the A300, went into service. The A300 was a twin-engined jet capable of carrying 220 passengers at a range of up to 1,668 km. By using new technologies Airbus was able to provide an aircraft with a lower noise profile, significant fuel efficiency and thus lower operating costs than its principal competitors (the market leaders). It was able to leverage launch orders through its European partners. The multi-government

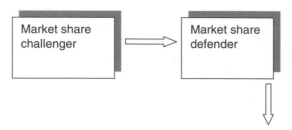

The Defender withdraws from part of the market to focus upon core business and/or develop new business areas.

Figure 7.24 Contraction defence

financing available at the time allowed Airbus to use easy credit terms and penetration pricing to enter the world market for wide-bodied aircraft.

In 1978 Airbus launched the next development in its A300 family, the A310. Further technical improvements increased its economic performance. The company had increased its market share from some 3 per cent in 1976 to 33 per cent in 1981, and by mid-1983 they had secured over 350 orders for the A300 and the A310 from 46 airlines (Eckles, 1990). By March 2003 the total orders of the A300 and A310 had reached 849, with 775 deliveries to 86 airlines. The A300 and A310 allowed Airbus to build both its resources and reputation to challenge the major players within the marketplace. Since the 1980s Airbus has increased its family of aircraft to include the A320, A330, A340 and the forthcoming A380 (superjumbo). Overall by March 2003, Airbus's order book totalled 4,668 aircraft, with 3,192 delivered to a customer base of 183 airlines*.

Airbus Industries' frontal attack successfully positioned them within the international aircraft market and virtually excluded rivals from market segments in Africa, Asia and the Middle East. (See Figure 7.25.)

Flanking attack

This is where a challenger will 'go around' the market leader's frontal defences to attack the point of weakness. Eckles (1990) suggests that a challenger identifying an unmet market need caused when markets shift, creating market gaps in the defender's business/marketing strategy, can achieve success. Japanese car manufacturers were able to use successful flanking movements to introduce small cars into the US marketplace, later followed by the Europeans. The US manufacturers had failed to see an increasing demand for smaller, more fuel-efficient (thus environmentally friendly) vehicles. This became increasingly so in the 1970s and 1980s when the OPEC nations increased the dollar price of a barrel of oil. Many US residents perceived that fuel would become excessively expensive, hence the need for improved performance

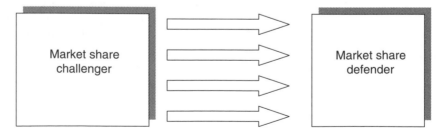

Figure 7.25 Frontal attack

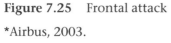
*Airbus, 2003.

efficiencies. The Japanese and European car manufacturers saw the market opportunities, while the majority of American manufacturers did not. (See Figure 7.26.)

Encirclement strategies

This is where a challenger surrounds a brand or company and attacks it at several points, capturing large sections of the market. Simultaneously the challenger is able to prevent the leader from reinforcing its position, thus avoiding the possibility of a counteroffensive move. It is critical that the challenger can deploy resources efficiently and effectively to overwhelm the market leader. If the challenger does not have the element of surprise and sufficient resources to consolidate its position within the market, the

market leader will counterattack often with overwhelming force. The challenger may thus be pushed further back, if not totally out of the market. (See Figure 7.27.)

Bypass attack strategy

This is an 'indirect' attack strategy, as the challenger seeks new markets rather than attacking the market leader directly. A tactic within a bypass strategy is dual marketing, where the company markets its product to both business and consumer markets. For example, Redken hair care products were originally only available though exclusive salons. However, the manufacturers saw a market opportunity to sell directly to consumers through department stores (Eckles, 1990). (See Figure 7.28.)

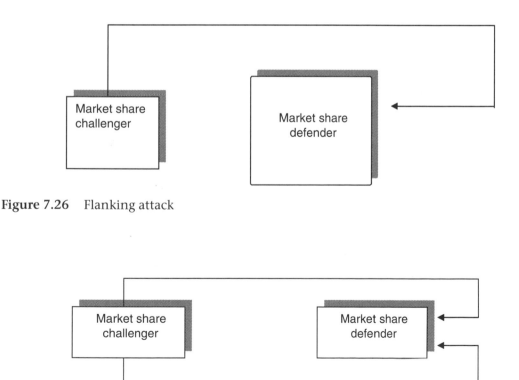

Figure 7.26 Flanking attack

Figure 7.27 Encirclement strategies

Figure 7.28   Bypass attack strategies

Guerrilla attack strategies

This type of strategy consists of small ongoing actions that are designed to frustrate market defenders. The objective is to gain a permanent slice of the market but without causing the defender to launch a full-scale counterattack. Such strategies tend to be used by micro and SME businesses, though not exclusively. The tactics companies use include merchandising to increase the appeal of the brand, selective price reductions, event marketing, issues advertising and intensive personal selling. (See Figure 7.29.)

Market follower strategies

As Eckles (1990) states:

> the leader or attacker must commit funds to the initiation (product design, engineering and testing)

and implementation (distribution, packaging, promotion and pricing) of its overt strategies. Some companies are willing to accept a follower's role that can provide high profits to avoid the high cost and trauma associated with market leadership and offensive competitive strategies.

The follower aims to develop a product that is similar to the market leaders/challengers, and to remain close to the market leader. However, it does not want to engage in battle: that would be catastrophic for the market follower. Often the market follower will develop an improved product and market it at a lower cost, perhaps into new market segments.

Niche market strategies

This is where an organization is a specialist within one narrow (single niche) or a few narrow (multiple niche) market segments.

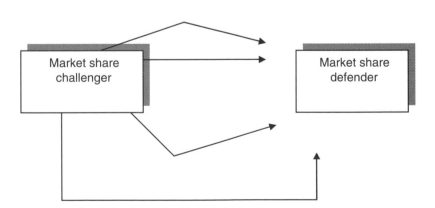

Figure 7.29   Guerrilla attack strategies

Anderson and Vincze (2000) suggest that 'marketers who pursue a niche marketing strategy must have a distinct advantage over competitors and must be able to satisfy customers with superior products or services'.

An example of niche marketing is Air Foyle, a specialist air charter company based at London's Luton airport in the UK. Air Foyle is the worldwide sales agent for Antonov Design Bureau, the Ukrainian designers, manufacturers and owners of the giant 150-tonne payload AN124 'Ruslan' cargo aircraft. This is currently the world's largest cargo freighter in commercial operation.

Environmental dynamics: forecasting and scenarios

In Chapter 2 we considered both the micro and macro environments, and concluded that both these environments experience turbulence of one form or another. The degree of complexity and turbulence will vary from sector to sector and from industry to industry. However, organizations need to consider and analyse these environments in order both to maintain an objective outlook on the business world, and steer an effective course for the survival/development of the individual business.

Lynch (2000) suggests that the environmental forces can be assessed according to two main measures.

Changeability

This is the degree to which the environment is likely to change. For example, there is relatively low changeability in the chocolate bar market, but the possibility of high changeability in the various Internet markets.

Predictability

This is the degree with which such changes can be predicted. For example, changes can be predicted with some 'certainty' (our emphasis) within the mobile telephony market. However, this is not the case with biogenetics.

Lynch (2000) suggests that these measures can be further subdivided. Changeability comprises:

Complexity

This is the degree to which the organization's environment is affected by the PESTEL factors (see Chapter 2). For example, the events of September 11 2001 and the US government's subsequent war on terrorism have increased the level of complexity within the global marketplace. Tour operators and airlines now operate within a very complex and dynamic marketplace.

Novelty

This is the degree to which the environment presents the organization with new situations. For example, this may be a change in legislation that could either open up or close a market.

Predictability comprises:

Rate of change

This is whether the environment changes from slow to fast. The events of 11 September 2001 created a rapid change of events for the world's major airline companies. For some the rate of change (involving new security measures and drastic reduction in passenger numbers) was too rapid for them to react effectively and predict suitable outcomes. For some airlines these events compounded an already weak financial structure, and they could not compete any longer within the market.

Visibility of the future

This is the availability and usefulness of information in order to predict the future. Market researchers can provide information on possible trends by surveying particular market segments. Equally, governments can provide information on changing demographics. For instance, the population trends in Europe suggest that because of improved health care among other factors there will be a dramatic expansion in the number of people of 60 and older over the next 10 years. This segment of the population will tend to be mobile and relatively financially stable. These factors can provide a range of marketing opportunities for companies who either have, or can create, suitable products for this target group, such as travel companies.

Defining scenario planning

Johnson and Scholes (1999) suggest the following definition of scenario planning:

> Scenario planning is not based on a hunch, but builds plausible views on different possible futures for an organization, based on groupings of key environmental influences and drivers of change which have been identified. The result is a limited number of logically consistent, but different scenarios which can be considered alongside each other.

Johnson and Scholes (1999) suggest that there are two key benefits to this type of approach. First, managers are able to examine various strategic options against the scenarios. From this they can address a series of 'what ifs': for example, what would be the effect on our product range if X or Y happened?

Second, the implications of scenarios can be used to challenge the status quo assumptions of the environment. Managers may be so focused on the day-to-day operations of the business that they fail to consider the possibility of an uncertain future. For example, some US airlines failed to realize the impact deregulation would have on their business. The 'opening up the US skies' allowed new low-cost entrants into the market, thus increasing the level of competition. Several

airlines could not compete with the newcomers, and had to restructure and redefine their position within the market. As a result some lost valuable revenue-generating routes because their product was unable to compete.

While scenario planning is not without its criticisms, such plans can influence decision making by identifying new critical success factors (CSFs) for an industry. If they are able to identify, for example, changes in customer behaviour and purchasing power, marketers can implement new approaches to meet customer expectations.

Strategic marketing plans

Dibb *et al* (1997) describe marketing planning as:

> a systematic process that involves assessing marketing opportunities and resources, determining marketing objectives and developing a thorough plan for implementation and control. A core output of marketing planning is the marketing plan, a document or blueprint that details requirements for a company's marketing activities.

An operational marketing plan should be viewed under the following terms.

One year duration

Marketing plans should be developed annually to take into consideration changing market conditions. Of course, the marketing plan should be monitored and adapted to reflect any dynamic changes within the market.

Blueprint or road map

As Dibb *et al* (1997) suggest, the plan is a blueprint to be followed. Other authors use the term 'road map'. It demonstrates to management how the marketing plan will be implemented and the direction it will take. By following the blueprint/road map, the organization should in theory reach its destination. Of course that will not always be the case. This makes the assumption that the organization has the right road map or blueprint in the first place.

Results oriented

The objective is to generate revenue. Thus the plan must reflect both the intended results and how they will be achieved.

Davidson (1997) suggests that there are seven steps or phases in the marketing planning process. These phases often vary, depending on the author's predilection for certain issues or analysis. We have chosen the Davidson model as our basis because it includes future thinking. This may be increasingly valuable

within a dynamic, global and turbulent business environment. However, we have added a few additional aspects because we feel that they make an explicit contribution to the planning process. Table 7.20 sets out the key parameters.

The information for this planning process is derived from the various analyses discussed throughout this chapter. From this planning process we must extract the marketing plan, and we consider that in more detail in the next section.

Developing a marketing plan

As you read around the subject area you will see that various authors will have different ways of presenting a marketing plan. Some are

Table 7.20 Steps in marketing planning

	Steps or phases	Issues
1.	Business and PESTEL analysis	Issues covered include the macro and micro environments, including the current and potential competition.
2.	Marketing mix analysis	This is an analysis of the previous marketing mix strategies implemented. Analysing what has gone before allows the organization to realize what works and what does not.
3.	Marketing research	This should be ongoing and the results should be fed back throughout the organization. Research may point a gap within the market that the organization can exploit using current resources. Therefore this has to be built into the marketing plan.
4.	Future thinking	Includes forecasting and scenario analysis.
5.	Opportunity identification	These will be the outcomes from Steps 1, 3 and 4 above. It involves identification and screening of the potential market and business opportunities.
6.	Set objectives	This involves setting the corporate strategy and plan. It is the outcome of Steps 1 to 5.
7.	Build strategies	This is the development of marketing mix strategies to implement the overall marketing/corporate strategy.
8.	Develop plans	This is the marketing plan that will show how the strategies in Step 7 will be implemented and over what timescale.
9.	Monitor results	Plans must be monitored and benchmarked on a regular basis to determine whether the strategies are being successfully implemented or not. By careful monitoring corrective action can be undertaken if the plan slips in terms of schedule, goes off-course or is affected by external factors.

Adapted from Davidson (1997)

more detailed than others. However, generally they all seek to analyse the same type of information.

Makens (1989) believes there are several key criteria that must be observed when companies formulate marketing plans. These are reflected below with additional comments:

▌ **Realism.** This could also be classified as objectivity. It is relatively easy to create a marketing plan that forecasts strong growth in specific sectors. However, how achievable is this growth? What happens when these targets are not met? Companies are often guilty of wild sales forecasts. When they do not materialize everyone within the organization suffers.

▌ **Detailed.** Marketing plans must be detailed and complete. As the saying goes, 'the devil is in the detail'. If it does not focus on both detail and completeness the marketing plan is unlikely to reflect true possibilities.

▌ **Regular planning.** A marketing plan is not an occasional plan. Marketing plans should be developed on an annual basis during the same period each year. The benchmarking of the plan against reality must also be on a regular basis. The ideal is perhaps on a monthly basis.

▌ **Commitment of senior management.** The organization's senior managers must be committed to supporting the plan. They must be aware of what the plan entails and the level of resourcing necessary to execute the plan effectively and efficiently. Their level of commitment to the marketing plan will be reflected in the level of commitment of the marketing team. If there is little commitment on behalf of both parties, then it is unlikely that the plan will be a success. In the long term the organization, and thus the staff, may suffer as competitors acquire increased market share.

▌ **Commitment of the marketing team.** The active involvement of the whole team in the development of the marketing plan helps to secure commitment to the plan. As it is the marketing team, in the main, who will have to enact the plan, the greater their commitment – both individually and collectively – the greater the opportunity for success.

▌ **Commitment from other functional units.** Marketing does not stand alone. It must interact with other functional units such as finance and operations. The marketing plan must be written in conjunction with these units. For example, it is the finance department that will underwrite the plan, therefore it must work with the marketing department on the development of the appropriate budgets.

▌ **Being prepared to modify.** Situations can change dramatically and suddenly. The effect of the terrorist attacks of 11 September 2001 on the international airline industry was significant. In the wake of falling passenger numbers, airlines had to review their marketing plans to seek ways of reducing the fall in passenger numbers, and persuade customers that airline travel was still safe.

▌ **Measurable.** One critical area is measurement of performance and how that is determined over the short and medium term.

Thus a marketing plan is a combination of:

▌ previous information/experiences;

▌ market analysis;

▌ environmental analysis;

▌ the direction in which the organization wishes to proceed based upon its goals/ objectives.

Table 7.21 illustrates the key components of a marketing plan.

Table 7.21   Key components of a marketing plan

	Component	Comment
1.	Marketing (including sales) objectives	This has to be the focus of the plan. The plan has to reflect the marketing objectives, which in turn have to reflect the corporate objectives of the organization. Marketing and sales objectives should be quantifiable: for example, achieving or maintaining (for highly competitive markets) X per cent market share for a particular product. Of course, the outcome of achieving X per cent market share must be profit rather than a loss. Companies can devote all their resources to achieving increased market share only to discover that the costs outweigh the profit they hoped to generate. Thus judicious financial analysis is vital throughout the marketing process.
2.	Sales projections or forecasts	The organization must project the level of sales to be achieved over the next 12-month period. These estimates must cover each individual product line and geographical territory.
3.	Target markets	The organization must be able to target the right customers within the right market segments. Failure to do so leads to wasted resources, declining revenues and lost opportunities.
4.	Marketing and tactical strategies	These are developed using the full power of the marketing mix. They must be responsive to changes within market conditions, to the overall marketing and business objectives, and generate revenues for the organization. They must operate successfully within the constraints of a budget.
5.	Marketing research programme	Marketing research helps organizations to understand their customers, markets, competition and changing trends. This information can be beneficial in determining which segment(s) of the market to target and with which product or service.
6.	People	People are an important resource within the marketing operation. They are also a cost that needs to be budgeted for within the plan. The objective is to maximize their value, to both the individual and the organization. There should be staff appraisals which link to training and promotional opportunities. It is one thing to have a brilliant marketing concept. However, if the right calibre of staff are not in place then there is an increased risk of the concept failing.
7.	Budget	Realistic budgets need to be allocated against the key areas of the marketing plan. The budget should reflect proposed costs associated with implementing the plan: for instance, the promotional activities on a month-by-month basis.
8.	Activities timetable	The various marketing activities need to be scheduled for several reasons: ▪ This presents a holistic picture of how the marketing plan will operate: for example, when the price decrease will coincide with the promotional push. ▪ It ensures that activities are implemented and completed. ▪ It provides the basis for benchmarking the plan against outcomes. ▪ It helps the marketing staff know what they need to accomplish by a specific time.
9.	Reviews and measurement	The marketing plan should not be reviewed at the end of every year, but continually throughout the 12-month period. If, for example, the plan is reviewed on a monthly basis this provides the organization with the opportunity to revise the plan in relation to changing market or environmental conditions. Predictions can be compared with outcomes to see if the marketing strategies are delivering effective results.

The marketing plan is the final outcome of the previous analyses. While there is probably no perfect marketing plan, a realistic plan can assist an organization in achieving a sustained competitive position.

Chapter summary

This chapter has illustrated some of the key, indeed critical, strategic analytical techniques that organizations can employ. It is important to remember this is not a stand-alone chapter. On the contrary, all the chapters within this text to a greater or lesser degree either influence or are the mechanisms by which strategies are implemented. For instance, the macro environmental factors discussed in Chapter 2 influence strategic decision making. Meanwhile, Chapter 9 reflects on the pricing strategies and tactics that can be implemented. We shall see elements of this combination in Chapter 15. There we bring together many of the issues raised within this and other chapters to show how organizations can and do react to changes within a product life cycle.

This chapter on strategy has demonstrated the possible techniques that companies can use to decide on marketing and corporate policy. It should be clear that no one model or technique is a panacea for all ills that befall a product, an organization or an industry. Often techniques will need to be combined to provide as exacting an analysis as is possible. However we now live in an extremely volatile period. We need thus to consider how techniques such as the balanced scorecard and scenario analysis can help organizations to be flexible yet still have objectives for the future. That is probably the most complex issue facing organizations today.

Exercises and questions for review and critical thinking

1. Evaluate the advantages and disadvantages of niche marketing for a company.

2. What are the limits of the BCG matrix and how far do other portfolio models overcome these?

3. Critically differentiate and explain the important elements of the three levels of strategy: corporate, business and functional. Then explain how marketing contributes to the development of each level.

4. 'Marketing plans are a theoretical exercise that is a waste of resources.' Discuss.

8

Products and brands

Introduction

In this chapter we explore three key areas. The first is the development of products, how they originate, are tested and launched into the marketplace. The second is how products are diffused into the marketplace. That is how well they are received or not, as the case may be, by potential customers. Third, we consider the role of branding, the different types of brand, and how important branding and brands are to the marketing of a product or service.

When reading this chapter reflect back on the previous chapters and consider how many of the techniques previously discussed contribute to the marketing of the product or brand. Obviously these are only a few elements of the whole picture that comprises the marketing mix. There are further elements of the marketing mix to consider: price, promotion, placement, physical evidence, process and people. These are discussed in the chapters that follow.

Once you have considered all these elements you should be able to bring them together as discussed in Chapter 15, 'Application'.

Learning objectives

On completion of this chapter you will be able to:

▌ explain why companies brand products and services;

▌ analyse how brands can be differentiated, and the advantages and disadvantages associated with such differentiation;

▌ evaluate how consumer and industrial products are classified;

▌ demonstrate an awareness of brand power in the national and global context;

▌ explain the process of new product development, and why some products fail to achieve success within the marketplace;

▌ explain the risks involved in developing new products, and adapting current products to new markets;

▌ identify and analyse why private brands have increased their share within certain markets;

▌ explain why companies terminate or cull brands, and the risks involved in such actions.

What is a product?

Here are a two definitions. The first is from Kotler (2000), and the second from Dibb *et al* (1997). In general terms they are similar; however Dibb *et al* (1997) have also stated that a product is 'everything, both *favourable* and unfavourable' and that it is a 'complexity of tangible and intangible attributes' (my emphasis). As you read through this chapter it will become apparent that the products and brands we often take for granted are complex in nature. Therefore the decisions marketers must take in order to develop and market a product or brand successfully will be equally complex. We must remember that, as Inwood and Hammond (1993) stress, a product (including a service product) exists to generate value, and this can only be achieved by fulfilling the needs of customers.

Kotler's definition is:

> A product is anything that is offered to a market for attention, acquisition, use or consumption and that might satisfy a want or need. It includes physical objects, services, persons, places, organizations and ideas.

Dibb *et al*'s is:

> A product is everything, both favourable and unfavourable, that is received in exchange. It is a complexity of tangible and intangible attributes, including functional, social and psychological utilities or benefits. A product can be ideas, a service, a good or any combination of these three.

Products come in a variety of shapes and sizes and perform different functions. Moreover, they are often composed of a range of other products. Consider, for instance, how many separate products are combined to form and operate a luxury twin-hulled cruise ship.

Market classifications

Products can be divided into two broad market classifications, consumer and industrial (also known as commercial). Within these two groups are a series of sub-sets that illustrate the different product types.

The classification of consumer products

These are products aimed at satisfying personal and family needs and desires, and can be classified into a number of groups. This classification relies heavily on understanding consumer buying behaviour (Dibb *et al*, 1997).

Convenience products

These are the basic frequently purchased everyday items that require little or no pre-planning or preparation on the part of the purchaser. These can be further divided into the sub-sub-sets of staple, impulse and emergency purchases.

Here brand awareness is particularly important, as manufacturers attempt to position their brand in the mind of the consumer. (Reflect back on Chapter 5 on 'Segmenting, positioning and targeting'.) Dibb *et al* (1997) suggest that manufacturers expect little promotional effort at the retail end of the chain, so they need to provide it themselves in the form of advertising and sales promotion. Promotion can be through a mixture of advertising and on-pack promotions. Memorable slogans also have their role to play in reminding consumers of the product's attributes. For example the UK promotion of the then Rowntree (now Nestlé) Kit Kat chocolate bar in the 1980s, 'Take a break, take a Kit Kat' is still used in advertising today (May 2003) and people knowingly react when they hear those seven words.

Let us consider the sub-sub-sets in more detail.

■ **Staple products or purchases.** These are products that are generally consumed on a regular, if not daily, basis. They include bread, tea, coffee, milk, fruits and vegetables and basic over-the-counter (OTC) medicines such as paracetamol, aspirin and other cold and flu remedies. This list is rather British-oriented: staples in other countries will not necessarily be the same, but in all places they are fundamental to the existence of the individuals and families that consume them.

■ **Impulse products or purchases.** These are products bought as a result of 'spur of the moment' decisions to purchase. Products within this category include low-cost confectionery, newspapers and magazines. In many supermarkets these items are displayed near the checkout counters or in newspaper kiosks. As Underhill (1999) states, we must not underestimate the value of impulse buying to the success and profitability of the business. Here the 'business' could be defined as both the manufacturer and the retailer.

■ **Emergency products or purchases.** These are goods purchased when the need is particularly urgent, such as an umbrella during a sudden rainstorm or an analgesic to reduce the pain of a sudden headache. Due to the unpredictability of the English weather, it is perhaps not surprising that numerous department stores in London's Oxford and Regent Streets (two main shopping areas) have compact umbrellas conveniently located near the entranceway!

Most consumers until recently tended to buy convenience products at retail outlets near their home. However with increasingly long working hours, and retail outlets such as supermarkets opening till late at night, some consumers shop near their offices. Increasingly, supermarkets are opening in or near busy office districts.

Linked to convenience products are convenience stores also known as C-stores. These stores trade primarily on the appeal of the convenience they offer to the local customer. In many countries these tend to be independent outlets (often family run businesses). Additionally, they can be chain stores, such as Londis in the UK or the US-based 7-Eleven which has expanded its outlets in several countries, including the UK.

Stanton, Etzel and Walker (1994) suggest that other products may be classed as convenience products, even though they are not purchased on a frequent basis. They suggest Christmas lights and Mother's Day cards. To this we can add products associated with Valentine's Day, birthdays, Easter and other religious festivities. These include cards, flowers and chocolates.

Shopping goods or products

This focuses on durable or semi-durable items that have a relatively long life span. There are several key factors associated with shopping goods: they include such products as clothing, furniture, televisions, video cameras, cars, washing machines and refrigerators. As such most people buy them infrequently. There are exceptions: think, for instance, of pop, sport and movie stars who are regularly spotted at their favourite designer clothes stores.

Shopping goods can be subclassified as homogeneous or heterogeneous. Homogeneous goods are those products that tend to be similar to each other in terms of performance, benefits and pricing. For example, most washing machines can be considered as homogeneous goods. They tend to have similar wash loads, wash similar types of clothes (cottons, delicates and so on), and have similar speed settings. However, brands attempt to differentiate themselves from the others within the marketplace. This is usually achieved through design, features and technical performance. Such additional features are usually reflected in a higher pricing structure. For example, the British company Dyson patented and launched the contra-rotating

washing machine drum. This was a radical design and performance feature.

Heterogeneous goods tend to be non-standard products where features, benefits and image tend to outweigh the price. In this case individuals' personal behavourial factors tend to influence their purchasing decisions. Goods such as handmade or handcrafted products and diamond bracelets are designed to appeal to individual tastes.

When looking to buy shopping goods, consumers might devote significant time to gathering a range of comparative information covering such points as features, performance, price, credit arrangements, delivery, guarantee and after sales service.

Brand awareness can be a critical factor here. Companies may engage in high profile promotional strategies that assist in creating strong brand awareness in the mind of the consumer. Therefore the consumer may be influenced to consider one brand over another. However, consumers are not necessarily brand loyal. Otherwise, as Dibb *et al* (1997) suggest, they would not devote significant time researching the different variables to assist them in their decision making. (We discuss brand loyalty later in this chapter. You may want to reflect back to Chapter 7 and consider Ries and Trout's work on positioning the product in the mind of the consumer.)

The quality of service received by consumers may be an additional (and important) factor in their decision to purchase from a particular store.

Speciality or luxury goods

As the name suggests these are products that possess one or more special or unique features. Like shopping products, consumers normally buy them infrequently. Consumers seeking speciality products normally devote significant time, and often resources, to obtaining the product of their choice. They will not seek out alternatives and make comparisons, nor will they accept substitutes.

Additionally, they are prepared to pay a premium price for the prestige associated with the particular product or service.

A significant number of different products can be classified as speciality goods. Here are a few choices:

▌ An Aston Martin Vanquish sports car, of the type featured in the James Bond movie *Die Another Day* (2002) (value: £158,000).

▌ The auctioning in 1999 of the 1953 painting *Going To The Match* by British artist L S Lowry (1887–1976) for £1,926,000.

▌ A bottle of Taittinger Comtes de Champagne Blanc de Blanc 1990 (£80–100, 2001 prices).

▌ A bottle of either The Macallan 1948 or The Macallan malt whisky (£2,000, 2001 prices).

▌ A suite on a luxury cruise ship for seven nights in the Mediterranean (approximately £5,000–8,000 per person, 2002 prices).

▌ A residence on *The World* (www.residensea.com). This is a luxury floating residence where an apartment costs from US $2 million.

As you can see from this list, both time and financial resources normally have to be invested in such buying decisions. Of course, the amount of time spent on decision making may relate to the level of personal wealth available. If a couple wanted to go on the dream cruise of their life – but had limited resources – they would most likely spend significant time in analysing the various options (especially in terms of price). However if money was not an issue, the time devoted to making the decision might not be so lengthy. There cannot be a hard and fast rule here. Such decision making is dependent upon numerous factors including the individual's behavioural characteristics.

Motorboats designed and built by the Italian companies Riva and Colombo have gained, over the years, an international reputation for style, image and elegance. Chosen by celebrities, entrepreneurs and business people they reflect a luxury lifestyle image.

Unsought goods

These are products or services that consumers had not considered purchasing until they were made aware of the need or benefits available. This can be divided into three sub-sets:

▌ To resolve a problem. For example, following a burglary someone might need to have a pane of glass, door locks or even a door replaced. He or she will look to use a glazier, locksmith or carpenter, but only to deal with the problem, assuming he or she had not previously been planning to replace the glass, have new locks or a door fitted. The need is a result purely of actions beyond the individual's own control. Another example is emergency car repairs.

▌ 'Hard sell' techniques. While many of these techniques are illegal in several countries, they still exist in others. A classic example from the UK is double glazing salespeople. Perhaps unfairly, the majority of double glazing salespeople have been tarnished with the actions of a few salespeople who opted for the hard sell approach. From the initial telesales call to the visit from the salesperson there is an attempt to 'sell' double glazing to the consumer, even though it is not the consumer's personal priority. Another example has been the hard sell tactics of insurance companies, especially in the UK in relation to pension provision. Consumer legislation has reduced the impact of hard selling techniques with the imposition of 'cooling off periods' which allow consumers time to consider whether they want to proceed with the transaction. Additionally, companies have been prosecuted and fined for using such tactics.

▌ We must also consider that unsought goods can satisfy a need. If we return to our example of the double glazing salesperson, the consumer might see genuine benefits from having double glazing installed. These could include:

- replacing rotting or decaying windows;
- improving the overall visual look of the house;
- improving security through additional window locks;
- reducing condensation during the winter months;
- improved insulation, thus reducing heating bills during the winter months.
- reduced exterior noise, especially if the house is near a busy road.

The same could also be said of insurance salespeople. Initially, their approach may be unsought. However there may be features and benefits of their policies that benefit the consumer: for example, savings policies linked to life insurance.

Catalogues that arrive via direct mail, or via door drops, often contain a range of products from furniture, picnic hampers and clothing to kitchen utensils, bathroom fixtures and children's toys. While many of the items are readily available in retail outlets, others are not. It is usually these items that attract the reader's attention.

Classification of industrial products

Industrial products or goods are generally purchased on the basis of the company's overall goals and objectives (Eckles, 1990). These products can be classified under the following categories.

Raw materials

These are the basic materials that contribute to the manufacturing process. They include natural resources (for example, minerals such as gold and iron ore, tin, coal, crude oil and sand) and agricultural products (for example cocoa for chocolate, fruits and vegetables). Some of these raw materials (such as cocoa) are bought on the Futures Market. Here contracts are struck where buyers agree to buy something in the future for a price that is fixed in the present.

In Chapter 2 we discussed the macro impact of environmental factors. It is important to consider here that if say there is a particularly poor harvest of cocoa, the price of this raw material will be affected. The chocolate manufacturer, for instance, faced with a higher price per tonne, would need to consider whether to absorb the cost within its margins or pass it on to retailers. They in turn might absorb the cost or pass it on to consumers.

Processed materials

These are materials that have been processed in one form or another before being sold for use in production processes. They may not be readily identifiable to the end user. Examples are various chemicals, lubricants, filters, plastics, sheet steel and hydrocarbons.

Component parts (also known as fabricating parts in the United States)

These are identifiable and distinguishable components that form part of a finished product. For example, a major car manufacturer does not produce all the components that go into the finished car. The vast majority are made by approved suppliers which are often themselves well known brand names, such as TRW Automotive (suppliers of car braking, steering, suspension and safety systems) and Michelin, the French tyre manufacturer.

A large part of a car engine comprises component parts. When one of these parts fails either the local garage mechanic or the owner buys and installs the replacement part. The computer upon which this textbook was written comprises several hundred components, from the microchips and wiring to the keys on the keypad. All these originated from specialist suppliers and were assembled into a computer by the brand manufacturer.

There are a few key factors to consider here:

▌ The components must meet the quality specification of the producer/assembler of the finished product. It is the assembler's reputation that is typically on the line if the system or product fails. If a computer fails to operate efficiently, the manufacturer will bear the brunt of the consumer's wrath, not the supplier of the microchip that failed prematurely.

▌ The supply chain logistics are important. Can the component manufacturer deliver the number of components required at the stated time and on the stated date? That might be not just locally, but also globally. Otherwise there could be delays in providing the finished product to distributors, and thus the end customer. (See Chapter 13.)

Installation: plant and machinery

These are major items of plant and equipment/machinery that are needed to produce the organization's finished products. They range from state-of-the-art computerized printing presses for the production of high-quality pictorial format books (art or photography books) to computerized car manufacturing lines.

Companies that need to install such facilities will consider the following:

▌ The long-term viability of the equipment. The often significantly high levels of investment mean that the company will seek to maximize its return on investment. As technology develops so the obsolescence lead time often decreases. This can place additional burden on a company whose cash flow may be under pressure. The decision to purchase is often linked to the long-term competitive viability of the organization within the marketplace.

▌ The organization will probably engage in an extensive search for alternative equipment that it believes will meet its needs, both now and in the future. Its final decision on what to buy may not be based on the cost of the equipment alone. It may be determined by the following factors:

  – Payment terms, for example a discount for full payment in advance.
  – The quality of the equipment, its features, benefits and performance.
  – The cost of operating the equipment, in terms of both human resources and material resources.
  – The quality of the after sales service should there be any operational/functional problems. If a component failure leads to down time in a factory, it could be prohibitively expensive for the company concerned. If the supplier cannot either repair the component or supply a new one rapidly, it could not only lose custom but also have to reimburse the customer for the down time.

Accessories (auxiliary equipment)

This can be described as equipment that does not become part of the finished product, but in some way contributes to its successful production and distribution. These items tend to be less expensive than capital purchases of plant, and include office and operational equipment such as computers, software packages and electronic test facilities.

Consumable supplies

These are supplies that facilitate operation and production, but are not strictly part of the finished product. Within an office environment they include pens, paper, laser and photocopying cartridges. Within an operation and production environment they include gloves, safety glasses, uniforms and hard hats.

Generally the products are homogeneous and therefore companies may use several suppliers. By using several competing suppliers they might gain competitive pricing and/or delivery times.

Industrial or business services

These are tangible services that companies and organizations use to achieve their overall business objectives. They include legal, financial, accounting, training, catering, market research, printing, advertising, security and management consultancy services. For the company or organization the decision is whether to develop internal services and/or employ external agencies.

The management consultancy services sector, for example, is rapidly expanding within the United States and Europe. The major players within this sector market their expertise heavily to target organizations.

New product development (NPD)

Why innovate?

Products can have very short or extremely long life spans. For many companies, new product development (NPD) is an ongoing operation. It is not purely to replace products that are in the declining phase of their life cycle, but to develop products that support the company's longer-term strategic objectives. Those objectives often include maintaining a technical-specific competitive advantage over rivals. An example is manufacturers of DVD players or televisions for the consumer market.

The development of new products is often essential if a company is to survive, let alone grow and prosper in the longer term. Many products become obsolete, affected by technological developments, competition and changing buyer behaviour (the typewriter and mechanical cash registers are particular examples). Declining markets affect sales revenues and hence the profit performance of the business. Therefore companies must be proactive in NPD.

As Inwood and Hammond (1993) illustrate, the 'new' in NPD can take on several connotations. The following are a few potential variations:

- The simple adaptation of an existing product or its packaging. (This may be particularly relevant to a product entering an international market. Various factors, ranging from government legislation in the host country through to customer preferences, may determine the level and scope of the adaptation required.)

- Minor or major redesign of an existing product (and/or its packaging) to extend its life span.

- Replacement of an existing product with a completely *new* product.

- The introduction of a completely new product, perhaps potentially for a new market sector.

NPD can significantly enhance a company's competitive edge. Merck, the world's largest pharmaceutical company, enjoyed significant success when it introduced two new products. Vasotee treated high blood pressure, while Mevacor reduced cholesterol levels. Merck's technological breakthroughs gained it competitive advantages and market share over its competitors (Kotler, 2000).

The processes involved in determining NPD

Based on their work with international clients, the management consultants Booz Allen & Hamilton proposed a cycle or sequence for new product development (Baker, 2000). This remains one of the most used sequences.

Generally there are eight stages in NPD, although some authors may combine or add stages.

1. Idea generation.
2. Idea screening.
3. Concept testing.
4. Business analysis.
5. Product development and testing.
6. Market testing.
7. Product launch.
8. Commercialization: the diffusion and adoption process.

Idea generation (also known as exploration)

Obviously all new products commence with an idea, which can be very simple or very complex. Ideas can emanate from a variety of sources and might require further exploration. These sources include:

▌ Further development of an existing product through a refinement or adaptive feature.

▌ External technology or scientific developments/discoveries. New developments in one technological field may lead to innovations in others. For example, the technological developments that led to placing a man on the moon have spun off into the consumer market. In this particular case, they range from non-stick coatings on cooking pans (developed from the wafer-thin coatings on the re-entry heat shields) to enhanced computer systems.

▌ Senior managers. They may see a potential opportunity or niche within the marketplace that they can enter relatively quickly and efficiently, possibly maximizing their return on investment.

▌ The sales team/sales force. In meetings with their customers, the sales team might hear suggestions for product improvements and developments. Equally, the sales team themselves might make recommendations for enhanced product development.

▌ Customers. These are customers who may not come into direct contact with a sales team. If they use the product on a regular basis they might decide to contact the company with suggested improvements. Equally, they might contact the company to complain about the product. Complaints, while potentially damaging to the company in terms of public relations, can also provide significant opportunities for development. It is all a question of how the company handles the complaint in relation to customer servicing, and relays the customer's views to the product development and operations departments.

▌ Competitors. By watching and analysing the action of competitors, companies may be able to emulate their success, or leapfrog them in terms of product development. This may be the way the company can gain a competitive edge within the marketplace. Of course, it is one thing gaining the edge; it is a very different proposition retaining or sustaining that advantage.

▌ Brainstorming sessions, ideally carried out by a mix of people (for instance not just the research and development team but also operations and marketing). Brainstorming often creates a rich variety of ideas. Many of these ideas may not be practical, at least at the time, but gems can be born out of such critical thinking processes. In a survey of Dutch industrial goods, over 60 per cent of companies claimed to use brainstorming to generate new product ideas (Inwood and Hammond, 1993).

- The employees. New ideas are not just the province of the senior management team. There are numerous examples of employees, at all levels within an organization, generating ideas that have either saved the company money, or helped it create a new range of products. Organizations often encourage idea generation amongst the workforce through financial incentive schemes.

Idea screening (also known as the initial screening process)

Developing new products is a highly risky and expensive operation. Therefore the company must undertake a series of screening activities to determine, even at this early stage, whether it is a viable proposition or not. Companies may state that they invest billions of dollars in R&D; however, they must seek a return on that level of investment.

The company will usually form a working group or committee to analyse and consider the viability of new ideas. Such a working group may comprise people from various departments – R&D, marketing, finance, production and operations. The function of such a working group is to determine the potential winners from the losers. This is never going to be an easy task, but a systematic approach aids the decision-making process.

Overall the company must determine whether the idea strategically fits its corporate objectives, considering also demand, resourcing and competitive forces. As you will see from the questions below the company must consider a range of issues, from production and operations through to finance and human resource management. Equally, there is a range of micro and macro factors that they will need to consider. The types of questions a company could consider include the following:

- Does this idea fit with the existing product range? Will the new product affect the viability of exiting products? (In other words, will it take sales away from exiting products?) What will be the likely impact on the business?

- What is the possible demand for this product? Who will buy it and why would they buy it?

- Does the company have the appropriate expertise to develop such an idea? If not, can it acquire that expertise, and how long will it take to acquire and assimilate that expertise into the business? What could be the possible negative effects of bringing that expertise into the company? For example, how will the current employees react? (As you can see this is not just a marketing, production and finance issue, it also very much involves human resource management, and all associated with it.) Should the company seek to outsource the manufacture of the product? If so, what will be the cost and quality implications?

- Does the company have the capacity to produce this new product, or will it need to consider building new facilities? What will be the cost and time lags involved? Again, should it outsource the manufacture of the product? If so, what will be the cost and quality implications?

- Will the company be required to invest in new equipment in order to manufacture this product? If so, what will it cost and how will it be financed (for example, through short or long-term borrowings or using liquid assets)? If there are substantial borrowings, how will that affect the business as a whole? What will be the impact upon the balance sheet in terms of retained funds and profits?

▌ What is the likely sales potential of this product? What is the potential size of the market, nationally, regionally, internationally or indeed globally? What are the possible risks involved?

▌ What are the likely costs involved in the development and production of this new product idea? Will the company need to seek additional funding from external sources? If so, what will be the costs involved in borrowing the additional funding? How will that funding be raised – share market, via the banking system or both?

▌ Is the idea technically feasible now? Or will it be in the near/distant future?

▌ Are there any obvious problems that can be foreseen in the development stage of this idea?

▌ What will the potential reaction of the current customers be? Does the idea meet a current market need?

▌ Should it be aimed at a new customer base? What is the potential size of that customer base?

▌ What is the possibility of substitution or product obsolescence? If so, are there any measures that can be taken to overcome these, or reduce their potential impact?

▌ What will be the potential competitor reactions? Could they be working on a similar idea? Could the competitors launch a similar product earlier? If so what will be the likely impact upon the market, and the company?

▌ Are there any negative/positive environmental considerations? Will the raw materials, the manufacturing process or the finished product harm the environment? Will the processes comply with current and possible future environmental legislation?

▌ Are there any potential legislative issues to be considered? For example, are there product safety implications, now and/or in the future?

▌ What are the potential advantages and/or disadvantages from the company's perspective?

▌ To what extent will the proposed product assist in reducing production or marketing costs of other products?

▌ What will be the impact on current distribution outlets? Will new distribution patterns need to be developed? If so, what are the potential cost and management implications?

▌ What are the estimated time scales from the ideas stage through to prototype and manufacture?

▌ Who is the potential competition? Are they current competitors or will new ones enter the market? Consideration must be given to potential international competition, not just local or national. With the growth in e-commerce, business is becoming very much a global entity.

As you can see from the above questions, they are very much interrelated, reliant on cost, and are to some extent future thinking. They also reflect the need to think across the organization. These issues do not affect only one department: they impact to a greater or lesser extent on all functional departments.

While it is impossible to predict the future accurately, there are trends that may provide some indication of what may happen in the near future, at least.

Concept testing

As part of the ideas screening process, marketers may have to test the concepts on potential customers. Here the objective is to gain customer reactions to the idea. However, while this may be a valuable exercise, there are inherent problems associated with concept testing. These include:

- Can the concept be communicated effectively to the potential customers so that they can make realistic judgments? A development team may be able to visualize the final product, indeed the whole production process. However can that be accurately translated into a language that the customer easily and readily understands?

- Will the potential customers' reaction to the concept be objective and rational? Will they, for instance, think it is a novel idea and state so, but in reality consider it impractical?

- Can such an exercise be cost-effective in terms of resource expenditure versus feedback, and the quality of that feedback?

- Companies will need to consider how far individuals are conditioned by what is called 'traditional'. Radical new ideas may be considered bizarre by traditionalists, but convenient and practical for others.

Business analysis

Based upon the outcome of the concept testing, management will need to consider the market and financial viability of the product. This will entail break-even analysis, market analysis, and forecasts of costs, sales and potential profit. (It is important to bear in mind that these are far from being exact sciences.)

In the case of a radical new product development, some of the forecasts can only be educated guesses based upon prior experience within the marketplace. Generally, companies conduct business analyses not only at this stage, but throughout all subsequent stages. At a later stage it may become overwhelmingly clear that the product is too expensive to develop, that it is not technically feasible to develop, or there is no market for it. Therefore the project will need to be either terminated or held back until it becomes feasible. (See the section on risks associated with NPD.)

Product development and testing

At this stage a prototype or working model has been constructed. This reveals the tangibles and intangibles attributed to the product. Products can be tested two ways. First, the company can run its own tests on the product. This is known as alpha testing. For example, the prototype of a new aircraft will be test flown by the company's own test pilots. Usually the aircraft will have additional computers onboard to test different elements of the aircraft, from the hydraulic control systems to individual engine performance.

Second, potential customers are also involved in the testing process. This is known as beta testing. The issue here is that the product should be tested in order to replicate reality as closely as possible. For example, computer software manufacturers will provide both consumers and business customers with beta test samples of their software to see how the products perform under user conditions. The feedback from such beta test sites is important for the incorporation of product refinements.

However, not all companies aggressively product test. There may be various concerns or issues that limit such testing. For example:

- Senior management may be committed to launch the product, and within relatively restrictive deadlines. Therefore limited or no testing may be undertaken to meet the deadlines.

- Only qualitative data rather than quantitative data might be available. Some organizations look upon qualitative data as 'soft' data. As a result the organization may be reluctant to halt the project if the qualitative data has signalled a negative response to the product. This will especially be the case if the project has enthusiastic support from the senior management team.

- Fear of competitive pressures can result in a company launching a product without concept (and market) testing. The view in the boardroom may be, what if the competition launches a similar product before we do? While there may be sound marketing and competitive strategies to combat such actions, the board may decide to develop the product without concept testing.

- Sometimes organizations are prepared to take the risk of backing a hunch. This is often in the absence of any real demand for the proposed product. This approach may work – it has in the past. However, the risks for a company can be enormous. Its very financial survival could be at risk if the product fails.

Market testing (also known as test launch)

Before the product is introduced to a wider market segment, it may be market tested. This is a 'sample' launch of the product into a limited area to determine the reaction of its potential customers. Market testing can provide the company with several benefits:

- It allows product exposure to a natural (rather than a controlled) market, and as such should reflect a real measure of performance.

- It provides the marketing team with an opportunity to test different aspects of the marketing mix. This testing can take place in different locations, allowing the marketers to experiment with pricing and promotional variations.

- It allows the marketing team to observe weaknesses in the product, and other components of the marketing mix. Therefore it provides them with the opportunity for corrective action prior to the actual launch. Such testing of the mix can lead to more effective use of the mix, and prevent embarrassments such as inappropriate advertising.

- Testing can provide additional information for cost, sales and profit forecasts.

- Sample launching allows supplies of the product to be accumulated over a longer time frame prior to the full market launch. However, there may be warehousing cost and potential depreciation cost implications associated with such actions.

Product launch

Once the product has successfully completed the concept and market testing stages, it is ready for launching into a wider marketplace. Generally, a product can be launched two ways. First, it can be launched nationally. On a given date the product is launched and available to customers across the nation. The product could be anything from a new washing powder to a new car. Such products are usually supported by intensive promotional campaigns. The important issue for companies is that appropriate quantities of product are available in the distribution outlets prior to launch date. Nothing is more frustrating for consumers than to go to buy a new product on launch date, only to find that it is not available, and may not be for several days or weeks.

The second option is roll out. This is where the product is rolled out area by area. This can mean geographically, area by area within a country, or regionally, perhaps progressing through several countries. A product could for instance be rolled out through Europe over a period of three months.

Commercialization: the adoption and diffusion process

This is the full-scale manufacturing and marketing of the new product. The adoption and diffusion process is how information and experiences of the new product are disseminated through the marketplace.

The stages of potential customer reaction to the new product can be described by the mnemonic AIETA. See Table 8.1.

Rogers (1983) devised a broad classification (based upon the 1930s/1940s sociological studies of Neal Gross and Bruce Ryan) for customers who adopt new products. See Figure 8.1.

Adoption characteristics

Innovators

A small group, these are the first customers to purchase the product. They generally tend to be younger, have access to financial resources, are reasonably well educated and confident in their outlook. They may adopt the product if it is fashionable and fits with their lifestyle. This group often acts as opinion formers for companies to drive the product into a wide marketplace. Equally, innovators are risk takers as there is no guarantee the product will ultimately be successful.

An example is the introduction of the mobile telephone into the UK in the late 1980s. These telephones were quite large and relatively heavy to carry. Additionally, the range of the network was limited to large cities such as London and Birmingham. However, the mobile phone was increasingly seen as a vital communications device for senior dynamic business people. It was not only a communications device, but clearly a status symbol as well.

Early adopters

This is a larger group than innovators (Rogers estimates some six times larger). Early adopters tend to have similar characteristics to innovators, being well educated with high incomes and self-confidence. However, they are not prone to take the level of risks associated with innovators. They can be seen as change agents. They are potential opinion formers and leaders, and so can strongly influence other people's views. Therefore companies target them with promotional campaigns to reinforce the features and benefits of the new product.

Table 8.1 AIETA model

Reaction	Description
Awareness	This is where the market (the customers) becomes aware of the product introduction. This usually happens through pre-promotion and the launch event.
Interest	Customers seek more information about the product. This may range from test reports undertaken by customer groups (for example, independent consumer associations) through to availability and pricing.
Evaluation	Customers evaluate the product's features and benefits to determine whether to purchase the product or not. This may be through in-store demonstrations of the product: for example, the latest in digital television or audio sound systems.
Trial	Customers test the product to determine its value to them. To help the consumer, for example, companies often create trial size samples that are either giveaway promotions (handed out in-store or through door-to-door drops – see the section on direct marketing in Chapter 10, page 346) or sold at special trial offer prices. Examples of products that use trial size samples are shampoos and soaps.
Adoption	This is the process by which customers incorporate the product into their buying patterns. From a first-time purchase they may become repeat buyers, and indeed advocates of the product.

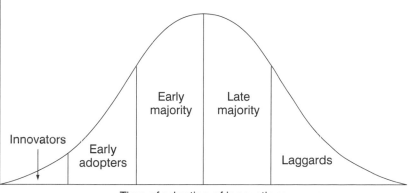

Figure 8.1 Diffusion of innovation curve

Zikmund and D'Amico (1999) suggest that early adopters filter the products accepted by the innovators and popularize them. This in turn leads to acceptance by the majority of buyers within the marketplace.

Early and late majority

Combined, these make up approximately 70 per cent of the total adopter group. They can be described as mass market consumers, and cautious in their approach to buying. Some customers (the early majority) want to see the products proven within the market before committing themselves to purchasing them. Others (the late majority) may be sceptical about the product's long-term value, and thus even more reluctant to purchase the product. Adoption comes via proof of the product's performance and value, and usually pressure from others to adopt. The latter may be in the form of social and political pressure: for example, in adopting unleaded fuels for the family car.

Laggards

This group can be characterized as reluctant to adopt any innovation. As Jobber (1998) suggests, the innovation needs to be perceived as almost a traditional product before they will consider purchasing it. They tend to be older, conservative and traditional in their outlook, avoiding risk taking where possible.

A general point on adoption theory

Rogers' model provides a valuable insight into how products are adopted by customers. However, not everyone purchases a product that can be described as an innovation. Therefore individuals or groups that fit this category could be described as non-adopters.

Risks associated with NPD

There are various risks associated with the development and subsequent launch of a new or modified product. The failure rate tends to be extraordinarily high: Clancy and Shulman (1991) estimate the failure rate of new packaged goods at 80 per cent, and believe it is similar in financial services. Moreover, Cooper and Kleinschmidt (1991) estimate that 75 per cent of new products fail at launch. So what are the reasons for such extreme levels of failure? The following provides some indicators; however it is far from an exhaustive list.

Competitor activity

A competitor may instigate certain strategies and tactics to maintain or capture market share. For simplicity we will assume that there are only two companies within the market, Company A and Company B (the competitor in this scenario). The tactics could include the following:

▌ Company B develops a similar range of new products or product adaptations to Company A, and launches early in a pre-emptive strike in order to capture market share.

▌ Following the launch of its product, Company B may reduce its prices, thus potentially further weakening the position of Company A. (However, it should be borne in mind that such a tactic can work against Company B. It might have the same level of costs to recover as Company A, and in doing this it could increase its debt burden. Equally, Company A might retaliate by reducing its prices below Company B's, or keeping its prices higher on the basis that it is delivering a product of particular quality to consumers.)

▌ If Company B does not have a new product or adaptation to launch, it may reduce the prices of its current product portfolio. The aim here is to compete more effectively against the product being introduced by Company A and retain market share. This could however only be a short-term strategy. It might be forced into modifying its products or launching new ones.

Customer behaviour

As was discussed in Chapter 4, numerous factors influence customer buyer behaviour, and the needs and wants of customers often change over time. As a result, by the time a product is launched (consider the years of R&D that may be required) the demand for that type of product(s) may be limited or virtually nonexistent.

For example, in 1957 the Ford Motor Company introduced the Edsel car, which subsequently lost it between US $250 million and US $350 million (Walters, 1997). As a result, the Edsel has been claimed to be the worst car ever built. Criticisms of the Edsel covered everything from the shape of the grille to its high, large tail lights. The real problem for the Edsel was that it was not considered sufficiently different from other cars (although in reality it had some relatively impressive features), and Ford had difficulty positioning it in the mind of the consumer. The company was aiming to create a mid-range market between the lower-end range – the Mercury – and top-end range – the Lincoln. The problem was marketing and creating that position in the mind of the potential customer (Walters, 1997). Interestingly, today Edsels are considered collectors' items, and command a high price at auctions.

In such cases the company has only a few options:

▌ Scrap the product and absorb the losses. The experience and knowledge gained from the development of the product could be useful in the development of further products.

▌ Hold the product in reserve. There is the possibility of resurgence in demand for the product or the development of a totally new market.

▌ Aim to create a market for the product through intensive marketing communications. Success in such an operation might however be short-lived.

Political change and economic factors

As we showed in Chapter 2, various macro factors can significantly impact on the marketing success of a product. Within the political environment, changes in legislation can impinge on the development, manufacturing, launch and/or distribution of a new or modified product. Such legislation could include:

▌ Introduction of improved safety requirements. An example is the European Union where all electrical appliances sold must have a moulded plug attached by the manufacturers. This is to prevent consumers from wiring the plugs incorrectly, thus risking electrocution and fire hazards as a result.

▌ The restriction of certain products. An example is the UK where particular types of fireworks are banned.

▌ The introduction of embargoes and/or sanctions that restrict the exportation of products to certain countries or regions.

Changes within the economic environment may include:

▌ Consumers being reluctant to spend because of increases in taxation and/or interest rates. This might, however, only be a short-term reluctance.

▌ The country or region might enter a period of recession, which (as demonstrated by the UK's recession of the late 1980s) could be deep and long. Such a recession will affect not only consumer buying power but the company's ability to raise capital and meet its potential debts. In such cases a company may decide to suspend some or all new product development to protect itself from too much financial exposure. While this is a totally understandable measure, such prudence might only provide a short-term advantage. When the country or region emerges from recession, companies that have been able to invest in some product development might be able to capture market share for competitors who did not.

▌ Either the domestic government or the government in a target market territory might impose a tariff barrier. This is likely to increase the price of the new product to the end user. In turn this might affect the level of demand for the new product.

Technical factors

There can be many technical reasons that a product either works efficiently, or completely fails within its operational environment. Here are a few examples:

▌ In 1949 the Bristol Aviation Company built the Bristol Brabazon, an enormous airliner weighing 130 tonnes and powered by eight propeller engines. However, the prototype aircraft was plagued by technical difficulties and never went into production. It was withdrawn in 1952. Additionally, the De Havilland Comet, the world's first jet propelled commercial airliner, was unveiled within months of the Brabazon's inaugural flight. It was clear that jet propulsion was the future for mass commercial air transportation. Interestingly the life of the Comet was also to be relatively short within the marketplace. It would also be plagued by technical difficulties (wing fractures), resulting in its withdrawal. The market would then be taken by the Boeing 707. Boeing held a commanding lead in civilian aircraft manufacture for the next 30 to 40 years. Its main rival in the 21st century is Airbus of Europe.

▌ Another in this league was Howard Hughes' ambitious project, the Hughes Flying Boat, the H-4 Hercules also known as the 'Spruce Goose'. The H-4, apparently the largest aircraft built to date, was a large wooden eight-engine seaplane which was completed in 1947 and designed to carry 750 passengers. On 2 November 1947, with Howard Hughes at the controls, the H-4 powered up for taxi tests. However, Hughes decided to embark on an unannounced flight. The H-4 lifted approximately 70 feet off the water, and flew for a distance of one mile before landing. This was to be its one and only flight. It simply did not meet the power and construction capabilities of its original designers.[1]

While controversy later surrounded its financing (the US government invested significant funds), the project apparently yielded valuable technical knowledge for the aircraft industry. Since 1993 the aircraft has been a museum exhibition at the Evergreen Aviation Centre in Oregon, United States where it is being restored to its full glory.

▍During the 1980s there was much debate in the media on whether some computers with small hard disk capacity (80 megabytes) required fans. The concern centred on whether fans were necessary to reduce the risk of overheating, and thus data loss. Consumers who were concerned that there was a risk of data loss tended to purchase computers with fans incorporated. As a result companies that did not incorporate fans failed within the marketplace.

Poor promotion

A new product may not develop a market share for itself because of poor promotion. Such poor promotion may be the result of a single factor or a combination of factors. These factors can include the following:

▍Insufficient budget allocation to maximize exposure of the product.

▍A lack of a coherent communications strategy that focuses on the product's features and benefits.

▍A lack of effective targeting of the appropriate media.

▍A failure to understand the market at which the product is aimed.

Levels of investment required

One of the major risks associated with cutting edge Research and Development (R&D) is budget overruns. It is virtually impossible to state at inception exactly how much a new product is going to cost. Technical problems during development will affect budget allocations. This risk, of course, is that the product in development becomes so expensive to manufacture that it becomes uneconomic to launch.

Equally, of course, some companies have inadequate levels of investment and this manifests itself in a final product that is of poor quality. The consumer who is aware of competitor products of higher quality might reject such a product.

Change in strategic aims

There are potentially two issues here. The first is that the product does not meet the current strategic aims of the business, and the second is that because of business dynamics, the strategic aims of the company change. If the product has had a long gestation period, then by the time of its introduction it might not fit the organization's strategic objectives. The company therefore has to take the difficult decision to launch, or not to launch. Either way the result may be costly for the company.

Minimizing the risk of failure

As we have seen, many companies face a significant risk of product failure. While it is impossible to eliminate the risk of failure totally, steps can be taken to minimize the level of risk. Various characteristics need to be evaluated in relation to the marketing mix and proposed target markets.

Relative advantage

Products that offer consumers real features and benefits over existing products tend to be more readily adopted.

Compatibility

An innovation will generally have an increased chance of success if it is compatible with current technologies, usage patterns and behaviour. Of course there are exceptions to the rule. In terms of technology, the introduction of the CD changed the face of music listening, superseding both vinyl LP records and turntable systems. CDs provided higher quality sound reproduction and easier storage. Meanwhile chip technologies enabled the miniaturization of CD systems, from the Sony Walkman™ through to midis. Now CD systems – whether standalones or integrated into computers – must be of a compatible format. That has created increased versatility for the consumer.

Trialability

If consumers have access to a trial version prior to purchase, there is an increased chance they will adopt the product. Earlier we mentioned the distribution of trial packs, through in-store promotion or door-to-door drops. Additionally, companies can organize demonstrations.

Let us take a computer system as an example. A consumer can visit a retail outlet and receive a free demonstration that also allows him or her some hands-on time. Within a business-to-business environment, the computer company might allow the prospective customer to use the system for a few days in order to trial and test its functions. After this limited trial period the business customer can accept or reject the system.

Some car companies are allowing prospective customers one-day test drives of their new models. This is especially so in the case of company fleet purchases where several cars are likely to be bought.

Observability

Adoption is more likely if consumers can see the advantages of the new product to their own lives. For example, consider the development of the mobile phone, where consumers can witness the benefits derived from communicating with their friends and family.

Complexity

Generally, consumers are more reluctant to adopt new products that are, or are perceived to be, complex. During the 1990s some VCRs were introduced with an array of innovative features. However they were perceived as far too complex to operate. Additionally the instructions or operation manuals were not written with the average consumer in mind, adding to the perceived complexity. The lesson here is for companies to show that complex products are easy to use. This will go some way towards stimulating adoption.

Risk

As we have seen from Rogers' (1983) analysis, consumers are reluctant to adopt a new innovation if a high degree of risk is perceived. This perceived risk can be monetary, psychological, physical, or a combination of these factors.

For example, in 1985 the electronics engineer and inventor Sir Clive Sinclair introduced, with much publicity, a small three-wheeled 'personal transport' buggy onto the market. The C5, powered by a washing-machine engine and rechargeable batteries, was developed as a serious on-road, single-seater vehicle for city or country use. However it was slow and fragile, and was perceived by consumers as unsafe and impractical, especially in heavy city traffic. Within two months of the launch production was halted, and the C5 rapidly disappeared from the marketplace (Tibballs, 1999).

Marketing insight: Airbus A380–100

In July 2000, at the Farnborough International Airshow in the UK, Airbus launched its plan to build a new generation of large aircraft. The A380–100 (formerly known as the A3XX) will be a long-range, double-decked aircraft capable of carrying between 481 and 656 passengers. Airbus Industries is a joint venture consortium formed by France's Aerospatiale, Germany's Messerschmitt Boklow Blohm, the UK's British Aerospace and Spain's Construcciones Aeronauticas, and is considered the major rival of the Boeing Corporation.

By the time Airbus announced its plans to build the A380–100 it had already invested 10 years of design development and US $1 billion. Its reasons for designing such an aircraft were based on the following predictions:

- Passenger numbers will continue to rise, as more people travel for both business and pleasure. Forecasts suggest that (from 2000) world air traffic is set to double in the next 15 years and triple in the next 22 years.
- Major airports are currently operating up to their limits. At London's Heathrow Airport, there is an aircraft movement every 60 seconds. There will be a need to alleviate this stress as the skies over major airports become even more congested.
- There is growing demand for lower-cost airline travel.
- There is growing demand from passengers for increased comfort on long-haul flights, especially in economy class.

Therefore an aircraft manufacturer needs to deliver a plane that will:

- Reduce airline operating costs. That means reducing weight and increasing fuel efficiency through improved engine performance, more aerodynamic lift capabilities and less drag.
- Fit within the box allocated by airports to separate aircraft during passenger loading and unloading.
- Be designed to speed the process of passenger loading and unloading, especially from two levels. The longer the aircraft is on the ground, the greater the cost to the airline, so faster turnaround times are becoming crucial to airline operating efficiencies.
- Not damage the runways on landing. The weight load, like the Boeing 747's, will be spread. However it will still be 600 tonnes of aircraft touching down.
- Be delivered on schedule and be affordable in airline terms. The A380–100 will cost (depending on configurations) approximately UK £160 million.

Overall there will be major technical challenges for the A380–100 manufacturers. They will need to push the boundaries of current technology. Again this is a major investment in research, design and manufacture.

The commercial airline manufacturing industry is highly competitive, with billions of dollars at stake. Airbus needs to convince airlines that there is a viable market for such an aircraft. On 24 July 2000 Sheikh Ahmed bin Saeed Al-Maktoum, Chairman of Emirates, signed a UK £1 billion commitment to buy five passenger and two freight versions with an option on five more. The airline is due to take delivery of the first A380–100 in February 2006. By March 2003 advance orders totalled 95 for eight airlines. However Airbus predict that the demand for aircraft with over 500-seat capacity will place 1,235 into service by 2019. Such a market could be worth over US $300 million over 20 years.

Questions/activities

These can be undertaken either individually or within groups.

1. Using Web resources, consider how the Boeing aircraft manufacturer has reacted to this competitive challenge. Do you think the market is potentially large enough for two large commercial aircraft? What do you consider to be the potential risks involved in this new product development?
2. Using Internet and other library sources, consider whether Airbus has correctly anticipated the development in air travel. Is there research that counters or contradicts the manufacturer's predictions?
3. Monitoring news channels, documentaries, the Internet and Airbus's Web site, consider whether the company is being successful in marketing the A380–100 to the world's airlines.
4. Consider the future of the A380 in light of the terrorist attacks on New York and Washington in September 2001, and their subsequent impact on the airline industry.

Sources: Channel 4 (2001); Apter (2000); Airbus Web site: www.airbus.com

Brands and branding

Brands are at the heart of marketing and business strategy.

Professor Peter Doyle (1998)

What is a brand?

Kotler (2000) describes brands as:

A name, term, symbol or design (or a combination of them) which is intended to signify the goods or services of one seller or groups of sellers and to differentiate them from those of the competitors.

The difference between a product and a brand has been described like this:

Products are tangible things that exist in the physical world. If everyone in the world died tomorrow, products would still be there. But brands exist in consumer perception, in people's heads. If everyone in the world died tomorrow, brands would die too. When enough people come to share the same perception of a product, it reaches a 'psychological critical mass'. Take the BMW badge. This stands for values beyond car values. It is a symbol of social success, of youthfulness, of sportiness – reaching the 'critical mass' in brand perception always seems to require consistency.

(Toby Hoare, Managing Director of the advertising agency Young & Rubican, quoted in Hindle, 2000)

I would view a Superbrand as one that can stand the test of time, a brand that can survive in an ever changing world is something extra special – Coca-Cola and Persil are two such examples. The secret to their success is innovation. Manufacturers of Superbrands constantly invest in the product to ensure it meets the ever changing needs of the consumers and fluctuating market conditions.

(Jim Rose, AC Neilsen, quoted in Hindle, 2000)

Brands and packages are part of a product's tangible features, the verbal and physical cues that help customers identify products they want and influence their choices when they are unsure. A good brand is distinct and memorable; without one, companies could not differentiate their products and services, and consumer choice would be arbitrary (Dibb *et al*, 1997).

To take a partial line of text from Kotler's (2000) definition of branding, we can see that there are some powerful images (many perhaps subliminal) that reinforce the brand:

A name, term, symbol or design (or a combination of them)

Let's consider a few examples, many of which are easily recognizable:

Coca-Cola

The combination of the unique typeface and bottle shape have made it one of the enduring brand symbols of the 20th and 21st centuries.

Pillsbury Foods

While Pillsbury diversified into other food products during the 1960s and 1970s, it remains famous for its refrigerated dough. In 1965 a small group of advertising executives sat around a table searching for a creative idea that would build the brand. Out of this meeting came the character 'Poppin Fresh' (widely known as the Pillsbury Dough Boy™). Within three years of his first appearance, more than 87 per cent of the American public recognized the symbol, and hence the brand. By advertising the company was able to reinforce the brand's qualities through this animated character.

By the late 1990s the Dough Boy™ often still ranked Number 1 on the list of America's most popular food product characters. However, such characters need refreshing from time to time to maintain that brand quality. In the 1960s the Dough Boy™ was seen in the family kitchen, followed in the 1980s by his playing an 'air' guitar, and the 1990s turned him into a rap star to appeal to the youth culture.[2]

HMV (His Master's Voice)

HMV has global recognition as both a CD label and a chain of music stores. In the UK it has more than 100 retail stores, and the HMV brand has been developed successfully throughout the rest of the world, with a further 200 outlets across the United States, Canada, Australia, Japan, Hong Kong, Singapore, Germany and Ireland.

His Master's Voice was originally the title of a painting by Francis Barraud (1856–1924), showing the artist's terrier cross dog, Nipper, looking curiously at the black horn of a wax cylinder phonograph player from which the sound of 'his master's voice' is emerging. The Gramophone Record Company agreed to purchase the work in 1899, stipulating that the picture had to be altered to show a brass horn and a more up-to-date gramophone. Nipper was first used on an advertisement in 1900 in America. In the UK Nipper appeared on records from 1909, and the phrase 'His Master's Voice' became part of the logo in 1910. By the late 1990s HMV, still incorporating the symbol of Nipper, began using the slogan 'top dog for music' to reinforce the brand image. It remains a highly recognizable symbol of the 21st century.

Real people and fictional characters

People are increasingly becoming 'brands' in their own right, although this is not really new: you just have to consider the movie icons of the 1930s and 1940s to realize that movie stars were considered as brands by the studios. Personalities such as Madonna, the Beatles, footballer David Beckham and the actor Leonardo di Caprio show many brand characteristics. Of course, the personality does not have to be real: for example, Ian Fleming's fictional secret agent James Bond presents a very strong brand image and identity. The actors who have played the character in a highly successful series of movies have reinforced this brand image.

Not-for-profit organizations

Equally, not-for-profit organizations are branding themselves in order to differentiate themselves. Even the charities market is competitive, as organizations compete for donations and voluntary support. Strong brand identities and images help in their quest to help the less fortunate in our communities.

Cities and countries are brands as well, often with structures being their symbols or logos. In the first picture the Eiffel Tower clearly represents Paris, and thus France. Meanwhile the traditional English cricket ground set against the sprawling backdrop of skyscrapers represents part of Singapore's traditional and contemporary business image and identity.

Business brands

The issues considered above were clearly focused on consumer brands. These are things that we are familiar with. However, what is often neglected is business brands. If we accept that there is a business-to-business environment, then there are B2B brands that have both reputation and value associated with them. We all know the names Boeing and Airbus – suppliers of aircraft (both military and civilian) – because we have seen them and flown on their aircraft. However, the aircraft they develop and manufacture are marketed to governments and airlines, not to the end users, such as the passengers flying British Airways to Sydney, Australia.

While most of us are aware of the names Boeing and Airbus we may not be familiar with the companies that manufacture the seats and avionics and provide the catering services, yet these will be brands with a reputation for service and quality. They are known to the airlines and aircraft manufacturers but not to the end users of the aircraft, the passengers.

Table 8.2 lists some powerful B2B brand names that you may or may not be familiar with. However, within their operational environment or sphere of influence they possess high brand awareness and valuation.

Of course there are brands that span both the B2C and B2B markets. For example, a hotel chain such as the Hilton Group

Table 8.2 A Selection of B2B brands

Brand	Functional activities	Country of origin
Fincantieri	Naval and commercial shipyard	Italy
Clays	Commercial printers	UK
3663	Food service company	UK
WPP	Advertising and other media services	UK
AC Neilson	Market research	United States
Hill & Knowlton	Public relations agency	United States
W G Gore and Associates. Gore Tex©	Waterproof fabrics	United States
Andersen Consulting	Management consultants	United States
Tetra Pak	Packaging	Sweden
Hilton International	Hotel group Main and subsidiary brands	United States Now UK owned

markets to both companies and vacation seekers. Where companies are concerned, the facilities provided can range from executive floors (with their own dining rooms and bars) to conference and exhibition rooms. For the vacation seeker there is the mixture of location and facilities such as swimming pools and fitness areas. The approach of the hotel's marketing team will be very different depending on the customer focus. The Hilton Group is one of several hotel groups that have developed a strong brand profile within both the B2C and B2B marketplaces.

How branding started

The word 'brand' is derived from an old Norse word *brandir*, which means 'to burn'. We can take this as imprinting an idea or symbol on a product. As we will see later in this section, livestock was branded as a means of identification.

If we look back over the centuries the vast majority of products were sold loose from barrels or glass jars. Indeed children in the 1950s and 1960s often bought their sweets loose from glass jars at the local confectioner. So many sweets would be scooped, weighed out and placed in brown or white paper bags. There are a few shops in the UK and United States where such practices still exist.

Branding can be traced back to the craft guilds. Merchant guilds were formed in England during the 11th century, with many becoming powerful forces within local government. Trade or craft guilds came into prominence in Medieval Europe during the 14th century, effectively controlling trade and commerce within many countries. These craftspeople's reputation was paramount, thus they controlled quality and production flow. These factors also impacted on the pricing of the ultimate finished product, much the same as today!

As transport improved during the 19th century, and the Industrial Revolution changed the face of business, travelling salespeople crossed continents with every known (and unknown) type of product. Slowly there was an awareness, first locally, then regionally and finally nationally, of recognizable brands. This provided the foundation for growth on a much larger and more impressive scale.

During the period of the American 'Wild West' and the opening up of territories, cattle ranchers faced the problem of identifying their herds, especially when they became mixed in with cattle from other ranches. We must remember that lands were not necessarily fenced, thus several hundred or indeed thousand hectares could belong to one ranching family. Cattle would often wander or be rustled (stolen). Thus the ranchers introduced the branding of their cattle with hot irons. The branding clearly identified whether the cattle were from the 'T-bar' or 'Circle O' ranches using the simple symbols 'T' and 'O'.

In the late 1920s Procter & Gamble (P&G) started developing a new system of brand management. In 1931 Neil McElroy, the company's Promotions Department Manager, created a marketing organization based on competing brands managed by dedicated groups or teams of people. The brand management system provided P&G with more specialized marketing strategies for each brand. P&G believed the most efficient way to organize brands, and its business, was to give responsibility for advertising, promotion and packaging of a single brand to a single individual. Thus a new function of business was born, the brand manager (Decker, 1999).

The world's most valuable brands

Table 8.3 lists the world's most powerful brands from 2000 to 2002. There are several points to note:

▌ The sheer value of the brands, both individually and collectively. Collectively the top 50 brands for the year 2002 had a value in excess of US $800 billion.

▌ With two exceptions US multinationals dominate the top 10 positions. The exceptions are number 6 in the 2002 rankings, Nokia (Finland) and number 10, Mercedes (Germany).

▌ Coca-Cola remains ranked first, yet the computer software giant Microsoft is relatively speaking not far behind, as is the computer hardware company IBM. All three companies have maintained their positions over the three-year period.

▌ The highest ranking European company for 2002 is the telecommunications giant Nokia in sixth position.

▌ There are eight European, five Japanese and one South Korean company on the list.

▌ While there have been climbers, some brands have fallen in value, namely Ford, Merrill Lynch, Compaq, Kodak, Nintendo, Merck, Nike, Volkswagen, Kellogg's, MTV, Gap and Apple.

So where are the other famous brands that we see virtually every day of our lives? First let us consider those who have fallen out of the Top 50 from 2000:

Xerox	51	Yahoo!	67
Gucci	52	Ericsson	71
Reuters	58	Motorola	74
Philips	60	Duracell	75
AOL	63		

Here is a snapshot of some other 2002 positions:

Kleenex	55	Burger King	90
Colgate	59	Barbie	94
Levi's	73	Jack Daniels	98
Amazon.com	80		

Table 8.3   The top 50 world's most valuable brands

Brand	2002	Value US $ bn	2001	Value US $ bn	2000	Value US $ bn	Country of Origin
Coca-Cola	1	69.63	1	68.94	1	83.84	United States
Microsoft	2	64.09	2	65.06	2	70.19	United States
IBM	3	51.18	3	52.75	3	53.18	United States
GE	4	41.31	4	42.39	6	38.12	United States
Intel	5	30.86	6	34.66	4	39.04	United States
Nokia	6	29.97	5	35.03	5	38.52	Finland
Disney	7	29.25	7	32.59	8	33.55	United States
McDonald's	8	26.37	9	25.28	8	27.85	United States
Marlboro	9	24.15	11	22.05	11	22.11	United States
Mercedes	10	21.01	12	21.72	12	21.10	Germany
Ford	11	20.40	8	30.09	7	36.36	United States
Toyota	12	19.44	14	18.57	15	18.82	Japan
Citibank	13	18.06	13	19.00	16	18.81	United States
Hewlett-Packard	14	16.77	15	17.98	13	20.57	United States
American Express	15	16.28	17	16.91	19	16.12	United States
Cisco Systems	16	16.22	16	17.20	14	20.06	United States
AT&T	17	16.05	10	22.82	10	25.54	United States
Honda	18	15.06	21	14.63	20	15.24	Japan
Gillette	19	14.95	18	15.29	17	15.29	United States
BMW	20	14.42	22	13.85	23	12.96	Germany
Sony	21	13.89	20	15.00	18	16.41	Japan
Nescafé	22	12.84	23	13.25	22	13.68	Switzerland
Oracle	23	11.51	25	12.22	NA	NA	United States
Budweiser	24	11.34	26	10.83	26	10.68	United States
Merrill Lynch	25	11.23	19	15.01	NA	NA	United States
Morgan Stanley	26	11.20	NA	NA	NA	NA	United States
Compaq	27	9.80	24	12.35	21	14.60	United States
Pfizer	28	9.77	30	8.95	NA	NA	United States
JP Morgan	29	9.69	NA	NA	NA	NA	United States
Kodak	30	9.67	27	10.80	24	11.82	United States
Dell	31	9.23	32	8.26	28	9.4	United States
Nintendo	32	9.2	29	9.46	NA	NA	Japan
Merck	33	9.1	28	9.67	NA	NA	Germany
Samsung	34	8.3	NA	NA	NA	NA	South Korea
Nike	35	7.7	34	7.5	30	8.01	United States
Gap	36	7.4	31	8.74	29	9.31	United States
Heinz	37	7.3	37	7.06	NA	NA	United States
Volkswagen	38	7.2	35	7.33	31	7.83	Germany
Goldman Sachs	39	7.194	33	7.8	NA	NA	United States
Kellogg's	40	7.191	39	7.00	33	7.35	United States
Louis Vuitton	41	7.0	38	7.05	34	6.88	France
SAP	42	6.77	43	6.30	39	6.13	Germany
Canon	43	6.72	41	6.58	NA	NA	Japan
IKEA	44	6.5	46	6.00	NA	NA	Sweden
Pepsi	45	6.3	44	6.21	35	6.63	United States
Harley Davidson	46	6.2	48	5.53	NA	NA	United States
MTV	47	6.078	40	6.59	37	6.41	United States
Pizza Hut	48	6.046	47	5.97	NA	NA	United States
KFC	49	5.346	51	5.26	NA	NA	United States
Apple	50	5.316	49	5.46	36	6.59	United States

Data © Interbrand.

Sources: Adapted from Interbrand's *World's 100 Most Valuable Brands* reports. Students are encouraged to visit Interbrand's excellent and exhaustive Web site on brands and brand valuation.

The UK-based company Interbrand has developed a formula for calculating brand values. It takes an objective measure of the brand's recent profitability, and multiplies it by a number based upon a subjective judgment of the following seven brand characteristics:

- the brand's leadership (or otherwise) within the marketplace;
- the brand's stability (or longevity);
- the nature of the market, for example, whether it is large and stable or subject to fast-changing fashions and fads;
- the brand's internationality. International brands are assumed to be more powerful (domestically and overseas), than purely national brands;
- the potential trend for the brand;
- the marketing support for the brand;
- the brand's legal protection through patent and trademarks.

Why companies and organizations brand themselves and their products

We have already gleaned some of the reasons companies brand their products from considering the historical aspect. Here we develop these themes further, and introduce new ones. As you will see many of these points are highly integrated. These make up the whole of what we can describe as a 'brand'. The more effectively and efficiently a company can deliver these elements, the greater the opportunity it has of positioning and developing the brand within the marketplace.

Brand differentiation

In Chapter 7 we considered Porter's generic strategies model, which suggests companies need to differentiate themselves to gain a competitive advantage. This applies to branding. Branding is a form of product differentiation that conveys information. This helps the consumer identify the goods, therefore creating an opportunity for customer loyalty to the brand. It is therefore a means of potentially (though not always) increasing and/or maintaining sales. It is perhaps important here to remember that a

company is striving for a sustained competitive advantage, and brand differentiation may assist in delivering that sustainability.

Brand advertising

Although it is called brand advertising, we can really consider this brand promotion in the widest sense. 'Promotions' need a brand name to sell to consumers. Therefore branding and advertising or promotions are very closely related. The more similar a product is to a competing one, the more branding is necessary to establish and reinforce a separate product identity.

Brand selection

This facilitates self-selection of products in self-service stores (for example in department stores and supermarkets). Again, this is about positioning the brand in the minds of consumers: some they recognize and feel emotionally comfortable buying, while with other products they will not feel so emotionally attached.

Brands remove price differentials

The stronger competitive brands tend to be similarly priced (though not always), thus removing any price differentials. In such cases differentiation appears in the form of perceived or real benefits (for instance, user friendliness).

Brand awareness

Branding assists in creating awareness, the ability of a consumer to remember or recognize a brand. This awareness can be either spontaneous or prompted (for example, through in-store advertising or point of sale). This is widely used in tests as a key indicator of brand management effectiveness.

Brand loyalty

Brand loyalty from consumers can provide a manufacturer with more control over marketing strategy and choice of distribution channels. However, brand managers must be aware that a consumer may be loyal to several competing brands, almost simultaneously. For instance, a consumer may be loyal to one supermarket because it is positioned directly opposite his or her place of work. At the weekend he or she may be loyal to another supermarket brand because it is positioned near his or her home.

Brand extensions

Other products can be introduced into the brand range. Adding products to an existing brand range is known as brand extension strategy. For example, SmithKline Beecham's painkiller brand Hedex (which is a global brand) is now available in several variations: Hedex, Hedex Extra and Hedex Ibuprofen. (See the section on brand extensions on page 292.)

New additions to a brand range can be beneficial for two reasons. First, they require a lower level of marketing investment (their image is already known). Second, the extension of a successful brand presents less risk to consumers who might be worried about trying something new. This could include a new model within a car range, such as a hatchback/convertible or an estate.

The Marlboro™ cigarette brand has been extended into clothing with Marlboro Classics™. As well as differentiating beyond cigarettes for the company, the clothing brand links into brand awareness, recognition and recall – the Marlboro™ name – as well as the potential loyalty factor.

Brand segmentation

Branding makes market segmentation easier. Different brands of similar products may be developed to meet specific needs of categories or users. (See Chapter 5.)

Brand recall

Branding facilitates memory recall. This is the extent to which a consumer can recall the names or images linked to particular brands. This in turn provides the opportunity to improve sales and reinforce brand loyalty.

Brand equity

Brand equity is the accumulated goodwill that exists within the market towards a particular brand. This gives the brand added value over similar unbranded or undistinguished products.

Brand recognition

Branding aids recognition: this is the extent to which a consumer can recognize a brand from a series of clues, particularly visual clues. Certain purchasing decisions require recognition. For example, when shopping in a supermarket, visual recognition of a particular brand may trigger purchase. Examples include a particular brand of chocolate or washing detergent, or even a family car.

Brand stretching

Brand stretching (also known as brand elasticity) is the concept that one brand name can be stretched over several quite different products. An example would be the UK's Virgin Group, where the brand has been stretched to encompass airlines, trains, mobile phones, finance and insurance. Already Virgin has lent its name to over 130 different companies. (See the section on brand extensions on page 292.)

Brand valuations

Brand valuation is the process of attaching a financial value to its brands, although in many countries companies cannot add this valuation to their balance sheet. Nevertheless the value of brands has become increasingly important beyond the realms of the marketing department. Now the finance departments of major companies actively value not only their own brands, but those of other companies. Today when companies seek potential acquisition targets they are analysing not only the value of the tangible assets such as plant and equipment but the intangible value of the brands. That valuation must consider not only their value today, but future potential as well.

When the American tobacco company Philip Morris bought the Kraft General Foods in 1988 it paid US $12.9 billion. That was four times the value of Kraft's tangible assets, therefore Philip Morris paid approximately US $10 billion for Kraft's intangible assets, in essence for its named brands (Doyle, 1998). This was not only seen as a valuable proposition, it also helped Philip Morris diversify. It was clear that there would be increasing global curbs on its core business, the tobacco industry (increased taxes on cigarettes, bans on promotional activity and litigation), and such acquisition could secure the future of the business.

Another example is the acquisition of the UK confectioner Rowntree Mackintosh by the Swiss-based food conglomerate Nestlé. In 1988 Nestlé, the world's largest food manufacturer, paid UK £2.5 billion for Rowntree Mackintosh. That was five to six times the stock market valuation, an extraordinary premium for any acquisitional venture. The reasoning behind the purchase decision was the power and reputation of the brands created, developed and nurtured by Rowntree Mackintosh since the 1930s (Doyle, 1998). These brands included Polo mints, After Eight mints and Kit Kat chocolate bars. The latter was perhaps considered the real jewel in the crown and worth the high acquisition price. Since the takeover the name Rowntree Mackintosh has disappeared; however Nestlé moved its international confectionary HQ to the UK. It could be argued that with such powerful UK-based brands in its portfolio, it was only logical for the company to position its HQ in the UK. This also reinforced Nestlé's market position against such players as Cadbury's in the European marketplace.

Brand protection

Branding is a means of obtaining legal protection for specific product features and/or benefits, and the brand name itself. The protection is enforced through trademarks, copyrights and registrations. This is a key factor in the long-term success of the brand. However, piracy is a fundamental problem for leading brands such as Nike and Microsoft. As a result of piracy significant sums are lost every year in terms of both direct revenue generation and reputational damage. Many who buy pirated products are unaware that they are illegal products, so if the product malfunctions they blame the legitimate manufacturer (whose product it is not). Piracy has become a multi-billion dollar issue, as companies seek to protect their legitimate rights, and thus in turn protect the rights of consumers.

Branding identity

This helps to build a strong corporate identity, especially if the brand name is also the company name: for example Heinz, Kodak, Pepsi-Cola and Microsoft.

Integrating communication

Branding makes it easier to link advertising to other marketing communication functions, such as public relations, point of sale and sponsorship (see Chapters 10 and 11).

Building brands

Kashani (1999) believes that powerful brands are built over time through a deliberate management process involving strategic decision making followed by corresponding (and appropriate) actions. Figure 8.2 shows Kashani's model for brand building. The process elements are shown along two dimensions: strategy implementation on the horizontal axis, and the values and attributes along the vertical axis. Within this arrow head or wedge there are six decision and action elements, and these are outlined below.

Anchor values

Kashani (1999) suggests that every brand needs to be based on values and attributes that are permanent, purposeful and fundamental to its strategy. These values could include being innovative, contemporary, dependable, easy to use, strong and ambitious.

Kashani (1999) contends that by creating such values the organization is providing a direction and thus a future for the brand. However, the difficulty for some companies is in accurately deciding on the values. An incorrect decision could lead to problems in defining a long-term brand strategy. Equally, companies have to react to unforeseen circumstances as well as longer-term changes in external environmental influences. As we saw in Chapter 2, societies are modified, altered or changed over time. People can become weary of a brand, for many reasons. Therefore it could be argued that some degree of flexibility needs to be considered when developing anchor brands. Clearly a company cannot go too far astray from the original values, but there must be some movement to react to change.

Customer value proposition (CVP)

This is the translation of the anchor values into specific functional and beneficial statements

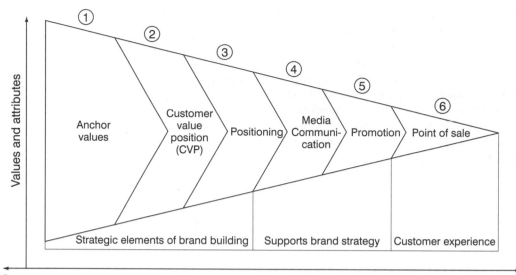

Figure 8.2 Kashini's model for brand building

that help inform the buying decision. These statements must focus on issues that are important to the customer. Differentiated products can normally rely on tangible and functional benefits. However, non-differentiated products and services often lack these tangibles, and thus must rely on intangibles. These tend to be emotional values. Increasingly, though, there is a view that branding has a more emotional content than was originally thought. Thus brands represent not necessarily just a product, but increasingly a way of life for many people. An example is the mobile phone that has become very much an emotional attachment for many people. Could you go several days without your mobile phone?

As a result of this phenomenon of attachment, companies are attempting to make their products stand out by emphasizing their emotional aspects, with the objective that the customer identifies with the set of values the brand represents or portrays (Kashani, 1999). Companies that can break through the 'promotional clutter' and connect directly with their customers may be able to create strong emotional bonds.

Positioning

This brand building element consists of two core components, target segmentation and differentiation. Segmentation identifies the customers who best identify with the anchor values and are best served by the brand's CVP. Targeting, though, should not just focus on current customers but consider potential targets for future brand building.

Differentiation is what makes the brand different from its competitors, and this, as stated earlier, may be emotionally driven. For example, the Nokia brand is perceived as youthful, exciting, fun, stylish, complex, yet easy to use. Nokia has communicated a youthful image through the use of different and colourful fascia, ring tones and technical features.

According to Kashani (1999), anchor values, the CVP and positioning are the three strategic elements of brand building.

Advertising media

This covers the range of advertising media available, from newspapers, magazines and television through to billboards and the Internet. Kashani (1999) suggests that for brand builders to succeed with such advertising media they need to break through 'clutter' and overcome 'message decay'. Clutter can be defined as the inordinate amount of messages the average consumer is bombarded with each day through advertising media. Decay is where the viewer cannot recall all or part of the message within a short time frame. Companies and their advertising agencies need to deploy techniques so that the customer first is more aware of the brand, and second, has a longer-lasting impression of the brand and its values, and improved recall.

Promotion

This is non-mass advertising media brand support, and can include sponsorship of events or good causes, public relations and direct marketing. Such promotions can be highly effective as they can be used to target specific individual customers and/or groups. Often one of the keys to brand success is an integrated marketing communications (IMC) campaign that brings together a range of marketing communication elements which can reinforce a brand's position within the marketplace.

Point of sale or point of purchase

This is the point where the customer makes the decision to either buy or not buy a particular brand. Many individual factors are often brought together here and focused, often for a very short time frame, perhaps a matter of seconds. It is what Kashani (1999) considers the 'moments of truth'. Consider for a moment the often numerous different brands of detergent on a supermarket shelf. A range of factors can shape the customer's buying experience and decision to purchase. These influencers include:

- the position on the shelf;
- the packaging: size, the imagery on the packaging and the wording;
- the ingredients (which might or might not be environmentally friendly);
- word of mouth, what the customer remembers of what others have said about specific brand(s);
- the price;
- any special offers.

However point of sale is not just linked to the product. It is the customer–seller interface as well that may drive the sale. This is equally true of B2B and B2C. For McDonald's the customer's experience is an important brand value: friendly, clean environment, consistent food quality and efficient service. These have all contributed to McDonald's global brand development.

We should also not forget the customer interface when buying via the Internet. Whether people are buying theatre or airline tickets, it is the experience of buying (for example, fast, clear and efficient) that creates a longer-term customer loyalty.

Brand types

There are various types of branding policy that a company can adopt for its products or services. The nomenclature varies significantly from textbook to textbook, and indeed from country to country. As this can prove confusing we advise students to read widely on this topic area. We have attempted to create as full a picture as possible within the bounds of this book.

Family brands

(These may also be referred to as masterbrands, manufacturing or umbrella brands.) These are strong powerful brand names which all contain the name of the company, which becomes the vehicle for promoting a range of products. Examples include both product manufacturers and service providers, such as Heinz, Sony, Virgin, Cadbury, and the Hilton and Paradores Hotel chains.

Advantages

Davidson (1997) contends that such brands can generate high volume and critical mass by spanning a wide range of markets. If advertising support and other media tools and techniques are used efficiently (taking advantage of economies of scale) the brand can be extended into new areas, minimizing risk.

Disadvantages

The main potential problem is over extension of the name. Some companies try to be 'all things to all people'. As a result the consumer may become confused or complacent about the brand name and image.

Adverse publicity from any one product may have significant impact on the family of brands. An example in the UK is Virgin Trains. The Virgin brand name, synonymous with its founder, the entrepreneur Richard Branson, had gained a powerful reputation for quality and service, first through Virgin Records, then Virgin Megastores, Virgin Atlantic (airline), Virgin Cola and Virgin Direct (financial services). In the 1980s the Virgin Group successfully bid for two railway franchises. However, they were inheriting from British Rail two of the most problematic sectors of the UK rail network, with older rolling stock than on other lines, poor overall services and low staff morale. While significant immediate investments were made, combined with a comprehensive investment strategy for the 21st century, Virgin Trains suffered from continued criticism from the travelling public, something the media were quick to seize upon.

The impact of this adverse publicity had an effect on the image of the Virgin Group. Even

Richard Branson admitted that, with hindsight, perhaps another name should have been chosen for the railway company in the first instance, with it changing to the Virgin banner at a later stage when systems and new rolling stock were successfully in place (BBC, 1999).[3] Since then Virgin Trains has introduced a range of state-of-the-art rolling stock on to all its lines. By 2002 the transformation had begun.

Individual brands

These are stand alone products that carry individual brand names and have clear and distinctive identities. For example, Procter & Gamble household products all carry individual brand names, so in the UK Ariel is a P&G laundry detergent and Flash a kitchen cleaner.

Within a policy of individual branding a company may adopt a multi-branding strategy. This is the practice of carrying several brands within one product line. A good example is the various washing detergents produced by P&G, which has some 24 different brands of fabric washing products. Obviously many of these individual brands are in competition with each other for market share. This strategy has several objectives:

- It is a means of the company obtaining greater shelf space in retail outlets, relative to its competitors. This is especially the case where the competitors are less known or less market established brands.

- It is a way of dealing with brand switchers. These are customers who either like to try a different brand from time to time, or dislike a particular brand (for example, because they feel it has poor performance) and thus switch to another. Equally they could be customers who dislike a particular company and switch to another brand, not realizing the other brand is marketed by the same company.

- It is a way of creating barriers to potential new entrants into the marketplace (see Chapter 7 and Porter's five forces model). It might leave no gaps within the market to penetrate at the same level. In order to enter the market a new entrant might have to go either downmarket or significantly upmarket. However if it did this it could still encounter barriers to entry, and it might not be within the potential entrant's corporate interests to go either down or up.

▊ It is a way of segmenting the market, providing brands that may develop their own loyal followers and thus supporters. (See Chapter 4, and reflect on buyer behaviour and advocates.)

▊ It is a strategy that can be used to create a degree of competition among a company's brand managers, and keep them alert and competitive.

▊ It is a means of delivering significant revenues to the parent company, assisting in building its strength. Consider, for example, the global power of companies such as P&G and Lever.

▊ If there is adverse publicity affecting one of the brands, it is unlikely to have a detrimental impact on others within the brand portfolio. Indeed, it might shift buyers towards another brand within the company's overall portfolio.

Own-label brands

These are also referred to as own brands, dealer brands, private labels, store brands, retailer brands, no-names, generics and distributor brands. Supermarkets and chain stores often have their own brands: for example the UK-based supermarket chains Sainsbury and Tesco have a wide range of own-brand products, from detergents to tins of baked beans, spaghetti and chilled ready-prepared meals.

The UK retail chain Marks & Spencer established (and trade marked) its own label St Michael in 1928. This remained its only own-label brand until the late 1990s. In 1999 it introduced a new own label, Salon Rose, designed exclusively for Marks & Spencer by the luxury lingerie company, Agent Provocateur. Since 1999 Marks and Spencer has introduced other own-label brands including per una, Blue Harbour, Autograph and View From.

According to work conducted by Kashani (1999) the market shares of private label brands in grocery products grew significantly across Europe during the 1990s. All this gain came at the expense of manufacturer brands. Moreover, many manufacturers supply their private label competitors to help make up for income shortfalls due to loss of market shares and pressures on margins.

The growth of own-label brands has been particularly dramatic in some national markets. Tables 8.4 and 8.5 give details of own-label grocery and household product share by both volume and value.

Table 8.4   Own-label market share by volume, 1999

Country	Volume (%)
UK	45.4
Belgium	34.7
Germany	33.2
France	22.1
Netherlands	20.6
Spain	20.5
United States	20.2
Italy	17.1

Source: Tomkins (2001)

Table 8.5   Own-label market share by value, 1999

Country	Value (%)
UK	43.5
Germany	27.4
Belgium	26.0
France	19.1
Netherlands	18.4
United States	15.8
Italy	15.5
Spain	14.8

Source: Tomkins (2001)

One of the possible advantages that own-label brands have over brands from mainstream manufacturers is that they can launch a product relatively quickly. They are not usually encumbered by the need to create major advertising campaigns and strategies to support the brand.

Marketing insight: The Co-Op Brio Actipods and McBride

Some consumers have often perceived own-label brands as inferior to the established power of well-known widely available big brand names. The thought prevailed that 'own label' tended to mean cheap, and often poor quality. In some cases it meant exactly that, but not in all cases. However, the stigma remained. Thus many consumers would not be seen dead buying own-label products when they could buy the 'real thing'!

Some retailers have created two tiers of own labels in order to boost their own-label products, one perhaps labelled 'premium value' and the other 'economy'. This differentiation is designed to say to consumers that if they are particularly price-sensitive they should buy the product labelled 'economy'. If they were not particularly price-sensitive, but still wanted to save some money, they should choose 'premium value'.

Manufacturer brands have had two key advantages over the own-label versions. The first was significant marketing budgets: the products could be advertised repeatedly to remind consumers of their various features and benefits. The second key advantage was innovation. The national brands led the game and the own-label brands were often reduced to being the imitators, the followers.

Traditionally, the national brands fought each other within the competitive arena, and the own-label versions were to some extent inconsequential within the overall market environment. Not any more: the market dynamics have changed and the own-label brands have now gained a significant slice of the market. Today the retail grocery market in the UK is dominated by a small but increasingly powerful group of companies. They have successfully built and extended their brand names and image, they are easily recognizable and they are increasingly trusted by the consumer. In order to gain that consumer trust, they have had to build a reputation for quality and value, and that includes their own-label brand ranges too.

Now they are beginning to demonstrate that they can be innovative, not only in packaging utility and design but also with the product itself. In February 2001 Britain's Co-Operative retailing group launched Brio Actipods, pre-measured doses (50 ml) of concentrated liquid detergent sealed in soluble sachets. The sachets are placed inside the washing machine drum with the laundry and dissolve during the wash cycle. This was an innovative product and launched before anyone else, including Unilever and P&G. P&G launched its Ariel Liqui-Tabs in March, followed by Unilever's Persil Capsules in April 2001.

Brio Actipods are made by McBride, a manufacturer of own-label products which supplies many of the store-branded laundry detergents, washing up liquids and shampoos sold by the major UK supermarket chains.

Questions/activities

These can be undertaken as either group or individual exercises.

1. Using an Internet search engine, investigate the latest statistics on the growth of own-label grocery products across a number of countries of your choice. Consider how the markets in those countries have changed over time. What could be the future for own-label products in those countries? Could there be potential market risk to manufacturer brands? If so, how could the manufacturer brands overcome or reduce that potential risk?
2. Study a major supermarket of your choice. Using Internet sources and direct contact with the company's head office, (a) list a selection of their own-label products, (b) list who makes these own-label products (some retailers may not want to divulge this information because of contractual arrangements with the manufacturers), (c) map or compare your selection of the supermarket own-label brands against those of the national or manufacturer brands, and list any differences/similarities between them.
3. Refer to the chapters on buyer behaviour (Chapter 4) and marketing research (Chapter 6). Then list, in detail, the reasons for consumers to purchase own-label brands over mainstream brands.
4. 'True, this is only one innovation amongst all the others that the manufacturers of the national brands launch. However, what it does signify is that consumers can no longer class the own-label brands as "second rate". The own-label brands have taken their place within the competitive brand battlefield. Now, they are no longer followers but must compete equally in an increasingly turbulent environment.' Critically evaluate this view.

Sources: Groucutt (2001), Tomkins (2001).

Brand extensions (also known as brand elasticity)

This is where the company decides to extend the range of its products within a specific category, all under a particular brand name. For example: the pharmaceutical giant SmithKline Beecham has extended several brands, including Veno's cough remedies available in various strengths and tastes, and Hedex painkillers, again in various strengths. If you look at Kellogg's brand list on its Web site (www.kelloggs.com), you will see several very successful brand extensions.

Aaker (1991) suggests that effective extension strategies have the following three key characteristics:

▌ The original brand has strong, positive associations that reinforce consumer expectations, reduce the communications task and help to establish differentiation.

▌ There is a high perceived quality of the original brand.

▌ The original brand is well known and easily recognized.

However there can be several disadvantages to extending the range of a brand. These include over-extension, where the value of the original product is diluted by a large number of extensions. Some washing powders have been associated with over-extension. Also, a problem associated with one product within the extended brand range can impact on the others. This can be considerably detrimental to the brand in terms of both image and subsequent revenue generation.

Brand image

A brand image distinguishes a company's product from competing products in the eyes of the consumer.

Brand image is how consumers actually perceive a brand. This can often go beyond a brand's physical properties, and includes a range of associated feelings and meanings. It can be quantified within a survey environment and thus tracked over time. It has also been described as the aura behind a particular brand.

Brand image endorsement is how consumers feel about a particular brand, in terms of liking or disliking it. This reaction is based upon many separate evaluations of the brand's individual characteristics. Macrae (1990) has distinguished the various images or auras that can be attached to brands: see Table 8.6.

Co-branding (dual branding)

This is the use of two or more individual brands on a single product item. Lamb, Hair and McDaniel (1998) believe that is a useful strategy when a combination of brand names enhances the prestige or perceived value of a product or service.

The use of co-branding is increasing. Two general areas of significant importance are banks and credit card companies, and affinity cards. Major banks such as HSBC and MBNA have co-branding arrangements with the VISA and MasterCard companies. Affinity cards were first issued in the United States in the late 1970s in a wide variety of forms to cater for different interest or affinity groups. An affinity group is a group of people sharing a common purpose or interest, such as a university alumni association, members of an exclusive club or society, or supporters of a charity.

It is important to consider the value of co-branding to the various partner organizations. Kapferer (1998) has identified 10 collaborative benefits:

▌ New product launches clearly identify the brands that cooperated to create and market them.

Table 8.6 Types of brand image

Brand image	Description
The ritual brand image	Usually associated with special occasions: champagne for an anniversary or wedding; cards, chocolates and flowers for Valentine's Day and Mother's Day; cranberry sauce for a Thanksgiving/Christmas dinner; Christmas pudding following an English Christmas lunch; greetings cards for different types of events, such as a student's graduation.
The symbol brand image	The symbol becomes the element of specific value to the consumer. For example: the alligator branding of Lacoste™ clothes, the CK™ logo of Calvin Klein, the interwoven YSL™ of Yves St Laurent, the swoosh symbol of Nike products and the unique lettering style of the words Coca-Cola.
The 'heritage of good' brand image	The brand establishes itself as providing specific benefits, for example Kellogg's breakfast cereals claim to provide 'a bright start to the day'.
Expense-wealth-aloof brand image	This is where the brand has very strong associations with wealth and perhaps power. We consider the following to be in this category: prestigious and expensive cars (Aston Martin, Ferrari), foods (caviar and certain brands of champagne and spirits), banking and credit facilities (private banks such as Coutts in the UK, platinum or black credit cards) and memberships (exclusive social and sports clubs, such as the RAC Club in London).
Belonging brand image (this could also be considered as 'me too' branding)	These provide consumers with a feeling of belonging. For example, the wearers of Benetton clothes might feel that they are all members of a multiracial, multicoloured global community. Consider also people who support local and international good causes, such as children's charities, UNESCO, the Red Crescent and Red Cross, and Médecins Sans Frontières. They feel that they are helping people much less fortunate than themselves, again a feeling that we are all part of a global interdependent community.
The legend image	For example the Levi 501™ jeans, the first ever jeans made by the Levi Strauss company. Other legends include Harley Davidson and Triumph motorbikes, Piaggio motorscooters, Aston Martin sports cars and Coca-Cola.

▮ Many product line extensions capitalize on a partner's brand equity.

▮ To maximize their brand extension success rates, many companies seek help from other companies' brands, whose established reputation might prove decisive.

▮ Co-branding may help develop usage extension. Kapferer (1998) quotes the example of Bacardi Rum and Coca-Cola advertising together. This illustrates how Bacardi can be drunk, and presents Coca-Cola as a mixer.

▮ Ingredient, fabric and component co-branding has developed significantly since the 1970s. Examples include Nutrasweet™ in foods, Intel™ components in computers and Gore-Tex™ fabrics in clothes.

▮ Image reinforcement: in the detergent industry, various white goods brands endorse various detergents: for example, Whirlpool washing machines endorse Ariel detergent.

▮ Co-branding can benefit sales promotions: Whirlpool has included food discount coupons in its refrigerator manuals.

▮ Helps to reinforce loyalty to a particular product/brand.

▮ Capitalizing on synergies within a portfolio of brands. Nestlé launched a breakfast promotion which highlighted a range of its brands under the banner 'healthy breakfast'.

▌ Co-branding can benefit B2B operations. Kapferer (1998) gives the example of how a product may be designed for a distributor and signed by both manufacturer and retailer.

Rebranding

There are occasions when companies seek to rebrand themselves. This might be for several reasons: to appeal to a more contemporary audience, restructuring of the business, the name is now inappropriate, or for legal reasons. There are of course risks associated with rebranding, most especially if there is a significant name and directional change. In many cases the rebranding is minor in customers' minds, although it could be one of the most expensive operations undertaken by the company or organization. Here are some examples:

▌ **The Spastics Society.** This UK-based charity was originally founded in 1952. However it came to be felt that the name was inappropriate and offensive, and it was changed to Scope. This national disability organization focuses on people with cerebral palsy. Their aim is that disabled people should achieve equality in a society in which they are fully involved and have the same human rights as everyone else.

▌ **General Post Office (GPO).** The UK postal and telephone services used to be government controlled under the GPO, which was renamed the Post Office Corporation on 1 October 1969. In 1981 the postal and telephone services were separated, with the telephone services being run by the newly created British Telecom (BT). BT remained state controlled until 1984, when it was privatized and floated on the UK Stock Market. Today BT is an international telecommunications company.

▌ **British Midland Airlines.** In February 2002 this European airline rebranded itself as bmi (essentially, British Midland International) in preparation for its first proposed scheduled transatlantic route (Manchester, England to Chicago).

The lifespan of brands

Over 75 per cent of the brands we know have been around for more than 40 years. This is how important brands are to consumers (Cooper and Kleinschmidt, 1991). Table 8.7 lists the longevity of some well-known brand names (as of 2000). You may be surprised by the age of some of today's most popular brands.

Table 8.7 illustrates the success of several brand names. However, we must consider the increasing dynamics of the business world. With increased globalization and subsequent competition, will these brands survive much longer? It is likely that many will increase their power base as they become more globally focused. However, companies cannot be complacent. Many of the top British companies (and brands) of the early 1960s no longer exist. They suffered financial collapse, mergers or hostile takeovers. Among other things they did not consider their competitive brand position in relation to the rest of the world. They became complacent, and as a result failed.

Brand culling or termination

Products and product ranges can be culled or terminated. Companies that cull products are seeking to focus their resources on the brands with the most potential. Among the reasons for brand culling are:

Table 8.7   Brand longevity

Brand	Manufacturer*	Type of product	Year of introduction
Beetle	Volkswagen	Car	1939
Bounce	Procter & Gamble	Fabric softener	1972
Bournville	Cadbury Schweppes	Chocolate	1908
Bran Flakes	Kellogg's	Breakfast cereal	1915
Camay	Procter & Gamble	Soap	1926
Corn Flakes	Kellogg's	Breakfast cereal	1894
Creme Eggs	Cadbury Schweppes	Chocolate	1923
Crest	Procter & Gamble	Toothpaste	1955
Crunchie	Cadbury Schweppes	Chocolate	1929
Dairy Milk	Cadbury Schweppes	Chocolate	1905
Dreft	Procter & Gamble	Detergent	1933
Fairy Liquid	Procter & Gamble	Washing-up liquid	1898
Flake	Cadbury Schweppes	Chocolate	1920
Flora	Unilever	Margarine	1964
Fruit & Nut	Cadbury Schweppes	Chocolate	1928
Gillette	Gillette	Safety razors	1903
Hoover	Hoover Corporation	Vacuum cleaner	1908
HP sauce	HP Foods/Danone	Spicy table sauce	1903
James Bond	Books: Ian Fleming/Jonathan Cape	Character	1953
James Bond	Films: Eon/Danjaq/MGM/UA	Character	1962
Kingfisher beer	United Breweries	Indian lager beer	1857
Kit Kat	Rowntree (now Nestlé)	Chocolate	1935
Kleenex	Kimberley-Clark	Disposable tissues	1924
Lego	Lego Group	Toy building bricks	1930s
Levi's	Levi Strauss & Co	Blue denim jeans	1873
Marmite	Best Foods	Yeast and vegetable spread	1902
Mars Bar	Mars	Chocolate bar	1932
Mickey Mouse	Disney Corporation	Cartoon character	1920s
Milk Tray	Cadbury Schweppes	Chocolate	1915
Nescafé	Nestlé	Coffee	1938
Pampers	Procter & Gamble	Disposable nappies	1961
Polaroid	Polaroid (The company was declared bankrupt in 2002; new company formed)	Instant camera	1947
Reader's Digest	Reader's Digest	Magazine	1922
Rice Krispies	Kellogg's	Breakfast cereal	1928
Rolex Oyster	Rolex	Designer watch	1926
Roses	Cadbury Schweppes	Chocolate	1938
Scotch tape	3M	Adhesive tape	1952
Tide	Procter & Gamble	Detergent	1946
Tupperware	Tupperware Corporation	Plastic containers	1948
Vimto	J N Nicholas (Vimto) plc	Soft drink	1908

* These are the current manufacturers/brand owners; however they may not have developed the product originally. In some cases the product was developed and marketed by smaller companies which have subsequently been acquired. All trademarks are acknowledged.

Source: Groucutt (2002)

▌ The brand is providing diminishing revenues, and thus profits.

▌ Product proliferation clutters supermarket shelves: there is literally too much competition for shelf space. This can prove confusing for consumers, and does not necessarily provide the best visibility for brands. As a result consumers might purchase either the cheapest product, or nothing.

▌ As we mentioned in discussing product life cycles, products in a declining phase will often be starved of promotion. This often results in the brand struggling against the existing and new competition (especially if barriers to entry are low), probably further hastening its decline within the marketplace.

▌ By focusing on core brands companies can increase production efficiency through improved use of resource investment.

▌ Large brand portfolios often cause promotional budgets to be spread thinly over the full brand range. This can be detrimental to all the products, most especially in highly competitive markets. By focusing on core brands, a company can concentrate larger promotional budgets on a small number of products. Thus there is a greater opportunity to maximize returns on that promotional investment.

Risks associated with brand culling

There are several risks associated with brand culling, which can be short, or potentially long term.

▌ Consumers may protest at a certain brand being culled. For example, in 1999 there was public outcry in the UK when Heinz announced that it was planning to 'kill off' its Salad Cream, because of increased competition from an array of other salad dressings. This may or may not have affected Heinz's reputation in the minds of consumers.

▌ Consumers might switch to rival brands rather than the company's alternative brand(s). If consumers become relatively loyal to the rival company's brand then long term revenue is lost.

▌ Brand culling on a large scale will reduce turnover of the company, and thus its size within the marketplace. The counter-argument to this is that the company should become more profitable.

▌ Companies may decide to sell their brands to new owners. However, they must achieve a reasonable sale price. This is to compensate in the short term for the loss of revenue, and where applicable profit loss. Companies will be reluctant to purchase brands at high prices if those brands have been starved of promotional investment, however. The buyer would have to invest heavily in promoting the brand to hold its position within the marketplace, and this would make the product less profitable. For the company trying to sell the brand, there is the cost of retaining the brand until it finds a buyer prepared to pay the purchasing price. This can be a lengthy process (Aaker, 1991).

▌ There might be legal restrictions that prevent the termination of a brand, especially if this impacts severely on the company's employees. For example, under the European Union's social protection laws the costs in closing plants include significant redundancy payments to employees. It could be more cost-effective for a company to pay another body to take over the plant and provide continuing employment for the workforce (Leonard, 1998).

▌ During the late 1990s companies were being formed, with significant financial resources, to buy culled brands. The risk for the major brand owners is the future potential of brands that they sell to these companies. If the new buyers are able to turn round these ailing brands, they will be able to compete effectively against the original brand owners. A company that is insignificant today could be a major competitor in the future.

▌ Research and development could also be reduced as companies perhaps strive to increase the number of brand extensions. As was mentioned earlier, there are risks attached with extending the brand too far. Additionally, if R&D budgets and activities are also reduced, where will the product innovation of the future come from?

▌ There is also a social impact. Job losses often come from heavy brand culling. As is explained in the 'Marketing insight', Unilever appears likely to close approximately 100 plants with some 25,000 redundancies. This can have a PR fallout on the company, which in turn may affect its share price and consumer attitudes.

Marketing insight: Unilever

In September 1999 the Anglo-Dutch multinational Unilever announced that it intended to streamline its 1,800 strong portfolio of brands. The five-year strategic plan was designed to accelerate growth and increase operating margins. This was designated the Path to Growth Strategy. The principal components of the plan remain:

▌ Terminating hundreds of products to build a core portfolio of some 400 leading brands, each number one or two in their market or segment. This was to be the cornerstone of the plan. By 2004 the leading brands represented over 90 per cent of the business compared with 75 per cent in 1999. By the end of 2003 Unilever was on target to achieve this goal, and had exited over 100 businesses.

▌ The core brands were chosen for first, brand appeal: the strength of their current consumer appeal and how well they would meet expected and emerging consumer needs over the next 5 to 10 years (from 2000), and second, brand scale: their potential to justify and sustain significant investment in technology, innovation and brand communication.

▌ The portfolio has been classified into three types of brand, which will determine the nature and degree of innovation and development expended upon them:
  – International brands: these have common appeal to consumers in many countries, enabling common brand positionings, advertising campaigns and other marketing synergies. Examples include Lipton tea and Magnum ice cream.
  – International brand positionings: these cover brands where the marketing mix is focused on achieving the same consumer positions; however the brand names, for many reasons, are different. For example PG Tips (UK), Bushells (Australia), Home Cup (Africa) and Ting Hua (China) are all positioned as main tea brands in their particular markets.
  – Local jewels: these are brands with an exceptionally strong and often unique position, and generally a long history: for example Oxo bouillon and Persil laundry care (UK), Wishbone salad dressing (United States) and Andrelon shampoo (Netherlands).

▌ The brands include Lux, Dove, Lipton, Magnum and the Calvin Klein fragrances. There has clearly been investment in brand extensions, especially in the Dove range, with the introduction of new additions during 2003 such as shampoo and conditioner.

▌ Within the slimmed down portfolio there are several power brands that have a worldwide reach.

- The group has invested a total of UK £1 billion in additional marketing support over a five-year period.
- Greater brand focus has reduced complexity, increased cost-effectiveness and enhanced productivity. Consequently Unilever expects to improve operating margins by 0.5 per cent per year over a five-year period.
- The overall view is that such focus will also lead to a simpler, more efficient supply chain, and Unilever targeted to have reduced costs by improved buying in this area by UK £1 billion by 2004. Of those savings, UK £750 million will be allocated to margin improvements, and UK £250 million to increasing resources behind the 400 leading brands. An additional UK £200 million currently supporting non-priority brands will be reallocated to the portfolio of leading brands, creating an increase in annual investment of UK £450 million by 2004.
- Central to the plans will be revised knowledge and information systems to support the brands and a redesigned supply chain. The costs are estimated at UK £1.3 billion, and will be provided as the various plans are implemented.
- The programme is estimated to cost UK £3.3 billion in total, the majority of which is expected to be exceptional restructuring cost.

By the end of 2003 (the time of writing) significant progress had been made to achieve the Path to Growth Strategy.

Other factors

- There have been and will be the closure of around 100 of Unilever's 380 plant sites. This will result in long-term job losses (through site sales, closures, redundancies, early departures and retirements) of 25,000 people, approximately a tenth of its total workforce over an approximate five-year period. This will be primarily in Europe and the Americas.
- During late 2000 and early 2002 Unilever concluded several high-profile acquisitions, namely Ben & Jerry's Ice Cream and Best Foods. While further disposals resulted, the overall company objective was to add value and improve the company's ability to market its leading brands.

Questions/activities

These can be considered as either individual or group exercises.

1. Monitor Unilever's press releases (this can be achieved via the company Web site). Critically review its acquisitions and disposals, and consider how they are adding value to its portfolio of brands. You may also want to cross-reference this by studying the company's annual report. Do you think that the group is achieving its objectives? State why.
2. Referring back to the discussion on brand extensions, critically review the Dove brand. Do you think the brand runs the risk of being over-extended? Why?
3. Consider how Unilever's key competitors, for example Procter & Gamble, reacted to this radical brand strategy. Here you should use Internet search engines to investigate both journal research and quality newspaper and magazine reports.
4. Do you think that Unilever has embarked on the right brand strategy? Create two equal groups and have one group state 'Yes' and the other 'No'. Both groups have to justify their views with reasoned argument and debate. (This is aimed at helping you consider both sides of the argument.)

Sources: Houlton (2000), *Economist* (2000), Bittar (2000), Bidlake (2000), *Advertising Age* (2000), Unilever (1999, 2000, 2003).

Chapter summary

In this chapter we have considered how products are conceived and developed, and the role branding plays in bringing the product alive in the mind of the consumer or business customer. Products and brands do not stand alone, though: they are part of a more complex marketing mix. It is therefore important for you to consider how the other elements within the mix will affect the purchasing of a product/brand over time. This interrelation often determines the success or failure of the brand.

Exercises and questions for review and critical thinking

1. Consider why product development is a cross-functional activity within an organ-ization. What are the potential problems associated with such cross-functionality?

2. Why is the image of a brand considered so important?

3. Using examples from this and other texts, consider the reasons a company decides to terminate the life of a product.

4. What potential value do you think a company gains from co-branding?

5. Consider Table 8.3. Using secondary research techniques draw up a list of what you believe will be the 10 most valuable brands in five years' time. Briefly state alongside each why you believe it will be in that position.

9

Price and pricing strategies

Introduction

Price is one of the major variables of the marketing mix, and the only one that is considered as pure revenue generating. Price can be defined as a measure of the value exchanged by the buyer for the value of the product or service offered by the seller. However, like all the variables it can not be considered purely independently, but must be related to the rest of the mix. It will be useful for you to bear in mind the issues raised in Chapter 2, especially in relation to inflation, interest rates, level of income, level of wealth/savings and the taxation system, and Chapter 4 in relation to price sensitivity and what motivates customers to buy products and services.

It is necessary to consider what constitutes price, the methods of determining what price could be charged, how price affects the other variables and how they in turn affect price.

Broadly, two objectives dominate pricing decisions:

1. maximizing profits (this is, maximizing the returns on assets and/or investments); and

2. maintaining or increasing market share. This involves maintaining (the basic option) or increasing (the preferred option) customer involvement.

These may require different, radical and competitive approaches to pricing. While a company or organization may have the largest share of the market, that does not mean it will be the most profitable within the marketplace. Other factors must be taken into consideration, including both financial and operational efficiencies.

Learning objectives

By the end of this chapter you should be able to:

▌ discuss why of the 7Ps of marketing price can have the most dramatic, and immediate, effect on the financial fortunes of the organization;

▌ outline why successful marketing strategies depend on carefully planned and executed pricing strategies;

▌ critically evaluate the different pricing tactics or techniques that companies, organizations and retailers employ.

Organizational policy

Obviously the overriding factor in setting prices must be the company or organization's overall corporate policy. If the organization sees itself as providing high value and exclusivity, it would not be in keeping with that policy to charge low prices. If however it is intending to appeal to a very broad market it will need to price accordingly. This is particularly so in the service sectors, and to some extent in the general consumer product market. Again it depends on how the organization tries to differentiate itself from others within the same potential market.

Companies and organizations must not only develop a framework for their pricing decisions, but also decide on their specific pricing objectives. These objectives will vary depending on the market the company or organization serves, the position in the market life cycle and the aims and objectives of the organization.

In extreme cases there is no expectation of a good return on investment (ROI), the policy turns into one of survival, and prices are set purely to maintain cashflow. In reality the company or organization is likely to go out of business, as the price charged often becomes less than the cost of providing the product or service. Larger organizations and especially those in mature markets may try to maintain a stable market condition. This is ensured by setting prices close to those of the market leader.

The market leader is unlikely to use price as a competitive weapon to maintain its position, so a price war is unlikely to happen. All competitors use non-price methods to enhance their share of the market and often build the total market in the process.

An organization's pricing objectives

Buttell (1986) believes that a company's pricing objectives depend on several factors. Each one in turn has an impact on the profit line:

▌ The cost of producing the product or service.

▌ The cost of marketing the product or service.

▌ The time frame in which the company requires a return on the investment in the new product or service.

▌ The profit margin level the company wants to achieve from the product or service. This is the amount above the cost of manufacturing and marketing the product or service.

▌ Whether the product or service will be offered as a single purchase, or could become a regular or repeat purchase. For example, a luxury car that could be a one-off purchase, while a bar of chocolate is likely to be a regular or repeat impulse purchase.

▌ The relationship between the new product's price and that of the company's other products.

▌ Whether the product or service is new to the market or already established.

▌ The level of uniqueness of the product or service compared with the competition.

▌ Where the product is located within it's life cycle phase.

▌ The kind of relationship the company wants to establish with its customers. Is it short, medium or long term? This may reflect the types and levels of discount available to customers.

▌ The kind of price comparison the company seeks to establish with their competitors in consumers' minds.

- The extent to which the company seeks to establish a major share of the market.

- The level of inventory for that product, the company's possible need to reduce it and over what time frame.

Key factors that influence price

As we have seen, price cannot be considered in isolation. There is a range of factors that can, and do, influence the price that can be charged for a particular product or service. It is important to consider these factors in isolation first; however, several factors may combine to influence the price an individual pays for a particular product or service. Before examining how to establish methods of price setting, we should first consider the influencing factors in some detail.

Cost

The first, and perhaps the major, factor is cost. The price charged must ensure all costs are recovered, even if this is not done immediately. Calculating the total cost may not be easy. A very careful watch must be kept on the cost of any product and service, as costs will change over time. For example, raw materials (like the cocoa in chocolate) might rise in price, and it is necessary to consider reflecting these changes in the price charged.

Government policy: local taxes and surcharges

When considering the pricing of a product or service the company must be mindful of the 'additionals'. These are costs added when the bill is finally presented to the customer. The additionals can include:

- local taxes (there might be more than one tax);

- service charges;

- surcharges (such as delivery costs).

Let us use the example of a five-star hotel in Trinidad. This is from an actual bill/invoice of February 2000:

Room rate	US $120.00
Utilities charge	US $1.95
	(this is a local energy tax)
Service charge	US $13.80
Government room tax	US $12.00

So while the daily room rate is stated as US $120.00, the actual daily room rate is $147.75, an additional US $27.75 per day. Equally any meals are subject to taxation. Room service meals are subject to service charges, taxation and a surcharge, so approximately an additional 25 per cent is added to the published rates.

In a B2B situation within the home country, value added tax (VAT) or purchase tax might not be a problem. Depending upon the balance of inputs (charges made by the company) against the outputs (charges made to the company), the company may be eligible for a rebate, and therefore benefit from the VAT. Of course this depends on the tax regime operating at that specific time. However, for the ordinary consumer such issues or benefits do not apply. Therefore the product or service may be significantly more expensive than first imagined. This might dissuade the consumer from purchasing the same product or service in the future, or persuade him or her to seek alternative sources for it.

In the example of the Trinidadian hotel, it too faces difficulties. It must abide by the laws that govern the imposition of local or regional taxes.

Economic worth

This relates extremely well to the basic marketing concept in so much as it refers to what is obtained when a product or service is bought. It is the benefit that is provided by the use or ownership of that product or service.

However, this raises the problem of how

economic worth is measured. The value of any particular product or service varies from person to person, and from time to time. On a very hot day in the middle of the summer a nice cold ice cream is likely to have a very high value to a potential purchaser. However that same ice cream might have no value at all to many people on a very cold day in the middle of the winter.

We can also link to economic worth the issue of scarcity. In the middle of the 19th century 1,200 million oysters were consumed in Britain per year. A century later demand had fallen to between 5 and 6 million because of a scarcity in supply which led to a price rise (Buttell, 1986). Today oysters are highly priced, and tend to be one of the most expensive dishes in restaurants.

Competition

Competition is another of the major influencers on the price that can be charged for a product or service. Potential customers perceive many products as very similar, so they expect the price to reflect that similarity. While any sensible organization tries to differentiate its products or services from its competitors', it is not always possible to do so

to any great extent: for example two bus companies covering the same route will probably provide much the same service.

While having a very good brand allows an organization to ask a higher price, there is a limit. If competitors' prices are much lower, it will lose sales to them. Much depends on the value customers feel they receive. Higher value is likely to command higher prices, but at some point this value must be real and not just perceived.

Market conditions

The next major concern is market conditions. The marketplace is not static, it is in a state of constant change. In general terms it can be seen from demographic data (Table 9.1) that the average age of the UK population is increasing.

A similar trend is also apparent in the rest of Europe. This is because fewer children are being born, smaller family sizes are becoming the norm and people are living longer. Older people (also known as the grey market) require different goods and services from younger members of society. Because they are a sizeable proportion of the population no organization can afford to ignore them. It also

Table 9.1 Population projection (UK) in millions

Age/gender	1996	2001
0–14	11,358	11,289
15–29	11,903	11,197
30–44	12,935	13,747
45–59	10,582	11,228
60–74	7,831	7,752
75+	4,193	4,406
Males	28,856	29,377
Females	29,946	30,241
Total	58,802	59,618

Source: Office of National Statistics (UK) (2002).

needs to be noted that the disposable income per household has in general increased over the past couple of decades (see Table 9.2).

This trend is likely to continue for the foreseeable future. The changing market and the trend of those changes will have a direct impact on the price that can, or should, be charged for any particular product. If the demand for a particular product or service is increasing, it should be possible to charge a higher price. However if the demand is falling the price will have to be reduced, or some suppliers will have to leave the market, or some way of stimulating the demand will have to be undertaken.

Geography

When considering pricing strategies and structures it is vital to consider the geographical implications. For example, the following questions and issues need to be considered:

▮ Is the product being exported to a particular region?

▮ If so, what costs are incurred in exporting this product?

▮ Can local consumers afford to purchase this product at the price charged in its country of origin?

▮ Will it be too expensive for the new market once transportation and other costs have been added?

▮ Should the pricing structure be totally rethought for this new market?

Some of these points are raised again later in this chapter. These issues are discussed in more detail in Chapter 14, which covers international dimensions.

Legal issues

Governments may impose legal restrictions on the prices at which companies can sell their products or services. One aspect of this is dumping. This is where a company sells its products on international markets at prices below their marginal cost. This implies that the seller is making a loss on each sale. This tactic has been used to penetrate markets and increase market share. There is then a price increase when the company is established in the marketplace. The European Union has

Table 9.2 Trends in households' disposable income (UK)

Year	Income (UK £)	Expenditure (UK £)
1970	15,002	14,290
1975	16,512	15,329
1980	17,410	15,799
1985	17,798	16,528
1990	20,297	19,152
1995	22,643	20,074
1996	23,082	20,716
1997	23,586	21,190
1998	23,043	21,395

Note: all figures are corrected by the Retail Price Index (1998 = 100)

Source: Office of National Statistics (UK) (1999)

imposed anti-dumping laws on the basis that they are anti-competitive.

Consumer tastes and preferences

Individual tastes and preferences often reflect the price people will pay for a product or service. Consider, for example, collectors of fine art and the prices they are prepared to pay for a masterpiece by Monet, Lowry or Hockney. Equally, individuals will pay high prices for limited edition/collectors' item records and CDs, whether they are by the Beatles, the Beach Boys, the Rolling Stones or composers such as Erich Wolfgang Korngold or John Barry. Would you pay £150 for a CD or a vinyl record? Collectors do, and the demand is reflected in the price charged.

Price sensitivity

Sometimes customers are particularly sensitive to price increases. For example, a 10 per cent price increase on a £1 product is only 10p, but it could deter some consumers. They will seek a lower-priced product, even if it is inferior, or not buy at all.

In most texts, price sensitivity is considered when discussing lower income groups where literally every penny counts. However, price sensitivity affects all groups. Even financially comfortable people are sensitive to price changes, for they are considering the relationship between price and the tangible/intangible value of the product or service.

Price setting tactics

Here we consider the different types of pricing tactics companies, organizations and retailers can employ. We consider them individually, but it must be borne in mind that a retailer, for instance, might use several or indeed all of them in different places, for different products or at different times.

Pioneer pricing

This is the 'base' price for a new product or service being launched. When determining a base price the organization must consider the following:

- Over what time frame it plans to recoup its development and launch costs. The shorter the time frame, the higher the base price will need to be. The question for the organization is whether or not it is the right price for the market, and meets all the legal regulations for price setting.

- The potential impact of a new competitor entering the market with a similar product or service, including how rapidly this could be done.

- Whether competitors have the promotional budget to launch an effective campaign against the product or service.

- Whether a low base price will discourage competitive action, at least in the short term.

Price skimming

This tactic is often used when a new product is introduced. New products tend to be price inelastic: that is, the demand for the product is relatively insensitive to its price. With price skimming, the retailer sets a relatively high price for the product during the early stages of its life cycle, to attract those customers particularly interested in acquiring a new product. (You may want to refer back to Chapter 8 where we discussed the adoption and diffusion process.)

When an organization enters a market with a new product it may well have high development and launch costs. An early recovery of these might be an important consideration, so the product might be launched into the market at a high price so as to achieve a fairly rapid return on the investment.

A 'skimming' price is only viable if it is difficult for other suppliers to enter the market, at least at an early stage. This means the product has to be unique, very difficult to copy or protected by patents. These high barriers to entry are often, but not always, short-lived. Even if competitors cannot copy the product (for example instant picture film from Polaroid, which is protected by patents), substitute products are likely to soon enter the marketplace. For example, one hour processing is a competitor to instant film, using ordinary colour film at much lower prices and not requiring special cameras. Where entry barriers are low, skimming prices are not realistic as competitors can quickly enter the market at much lower prices. The producer of the new product might suffer so much competitive pressure that the product or even the company fails.

Of course, the price might not always remain high. As the product matures, technology develops and sales begin to slow, the price will be lowered to attract new buyers. Consumer examples include:

▌ Mobile phones, which when first introduced were prohibitively expensive. They tended to be used only by senior executives of large companies in big cities. Over time they have become relatively cheap, and today children carry them to keep in touch with family and friends. The networks have expanded rapidly, the technology has developed and the purchase price, rental and line charges have fallen. The mobile phone has gone from being a status symbol for senior executives to an everyday item.

▌ At the time of writing (2003) mini disk players in the UK were still relatively highly priced. However, if the technology catches on, and is not rapidly superseded, their price is likely (though not guaranteed) to fall.

▌ In the B2B context Eckles (1990) quotes the example of the multinational Du Pont. It used price skimming when it introduced each of its innovative products,

Cellophane™, Nylon™, Teflon™ and Corlon™. Now they are relatively cheaper and part of everyday life.

Penetration pricing (predatory pricing)

This is a tactic used to achieve the following aims:

▌ to gain a large proportion of the market;

▌ to open up a new low-price segment of the market;

▌ to gain market entry by very low prices set against the average product or service price.

In markets that have low barriers to entry it is more usual to enter with a market penetration pricing policy. Prices are set deliberately low to ensure that a high level of sales is achieved, and thus allow full economies of scale. This policy also tends to deter smaller competitors from entering the market, which allows much larger shares to be established by the first (pioneers) in the market.

The concept of the first into the market gaining market leader position is not new, but to take advantage of the position the price must be set accordingly. An example of this is the changing airline business within the UK market. During the 1990s several low-cost airlines received permission to operate from the UK into Europe. Their objective was to provide a low-cost no-frills service that would give customers efficient transportation to a variety of European destinations at much lower cost than the regular airlines. EasyJet, founded by entrepreneur Stelios Haji-Ioannou, has made a dramatic impact on the market through aggressive pricing. This has proved a highly competitive market, with other players including Ryanair vying for market share. Since 1995 there have been casualties in this marketing battle, the most prominent being Debonair, a company that invested significant amounts in advertising and aircraft expenditure.

Price matching

This tactic is often used in highly competitive markets. Retailers closely match the prices of their nearest competitors. In 1997 the petroleum company Esso launched a PriceWatch™ campaign in the UK, which is still active at the time of writing (2003). The essence of the campaign was that Esso would match the lowest price within a certain distance of its petrol stations. This has proved a highly successful campaign.

Variable or flexible pricing

Pricing can be flexible or variable to reflect the differing competitive, market, time and value added environments. Here are a few examples:

▌ **Travel.** London Underground is the largest and most complex rapid transit system anywhere in the world. During the week several million people are moved around London each day. Many are on their way to work, others to school, college and university, others shopping or visiting the many tourist attractions. London Underground operates on a zonal system, with fares reflecting the number of zones crossed.

   The cost of a return ticket, say from Euston (a mainline railway terminal) to Oxford Circus (a shopping district) is standard at any time of the day. However, for a day travel card (providing unlimited travel on any day from Monday to Friday) covering one or more zones the charges vary depending on the time of day. Before 9.30 am there is a peak hour charge; after 9.30 there is a lower off-peak charge. At weekends the off-peak fare applies all the time.

▌ **Cinemas.** Cinemas and theatres may charge different rates according to the time of day. A Wednesday matinee might be far cheaper than a Friday or Saturday evening performance when demand is at its highest.

▌ **Holiday companies and airlines.** These charge different rates according to the season. Often consumers can negotiate good deals on travel at the cross-over point between the peak and off-peak seasons.

Psychological pricing

▌ **Prestige pricing.** This is a tactic where the price is set high to attract the wealthy. Prestige pricing aims at sustaining an often extreme image of the product or service, which separates it from the general marketplace. The aim here is to convey high quality and exclusivity, high status items. Prestige pricing is also known as high ticket pricing.

   We can consider a wide range of products and services here. For example:

– A 14-day luxury cruise might cost between £8,000 and £18,000 per person (2003 prices) depending on the level of accommodation. Of course, in order to maintain such prices and reputation the level of service and facilities needs to be exceptional.
– Russian and Iranian caviar. While this is relatively inexpensive in the countries of origin, it is not so elsewhere. Even within duty free areas such as Dubai Airport both Russian and Iranian caviar are prestige priced. In many countries caviar has a prestige value and so carries an associated price. In England a small jar of Beluga Russian caviar may cost several hundred pounds.
– Luxury sports cars. The prestige value of Aston Martins and Ferraris is reflected in their pricing. However, it must be borne in mind that this is a highly competitive market, and some car manufacturers have been significantly more successful

than others. It was not until the Ford Motor Company purchased Aston Martin in the late 1990s that it was able to return a reasonable profit.

- Certain types of drink. For instance fine champagne or Napoleon Cognacs may be priced at £500 or more a bottle.

■ **Pricing points/odd–even pricing.** The product is priced at an odd number rather than being rounded up to a whole number. For example, a CD might be priced at £4.99 or £4.75 rather than £5.00. While it is obvious that a CD costing £4.99 is only 1p cheaper than one costing £5.00, the perception is that it *is* cheaper. Consumers might focus on the '4' or even the '99' rather than round up the number. This method of psychological pricing might entice the consumer to buy more.

■ **Single price/double pricing.** A retailer might sell all products at one or two set prices. When Frank Winfield Woolworth (1852–1919) began his successful retail venture Woolworth, it was known as a five and dime store because products were priced at either 5 or 10 cents.

During the 1990s some general retail stores in the UK sold a range of products at 50p and/or 99p. While some of the products were by brand leaders, many others were unbranded. However, some customers seek low prices in the knowledge that the quality is reflected in the price. While there might be a perceived or psychological discount on the items, some products are cheaper in major retail outlets. This is especially the case with soap products and detergents. While priced at 99p in these discount outlets, they are sometimes priced at 85 or 95p in the major chain stores.

Similar types of stores operate in North America. However, as Stanton, Etzel and Walker (1994) state, some analysts doubt whether such stores can be successful not just at a time of recession but during upturns in the market.

Promotional pricing

Bundling or bunching pricing
Bundling or bunching pricing is where several products or services are offered as a package at a single price. As Churchill and Peter (1998) state, bundling assumes that the consumer will appreciate receiving a variety of products or services by making a single purchase.

We can consider two examples. First, the travel industry has for years used bundling pricing techniques. Holiday packages today generally include air travel, accommodation, entertainment, car rental (or transfers), all meals and the services of a tour guide, all for one overall price. Second, various computer suppliers have opted for price bundling. These bundles might include the computer, video/photo camera, printer, scanner, educational software, home software, business software, modem and Internet access and games software.

Trade-in allowances

This is a price reduction for trading in an old item when a new one is purchased. It has been used extensively in the car retail business. The car owner trades in a used car for a new or another used car, and the trade-in price for the old car is offset against the price of the new purchase.

Discount pricing

There are various types of discount pricing tactic. We have briefly illustrated each below.

■ **Quantity discounts.** This is a price reduction to those who buy in large volumes. It is a pricing tactic mostly used within B2B environments. The 'Marketing insight' gives an example from a UK-based stationery and office supplier.

■ **Seasonal discounts (also known as differential pricing).** This is a price reduction for

---

Marketing insight: Economy white photocopy paper

List price	Price per ream for a purchase of:			
	1 ream	10 reams	30 reams	50 reams
£7.00	£2.95	£2.29	£1.99	£0.99
Totals	£2.95	£22.90	£59.70	£49.50

Prices are as at 2000. (The list price is generally the manufacturer's recommended selling price.) As you can see there are significant price differences. It is cheaper to purchase 50 reams than 30 reams. The cost of 50 reams at £2.95 is £147.50, compared with the bulk discount price of £49.50, a saving of £98.00. Also look at the per ream prices, and you will see not only discounting but pricing points. Psychological pricing is used in the B2B environment as well as in the consumer marketplace.

---

those who buy the product or service out of its normal season. Here are two examples:

- Winter fashions that are discounted just prior to the arrival of the spring/summer collections. The discounts are normally higher for women's fashion than men's. This is usually because men's clothes span several winter seasons, whereas women's fashions change more rapidly.
- The price of garden furniture and barbecues may be discounted during the autumn/winter from the spring/summer prices.

▌ **Trade discounts (also known as functional discounts).** These are B2B discounts. A builder's merchant or materials supplier often has one price for retail customers, and another for trade customers, such as carpenters, general builders, painters and bricklayers. The prices are usually clearly marked as 'trade' and 'non trade'.

▌ **Promotional discounts.** This is a technique where discounts are provided on products/services for a limited period. Here are two examples:

- Buy one get one free (also known as BOGOF promotions: see Chapter 11). This is generally used within the retail sector as a means of promoting own-label products. There are several variations on this theme, such as three for the price of two or one item given free with the purchase of another (can be used as a co-branding exercise).
- Travel companies use this technique to sell holidays several months in advance. A holiday booked for July but paid for in January might command a significant discount for the buyer.

▌ **Special event pricing.** This is a special price set for a product or service for a limited time frame and event. For example, a retailer or supplier might be celebrating an anniversary and advertise special discounts for the anniversary week or month. These discounts could be based on the length of the anniversary, such as '25 per cent off all products to celebrate our 25 years in business'. A more adventurous company had a one-day event in 2000 when it sold products for the prices charged in 1960 when it opened.

▌ **Direct payment mechanisms.** Companies often offer a price reduction to customers who pay using a direct debit system. For example, in the UK utility companies offer discounts to customers who opt for direct debit payments. This allows the utility to withdraw the invoiced amount directly from the customer's bank account on a specific day each month or quarter. This reduces potential payment delays for the company (provided there are sufficient funds in the customer's bank account), and provides an incentive to the customer.

Business-to-business pricing

Many of the pricing strategies considered earlier are applicable to both consumer and B2B markets. There are, however, pricing strategies that are confined mainly to the B2B and industrial sectors. The following is an overview of the key strategies within these sectors.

Professional services pricing

This can operate in both B2C and B2B environments. For example:

▌ A solicitor acting on behalf of a family buying a house might offer an all-inclusive price for undertaking the conveyancing (the legal transfer of title/ownership) of the property.

▌ A barrister or lawyer acting on behalf of a defendant in court might agree a no-win no-fee arrangement. If the case is won the barrister charges for the time spent preparing the case and in court. All correspondence is also charged.

▌ Private medical facilities. A doctor or medical centre might charge on the basis of the time of visit (normal working hours or unsocial hours), the type of medication and treatment.

▌ A marketing or PR consultant might charge a client a monthly fee plus agreed expenses. This is usually for a set time frame, for instance 12 months, after which the contract might be renegotiated.

Competitive bidding (also known as competitive tendering or pitching)

There are two types of bidding processes, open and closed bidding or tendering. Bidding or tendering tends to be used by governments to secure the right price and service requirements. In the bidding or tendering process a company attempts to meet the published specifications with a tailor-made proposal that includes the price.

The US government is probably the largest buyer of goods and services in the world. Its purchases include everything from stationery supplies to nuclear-powered aircraft carriers (among the largest ships afloat).

It is important to remember that contracts are not always awarded to the lowest bidder. The buyer seeks reassurance that the proposed supplier can actually deliver the products/services by the deadline, and often looks to obtain further information about the bidder. This includes the bidder's reputation in the marketplace, its ability to meet the desired project specifications and deadlines and any past business experiences with the company or individual. However, even with such information projects do not always run to schedule. With this in mind buyers may build into the agreement financial safeguards or penalties against cost over-runs or delivery delays.

For example, a major shipping line sought tenders from shipyards for the refurbishment of its flagship cruise liner. British shipyards lost out on the multi-million pound project to a German shipyard. The German yard agreed to a tight deadline and offered a lower bid. However, it was unable to meet the deadline. The liner returned to its home port for its first passenger voyage with shipyard workers still onboard. Its subsequent sailing was a public relations nightmare. Passengers complained about facilities not working and the noise from ongoing work. The passengers received refunds, the shipyard was charged financial penalties for the over-run and the shipping line faced a storm of bad press, which in the short term damaged its image and staff morale.

Eckles (1990) describes open bidding (also known as open tendering) as an informal process where bids (often negotiated) are submitted by the seller by a given deadline. Closed bidding (also known as sealed bidding) is a formal process where suppliers are invited to submit written sealed bids that meet the required product/service specification. All the bids are opened at the same time with the contract being awarded to the supplier with the lowest priced bid. This type of bidding is generally reserved for standardized products such as stationery where price is the major differential (Eckles, 1990).

Leasing

This is a contract where the owner (lessor) of the equipment extends the right to a customer (lessee) to use the equipment in return for periodic payments over a specific time period. Companies tend to use leasing rather than purchase equipment through capital expenditure. This allows them the flexibility of upgrading the equipment without significant investment and write-off costs. Leasing is increasingly used for a wide range of products including computers, photocopiers, company cars, trucks, passenger/cargo aircraft and construction equipment.

Geographical pricing

This issue should be considered in relation to the points raised in Chapter 14 on the international dimension. When a company sells a product internationally it has to consider the extra transportation cost, tariff charges, local taxation/duty charges and insurance costs. These may be borne by the seller, the buyer or both. The impact of these additional costs is reflected in the final price charged for the product to the end user.

Price setting models

Economic pricing: supply and demand

It is important to understand the basic pricing models that are available and their usefulness under given circumstances. It should be noted that none of the models guarantee the 'correct' price. It is very unlikely that such a model could ever exist, but the models available highlight the problems that are experienced when trying to set prices for a service or product.

Perhaps the best known model is economic pricing. This is based on the concept of equating supply and demand: that there is a price at which these two variables are equal. This model of pricing makes two fundamental assumptions, and can only really work when these assumptions are met.

The first assumption is perfect competition: a situation where competing products are identical and customers have details of these identical products. As we have seen, one of the major concepts of marketing is differentiation: that is, each supplier tries to make what it offers different in some way from all the other offerings. The fact that the product or service fulfils the same basic functions or even benefits is of no concern: provided it is perceived as different in the minds of potential customers, it is different. This means that the different suppliers can charge different prices because the products are not the same. Therefore this assumption does not work in the real world. There is no such thing as perfect competition.

The model also assumes perfect markets. This is where all the potential customers are aware of the product and have access to all the relevant details about it. This of course ignores the basic concept of segmenting markets and the way in which advertising and promotion actually work. An organization may only want its products to be known by people with certain lifestyles. Therefore it needs only advertise in the media it knows these customers read or see. This allows the company to price the product accordingly. It could be higher or lower than similar products aimed at different market segments.

The model is, however, useful for explaining what might happen with price movement. It certainly does provide an explanation of the concept of equating supply and demand to make the best use of limited resources. However it tends to ignore the real business environment.

Cost plus model

This is the model generally favoured by accountants. Simply, it means that the price must always equal fixed plus variable costs plus some margin that represents a return that is acceptable to either the management or the owners (including all shareholders) of the supplying organization.

The basic assumption here is that it is possible to calculate the costs *accurately*. It also assumes that the cost cannot be changed, perhaps by different production methods. With a single product it might be possible to calculate the cost, but with multi-product lines or complex operations the whole task becomes virtually impossible. Levitt (1960) makes the point that if Ford had used this basis then there would not have been the cheap mass-produced motor car. As Ford so eloquently said:

> Our policy is to reduce the price, extend the operations and improve the article. You will notice that the reduction in price came first. We have never considered any costs as fixed. Therefore we first reduce the price to the point where we believe more sales will result. Then we go ahead and try to make the prices. We do not bother about the costs. The new price forces the costs down.

As Levitt (1960) points out in his article, Ford's real genius was his marketing. The assembly line was a result of his realizing that he could sell cars at $500. Mass production was the result, not the cause of the low prices.

The major advantage of the accountants' pricing model is that it is very easy to calculate if the company is prepared to accept that the cost calculations are right and that the margin suggested is acceptable. However it tends to ignore market conditions. The actual cost to provide a particular type of leisure pursuit, for instance, might be quite cheap, especially within a fairly large leisure complex. However, it could be in the organization's best interest to charge a higher price for this particular activity, perhaps because of its popularity, and the possibility of using the extra revenue to subsidize other less popular, and perhaps more costly, pursuits.

This is a quite normal practice in the travel business where popular routes are used to subsidize less popular ones to ensure they stay open. Also if the popularity of one product changes it is possible to adjust the price to make the best use of the changing market. The costs may not have changed even though the market has been modified. So it can be seen that the accountants' model of pricing tends to be rather inflexible, and in a dynamic market organizations cannot afford to be inflexible.

Despite its shortcomings, this model is still one of the most common ways of setting prices in some industries. There are some exceptions where the model is modified to set margins for each product rather than a fixed margin across a range of products, but even this does not really go far enough to allow the organization to respond to all the changes within a dynamic marketplace.

Competition based pricing (also known as going rate pricing)

In this model the company sets prices near to those of its immediate competitors. This price may be either just below the perceived nearest competitor, or just above, if the company believes it offers some perceived added value to potential customers. This model tends to assume that there is a going or normal rate, and in general does not fully take into account the concept of differentiation. Overall, this pricing model tends to lower general pricing levels, as all suppliers try to offer the lowest price within the marketplace. This often leads to the problem of organizations making very little or perhaps no profit on a product or service.

While many economists argue that competition-oriented prices are in the best interests of consumers, this can only be in the short term. In the longer term the number of suppliers will be reduced, which will reduce choice and will eventually cause prices to rise as the market becomes more monopolistic.

Economists relate this model closely to the supply and demand model, saying that the market forces cause supply and demand to equate. While this may be partially true in the commodities market (for instance, cocoa) where it is difficult to differentiate what is being offered, it does not help the development of other types of market.

Again, if the basic concept of marketing is deployed and the products being offered are differentiated, different prices can be charged by different companies, especially if they are offering products or services that are perceived by the potential purchasers as being different.

Market pricing

In market pricing the price should equate to the consumer's assessment of the economic value of the benefits derived from the product or service. It is based on the idea that consumers perceive that what is being offered has a specific or intrinsic value to them. Therefore, they are prepared to pay a specific price to obtain that benefit. Quite simply, the price completes the product offering.

When you purchase a product or service you do not just obtain the tangible item, you also receive the intangibles that go with the product, and this of course includes the price. Consider the perfume Chanel No 5. Here the price is one of the major intangibles. It is the price that makes the product what it is: exclusive. The same could be said for a luxury vacation in New York.

This method of pricing means that several variables need to be considered when setting the final price.

▌ The first consideration must revolve around the structure of the market. It is necessary to give careful consideration to the population that contains the company's potential customers. The company must fully understand the movement of the population: not only immigration and emigration, but perhaps more importantly the age spread and mix of sexes. These will change over time.

▌ Details must be considered of the target market's disposable income, especially as this varies not only with age and sex but also across the country.

▌ The lifestyle of the target population will also have a profound effect on the level of disposable income. The level of disposable income will affect the price people are prepared to pay for the particular benefits they perceive they will obtain from the product or service on offer. It is very important that potential customers' wants or needs, perceived or real, are satisfied. A part of these wants and needs is to do with the price they are prepared to pay to obtain the need or want satisfaction. Each segment of the market is likely to have a different level of price it is prepared to pay. This is why many companies offer a range of products so they can have a range of price levels to meet the needs of different market segments.

▌ The organization itself plays a key role in the price charged for its products or services. The reputation of the company and its product/service reputation are of prime importance to customers' perception of the value of the benefit they will receive. Why should a round of golf on one golf course cost more than a round on another? Why is one well-known brand of baked beans, for instance, more expensive than other brands? The reputation of both what is being offered and by whom has a direct bearing on the price that potential customers are prepared to pay. Often this reputation is linked to the type of promotion that is undertaken by the organization.

▌ A heavily promoted product or service can often be charged at a higher price than one that is less well supported. The promotion not only ensures that more potential customers are aware of what is being offered, but also tends to enhance the desirability of the product or service within the marketplace. In theory, this should become a spiral because as income increases with the higher prices then more can be invested in promotion. This will in turn allow the company to charge a higher price, and so on ad infinitum, but not in the real world as a time must come when the value that can be added by promotion is insufficient to increase the benefit value. This is one of the major problems faced by all organizations. They must calculate the optimum promotion for the price they can charge.

▌ Obviously for the value of promotion to be realized the promise indicated in the marketing communication must be

delivered. The service and product offering must match, and if possible exceed, potential customers' expectations. If the product or service does not meet the expectations indicated by the price, the customers will not use that product or service again. What is more, they will make sure that other people are aware of its shortcomings. This perception effectively sets the ceiling on the price that can be charged.

▌ Another variable that must be considered when setting market prices is the demand for other products. There may or may not be cross-elasticity of demand between the various products that are offered in the marketplace. However, there will be derived demand. This is where the demand for one product is derived from the demand for another. Careful pricing of the products concerned can lead to an overall increase in profit, even if one of the products is sold at a loss. It may be worth having a very small margin on the sales of, for example, computer printers if a better return can be made on the sales of the consumables (such as print cartridges) required for the printer.

It is also necessary to remember that potential customers have choice. This invariably means that there is more than one organization providing a way of satisfying a particular need or want. Customers are free to choose which particular product or service they buy or use. Demand is often influenced by peer pressure, so an understanding of how peer group pressure influences purchase within a given segment will help to establish a price that is likely to be acceptable to that particular segment (see Chapter 4). There are other influences on choice, and each of these needs to be considered before a price can be set. In general, it is necessary to consider a number of factors before a market acceptable price can be established.

Pricing: a systematic approach

A number of models of pricing have been considered, but it is necessary to work systematically through a procedure actually to arrive at a price. The most common model is that developed by Oxenfeldt (1960) in his *Harvard Business Review* article entitled 'Multistage approach to pricing'. This model has six stages, and while now rather dated still provides a systematic approach to calculating the price that should be charged. This model is depicted in Table 9.3.

Davidson (1997) postulates eight key principles for what he terms 'offensive pricing'. These are outlined in Table 9.4.

Organizations are faced with a number of situations in deciding the most suitable pricing strategy. Often the first problem they have to consider is how to price a new product. While this can be difficult when entering an existing market, it becomes more so if the organization is trying to enter a new market with its new product. The problem of trying to reposition a product usually requires a modification to the price to maintain or establish credibility in the new position. It is also sometimes necessary to consider a price change in response to threats from close competitors. Also, as we have seen, it will be necessary to modify the price as the product passes through the various stages of the life cycle.

As Oxenfeldt (1960) points out, it is necessary to undertake a product–market analysis. This should specifically consider the

Table 9.3 Systemic pricing model

Stages	Description/action
Market opportunity analysis	It is necessary to select the specific market segments that the organization wishes to target. As we have already seen, different segments expect different levels of price. Therefore a clear policy on which market segments are to be targeted is crucial to ensure that an acceptable pricing strategy is developed.
Company image	The second stage is to consider the sort of image the organization wishes to portray, for both itself and the product or service in question. The image and reputation will have a direct effect on the price that can be charged and it must, of course, be compatible with the chosen segment or segments.
Marketing mix strategy	It is then necessary to develop the marketing mix strategy for what is being offered. The price is affected by and in turn affects all the other elements of the marketing mix. Therefore all the variables must be considered together. The components must blend and portray a consistent image in the minds of potential customers.
Pricing and the marketing plan	Once you have worked through the initial stages of this model, it is then possible to start considering the most suitable overall pricing policy. This must, of course, fit with the overall marketing plan.
Develop and implement pricing strategy	The next stage is to develop and implement a pricing strategy. We have seen that prices are likely to change during the various stages in the product life cycle, so it is important that this is planned in advance. The other elements of the marketing mix will also change, so care must be taken to ensure that consistency of the overall image of the product or service is maintained.
Specific price for product or service	The final stage is to choose a specific price that will be charged for the benefits that are being offered to the market segment. Provided the groundwork has been undertaken, this price will be the market price and will result in the optimum sales for the product.

Table 9.4   Offensive pricing

Principles	Description/action
Know the price dynamics of the market	It is important to get a feel for what might influence price. Consideration of such factors as frequency of purchase, degree of necessity, unit price, degree of comparability and degree of fashion or status all contributes to the price sensitivity of the company's product or service.
Choose price segments	Price bracket segments of all markets. In general the strong brands are in the upper pricing segments while the commodity products and less known brands are in the lower segments. It is important that an organization can clearly define the segments in which it operates.
Achieve clarity of pricing	Potential customers must understand a company's pricing system. If it is not logical then they will not trust the brand or organization. Currently (2003) much of the UK's privatized railway system is suffering from this problem, with extremely complex and illogical ticket pricing systems.
Always consider the alternatives	Pricing is often considered as a rather mechanical aspect of marketing. Davidson (1997) says that it is necessary to be more creative. Price is only one part of the marketing mix, therefore the whole mix must be considered when analysing the pricing strategy.
Target price changes	Remember that price elasticity varies by type of consumer, shopping environment and occasion of use. Companies must make sure that they understand the way price elasticity works and use price promotions, not only to stimulate new sales but also to reward loyal customers.
Avoiding profit cannibalization when pricing new products	Companies should ensure that new products take profits from their competitors, and not from other products in their own product lines.
Using pricing to optimize return on capacity	This is especially the case with perishable products such as fresh food. It means using all the available demand forecasting tools, and having a good understanding and being able to act upon price elasticities of different customer types. It also involves analysing capacity utilization and using price to maximize it. A company must also make sure its cost allocations are efficient.
Pricing mistakes/errors	If a company makes a mistake on pricing, it must admit it and remedy it fast. It is easy to make mistakes. Normally they do not really matter as long as they are spotted and efficiently and effectively adjusted.

following major areas, as defined by Cravens (1982).

▌ How large is the product-market in terms of buying potential? A thorough understanding and evaluation of the potential market is required before any consideration can be given to the pricing of the product.

▌ What segments exist in the product-market and what market target strategy is to be used? We have seen that different market segments seek different benefits and hence expect to pay different prices. A clear identification of the segments and their profile is vital in price setting.

▌ How sensitive is demand in the segment(s) to change in price? This relates to price elasticity, which was discussed earlier. It is very easy to get this wrong and misjudge the acceptable price range. Prices set outside the acceptable range of price levels in the potential buyer's perception will result in the loss of sales.

▌ How important are non-price factors such as features and locations? This is an area often missed by organizations when considering price levels. Products must be differentiated, and it is often better to enhance the product or service features as a competitive tool rather than use price.

▌ What are the estimated sales at different price levels? Davidson (1997) clearly indicates that there are a number of alternatives when it comes to setting prices. Levels of promotion will also affect sales, so all these factors must be taken into account when looking at setting price levels.

To conclude this chapter on pricing it may be worth highlighting some of the most common mistakes made in pricing strategy. These are put forward by Wilson and Gilligan (1997):

▌ Pricing decisions are too often biased towards cost structures rather than market considerations.

▌ Prices are set independently of other marketing mix elements.

▌ Too little account is taken of opportunities to capitalize on differentiation.

▌ Prices do not vary greatly between different market segments.

▌ Pricing is defensive.

Chapter summary

In this chapter we have seen that price can be one of the most effective marketing tools available to an organization. Of the seven Ps (the marketing mix), it is price that can have probably the most dramatic impact on the financial bottom line. Therefore, price can be

a determinant (not necessarily the only one) of whether a product or service is a success or failure within the marketplace.

Price is influenced or determined by several internal and external factors. These include costs (which are in turn influenced by numerous variables), the competition (local, regional, international and global), general and changing market conditions (influenced by demographics and economics), the product's life cycle position, and people's sensitivity to the prices.

Successful marketing strategies depend to a large extent on well-developed pricing strategies. In turn, successful pricing strategies depend on careful analysis, which is ongoing to take account of changing market conditions.

The overall influencing factor is the potential buyer. If, at the end of the day, the customer is not prepared to buy at the price being asked then the sale is lost. If customers perceive the price as too high they will not make the purchase. Likewise if they perceive the price as too low, they will consider the offering as inferior and the sale could be lost. It is therefore very important to ensure that the price charged equates with the potential customer's perception and possibly lifestyle. The understanding of consumer behaviour is as important in setting prices as is understanding of costing and accounting.

Exercises and questions for review and critical thinking

1. State, in detail, the key factors that can influence price. Cite examples.

2. Outline the pricing tactics or techniques that are used in the consumer marketplace.

3. What do you think are the potential advantages and disadvantages of the competitive bidding process from the buyer's perspective?

4. Contact a company that supplies computers, photocopiers or cars on a lease basis. See how the leasing agreement is structured in terms of periodic payments over a specific period of time. Together with additional research, consider what could be the possible advantages and disadvantages of leasing plans.

5. Revise the example we quoted regarding the Trinidadian hotel and the additions to the bill. Consider the indirect taxation systems within your own country and consider how they may impact on the room rate of a four or five star hotel. You could visit a hotel and collect its rate card. Alternatively you could log onto its Web site, especially if it is part of an international chain, and obtain details. If it is an international hotel chain you may want to compare room rate prices and the impact of local taxation policy.

6. When videos to buy were first introduced into the UK (early 1980s) they were priced at between £30 and £40 each. At that time it was very much a rental market. In 2001 it was very much a buyer's market with videos priced at between £4.99 and £15.99. Consider the possible reasons why over a period of some 20 years the prices have reduced rather than increased. You will need to consider other marketing mix factors in answering this question.

10

Promotion 1

Communication is the most important form of marketing.
Akio Morita (1921–1999), founder of the Sony Corporation

Introduction

As the Morita quotation above suggests, communication (or promotion) of a product or service is a critical element in marketing. Such is the scale of promotion, or marketing communications, as it is often known, that we have divided the subject into two chapters. In this chapter we consider the background of marketing communications, then advertising, direct marketing and the sales force. In the following chapter we examine public relations, sales promotion, merchandising, product placement, exhibitions and word of mouth or viral marketing.

While these elements are discussed in isolation over two chapters, and can function in isolation, they should be viewed as integrative. This is a point discussed in this chapter, but you should reflect on this across both chapters.

Learning objectives

On completion of this chapter you should be able to:

▌ demonstrate the role of promotion within the overall marketing mix;

▌ identify some of the core elements of the promotional mix, and explain their role within the overall promotional and marketing mix;

▌ demonstrate how advertising can be used to promote either a product or service;

▌ explain how Internet advertising can be used to support other marketing initiatives;

▌ examine how the role of the salesperson has developed and changed to meet the demands of 21st century business.

What promotion and marketing communications are

Perrault *et al* (2000) describe promotion as 'communicating information between the seller and potential buyer or others in the channel to influence attitudes and behaviour'. Following on from this quote we can see that marketing communications can be used to achieve several different, although linked, objectives. We can define these objectives as:

▊ Creating, maintaining and reinforcing brand awareness.

▊ Creating, maintaining and reinforcing a positive image of the brand in the mind of the customer. This is equally as important in a B2B scenario as it is in a consumer one.

▊ Influencing the views and decisions of key opinion formers. These range from government officials and politicians through to individual consumers or business customers.

▊ Creating the environment for the customer to purchase the product or service. We can include here ease of purchase.

▊ Providing after sales communications in order to create customer retention. Linked to this is the ongoing development of relationship marketing.

Communications theory

As Smith (1993) suggests, there are three fundamental elements in communications: the sender (the communicator or originator of the information or message), the message itself and the receiver (the collector of the message). This is illustrated in Figure 10.1.

The basic communications model suggests that the Sender is active, whilst the Receiver is passive. It also suggests that there is no 'interference' in the communication of the Message. However, the real world is not as simple as the illustration suggests. Schramm created a communications model in 1955 that still has significant value today in understanding the complexity of communications (Smith, 1993). Figure 10.2 illustrates several more stages in the communications process.

The sender/the communicator

When senders communicate they encode (or as Smith (1993) suggests, 'dress up') the message. For example, this could be the visual imagery, words and/or music used in a television commercial (channel of communication) to promote a new car.

Sender → Message → Receiver

Figure 10.1 Basic communications model

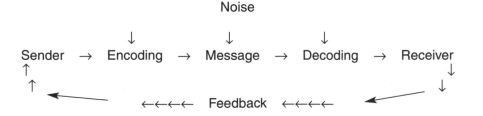

Figure 10.2 The communications process after Schramm

The receiver

The receiver (that is in this case, the viewer) then decodes the message. This can be interpreted, in our example, as understanding the features and benefits of this new car. The receiver evaluates or analyses the actual message and the source of that message. The evaluation of the source of the message will relate to trustworthiness, credibility, reliability and ethical stance. In our example of the launch of the new car, the receiver might consider whether it is from a well-respected car manufacturer, and who appears to be endorsing it. For example, a movie star might appear in the television commercial saying what a wonderful drive it is. This celebrity endorsement could add credibility in the mind of the receiver to the product.

The receiver then provides feedback, or responds, to this communication. This can take the form of seeking further information/ details (for instance, by telephoning or accessing a Web site) or rejecting the communication.

Noise

However, as depicted in Figure 10.2 there is a further influencer, and that is noise. This can be described as something that affects the understanding or actual receiving of the message. There are two sub-sets of noise, physical and semantic noise.

Physical noise

As the name suggests this is anything that physically reduces the effectiveness of the communication. This may range from audible noise, to physical movements (someone walking in front of the television set while you are watching the commercials) to literally just too much communication (known as clutter). For example, imagine standing at the end of a runway and talking on your mobile phone as a Boeing 777 comes in to land over your head. It is unlikely that the person trying to listen to you will hear you.

Clutter can be described as the high intensity of competing messages that are vying for the consumers' attention. As a result of this clutter the receiver may not 'see' the advertiser's message.

Semantic noise

This relates to misunderstanding the message, even though it was received exactly as it was transmitted. This breakdown of communications may be created by differences in social, economic and educational backgrounds (for instance, language/reading skills).

One of the biggest challengers for marketing communicators is how to cut through the noise and communicate effectively and efficiently with the target audience.

Overcoming communications breakdown

Once there is a realization that there has been a communications breakdown, various actions can be taken to remedy the situation. However, it cannot be taken for granted that, individually or collectively, these remedies will overcome the communications breakdown in its entirety. One factor that must be taken into consideration is the receiver's reluctance to accept the communications message as sent. Receivers might seek to distort or alter the message to suit their own views or ambitions. This point is not purely confined to marketing communications. It is prevalent throughout business and social interactions.

Potential methods of overcoming communications breakdowns

▌ A company can use more than one channel of communications: for example, a combination of visual, aural and written communications. In our example the features and benefits of the new car could be communicated by posters, television, radio, magazine advertising and editorials, direct mail to existing customers, face-to-face contact via the sales force or e-mail alerts to targeted customers (the use of permission marketing).

▌ The use of different 'devices' to capture the potential customers' attention. These can include colours, shapes (3D posters, for instance), humour and music (for instance, pop songs and classical music).

▌ Through improved segmentation, targeting and positioning reach the key audience.

▌ In addition to using more channels of communication (as stated above) there needs to be careful channel selection. This keys into targeting the right audience for the message.

▌ Improved understanding of the potential and current customer base. This can be achieved through market research and relationship marketing activities.

The marketing communications mix

This can be described as a combination of several major promotional techniques or elements. These elements can be either stand-alones or integrated to a greater or lesser degree. They are:

▌ advertising;
▌ direct marketing;
▌ sales promotion;
▌ sales force;
▌ sponsorship;
▌ product placement;
▌ merchandising;
▌ public relations;
▌ exhibitions;
▌ word of mouth.

Integrating marketing communications

Before we study the elements of the communications mix in isolation, we should consider the role of integration. Integrated marketing communications (IMC) is the coordination of the communications mix from the organization to the target audience. The objective is to create and convey a consistent complete message. As you work your way through this and other chapters, do not only consider the individual communication elements or channels, but think how they can be integrated.

However, there are both advantages and disadvantages to IMC. Here we briefly outline them. Again, when you consider the overall communications mix bear these positives and negatives in mind.

Positive aspects

▌ IMC can assist in building a long-term relationship with the customer. Companies and organizations (charities, for instance) seek to build a long-term relationship with their customers. Reflect back to Chapter 4, 'Buyer behaviour'. In that chapter we considered how companies seek to move individuals from prospects to first-time buyers and then repeat buyers. If companies can use a range of channels to communicate successfully with their customers, then they may achieve a competitive advantage over their competitors.

▌ IMC can increase sales by stretching the message across several different communication channels. This creates diversity and the opportunity for the customer to become aware and interested in the message. This may ultimately affect or change behaviour. This could lead ultimately to a purchase.

▌ IMC can provide consistency of brand message. This in turn can significantly aid brand awareness and identity – thus recall and retention. This feeds back to Point 1 above and building that long-term relationship, and brand loyalty.

■ By focusing on an integrated message, IMC can significantly reduce or eliminate duplication of effort. For example, several different communication specialists (advertising, sales promotion, public relations and so on) are not developing different campaigns for the same client. They are seeking a commonality, thus reducing effort and ultimately costs.

Negative aspects

■ Resistance to change. This not only affects certain aspects of marketing, it can be seen throughout business. Change is probably inevitable in all aspects of business. After all, we now live in a highly dynamic business environment – a global one. IMC means that different groups within different agencies and consultancies must work together. In an ideal world they would work towards the common goal of benefiting the client's aims and objectives. Unfortunately reality is not always so accommodating and focused. People are often afraid of change, because they may need to think differently and use their skills differently.

■ Organizational structures. This also relates to the above point. Managers within the same organization, let alone external agencies, may be protective. This protectiveness can range from budgets through to the actual project and, of course, power. Again, this is an HRM issue. However, it can greatly affect the outcome of an IMC project.

■ Restriction of creative freedoms. The issue here is, who is the creative driving force behind the integrated communications project? From where does the creative brief emanate? Creativity does not necessarily reside only within an advertising agency. It

can originate from any of the marketing communication tactical agencies or consultants. Thus there can be creative conflicts and restrictions.

■ Difficulties of planning over different timescales. Lead times can vary enormously from magazine advertising through to PR deadlines. Thus careful planning is necessary so that sales promotions can be achieved without detriment to longer-term advertising objectives.

■ Budget restrictions. IMC may best suit large corporations with equally large budgets. However, it may be impossible for micro businesses or SMEs to stretch their budgets over so many communications channels. Equally, their frequency of exposure will be greatly reduced. An SME could achieve more effective coverage by focusing on a very narrow range, for example, PR and sales promotion.

Advertising

Advertising is the greatest art form of the twentieth century.
Marshall McLuhan (1911–1980)

You cannot bore people into buying your product; you can only interest them in buying it.
David Ogilvy (1911–1999), founder of the agency Ogilvy & Mather

Advertising is any paid for communication overtly intended to inform and/or influence one or more people.
Jeremy Bullmore, Chairman of J Walter Thompson (1967–87), Non-Executive Director of WPP

The various points of this last statement are considered in Table 10.1.

The role of advertising, as one of a number of variable elements in the communication mix, is 'to sell or assist the sale of the maximum amount of the product, for the minimum cost outlay'. Advertising is more

Table 10.1 Key elements of advertising

Key element	Description
Paid for	An advertisement that is not paid for is not an advertisement, it is rather editorial of some sort. The payment is made to the provider of the medium, for example a magazine or newspaper. However, also consider a handwritten note placed in the window of a local shop. Here the advertiser is the person who wants to, for example, sell an item or rent out a room to a student. He or she pays the shop owner a small fee for advertising.
Communication	Every advertisement is attempting to bridge the gap between the sender of the message and the potential receivers of that message. The bridging is the communication. However, consider here the 'noise' that may prevent the message being accurately received. Reflect upon what could cause that noise and how it could be overcome.
Overtly	Advertising can be 'upfront' and dramatic, whereas product placement or public relations can be subtle (though not always) in its approach. (See later sections on product placement and PR.)
Intended	Not all advertising appears to work in the sense of achieving its objectives. Nevertheless it remains advertising. Consider for example advertising that you instantly remember. Why do you remember it?
Inform/ influence	Some advertisements inform and influence, while others purely inform: for example: the government announcing that there will be a Census taking place during the year. Equally, a government may use advertising to advise its citizens on how to act during a crisis – for example the British government's advice in the 1990s on preventing the spread of AIDS.
One or more people	Depending upon such factors as targeting and segmentation tactics an advertisement can address small or significantly large audiences. An advertisement within a major tabloid newspaper will have a potentially large audience, while an advertisement in a small trade publication will have a significantly smaller one. However, that does not detract from its potential effectiveness. The key is placing the advertisement in the right publication to reach the right target audience at the right time.

than a series of individual advertisements. It reflects, or should do, an overall game plan – a strategy, which coordinates what is done, producing a cohesive whole directed at achieving the desired results.

Advertising needs to be designed and produced in a way that reflects an analysis of the market and a subsequent sensible choice of media and of advertising strategies. This means those involved – more than one person is often involved – must be in close communication.

If advertising effectiveness is to be maximized, it must be planned and originated carefully. It may help to spell out what needs to be done in a simple strategy document. At

its best, such an advertising strategy statement is brief and economical, and does its job in three paragraphs, which describe:

▌ the basic proposition: the promise to the customer and the statement of benefits to the customer;

▌ the 'reason why' or supporting proof justifying the proposition, the main purpose of which is to render the message as convincing as possible;

▌ the tone of voice in which the message should be delivered: the image to be projected, and not infrequently the picture the customer has of himself/herself, which it could be unwise to disturb, or rather, wise to capitalize on.

In various fields some of the finest and most effective advertising has sometimes been produced without reference to any advertising strategy, or for that matter without knowledge of real market facts. However, although research or objective thinking cannot always give all the details, or for that matter always be infallibly interpreted, it can give strong indications and reduce the chances of failure.

Most executives, when faced with a rough or initial visual and copy layout, have an automatic subjective response, 'I like it' or 'I don't like it.' And while the creator may attempt to explain that the appraiser is not a member of the target audience, it can be genuinely difficult to be objective. Nevertheless, while an attempt at objectivity must be made, there are few experienced advertising or marketing executives who can say that their judgement has never let them down. Advertising remains as much an art as science. (The most famous saying about advertising by a company chairman: 'I know half the money I spend on advertising is wasted, but I don't know which half' – a remark that contains a good deal of truth, and a sobering thought with an eye on budgets, every penny of which has to be fought for in many organizations.)

Another possible problem in any business is what is called 'me-tooism'. Advertising gets into a rut, with those producing it simply reiterating an established formula and ceasing even to try to think creatively. This gives rise to so-called 'tombstone style' advertisements, saying little and saying it non-creatively. Easy to produce, low cost, yes – but hardly likely to have major or striking impact. They might be judged fine as announcements to the faithful (those who will buy the product almost automatically), but surely much advertising is, or should be, designed to do more than that. It is one thing for it to be there and visible, it is quite another for it to be persuasive.

There is a danger also of confusing creativity, the process that makes something both appropriate to customers and memorable, with cleverness. Sometimes a clever idea – a play on words in a headline, perhaps – can act not to increase the power of the advertisement, but to dilute it or obscure what should be a clear message. Advertising must never fall into the trap of confusing cleverness with clarity of communication.

All companies must ask straight questions about their advertising generally and also about particular advertisements:

- Does the advertisement match the strategy?

- Does the advertisement gain attention and create awareness?

- Is it likely to create interest and understanding of the advantages of what it offers?

- Does it create a desire for the benefits and really prompt the need to buy?

- Is it likely to prompt potential customers actually to make a purchase, now or in the future?

- Can it be linked to tangible action (with a coupon to be completed and returned, a 'hotline' to be telephoned, for instance)?

- Is it concentrating on the features of the product, rather than benefits to the reader/purchaser? In other words, does the advertisement communicate? Will people notice it, understand it, believe it, remember it and buy as a result of it?

Therefore, advertising needs to be creative. Often its task is to make something routine, or even potentially dull, 'interestingly different'. Just occasionally the product really is interestingly different, more often the essential qualities of the product need presenting in whatever way allows the presentation to persuade.

Forms of advertising

There is a variety of forms of advertising, in terms of both the type of advertising and the target to which it is directed. These include, by way of example:

▌ national advertising;

▌ retail or local advertising;

▌ direct mail advertising (direct response advertising and leaflets inserted in publications);

▌ business-to-business (also known as trade advertising);

▌ sector advertising (for instance to a particular sub-division of a market such as the SoHo market (the small office/home office, part of the market for computers and other office equipment)).

▌ Internet advertising via Web sites.

A more specific way of understanding what advertising can do is to summarize some of the major purposes of advertising: that is, the various and different objectives that can be achieved through advertising in particular ways. The following is a representative list, which is by no means exhaustive:

▌ Inform potential customers of a new offering. This can range from a new product to a product revision. You may want to reflect on Chapter 8, and consider Lucozade as an example.

▌ Through advertising it may be possible to expand the market for a particular product or service, for example, advertising cars to the fleet car market. Another example is medicines that were previously only available on prescription, but have become available over the counter (OTC).

▌ Announce a modification or an enhancement of the product. Examples include computer software (MS Windows 95, 97, 98, 2000, and XP – home and professional), improved detergents and additional safety features on a particular car model.

▌ Announce a price change. Examples include price reductions that may be for a limited period only – this has often been used by various fast-food outlets. Equally, banks advertise increases or decreases in interest rates to borrowers and savers.

▌ Announce a new form of packaging. Examples include new handipacks (smaller travel sizes of toothpaste, mouthwash, tissues), liquid forms available in addition to traditional powdered varieties, and easier opening cartons.

▌ Announce a special offer: examples, are 'buy one and get one free' limited offers, money-off coupons or vouchers, and special limited holiday offers.

▌ Invite enquiries, for either consumers or B2B: for example, requesting a catalogue of the latest CD release from a music company. There is normally a response coupon attached to the advertisement.

▌ Selling direct. This is also known as 'buying off the page'. Buying direct from an advertisement can cover virtually any product from vitamin capsules to CDs, books and garden furniture.

▌ Announce the location of stockists. This is to support dealers or general stockists of the product and/or service.

▌ Maintain sales/remind customers. Here the objective is to maintain sales by keeping the product/service prominent in the buyer's mind.

▌ Retrieve lost sales. Advertisements can be positioned and devised to retrieve lost sales because of, for example, weather conditions (long hot summers and their impact on chocolate consumption), product recalls, or product withdrawal then reintroduction.

▌ Recruit new staff to the organization. Job advertisements for particular sectors tend to appear together on specific days. For example, the quality broadsheet newspaper the *Guardian* in the UK has a section devoted to sales and marketing jobs on Mondays, with educational jobs on Tuesdays.

▌ Announce trading results. Major Stock Market listed corporations announce their annual results through advertising in key publications.

▌ Increase the frequency of purchase.

▌ Increase the use of a product.

▌ Increase the quantity purchased.

▌ Increase the frequency of replacement.

▌ Lengthen the buying seasons. Cadbury has been very successful in selling its Creme Eggs beyond the Easter period for which they were originally introduced.

▌ Present a promotional programme.

▌ Bring a family of products together.

▌ Attract a new generation of customers.

▌ Support or influence a retailer, dealer, agent or intermediary.

▌ Reduce substitution by maintaining customer loyalty.

▌ Make known the organization behind the range of offerings (corporate image advertising).

▌ Stimulate enquiries (from consumers or B2B customers).

▌ Provide reasons for wholesalers and retailers to stock or promote a product.

▌ Provide technical information about something (this may be actually technical or more general information).

There are clearly many reasons behind the advertising that you see around you. The purposes listed above are not mutually exclusive, of course, and many of those listed apply, or could apply, to a single advertising campaign.

Whilst these are two very different advertising styles they are both reflecting 'discounts' and attempting to make themselves 'heard' within a crowded marketplace. The advertisement for Spar stores is an announcement of a special limited 'three for two' offer on branded milk products between 22 August and 3 September. The emphasis is on the offer and the 33 per cent saving. The poster is very bold – the discounts in essence 'shout out at you'. The second advertisement is stating that there are discounts available at a clothing outlet village. The imagery here is of a beautiful woman posing a question (the limited text). However, there is also a sexual undertone to the advertisement. Such imagery is often used to make an advertisement overt, standing out against others it is located near.

Whatever specific objectives the use of advertising seeks to achieve, the main tasks for it are usually to:

▌ gain the customer's attention;

▌ attract customer interest;

▌ create desire for what is offered;

▌ prompt the customer to buy (either at once or some time in the future).

Advertising is, therefore, primarily concerned with attitudes and attitudinal change. Creating favourable attributes towards a product should be an important part of the advertising effort.

Business-to-business advertising

This is certainly important, and in many industries advertising is split between that directed to ultimate customers and that directed at those in the channels of distribution. It is often not sufficient to advertise products to consumers alone, particularly where it is important that distributors/retailers are willing to stock and promote a product.

For example, a publisher might advertise the launch of a new novel to the public. Additionally, through trade media it will advertise it to retail and Internet booksellers. Although the sales force has a primary role in ensuring that stocking and promotional objectives are achieved, trade advertising has a supportive role; indeed it sets the scene for such sales visits:

▌ It can remind retailers/distributors about the product/product range between sales visits.

▌ It can keep them fully informed and up to date on developments and any policy changes.

▌ It can alleviate problems associated with the cold-call selling of less well-known products.

▌ It can indicate the support, and weight, being given to a product. This is disproportionately important within many trades. It is used as both an objective measure of assessing what stock to buy, and an easy – albeit subjective – way of making a quick decision to stock.

Often B2B advertising occurs prior to, or linked with, consumer advertising campaigns. This is to help prompt the buying-in of stock in anticipation of future demands created by the consumer advertising. Other tactics also feature. For example, when new products are launched, or special promotions introduced, trade support may be achieved through special offers or increased (introductory) discounts. All these factors can be emphasized through trade advertising.

This type of advertising can also communicate to the trade the detail of the moment – why they should stock forthcoming lines or reorder existing ones – as well as flag the timing and weight of any advertising or other support (such as editorial coverage) that is to come.

Curiously perhaps, one of the most important aspects of B2B advertising is not what it says. The commitment (and cost) of taking such space is seen by many as a commitment to particular products or promotions. If a sales representative is pressing a shop to take good stocks, mount a window display or generally take a product seriously, then buyers are apt to ask, 'What are you doing for it?' This is a reasonable enough statement from their point of view. Even so, the advertising mix that is deployed here, whether it is directed to individual products, the company, the range or any combination, must accommodate this fact. The more that retailers feel a supplier is matching their views of potential success with action, the more they are likely to respond positively to stocking suggestions.

Advertising effort needs to be spread amongst the various target audiences that match a particular product. B2B advertising may take a large share of this on occasion. It must be tailored to the trade, who probably want to hear different things from the ultimate public and potential customers, and be spoken to in a different way. The basic principles of what makes advertising work and the strategy involved are similar for all types of advertising.

Advertising objectives

Fundamentally, however, advertising also aims to sell, usually with the minimum of delay, although a longer time period may be needed in the case of informative or corporate (image building) advertising. Every advertisement should relate to the product or service, its market and potential market. As a piece of communication, each can perform a variety of tasks. Table 10.2 considers advertising objectives.

Table 10.2 Advertising objectives

Objective	Description
Provide information	This information can act as a reminder to current users or it can inform non-users of the product or service's existence.
Attempt to persuade	It can attempt to persuade current users to purchase again (repeat purchasing), non-users to buy for the first time and new users to change habits or suppliers (brand switching).
Create 'cognitive dissonance'	This memorable piece of wording or jargon means advertising can help to create uncertainty about the ability of current suppliers to satisfy needs best. In this way, advertising can effectively persuade customers to try an alternative product or brand. (Extreme versions of this are used sometimes by, among others, car manufacturers that are openly critical of the competition.)
Create reinforcement	Advertising can compete with competitors' advertising, which itself aims to create dissonance, to reinforce the idea that current purchases best satisfy the customer's needs. This is maintaining awareness and aiming to continue to prompt ongoing purchases.
Reduce uncertainty	Moreover, advertising may also act to reduce the uncertainty felt by customers immediately following an important and valuable purchase, when they are debating whether or not they have made the correct choice. This is perhaps most important with significant types of products and levels of spending (for example: a car or refrigerator/freezer). Advertising remains a constant reinforcement of their decision to purchase.

Five points that need to be considered prior to advertising

▌ Who is the company trying to influence? Who is its target market? What does it do? Who are the decision makers?

▌ What is the company selling: a product, service or both? What is the company name and corporate image?

▌ Why should prospects buy? What makes the product or service special? What are the USPs (the unique selling points or proposition)?

▌ Where will the company find prospective buyers? What does the potential audience read/watch/listen to? Can the company place an advertising medium in front of them?

▌ When should the company communicate with them? Should the company communicate with them on a regular basis? Is the company's product/service seasonal? Thus will this affect the times when it communicates with its customers?

The company's overall objective in advertising

This can be expressed as AIDA; that is:

get **ATTENTION**
hold **INTEREST**
arouse **DESIRE**
obtain **ACTION** ➜ purchase (may be a long-term objective).

Let's consider these points in terms of the layout of the advertisement.

Attention

In a highly competitive business market an advertisement needs to stand out from the rest of the crowd. This is often described as 'breaking through the clutter'. This may be achieved through the words of the banner headline, size and position of the advertisement, type of illustration and typography.

Interest

Here we can consider a number of factors:

▌ **Originality.** It is very easy to fall into clichés and copy other advertisements. Imitation may be a form of flattery; however an advertisement needs to differentiate itself.

▌ **Focal point.** The aim here is to bring the prospective buyer's eye to a major point of interest. Clarity is important. 'Busy' or 'noisy' advertisements tend to distract.

▌ **Comprehensibility.** Again clarity is important. Is it immediately clear what the company is selling?

▌ **Logical sequence of events.** Are buyers carried through the advertisement, or is it too disjointed, too confusing for them to understand and appreciate?

▌ **Unity.** There needs to be a union between all the elements of the advertisement, from the heading through to the illustration, logo, text and even the clip coupon (important in direct marketing).

Desire

This is the translating of a liking, for a particular product or service, into the wish to own it. Holiday advertising is an example.

At this stage it is worth linking attention, interest and desire through the text used within the advertisement. The flow of reading should not be interrupted, thus it is important to consider the wording and presentation of the text or copy.

▌ **Attractive copy.** The copy or text needs to be legible through the use of appropriate typefaces, type sizes and layout.

▌ **Interesting copy.** A large body of text can be uninteresting to read. Prospective buyers may 'switch off' if they have dense text to read. The use of italics, bolding, indents and colour can break up the text so that it is interesting to read. Again, making it eyecatching helps to retain interest.

▌ **Writing style.** Advertising often breaks writing conventions in order to make the words and phrases more interesting, or more powerful. However, the copy should not be difficult to read – it has to involve readers and maintain their interest.

▌ **Using slogans.** The right slogan can make both the advertisement and the product memorable. Ones that have stood the test of time include:

– Beanz Meanz Heinz™
– Don't just book it – Thomas Cook it™ (Thomas Cook Travel)
– Diamonds are forever™ (DeBeers)
– Just do it™ (Nike)
– The breakfast of champions™ (Wheaties)
– Let your fingers do the walking™ (Yellow Pages telephone directories).

There are various reasons slogans can be successful. They include:

– providing a simple, very direct form of communication;
– being easily remembered, thus easily recalled when there is a purchasing decision to be made;
– becoming characteristic of, or synonymous with, the product or service;
– supporting the selling points of the product or service.

Action

Here the advertiser needs to create some form of response mechanism. This may take the form of:

- a direct purchase;

- request for further information by post, fax, telephone or e-mail;

- request for a visit, for example in the case of financial services;

- request for a quotation, again this could be related to financial services;

- direct telephone conversation with the advertiser.

The objective is to make it as easy as possible, and as convenient, for the prospective buyer to make contact. The mechanisms by which this can be achieved include:

- a named contact person with a direct-line telephone number;

- a freephone number;

- a hotline number that allows for quicker purchasing;

- a fax number so to fax over the order;

- e-mail address;

- a Web site address, which can provide more information on a range of products and the company itself;

- a clip coupon whereby the prospect can request either a range of items or specific information;

- a freepost address.

A variant on the AIDA model is the SPIS (sales, persuasion, involvement and saliency) model, which is outlined in Table 10.3.

Table 10.3 The SPIS model

Technique	Description
Sales	The objective of promotion or marketing communications techniques is to influence positively the sale of the product or service. We should also consider sales in terms of not-for-profit organizations. Here a sale could be defined as a donation to a charity, for instance.
Persuasion	The various promotion and marketing communication techniques aim to persuade the customer to purchase the product or service. Marketing communication specialists (for example, advertising agencies) devise messages that assist in persuading a customer to buy into the product or service being offered.
Involvement	Links or associations are made, through the persuasive message, between the product or service provider and the potential customer. For instance, consider a charity seeking donations to help starving children in a famine-ravaged country. The charity could create a message that links the audience's average weekly grocery bill to the plight of the starving children, by stating that a mere small percentage of that weekly bill could save numerous lives. Thus an emotional involvement is created.
Saliency	One of the biggest problems in promotion or marketing communications is clutter (literally, too much communication). There are numerous companies and organizations vying for the customer's attention. Here saliency refers to the ability to stand out above competitors in the marketplace. It can be argued that Toscani's controversial advertising for Benetton was instrumental in pushing the brand to new heights. However, as Benetton discovered to its costs, there are limits to the techniques used to break through the clutter (refer to the 'Marketing insight' on page 74).

As stated earlier in this text we are currently bombarded by an array of images. You may want to consider how these three images link back to the AIDA and SPIS models described in the text.

Types of advertising

There are several basic types of advertising, which are distinguished in Table 10.4.

Types of advertising media

There is a bewildering array of advertising media available. As the 'Marketing insight' illustrates, the range of media potentially available in the UK is significantly broad. All are potentially appropriate in any business, although the right mix for any one business will vary. For example, not every company can afford television advertising or wants the broad coverage it provides.

Equally, in some countries television is government controlled (to a greater or lesser extent), thus it may not be permitted to generate advertising revenues. Additionally, certain types of advertising may be banned. For example, in the UK tobacco advertising is banned on television and in newspapers.

Table 10.4   Types of advertising

Type	Aim
Primary	This aims to stimulate basic demand for a particular product type – for example, insurance, books, tea or wool – and includes advertising by overall trade bodies rather than individual suppliers.
Selective	This aims to promote an individual brand name, such as a brand of car, soap or washing powder, which is promoted without particular reference to the manufacturer's identity.
Product	This aims to promote a product or range of related brands, where some account must be taken of the image and interrelationship of all products in the mix.
Institutional	This covers public relations-type advertising, which in very general terms aims to promote the company name, corporate image and the company services: as an organization might advertise overall, without mention of its products or services. For example, corporate advertising for the petrochemical multinational ICI, the management consultants Accenture and the UK's Automobile Association.

Marketing insight: UK media

National daily newspapers	14
National Sunday newspapers	11
Regional morning newspapers	18
Regional evening newspapers	72
Regional Sunday newspapers	7
Local weekly newspapers	477
Free distribution publications	These are newspapers and magazines that are distributed free and delivered door to door. Distribution is usually confined to a specific locality, for example districts of a city. The number is in excess of several thousand.
Consumer magazines	Over 3,500 ranging from the *Radio Times* with a circulation over 1 million to hobby/leisure publications which sell a few thousand copies.
Business, professional and controlled circulation magazines	Over 6,300 titles. These cover everything from the grocery business to biochemistry.
Television	13 regional stations, plus GMTV (breakfast programming), and two national commercial stations, Channels 4 and 5. Then an array of cable and satellite broadcasters.
Radio	241 commercial radio stations.
Cinema	2,680 screens (some grouped in cinemas with more than one screen).
Poster panels/billboard sites Transport sites	Roadside: approximately 120,000. Rail 11,000, buses 37,000, London Underground 151,000, taxis 36,000. Total: 235,000

Sources: Advertising Association (www.adassoc.org.uk), Outdoor Advertising Association UK (www.oaa.org.uk). Details as of 2003.

Print media

There are two key issues with print media: readership and readership buying power. Readership is the total number of people who read each issue. Magazines can be passed onto others outside the household, friends and neighbours for example.

The buying power of a newspaper or magazine is also very important. For example, luxury items would be better suited to the weekend *Financial Times*, a business-based broadsheet, than a tabloid newspaper. The *Financial Times* may have a lower circulation than a tabloid, however it is the level of buying power that is crucial in this example. See Table 10.5.

Table 10.5   Types of print media

Print medium	Description
Daily newspapers	These can be national or regional. They often enjoy reader loyalty and hence high credibility. Consequently, they are particularly useful for prestige and reminder advertising. As they are read hurriedly by many people, lengthy copy may be wasted.
Local newspapers	These are (obviously) particularly useful for anything local, but are relatively expensive if used *en masse* for a national or broader campaign. They are sometimes used for test market area advertising support where a product is initially only made available on a limited basis. Local newspapers can be either free (via door drops) or be paid for by the public.
Magazines	These vary from quarterlies to weeklies and from very general, wide-coverage journals to many with a specific focus and often linked to very specialized interests. Similarly, different magazines of the same type (for example, women's magazines) appeal to different age and socioeconomic groups. Magazines are normally colourful and often read on a regular basis.
Customer magazines	These can either be free or paid for. They may be published through the company's own marketing services department or through a contract publishing company. While these magazines reinforce the image of the company they can also provide opportunities for other companies to advertise their products. This creates revenue for the publication, and allows the advertisers to target specific groups.
	Major insurance companies often use them to illustrate their different ranges of products: everything from insurance for pets, travel, cars and home to family savings plans. As incentives, gifts or prize draw competitions may be included. Virtually every airline has its own inflight magazine. An example is *Going Places* which is published by the Marketing Services Division of Malaysia Airlines. As well as providing an advertising medium for credit card companies, partner hotels and designer wear, there is promotion of the airline's services, routes and merchandising. In the UK one of the most successful paid-for customer magazines has been *Sainsbury's Magazine*. This is contract published on behalf of the Sainsbury supermarket chain. Published monthly, a typical edition covers general lifestyle features, food and drink, and gardening. All the food and household products advertised are available through the supermarket, whilst other advertisers take advantage of the target audience. In addition, money-off coupons are included.

Television, cinema and radio

The use of sound and/or visuals can enhance the impact value of a product or service. Table 10.6 provides a brief summary of television, cinema and radio media.

Outdoor advertising (posters, billboards and hoardings)

Outdoor advertising is generally considered the first advertising medium, dating back over 5,000 years when hieroglyphics appeared on obelisks to direct travellers. Nearly 2,500 years ago, Egyptian merchants inscribed sales messages on stone tablets, placing them along the roadside.

Strategically placed posters near high-density populations, busy thoroughfares or at commuter stations can offer very effective, long-life support advertising. Collaboration between suppliers and retailers can sometimes be used to link these to strategic locations designed to support local activity.

Posters are considered a passive medium. While a person may walk or drive past a poster

Table 10.6   Television, cinema and radio advertising

Medium	Description
Television	This is regarded as one of the best overall media for achieving mass impact and creating an immediate response mechanism. It is arguable whether or not the audience is captive or receptive, but the fact that television is being used is often sufficient in itself to generate trade support. Television allows the product to be shown or demonstrated, and is useful in test marketing new products because of its regional nature. However, it is very expensive, and therefore ruled out for most SMEs. In the UK advertising time is sold in 'spots' which range from seven seconds to one minute. The costs vary depending upon the time of day or night the commercial is being shown. Programmes which receive high viewership (for example, *Baywatch*: see Chapter 14) tend to attract prime-time costs.
Cinema	With its escapist atmosphere it can have an enormous impact on its audience of predominantly young people; but without repetition (people visiting the cinema once every week, or a tie-in with other media) it has little lasting effect. It is again useful for supporting press and television, however for certain products only, bearing in mind the audience and the atmosphere. Another medium where cost rules out the smaller company, although local advertising is possible by booking space in one individual cinema.
Commercial radio	Commercial radio, playing music for every conceivable taste, or focusing on interest groups (for example, news and current affairs) offers repetitive contact, has proved an excellent outlet for certain products, and is expanding its users all the time. It is becoming apparent that local and regional radio stations appeal to a wide cross-section of people. Thus they offer support potential to a wide range of products. Many smaller companies are included among those who have tried this medium.

on a regular basis, that does not mean he or she has necessarily noticed the poster, or reacted to it.

Developments in technology, combined with imagination, have provided for the creation of unusual and eye-catching advertising. For example:

▌ Bus backs. These have progressed from small rectangular advertisements (usually uninspired cardboard within a clear plastic holder) to transfers which cover the whole of the bus back, or indeed the whole bus. These are now the norm in cities like London, Singapore and Paris. (See page 335.)

▌ Car manufacturers have used car sections to create a three-dimensional effect to poster advertising.

▌ Mobile billboards: billboards do not need to be static. Increasingly billboards of varying sizes are mounted on vehicles. This provides advertisers with the opportunity to display their messages in places where normal billboard advertising would be difficult and/or ineffective.

Ambient media

'Ambient' can be described as 'in the surroundings or in the background'. As we shall see, ambient media are very much absorbed into the background, as opposed to the often boldness of traditional advertising methods. Originally called fringe media, ambient media may be classed as non-traditional advertising. In the United States it is often referred to as out of home media. Table 10.7 gives a few examples:

Table 10.7   Ambient media

Medium	Description
Taxis	A full range of interior and exterior advertising opportunities can be offered. These range from full and partial company liveries emblazoned on the cab (newspapers and airlines are examples) and exterior door panels to small interior advertising panels. The advertising varies depending upon the aims of the campaign. Taxis in Singapore, for example, have sign boards on top of the cab, many of which are illuminated at night.
Aerial	This covers airships and aircraft. Airships flying over cities or strategic locations often carry giant illuminated signage along their length. Similar in idea to airships, aircrafts can tow banners advertising a product or an event, such as a pop concert.
Tickets	Often the side, or reverse of a ticket for a concert or transportation advertises a product, service or event. Here are two large-brand examples from London Underground tickets. In June 1999 the Kellogg Company used the tickets to advertise the Nutri-Grain™ bar with the copyline 'Missed breakfast? Seek assistance.' In August 1999 Pizza Hut with the copyline 'Your meal ticket' used them to advertise the 'Pizza Hutline™', a telephone number for delivery and takeaways within selected areas of London.
Giveaway postcards	These are postcards that feature either an event or a product. They look like any ordinary postcard and can be mailed if the user so wishes. They can be located in racks inside cinemas or restaurants, for example.
Trolleys	Airport, supermarket and railway station trolleys often feature advertising signage. This can range from duty free products and credit cards to local taxi services and hotels.
Washrooms	Washroom walls have become one of the fastest growing advertising media in the UK. The washroom environment can be divided into two: pubs, wine bars and clubs, and shopping centres. In pubs, wine bars and clubs, the most commonly seen advertisements are for drinks, condoms and anti-drink driving messages. In shopping centres the advertisements often feature nearby stores and/or the various products they sell. Additionally, specific groups can be segmented and targeted depending on the venues: everyone from young clubbers to mothers with babies.
Maps	Local tourist maps often feature small advertisements for a range of local products and services. These can range from restaurants and sightseeing tours to car rental and hotels.
Other sources	These include rubbish collection bins, lamp posts, petrol pump nozzles, fast-food cartons, carrier bags, airline seat tables and even pavements.

Research by Alvern Forecourt Media/MRSL shows that a chocolate brand advertised on a petrol pump nozzle can create a sales lift by 54 per cent during a promotional campaign. However, more industry-wide research is needed to assess the impact on sales and brand awareness once the advertising has stopped.

As Ambient Media suggest 'it is in the background'. Here we see two examples. Firstly, a series of tables with serviette holders and ashtrays, all of them promoting the fruit drink Derby Blue™. The second example shows how the 'humble' carrier bag plays an important role in promoting a strong brand image and identity.

Internet advertising

There are several types of Internet advertising currently available:

▌ banners of various forms;

▌ skyscrapers;

▌ pop-ups;

▌ buttons;

▌ classified.

Table 10.8 considers the options.

Advertising: general points

Not all these are right for every product or in every circumstance. Some are simply not cost-effective in certain circumstances; you are unlikely to see an individual small retailer advertising on television, but it could advertise in a local newspaper or on a poster in a shopping precinct. Others assume greater importance because of their linked characteristics: an advertisement alongside an editorial mention may work much better than one without this editorial link.

Table 10.8   Types of Internet advertising

Technique	Description
Static banner advertising	This is a rectangular graphic that normally appears at the top of the page or along the bottom of the page. Banners can either be static or animated. As more consumers become comfortable with Flash and other animated technologies, companies will use banner advertising to create something different and eyecatching.
Animated banner advertising	By using such technology as Flash, banner advertising can comprise several different images in a sequence to attract the viewer's attention. The different 'layers' help to build an image that can lead the viewer to a state of action – clicking on to the advertisement. This direct response mechanism leads them to the Web site. There are numerous examples ranging from online bookstores through to cosmetic companies and insurance companies.
Interactive banner advertising	This is one step beyond purely animated banner advertising. In addition to attracting the viewer's attention, the advertisements adds value by allowing the viewer to input information. This will then lead to a further, more personalized response. Examples of advertisers are travel and credit card companies.
Skyscrapers	These are, in essence, a vertical form of banner advertising. The same interactivity and animation potential exists.
Pop-up advertising	These are also known as interstitials. These are advertising windows that 'pop up' in between screens of information as a new page is displayed. Once displayed the advertisement can only be removed by the viewer closing the specific window. Thus pop-up advertising has the advantage of being highly visible, and the viewer has to close it down. However the negative of this is that pop-ups are often deemed intrusive, getting in the way of the page the viewer wants to see. Equally, the physical action of having to close down the window costs time, if only a few seconds, and can be irritating for the viewer.
Buttons	As the name suggests these are small circular, oval, square or rectangular objects that display an image. That image is usually a company name and or logo. This provides a click-through opportunity to the company's Web site.
Classified	As with their print media counterparts, these are small, normally text only advertisements that typically appear in online magazines and newspapers. They can cover everything from business opportunities through to individuals seeking friendship and marriage.

Every advertiser must make its own decisions (advertising agencies that handle the larger advertising budgets have sophisticated media buying departments), not only about different methods, but about exact media, one newspaper versus another and so on.

However, not all advertising is aimed at potential consumers, some is directed at intermediaries. The objective here is to influence the intermediaries to buy the products and services, and then push them to the end users. For example, a manufacturer will advertise to retail outlets such as major supermarkets. They in turn advertise to the end user – the consumer. In Chapter 13 we consider placement and distribution channels that explore the relationship between the various groups involved in the supply and management of products and services. When you read that chapter it would be worthwhile reflecting upon the different marketing communication links within the supply chain.

Measurement

Here we need to consider how a company can measure the level of success achieved by its advertising campaign.

We can initially measure the value of the advertising by:

▊ The number of responses. It is important that any telephone enquirer is asked, 'Where did you see our name?' or 'Where did you hear about us?' The response has to be noted in order to obtain a reasonably accurate analysis of advertising success.

▊ In a B2B environment, are people talking about the advertisement? Especially competitors?

▊ The quality of responses. This is especially important in a B2B environment. Are they the true decision makers? Could they be potential long-term customers? If so, what levels of expenditure from them are possible?

▊ The final test is conversion. The role of the company is to convert the prospective buyer into an actual buyer.

If the response to the advertising campaign is poor, the following questions should be asked:

▊ Is the message the company wants to communicate being communicated?

▊ Is the message the right one for the product or service?

▊ Is the design of the advertisement right for the market?

▊ Is the design and layout of the advertisement clear?

▊ Is the design professional?

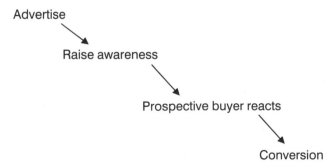

Figure 10.3 Objectives of advertising

▌ Was sufficient invested in design/layout to achieve a quality advertisement?

▌ Is the advertisement eyecatching enough in relation to competitors' advertising?

▌ Is the copy clear, interesting and readable?

▌ Was enough advertising done? Was it a sustained campaign or did it only select one or two slots? If the latter, was it really effective?

▌ Were the right media chosen?

▌ Were the right times of the year to advertise chosen?

Direct marketing

In this section we investigate the contribution that direct marketing has made to the marketing communications and transaction process, and possible future developments. Direct marketing is often, and rightly, considered as one-to-one communication. As we have already seen in previous chapters there is a potentially strong interrelationship between the various marketing communications elements, and perhaps none more so than with direct marketing. There is clearly a relationship, as we shall discover, between advertising, direct mail, the sales force and e-marketing.

As both Rich (2000) and Mitchell (1998) state, 'what many people call one-to-one marketing is actually nothing more than database marketing – personally addressed marketing communications. The difference between the two is that one-to-one marketing is nothing without customization. It is about generating feedback so that marketers can learn more about customers' preferences with future offers being tailored to those preferences.'

As well as this relationship between media, paramount to direct marketing is the relationship between the producer/retailer and the customer. Direct marketing is about relationship building, operating within an interactive environment and conducting a dialogue with the customer. As Grönroos (1990) suggests:

> Marketing is to establish, maintain, and enhance relationships with customers and other parties, at a profit, so that the objectives of the parties involved are met. This is achieved by a mutual exchange and fulfillment of promises. This perspective departs from the traditional view of marketing that emphasizes only 'exchange' and moves toward the notion of 'exchange in relationship' and, thus called the emergence of relationship marketing a paradigm shift in the marketing discipline.

Indeed, during the early 1990s several direct marketing agencies in the UK began calling themselves relationship marketing consultancies.

Direct marketing brings with it several advantages:

▌ Companies can track a single customer from the millions that they may have on their database. As a result they can better understand buying behaviour and purchasing history.

▌ There can be an interactive dialogue between the company and the customer, allowing for greater feedback. As Peppers and Rogers (1997) state, 'Dialogue and feedback are indispensable elements of a customer relationship. Communication *with* [their italics] the customer (rather than *to* [their italics] the customer) plays an essential, integrating role in the customer-driven dynamics of competition. Each interaction gives the enterprise access to information about that particular customer that would otherwise be completely unavailable.'

▌ There can be further development of mass customization, where products and services can, through modularization, be tailored.

What is clear is that direct marketing has revolutionized marketing communications and has demonstrated phenomenal growth in recent years. In 1999, US direct marketing produced some US $1.5 trillion in sales (approximately US $0.5 trillion increase from 1994 sales). By 2004 this is expected to be US $2.3 trillion, with an industry growth nearly double the overall US economy. Of course, that is just the United States. Now consider the growth potential in Europe, Latin and South America, and the burgeoning potential in China and other Far Eastern nations.

While we discuss advertising, the sales force and the Internet within this chapter it is important that you investigate the contents of the other relevant chapters. This will reinforce the relationships and integrative aspects.

What direct marketing is

> One of the future aspects of advertising is the custom-made, the tailor-made. Instead of peddling mass-produced commodities, advertising is going to become a personal service to each individual.
> Marshall McLuhan (cited in McCorkell, 1997)

This statement by the Canadian communicator and scholar Marshall McLuhan in the early 1960s in many ways foretold the significant development in direct marketing. In this quote McLuhan was already expressing the concept of one-to-one marketing. As we will see, though, he was not the only one who considered the one-to-one marketing relationship.

The key to successful direct marketing is in its targeting, although this can also be its weakness. The ability of direct marketers to find the right audience for the product at the right time is crucial to success. An enormous benefit in this quest has been the development of powerful computer hardware and sophisticated software systems. Linked to direct marketing therefore is the database, and the successful manipulation of databases

helps companies refine their targeting of customers. However, as we will see, if the targeting is not precise, depending of course on the definition of precise, the direct marketing operation may be ill-conceived and thus costly.

Definitions

Many definitions encapsulate direct marketing. Here are a few which should provide you with both the flavour of direct marketing, and the complexity of direct and database marketing. The Direct Marketing Association in the United States defines direct marketing as 'An interactive system of marketing which uses one or more advertising media to effect a measurable response and/or transaction at any location', while the National Center for Database Marketing in the United States defines database marketing as follows:

> Database Marketing involves at least the following elements: (1) managing (2) a computerized (3) relational database system, (4) in real time, (5) of comprehensive, up-to-date, relevant data on customers, enquiries, prospects and suspects, (6) to identify your most responsive customers (7) for the purpose of developing a high-quality, long standing relationship of repeat business, (8) by developing predictive models (9) which enable us to send desired messages at the right time in the right form to the right people... (10) all with the result of pleasing our customers, increasing our response rate per marketing dollar, lowering our cost per order, building our business and increasing our profits.
> (Davies, 1992)

As you can see this is a somewhat complex and burdensome definition. Tapp (1998), however, illustrates the relationship between direct marketing and database marketing in two succinct definitions:

> Database marketing: This is using a database to hold and analyze customer information, thereby helping create strategies for marketing. There is a big overlap with 'direct marketing'. [It is also

referred to as data-based marketing and data-driven marketing by some authors and researchers.]

Direct marketing: This focuses on using a database to communicate (and sometimes distribute) directly to customers so as to attract a direct response. There is a big overlap with 'database marketing'.

Tapp (1998) encapsulates these definitions in a direct marketing system, where he states:

Database and direct marketing can be brought together to provide a complete, alternative method of marketing analysis, planning, implementation and control. These words have been carefully chosen... direct marketing systems have distinct strengths in all four of these marketing activities.

In essence direct marketing is about building a long-term relationship with the customer, and in order for that to be successful a company must know about its customers. It is of little value attempting to persuade someone to join a pop music CD club if he or she likes only opera. The long-term value is in gaining knowledge of customers in order to place before them something they might be interested in purchasing.

Creating lifetime values (LTVs)

Sheth and Parvatiyar (1995) suggest that financial benefits and/or competitive advantage can be gained by a company only if customers are willing to engage in relationship patronage, while Moorman, Zaltman and Deshpande (1993) conclude, 'commitment to the relationship is defined as an enduring desire to maintain a valued relationship'.

With the support of various database/data mining tools and techniques the direct marketer is seeking to build a long-term relationship with customers. The customer pyramid (Figure 10.4) illustrates an important concept in direct marketing: the lifetime value of the customer. What direct marketers are aiming to achieve is repeat purchases on a reasonably regular basis, combined with the 'advocate' concept where repeat buyers also market – by recommendation – the products/ services to their friends and colleagues.

Through analysis of purchases direct marketers can assign values to their customers. What they are considering are the total net revenues each customer contributes to the business. The abilities to produce

Figure 10.4   The customer pyramid: the different types of customers

management information and analyse it are fundamental. As we have previously discussed it is more cost-effective to develop sales from existing customers than to acquire new ones. Therefore if we consider Figure 10.4, direct marketers need to develop first-time buyers into repeat or regular buyers, then advocates (those who recommend to other potential customers, usually family, friends and work colleagues).

The premise for LTV is building loyalty (a relationship) with the customer. However, Jenkinson (1998) postulates 13 laws of loyalty which he believes direct marketers need to observe:

▌ Rewards (that is, gifts or bonus points) do not buy loyalty, they only buy data. (However, that data can be extremely valuable if accessed efficiently and effectively.)

▌ Loyalty to customers creates loyalty from customers.

▌ Relationship efforts must respect the preferred boundaries of customers. (As you will see later in this chapter there are aspects of direct marketing that can be intrusive.)

▌ Loyalty is not a behaviour, satisfaction or attitude. It is best summed up as 'active affection' (Jenkinson's emphasis), but arises from the integration of thinking, feeling and action based on trust.

▌ Loyalty is personal and individual and arises out of the holistic experience of a succession of 'moments of truth'.

▌ Loyalty is generated through the deployment of financial, social and structural bonding processes (or programmes).

▌ Not all customers are equal. However, not all companies recognize the fact. (Here Jenkinson is referring to the mixture of customers. These range from highly active, high-spending customers through to lapsed customers. The key for any company

is to focus on the customers that are currently or potentially most profitable.)

▌ The attitudes of all stakeholders are mutually reinforcing.

▌ Loyalty is a journey, not an arrival.

▌ Loyalty is a moral issue. Its deployment will emphasize marriage over military metaphors.

▌ Loyalty stems from loyalty values. Company and customer share a set of values based upon fair sharing, the everybody wins principle.

▌ Over-hyping loyalty programmes can itself lead to dissatisfaction. (For example, a customer might be inundated with e-mails promoting special offers. After a while the customer either cancels his or her e-mail alerts or just deletes (without reading) any e-mails from that particular company or organization.)

▌ The best customers are those with the propensity to loyalty and to spending. They are already somebody's best customers. Before a company seeks them, they should be sure that they are already looking after the customers they already have.

A brief history of direct marketing

Direct marketing is often considered a phenomenon of the latter half of the 20th century. This is a falsehood. In fact it has its roots in the mail order industry, mail order primarily being a business where customers order from illustrative catalogues. Evans (1999) cites the work of the Venetian scholar and printer Manutius Aldus (the Latin name of Aldo Manucci or Manuzio, c1450–1515). Aldus, the founder of the Aldine Press, produced the first printed editions of many Greek and Roman classics. In 1498 he printed a catalogue describing this collection of works and their availability.

In the UK it was the pottery manufacturer Josiah Wedgwood (1730–1795) who was probably at the forefront of developing advanced marketing techniques. He clearly adopted branding for his porcelain, devising different products for different markets. Additionally, he showed his marketing flair by using a range of techniques to maximize sales, including catalogue marketing with free delivery, money back guarantees and free replacement on breakages (Dugan and Dugan, 2000).[1]

However, it was not until the 19th century that catalogue marketing really expanded. In the United States, retail mail order was developed primarily for rural customers, who rarely travelled into the larger towns and cities. Montgomery Ward (1844–1913) was a manager of a general store in Michigan. He became aware of how farmers resented the profit made by intermediaries or 'middlemen', so he developed the idea of buying goods wholesale then selling them by mail, at a low margin, for cash. In August 1872 he issued his first catalogue, a single sheet of paper, with about 150 items. By 1875, just like Wedgwood before him, Ward was offering money back guarantees. Within 16 years of Ward launching his mail order business annual sales had reached the US $1 million mark. At the time of his death in 1913, annual sales had grown to over US $40 million (Britannica, 2002).

Another proponent of mail order was Richard Sears (1863–1914) who started a watch business in Minneapolis in 1886. Within a year he had hired Alvah C Roebuck (Britannica, 2002) as a watch repairer and moved his business to Chicago, where in 1887 he published a mail order catalogue offering watches and jewellery, all with money back guarantees. Two years later he sold the business, but became restless and returned to Minnesota and established a new business with Roebuck which was later to transform itself into Sears, Roebuck and Company, moving back to Chicago in 1893. In that year he marketed a 196 page catalogue which contained a much wider range of products. A year later it had dramatically expanded to over 500 pages (Britannica, 2002).

The expansion and success of the mail order business was aided by the development of more efficient postal services. This included the introduction of parcel post systems, and later an improved transportation distribution system.

During the early part of the 20th century, because of population shifts in the United States, mainly to urban areas, many of the mail order companies opened their own retail stores (Ward and Sears being prime examples). By the middle of the 20th century, however, these companies' retail sales outlets outperformed their mail order businesses. To overcome this, many stores included their catalogues in-store as well, providing their customers with a choice.

In the UK, mail order developed at the start of the 20th century. However, it was not until the late 1940s that the mail order business truly expanded. Howe (1992) suggests that consumers were attracted to mail order for several reasons:

- the convenience of shopping from home;

- the convenience of free home delivery;

- the wide product choice within a single catalogue;

- the ability to order goods on approval and return them if they were unsatisfactory (the mail order business was at the forefront of introducing guarantees for the consumer);

- the availability of credit spread over an extended payment period.

O'Malley, Patterson and Evans (1999) suggest that it was the increasing availability of credit which has, to some extent, caused a decline in the mail order business. The ability to spread payments over a period of time was one of mail order's unique selling points (USPs). However, the increasing availability of credit through normal retail outlets and more competitive pricing provided the consumer with a wider choice.

The mail order business is however not dead. Now there is an increasing blurring of what is direct mail and mail order. Indeed, the mail order businesses have grasped technology and have established powerful Web sites, through which they sell their products.

While catalogues signify a direct relationship with the customer, the term 'direct marketing' did not become common language until 1961. It was marketing innovator Lester Wunderman, the co-founder of Wunderman, Ricotta and Kline (WRK) in 1958 who first expressed the term 'direct marketing'.[2] Since then agencies and other marketing specialists have sought to develop the concept of direct marketing. Indeed, relationship marketing is very much a derivative of the direct marketing approach.

Today, the dramatic development of computer technology has provided the catalyst for the movement away from mass production to mass customization in manufacturing. This, linked to the ability to collect, store and critically analyse vast amounts of customer profile data, provides direct marketers with sophisticated tools with which to communicate to their customers.

Reasons for the expansion of direct marketing

Tapp (1998) and Evans (1999) have extracted from several sources the various factors that led to the burgeoning of direct marketing. These have been adapted, developed and added to below under both social and business conditions.

Social conditions

Fragmentation and diversity of society

Throughout many countries (most especially Western nations) there have been significant demographic changes. Markets have become demassified. The UK-based Henley Centre during the 1970s predicted that households would become cellular in behaviour rather than the traditional nuclear format (Tapp, 1998).

In Western nations particularly, society has become heterogeneous as the more traditional nuclear family tends to account for a small fraction of households. There are, for example, more couples who have decided not to have children, focusing on their careers and accompanying lifestyles. There are a greater number of working women, both single and in relationships. They now choose independent lifestyles, very different from the lifestyles of many women of the 1950s and 1960s, when there were few women in prominent working roles. The stereotypical woman then was a housewife and mother. That is often reflected in the advertising of the period (although it can still be argued that there are still advertisements of this type today).

There is a greater ethnic mix of populations, especially within urban areas – we now live in a multicultural society that adds to diversity of lifestyles and product ranges. This, in turn, has opened up a range of niche markets that previously did not exist.

Equally, there has been a move towards individualism, that is, a focus on the beliefs and desires of the individual person, rather than groups. Today, households are comprised of almost separate communities, with increasing numbers of people choosing their own lifestyle within the confines of their home. For example, it is increasingly common for each member of a family to have his or her own brand of breakfast cereal. There is no longer one large box of one type of cereal.

Today, it is about taste, goodness, ingredients and style.

Proliferation of media

During the second half of the 20th century there was an explosion of media, both regionally and globally. This ranged from a proliferation of newspapers and magazines (benefiting from the cost-effectiveness of new computer print technologies) through to the development of cable, satellite, digital television and Internet systems. Images could be dispersed globally with immediate impact on people, businesses, and even nations. The last five years of the century witnessed the rapid expansion of the Internet. There is no doubt that this medium, whatever guise it takes, will have a tremendous impact on society in the 21st century.

With such an expansion of media, there is a significant risk of 'clutter', an issue we considered earlier in this chapter. Therefore while these new media expand the range of possibilities, there needs to be a note of caution. No matter the medium, sheer proliferation can exacerbate the clutter, thus confusing the intended target. As we will see, with careful planning direct marketing provides another opportunity to break through media clutter.

Dynamic technological developments

The invention of the printing press provided the opportunity for mass circulation leaflets, then later mass-produced mail order catalogues. The radical development since the 1940s of computer technology has given direct marketers the opportunity to produce a range of printed material cost-effectively, then sort and bulk mail to thousands of people in a matter of a few hours.

Now the combination of computer technology and digital communications provides, through the Internet, the opportunity to communicate directly with customers and potential customers almost anywhere, at any time.

Cashless transactions

Since the 1980s there has been a significant global rise in the use of credit and debit card transactions. Whereas before cash and cheques dominated, now debit and credit cards have gained the advantage. Whether the world becomes a cashless society is the subject of lively debate. However, the greater acceptance of credit and debit cards has increased consumer freedom. Whether the payments are by post, telephone or Internet, this provides a 24 hour opportunity for the consumer to purchase.

Additionally, using data warehousing and data mining techniques, companies can track such transactions and build a profile of their customers. While there are advantages, for example, from the perspective of meeting customer needs through improved and focused targeting, there are also ethical issues.

Greater consumer sophistication

Generally consumers since the late 1950s have become increasingly demanding of both manufacturers and retailers. The demand for quality and the right to choose has been supported by the easier access to information and knowledge. Today, in most countries, more young people enter tertiary education than previous generations thought possible. As a result, there is an increasing awareness of brands, ethics, culture/societal issues, political issues and economics. Therefore consumers seek to be informed about the brands/services on offer. They are also prepared to ask questions (often challenging ones) and expect reliable fact-based answers, otherwise they may buy elsewhere. Companies that operate within competitive environments must face the challenge of possible brand switching if they do not meet customers' expectations.

Consumers in control

Today, consumers seek to have greater control over aspects of their lives. This includes having the facilities to contact companies direct to seek further information, and to complain. The development of the 24 hour society means that individuals who work shift patterns or work late want to be able to make contact when they are free to do so. Hence, companies have been quick to develop 24 hour helplines to support customer communications.

Linked to this is the greater use of the Internet as both an interaction and purchasing mechanism. Again, this provides the customer with the advantage of contacting the company at any time of day or night. Thus everything from CDs to groceries can be ordered and paid for at the customer's convenience.

Business conditions

Increased global competition

Since the 1980s there has been a dramatic increase in local, national, regional and global competition. Organizations have sought ways of adding value to their products and services through the use of technology. The use, for example, of telemarketing and improved logistics has assisted companies in improving their product delivery times. It is now not uncommon to have same-day deliveries within certain defined geographical locations, such as central London.

It is clear that while the use of new technologies will provide added value to customers, it will also increase the competitive environment. The Internet and its future potential are good indicators of this.

The drive for cost-effectiveness

The deep recession of the late 1980s, and the subsequent collapse of Far Eastern economies in the late 1990s, highlighted the need for cost-efficiency. It became apparent that many companies were not efficient managerially, financially or operationally. Thus, over time, any cost-effectiveness was further diluted by the competitive environment.

Increasingly companies are seeking cost efficiencies. Improved targeting of potential and active customers, supported by measurement, has assisted marketing departments in achieving greater cost-effectiveness.

The development of customer retention and loyalty

Developing relationships with active customers is now considered paramount for many companies and organizations. The objective is now to create advocates from repeat customers. However, within a highly competitive and dynamic environment it may become increasingly difficult to retain customers' loyalty to a single brand. There will most likely be some increase in brand switching and multiple brand buying. The key for companies is to find the communication (and product quality) that keeps the brand in the mind of the customer. Even if people buy more than one brand of, say, washing powder, then it is necessary for the product to remain one of the several they switch between. The key is to reduce customer defections. A particular example is how consumers are switching their credit cards on a regular basis to find the best service.

Increased computing power and reduction in computer costs

According to Peppers and Rogers (1997), the actual cost-efficiency of information processing doubles every 12 to 18 months. In 1978 the Cray 1 supercomputer processed 160 million instructions per second, making it the most powerful computer in the world (cost: US $20 million). In 1995 Sony introduced the Playstation™ game system which was capable of 500 million instructions per second (cost:

US \$299). By the end of the year 2001, 2 GHz speed computers were readily available to the home market. By the beginning of the 21st century there was more computational power in the average home computer than there was in the US Apollo Eagle spacecraft which landed on the moon in 1969!

As we shall see, such advances in computing power have placed the marketing database at the heart of direct marketing. As Evans (1999) states:

> At a strategic level, decisions will need to be taken with respect to segmentation and targeting. In this sense the marketing database can focus on a whole range of different categories – for example, new prospects, best prospects, loyals and so on – perhaps essentially, these can be boiled down into acquisition and retention strategies.

In the next section we discuss the development and use of data warehousing and data mining. As previously stated, the database is at the heart of direct marketing. For example, by 2001 the US grocery chain Wal-Mart held more than 100 terabytes of data in its data warehouse. Consider how that could drastically increase in the years to come. Thus it becomes a powerful tool in marketing to their customers.

The customer database: data warehousing and data mining

O'Malley *et al* (1997) describe a good database as:

> one which allows for flexibility, accurate and quick access to the stored records. Flexibility implies the ability to interrogate the database in new ways as new questions or opportunities present themselves. The key to flexibility is data structure. Accuracy results from quality name and address management, while the ability to generate information quickly relates to the power and speed of the technology being used. This is particularly important when we consider the vast amounts of data held on databases today.

To support this view Evans (1999) writes:

> Once created the database has a variety of uses. It can clearly be used as a list from which to target customers via direct marketing activity. But in addition, it can provide a wealth of information on the market and on customers and potential customers within it. In this context, the database provides data for both planning and analysis purposes: the database can be analysed for most attractive segments, for campaign planning and predicting campaign responses.

It is clear that a database can be used as a tactic within an overall competitive marketing strategy. This is outlined in Table 10.9.

Sources of customer information

It is clear that customer information is vital to the successful execution of direct marketing. In this section we cover the key areas of customer information provision. However, the collection and analysis of information is an ongoing and developmental process. Consider the current and future potential development of such sources.

There are two basic sources of customer information:

Internal company sources

This is information processed from internal sources. This data includes general customer files, marketing and sales information (for example, sales receipts, sales leads) and accounting information (for example, invoices). Once this information is collected and accurately processed it can often provide a detailed profile of the company's customer base.

Often this information is not centrally located, but rather filed in disparate locations throughout the organization. If it is computerized, the software may be incompatible, requiring significant levels of investment to create compatibility. Fortunately, many companies are investing heavily in data systems that can efficiently link all elements

Table 10.9 Databases as a competitive tactic

Competitive opportunity	Marketing strategy	Role of information
Change competitive basis	Marketing development or penetration. Increased effectiveness. Better margins. Alternative sales channels. Reducing cost structures.	Prospect/customer information. Targeted marketing to key individuals. Better control of the use of that information.
Strengthen customers	Tailored customer service. Providing value to customers. Product differentiation. Create switching costs.	Know customer needs. Individual promotions. Response handling. Identifying potential needs. Customers as 'users' of the company's service.
Strengthen buyer/supplier position	Supermarket information. Decreased cost of sales. Providing access to supplier. Pass stockholding on to supplier.	Internal/external data capture. Optimization of sales channels. Measure supplier performance. Identify areas of inefficiency.
Build barriers	Unique distribution channels. Unique value services. Create entry costs.	Knowledge of market allows for improved service/value. 'Lock in' customers, suppliers and intermediaries. Immediate response to market threats, including new entrants to the market (see Chapter 7).
Generate new products	Market-led product development. Alliance opportunities (both upstream and downstream). New products/services can be developed (includes enhancements of existing products and services).	Market gap analysis. Customer dialogue. Building the relationship with customer, thus increasing loyalty and advocacy. User innovation. Information as a product.

Source: Fletcher *et al* (1990)

of the business, thus allowing for a more efficient use of data in the future.

External sources

Geodemographics

Geodemographics are covered in detail in Chapter 5. Here we provide a brief refresher description. Geodemographics is a combination of geographic and demographic information to help build profiles of individuals or groups of people. It forms the basis of a consumer targeting system based on the concept that where someone lives indicates something about his or her lifestyle, and perhaps the products he or she buys.

Since the 1970s several companies have developed sophisticated geodemographic models, for example, CACI with ACORN™ and Experian with MOSAIC™. Originally introduced in 1977, ACORN (A Classification Of Residential Neighbourhoods) identifies key clusters of the population within a region or country. The objective is to discover geographic areas where people are likely to have similar lifestyles and purchasing habits.

ACORN™ comprises six categories, 17 groups and 54 types. It allows a company or organization to perform several different types of analysis:

▌ site location analysis: the evaluation and selection of sites for new stores or branches;

▌ sales planning: the identification of sales territories best suited for various products and services;

▌ database analysis: the planning of a company's marketing campaigns by using ACORN™ profiles of customer lists;

▌ media planning: identifying the media types (television, radio, cinema, newspapers and magazines) most effective in reaching specific customer segments;

▌ direct mail: identifying prospective customers from rented, purchased or own lists;

Marketing insight: Lifestyle Plus™ and People UK™

In October 1997 CACI launched a new lifestyle database, Lifestyle UK™. This featured information on over 44 million individuals, each one selected by over 300 lifestyle attributes. The database contains lifestyle information on individuals and not households, with over 90 per cent of the data being less than two years old. Each of the 44 million consumers on the database is scored from 0 to 99 on the propensity he or she displays for each of the 300 lifestyle variables. This allows companies to rank their entire database on any given set of characteristics, based on how well they match their requirements.

Each section of the system is completely tailored, recognizing that a company's database is unique. For example, a company or organization may want to select individuals using a combination of income, leisure interests and known purchasing power or behaviour. Or a company may want to target suspects who most closely match their existing client base.

People UK™

In October 1998, CACI launched a new product into the UK market. People UK™ is an individual-level, geodemographic lifestyle segmentation system that is not specific to any market sector. Unlike previous systems that have worked at post code level, People UK™ was designed to assign different people, within the same household, to different types, the objective being to bring a new level of precision to individual consumer targeting.

This targeting tool focuses on life stages, or age/family status along with key lifestyle characteristics. It summarizes individual lifestyle characteristics into 46 discrete types. The characteristics are taken from CACI's Lifestyle UK™ database, which includes 300 pieces of lifestyle information for each individual.

Questions/activities

1. Log on to the CACI Web site and consider its development of these and other analytical tools. Also view its case study examples.
2. Consider, then discuss within your group, the potential ethical issues that might arise from the accumulation of such levels of data.

Source: CACI.

new product lines: determining which additional products or services the company wants to develop, or enhance, based on its current client base.

As well as ACORN™ there are other means of customer profiling. They include targeting by age and the value of the individual's home or street value. What these geodemographic tools illustrate is that the analysis is becoming ever more sophisticated.

Lifestyle analysis
This is the analysis of the way people choose to live their lives. People's feelings, beliefs, needs and desires influence their buying behaviour. We must realize that the factors that determine an individual's lifestyle are often immensely complicated. Marketers attempt to gain a greater understanding of potential and actual customers by analysing different types of lifestyle.

Through detailed surveys it is possible to collect and collate a wealth of information. Companies often sponsor research companies to undertake such data collection. In the UK, for instance, surveys are regularly conducted to discover people's purchasing habits, likes and dislikes.

The role of data warehousing and data mining in direct marketing

This is a brief introduction to the techniques of data warehousing and data mining. These are relatively new tools in the direct marketer's armoury; however, indications are that these, and other analytical techniques, will have an impact on the effectiveness of direct marketing during the 21st century.

Data warehousing

This is the process of creating a large collection of data in a single location. The system collects data from various applications throughout the organization, integrates that data, stores it and then exploits it to deliver information throughout the organization.

From data warehouses, data marts can be created. These are decentralized sub-sets of data from the data warehouse, designed to support a unique business unit, for example, sales and marketing (Welsh and Heyworth, 1996).

Data mining

While data mining is an evolution of the analytical fields of statistics, artificial intelligence and machine learning, the term itself was really only introduced in the early 1990s. Data mining can be described as a complex process of extracting hidden or previously unknown, comprehensible and actionable information from a large computerized database. By using appropriate analytical software, a data analyst can drill down and across through the vast amounts of data, following a particular line of enquiry to extract relevant information.

As a simple example, a company might be about to celebrate its centenary, and decides to send gifts to all customers who have their birthday on the same date. Data mining tools would be able to extract the relevant names and addresses.

What direct marketing can provide to businesses

Direct marketing can provide companies with several benefits. However, they should not be considered in isolation, but viewed in conjunction with other marketing communication techniques.

Direct marketing techniques

Direct marketing consists of several interrelated tools or techniques. It should be borne in mind that these are often integrated with other marketing techniques such as sales promotion and public relations. Table 10.10 lists the different direct marketing techniques.

Table 10.10 Direct marketing techniques

Technique	Description
Door drops (also known as door-to-door distribution or household deliveries)	This is a basic form of direct marketing, often linked to sales promotions (refer to Chapter 11). An item is placed through the letterboxes of a particular area, but not personalized to the residents of those households. However, a company might choose specific geographically sensitive coverage, identifying a particular area or areas that are populated by people with the right lifestyles for the product. This is another method of getting suspects to step forward and be identified. As with other forms of direct marketing there may be direct response opportunities, perhaps through telemarketing or pre-paid response cards. Examples of door drops are: ▌ menus from local restaurants advertising their take-away meals, often associated with free delivery; ▌ flyers for local taxis and van hire services; ▌ flyers for local tradespeople, such as painters and decorators or carpenters; ▌ local supermarkets might promote a range of special offers with money-off coupons/vouchers, ▌ samples of new products from major companies.
Inserts	These are single, folded sheets or mini-catalogues inserted into magazines or bank/credit card/club statements, also known as statement stuffers.* They often double as door drops. However, the advantage of using them as inserts in magazines or statements is that some elements of the targeting can be improved. For example, a company might target platinum credit card holders for private health care.
Door-to-door selling (also known as personal selling, face-to-face selling, direct selling or home calling)	This provides direct face-to-face contact with the suspect, first time buyer or repeat customer (refer to Chapter 11). This can be separated into two types: First, a salesperson visits a neighbourhood knocking on every door in an attempt to interest the occupant in a particular product or service. An example is the selling of insurance or encyclopedias in some parts of the UK and United States during the 1950s and 1960s. With hindsight, this was not necessarily a cost-effective and efficient method of selling. While it has virtually died out in many countries, it is still prevalent in others. We must therefore consider it in the wider global context. The second type is arranged and regular meetings. Various companies have developed operations where their products are only available through their sales representatives. An excellent example of this is the cosmetic giant Avon.
Direct mail	This is the despatch of mailed items from the producer or retailer direct to an individual's residence or office. These can be a vast range of items from clothing catalogues through to introductory offer letters from credit card companies. The key here is that marketers can target their audience with the use of databases. Direct mail can be one of the most flexible tools in an integrated marketing communications campaign. It can be used to reinforce the effectiveness of other marketing techniques through the targeting of specific and relevant groups.

Table 10.10 *continued*

Technique	Description
Telemarketing	Since the 1980s there has been rapid growth in the development in fibre optics, microwave links, digital telecommunications and high-speed data storage and transmission. This technology has enabled the subsequent development of telemarketing as a marketing communication technique, and call centres as a means of delivery of that technique. While there has been for many years an element of telephone sales, the introduction of telemarketing has revolutionized the relationship between customer and seller. No longer is it purely a one-way approach, seller to customer. Now it involves two-way communication. Key aspects of telemarketing include: ▌ Outbound telemarketing, where a company makes a planned and structured telephone call to a prospect or customer. It is important that the call is structured so the response can be measured. It is not simply 'telesales', it has become much more sophisticated in its operation. ▌ Inbound telemarketing, where a company or organization invites a telephone call from a prospect or a customer. This call may be a freephone/toll-free call (increasingly so in developed countries) or paid for by the customer. Inbound telemarketing is used increasingly for both consumer and B2B operations. ▌ In the consumer environment it is used as part of the response mechanism to direct response advertising (print, television and radio). ▌ It also acts as a response mechanism to product and supermarket carelines. For example, many branded margarines and shampoos carry customer freephone/toll-free helpline/information line numbers. These encourage customers to seek further product information. According to Tapp (1998), Procter & Gamble in the United States receives in excess of 500,000 calls annually from its various product carelines. The data collected from its customers, during these calls, contributes to the development of its customer database and promotes communications. ▌ In the B2B environment inbound telemarketing allows business customers to contact suppliers easily to place orders.

*The use of 'statement stuffers' was pioneered by the Chicago advertising executive Homer J Buckley (1881–1953). He also formed the forerunner of the US Direct Marketing Association in 1917.

Marketing insight: Office Deport® and Viking Direct®

Founded in 1986, Office Deport® is the world's largest supplier of office equipment. It uses various distribution channels: stores, direct mail, contract delivery and the Internet. Viking Direct® is its wholly owned subsidiary and one of the industry's leading direct marketers of office products. It operates on an international scale. In 1998 sales outside the United States generated some 65 per cent of the company's total US $1.3 billion revenue (Witthaus, 1998).

Viking Direct® seeks to provide customers with a superior service: ease of ordering, fast delivery and 30 days risk-free trial. In the UK the company rapidly established itself through discounts of mainstream products and own brands, and regular mailings (fortnightly) to its customer and potential customer base. Through such marketing activity it soon achieved high visibility.

In 1998 the UK operation was taking up to 35,000 calls per day, all on 0800 freephone lines, and shipping orders before 6 pm the same day it received them (Witthaus, 1998). In central London companies that placed orders by 11 am would receive the delivery by 5 pm that evening (subject to availability of the products).

The company's drive for effective direct operations is reflected in its allocation of staff resources. In 1998 total UK staffing was approximately 850, with the majority (480) in its call centre. A further 280 were based in the warehouse, with 25 in finance, 30 in product buying/marketing, 8 in inventory, 10 in personnel and 10 in data processing (Witthaus, 1998).

Questions/activities

1. From the information stated above it is clear that the company has focused on a mixture of direct mail and inbound telemarketing. How important do you think segmentation tools are to this company? What role do you think data warehousing and data mining play in the development of this business?
2. Undertake a literature search on the company and chart its development since 1998. Has it remained, for example, a significant player within the direct marketing of stationery? Where does it see its future: in a further integration of marketing communication tools, or solely through the Internet?
3. If you were the CEO of Viking Direct® how would you develop the business within an increasingly competitive environment?
4. What lessons do you think companies could learn from the Viking Direct® operation?

The 'Marketing insight' above illustrates the role of telemarketing within a B2B environment.

Direct response advertising

This is also known as direct response marketing or direct action marketing. It can occur in several ways:

A telephone number is advertised, in a magazine, newspaper, on the radio or on the television. The television advertising spot might be an ordinary 15–30 second commercial or an infomercial (these are extended television advertisements which last 20 minutes or more). Infomercials have their roots in the United States, where blue-chip companies use well-known actors and actresses to demonstrate (and thus to an extent endorse) products.

The highlighting of a 24 hour telephone number allows the prospect/customer to request further information (for example, an insurance scheme or pension plan) or order goods. It can also be used for charities, voluntary or not-for-profit organizations to raise extra funds (telethons are a case in point). Thus it is an example of inbound telemarketing.

Off-the-page advertising: Here the potential customer clips and posts a coupon in order to seek further information or to purchase the goods direct. This method has been used by a wide variety of companies and organizations: charities, universities (for courses), insurance and pension companies, banks and mail order only companies.

An insert (this can be, for example, included with a bank or utilities statement). It is often a pre-paid response card/envelope that provides for either a purchase or a request for further information. An example is a book or CD club promoting an introductory offer (such as five CDs for UK £10.00).

Advantages

It creates a potential integration between different media: newspapers, magazines, radio and television. Thus a common identity or purpose across the media is promoted.

It is measurable, since a company can track the response rate. Freephone responses can be measured as immediate responses, delayed responses, and by the length of delay. For example, was contact made after the television programme in which the commercial appeared or later still? It is also possible to track the level of response at different times, perhaps to see if a commercial performed as successfully during off-peak times as it did during peak scheduling periods.

The customer is in control. He or she decides whether to call in or send the freepost coupon.

Disadvantages

As Foster (1998) states, 'it requires more than the presence of a phone number for five seconds to make a DRTV commercial generate cost-effective volume response. It requires the application of a clear response-base philosophy which affects creative and media aspects of the campaign.'

In the case of DRTV there may be limited coverage, especially if the commercial is aired off peak schedule and regionally.

There can be a proliferation of direct response advertising through television, radio and the press. The problem is once again clutter and potential customer irritation.

Cost-effectiveness is an issue, and this can especially be the case with DRTV. The combined production of the commercial and the airtime costs may make this prohibitively expensive. This is especially so if response and conversion rates are low in comparison with other direct marketing techniques such as direct mail. A word of caution should be added here. Advertising rates vary from media source to media source, from region to region and from country to country. For example, in late 2001 many UK publications and commercial television companies were discounting their rates in order to encourage media buying. The fall in the market was caused by a combination of factors: media buyers seeking other avenues of customer

Marketing insight: The Great Indoors®

The brief

Owned by Sears, Roebuck and Co, The Great Indoors® is a one-stop shop for furniture, electrical appliances and decoration materials. It wanted a campaign that would help it stand out from the crowd of the more established DIY stores, and in addition, enable it to break into the electronics and home furnishing niche market. More specifically, the campaign had to generate awareness, drive traffic into the newly opened store and create consumer excitement with a mixture of special events and offers.

The campaign

Wunderman Cato Johnson (now called Wunderman) was appointed to generate a pool of prospective customers ready for the store when it opened. The agency devised a two-pronged action which ran from February to March 1998.

First, a self-mailer with a discount offer was sent to 25,000 households within the catchment area of the new store. To qualify, households had to meet various demographic criteria, including a house value of at least US $175,000 (UK £107,000). Second, double page spread advertisements, complete with detachable discount coupons, were inserted into local magazines with an appropriate circulation. Point of sale (POS) material reflecting the direct mailer and the advertisement was placed in store to reinforce the marketing message.

The message, used across all media, was developed after exhaustive research of the target audience: females with a household income of US $50,000+ (UK £30,000+). As well as conveying the store's main point of difference – its breadth of products and services – it adopted a 'woman to woman' language that created instant empathy through shared experience. A brand personality was created that combined confiding humour, logic and a stylish look.

The results

With a budget of just US $57,000 (UK £35,000), the campaign exceeded all its targets. On opening day, the store attracted over 15,000 visitors. Individually, the self-mailer resulted in 642 customers who generated sales in excess of US $238,000 (UK £145,000). This equates to a 2.6 per cent response rate, with a cost per response of US $34 (UK £21). The average order was US $371 (UK £226). Similarly, 2,171 customers responded to the magazine coupons, generating sales of US $792,000 (UK £484,000). This 1.3 per cent response rate cost US $21 (UK £13) per response and generated average orders of US $365 (UK £223), a significant return on investment.

This campaign won a Bronze award in the Retail: Traffic Building category of the 1998 International Echo Awards.

Source: *Direct Response Magazine*, March 1999, p 35.

communication, fear of recession and an economic slump, and the aftermath of the 11 September tragedy.

Kiosks

This is a relatively new direct marketing medium. Using touch-screen technology, interactive information kiosks allow in-store customers to search for and retrieve information. Increasingly located in supermarkets, busy shopping malls and offices, electronic kiosks allow the customer to browse catalogues and order online. In Singapore, for example, they are also located along the main street in the heart of the shopping district.

It is too early to determine the effectiveness of kiosks. However, as computer power continues to expand rapidly, the future could hold enormous potential for this new marketing medium.

The future

In considering the future we focus on certain areas.

Data

The English philosopher, lawyer and essayist Francis Bacon (1561–1626) said, 'For also knowledge is power'. The same can be said for direct marketing. Information is critical to a company's success. For most companies, even those using direct marketing, the information is not usually analysed in any great detail, thus not fully exploited. However, by using data mining tools and techniques companies will be able to increase their opportunities to build added value services for their customers, thus increasing the possibility of improved lifetime values.

However, all data or information must be used in a proactive manner. Consider the amount of information a bank holds on an individual customer, especially one who has been with them for several years. However, many banks still treat established customers as perfect strangers. The message is clear: companies must be able to use data as a means of making it easier for customers to stay with them. This, however, may mean a rethinking of how companies currently undertake business.

Profiling and modelling

It is clear that modelling of customer profiles through both geodemographic and lifestyle analysis will become more sophisticated. Much has been achieved in this area since the mid-1990s. Such profiling systems have contributed to the improved targeting of products and services to customers. This in turn has greatly improved the reputation of, for example, direct mail, which had been previously criticized for lack of focus.

Modelling or profiling techniques, combined with advances in computer software and hardware, will create a platform for increased mass customization of product and service offers.

The Internet: e-marketing capabilities

In many ways the Internet is the perfect medium for both conducting business, and building and managing relationships. It is a global medium, immediate, dynamic and relatively inexpensive. The Internet remains open 24 hours per day, seven days per week, 365 days per year. Therefore customers can do business on their own terms, when it is most convenient or urgent for them. Equally, it allows the direct marketer to update information in real time.

E-marketing has the potential to make a tremendous impact on direct marketing activities. It will not negate the marketing fundamentals of segmentation, positioning, the marketing mix, customer satisfaction and value. However, it will create radically new challenges for marketers, even direct marketers who generally have been more adventurous and daring than some of their counterparts. E-marketing will provide direct marketers with another means of developing a one-to-one relationship with their customers. Companies such as Dell Computing are placing the Internet at the heart of their business, thus allowing them to tailor offers to the customers, and deliver them efficiently.

Customer relations management

In early chapters we referred to relationship marketing. In many ways customer relationship management (CRM) takes this a step further. It is about the management of that relationship. McDonald (2002) defines CRM as 'The IT-enabled integration of data across multiple customer contact points to enable the development of offers tailored to specific customer needs'. He continues by emphasizing the need to focus on 'customer profitability' rather than just 'product profitability'. This links back to Chapter 5 where we emphasized the importance of effectively and efficiently positioning a product or service to the most appropriate targeted and segmented market.

As we have seen in this chapter, the use of IT systems allows companies and organizations to store vast quantities of data, with the potential to drill down into that data and extract valuable information to support the customer relationship. Although the IT facilities are available to achieve this, there are numerous problems with CRM. These can be summarized as follows:

▌ Companies may have bought into data warehousing and data mining. However, there needs to be a cultural change or cultural awareness as to the potential long-term value of CRM. It is one thing collecting vast amounts of data, it is very much another being able to translate that data into something that is meaningful for both the company and the customer.

▌ Linked to the above is an over-focus on IT. While IT will enable CRM, CRM is not IT driven – it is people driven. Clearly there is the need to invest in IT, but not at the expense of management and the employees. It is the IT that enables the people within the organization to drive CRM.

▌ Hype! As probably with all new systems or ideas, there is a certain amount of hype. While there is the need to promote the value of CRM, there also needs to be an element of caution. If a company has not tested the system 'to destruction' and invested in the people element, then there is the risk of failure. This failure will most likely have a direct impact on the customer relationship, resulting in dissatisfaction. So instead of enhancing the relationship, CRM could potentially destroy it. The customer might well brand switch as a result.

These problems with CRM are not issues of rocket science: they can be resolved with initiative and willing. If both the IT systems and the organization's people are enabled, CRM will make a potentially enormous contribution to the marketing of products and services in the future. To quote McDonald (2002), 'In the future, the most powerful brands will be customer-centric. Successful companies will know the customer and will be the customer's advocate.' If his view is right, CRM will be a focal point of developing this customer centricity.

Logistics interface

While the Internet and other means of telecommunication open up the opportunity for real-time purchasing 24 hours day or night, the issue of logistics remains. Ordering is one thing, delivery another. As we truly enter the 24 hour society, companies will need to make radical changes to meet the delivery demands of the future customer. This will obviously have an impact on supply chain management systems.

If a customer can order at 3 am, why cannot products be delivered at that time, or so the argument goes? The Internet has broken the 9 am to 5 pm Monday to Friday barrier. In the future companies will have to reappraise their delivery policies. How long before you can have products delivered at the time and day you want them delivered? It may not be as far away as we imagine.

Ethical dilemmas

As indicated in Chapter 3, ethics clearly exercises the mind of the consumer. Of course, many consumers are not aware how technology can be used to track their purchasing habits and profile their lifestyle. Some consumers will not mind this 'view of their life' if it delivers sound benefits to their lifestyle. However, others will consider this a breach of trust and be concerned that their privacy has been invaded. This poses an ethical dilemma for all concerned. The key issues focus on government intervention to protect citizens and the level of corporate responsibility. Of course, if a company is seen to violate the privacy of its customers then external stakeholder action may be swift and unforgiving.

Selling and the sales force

The sales force is inherently a part of the promotion element of the marketing mix, and must be deployed appropriately. That means that those undertaking the selling must be professional. They should have product knowledge, customer knowledge, be ethical and able to communicate persuasively and create the necessary relationship with customers. It also means that the efforts of the sales force must be properly deployed and managed. Thus sales management is therefore important to the success, or otherwise, of the operation.

A successful sale on one occasion does not guarantee that a person will necessarily make a repeat purchase. As we stated in Chapter 4, the objective is to encourage the customer to become a repeat buyer and later an advocate for the product or service. One of the key values of salespeople is their potential to build long-term relationships with their customers. Here we consider customers in the widest context including B2B and B2C. We consider the various differences within this chapter. However, it is important here to consider the relationship building aspects.

Definition and functions of the sales process

Selling can be defined several ways. For example, the UK's Chartered Institute of Marketing (1996) defines selling as 'the process of persuasion leading to a continuing trading arrangement, initiated and perpetrated at either a personal or impersonal level but commonly confined to oral representation supported by visual aids'. However, as Miller (1999) points out, such a definition does not cover all the various roles and tasks that salespeople often undertake. As you will see as you work through this section, the salesperson often undertakes roles beyond what most people would consider purely that of selling. That is why we must consider the role of selling within the wider marketing function. These added value roles could include the following:

- Working closely with distributors and retailers. To some extent this is a negotiation/public relations role.

- Organizing in-store displays. Consider, for example, the launch of a new book, which may have specific point of sale (PoS) material.

▮ Training and recruitment. These roles may be split over different management levels, but new salespeople need to be recruited and trained (often on the job). While external agencies and consultancies can be used, this is usually internally organized.

▮ Administration. This can range from daily or weekly sales activity reports through to taking orders via telephone, fax, and e-mail. The administration not only provides a record of activity, it also forms part of the processing function (order – delivery – billing).

▮ Market information processing. Field sales personnel in particular are ideally placed to gather market information. As they visit customers they often receive feedback on a range of issues. These cover their own company's performance (product quality, pricing, delivery times and billing operations), their competitors' performance and market dynamics. While all these point are important, the last one can provide particularly vital feedback. Such information can assist in medium to longer-term planning.

▮ Maintaining relationships. Within dynamic business environments, it is vital to build and maintain long-term relationships with customers. This is an increasingly important role for the salesperson. It is not just about product knowledge; the salesperson's personality and communication skills are equally important.

The relationship between sales and marketing

Marketing and sales are often considered very separate entities. In many companies and organizations this can lead to conflict between the two groups. We strongly believe that while marketing and sales have different functions, they are inextricably interrelated.

However, a broader view of selling must be taken if the overall effectiveness of the sales resource is to be maximized successfully. Specifically looking at the sales resource from a broader perspective means viewing it as essentially a marketing technique – one that needs to be regarded as a variable like any other. The sales resource must play an appropriate part in whatever overall marketing mix an organization decides to use (something that may well vary over time). This will not just happen, it needs planning and organizing. Above all it needs regular fine-tuning if the sales resource is to act continuously to achieve planned results in the marketplace, and do so with some certainty.

There is no straight formula for the creation and structuring of a marketing department (sometimes called a sales and marketing department). The specific format depends on the particular business aspects of the company or organization. Here we present several examples; however we caution students that these are generalizations only.

Although every organization and company is different, there are usually common patterns in their structure. Traditionally all marketplace issues were the responsibility of a sales director who reported directly to senior management – normally the managing director or another member of the board of directors. Most organizations were oriented to production or sales, rather than marketing. When the need for a marketing-oriented approach became more widespread, a marketing director was sometimes appointed in parallel with the sales director, but there were two distinct functional departments.

Organizational structures have generally moved from a sales department to a marketing department function as business philosophy changed. With a greater recognition of the marketing approach to business, sales and marketing may become a single department, with sales as a sub-group within

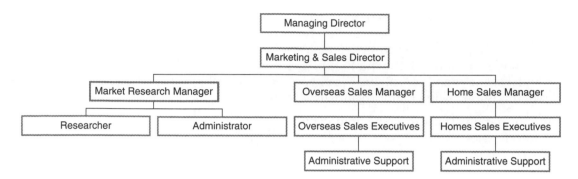

Figure 10.5 Possible structure of a marketing and sales department

the marketing department, as opposed to marketing being a sub-group of sales. Today the marketing department plays a key role in coordinating marketing activities.

Figure 10.5 illustrates the possible structure of a relatively large marketing department. As you can see we have included a range of marketing functions from market research manager to overseas sales manager. In some organizations, as in the one depicted, these are separate roles. In others, elements of roles and responsibilities may be combined. For example, the overseas sales manager might be responsible for undertaking market research as well. In other organizations market research might be contracted in from external consultants who are experts within this field (refer to Chapter 6).

The size of the marketing department depends on several factors, including the size of the company, range of products, size of overall market including competition and budgetary constraints. While size may be important for large organizations where there is product/service volume, this does not mean that small marketing departments are any less efficient and effective than large ones. On the contrary, lean marketing departments can often outperform their larger counterparts, simply because they are proactive rather than reactive to events within the marketplace.

There is no one best way of organizing a marketing department, it varies from company to company and industry to industry. The existing organizational structure, management roles and the physical spread of the company's product and geographical interests will all play a part in determining how the marketing department develops.

It is important to note the meaning of the word 'director'. In UK company law, strictly speaking a director or executive director is responsible for the operation of the company, and holds a 'directorship' of that company. He or she is responsible for good stewardship of that company. If there is a serious breach of company law, he or she can be prevented from holding directorships in future. The terms 'Sales Director' and 'Marketing Director' do not necessarily mean the individuals hold a directorship in the company law sense – it is more a title of seniority. In many advertising agencies there are 'account directors' who are not legally responsible for stewardship of the company.

Selling channels

We often do not consider the number of salespeople involved in a single selling operation. In the example below, from publishing, you will see that some people take on the role of salesperson although that is not necessarily their job title.

The writer

A writer approaches a literary agent to handle the sale of her synopsis. While she is not a professional salesperson, she needs to 'sell' her idea to the agent. This may be achieved through 'product knowledge': that is the substance of the work, the synopsis.

The agent

The agent approaches several publishers to 'sell' them the synopsis idea. Her objective is to obtain a book deal for the client. Her financial success is dependent on the success of the negotiation (another selling skill). If the agent is successful she might secure the writer a two-book deal. Thus the writer has an improved contract and writing future (potentially more secure) and the agent has received a larger fee for her selling skills.

The printer

The printer, as part of its normal operations, sells its skills to the publisher. If it is successful it will receive a continual supply of orders throughout the year, and even beyond.

The publisher

The publisher's sales team sells the new novel into bookshops and book clubs. It is often supported by advertising and point of sale material.

Logistics and distribution company

This company sells its expertise to the publisher. Distribution may not be within one country, but over several. Thus there may also be subcontracting to airlines, for example, for delivery. Again, several salespeople may be involved.

The retailer: the bookshop

Through one-to-one contact and PoS material the bookshop sells the book to customers. Again, the retail salesperson must be skilled and knowledgeable about the book.

The customer

Once the customer has purchased the book he or she too can become involved in the 'sales' process. Reflect back to Chapter 4, where we considered what influences people to buy. One influence is recommendation, where the customer becomes an advocate for the product and the company. This is not professional sales force activity, but it is part of the promotional and sales process.

Of course, the distribution channel can be shortened (see Chapter 13, 'Placement, distribution and logistics'). In this example, the publisher could have a direct sales network (via direct mail and the Internet) and sell directly to the customer, completely bypassing the intermediary.

Types of selling

There are many types of selling, some face to face, others not. Here we consider each, and the main functions of the role.

Retail sales

This is also known as across-the-counter selling and over-the-counter selling. There are numerous aspects to selling within the retail environment. Here you will need to consider more than the personal selling role. Retail selling also includes:

- Imaginative use of point of sale (PoS) material, which includes window displays.

- Effective store layouts which are welcoming, easy to navigate and provide easy access to payment areas. Consider here bookshops which have sofas so you can relax and read through books prior to purchase. It is an unhurried approach to selling. The point is that customers often purchase more books because they are in such a relaxed, peaceful environment.

▌ Additionally, stores need to be well sign-posted to help direct customers to products, salespeople and customer support.

The retail sales staff provide the face-to-face contact with consumers. It is often their knowledge, advice and enthusiasm that turns a prospect into a repeat customer and then an advocate. Consider stores you visit on a regular basis. Why do you visit them? Is it because they are the only ones selling goods you need, and you have no choice? Or is it because of the sales staff?

Technical sales support

It is important to notes that technical sales support is needed in both B2B and B2C environments. In both situations the salesperson is providing advice, information and reassurance to the customer. The types of area where such support is necessary are car dealerships, estate agencies, washing machine and computer suppliers.

Within the B2B environment salespeople might not only be trained in selling skills, they could be highly trained in another discipline. For example, consider the computer market. A company might seek to purchase a whole new network with associated software. This will be a significant investment. The salesperson will need to be able to determine, in discussion with the customer, the exact specifications required. Thus he or she must have a high level of technical knowledge and effective consultative skills.

Delivery salespeople

Delivery teams do more than deliver products, whether they are food, technical components or parcels. If well trained, they can also provide advice to customers which could lead to additional purchases. For example, in the UK milk is still delivered directly to consumers' doors, although this service has much declined. These delivery teams carry much more than milk varieties on their electric-powered vehicles: they typically also sell butter, eggs and cheeses.

A delivery representative from an international courier company, for example, could advise on more effective means of delivering documents or parcels. It is important to change the mindset that delivery people are just what the title suggests. They can make an important contribution to the company through efficient customer service.

New business development

As the title suggests, the salesperson is charged with seeking out new business opportunities. He or she could have this role as a specific task and only seek out new business, or combine it with a daily ongoing sales role. Building long-term relationships with existing customers is vital for the continuing operations of any company. However, from time to time customers stop or reduce their purchases from specific companies. This may be for numerous reasons: lack of finance, the customer has relocated or indeed died. Lost customers need to be replaced in order for the business to continue, grow and prosper, so new business development is significant. However, seeking new business should not be undertaken at the expense of existing clients. If existing customers are not supported, then they may switch to a rival. Thus the business can be sorely damaged.

Ongoing or existing business

Salespeople must maintain their relationships with existing customers. This can be achieved through regular visits, via the telephone or increasingly through e-mail, especially within the international context.

Direct selling: telemarketing, telesales and Web-based selling

As stated earlier in this chapter, direct selling has been around for centuries. The difference is that today technology has provided a platform for the communications process. A vast range of companies from banks and credit card companies to insurance houses have developed call centres as a means for customer contact. While customers can participate in inbound telemarketing, we are concerned here with outbound telemarketing. With digital telephony call centres can be based virtually anywhere. The technology enables vast numbers of calls to be made and received from one location, and call costs are significantly reduced. During every communication there is an opportunity for the sales person to 'add value' to the call. For example, in order to active new credit cards customers have to contact the call centre. Once the credit card is activated the salesperson could, for instance, encourage the customer to transfer balances from existing cards to the new one by emphasizing an introductory deal (reduced APR).

As technology develops it will not only be telemarketing that provides selling opportunities. The Internet, through permission marketing, allows salespeople to contact customers on a regular basis with special offers. These might be only available via the Web.

Personal selling skills

As indicated earlier, the salesperson is not purely an 'order taker'. He or she must display a range of skills that contribute to the successful marketing of the product or service. In this section we consider the key personal aspects that salespeople need within today's dynamic business environment.

Interpersonal qualities

We can define these as the ability to communicate effectively with other people. This does not mean that the salesperson has to be an extrovert; often that is not what is needed. He or she needs to be able to build a rapport with the customer. Often that involves understanding the deeper aspects of what drives or motivates the customer. For example, a customer might as a subtext to a meeting express a concern regarding stock levels. By understanding these concerns, the salesperson can work with the customer to alleviate them, perhaps by organizing a different delivery regime. While this is linked to problem solving (see below), the salesperson needs the interpersonal qualities to understand the customer's concerns in the first place. Like so many aspects of marketing, understanding human psychology is a key success factor.

Honesty and an ethical approach are vital. The literature is filled with examples of unethical and dishonest salespeople and selling schemes. Such a litany has given salespeople generally highly negative public relations. However, most likely the minority have tarnished the reputation of the majority. There are several key points to consider here. Dishonesty usually leads to being caught by either the company and/or the authorities. During the 1990s there were some high-profile prosecutions with resulting prison terms. Also, dishonesty and unethical activity are very short-termist. If a company has promoted such activity, its future will be very limited. Again the authorities might prosecute depending on the circumstances.

Adaptability

Salespeople need to be adaptable and flexible in their approach. As outlined earlier, they have to undertake tasks beyond pure selling, therefore they need to be adaptable to such circumstances. Flexibility can be associated with two areas: first, arranging meetings to suit the customer where possible, and second, devising sales processes to assist the customer where possible, for example by extending payment periods. Again this links to the issue of problem solving.

Personal character and self-motivation

Selling is not an easy task, so a salesperson needs strength of character. For example, he or she will have proposals rejected, and this can be disheartening, but he or she must rise above the disappointment in order to continue in the role.

Problem solving capabilities

As indicated earlier, salespeople must be able to solve often complex problems for the mutual benefit of their company and their client. For example, a customer might consider the front-loaded cost of a product or service to be too high. The salesperson, if empowered, could solve the problem by proposing payment spread over a specific time frame. In this case the solution provides a sale for the company, and the customer with better cash flow.

Product knowledge

All salespeople, whether they are selling the latest detective novel or a fleet car service, must know their product or service. There are several areas for consideration: features, benefits and potential market demand.

Customer knowledge

The company must build a picture of its customers through its market information systems. By understanding their customers, salespeople can consider the most appropriate approach to take when meeting them. For example, the customer might be very formal in his or her approach, and the salesperson would need to reflect that. Similarly, if the salesperson knows the customer is not interested in some products, he or she knows which to discuss and which to ignore, and avoids wasting time and money.

Presentation skills

This is a critical skill, whether the salesperson is working on a one-to-one or one-to-group presentation basis. It can be considered as part of the 'promotion' aspects of selling. Good presentation skills not only communicate confidence and product knowledge, but promote the organization as professional and knowledgeable. Ask yourself, would you buy from someone who could not communicate how a product or service would help you?

Key account handling

Large accounts, in terms of volume, revenue generation and profit, often require special handling. A key accounts manager or major account executive usually undertakes this role.

Key accounts are often powerful. For example, as with certain other businesses, a large proportion of total UK publishing business goes through a small number of large distributors and retailers, such as W H Smith and Borders. To exploit the market to any real extent, any publisher has to trade with these clients. Food products and major supermarket groups are another well known example.

Sometimes the distributor or retailer exploits its power to (Miller, 1999):

▌ Negotiate for preferential – and ever larger – discounts. These are sometimes used to facilitate price reductions.

▌ Force suppliers to produce own-brand products. The distributor then sells these own-label brands at a lower price. They are a major feature of many consumer goods markets: for example a supermarket's own-label chocolate bars.

▌ Limit the supplier's role to producing goods to the distributor's specification at the lowest possible margin. In some businesses, trends are most influenced from the retailer end.

It is sensible for companies to manage their dealings with major customers on a different basis from smaller customers, as major customers are different not just in scale but in nature, demanding different skills, such as negotiation, and the ability to handle them diplomatically. The sales role here is characterized by the desire of the supplier to create an effective ongoing business relationship, and to characterize that as something the customer wants.

In a highly competitive dynamic environment the pressure here is considerable. Not all relationships are equally well regarded by customers, and some suppliers do better than others.

Current and potential trends

Since the 1990s markets have been particularly volatile, in the main as a result of dynamic competition in the wake of the internationalization and globalization of markets. However, this has been compounded by the events surrounding the terrorist acts of 11 September 2001 in New York and Washington DC, and subsequent terrorism in Bali, Morocco and Saudi Arabia, which added significantly to market volatility.

All aspects of a company need to be more effective and efficient if it is to develop and maintain market presence. Sustainable competitive advantage comes only from innovation, and that is derived from many aspects of the company's operations: organization, product development and sales.

Furthermore, one of the most pertinent changes of recent times has been with B2B customers. Because they have had to react to protect and secure their future, their attitudes to suppliers have changed markedly with economic and political fluctuations. The expectations are now better defined than perhaps ever before. They know the type of service and the technical standard required. Thus they seek suppliers who can match their demands and be problem solvers when necessary. Not least, they want to deal with professional people representing a professional company or organization.

Success on one occasion does not necessarily mean that people will buy again. There has been a move towards Customer Relationship Marketing in order to build longer-term relationships with customers.

The impact of technology

Technology has provided immense benefits to salespeople. The use of laptop computers, faxes and mobile phones has proved a benefit in both the field and the office. The technological benefits include:

▌ An opportunity for improved flow and storage of information.

▌ Using sophisticated yet easy to use software programmes, a salesperson can analyse stored information. This analysis typically includes customer values, budgetary and forecast information. This type of information contributes to monthly departmental reports.

▪ The salesperson can produce a contract, order form or statement for the customer on the spot. He or she does not have to return to the office to complete the documentation. This is particularly important for field sales staff who may not visit their office for weeks at a time.

▪ Improved communications: both salespeople and customers are contactable via mobile phone and e-mail. This has been further enhanced by the introduction of mobile Internet capabilities. The use of such technology should significantly expand in the near future.

▪ The ability to change laptop computer presentations in the field, thus being able to address changes within the marketplace, and tailoring to customers' needs. Consider, for instance, an international manager visiting several customers in different geographical locations. While he is travelling the technology (both laptop and Internet) allows him to adapt or refine his presentation.

▪ The compactness of the hardware technology allows for easy transportability.

E-sales and the Internet

As indicated earlier in this chapter (with reference to permission marketing and CRM), the Internet can be the medium for customer relationship building. This can be delivered through exclusive Web-based only offers. Additionally, B2B companies are seeking to develop an environment where they can buy and sell via e-marketplaces. These can be described as online portals that function as information brokers and gateways to services. The e-marketplace offers the expertise of a particular vertical sector. The aim is to ensure that information and services offered are of a high value to the participants within that e-marketplace. Maciver (2001) suggests that 'procurement through e-marketplaces is just

the start of what many believe is the single biggest change in business opportunity for over a century'.

E-marketplaces can be divided into three basic types of operation: public, consortium-based and private exchanges.

Public exchanges

These are also known as independent trading exchanges or ITEs. They are independently operated B2B trading platforms that any relevant business or group of businesses can join. The objective here is to establish online interaction and transactions with a community of trading partners. As Masood (2001) indicates, 'they capture the most obvious advantage of the web – the ability to contact and share transactions with a wide network of business partners across the globe'. Thus they are truly global players. An example is CheMatch (www.chematch.com), the chemical industry exchange.

Consortium exchanges

These are owned and operated by a group of competitors, bringing them into contact with suppliers. Although this may work against normal thinking (that is, competitors collaborating), the overall aim is to lower the buying costs of the companies by consolidating their overall buying power. The key issue for such consortia, though, is the transference of information. On occasions commercially sensitive information could be revealed, giving rival companies an unfair advantage. In order for such consortia to survive and prosper in the future there may need to be a radical restructuring and rethinking on how industries operate within such fora.

Private exchanges

These are exchanges that are owned and operated by a single company or organization.

Marketing insight: Prudential plc

This 'Marketing insight' demonstrates several points. First, it shows what effect issues surrounding mis-selling of products and regulatory breaches can have on a company. Even highly regarded and well established companies such as Prudential have been affected by such actions. Additionally (the main point of including the study at this point) there are the changes taking place as a result of technology.

The company was originally formed in 1848 as the Prudential Mutual Assurance, Investment and Loan Association, to help the working class to save with penny policies. Today it is one of the world's largest insurance groups. 'With his battered trilby hat the Man from the Pru was once a familiar sight to generations of post [World War 2] families as he trod the streets of Britain's industrial heartland collecting premiums.' However, accusations of pension mis-selling and lack of regulatory compliance in the 1990s led to a drastic reduction in the number of direct sales staff, and retraining of those remaining. In early 2001 the company announced it would phase out its main UK direct sales force by 2002. After allowing for redeployment it believed this would lead to approximately 2,000 redundancies, including those in sales support operations and central back-office and administrative support functions. The company planned to focus its sales efforts on the Internet and telesales. A small direct sales team would be retained to focus on specific affluent customers.

Prudential believed it was increasingly uneconomic to retain a direct sales team, as more than 90 per cent of customers interacted with the company via mail, the Internet and the telephone. In 1998 the direct sales force had accounted for 27 per cent of UK sales, but by 2000 this had dropped to 13 per cent. In 2001 over 70 per cent of general insurance business, including all customer service handling of claims, was conducted over the telephone.

However, there are costs associated with such restructuring. The group expected to incur a charge of UK £110 million of which UK £13 million would impact directly on shareholders. However, from 2002 it expected to achieve annual gross cost savings of UK £135 million.

Questions/activities

1. By visiting the company's Web site and checking your university's online databases update the Marketing insight. Have any further relevant developments taken place since the case study was written?
2. In moving towards Web-based and telemarketing sales do you believe that Prudential has taken the right decision? Why? (You may want to debate this as a group exercise.)
3. Do you think other market sectors could reduce their sales force in favour of Web-based and telemarketing activities? Why? (You may want to debate this as a group exercise).

Sources: Croft (2001), Prudential (2001).

These sites are specifically tailored so that the company can link its trading systems directly to its suppliers, which provides a potential strategic advantage. However, it is not without cost. These sites are expensive to develop and operate. The critical factor is whether or not they are cost-efficient over the longer term.

In theory, the efficiencies and greater transparency through the demand and supply chain lead to significant benefits. These potential benefits, for companies who engage in these exchanges, include:

▌ increased speed of transactions;

▌ access to more information;

▌ enhanced customer relationships;

▌ optimization of the supply chain, achieved though the use of sophisticated planning and forecasting tools, which assist in the automation of business processes;

▌ improved overall branding of products and services;

▌ a reduction in processing costs;

▌ increased speed in settling payments.

Chapter summary

The chapter has illustrated the role a wide range of marketing communications techniques plays in promoting both products and services. Since the early 1990s markets have been particularly volatile, and this has compounded increasing competitiveness. All aspects of marketing need to be effective and efficient if an organization is to develop and maintain market position. Sustainable competitive advantage comes through innovation, and that can be derived through many aspects of a company's operation: organization, product development, logistics and distribution and, of course, marketing communications.

Exercises and questions for review and critical thinking

1. 'In a technologically driven world the way we communicate with B2B customers makes the role of the individual salesperson outdated.' Critically evaluate this statement.

2. Critically evaluate the contribution that salespeople make to the communications mix and marketing overall.

3. How can a company use loyalty cards, and the information they provide, as an effective means of creating customer satisfaction and retention?

4. The use of direct marketing techniques in both the United States and the UK has become increasingly sophisticated. However, in many other countries direct marketing is still in its infancy. (a) What have been the limiting factors in its growth within these other countries? (b) In your opinion, what is the market potential within these countries and why?

5. A director of a large FMCG company stated, 'I have no need for direct marketing. Ours will always be a mass marketing industry.' Do you consider this company director is right? Support your answer with a well reasoned argument.

6. Direct marketers seek to obtain a significant amount of lifestyle information on individual prospects and customers. As a result, concern has been expressed in several countries about the amount and type of information a company should have on individuals. In the light of these concerns consider the potential ethical

and legal issues associated with obtaining detailed lifestyle information on individuals.

7. Consider the future of direct marketing. How do you think it will impact on your life and why?

11

Promotion 2

Introduction

This chapter is a follow-on from the previous one. Here we consider the roles of sales promotion, public relations, sponsorship, product placement, merchandising, exhibitions and viral marketing as part of an organization's promotional mix. When reading through this chapter, consider how these promotional mix elements can be combined with those in the previous chapter to create an integrated marketing communications campaign.

Learning objectives

On completion of this chapter you should be able to:

▌ outline the different sales promotion techniques, and explain which techniques you might use to promote certain products;

▌ examine the contribution public relations can make to the promotion of a product or service;

▌ debate the case for and against product placement as a vehicle to promote a product within a blockbuster movie;

▌ examine the potential value that sponsorship can bring to both the sponsoring organization and the sponsored;

▌ explain how viral marketing can be used to promote a product or service;

▌ develop an outline plan for an integrated marketing communications campaign to promote a product, based on what you have read in Chapters 10 and 11.

Sales promotion

This can be defined as an offer created to launch or relaunch a product or service. Effective planning is, therefore, essential whether sales promotion is to be used as a support activity for the organization's long-term objectives, or as a short-term tactic.

Table 11.1 lists the criteria that illustrate the objectives of sales promotion. It must be emphasized that this list is not definitive.

Table 11.1   Sales promotion objectives

Criteria	Objectives
The introduction of new products	The introduction of new products, by motivating customers to try out a new product, or retail customers to accept it for resale.
Attracting new customers	Attracting new customers, by motivating people to try out a new product, or retail customers to accept it for resale for the first time.
Maintaining competitiveness	Maintaining competitiveness by providing preferential discounts, or special low prices to enable more competitive resale prices to be offered.
Increasing off-peak sales	Increasing sales in off-peak seasons by encouraging consumption out of season.

There are always numerous options and circumstances where sales promotion can make a significant contribution to the marketing of a company or organization.

Marketing insight: Vacation promotion

A holiday company may offer lower prices at Mediterranean resorts during the period November to April. This is because it is generally outside people's main holiday period (in the UK the holiday period tends to coincide with the summer months and the school holidays), the weather is milder and some restaurants may be closed.

For holiday companies, especially those that completely or part own hotels, offering special rates can still provide a fair level of occupancy, and thus a fair return on investment.

This is an example:

Location: Northern Tuscany in Italy. Property: Small villa.				
Seasons and departure dates:				
Low season	Shoulder season	Mid season	High season	Peak season
April 4, 11, 18, 25	May 2, 9, 16	May 23, 30	June 20, 27	July 11, 18, 25
	Oct 3, 10, 17, 24	June 6, 13	July 4, Aug 29	Aug 1, 8, 15, 22
		Sept 19, 26	Sept 5, 12	
Prices for two weeks per person:				
£665	£745	£995	£1,486	£1,508

This information is based on a real travel brochure and 2002 prices.

Types of promotion

It should be borne in mind that there are no concrete rules for selecting the right sales promotion tactic. What is successful in achieving the marketing objective in one situation might not necessarily be successful in achieving a similar objective in another. Equally, the same promotion tactic might be suitable for meeting different objectives. Selection may be made easier by the analysis of the following issues:

▌ Which sales promotion tactic best fits the profiles of the target audience?

▌ What are the advantages of each sales promotion tactic?

▌ What are the disadvantages of each sales promotion tactic?

▌ Which is likely to provide the maximum return on investment in relation to overall budget spend?

▌ Which promotion best lends itself to accurate measurement of its overall effectiveness?

Table 11.2 lists the different types of sales promotion tactics that can be employed. As you will see some have similarities, and thus may be used in conjunction with each other.

Promotions direct to the consumer's home

These are also called 'in-home' promotions. Companies deliver direct to the suspect/first time buyer special promotional items and/or coupons.

Free samples – door drops

The objective here is to persuade recipients to try out the trial sample, then purchase the product the next time they visit, for example, their local supermarket. Clearly the items have to be suitable for home delivery. Here are a few examples of samples that have been delivered to UK homes:

12 ml sachets of L'Oréal Elvive revitalizing shampoo;
25 g bars of Dove soap;
pyramid shaped or round Tetley tea-bags.

Free samples inside magazines

This is a highly developed area. A free sample is attached to a magazine advertisement stating the benefits of the particular product. The majority of these samples are for women's beauty products.

Table 11.2   Types of sales promotion

Promotions direct to consumer	In-store promotions
Free samples – door drops	Product demonstrations
Free samples inside magazines	More for your money/extra value offers
Money-off coupons/vouchers	Buy one get one free
Door-to-door drops	Privilege/patronage/loyalty cards
Magazine/newspapers	Special offer bins
Free sendaway premium	Bundling
Competitions	

Money-off coupons/vouchers

According to research published by the US Coupon Council in 2003, US shoppers saved in 2001 an estimated US $3 billion by redeeming 3.9 billion coupons. That equates to approximately US $800–1,000 per shopper. Additionally 77 per cent of US shoppers used coupons to save on their weekly shopping, thus making it an integral part of shopping within the United States. They can be delivered to the potential consumer via several distribution mechanisms.

Door-to-door drops

These are used for a significant range of products and services, such as taxi services, restaurants, house repair services, estate agents and takeaway/home delivery foods. In the case of a fast-food restaurant, as well as providing a snapshot of the menu it may also contain price-reduction vouchers with a time limit on their redemption.

Magazines/newspapers

These can be delivered on subscription direct to the consumer's door.

On-pack distributions are free gifts that come with the magazine. Good examples of these are computer and classical music publications. In the case of computer magazines, CDs containing demonstration and fully working programmes are attached. With classical music magazines there are one or two CDs containing either extracts from new issues or a full recording of a particular work. Other examples include women's magazines carrying an abridged edition of a new novel and gardening magazines with packets of seeds or a small plastic fork or trowel.

Newspapers may run special reader offers. For example, during the late 1990s the *Sunday Times* ran a series of CD offers which were exclusive to the newspaper. CDs which featured well-known jazz artists and selections of classical music could be purchased from the newspaper for UK £1.99 each.

Free sendaway premium

This is a free gift that the consumer receives after sending to the promoting company a stated number of, for example, packet tops or ring pulls from cans. A soft drinks manufacturer might offer free sweatshirts or a CD music compilation in return for so many ring pulls.

Competitions

Prizes often consist of the chance to win cash, holidays to exotic locations or merchandise. The type of competition can vary from a prize draw (a name or a series of numbers are chosen at random) to a contest where the consumer needs to submit a completed entry, or a game.

There are various reasons for companies to develop competitions. It can be a means of selling more newspapers, especially if the competition runs for several weeks. In the case of *Reader's Digest* it is an opportunity to promote the value of the magazine to potential readers/subscribers. In addition, if the entrant needs to submit personal details to enter the competition, for example name, address, age, telephone number and so on, the company can capture this data. Subsequently (subject to data protection laws) it can be sold on to other companies, or used for the company's own direct mail/telemarketing purposes.

In-store promotions

Clearly not all products are purchased within a retailing environment. However, this type of promotion has the major advantage of featuring the location where many of the final decisions to purchase (as well as the actual purchase) are made.

Product demonstrations

These can take place within a retail outlet or at an exhibition. Demonstrations can take many forms, ranging from sampling food products to using kitchen appliances and even jewellery. With the development of audio-visual systems, the demonstrations can be videotaped and the tape placed on a loop. This provides continuous and automatic playing of the tape on television monitors at various locations within the store. This maximizes 'the opportunity to see', in other words the potential of customers viewing at least some sections of the tape. This would not be possible with a live demonstration every few hours.

More for your money/extra value offers

These are pack promotions where the pack contains extra of the designated product. For example, Gillette® shaving foam has been marketed with 20 ml extra – 'get 220 ml for the price of 200 ml'. Another example is a wine store that will offer 12 bottles of champagne for the price of 10. This may have a time limitation, say for one month only.

Buy one get one free/banded packs/price packs

Within the advertising and promotion industry this is know by the acronym BOGOF. There are variants on the theme, for example a retailer may offer three for the price of two. An example is a chemist or drugstore that promotes three packs of its own-brand toothpaste for the price of two. A supermarket could do the same for prepackaged potatoes, especially if they near their sell-by dates.

Another variant is the 'banded pack'. This is where two related items are banded together. Examples are toothpaste with a toothbrush, or a free tube of conditioner with a bottle of shampoo. However, the retailer's competitors can easily emulate such promotions. This can be seen in the UK where rival chain store chemists promote their dental products in this way. Some academics believe that such promotions are really only effective in holding regular customers, and not attracting

new ones. This may not be the case. Such promotions could attract new customers, thus adding to an established customer base. Depending upon the offer, it could be profitable for the company concerned. However, the company will still have to find some means of differentiating its offer and/or product from that of its rivals. This is often easier said than done.

Privilege/patronage/loyalty card schemes

These could also be classified as 'extra value offers'. Major supermarket chains use loyalty cards as a means of developing customer retention. Points or bonuses are gained from the purchase of a range of items. These can be later redeemed as a cash equivalent against future purchases.

Airlines, most especially US domestic carriers, have used frequent flyer promotions as a means of retaining and developing customers. They are now a standard feature with many international carriers. The more miles travelled with the particular airline, the more opportunity there is to redeem frequent flyer points later as free flights.

Special offer bins

These are also called dump bins or dumpers. Placing the product in these bins suggests a bargain offer, thus attracting potential buyers. In the UK these are often seen in newsagents and small grocery stores promoting low-priced videos. They can also be seen in some cosmetic stores where they are promoting the end of a particular range or where the product is near its sell-by date.

Bundling

This has been used extensively within the UK computer hardware market. Both retailers and direct-to-door distributors advertise pre-loaded bundled software as part of the overall offer. The offer may read '£1,000 of software free'. The software may range from games to word processing and graphics packages.

Public relations

Public Relations, often abbreviated to PR (be careful here: the same initials are used for 'press relations'), is concerned, in a word, with **image**. No organization can afford to overlook the power of effective and efficient public relations, or to neglect how damaging negative public relations can be to that very same organization.

Unless it is completely invisible, every organization has an image. Even elite special forces groups and government agencies such as the British Army's SAS (Special Air Services), the UK's Security Service (MI5) and the US Federal Bureau of Investigation (FBI) and Central Intelligence Agency (CIA) all want to project an image, and a positive contemporary one.

The Institute of Public Relations in the UK defines public relations as 'the planned and sustained effort to establish and maintain goodwill and mutual understanding between the organization and its publics'.

The scope of public relations

PR is about reputation: the results of what the company does, what the company says and what others say about the company. Public relations practice is the discipline that looks after reputation, with the aim of earning understanding and support, and influencing opinion and behaviour.

Every organization must ask itself how all the people to whom it must relate think of it. In seeking to create (and then maintain and develop) an image, it helps to have, as a starting point, a clear idea of how customers see the company. This is something that can be researched (perception surveys are important here). However, people often say what they think is expected, or worse, what is heard only confirms the existing view, and perhaps existing prejudices.

The effect of PR is cumulative and a host of factors, perhaps individually seeming of no major significance, are therefore important. These include the quality of business cards and letterheads (indeed the whole graphic image), of reception, of all printed promotion, of staff appearance and service, and so on. A major influence is exactly how people are

---

Marketing insight: The story of a security service, MI5

MI5 is the historical name for the British Security Service. Founded in 1909, MI5's role has been one of counter-intelligence operations within the UK. Until the late 1990s it was generally cloaked in secrecy, even though there have been several official and semi-official histories written about the service. It was Prime Minister John Major's government, and the then Director General Stella Rimmington, who became the public face of MI5 when it took a more enlightened approach.

Indeed, the MI5 Web site has been developed to dispel many of the myths that previously surrounded that organization, such as whether knowing the colour of the carpet was a national secret or not! Equally, MI5 uses the Web site as a means of explaining the type of people – from all aspects of society – that it needs to recruit, how to join the service, its history, its function and its role in modern-day Britain, most especially combating terrorist threats.

Source: www.Mi5.gov.uk.

dealt with, whether it is appropriate and corresponds with their image of good customer service; in this respect what one might call the 'image climate' is affected every time someone within the organization has contact with a customer.

Consider any company you know of, one that has a strong image and of which you think well. Then ask yourself **why** this is so. Unless you have direct experience of the organization, it will be largely because of what it tells you about itself. Such messages can be powerful. Large companies invest significant amounts of money on their corporate image, something that hits the headlines occasionally (as with British Telecom and British Airways, or the Pepsi-Cola colour change which was implemented on a worldwide basis). However large or small, the image matters, on everything from the overall logo (company symbol) in all its manifestations to an individual's calling card.

PR must provide a planned, deliberate and sustained attempt to promote understanding between an organization and its audiences. In fact, it must promote not just understanding, but a positive interest in the organization which whets the appetite for more information, prompts enquiries, re-establishes dormant contacts and reinforces image with existing customers.

Not only is PR activity potentially a powerful weapon in the promotional armoury, some aspects of it are also free – at least compared with advertising, which is a paid-for medium. However there is a catch. It takes time, and perhaps particularly in any small business, time is certainly money. Therefore in too many organizations PR is neglected because staff are busy, even overstretched, and opportunities are missed. Yet if the power of PR is consistently ignored, at worst not only are opportunities missed but the image that occurs by default may actually damage business prospects.

In many ways, therefore, time spent on PR is time well spent, and, while for smaller organizations it can produce good low-cost results, a larger organization able to subcontract the activity to a PR consultancy may well spend substantial sums to create a continuity of visibility in this way. If so, it will expect to see larger-scale results, and much of that potentially comes through the press. (See Table 11.3.)

Trends in PR analysis

Evaluation is the practical conclusion of objective planning. Either the objectives have been achieved or they have not, although there may be degrees of success or failure. PR should not be tied directly to sales and profits as it has potentially a more global impact. The total picture of the organization should be considered: industrial relations, internal communications, customer relations, stock market quotation, growth, future prospects, corporate image, reputation and so on.

The contributions made by PR to an organization's success are varied and numerous, and enhance the other contributors to the marketing mix. PR is mostly about affecting change, in one form or another. The question is whether this 'change' can be measured. Table 11.4 outlines some of the analytical methods that can be used.

Sponsorship

Sponsorship is simply a specialized form of advertising; however it can create significant exposure for companies and organizations. It works by associating the product with another specific area of activity. Many examples come from the world of sport, with whole sports or individual events linked to commercial companies. In this kind of area most companies involved are large, often FMCG, and with substantial budget allocations.

The 2002 Winter Olympics in Salt Lake City graphically illustrate the level of such

Table 11.3 The scope of public relations activity

Activity	Description
Public affairs	Working with governments, non-governmental organizations (NGOs) and opinion-forming groups that help determine public policy and legislation. Specifically the work of the lobbyist.
Promotion	Special activities, such as events or exhibitions designed to create and stimulate interest in a person, product, organization or worthy cause.
Publicity	Dissemination of planned and executed messages through selected media to further the particular interest of an organization or person without any payment to the media.
Issues management	Systematic identification and action regarding public policy matters of concern to the organization. Building mutually acceptable common ground on issues that typically relate to human resources, environment and government: for example a crisis management situation such as an oil spill. There is a branch of PR known as crisis public relations management. You may want to reflect back to Chapter 3 where we discussed the Tylenol crisis and how the parent company Johnson & Johnson successfully managed that crisis.
Media relations	Ongoing communications with the media in seeking publicity, or responding to their interests in the organization. An active and reactive approach.
New product and service launches	Using a range of PR techniques to launch a new product or service into the marketplace. An example is the launch of a new movie to both film critics and the movie-going public.
Industry-wide communications (sometimes known as industrial relations)	Communicating with firms operating within the same industrial sectors. Improving levels of cooperation. For example, greater air safety for passenger aircraft, improving pollution control for the off-shore oil industry, and standards in food preparation safety.
Employee relations/ internal communications	Communicating with the employees of the organization, both on a one-to-one and one-to-group basis. This can also include communication with ex-employees such as retirees who benefit from a company pension scheme. Additionally, they may be customers of the company. Good internal communications can encourage employee involvement which in turn can develop morale and enhance a motivational environment. This can also be considered as part of the internal marketing process.
Investor relations	Communicating with the shareholders of the organization and the investment and banking communities in general. These groups include stock exchange member firms, shareholders' brokers, branch office managers, unlisted and over the counter share dealers, investment bankers, commercial bankers (trust departments), insurance companies and pension funds, mutual funds and investment funds, trustees of estates and institutions, financial statistical organizations, financial media, debt ratings agencies such as Dun & Bradstreet, Standard & Poor, and Moody's, and portfolio managers.
Government relations	Communicating with legislatures and government departments on behalf of the organization, for example the UK Department of Trade and Industry on export-related initiatives and trade developments.

Table 11.3   *continued*

Activity	Description
Community relations	Communicating with individuals and groups within the organization's operating area or location, for example the British Airports Authority and the local community regarding low-level flying and night flights, the Royal Air Force and very low-level flight training exercises over the Welsh and Scottish countryside, chemical companies with plants and facilities in close proximity to housing estates.
Corporate relations	This links into both investor relations and internal communications. It includes live events (annual general meetings for shareholders and sales conferences), corporate advertising, corporate literature (brochures and annual reports) and business television (live and pre-recorded material delivered via satellite to dedicated private business networks).
Minority relations	This is the building of positive relationships with individuals and groups who are perceived as minorities within a particular community. These range from pensioners or retirees to ethnic and gay people. Although they may only form a small part of a particular community they have a valuable contribution to make to the development and sustainability of that community.

financial investment. The organizers raised over US $860 million in sponsorship, more than twice the amount raised for the 1996 Atlanta Olympics.

Another area where sponsorship is prevalent is in the arts. Programmes in theatres and concert halls bear witness to the fact. Sponsorship links to corporate entertaining. Companies do not just sponsor an event, they make use of it by inviting customers or distributors to events and providing hospitality.

There are dangers to this approach. Some companies may owe their decision to sponsor something less to objective thinking than to their chairman's fanatical love of, say, athletics or the opera. Despite these reservations sponsorship can work well, and is responsible for providing much-needed investment into areas that might wither without it.

In terms of sport, as Table 11.5 shows, such sponsorship in the UK has grown significantly over recent years.

Table 11.4   Types of PR analysis

Evaluator	Description
Observing change	We can observe change in individuals' attitudes whether that is the result of internal communications, a particular management approach, increased overall business performance, greater employee involvement or workforce stability. Many aspects can be categorized under this heading.
Experiencing change	The concept of experiencing change can be witnessed by the relationships that develop, within a dynamic business environment, with suppliers, dealers, opinion leaders (these could be stock exchange dealers in London, New York or Tokyo, the local community, employees and, of course, the customer).
Using research to measure change	Several potential information sources can be considered here. These can be analysed using a variety of different techniques depending on resource availability. They are generally easy to track if an effective monitoring system has been set up. For example, the type of complaint can be listed and checked for frequency. Consider a delivery service. The potential complaints could cover (1) Attitude of the delivery drivers. (2) Whether the service is only provided 9 am to 5 pm Monday to Friday. This is obviously of little value to someone who works those hours. (3) When customers can receive a delivery. (4) Customer helpline, which might be continuously engaged or not operate outside office hours. (5) Goods not being delivered on the stated day. (6) Poorly written communication left for the person to receive the parcel. (6) Poor written communication in terms of explanations for lack of quality service. (7) The customer may not only be receiving a poor service but may be receiving a lack of quality written and verbal information, as well as general misinformation. These factors once known can be remedied, however only if management has both determination and the skill. Otherwise the company's PR will continue to be negative. That may well cost it its position within the marketplace. If it is in a particularly volatile marketplace it may cost it its very existence.
Focus groups	These are groups of customers invited in to discuss their views on the service being provided. Individuals who are not directly employed by the company usually chair them. They are usually specialist consultants who understand consumer behaviour patterns and demands. Focus groups can work equally well for B2B operations.
Telephone surveys	These can be useful when respondents are scattered over the country and an urgent response is required. They can be inexpensive to implement and useful for gauging the response to, for example, a crisis management campaign. Such feedback can help direct or modify the campaign to overcome negative impact.
Polling	Opinion polls have been used for a wide variety of subjects, from politics, the popularity of political and business leaders to whether an individual intends to buy a new car within the next 12 months and who is the favourite television personality or football player of the year. However, as is seen with political polls, what people say, and what they do (for example, who they vote for) can be completely different.

Table 11.4   *continued*

Evaluator	Description
Media coverage and tone	Some PR consultants say that 'all coverage is good coverage'. That is far from the truth. Some coverage can be highly detrimental to the survival of an organization. The study of the media can reveal a great deal of vital information, for example whether there is misinformation, prejudice, ignorance of the facts or simple hostility. It is vital if information is misquoted or facts are misrepresented that there is a fast and effective response. Otherwise the public will draw their own conclusions, potentially further damaging an organization's reputation.
Which areas receive coverage	If the organization operates within more than one area, the level of coverage and tone of that coverage can be analysed from one sector to another. This can act as a performance indicator to see which areas, or issues, are receiving coverage.
Rating media and coverage	▌ Ratings: media coverage can be rated according to whether it helps or hinders the organization's corporate objectives. This could be on a rating scale of 1 to 5 with 5 being the most beneficial. ▌ AVE: some organizations use advertising value evaluation, that is a measurement of editorial coverage in terms of equivalent advertising costs. However, in terms of communicating the message, and the process by which this is undertaken, there can be no relationship between advertising investment and editorial. This is a negative means of attempting to evaluate PR programmes. ▌ Readership/audience listening and viewing figures: virtually all publications provide detailed analysis of readership, from total number of readers to industry sector that purchases the magazine and decision making power of the readership. Similar systems, relating to potential audience numbers, also exist for radio and television.
Effect of media coverage	What impact did the level and tone of media coverage have on the company, the company's brands or the organization? For example, did more consumers telephone or write in for more details? Did they stop buying the brand? Have people bought more shares in the company? Did customers complain? Has the reputation of the organization been severely damaged? Such analysis can be critical at any time within a product life cycle, or at times of crisis management.

Table 11.5   Spend on sports sponsorship agreements in the UK

Year	Value (UK £ million)
1981	50
1991	238
1992	239
2000	401
2001	422

Source: Institute of Sports Sponsorship (2002) in Clark (2002)

Marketing Insight: Ellen MacArthur and Kingfisher plc

Kingfisher plc, the international retailer, sponsors yachtswoman Ellen MacArthur. In 1998 Kingfisher began a trial sponsorship for MacArthur's solo race Route du Rhum. In the monohull yacht *Kingfisher* she won her class and took fifth overall place.

In 2001 MacArthur came second in the Vendee Globe race. As a result Kingfisher found itself in the middle of the 'media frenzy' that surrounded her success. The original three-year UK £1.8 million sponsorship deal brought the company and its corporate brand name significant media coverage. It demonstrated that sponsorship can cut through the clutter, as discussed in the previous chapter.

In January 2002 Kingfisher announced a five-year sponsorship deal. The key objectives of the sponsorship are to build familiarity of the Kingfisher brand with its international audiences, and to create an association between the Kingfisher corporate brand and its operating companies within the UK. Andrew Mills, Director of Corporate Affairs, commented:

> Ellen's remarkable achievements over the past three years have exceeded all our expectations. We strongly believe that Ellen represents the qualities we value highly as a company – determination, skill and professionalism, combined with the ambition and ability to succeed. She is a constant inspiration to our 90,000+ employees around the globe, and we see parallels between her international ambition and our own. We are delighted to continue to support Ellen through the highs and lows of racing across the oceans.

Kingfisher Challenges has its own multilingual Web site which covers the events and provides opportunities to purchase merchandise. There is also a link to Ellen MacArthur's own Web site.

Sources: Clark (2002), Web site www.kingfisherchallenges.com

This poster advertises the major events at the annual classical music festival in Salò, Italy. The festival was sponsored by several companies (logos bottom left of the poster), including the mineral water company Fonte Tavina. Without such sponsorship many such festivals would not be able to stage major events. For the sponsoring company there is high visibility of their brand.

Product placement

This is also known as alternative advertising, entertainment marketing and product integration. Product placement is where a product, or indeed a service, appears within a television programme or a movie. This type of product integration has become prevalent over recent years, especially in US movies because it has three key advantages: local and global reach, opportunity and cost-effectiveness/frequency.

Local and global reach

Movies have for many years been a popular form of entertainment. With the development of improved wide screen and sound systems, and digital effects, there has been a dramatic increase in audience figures. It is estimated that in 1997 some 2 billion people worldwide saw Hollywood-made movies (Marshall, 1998). Additionally, the growth of video purchasing and rental markets and the expansion of the television market (satellite, cable and terrestrial) have increased audiences. Thus product placement in a box-office hit can be a powerful communications tool for an advertiser.

Opportunity

In forming strategic alliances with major film production companies, consumer product companies can develop entertainment-based tie-ins. This can be in the form of advertising or in-store promotions. The latter is especially the case with fast-food outlets.

Cost-effectiveness/frequency

Product placement demonstrates diminishing costs per thousand. Here there are three key points:

▌ The original cost to place the product into the movie may be significantly lower than developing a major advertising campaign to reach the same global audience. Support advertising can be localized to key markets.

▌ The movie will be released to video/DVD/Internet. It will have both a new audience and a repeat audience.

▌ It will be released to television and repeated over the years. Even if it is shown on a non-commercial broadcast channel such as the UK's BBC the products are still seen. Thus over many years the product or service is seen without any further costs to the company.

Product placement objectives

A means of overcoming physical noise

This is an alternative form of advertising that may assist marketers in breaking through the physical noise (clutter) of competitive advertising. With product placement there will be no major rival within the movie.

Building brand awareness

Such exposure can help build brand awareness of a new product or service (see the 'Marketing insight'). Equally, established brands can benefit from reinforcement of the product's features and benefits. In the 1955 classic movie *Rebel Without A Cause*, teen icon James Dean played a rebellious young man. In the movie he often combed his hair with an Ace comb. This in itself became a classic comb used by the youth of the day to symbolize their affinity with the James Dean character. This was an early example of mainstream product placement.

Positive association/brand loyalty

As well as building awareness, product placement can create positive associations and elements of brand loyalty. The image of BMW cars may be reinforced in the minds of owners when they see James Bond driving the latest version.

Marketing insight: Shaken, but not stirred; James Bond as a marketer

Product placement in movies has become increasingly important to companies. The James Bond movies have a long history of product placement. Who can forget when James Bond had his first outing in his Aston Martin DB5 sports car in *Goldfinger* (1964)? Even all these years later there is a new generation of James Bond fans who watch the DVDs and the television repeats. Product placement has significantly developed since then.

In *Goldeneye* (1995) BMW were able to introduce their new two-seater convertible, the Z-3. This greatly assisted the introduction of the car into the marketplace. It has been cited as one of the most successful car launches to date. The BMW Z-3 was launched three months after the movie's release and was supported by a series of James Bond-themed television advertisements. These further reinforced the brand. The result was 12 months' worth of orders (Stewart-Allen, 1999). The Z-3 brand achieved global recognition.

In the movie *Tomorrow Never Dies* (1997) there was some UK £20 million worth of product placement (BBC, 2001b). This included BMW, Ericsson mobile phones, Avis car hire, Omega watches and Bollinger champagne. Some however argue that this movie became more like a long commercial break than an action-packed adventure. However, the value to BMW from *Tomorrow Never Dies*, where James Bond used a variety of products – the Z-3, the 750iL and the R1200c motorbike – has been estimated at over US $100 million (Stewart-Allen, 1999).

In the most recent James Bond movie, *Die Another Day* (2002), Bond returns to driving an Aston Martin – the V12 Vanquish – with an added array of special features, of course. Additionally, Bond's adversary is equipped with the latest Jaguar. Both Aston Martin and Jaguar are part of the Ford Motor Company.

Questions/activities

1. Research Land Rover's vehicle product placement in the live-action version of the computer game *Tomb Raiders* (2001). Also determine how Land Rover reinforced its placement through support advertising.
2. When you next watch a video, attempt to note all the possible examples of product placement.
3. List the products placed in the new James Bond movie. Consider the comment in the text above regarding the level of product placement within a movie. Do you think it can be too much? If so, why, and how could it affect the brand?

Sources: Stewart-Allen (1999), BBC (2001b), Aston Martin, MGM/UA (www.jamesbond.com).

Merchandising

The term 'merchandising' can have several interrelated meanings. It can simply mean selling products, being derived from the word 'merchant'. Here it can refer to a full range of products. In a narrower sense it can be used to describe products related to a specific event or organization.

In the first instance we consider merchandising in its broadest sense. Have a look around you next time you go shopping. Are there shops with window displays that make you want to look inside? Do you notice, in a supermarket, that essentials, such as say bread or sugar, are very often at the back of the store? This necessitates customers passing many other, less essential items en route to those they really want to buy. This is not a way of making people buy something they do not want, so much as a way of making sure they buy sooner, rather than later and from somewhere else. So, items likely to attract people in get prime display, essential items that people must have go at the back.

Let us now consider merchandising in its narrowest sense: the focus on particular products. Virtually every company and organization is involved, to a greater or lesser extent, in merchandising its brand identity. The value of merchandising within this context should not be underestimated. Probably one of the best examples is the UK football club Manchester United plc. It formed a wholly owned subsidiary Manchester United Merchandising Limited to further develop global brand awareness through merchandising the club. Table 11.6 illustrates the value of merchandising to Manchester United. Even though there was a decrease in the year 2001, as a result of exceptional items, it remains a significant percentage of the club's total turnover. To support its merchandising activities Manchester United plc has opened retail outlets at its Old Trafford stadium, as well as in Dublin and Singapore.

Let us consider a few other examples:

- **A university.** A range of products may be made available for sale to current students and alumni. These could include paperweights, clocks, ballpoint pens, ties, cuff links, brooches, scarves, mouse mats, china mugs, pencils, folders, jumpers, sweatshirts, caps, postcards and even teddy bears sporting their own university jumpers! Some universities have opened their own stores to sell their merchandising to both student and non-students. Additionally, products may be available via mail order.

- **A movie.** The *Star Wars* sagas are an excellent example of how merchandising can significantly increase revenue generation and the marketability of a movie. For the movie *Phantom Menace* (1999), Lucasfilm organized multi-million dollar merchandising contracts with companies such as the toy makers Hasbro and Lego. Virtually every toy shop in the world has displayed and sold characters from this highly successful movie.

- **Food manufacturers.** Heinz Foods sells a range of non-food products that carries its distinctive logo and brand name. They range from watches and nightshirts to a baked bean tote bag and a soccer ball.

Table 11.6 Merchandising at Manchester United

Year	Value (UK £ million)	Percentage of turnover
2000	23.6	20
2001	21.9	17

Source: Manchester United Annual Reports, 2000 and 2001.

▌ **A city.** Countries, regions and cities are all involved in the branding process. Thus a city authority, for example, will create official merchandise to reflect the city's history, culture and icons. In London, for instance, everything from 'I love London' t-shirts and plastic police officers' helmets to guidebooks on the Tower of London and the River Thames is available.

▌ **An airline.** Most airlines have some form of merchandising that reinforces their brand image and name. Products can range from model aircraft in the corporate livery to videos and books of their history and aircraft (British Airways have, for example, a video of the supersonic aircraft *Concorde*) to postcards, key rings, business folders and children's teddy bears dressed as pilots.

Merchandising can be both purchased and free. The luxury Spanish hotel chain Paradores produce a range of merchandise. Items ranging from Paradores branded men's and women's clothing to beach towels can be purchased. In-room merchandise feature own-branded shampoos and soaps. The Paradores Group, as with so many major hotel chains, seek consistency in their branding from reception areas through to merchandise. This reinforces their identity as a major hotel group.

Exhibitions

These are an important communications technique affecting both consumer and B2B marketing. Exhibitions demonstrate marketing in action in microcosm. They involve analysis and planning, demand a creative approach and ultimately are only made effective by the way the people aspect of what goes on works. A visit to one can give you an opportunity to observe how marketing works, while being an exhibitor means utilizing many marketing techniques.

The range of events under the exhibition heading is substantial, and includes many smaller – and local – events from country shows and fairs to events organized by local chambers of commerce and industry. What matter are not simply the overall costs, which are always important, but also the cost per enquiry or per order.

Every exhibition possibility must be considered carefully. Exhibitions produce a unique environment. A significant amount of research has been undertaken on the exhibition industry, and includes the following indicators:

▌ Attendees are receptive to what exhibitors have to sell. They have given up time to check out specific areas and there are none of the usual distractions of the office, telephones and other interruptions.

▌ The cost of a lead generated at an exhibition is low (certainly compared to salespeople's time) and they require, on average, less follow-up contact to convert.

▌ They provide a quality audience. The great majority of B2B visitors have buying influence, more than half are middle management and above, and special categories are useful too. For example, a third of those visiting exhibitions are new to their job, needing to check things out fast and actively looking for new suppliers.

▌ The average visitor spends five hours at an exhibition, and in addition to seeking new contacts, spends much of the time talking to people he or she knows (so it is a good way of maintaining contact with existing customers).

In addition, exhibitions are of course interactive. Products can be touched, tried and demonstrations watched; feedback is immediately available, and the progress possible towards a decision can be certain and fast. Further, many exhibitions are specialist; in fact, the fastest growing section is that where exhibitors are all from one industry.

Word of mouth: viral marketing

Also known as contagion marketing, word of mouth advertising or marketing is nothing new. Individuals and groups have for centuries expressed their views on subjects. Of course, those views are not always positive. The same applies today. Yet word of mouth marketing, or Buzz as it is increasingly being called, is increasingly important to marketers. Reflect for a moment back to Chapter 4, where we considered the various factors that influence a person to buy a product or service. Among those 'influencers' are family, friends and the media. In all these cases they can recommend or discourage purchase. Thus they are powerful influences that can lead to the success, or indeed failure, of a product or service.

As indicated earlier, the power of word of mouth is not new. Independent film makers with small marketing budgets know the value of word of mouth. Even mainstream film makers have gained significantly from the personal comments of others cutting through the clutter of media advertising. As Dye (2000) suggests, 'people like to share their experiences with one another... and when those experiences are favourable, the recommendations can snowball, resulting in runaway

People, both as groups and individuals, remain the most powerful influencing force in marketing. Their opinion can make or break the reputation of a product or service. Thus capturing the positive 'voice' is critical to companies and their brands, most especially in a highly competitive 'noisy' global market.

success'. Dye (2000) has dubbed this 'explosive self-generating demand'.

Today though it is not just a question of a company waiting and hoping that there will be positive word of mouth. Companies are actively seeking word of mouth actions through viral marketing (or contagion marketing). As the term suggests, word of mouth spreads like a virus or contagion through the community, infecting virtually everyone that comes into contact with it. Blackshaw (2001) suggests that 'these talkative, influential consumers will play a critical role in the future of your marketing schemes, loyalty programs, customer service efforts, public relations outreach, brand management, privacy policies and bottom line'. He continues to suggest that 'these [viral] ambassadors can be valuable, low-cost avenues for building existing relationships, recruiting new customers and keeping old customers happy for life' (Blackshaw, 2001).

While there may be positives, we must also consider those customers who disseminate their bad experiences to others. People tend to be negative rather than positive. Thus companies must consider that this is more than advertising, it encompasses a range of communications mix tactics.

McKinsey & Company estimate that two-thirds of the US economy has been influenced by word of mouth marketing (Dye, 2000). It suggests that:

- 13 per cent is largely driven by word of mouth: toys, sporting goods, movies, broadcasting, reaction services and fashion.

- 54 per cent is partially driven by word of mouth: finance (investment products), hotels, electronics, printing and publishing, tobacco, automotive, pharmaceuticals and health care, transportation, agriculture, food and drink.

Marketing insight: Lee Jeans and viral marketing

With the introduction of the Internet, companies have been devising methods to aid viral marketing. Lee Jeans is a good example of this approach. By the late 1990s Lee Jeans had rejuvenated its brand identity to appeal to the new youth generation. It wanted to influence its target audience of males 17 to 22 who played video games and actively surfed the Net. Lee Jeans created a list of 200,000 potential influencers within this target group and sent them video clips. These were not of jeans but scenes supposedly from low-budget thrillers, which were of poor quality, reminiscent perhaps of some of those dreadful 1950s B movies that did little to scare the audience. Intrigued, though, the target audience sent them on to their friends, estimated to be six per person.

Lee Jeans with its advertising agency created a Web address where the influencers could feed back their views. As a result some 100,000 unique visitors logged on to the Web site. This then linked into a television and radio campaign, where the video clips were linked to an online computer game. To play the game at an advanced level the target audience of 17–22-year-olds had to buy Lee Dungarees in order to obtain the product identification number on the jeans. This viral marketing exercise increased US sales by 20 per cent in 2000.

Source: Khermouch and Gree (2001).

▌ 33 per cent is largely immune from word of mouth: oil and gas, chemicals, railways, insurance and utilities.

You may want to reflect on your own country and how word of mouth may affect these products and services.

Chapter summary

In this chapter we have considered a wide range of marketing communication techniques and tools: advertising (in a variety of forms), sales promotion, product placement, exhibitions, merchandising, public relations (also in a wide variety of forms) and word of mouth (viral marketing). In terms of marketing, although the other 'Ps' influence our decisions to purchase (for example, price), it is the promotional elements that have a visual, spatial and aural impact on us as individuals and groups. Just consider how often a television or cinema commercial becomes a

---

Marketing insight: *Longitude* and *The Diving-Bell and the Butterfly*

Publishing companies can spend significant resources on marketing both fiction and non-fiction titles. In some cases these become international bestsellers; perhaps in most cases, though, they deliver only a small profit for the publishers. The following two examples demonstrate how word of mouth turned two non-fiction books into bestsellers. Both books have similarities. First, the same publisher – Fourth Estate, now an imprint of HarperCollins – published them in the UK. Second, both focus on the struggles of their central characters.

Published in the UK in 1996, *Longitude* by Dava Sobel is the 18th century story of John Harrison's 40-year obsession to build a timepiece (known today as the chronometer). The timepiece was devised to calculate longitude accurately for sailors. Without an accurate reading of longitude, ships were often lost at sea. To nations this meant not only the loss of crews, but of ships and often immense wealth in terms of cargoes.

The Diving-Bell and the Butterfly by Jean-Dominique Bauby is the moving story of his struggle to survive against impossible odds. To quote the book's jacket:

> On 8 December 1995, Jean-Dominique Bauby, a 42-year-old father of two and editor-in-chief of *Elle* magazine in Paris, suffered a massive stroke and slipped into a coma. When he regained consciousness three weeks later, he was paralyzed, speechless and only able to move one muscle: his left eyelid. Yet his mind remained as active and alert as ever. By signalling with the eyelid he 'dictated' this book, blinking to each individual letter as an alphabet was repeatedly read to him. Trapped inside his own body his dispatches are poignant and often wryly humorous.

When the book was first published in France in March 1997, it became an immediate success. Two days later, on 9 March 1997, Bauby died. *The Diving-Bell and the Butterfly* was published in the UK shortly after its publication in France.

In both cases the limited marketing budgets prevented a major promotional campaign. That meant no advertising to either the booksellers (the trade) or the end consumer. However, copies of the books were sent to book editors of major newspapers and key magazines with book review sections. Additionally, the sales force had copies and background material to present to key booksellers. Both are part of the normality of selling books. The reviews for both books were excellent, often outstanding, yet these alone do not necessarily sell books. Word of mouth however propelled both books into the Top 10 bestseller lists. They were both to become international bestsellers.

Longitude was translated into more than 20 languages, and won several awards including the Harold D Vursell Memorial Award from the American Academy of Arts and Letters, Book of the Year from the British Book Trade, Le Prix Faubert du Coton in France and the Il Premio del Mare Circeo in Italy. In addition, Dava Sobel was awarded a Fellowship of the American Geographical Society. In 1998 *Longitude* was made into a television drama, which itself scooped several awards.

Questions/activities

1. Consider other books that have become bestsellers through word of mouth. Do not confine your research only to recent books.
2. Do you think that academic textbooks can be marketed through word of mouth/viral marketing? How and why?
3. Do you think, based on the information above, that either *Longitude* or *The Diving-Bell and the Butterfly* would have been so successful without word of mouth? Why? Of course, it will depend upon your definition of success. Obviously, the publishers thought that both books would be successful, however perhaps not to the extent that they were.
4. Consider how you might generate word of mouth marketing for either a college sports team or college newspaper. You may want to undertake this question as a group activity.

focus of conversation. It may be because of its sheer power or beauty, or because of controversy, for example the Benetton campaigns of the 1990s. Whichever, messages are being communicated.

While marketing communications campaigns can often be very expensive to implement, effective and efficient campaigns can, in turn, create significant returns on investment. However, they must commence with a clear set of objectives. Exactly what is the organization trying to achieve and why? How it then works with the agencies and consultancies involved is also crucial to success. How people interact with others can also have an impact on the final campaign. While there is clearly a skill in creative advertising design, there is also a skill in motivating a diverse group of individuals into achieving the client's goals. Again, this is a perfect reason why objectives really need to be understood and effectively disseminated to target groups.

Although these techniques can be used in isolation, a company will often gain competitive advantages and synergies by creating an integrated marketing communication (IMC) campaign. Here a common theme runs across several media simultaneously. They may include television advertising, print media and door drops. These can be supported by a press and public relations campaign that picks up the theme and translates it into editorial coverage. For example, a company could use such techniques for the launch of a new product or service, especially if it was revolutionary.

Exercises and questions for review and critical thinking

1. When you next see a major movie, consider the potential product placement and merchandising opportunities it may or may not have. What do you consider to be the potential dangers in product placement?

2. Select a company or organization that you are familiar with, either personally or through your studies. Examine how it uses public relations to communicate its product or service values to its target markets.

3. Word of mouth or viral marketing is being hailed as the technique that could make or break a product or service. What do you think, and why?

4. You are responsible for the marketing of your college. Devise a marketing communication strategy to increase the recruitment of local students. What communication tools would you use and why?

12

People, physical evidence and process

Introduction

In Chapter 1 we discussed the ongoing debate regarding the relevance of the marketing mix. We contended that there was a generic marketing mix comprising the traditional four Ps and the three Ps, generally postulated as the service mix. In this chapter we evaluate the three Ps of people (also known as participants), physical evidence (also known as physicality) and process. These are linked to both the product and service environments, reinforcing the view that they are integral components of a generic seven Ps marketing mix.

Learning objectives

On completion of this chapter you will be able to:

▌ understand the role people, physical evidence and process play within marketing of products and services;

▌ apply the concepts of people, physical evidence and process to a range of contemporary business environments and scenarios;

▌ investigate and evaluate the link between these three Ps and the classic four Ps (as analysed in Chapter 1);

▌ evaluate both the positive and negative aspects that can be associated with people, physical evidence and process.

The debate between services and products

There are those that think that a service is just a little different from a product and therefore should be considered in its own right. The concept is not new, and one definition by Stanton, Etzel and Walker (1994) encapsulates the concept:

> Those separately identifiable, essentially intangible activities that provide want satisfactions and which are not necessarily tied to the sale of a product or another service. To produce a service may or may not require the use of tangible goods. However, when such use is required, there is no transfer of title (permanent ownership), to those tangible goods.

This definition of services in many ways

supports the idea that services are products because they satisfy a want or need. The only thing under consideration is whether or not a tangible or intangible item satisfies the need, and if a transfer of ownership takes place. This leads to the conclusion from a marketing view that both goods and services provide benefits and satisfactions. If this is accepted, both goods and services are products. Levitt (1972) emphasizes the concept in saying 'That there is no such thing as a service industry. There are only industries whose service components are greater or less than those of other industries. Everybody is in service.'

However the emphasis changes in the use of the marketing mix. This may make it necessary to consider how the marketing mix is relevant in industries where there is a high level of service content. While the original work of Borden (1964), which was further developed by McCarthy (1981), has been adopted by most academics, it needs to be considered whether, in its basic form, the marketing mix is really suitable for organizations with a high propensity to service provision.

As we considered in Chapter 1, Booms and Bitner (1981) developed a modified and extended version of the marketing mix containing three additional elements or variables. Table 12.1 summarizes these variables. The consideration of the extended mix containing the seven elements should, they proposed, now form the basis of the marketing mix when developing marketing strategies.

However, the three elements are inter-related. As Fisk, Grove and John (2000) contend:

> Any effort to affect customer response by stressing aspects of one element may require or result in changes in the other elements. Redesigning the process of service assembly to emphasise more customer participation in the service production will require a change in the participant's role and the physical evidence.

People (participants)

The first of the elements to be considered is people or participants. While Borden (1964) indicated the importance of people in his original research article, it was only in specific instances. However people are invariably required to provide support for both products and services. It is also easy to fall into the trap of only considering those that are in direct contact with the customer. Cowell (1984) raises this, and points out that the customer does not see many of the people involved in providing the product–service interrelationship. Equally, as pointed out earlier, it is not just the 'service' provider or employee within this equation, it is also customers. They must be considered a focus of attention.

For example, let us consider those involved in food manufacture. The simplified Figure 12.1 illustrates some of the people involved in delivering the product to the customer. (At

Table 12.1   The extended marketing mix

Mix variable or element	Description
People (participants)	This includes customers, employees and suppliers. It can be described as the 'communities' involved in the marketing relationship.
Physical evidence (physicality)	This is the tangible (or physical) aspects of the 'delivery' of the product or service, for example, the layout of a supermarket or a restaurant.
Process	This is the assembly or flow activities that support the fulfilment of other elements of the marketing mix, for example, credit card transactions.

Seed manufacturer
↓
Distribution/logistics
↓
Farmer
↓
Distribution/logistics
↓
Processor
↓
Distribution/logistics
↓
Packager
↓
Distribution/logistics
↓
Retailer
↓
Consumer (important to consider the consumer's reaction to the process of delivery)

Figure 12.1   People involved in delivering food products to consumers

People are the key to success of any organization. Through their actions, attitudes and appearance they both provide the public face of the organization and help to generate revenues. Tourists probably take the tying up of their ferry for granted, however it is the expertise of both the onboard and shore crew that make it an efficient, comfortable and, most importantly, safe part of the journey from A to B.

various stages in this chain a marketing department is involved, promoting the product/service to the next in the chain.)

People are important in all organizations. They often provide the initial impression of the whole organization, from their behaviour and general attitude. It is therefore clear that companies depend upon people and their interaction with clients or customers for successful business transactions. So it is important that the organization's staff have the skills and knowledge to be able to present the right image and level of service quality. Yet as Hoffman and Bateson (1997) point out:

> Consider any service industry, and look to the individuals who are the most responsible for customer interactions and customer perception of quality delivered, and you will most likely see the lowest paid and least respected individuals in the company. It makes no sense!

You just have to consider receptionists and waiters in hotels to realize that these people are fundamental to the successful delivery of customer service. Yet, as Hoffman and Bateson say, they may be the poorest paid, and in some cases the poorest trained.

Cowell (1984) develops the point by emphasizing the importance of carefully selecting and training customer contact personnel. The major role of these employees is in 'boundary spanning'. They are often the only link between the organization and the customer. They need to be able to cope with that role, which often means that they need to be more flexible and adaptive than other employees. Even in organizations like the fast-food chain McDonald's, it is recognized that customers are not all the same and therefore the offering and the way of providing it may have to be adapted from customer to customer. This invariably means careful selection and training of customer contact people, as this is crucial to the well-being of the organization.

McLean (1995), considering the marketing of museums, raises some of the problems

when she asks which comes first, the collection (in the museum) or the cleaning of the washrooms? She continues to develop the role of people in this context:

> As with most service organizations, frontline personnel, such as attendants and shop assistants, are a crucial factor in marketing where they are often the only visible representative of the museum, the curatorial staff usually working behind the scenes.

The concept of people being a major component in the marketing mix has, in many ways, led to the development of the concept of internal marketing. Bateson (1989) uses an article by Benjamin Schneider to propose the view that it has the task of creating service enthusiasts: 'These are the individuals who are able to strike the correct balance, when dealing with customers, between the demands of the organization and the needs of the customer.'

Varey (1995) develops the concept of the internal market, and proposes that it is the basis for improving internal working relationships between functional specialists by taking a social process perspective. He concludes,

> Internal marketing is a process and mechanism for ensuring effective responsiveness to environmental changes, flexibility for adopting newly designed administrative arrangements efficiently, and continuous improvement in performance. Internal marketing can assist the organization to match its responses to environmental change and to enhance its capability continuously.

It could be argued, therefore, that all the people employed by any organization are part of the provision of the organization, and as such their role is primarily one of serving the clients or customers. This role is an integral part of the satisfactions sought and the benefits offered by the product offering of the organization. It is a fundamental part of the marketing mix which is pertinent to all industries, as clearly stated by Levitt (1972). Yet without a specific reference to the people aspect of the mix, all the emphasis is given to the tangible product, and any augmentation realized from the support by the people is overlooked.

However, although people are important to the delivery of the marketing mix, we cannot assume that there is homogeneity in delivery. Standards in delivery vary for many reasons, for example:

▌ Individuals' personal attitudes to their roles/job. They may like or hate their jobs, and this may be reflected in their attitude and delivery. Their negative attitude may be a result of several issues, including a poor motivational environment and/or poor payment for their input.

▌ The quality of the motivational environment. This relates the point made above. While motivation comes from within the individual, there needs to be a positive motivational environment to support an individual's personal ambitions and goals. If for example, there is a 'blame culture', individuals will not be motivated beyond the basic standard enforced on them through fear. Such an environment will not retain the best employees, as they will seek alternative employment. Equally, customers will be quick to pick up on the feelings, or to use a slightly archaic word, 'vibes' given off by the staff. This will have a negative effect on customer relations.

▌ Individuals' lack of training. This may not be their own fault, but the fault of management who have neglected to implement an effective training programme.

▌ A poor training programme. This links to the point above, and can be equally damaging to an organization. Training for the sake of training has little or no value. Training must be effective, efficient and relate to the individual's job within the organization.

As you can see from the above points, the quality of human resource management has an impact upon the marketing and delivery of a product or service.

Physical evidence (also known as physicality)

This element is what the client or customer can see or feel that is supporting the actual product/service. Churchill and Peter (1998) suggest that physical surroundings influence buyer behaviour:

> An attractive display may influence need recognition by stimulating a desire to try something new. A quiet, elegant bank lobby may signal that the institution is stable and professional, thereby stimulating a decision to open an account there.

For example if we consider a major supermarket, the following would define 'physicality'. It is important to consider all the human senses when looking at store design and layout, and the use of smell should not be overlooked when the whole notion of atmospherics is considered.

Aisles and sections

The aisles and sections within the store will be laid out or regimented in a particular way. Products will be displayed at key points throughout the supermarket to maximize the opportunity to 'see' and thus purchase.

Checkout counters

The way the checkout counters are organized is another element. Consideration of payment areas should be seen as part of the image making of the outlet. These need to be positioned where they will be easy to see and reach, but must also be secure. The potential problem of crowding around the cash desk must be taken into account, and extra cash points should be available to bring into action at busy times. Having made a choice customers do not want to be kept waiting around to pay for their purchases. Equally the number of checkouts can provide a distinct physicality:

▌ Express checkouts: those for shoppers with a small number of items in a basket, usually six or less.

▌ Wide sections: these are for shoppers with special needs, for example those with children's prams and buggies, or for the disabled so they can move far more easily. Additionally, there may be additional assistance provided by staff who will pack and carry to the customer's car.

▌ Standard sections: for the remainder of the shoppers.

Ease of access

Easy access to the goods or displays will encourage people to get involved, then possibly purchase the products. The displays are the centrepiece of the store's atmosphere. They need to reflect both the store and the products being offered. With some product ranges the supplier organizes the display for the retail outlet as part of the sales service. However, care must be taken to ensure that the overall impression of the store is not compromised by one particular range of products.

The products themselves will be displayed within distinct categories, for example cereals. The cereals themselves will be ordered or positioned in a particular way, for example, the well-known brands on the middle to top shelves (at average eye level), the store's own-label product on the middle and lower row(s), then on the lowest shelves normally the cheaper unbranded products.

Customers select most readily from goods displayed at eye level (generally 60–62 inches for a woman, a little higher for men). This puts very high or low shelves at a corresponding disadvantage, and many shops have plenty of both in order to maximize utilization of space. There are problems here with the volume of stock to be carried and displayed, but customers may resent having to shop on their hands and knees. Manufacturers must spend part of their promotion and sales effort on securing space for their products in the prime locations.

Customers are less likely to pick up, or browse, from any layout that appears accident-prone, for instance if they think they might not be able to balance an item back in position or that other items may fall, especially if they fear damaging something, especially if it is fragile, valuable or both. This is important because in certain shops customers need to pick up and inspect the product, indeed they may not be prepared to buy without doing so.

Relationship between product types

Customers expect to find related items close at hand (for example, pens, pencils and paper go naturally together; products like strawberries and cream might seem to go in different areas – fruit, and dairy products – but will sell well together).

Colour

Colour has a fashion, and an image connotation – bright may be seen as brash – so it must be carefully chosen. This applies to display materials, for example a backcloth in the window, as well as decoration. Too dull, however, and it is not noticed.

Lighting

The lighting must be good, perhaps especially in shops where clear vision of, say, colour of a product is important. If something cannot be found or seen clearly no one will buy it, and people's patience is limited.

Seating

Some stores want to encourage browsing, so if lack of space does not prohibit, they provide some chairs and perhaps a stool near the till for older customers.

Background music

This can arouse strong opinions. Some people like it while some hate it, even loathe it. However the reverse, a library-like silence, can be equally irritating for some. Certainly careful choice and consideration of volume level is necessary. Some companies seem to favour relaxing, predominantly classical and soft jazz, music that becomes very much part of their overall style. Others go for a much brasher approach.

Signage and corporate identity

Again, as people are reluctant to ask, there must be sufficient signs, and all must be clear and direct people easily to everything in the shop. In addition, many signs are virtually in-store advertisements, and these can be used to good effect. This is an area first for clarity, but that can also be used creatively in a shop. It is another area where simple ideas and variety can be useful. With control of image in mind some retailers go their own way and have their own signs and posters in their stores. Others take and use material from their suppliers (another aspect of marketing is to make what is offered attractive and desirable).

The staff may be dressed in uniforms that reflect the corporate identity of the company.

The company's corporate identity will be reflected in the colours used on the company's own branded products, the fascia of the buildings, the shelving units, the customer service desk and any information leaflets (these may include recipes using produce from the store).

Security

This is now a critical aspect of any retail environment in most countries, providing visibility through, for example, closed circuit television (CCTV). So too is simple vigilance by both the retail and security staff. Retailing is unfortunately rarely sufficiently profitable to sustain a high level of theft without concern. Thus security measures become part of the physical characteristics of the supermarket. Beyond theft, the risk of terrorist attacks must be considered, especially within the United States and Europe. Such atrocities not only kill and injure innocent citizens but also damage businesses, and in turn have a detrimental impact on their stakeholders. Paramount amongst these are the retail staff.

Shostack (1977) raises the idea of focusing on the evidence. With product marketing it is not always possible to control much of the evidence, so emphasis is given to creating abstract associations. However:

> Service marketers, on the other hand, should be focused on enhancing and differentiating 'realities' through manipulation of tangible clues. The management of evidence comes first for service marketers, because service 'reality' is arrived at by the consumer mostly through a process of deduction, based on the total impression that the evidence creates. Because of product marketing's biases, service marketers often fail to recognize the unique forms of evidence that they can normally control and fail to see that they should be part of marketing's responsibilities.

Cowell (1984) identifies two kinds of physical evidence, and considers that a distinction should be made between them.

Peripheral evidence

He describes this as the evidence actually possessed as part of the service. In itself it has no value, but it is used to confirm the service.

This can be as simple as a bus or train ticket. However, it may include items available for the use of guests in a hotel, for instance guides to local attractions.

Essential evidence

This cannot be possessed by customers but only used by them to obtain the core service element. Examples of essential evidence are available in the entire business environment, whether it is your college library, a concert hall or luxury hotel or cruise ship. Bateson (1989) explains the concept by stating that the physical environment encompasses more than just the housing for the operation process. 'The configuration of the room, the decor, the lighting – are all part of the "tangible clues". Many of these physical characteristics are seen by the consumer and must therefore be viewed as part of the product.'

The form of physical evidence is not just limited to the decor and so on: it is extended to all aspects of the service provided. The UK-based long-haul transportation company Eddie Stobart is an example. It not only has all their vehicles in corporate colours but also has its drivers wear company uniforms. The vehicles are regularly cleaned. Additionally, the whole concept has been extended by the use of scale model vehicles produced in the company livery. This form of physical evidence is used to build and sustain a differential advantage in the marketplace.

The physical evidence must, however, be tailored to the customer target. Different things will appeal to different consumer profiles, and the use of shape, colour and even sound can alter the appeal and hence the perceived value. The actual location of the organization can also alter expectations, and it is important to ensure that the physical evidence being offered is in keeping with the general location from which it is being provided.

Hoffman and Bateson (1997) adequately sum up the range of physical evidence that a potential customer will use to try to formulate the evaluation of the service that they may receive.

> A firm's physical evidence includes, but is not limited to, facility exterior design elements such as the architecture of the building, the firm's sign, parking, landscaping and the surrounding environment of the firm's location; interior design elements such as size, shape and colours, the firm's entrance and foyer areas, equipment utilized to operate the business, interior signage, layout, air quality and temperature; and other physical evidence that forms customer perceptions, including business cards, stationary, billing statements, reports and the appearance of personnel and the firm's brochures.

However, negative aspects can be derived from physical evidence. For example, consider supermarket aisles partially blocked by in-store promotion bins. This can hamper customers, especially the elderly and those with small children, moving along the aisles safely and efficiently. As another example, the fascia of a hotel may look stunning when first constructed. However, the impact of weather and age may have a detrimental impact on the look. This could impact upon people's perception of quality standards once inside the hotel. It is therefore important to ensure that all the physical evidence surrounding the service package reinforces the image or perception of the product and company.

Two very different clothing stores, one marketing sports clothes (above), the other upmarket women's clothing (below and over the page). However, in both cases their signage and window displays provide physical evidence for the prospective customer.

Buildings portray identities and images, and present guests with 'physicality'. These photographs show how structures can provide both a sense of history as well as privacy and seclusion for their guests. The design of this Marrakech hotel (previous page and above) not only portrays a Moorish history but luxury as well. The grounds of this Spanish hotel (below) provide space and views as well as seclusion. Again, these are physical evidence factors that assist in the marketing of these and many other hotels globally.

Process

This element forms what may be described as the backbone of the way the service is offered, or indeed delivered. Consequently it has a direct influence on the quality of the service that is offered to the customer. It is important to consider here the influence of technology. By the time this text is published there may have been a further technological revolution. We suggest that you reflect on the points discussed within Chapter 2 and this chapter, then investigate further.

Booms and Bitner (1981) in their original thesis suggested that this was the 'process of service assembly'. Cowell (1984) explains that the process element has been derived from operations management. The traditional emphasis on manufacturing has now changed, and specialists in operations management are transferring their skills and knowledge into the service functions. The type of process being used will depend in many ways on the degree of contact between the processing system and the customer. This obviously portrays an image of the service quality in the minds of both the providers of the service and their customers.

The quality perception then forms the basis of the acceptability of the service being offered. Ballantyne and Payne (1995) point out that:

> The difficulty is that customers are continually experiencing and evaluating service performance in particular settings. They are continually "adjusting" their perceptions of customer service. Once something is "fixed" or "improved" other important service issues will naturally emerge. And when one among many critical service issues is resolved, the priority levels naturally change places.

This problem is exacerbated by the fact that customers tend to demand service at unpredictable intervals. While some work has been done in attempting to forecast demand patterns on service organizations, the results are not always useful. This is mainly because the sudden change in demand can be caused by an uncontrollable external incident. A clear example of this is when five or six coachloads of people arrive at a motorway or highway service centre area within a short time frame. This closeness of arrival is unlikely to have been planned and might have been caused by a minor accident blocking one carriageway of the motorway 10 miles from the service area. But still, all of a sudden the outlet has to contend with 300 customers all arriving within a five minute time span, and demanding some form of service: food, newspapers/magazines and/or washroom facilities.

Hoffman and Bateson (1997) specifically raise this issue when they discuss the service delivery process and some of the operational problems. They consider the inputs to the service system, the physical environment, contact personnel, other customers and the individual customer. They state that the environment may remain constant, however the three other inputs (or elements) are totally variable in their quality and rate of arrival into the process. They continue to explain the problems facing the service provider:

> Moreover, contact personnel are individuals, not inanimate objects. They have emotions and feelings and, like all other people, are affected by things happening in their lives outside work. If they arrive in a bad mood, this can influence their performance throughout the day. And that bad mood directly affects the customer, since the service worker is part of the experience being purchased.
>
> Customers can also be subject to moods that can affect their behaviour toward the service firm and one another. Some moods are predictable, like the mood when the home team wins and the crowds hit the local bars. Other moods are individual, specific and totally unpredictable until after the consumer is already part of the service system.
>
> (Hoffman and Bateson, 1997)

The process therefore has a very direct effect on the perceived quality of the service that is being offered, and is probably the most difficult element of the marketing mix to control or manage.

Types of process

We suggest that there are two main types of process, technological and non-technological.

Technological impact upon processes

Perhaps the three interlinking areas that have impacted process are computerization, electronic point of sale (EPOS) and barcoding. The three are very much key to the technological revolution. The rapid development of computer technology, especially microchip technology, in the 1980s led to increased speed and the ability to store large amounts of data.

Barcodes

The Westinghouse Corporation introduced the original concept of the barcode as early as 1929 (Hillman and Gibbs, 1998).[1] The original intention was to use them to sort electricity bills, however the system was not fully developed. Between 1932 and 1948 various researchers including Wallace Flint and his team at Harvard Business School, and Bernard Silver and Norman Woodland at the Drexel Institute of Technology in the United States worked on the development of a barcode system. Silver and Woodland filed a patent application in 1949, which was eventually issued in 1952. Several companies ranging from NCR, IBM and RCA were involved at different stages trying to create a reality out of the concept (Hillman and Gibbs, 1998).

However, it was not until 1974 that the first fully effective grocery store barcode scanner was introduced. On 26 June 1974 a 10-packet of Wrigley's Juicy Fruit chewing gum with a barcode was scanned in the Marsh Supermarket, Troy, Ohio (Hillman and Gibbs, 1998). (This pack of chewing gum was not consumed. It is on display at the Smithsonian Institution's National Museum of American History.) This was the beginning of a computerized shopping revolution that has impacted on both retailers and shoppers. IBM and other computer companies later developed the barcode that we now see on virtually all products.

The 13 internationally recognized lines and spaces on the barcode represent the manufacturer's identity and product number. This information is read by a laser-beam scanner at the checkout, which transfers it to the checkout till and the retailer's in-store database. From the barcode not only can the price be recognized, but the product description, size and stock location.

The advantages of the link between EPOS and barcodes include:

For the customer:

▌ an itemized receipt;

▌ faster and more accurate check through of items than conventional methods.

For the retailer:

▌ more efficient use of checkout staff;

▌ a real-time analysis of stock purchases and stock levels. This aids the replenishment of stock to the benefit of both the retailer and the customer;

▌ the ability, linked to a loyalty card system, for the retailer to build a profile of customers and use direct mail, for instance, to target key customers with special offers or other marketing incentives.

For the staff:

▌ reduces the error of margin, especially during a long day;

▌ automatically calculates the amount of coins/notes that need to be handed back to the customer in change.

Today scanning devices do not have to be stationary. The new generation of barcode scanners increase customers' control. Consumers can collect a barcode self-scanning reader as they enter the store. As they walk around the store with their trolley, they scan the products and place them in their trolleys. The scanner monitor displays information including the customer's name and any special promotions/incentives designed for him or her (in real time), and calculates an ongoing bill. The scanner already has customers' loyalty card details, so points are added to their account and their individual shopping profiles are updated. When customers complete their shopping they enter their credit/debit card details into the scanner to pay the bill. The shopping remains in the trolley, thus removing the time spent unloading and reloading the trolley. The overall aim is to personalize the shopping experience.

Barcodes are however not only the domain of retailers. With digital convergence of technology barcodes can now be placed virtually anywhere. Barcode readers are increasingly incorporated into pens and mobile phones. Technology will allow customers to pay their bills by scanning with their mobile phone or laser pen.

As indicated earlier, the aim of process is to deliver additional benefits for the customer. In Chapter 4 we considered how the low-cost airline easyJet operates. It and other airlines allow customers to book online. EasyJet operate a ticketless travel system. Passengers receive an e-mail containing their travel details and confirmation details. This is all the ticketing passengers require for their journey.

As this is an academic textbook, it is perhaps appropriate to close this section with a university example. To speed applications from both international and nationally based students, universities are increasingly developing online application forms. Your college or university might already have adopted such a system; indeed, you might have prepared and submitted your application by this means.

The technological future

Ever since the 1950s there has been a view of a technologically advanced home. In the early perspectives the home would be serviced by a robotic maid. Technology has developed significantly since those early experiments.

Several companies such as LG Electronics of South Korea have invested in the development of home networks, creating a digital home. For example, LG Electronics announced in June 2000 the introduction of its Internet Digital DIOS Refrigerator. Through its LCD information window it can display details on its temperature, use-by dates, and cooking instructions for the products stored inside.

Again, such appliances use scanner technology to read the barcodes of the products as they are placed in the refrigerator. The next step in the development of this technology is systems to alert the owner, via Internet or WAP technology, what should be consumed that day. Once the refrigerator's supplies become low, its on-board computer will be able to order more groceries via the Internet. Thus there will be links, via the Internet, from the household refrigerator to the grocery supplier. The technology aims to create a process that relieves the consumer of the shopping burden. The various elements of this technology are already available. While initial home network systems will probably be premium priced, it will not be many years before they are readily available.

Non-technological processes

Generally the literature focuses on technology as an aid to process. However, it need not be so. Completing forms, for instance, can be an irritation for many people. You just have to consider the average credit card application, for example. In the 1990s American Express instigated a personalized direct mail campaign in the UK with very much a minimalist card application form. The introductory letter invited those who had received the direct mailer to consider the benefits of an Amex card. If they decided they wanted to apply for the card, all they had to do was complete three boxes: their requested credit limit (minimum and maximum were stated), signature and date. American Express would undertake the rest of the processing, and that would include the appropriate credit reference checks. It is clear that American Express had carefully selected its target audience and made it as easy as possible to apply. Such simplicity can be applied to other application forms, whether they are submitted by post or via e-mail.

There are also potential negative aspects to the process element. They include the following:

■ Customers are increasingly dependent on computer technology. Any failure within the system could severely impact on them. For instance, the shutdown of a bank's ATM system impacts its customers' ability to obtain funds, especially outside normal banking hours.

■ Barcode scanners provide a system for the rapid identification of produce. However, in a supermarket, this can mean that the produce piles up at the end of the counter as the customer tries to bag it. This can cause delays to the customers following, who want to check through their produce. Depending upon the amount that they have to check through, they may encounter exactly the same problem. To counteract this type of log-jam, many supermarket chains have trained packers who assist customers, especially the elderly.

■ With self-scanning devices there may be an assumption that everyone is pro-technology or technology literate. While many children of school age are exceptionally computer/technology literate, not everyone is. Thus it may be some time before consumers are prepared to adopt such technology. (You may want to consider Rogers' diffusion of innovation research here. See Chapter 8.)

■ We perhaps have all experienced computer failure or 'lockout' at some time or other. Nothing could be more irritating for a customer who is ordering or buying online to see the system crash half-way through an order placement. Systems are much improved today from a few years ago. However, that does not totally prevent the system from 'crashing'.

Marketing insight: Hilton Hotels

In 1919 Conrad Hilton purchased his first hotel in Cisco, Texas. However, the first hotel to carry the Hilton brand was not built until 1925, and situated in Dallas, Texas. In 1943 Hilton became the first US coast-to-coast hotel chain, and by 1949 it had opened its first overseas hotel in San Juan, Puerto Rico. Over the following years it built itself into one of the leading international hotel brands.

In 1964 Hilton Hotel Corporation sold the rights to the Hilton brand outside the United States. Now the Hilton Brand, outside the United States, is owned by Hilton Group plc. This is a separately traded company based in the UK and listed on the London Stock Exchange. The Hilton Group plc and its wholly owned subsidiary Hilton International Company own the rights to the Hilton brand outside the United States.

However, since 1997 a worldwide strategic marketing alliance, which unites the brand on a global basis from the customer's perspective, has existed between the two companies. This cooperation includes loyalty programmes and central reservations. This strategic alliance has created a worldwide network of over 2,000 hotels in over 60 countries. In all that is approximately 400,000 rooms. In 1999 over 8 million guests stayed at Hilton International hotels.

Physical evidence

What is important to the success of any hotel is its 'physicality'. This includes the layout of its entrance, public spaces, washroom facilities, the design and amenities of the bedrooms, suites and executive rooms. Hilton Hotels has created a range of brands to cater for different segments of the market. These range from international business travellers through to families who seek highly cost-effective accommodation. In all cases the physicality of the hotel must be supportive of the customer. This is important to the overall brand image of the business.

People

A hotel is very much more than bricks and mortar. Without its staff it literally could not function. No matter what their role within the hotel, cleaner, concierge, chef, waiter, valet or general manger, they all have a significant role in the effective functioning and image of the hotel. Additionally, many international hotels such as the London Hilton have multilingual staff.

Process

Selection and reservation can be achieved by telephone, fax and the Internet. Using the Web site the potential customer can search availability by hotel and room type/price. Reservations can be made over a secure connection. Currently (2002) the US Hilton's wireless reservation system provides access through internet-accessible palmtops or WAP-enabled mobile phone systems. This allows the customer to:

- find a Hilton, Conrad or Garden Inn hotel worldwide;
- review descriptions of the hotel;
- display room availability;
- reserve a room;
- retrieve/cancel a room.

Loyalty card scheme: Hilton Honors (HHonors)

This loyalty scheme operates worldwide and allows business customers to accrue points against their hotel stay. The more a customer uses a Hilton and related brand hotels, the more bonus points he or she collects. This can also be linked into Air Miles if the person is a frequent flyer. Thus regular travellers are automatically rewarded for their stay.

Payment mechanisms

Like all international hotels, the Hilton chain operates a range of payment mechanisms from corporate accounts through to individual credit cards.

Questions/activities

1. Visit a Hilton or similar ranking/standard hotel and consider how the people (employees), physical evidence and processes add to the overall marketing of the hotel. For this exercise you may also want to log into the company's Web site.
2. The Hilton chain, for example, is an internationally renowned hotel brand. What do you consider to be the potential difficulties in providing consistent service standards globally? Consider this in terms of people, physical evidence and processes.
3. On a regular basis log on to the Hilton.com Web site and consider any new developments in processes to assist customers further. Consider how these developments are influenced by technology.

Sources: Hilton Group plc Annual Report 1999, www.hilton.com.

Chapter summary

In Chapter 1 we concluded that there was still a significant role for the marketing mix. The three Ps of people, physical evidence and process had previously been the domain of the service industry or service marketing. However, it is clear that these three Ps have a significant impact upon the marketing of both products and services. Therefore we conclude that there is a generic mix that includes people, physical evidence and process.

People are clearly an integral element within any marketing operation. This was a focus in Chapter 2 when we considered the micro environment and stakeholders. In Chapter 10 the role of the sales force provides a clear indication of their proactive and reactive roles within an organization. Equally, in this chapter the importance of people has been explored.

Physical evidence is increasingly being extended from the sheer physicality of a building through to elements within the structure. Consider, for instance, your college buildings, the elements within (the books on the library shelves) through to the surrounding environment: for example the sports fields, embankments, fountains and car parks. All add to the physicality and the marketing of the college.

In process, computer technology has rapidly changed how products and services are processed for the customer. The change is far from over. Self-scanning equipment and the Internet are yet to impact fully upon this aspect of society.

What is clear though is that people, physical evidence and processes are vital to the overall cohesion of the marketing mix.

Exercises and questions for review and critical thinking

1. Generally, when marketing literature covers people, physical evidence and processes it tends to focus on the positive aspects. What are the possible negative aspects of these three Ps and how do you think that they can be overcome?

2. 'People, physical evidence and processes – individually and collectively – can deliver significant competitive advantage for a company.' Discuss.

3. Process appears to be increasingly focused on technology. Consider possible non-technology-driven methods of improving processes that will benefit customers.

4. Reflect back to Chapter 1. Again consider the various arguments for and against the marketing mix. Having read both this chapter and Chapter 1, do you consider the marketing mix to be relevant? Why?

5. In this chapter various individual examples have been introduced, culminating in an end of chapter case. Using the three elements of people, physical evidence and process seek out and detail two other examples. They must be from two separate business sectors.

13

Placement, distribution and logistics

Introduction

As Davidson (1997) states, marketing channels exist to link producers to customers, whether they are businesses or individuals. Products, whether they are *Harry Potter* books, medicines, technical equipment or raw materials, have to be moved to the marketplace and direct contact created with potential buyers. The scale of material and product movements should not be underestimated. For instance, the supply-chain management company Exel coordinates the delivery of materials/products from over 300 separate collection points worldwide for the UK retailer Marks & Spencer (Exel, 2002). In order for a retailer (physical and online) to be successful within a highly dynamic and competitive market, materials and products must reach the right destination at the right time.

Placement, distribution and logistics allow such operations to happen. There are two aspects to this operation. One is concerned with the physical movement of the products from the supplier through intermediaries to the end user. The other is concerned with the channels that are used. Marketing tends to be more concerned with the channels, rather than the physical movement of the product, as the channel has more to do with the way the products are actually offered to the marketplace, and the channel is viewed as part of the overall offering of the benefit. However, it is crucial that marketers also have an understanding of the mechanisms and technologies that allow products to be delivered to the marketplace.

In Chapter 7 we considered the relationship between strategy and marketing. One of the key elements discussed was Porter's value chain model. Both inbound and outbound logistics are primary activities that contribute to the successful placement of a product in the marketplace. When reading this chapter, reflect back to Porter's model and make the links between the model and the importance of effective and efficient distribution.

Learning objectives

On completion of this chapter you will be able to:

- link Porter's supply chain model to the concept of channel management (see Chapter 7);

- explain the concept of marketing channels and the various functions of channel management;

- analyse the role of intermediaries as part of the marketing channel;

- evaluate non-retail methods of distribution, including the Internet, within consumer markets;

- explain how physical distribution integrates with marketing channel management.

Placement

In marketing texts the term 'placement' is used to cover distribution and logistics. This can be seen as putting a particular item or product in a particular place or state/situation, for example placing a product within a supermarket to be purchased. However, it is not as simple as it is often portrayed. The product has to reach the supermarket at the right time, either directly, or through intermediaries. This is the function of logistics, and increasingly a vital component within dynamic competitive environments. We return to the role of logistics later within this chapter.

Logistics

The US Council of Logistics Management (2003) has defined logistics as:

> that part of the supply chain process that plans, implements and controls the efficient, effective forward and reverse flow and storage of goods, services, and related information between the point of origin and the point of consumption in order to meet customers' requirements.

Contemporary logistics was born out of the military campaigns of the Second World War and Korean War. In order to sustain battles and move the offensive forward, military planners needed to be efficient and effective in moving the supply of men, equipment, armaments and support facilities. The military planners achieved this through procurement, maintenance and transportation. Today the movement of materials and finished products is often conducted with the same military precision.

Efficient logistics is vital in the quest for profitable supply chain management.

Channel principles

Let us take the general principles first. It does not matter how well any product or service is promoted and how much customers – and potential customers – want it, it has to be placed into a position which provides them with easy access to it. In other words, it must be distributed. This can be a complex operation, and it is certainly a marketing variable, referred to in the marketing mix as the PLACE (or placement) variable, albeit one that many regard as rather more fixed than it usually is (Forsyth, 1998).

It is necessary to consider the variety of ways in which products are made available to customers. Consumer products can be sold through retailers. These vary enormously in nature, from supermarkets, hypermarkets, shopping malls and department stores through to specialist retailers, general stores and even street market traders. These may, in turn, be variously located: in a town or city centre, in an out-of-town shopping area, in a multi-storey shopping centre or mall, or in a village in the case of a corner shop.

Consumer products can also be sold direct to the consumer. In Chapter 10 we considered direct marketing, and how this can remove the retailer, as companies sell direct to their market. Through direct mail and telemarketing consumers can order products that are then delivered directly to their home or office.

Increasingly businesses are using such direct marketing facilities. Equally, the Internet can provide a direct distribution service. Consider for example how the low-cost airline easyJet provide tickets directly to its customers via the Internet, or Amazon.com supplying a range of products from books to home appliances (see Chapter 4).

Marketing insight: Movies

Most of us enjoy visiting the cinema or watching a DVD. While we may look upon a movie as entertainment, for others it is a business. If a movie costs US $100 million to produce and promote, there has to be significant returns on that investment in order for the product (the movie) to make a profit. Also, whether a movie does well or not could make or break a production company, whether it is large or small. Thus companies seek the widest distribution deals possible.

The multi-million dollar production of *The Lord of the Rings Part 1*(2001) was released in December 2001 through some 10,000 cinemas globally. In addition to cinema or theatrical release companies also seek earn-out through other distribution media. These can be summarized as:

Television – terrestrial
　　　　　　　satellite
　　　　　　　cable
Video – 　　　DVD
　　　　　　　VHS format (PAL, SECAM and NTSC)
Internet.

Internet distribution is currently limited. However, it is clearly possible that this will become a medium for distribution in future. The keys for companies will be payment mechanisms (royalties) and security to prevent piracy.

Of course, this scenario assumes that a movie is a success, at first on the theatrical or cinema circuit. This is not always the case, nationally or internationally. The movie may be made but not find a theatrical distributor, for one reason or another. If so it could go straight to television or video, potentially limiting its distribution and revenue-generating potential. However, there needs to be a word of caution. Movies that have failed at the theatrical box office have become successes through their distribution via television and video.

Questions/activities

1. Outline the possible distribution channels for a new pop record.
2. By analysing press coverage note the distribution channels for both the *Harry Potter* and the *Lord of the Rings* movies.

Business-to-business (B2B) and industrial products are similarly complex in the range of distributive options they use.

Davidson (1997) suggests that consumers seek eight key qualities to be delivered through the marketing channels. These are adapted and detailed in Table 13.1.

Organizing distribution: channel management

How a company analyses the distributive possibilities and organizes to utilize a chosen method, or methods, effectively is certainly important to overall marketing success. This is really about channel management. The examples below illustrate some of the potential links between the manufacturer or producer and ultimately the buyer and/or consumer (the buyer may not necessarily be the consumer – think, for instance, of birthday gifts).

In many cases there is an intermediary. As Stanton, Etzel and Walker (1994) state, it can 'either own the product at some point or actively aid in the transfer of the ownership'. In some cases the intermediary has physical ownership of the product. You need to consider this aspect when you read Chapter 14 on the international dimensions of marketing. Often companies seek to use a range of intermediaries before they venture directly into the global marketplace.

Intermediaries can be described as wholesalers and/or agents. In some texts, and in some countries/cultures the intermediary is referred to as the middleman.

B2C environment

Within the B2C environment several channels of distribution exist. This covers both product and service environments. See Figure 13.1 for one example.

Table 13.1 Eight key consumer needs from marketing channels

Need	Description
Clarity	What does the channel sell and actually mean (this could be a value)?
Convenience	Is it easy to obtain the product, via a visit to a store (parking, ease of access, opening hours) or delivery services (physical or online)?
Range	A choice of relevant products and services that meet the need of the customer.
Price	Range of pricing points and methods of payment that suit customers' needs.
Quality	Does the price relate to the quality of the product or service? In other words, is the customer receiving value for money?
Service	Level of support received by the customer. Transaction time – the time that elapses between the order placement and delivery of that order.
Environment	This relates the product or service to the environment in which it is to be consumed. For example, is it easy to use? Consider, for instance, the delivery of a pizza. The customer will ask, is it hot enough? Has it been delivered in suitable packaging to retain both its heat and freshness for the customer to consume on delivery? If not, it is probably going to be a far from enjoyable experience.
Image	What is the image of the product or service? Does it match other factors such as price and quality?

The manufacturer/producer

↓

The intermediary
(the retailer)

↓

The consumer

Figure 13.1   B2C distribution channels:
example 1

In this example, the intermediary (in this case a retailer) has purchased the product directly from the manufacturer/producer and sells it to the consumer. Reflect back to Chapter 8, where we discussed own-label brands. An example here is the Co-Op Brio-Actipods outlined in the 'Marketing insight' on page 290. McBride manufacture the Liquid Tabs on behalf of the Co-Op which then (as retailer) sells them directly to the consumer.

Another example is the purchase of an airline ticket through a travel agent which, in turn, has to contact the airline to make the reservation. The reservation may be made there and then; however, the ticket might not be delivered for several days. Then the customer has to arrive at the airport and board the aircraft. Subsequently, the aircraft must take off and reach its destination for the transaction and service to have been fulfilled.

The manufacturer/producer

↓

Intermediary
(a wholesaler)

↓

Retailer

↓

The consumer

Figure 13.2   B2C distribution channels:
example 2

The example in Figure 13.2 depicts the traditional distribution route from the manufacturer through to the consumer. For many retailers throughout the world this is (currently) the only means by which they obtain products to sell to their consumers. You may want to consider how your local grocery store obtains the products it sells to you.

The manufacturer/producer

↓

The consumer

Figure 13.3   B2C distribution channels:
example 3

The route in Figure 13.3 is portrayed in the standard literature as the most direct route for a producer to interact with a consumer. While we outline some possible combinations below, we believe there should be some consideration as to the level of directness. In the following examples there is still some form of intermediary involved (although perhaps in the background). In direct marketing there are such services as couriers and the national postal service involved. They should be considered within the distribution equation, most especially in terms of logistics. The efficiency of the logistics might gain a company a competitive advantage, not just locally but internationally as well.

From a service perspective, the 'manufacturer' to consumer activity could include banking and other financial services, legal assistance, health care and household repair work. Increasingly, universities are exploring delivering both short courses and MBA programmes via the Internet. These vary in terms of whether they are fully online or online-supported programmes. However, the issue is that it is direct between the producer (the university lecturer) and the student, although via an Internet connection. Later in this chapter we consider how a UK supermarket chain has developed an efficient online grocery business alongside its traditional 'bricks and mortar' store business.

Marketing insight: the *Financial Times*

The *Financial Times* (*FT*), published in Britain, is one of the world's leading business broad-sheet daily newspapers. It has distinctive pink pages. There are several ways the *FT* is delivered to its customer base:

1. Through retail outlets. This is not only in the UK but internationally as well. However, the range of intermediaries depends on whether it is UK retail or international.
2. Through subscription. Receivers include individuals as well as corporations and libraries (business and universities).
3. Via its Web site, www.ft.com. The Internet site covers not only the day's main events but also special reports and surveys. Thus the *FT* is available to anyone, at any time, via the Web. In addition to general business news and features, the *FT* Web site also has an online subscription service which provides access to further business information and sources, depending upon which level of subscription is chosen.

Questions/activities

1. In point 1 above we suggest that several intermediaries are involved in the international distribution of the *Financial Times*. Outline who these intermediaries might be and their function in distributing the newspaper.
2. Consider a quality newspaper in your own country. How many methods of distribution can that newspaper use in order for it to reach its target audience?
3. Do you think Internet distribution will eventually eliminate the more traditional methods of newspaper distribution?

The manufacturer/producer

↓

Intermediary
(agent)

↓

Retailer

↓

The consumer

Figure 13.4   B2C distribution channels:
example 4

In example 4 an agent (this can be an individual or a company) markets/sells a product (which it has purchased and perhaps branded) to a retailer. This is often the case when manufacturers or producers want to break into the international marketplace. Refer to Chapter 14 on the international dimensions of marketing.

The manufacturer/producer

↓

Intermediary
(agent)

↓

Intermediary
(wholesaler)

↓

Retailer

↓

The consumer

Figure 13.5   B2C distribution channels:
example 5

In the example in Figure 13.5 there are several distribution links between the manufacturer/producer and the end consumer of the product. A company might manufacture a product (a generic hair shampoo, for example), and then enter an agreement with an agent. It, in turn, finds the most appropriate wholesaler for the product. The wholesaler might then brand this generic shampoo with its own label and sell it on to a retailer who then markets and sells it to its customers.

B2B environment

This covers both product and service operational environments.

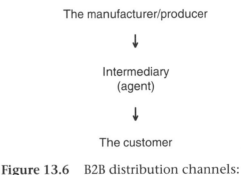

The manufacturer/producer

↓

Intermediary
(agent)

↓

The customer

Figure 13.6   B2B distribution channels:
example 1

In the example in Figure 13.6 the intermediary is the agent. Again this could be an individual, or perhaps more likely a company. There are several possible examples here. For instance, a company might manufacture industrial power tools. These are then sold through specialist trade-only outlets to the end users, in this case builders. The same applies to the purchase of paint and wallpaper by professional decorators. The professional decorators might then be engaged in work for companies (B2B) and/or consumers, as in the example quoted earlier.

Another example, this time service focused, is a business travel broker that arranges travel on behalf of a business customer. The business customer might range from a multinational publishing company, such as HarperCollins, through to a university that has international partnerships. A further example is a sales agent involved in the placement of a service. Later in this chapter we consider the role of Air Foyle and the Antonov Design Bureau in terms of logistics. However, Air Foyle act as worldwide sales agents for the Antonov specialist cargo aircraft.

The manufacturer/producer

↓

The customer

Figure 13.7 B2B distribution channels: example 2

As with the B2C example above, in example 2 there is still a physical logistics issue of moving or delivering the product to the customer. Possible examples are custom-designed turbines for generating companies (which would need transportation expertise, even if it is the company's own transportation service or subsidiary). Perhaps a more direct manufacturer–customer relationship is an aircraft manufacturer (Boeing or Airbus Industries, for instance) that delivers, often to customer specifications, directly to the customer. Either the manufacturer's pilots or the airline's own aircrew would fly the aircraft to the airline's home base.

On the B2B service front, this applies to professional services such as legal, banking, marketing, training and accounting advice.

Multiple distribution channels (dual distribution)

In the examples above we focused on a single distribution channel, for instance B2B. However, some companies' products are ideally suited to both B2C and B2B markets.

How they promote to those markets might be different. For example, the major computer manufacturer and supplier Dell markets its systems directly to both household consumers and businesses via the Internet. The difference is not necessarily in the distribution, but in the specification and quantity required.

Another example is the chartering through specialist companies (ship brokers and charter management consultancies) of luxury motor and sailing yachts. These are often aimed at both the B2C market (the super wealthy) and B2B (corporate hire for special events and client hospitality).

The channels effectively 'bridge the gap' between the manufacturer, the intermediary and the consumer/customer. The main reason that this is necessary is the requirements of economic manufacture in relation to consumer requirements, which are very different. Production often has to be concentrated in one particular location, and needs to be as far as possible on a continuous operational basis or in large volumes. Consumers on the other hand tend to be scattered across a large geographical area, purchase very erratically and usually only want to purchase in relatively small quantities. The use of intermediaries helps to resolve this conflict.

The role of distributors and intermediaries

There are, in fact, a number of good reasons for delegating what is an essential element of the marketing mix, for example (Forsyth, 1998):

▌ Distributive intermediaries provide a ready-made network of contacts which would otherwise take years to establish at what might be a prohibitive cost. Clearly even a large company might balk at the thought of setting up its own chain of specialist shops, especially because of the significant investment in time and other resources. Therefore the incidence of this is very low.

▌ Distributors are objective and not tied to one product. They can offer a range that appeals to their customers, electing to pitch this wide or narrow (some shops sell very narrow ranges, for example only ties, socks, books on sport or blends of coffee). Also they provide a full range of complementary products, which can make sourcing easier for the smaller retail outlet.

▌ Distributors provide an environment that the customer needs in order to make a choice. If different competing brands need to be compared, the customer in the store can conveniently do this. If a distributor stocks a product, and is itself well known and has an attractive image, this might enhance the overall attractiveness of the experience in the eyes of a consumer. In many fields, allowing potential customers to view a wide choice – as in, say, selecting a television set – is in fact an important aspect of encouraging sales.

▌ Distributors can spread the costs of stocking and selling products over all the items they carry, thereby doing so at a lower cost than a manufacturer/supplier operating alone.

▌ The cost of bad debts is sometimes lower than would be otherwise the case. This is because the distributor effectively shares the risk. (However, it may seem otherwise sometimes! Slow payment seems endemic in so many industries and countries.)

▌ Since the distributor is rewarded by a discount off the selling price, no capital is tied up in holding local stocks, though overlong credit can dilute this effect.

▌ Distributors tend to have good specialist knowledge of retailing or distribution, which the manufacturer might not possess. This clearly varies across different kinds of distributor and retailer.

▌ Distributors might also offer to assemble the product before moving it on through the channel, usually in the form of adding on accessories.

▌ They might also display and promote the product in their own showrooms. They provide information both to manufacturers about comments received from their customers and to the customers about the product ranges on offer. Often they supply various forms of after sales service that others in the chain cannot offer.

So far so good, but (there is always a but) there can be conflicts of interest between manufacturers and distributors (Forsyth, 1998):

▌ Distributors may not be as committed to a particular product as its producer is. If the customer prefers another (similar) product, the distributor will often substitute it. For example, if a customer asks a travel agent for advice – 'I want to arrange a weekend break and I see there are some good deals in France' – he or she might instead end up going to the Channel Isles. As the conversation progresses, the travel agent does not necessarily have any particular personal view to support in selling one destination rather than another. In some cases, however, discount structures might lead the travel agent to make particular recommendations that benefit it because it makes more commission selling one destination rather than another.

▌ Distributors might use the manufacturer's product for their own promotional purposes. This is often linked to price cutting, although not every product whose price is cut needs it (a manufacturer may feel it dilutes image, but be powerless to stop it being done).

▌ Distributors might remove the product from their list if they believe they can obtain a better profit with another line (this is known as delisting in the retail trade). This will clearly affect directly competing product lines.

▌ Many distributors expect the manufacturer to stimulate demand for the product, for example by advertising or providing display material. Publishers, for example, supply retail bookshops with posters, dump bins and leaflets to promote particular titles.

▌ Many distributors are tough on business agreements and arrangements. Additionally, distributors can have complex ordering procedures.

The question whether to deal direct with the consumer is therefore dependent first on the availability of suitable channels and their willingness to add additional products to the range they sell. Second, it depends on balancing the economies of the distributors' lower selling and servicing costs with the disadvantages of not being present at the point where customers are making their decisions, and having less control over the selling process.

Realistically, many companies have no option but to go through existing channels (whether these involve retail outlets or not). Exactly how this is achieved and the mix involved can be varied. In addition, more radical variants may need to be found and run alongside (and without alienating) the retail chain; this can certainly be a way of increasing business.

From this we can see that distributors do play a significant part in the marketing of any product or service. The channels carry:

▌ products;

▌ ownership (title);

▌ communication;

▌ finance.

What channels of distribution a company should choose

Although this is, as we have already seen, a decision involving some complex, interlocking issues, six main factors normally influence the route taken (Forsyth, 1998).

Customer characteristics

Distributors are generally required when customers are widely dispersed, there are a large number of them and they buy frequently in small amounts. This is certainly true of many sectors of everyday product purchasing, for example FMCGs. This is less so, or not at all, with regard to more specialist items.

Product characteristics

Direct distribution is required when bulky or heavy products are involved. Bulky products or outsized items (generators and turbines, for instance) need channel arrangements that minimize the shipping distance and the number of handling operations (see the 'Marketing insight' on Air Foyle – Antonov). Even a brief examination of physical distribution costs illustrates the importance of this factor.

Where high unit value can cover higher unit selling costs, any manufacturer can keep control over distribution by dealing direct. This is applicable to certain off-the-page advertising, or at the far end of the spectrum, the companies who sell door to door. Finally, products requiring installation or maintenance are generally sold through a limited network, such as sole agents. For example, in the UK gas central heating systems have to be installed by registered firms for safety reasons.

Marketing Insight: Air Foyle – Antonov

This 'Marketing insight' illustrates the complexity in moving outsized or heavy products. When companies undertake the movement of specialist cargoes they have to consider the product's special characteristics.

Air Foyle is a specialist aviation support company. In addition to operating a fleet of five AN124–100 Ruslans (which is the world's largest commercially operated freighter), they also have available AN12s, AN22s, IL76s, L-100s, nine BAe146 freighters and two Airbus A320 passenger aircraft. Air Foyle provides advisory and management services, air broking, aircraft leasing, sales and operations, aerial survey and executive flight services.

The development of heavy commercial aircraft, with unique handling capabilities, has become invaluable in moving specialist outsize and bulky cargoes. One such aircraft is the AN124–100 Ruslan, designed by the legendary Oleg Konstantinovich Antonov who, together with his company the Antonov Design Bureau, became the master of heavy transport aircraft design and production. With a wing span of 73.3 metres and a length of 69.1 metres, the AN124–100 Ruslan is officially described as the world's largest commercially operated freighter.

The characteristics of this aircraft were ably demonstrated in June 1994 with the transportation of a 109 tonne diesel locomotive from Ontario in Canada to Dublin, Ireland. Following the Irish government's approval in 1993 for an expenditure of IR £20 million (approximately US $41 million), Iarnrod Eireann (Irish Rail) ordered the first of ten newly designed 201 Class Model JT42HCW locomotives from the General Motors Locomotive Group in London, Ontario, Canada. The 201 Class locomotive is capable of over 100 mph with a capacity of hauling 1,500 tonnes at speeds up to 60 mph.

Delivery of the first locomotive was to be made by air in advance of the remaining nine – which were later transported by sea – to allow early proving trials, driver and maintenance training, and systems performance checks. General Motors Locomotive Group, one of the world's largest builders of diesel-electric locomotives, agreed to undertake the airlift in order to meet Irish Rail's urgent training and testing requirements. The use of early proving trials would thus permit the remaining locomotives to go into service immediately after arrival in Ireland.

The AN124–100 Ruslan has particular characteristics that allow it to load and transport unusual and outsized cargoes. Both ends of the aircraft can be accessed by fold-down hydraulic ramps, offering, in effect, full roll-on roll-off capacity. Front-end loading is further enhanced by a large flip-over top nose door, providing clear cargo access which is greater than the Belfast, Boeing 747 or C130 Hercules aircraft. With no restrictions caused by either the nose or tail doors, the entire width and height of the fuselage is available for cargo access.

Consideration was given to using an American C5A Galaxy. However, they are unavailable for commercial use without special permission from the US Defense Department. In addition, the interior was not large enough to accommodate the loading height of the fully assembled locomotive, therefore it would have had to be transported in separate units. In addition, the Ruslan has the unique ability to 'kneel', almost to ground level, on its front undercarriage to enhance drive-on access.

At the General Motors manufacturing plant at Locomotive High Bay, the locomotive was lifted onto skids located on a special 96-wheel, 12-axelled flat-bed transporter platform. Under the supervision of ETARCO (Engineered Transportation and Rigging Company), the transporter was hauled by a powerful 600 horsepower MACK tractor unit for its one and half mile journey to London Airport. In order to minimize delays to local traffic, the load, under police escort, left the plant at 8:00 pm, taking approximately one hour to complete its short journey.

Early the following morning, the transporter platform was guided onto a temporary steel extension ramp and bridge that had been precision mounted to align with the base of the aircraft's cabin. In the cargo cabin broad gauge railway tracks had been bolted to the floor. Once the transporter platform had been aligned, hydraulic jacks were inserted under the locomotive, raising it, then rail tracks were placed underneath the locomotive's wheels. A reverse process was used on arrival at Dublin International Airport. Using the two powerful 30 kN internal winching systems of the AN124–100 Ruslan, the locomotive was then winched, slowly and precisely, from the transporter platform along the rails into the aircraft's fuselage.

With the incorporation of powerful on-board winch systems, heavy loads can be positioned accurately without the need for specialist airport ground-handling equipment. Such internal facilities are vital when using airports that have limited ground-handling equipment and support staff.

Another unique feature of the AN124–100 Ruslan is the double overhead travelling gantry crane utilizing four 5 tonne electrical hoists deployed in pairs on two lifting beams located crosswise inside the fuselage on two rails mounted underneath the ceiling of the aircraft. The gantry can move the length of the fuselage, therefore loading can take place over the rear ramp in the tail of the aircraft as well as the nose. The gantry provides an internal lift capacity of 37 tonnes and allows heavy cargoes to be lifted with minimum preparation. In this particular operation, they were utilized for two specific tasks: first for moving the track sections within the cargo cabin for bolting to the floor, and second for supporting ballast at the rear of the aircraft during both the loading and unloading procedures.

The 201 Class locomotive, measuring 20.5 metres long and 4.014 metres high, comfortably slid into the cargo cabin which is 36.5 metres in length, 4.4 metres high and 6.4 metres wide. Once in position on the aircraft's deck, it was secured for its transatlantic flight by 120 chains hooked over the locomotive, at predetermined slots, and bolted to the cabin floor.

Weight is a crucial factor in transporting such a heavy traction unit. The AN124–100 Ruslan is unique in that it has a reinforced titanium floor which can sustain a floor-loading capacity of 1 kg/sq cm. The aircraft payload capability is 150 tonnes; the locomotive, with its associated bridging sections and equipment, brought the payload to in excess of 146 tonnes. Both the loading and unloading operations took over 12 hours to complete at each location, such was the overall complexity of the task.

Operating with a standard crew of 18, of which 7 were flight crew with the remainder composed of technicians and loadmasters, the flight took some 12 hours to complete with the AN124–100 Ruslan cruising at 750 kph. Because of the load size, refuelling stops had to be made at Montreal, Gander, Newfoundland and Reykjavik prior to final touchdown in Dublin.

UK-based Abnormal Load Engineering, together with Irish Rail, handled the transportation of the locomotive for the seven miles from Dublin International Airport to Irish Rail's Inchicore Yards. Once again, road transportation was undertaken late at night to minimize delays and congestion to local traffic. The combined load of the locomotive and the bridging equipment set a new world record for the heaviest combined commercial airlift. (The previous record was already held by Air Foyle and the Antonov Design Bureau with a combined single airlift of 142 tonnes in 1990).

Sources: Air Foyle/Michael Johnson at Barrington Marketing Services.

Distributor characteristics

Distributors are useful when their skills of low-cost contact, service and storage are important. Few retailers will even consider taking on a new product unless they can be convinced that the demand exists. They need to know which market segment the product is aimed at and whether it fits with their customer profile.

Competitive characteristics

The channels chosen may often be influenced by the channels competitors use, and there may be dangers in moving away too far and too fast from what a market expects. The competitive interaction in this way between retailers is another variable. In the area of fast food, Burger King, for example, try to obtain sites near to McDonald's. On the other hand some manufacturers, such as Avon Cosmetics, choose not to compete for scarce positions in retail stores and have established a highly profitable direct selling operation instead. (Note: in certain markets, for example China, Avon has for regulatory reasons established retail outlets. See Chapter 14 on the international dimension in marketing.)

Similarly, major chains may seek to open branches near existing smaller independent retailers, not only to take advantage of their market knowledge – they are in an area where there is a demand – but with the aim of replacing them all together. This last may well not be entirely in the customers' best interests, and illustrates one aspect of the sheer power of major retailing groups.

Company characteristics

The size of a manufacturing company often, though not always, correlates with its market share. The larger its market share, the easier it is to find distributors willing to handle the product. Thus even a small shop is likely to find a corner for major brand names such as Heinz and Cadbury, and will be selective about what else it stocks. It will not be able to stock everything; however it will find space for anything it believes in. Where there is clearly profit to be made, no one wants to miss out on it. Similarly, a supplier may be innovative (and/or build on a strength) and seek ways of becoming less dependent on the normal chain of distribution.

Creativity can have a role to play here. For instance, cosmetics may sell well in outlets that simply display them, but stores that organize make-up demonstrations (or provide facilities for the manufacturer to do so) create a competitive edge. The next time you are in a major department store, walk around the cosmetic department and study the range of in-store promotions and demonstrations. Some are clearly organized by the store itself, perhaps to push a new range. Others are designed and implemented by staff from the cosmetics companies. Additionally, there may be giveaways or samples for customers. Reflect on the direct marketing or promotion activity taking place.

Additionally, a policy of fast delivery is less compatible with a large number of stages in the channel, and there is a danger that slow delivery (measured in market terms) will dilute marketing effectiveness. As customers expect increased standards of service, there is less room for anyone that lags behind. Slow delivery is increasingly unacceptable to customers, as are restricted delivery times.

Macro environmental characteristics

Changes in the macro environment can also bring about changes in distributive structures. (Refer back to Chapter 2.) For example, when the market is depressed, manufacturers want to move their goods to market in the most economical way possible. Thus they may cut out intermediaries, or unessential services, to compete on price and deal direct with the end user. Again, legal restrictions have been introduced in the UK in recent years to prevent channel characteristics that may weaken the competitive environment.

Overall trends within retailing also influence how things are done. Out of town shopping, the use of the car (or restrictions on it), and everything from the rental cost to the desirability of an area influences the likelihood of shoppers patronising a particular area, and thus a particular shop. Certainly this influences where a range of products can be bought, and this in turn can influence what is bought.

An example is the development of Covent Garden market in London. This is a former vegetable and fruit market. It is now an attractive area of restaurants and entertainment as well as shops, which attracts people from far and wide. Someone buying perhaps a present in a shop there might choose something different from what they might have bought elsewhere. Such decisions are based on what is there, how it is displayed and more.

A major retailing trend in some countries has been, and remains, a focus on out of town shopping centres. In some, small, independent shops fit in well. In others, branches of large retail chains predominate, so the environment might not be right for the small shop owner.

The more expansive the environmental change, the more likely it is to have repercussions. And there are doubtless plenty of changes still to come in this area.

Usually it is possible to identify several different types of channel or distributor. In certain sectors some of the alternatives may be farther from standard practice than they are in other sectors. However, that does not mean they are not worthy of consideration, or cannot be part of the distribution mix. Situations that are normal now might originally have been difficult to establish.

Some companies are, of course, bound to the standard form in their field. However the point here is that it pays to remain open minded. Channels might change little, and

traditional routes might remain the most important, creating the greatest volume of business, but other possibilities could still create significant growth.

There are still without doubt many possible innovations in prospect for distribution (the Internet is just one of current interest), and things that seem unlikely today will no doubt be looked back on in years to come as entirely normal. We all have 20/20 hindsight. The key for suppliers is to make sure some marketing time, effort and thinking goes into exploring and testing new methods. This is, of course, true of most things; however distribution is a prime candidate, for the very reason that many see it as essentially static, at least in the short term. Perhaps this just means there is all the more possibility of using it to create a competitive edge over more conservative competitors.

So alternatives need be explored to see which channel or combination of channels best suits the company's objectives and constraints. However, the best choice of channel must take into account the degree to which the company can control, or at least influence, the distribution channel created.

Technology

This has had a significant impact on the ability to move products by road, rail, sea and air. As was outlined in Chapter 2, technological advances especially since 1960 have significantly enhanced the speed and the range of products that can be delivered within regions and across national boundaries.

As well as the physical methods of distribution – road, rail, sea and air – technology has made a significant impact through information technology (IT). IT systems provide the facilities for the global tracking of shipments, not only by freight forwarders but also by their customers through Internet sites. Therefore the freight forwarder's customers know when their own customers will be receiving their products. In addition to improving the flow of goods this can also be used to enhance the customer relationship. For instance, the seller can contact the buyer via e-mail stating that the purchase will arrive on a particular day, even though the seller is not directly involved in the physical movement of the products.

The development of IT systems has dramatically overhauled the operation of channel and distribution management. (See the 'Marketing insight' on fleet management systems and tracking on page 436.)

Distribution management

Chosen distributors are likely to work better on behalf of any manufacturer if communications, support (for example, information, training and service) and motivation are good. However, they will have their own ideas, and a good working relationship must be adopted if both are to profit from the partnership.

At best, all this takes time, and often it is easy to see people simply as suppliers, rather than colleagues to work with. Yet the best can only be extracted from a market when the two parties do work, and work effectively, together.

Although distribution is a key element in marketing, it sometimes goes by default because existing methods are regarded as fixed. However, making existing arrangements work well – and seeking new or additional ones – can create further sales and overall marketing success. Distribution is a vital process that links the company to customers, and thus marketing activity can be made or broken by its performance.

The right methods must be chosen, and then everyone down the line needs to work together effectively. Working through any channel of distribution demands clear policy. All parties should have clear, understood and agreed expectations of each other, and clear agreement on their terms of trade (discounts and all financial arrangements). Sufficient time and resources need to be invested in the ongoing process of managing, communicating with and motivating those organizations and people upon whom sales are ultimately dependent. There is always a range of options.

Some are seen as the norm, others as peripheral or unlikely to work; still more we can not as yet anticipate. However, whatever is done, whatever range of ways is used, this is an area that marketing must aim to influence. It is at the interface, whatever form that takes, that sales are ultimately made. So suppliers must work effectively with what is necessarily a given (and this includes dealing with difficult aspects of the business). They must also seek new approaches and methods where appropriate, and take an innovative and creative approach to the whole process of distribution.

Vertical marketing systems (VMS)

One development in distribution management is the concept of vertical systems, or the vertical marketing system (VMS). Companies have embraced this type of distribution to try to remain in control of what is happening to their products between them and the final consumer. The various ways to maintain control are summarized in Table 13.2.

The advantages of such vertical systems are that they can be very efficient, control of the distribution chain is easy, so conflict is less of a problem, and they tend to give stability to the supply of products, which benefits the producer and retail outlet.

The disadvantages are that there is a larger financial commitment required, usually by the producer, and the systems tend to be inflexible, which can prohibit the growth of new markets for the product, or restrict the retailer in the markets being served.

Table 13.2 Vertical marketing systems

Control mechanism	Description
By ownership	Companies such as Shell, BP and Esso Petroleum not only extract the oil, they refine it and deliver it to their own garage forecourts.
By power	Large retail organizations such as the UK supermarket chains Sainsbury, Tesco and the US Wal-Mart group have very powerful buying departments, not only for their own-label goods but also for branded goods. Because of the large purchase quantities and their very large turnover of products, they are able to control the whole of the distribution chain from the manufacturer through to the final consumer.
By legal contract	This is usually through a franchise agreement, where the retailer is allowed to use the manufacturer's brand name in return for only selling that brand. The brand is usually displayed in a way that reinforces the brand image. Highly successful organizations such as Body Shop International trade in this way. This allows Body Shop to open outlets, and control the flow of products and the presentation of those products.

Channel management

The actual management of the channel will go some way to ensuring that it runs efficiently and effectively. A number of issues need to be addressed when considering distribution channels. Wheeler and Hirsh (1999) suggest that there are three key elements that underpin effective channel management. These are developed in Table 13.3.

Table 13.3 Factors underpinning channel management

Factor	Description
Information flow	This is central to the channel management process. Information flows in two directions, outbound and inbound. Outbound is from the manufacturer/producer through a range of communication/distribution channels to the end user of the product or service. Equally, there is an inbound information flow where the end user feeds back to the manufacturer/ producer. This inbound information flow can be through the use of marketing research services or through much more direct contact. Equally, there is a potential relationship with value-added services (see below). For instance, feedback from customers should help a company to position, target and thus deliver a product to them at the right time. Information is vital in determining what customers want, when they want it and how they want it. These are factors that can lead an organization towards gaining a competitive advantage within the marketplace. In addition to using this two-way information flow to determine customer needs, information is also obtained through tracking the products while in transit. This has increasingly been seen not only as part of the information flow, but as value added to the customer.
Logistics	The process of moving the product to the place where the end customer can either buy it or receive it, for instance a supermarket or home delivery, physically via a vehicle delivery or virtually via the Internet, as in the case of an airline ticket booked at an online site. Earlier we considered how the European airline easyJet delivers its ticket confirmations via the Internet. In this example, the relationship between the manufacturer and the end customer is very much a direct one, although via the medium of the Internet. Wheeler and Hirsh (1999) describe how Frito-Lay considers the value of logistics to its business: 'By combining [field] information with each stage of the value chain, Frito's managers can better determine levels of inbound supplies of raw materials, allocate the company's manufacturing activity across available production capacity, and plan truck routing for the most efficient coverage of market areas. The company's ability to target local demand patterns with just the right sales promotion means that it can continuously optimize margins in the face of inventory risk.'
Value-added services	These are services that augment the manufacturer's product. They can be linked back to Porter's model of the value chain. For instance, they can include next day delivery from a customer's local store, or a delivery convenient to the customer. This could be any time during the week. Indeed as society moves more towards a 24 hour pattern, product delivery times could include evenings, late at night and early mornings. Companies that focus on such value-added services could gain competitive advantage over their rivals. At the time of writing (May 2003) some UK companies only deliver Monday to Friday 9 am to 5 pm. Unless these companies change their delivery patterns they are unlikely to maintain market share over the longer term. Indeed, they may be totally overwhelmed by their more dynamic competitors.

Marketing insight: Fleet management systems and tracking

Exel is a supply chain management company with a turnover in excess of UK £4 billion (US $6 billion), employing more than 55,000 people in 1,300 locations in over 120 countries. Companies such as Exel employ technology to enhance warehouse management and fleet management communications. Both aid in the tracking of products and reporting back to customers.

Exel has developed its own process management tool, Timesmart™. This delivers management information (including warehouse utilization) based on real-time activity measurements within warehouses. This information is processed through a data warehouse that identifies cost control opportunities and assists in troubleshooting potential disruptions within the supply chain.

In 2001 Exel introduced fleet management technology developed by Isotrak™ into vehicles serving its multi-user centre at Bawtry (near Doncaster, Yorkshire, England) as part of a 500 vehicle roll-out. Linked to its managed transport system, this provides Exel's transport managers with the tools for resource planning, real-time fleet management and in-cab communication as well as management reporting facilities. The Customer Services Department has real-time visibility of the delivery status and ongoing communication with drivers. This allows response times to customer queries to be reduced substantially. If, for example, a vehicle is unable to complete an allocated job, other nearby vehicles can be diverted to complete the delivery. Equally if there is traffic congestion or in-store difficulties, the company can take action to prevent or reduce delays within the supply chain.

Sources: Exel/Isotrak Web sites.

Key factors in channel management selection

Selection

The first of these must be the selection of the retail outlet by the producer, or of the producer by the retail outlet. Small retailers may have little if any choice of distribution channel, but larger retailers certainly need to consider the various channels and sources of produce. On the other hand, the producer may wish to have its product handled by specific types of retail outlet. Whichever, it is important that the criteria for selection are carefully thought through before the search and negotiations commence.

Motivation

The second issue is motivating the various members of the channel. Careful consideration should be given to the best methods, remembering that not all channel members will be motivated by the same issues. Consideration should also be given to the type and level of training required for the various channel members. This is especially important with complex products. All the channel members must be familiar with not only the products they carry, but also the policies of the companies that supply those products.

Channel evaluation

It is also necessary to consider how the efficiency of the channel will be evaluated. Full details of the criteria for success must be clearly stated and agreed by all in the channel. Agreed methods of measurement and how deviations will be corrected must be part of the channel contract.

Dispute resolution

Consideration must also be given as to the likely areas of conflict within the channel, what might cause these conflicts and how they are to be resolved to everyone's satisfaction.

Logistics and physical distribution

Marketing and sales create demand. The process of making sure goods get to the customer on time and in perfect condition is called physical distribution. A comprehensive definition is:

> Physical distribution management is the term describing the integration of two or more activities for the purpose of planning, implementing and controlling the efficient flow of raw materials, in-process inventory and finished goods from point of origin to point of sale and consumption.

These activities include, but are not limited to, customer service, demand forecasting, distribution communications, inventory control, material handling, order processing, service support, plant and warehouse site selection, procurement, packaging, return goods handling, transportation, warehousing and storage. From this list it will be obvious how closely marketing/sales and physical distribution should work together to ensure maximum efficiency in achieving results and maintaining reliability in meeting orders. Each link in the chain between initial enquiry, order placing, manufacturing or obtaining goods from stock, packaging, transport and delivery to the customer must be under constant scrutiny, or costs and prices will quickly spiral out of control. And customer service is always paramount.

Ellinger, Daugherty and Keller (2000) reinforce the above view that integration between marketing/sales and distribution/logistics is particularly critical for achieving maximum customer value. However, as they and others indicate, managers in these areas have tended not to consult and coordinate activities. Thus marketers have been slow to recognize the value of logistics (Murphy and Poist, 1994; Stock, 1990). It should be clear that distribution and logistics play an increasingly important role in the value chain. Efficient and effective distribution and logistics management can be a significant competitive advantage driver.

Customer service is clearly inherently linked to marketing, and may come under its control, usually as part of the sales department. Other factors, in part an element of physical distribution, have a dual role. Packaging has to protect the goods, meet additional specifications such as a facility to be stacked safely and conveniently on a display, and may also perform a promotional function. The pack is a mobile advertisement (and a purveyor of information). This applies to a range of factors from product labelling to display material. There are also certain legal requirements for packaging, with regard to both what is printed on the label and the type of materials used (refer to Chapter 2).

In most organizations marketing does not directly manage the physical distribution process. The overlap and the importance of this area to marketing success however are clear. Something arriving late or damaged will not begin to persuade the customer to buy again, and creates administration hassle and costs. Something arriving promptly, safely and in a way that adds to the attractiveness of the whole deal well might encourage repeat purchases. The impact on customers and their view of the company may be long-lived.

Materials handling

Raw materials, components and finished products display a range of physical characteristics, including size and shape. Depending upon the materials (for example, with the movement of valuable and dangerous cargoes), special handling and distribution systems may need to be employed.

The type of equipment, containers and facilities used can minimize the losses from spillage, breakage and theft, while also reducing handling costs. Cost reduction can be a critical issue, especially if the company is operating on reduced or narrow margins. In order to gain competitive advantage, retailers for example increasingly require reduction in upstream costs and more efficient handling processes.

In the following section we briefly examine the key areas of material handling.

Bulk materials (loose cargo)

Bulk materials can be liquids, gases or solids. They include:

▌ oil;

▌ petroleum;

▌ liquid gases;

▌ acids;

▌ coal;

▌ ores;

▌ fish.

Unrefined and untreated bulk raw materials tend to be moved by sea: for example, oil from the Middle East to the United States. Land movements by road and rail tend to be used for the breaking down of bulk raw materials such as ore and coal into manageable units. For example, long coal trains move coal from ports to power stations. This is almost a 24 hour operation in many countries. They are also used for refined or semi-processed materials, for example, petroleum from the oil refinery to the petrol station that serves the end consumer.

Oil can also be moved from oil fields direct to a port or a refinery via a pipeline. An example of a pipeline from source (drilling wells) to a port is the Alaskan pipeline which opened in 1977 and runs from Prudhoe Bay in the north to Valdez in the south. From here tankers ship it to refineries elsewhere in North America.

Distribution directly to an oil refinery removes the need for oil tankers and port facilities for both loading and unloading. Pipelines provide the following advantages:

▌ Generally low operating costs. The original cost of construction may, however, be significant. A case in point is the development of the Alaskan pipeline, which had to overcome severe weather conditions (permafrost) and ecological issues (preventing spills and not disturbing the migration routes of Caribou reindeer).

▌ No packaging or empty transport containers (tankers) on the return journey. Empty return journeys deliver no revenue, only costs (for example, fuel).

▌ No trans-shipment problems from the point of unloading at the refinery port.

▌ A 24 hour operation, 365 days per year.

▌ They are generally not affected by adverse weather conditions. A tanker may have to change route or seek shelter from fierce storms. This can severely affect the delivery of the raw material to the refinery.

Containerization

A container is basically a steel-framed box that is strong enough to support several others stacked above it, whether located on the deck of a ship or on train wagons. The introduction of containers revolutionized the design of ships, railway wagons, flat-bed vehicles, ports and handling facilities (including cranes).

The concept of containerization was first developed in the 1920s (Benson and Whitehead, 1975). However the first container port was not opened until 1956 at Elizabeth, New Jersey (Gilbert, 1999). Since then the use of containers and container ships and trains has come to dominate the transport of products. International agreements regarding the dimension of containers have made it possible for them to be transported virtually everywhere on earth (Gilbert, 1999).

Containers enable truly efficient and effective inter-modal transport from sea to rail and then to road. Containerization provides several key advantages:

This double-decked container train in Washington State, USA was over 100 rail units long. By running such trains on a 24 hour basis freight companies can maximize the distribution potential for their clients.

- The consolidation of several loads into one. Thus several packages of various sizes are brought together into one load.

- They significantly improve handling efficiency. This reduces both loading and unloading time, which in turn have an impact upon costs. The longer a ship is in port, the higher the port costs to the shipping company.

- Containerization provides companies with the opportunity to gain an advantage through the relatively rapid movements of basic goods and finished products across borders, through warehouses and to the end consumer.

- Less packaging is required as the products are being stored within the container. Fragile goods still need to be packed appropriately to prevent breakage, but overall less packaging is required than for previous distribution methods.

- The risk of theft is significantly reduced.

- Containers make through-transit a logical and economic way of moving cargo. Integrated systems can take the containers from, for example, sea to rail and then to road, without their being opened before they reach the distribution warehouse.

Specialist cargoes

There are various types of these. Some examples follow.

Valuables

These range from diamond and bullion deliveries to bank notes. Prior to the launch of the euro in 12 European states on 1 January 2002, several million euro notes and coins needed to be delivered to banks and ATMs. This logistics feat apparently posed few difficulties to the end users, the ordinary citizens of the euro zone. This was an enormous feat for the governments of the 12 nations and some 350 million people.

Hazardous materials

Obviously these pose a risk to both the natural environment and/or human health. Crude oil and natural gas come into this category. As stated earlier, oil is moved using a variety of methods. Oil spills can have significant impacts on wildlife and on local employment (for instance, in fishing and tourism).

Nuclear materials pose particular hazards. Britain is one of the world's leaders in nuclear reprocessing, which is actively marketed through British Nuclear Fuels Limited (BNFL). Specialist containers, ships, rail and road vehicles have been designed or modified to handle such hazardous, and potentially lethal, cargoes. Like any business, BNFL has marketed its expertise to the international community.

The nuclear material has to be transported to Sellafield in the north-west of England for reprocessing and then returned to its country of origin. Although it deals with highly toxic materials, reprocessing remains a business that has to deliver the final product and service to its clients. While safety must not be compromised it still remains a competitive market, as other countries have the ability to reprocess nuclear material.

Transportation

A key function of physical distribution is transport. The development of modes of transport and transportation routes has revolutionized the marketing and distribution of products across borders. The technological impact of transportation systems cannot be underestimated. The major methods of transportation are:

- road;

- rail;

▊ air;

▊ sea/waterways – includes canals and rivers;

▊ pipelines.

However, a single mode of transport is rarely used. Generally companies operate on an inter-modal basis: that is, more than one mode of transport is used for raw materials, parts or finished products. In our earlier example the material is moved by sea freight, then by road and rail. In some cases the various modes of transport are owned by the same company; in other cases several separate companies are involved. Whichever, logistics are a key requirement in delivering the materials/products to the customer at the right time and in the right place.

The role of freight forwarders

These companies provide a broad range of facilities, including the coordination of shipping from the manufacturer's plant to its markets. Freight forwarders are particularly beneficial to SMEs which, because of their size, do not have the resource capabilities to undertake such operations in-house. Without freight forwarders their ability to participate in international business would be severely limited. Table 13.4 lists the range of services provided by freight forwarders.

Warehousing and regional distribution centres

As Benson and Whitehead (1975) state, a warehouse exists mainly as a storehouse where either goods (for example, components) or finished products can safely be stored and cared for until required. The functions of a warehouse are:

▊ To store materials or goods (components) that are not in phase with the production process – that is, not currently required.

▊ To store finished products that are not immediately required by customers.

Table 13.4   The roles of freight forwarders

Activity	Description
Warehousing	Product storage over the short, medium and longer term. The longer products are kept in a warehouse, the greater the storage and inventory costs to the manufacturing or selling company.
Documentation	This ranges from booking of cargo space to preparing export declarations, airways bills and bills of lading, consular documentation in the language of the country to which the products are to be shipped, shipping documentation, and sending them to banks, shippers or consignees as directed. It also includes certification of receipt of goods.
Insurance	Insurance of goods during transit and storage.
Transportation	The physical movement of the goods/products from the supplier/manufacturer to indicated destination. Freight forwarders usually have their own fleets of road or rail vehicles, ships or aircraft. In some cases they supplement their fleets by hiring facilities from third parties, for instance a commercial airline company that also has air cargo facilities.
Tracking	Satellite and IT facilities provide freight forwarders with the systems to track the shipment of their customers' goods/products from the warehouse to final point of delivery. As well as advising their direct customer, they can also update their customer's customer on the delivery time and date.

Adapted from Stock and Lambert (1983)

- To build stocks (or inventory) against possible interruptions in production (for example, a strike either by delivery companies or the company's own workforce).

- To cater for seasonal demand and supply (for example, in the UK, chocolate for Christmas, Easter and Valentine's Day).

- To assist in creating economics of scale in production. By manufacturing in bulk the company reduces its production costs.

However, the savings are offset against the costs of warehousing the finished products.

As is shown in Figure 13.8 and expanded on in Table 13.5, companies may have central warehouses from which products are distributed to regional warehouses, and then to individual retail outlets. It depends upon the size of the company, the geographical distances and locations, and the type of product sold through the retail outlet.

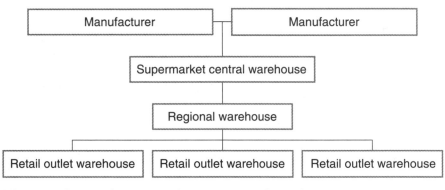

Figure 13.8   Distribution from manufacturer to retail warehouses

Table 13.5   Warehousing and distribution

Stage	Description
Manufacturers	In this example manufacturers produce everything from cosmetics through to ready-made meals and tinned foods. They store goods for a brief period in their own warehouses ready for distribution to the supermarket's main warehouse facility.
Supermarket's central warehouse	The products are delivered to a central warehouse in bulk shipments. These are subdivided for onward delivery (when required) to regional warehouses.
Regional warehouses	These handle the supplies to the region's retail outlets and operate on a just in time system (JIT).
Retail outlet warehouse	Land for supermarkets in the UK is at a premium. The objective is to use the combination of technology and good transportation links to maximize the retail aspect of the store rather than having a massive warehouse complex. Using JIT the retail outlet can request more stock within a very short time frame, thus reducing the need for a massive warehouse facility. Such operations have allowed chains such as Marks & Spencer and Tesco to establish relatively small food outlets in busy high streets and at railway stations. At these outlets stocks are replenished on a daily basis, usually overnight. The use of regional warehousing also allows the retail outlets to order truly FMCGs, rather than have to accommodate slow or non-moving stock. Stock that remains on the shelves is a waste of limited resources – the actual shelf space. This in turn affects revenue generation for that store.

Time management: JIT solutions

As we saw with the example of supermarket distribution, just in time (JIT) systems can play an important role in the efficient movement of produce. JIT is an approach to operations planning and control based on the view that materials (components) or finished products are only produced or delivered when they are needed. The objective is to deliver at the right time to the right location. Delivery too early leads to additional warehousing, and thus increased inventory costs. A delivery that is too late impacts on the customer who will be left waiting to either use the component within the manufacturing process or consume the product. Therefore it is important to note that a disruption in any part of the system can become a problem for the whole system to resolve.

To meet the overall JIT objective companies will seek operational requirements outlined in Table 13.6.

Table 13.6   JIT operational requirements

Requirement	Description
High quality	The manufacturer must seek high quality standards throughout the production and distribution process. Any disruption in terms of product quality will reduce dependability of the internal supply chain.
Speed	The operation must be designed to be fast yet efficient. The idea is to deliver the product direct from production rather than via an inventory.
Reliability	Reliable systems must be in place to maintain high quality standards and prevent distributions.
Flexibility	There must be flexibility in order for the manufacturer and/or distributor to respond to a customer's immediate needs.
Lower costs	With fast and reliable throughput there should be a reduction (or elimination) of waste. These factors should be reflected in lower costs.

Marketing insight: Renault

In 2000, the manufacturing division of the French car maker reorganized its logistics operation to reduce delivery times to a maximum of 15 days, across its six main European assembly plants: Flins, Douai and Sandouville in France, Palencia and Valladolid in Spain, and Novo Mesto in Slovenia. The aim was to integrate information flows (this includes customer ordering through to manufacturing and supply), finance and logistics (production control, planning, parts procurement from suppliers and delivery).

The company uses kanban (a just in time process system) with the objective of providing suppliers with accurate and detailed schedules to manufacture and deliver components to the various assembly plants. The 15 day operation and distribution schedule is segmented as follows:

1. A maximum of six days for suppliers to deliver components to the various plants from receipt of requisition. This, of course, could be a problem area which impacts down the chain to the delivery of the vehicle, so there must be clear and accurate information flow

between the company and its many and varied suppliers. However, Renault is responsible for its own components transportation. The company hires or charters some 3,000 vehicles and three trains every day in Europe to distribute thousands of components to its plants. Two trains operate between France and Spain, while one operates between France and Slovenia.
2. Two days for vehicle production.
3. Five days for the transportation of the vehicle to the dealer. New vehicles are transported by Renault's subsidiary Compagnie d'affretement et de transport (CAT), which in 1999 delivered some 1.9 million vehicles.
4. A two-day window or margin to compensate for potential problems in any of the three operations above.

Source: Farhi (2000).

Retailing

Retailing is a way of performing the major function of distribution. Retailers form the final outlet for the products and services offered by organizations, and really provide the satisfaction of consumers' needs and wants. Table 13.7 details the different types of retailers and their special characteristics.

From our earlier comments we know that products themselves have no real value, it is only when they are consumed that any value is assigned. As we indicated earlier, there are often conflicts between retailers and manufacturers.

Table 13.7 Retailer types

Retailer	Description
Independent	Generally these are considered as single small corner shops. For example a confectioner/tobacconist/newsagent (CTN) on a town's high street may be the only shop owned by that individual or family. However, the family could buy other small shops in the neighbourhood. Although it has increased its property ownership it remains an independent retailer. Thus 'independence' can mean more than a single outlet.
Multiple chains	Both their size and the range of products offered can vary. Again they may be small retailers, extended over a wider geographical location – that is, beyond a single neighbourhood. They might focus on one class of product or hold a variety of different stock. An example is a hardware or clothing chain.
Multiple stores	Supermarkets are a good example of multiple stores. They buy direct from producers/manufacturers (see Figure 13.8). In most cases as well as marketing branded products they market own-label products. (See the 'Marketing insight' on Co-Op Brio Actipods, page 290.)
Online retailers	Although they are not traditional retailers in the sense of 'bricks and mortar' they are still retailing products. Companies such as Amazon in the B2C market and Viking Direct® in the B2B market retail their products through this different medium.

During the development of mass marketing, large manufacturers with strong brands held power over retailers. As customers demanded such high-profile brand names, it would have been unprofitable, if not suicidal, for stores not to stock such brand names. During this period, manufacturers conducted market research whereas retailers did not. Equally, the manufacturers' sales teams knew everything about their products and their market, whereas retailers did not.

However, with changing demographic structures and the development of supermarkets and hypermarkets, the developing retail chains have significantly improved their knowledge base. With increasing numbers of competitors entering the marketplace, in order to survive retailers needed information, on both stock movements and customers. With the introduction of information technology, large retailers are better able than manufacturers to find out about customers' buying habits. From such in-store research, retailers were able to develop their own-label brands and sell them competitively against major brand names. This provided consumers with the opportunity to substitute the store's own-label products for the branded ones. Whether the consumer purchases a branded or an own-label product, the retailer gains a sale.

Thus the balance of power shifted from manufacturers to retailers. At the beginning of the 21st century the power of the food retailers, for instance, has increased significantly. The acquisition of the UK supermarket retailer Asda by the US giant Wal-Mart, and further mergers and acquisitions, could lead to there being only five or six global food retailers, giving them further dominance of the marketplace.

From this concept we can see that if manufacturers want to achieve sufficient bargaining power, they too must be truly global, in both size and power. Only by building very powerful brands can they force retailers to stock them. Major manufacturers may need to seek out suitable acquisitions in order to build both brands and a global reach.

In 1999 Unilever announced a culling of brands which would reduce its portfolio from approximately 1,600 to 400. This strategy allowed it to focus on core brand building. In June 2000 the company bought the American food giant Bestfoods for US $20.3 billion (UK £13.5 billion) (Unilever, 2001). Bestfoods has among its portfolio Knorr soups and sauces and Hellmann's salad dressing. Both these product ranges have already achieved global reach, and Knorr will immediately become Unilever's largest brand. This acquisition therefore provides Unilever with leverage within the marketplace.

As we shall see later, the Internet presents retailers with both challenges and opportunities. It also provides manufacturers with a further opportunity to sell directly to consumers. However, as with retailing, such direct selling is most unlikely to replace the need for manufacturers to have their brands displayed in retail outlets.

Location

The main concern for retailers and producers is to ensure that they are located in places where consumers wish to purchase the products. The growth of large out-of-town shopping complexes was caused by a change in lifestyles.

In some countries shopping is often now a family affair, almost a leisure activity, and all the week's shopping tends to be done in one go. This almost invariably means the use of a car, as it is difficult to handle large quantities of groceries and the like using public transport.

Even the companies that lay on their own buses to the store can only really cater for relatively small loads of shopping, and hence tend to cater for retirees/pensioners, single people or two-person families, rather than the average family.

These large out-of-town stores have now tended to develop into the concept of one-stop shopping centres, with customers being able to obtain all their needs from one location and probably have lunch on the premises as well. There may be some restrictions, such as opening times, but this is rapidly changing. In the UK there are examples of centres continuously open 24 hours, most especially at weekends and before Christmas.

This has caused some major problems for some towns and cities as fewer and fewer people are now visiting these areas. This has led to a predominance of service oriented outlets in city centres, for example estate agents/realtors, rather than traditional shops selling a variety of goods.

Issues for retailers

Perhaps the major issue faced by any retailer is the location of its outlets. They need to be close to large population centres but must also offer the convenience of easy access, which usually means good car parking. They must also offer access to suppliers, which means they must be accessible by large vans or often articulated trucks weighing upwards of 30 tonnes.

While much has been debated on the pros and cons of large edge-of-town shopping complexes, it usually depends on the type of product and service being offered. Large speciality stores do quite well in city centres, which are often pedestrian only. People tend to use these stores almost as a leisure activity, and enjoy browsing and taking their time to select their purchases. Often these outlets are located near complementary outlets, so a whole range of products is available within one area. This often enhances the shopping experience and in many ways has led to the development of not only pedestrian-only areas in town centres, but fully enclosed shopping malls.

Grocery outlets, such as supermarkets, are used mainly to purchase the necessities of life, so the whole shopping experience takes on a different dimension. The underlying motivation is to get what is necessary as quickly and effectively as possible, and then get the rather large trolleyful of items home with the minimum of delay, especially if frozen produce has been purchased.

With smaller outlets, such as convenience stores, it is again important that they are close to centres of population, although in this case it is a population that is actually living close rather than just being in the location for other reasons such as work or recreation. Convenience stores have to offer the 'fill-in' types of product that customers either forgot to purchase during their main weekly shop or have run out of during mid-week. These are usually supplemented by a range of short-life items such as newspapers and confectionery.

Retail outlets also have to consider the assortment of products that they will offer to their potential customers. We have already mentioned this with regard to convenience stores. These usually carry a reasonable breadth of products but very little depth. Breadth refers to the number of product lines, for example soup, sauces, confectionery and bread products. Depth refers to the choices within each product line. A small convenience store might only offer three or four varieties of soup. A supermarket might stock 20 or more different varieties, and ranges from different manufacturers as well.

The relationship between breadth and depth differs depending on the type of outlet and the type of products. It is sometimes possible to get greater product depth by the use of technology. Many DIY outlets now have paint mixing apparatus which means they need only carry the base paint plus a range of pigments to be able to supply customers with virtually any colour. Because the mix is computer controlled it is possible to replicate the colour at a later date from the unique identification code which is produced at the time the paint is mixed. This also means a different outlet can replicate the colour provided it uses the same equipment.

While this is not possible with all product lines, there is a move to this type of solution, as outlets need to ensure that the depth of product offered meets customers' requirements. Organizations are also offering rapid order facilities, so if a particular colour or size is not in stock it can usually be obtained from the supplier within 24 hours. The outlet may also offer a delivery service for products that are not in stock.

The issues of what to stock need to be analysed very carefully. When considering the operation of marketing channels Walter and Bergiel (1982) postulated three areas: purpose, status and completeness. (See Table 13.8.) These three concepts allow the retailer to carefully analyse what type and depth of product lines to stock.

As with all concepts in marketing, positioning is very important in retailing. As we know from our previous analysis this is how what we offer is considered in relationship to our competitors. With so many retail types in the marketplace it is helpful if a retailer can position the outlet to occupy a particular place in potential customers' perceptions. All the large outlets do this, although with many of the large supermarkets the boundaries are becoming very blurred.

Positioning is about the image portrayed to potential customers. The outlet might want to position itself as a provider of high quality goods that only offers premium brands and the service to support them. This will initially be reflected in the location of the store, but will be supported by the range of goods stocked and the deportment of the staff. Often the staff will be provided with uniforms and will be taught how to approach potential customers. Goods purchased will be wrapped and supplied in good quality bags with the store logo clearly displayed. The service level will be very high and many regular customers will be addressed by their names. Details of all customers will be kept on a database, they will be contacted at regular intervals with details of new products, and so on.

Table 13.8 Purpose, status and completeness

Stocking decision	Explanation
Purpose	The retailer must consider the type of customer who is likely to visit the outlet. This will, of course, depend on the location and the type of outlet. It is important that the range meets the wants and needs of customers. The products need to be ranked to establish which rate highest in the order of customer wants. It is important that the breadth of products is wide enough to satisfy customers but not so wide as to be impossible to stock or manage.
Status	Items considered to be of low 'status' by customers might have to be removed from the range. The 'status' of products needs to be monitored and the assortment of products modified over time.
Completeness	The range offered also needs to be 'complete'. Again this can be established from what customers expect to be offered. A DIY outlet is expected to carry a range of the most popular size and types of nails, and would not meet the requirements of its customers if these were not available. The retailer must be fully aware of customer needs and the introduction of new lines to the marketplace. Constant monitoring of the customers' preferences is necessary, and modifications to both the breadth and depth of the product range must be in response to changes in customer needs. The main aim must be to have a product mix that generates the maximum sales that will realize the maximum profit.

Other images, and hence position, might be better for a particular outlet. However, it is important that the image to be portrayed is carefully thought about, and that a strategy is developed to ensure that the required image is communicated to potential customers. This image is the picture that the retailer wants to project into customers' minds whenever the store name or logo is seen.

If a number of markets are being targeted, the retailer may wish to create different atmospheres in different parts of the store. This is especially likely in department stores and many of the bigger supermarkets and hypermarkets, where a very wide range of product types is made available. The image being promoted must be carefully considered and then maintained. While it is possible to reposition the outlet this can be very time-consuming and costly. The position will tend to drift over time as people's perceptions change, so these must be monitored and minor changes made to the atmospherics to maintain the desired perception.

Product considerations

Retailers may wish to expand their customer base, and this is usually done by the addition of products that are not related to their existing lines on offer. Usually they move into goods that are likely to be fast selling, so additional revenue can be generated easily. Problems may arise from the need to deal with a more diverse market, and this may lead to their losing some expertise across all the markets they are trying to serve. However, if retailers are to grow it is often necessary to diversify into other products. The diversification might change the store's competitive position, and certainly it will face new competitors who are already in the proposed markets. Often the retailer with a diverse range of products allocates store space to reflect buying priorities during the year. Christmas time will see most of the selling areas given over to toys and gifts, whereas during the summer months it could be predominantly DIY and gardening products.

Most retail markets are now saturated, so the only way that retailers can grow is by offering a greater choice of products to their customers. The core choice is whether to increase the product depth, and therefore become more specialized, or increase the product width to attract a wider range of customers. Take the example of a small model store that has specialized in model railways and has a reputation for expertise in this area. To grow the business the retailer could either increase the range of model railway accessories, perhaps offer a greater range of kits or specialized parts for the models, or broaden the range of models on offer by stocking model aeroplanes and boats. This is not an easy decision but it is one that all retailers face.

Retailing, like all markets, is dynamic. The basic structure develops over time. This constant movement has been called the 'wheel of retailing', and is based on the hypothesis that the retailers start as small low-price operations. As they develop they increase their service levels, which inevitably means an increase in the prices charged. They then become vulnerable to new entrants into the market and so go into decline. The cycle is then repeated with the new entrants. While this might work in some sectors of the market, retailing is mainly influenced by the balance of power between suppliers and retailers. This balance tends to change over time, and hence influences the price that can be charged by the various outlets. Many retailers are now also part of a vertical marketing system, so control over the prices is not with the final outlet.

Retailing is also going global. Many large retail organizations are part of multinational organizations; this gives them immense buying power on a global basis, and they are therefore not so affected by changes in the various domestic markets.

Non-store retailing

Products and brands can be sold to the public without the use of a retail outlet. This method of selling has grown as it is often convenient for certain types of customers who do not have the time or inclination to go to their nearest town to shop for certain items. We briefly revisit some of the key elements in this section.

The key issues here are the combination of placement (making the product available to the customer) and the various physical distribution activities. When reading the section on automatic vending consider how, for instance, a chocolate bar brand is distributed to the numerous vending machine outlets in a large city.

Catalogues

One of the most popular methods is catalogue selling, which is a form of direct marketing. These can work on two levels. First, individuals can have their own catalogues, which are usually published twice a year, and operate an account with the catalogue supplier, ordering direct either by phone, post or the Internet when they wish to buy from the catalogue. Payment is often made by regular four-weekly instalments, and the cost of the item(s) purchased can be spread over a period of time. Interest may be payable if the repayment period is long. Commission is received against the purchases made, which can be 'cashed in' at any time the customer wishes and used against further purchases.

Alternatively an agent runs the catalogue, collecting money from customers and keeping the commission. Each agent has a number of customers who do their purchasing and payments through the agent and not directly with the company.

A number of other suppliers have entered this method of retailing, and it is now possible to purchase a whole range of goods from a variety of different companies. Stationary

suppliers often a whole range of products by direct mail, supplying catalogues and leaflets at regular intervals. Suppliers of DIY materials have also joined the ever-increasing companies offering to supply direct by mail order, and offer anything from a box of screws through to specialized welding equipment and power tools. Many organizations specialize in limited ranges of special or unusual items, or perhaps clothing for particular sizes or market segments that are not adequately served by the major catalogue retailers. It is also possible to purchase directly from advertisements in magazines and newspapers.

Automatic vending

Automatic vending has also become more popular in the past decade, initially starting with consumables such as confectionery and cold drinks. Today it is now possible to obtain a whole variety of goods, including hot and cold snack meals, mini travel kits and contraceptives from vending machines. They have the advantages of being available 24 hours a day and at locations where normal retailing is not viable. Locations range from railway station platforms to university common rooms.

Direct selling (door-to-door)

The oldest method of non-store retailing is door-to-door selling. Although it is less popular in some developed countries than two or three decades ago, some companies still use this method. The process has changed and the tendency is to provide salespeople with small catalogues which they deliver one day and collect two or three days later, hopefully with an order. The two most well-known users of this technique are Betterware and Avon Cosmetics.

Telemarketing

Telemarketing has grown rapidly since the 1980s. This is the result of technological developments (fibre optics, microwave links and digital communications) and buyer behaviour/cultural changes. While there had been some telephone selling for many years, the introduction of telemarketing has revolutionized the relationship between customer and seller, in both the B2C and B2B sectors.

Internet

Non-store retailing could not be considered without reference to using the Internet as a marketing medium. This is, and will continue to be, a technical and cultural challenge for retailers who need to reconcile a virtual presence in cyberspace and their existing bricks and mortar presence on the high street or in the shopping mall.

The notion of e-commerce is gaining popularity as the use of encryption codes becomes more sophisticated. The major fear is unauthorized or fraudulent use of credit or debit cards when details are sent over the Net. However, the notion of buying computer hardware and software over the Net has been extended into many other areas, notably books, CDs, groceries, holidays, flights, train tickets and even cars.

The development of the Internet as a marketing medium presents retailers with both a threat and an opportunity. While some take the view that in the future the Internet will replace stores, there is a counter-argument that the two can work together. The Net provides customers with a choice. They can browse and buy over the Web site, and/or walk around the store. We can consider this as a 'clicks and mortar' approach to retailing. Such retailers may therefore gain an advantage over retailers who are purely either store based or Internet based.

Marketing insight: Tesco, grocery retailing via the Web

Tesco is the UK's largest grocery retailer. It has stores throughout the UK, Europe and in Thailand and South Korea. While it remains very much a bricks and mortar retailer, it has added value to its business through e-tailing. It has become an excellent example of 'clicks and mortar'.

Tesco has now become the largest Internet grocery retailer in the world. It allows customers to purchase a range of products via the Internet and arrange a suitable time for delivery to their home or office. Tesco has introduced a virtual store that allows it to make further increases in product offers, especially on non-food items. It offers a wider range of items than can be housed in local in-town supermarkets, for example books, CDs and DVDs. Online it has created separate areas for electrical goods, clothing, gifts, wine and Tesco Personal Finance. It has also embarked on a joint venture with iVillage.com, which provides a UK-based version of the successful US-based women's interest Internet portal.

In 2001 Tesco announced that it planned to launch Tesco.com in South Korea.

Tesco Internet UK statistics as of April 2002 are:

Sales:	85,000 orders per week
Area covered:	692 stores, 94 per cent of the population
Products on offer:	Over 10,000
Delivery charge:	UK £5.00
Registered users:	Approximately one million
Turnover:	UK £356 million
Average sales per customer:	UK £85.00

Sources: Tesco.com and MediaGuardian.co.uk (10 April 2002).

The future

Placement has often been seen as a poor relative of the other marketing mix elements. Perhaps it has not been considered as glamorous as, for example, the array of promotional tactics that can be used to market a product or service. However, it is clearly an integral component of the whole marketing operation. Without placement there would be no products or goods in stores or warehouses for customers to purchase.

The future of distribution will probably be driven by the following three interrelated factors.

Information technology

As we have already witnessed, IT has driven radical changes in the distribution and logistics business. Today, organizations from the comfort of their office computers can track their products en route to their customers. This process will be further refined with the installation of micro chips in packaging, and refinements to tracking devices and monitoring systems. Moreover, it will not only be the freight forwarders and the sellers tracking the progress of the goods. Buyers can also track the goods as they leave their original destination en route to their warehouse, retail outlet, office or home.

Transportation technology

Working hand-in-hand with IT will be transport technology. Since the 1990s we have seen a radical development in specialist containerization facilities, for example in the transportation of everything from garments to fresh fish and fresh flowers. Fish caught today in the Pacific Ocean can be on a diner's plate tomorrow in a fashionable San Francisco Bay restaurant, such is the ability to chill and freeze foods and transport them over longer distances without the loss of flavour and texture. It is most likely that there will be further refinements to specialist containerization facilities, speed of aircraft and road movements and the logistics or planning behind such operations.

JIT demands

These demands will emanate from two key sources, companies and customers. First, companies will want to minimize any warehousing and thus want rapid delivery turnarounds. Second, consumers or customers will increasingly want both rapid availability of products and service, and products and produce that have not been readily available in the past. For instance, Dutch tulips in a flower market in Seattle, Washington State were a rarity in the 1970s. Now they are a common sight. Technology has made that possible. In the future a wider range of produce will be demanded, and at a lower cost. This will be the real challenge.

Chapter summary

This chapter has outlined the different aspects of distribution, channel management and retailing. Since the 1960s there have been significant developments within these areas, driven by changing consumer behaviours, the introduction of sophisticated technologies, changing business relationships and a move towards global businesses.

While the basic concepts currently remain the same, dynamic business environments will impact on how products are marketed and distributed to end users in the future. The Internet has brought distributors both threats and opportunities. The opportunities may, in the longer term, bring significant advantages to customers, especially in terms of information, real-time online purchasing, improved distribution logistics and innovative store layouts.

Exercises and questions for review and critical thinking

1. Consider, in detail, the potential advantages and disadvantages of a manufacturer using an intermediary to distribute its products.

2. Explain how the key account process can be developed to improve overall market efficiency/penetration of a product, and thus generate higher revenues.

3. Consider the potential advantages and disadvantages of manufacturers removing intermediaries and selling their products direct to the end user. Use practical examples in your analysis.

4. Compare and contrast the different and various functions of marketing channels.

5. Compare and contrast the different types of retail outlet.

6. How can different display systems assist in marketing a store's product range? Cite practical examples in your answer.

7. There has been an increasing number of takeovers and mergers within the international retail sector. Consider the reasons behind such actions, and how they will have an impact on the marketplace.

8. In your opinion what will be the impact of the Internet on store retailing over the next five years? Support your views with evidence.

Marketing across borders: the international dimension

We used to be an American company with a large international business. Now we're a large international business with a sizeable American business.
The late Robert Goizueta, former CEO of Coca-Cola

Introduction

Two decades ago, the phrase global marketing did not exist. Today, businesses look to global marketing for the realization of their full commercial potential.... But there is another, even more critical reason why companies need to take global marketing seriously: survival. A company that fails to become global in outlook risks losing its domestic business to competitors having lower costs, greater experience and better products.

(Keegan and Green, 1997)

Since Keegan and Green made this statement there has been a significant move towards globalization, but it has not been without its critics and problems. In Chapter 2 we discussed some of the concerns raised in terms of political power and influence as companies increase their global reach.

However an international approach does not necessarily mean a standardized product across all markets. The former CEO of Sony, Akio Morita, used the term ' global localization' (Ohmae, 1990). This is a point Ohmae discussed in his groundbreaking book *The Borderless World* (1990). He considered how a company could serve local customers in markets globally in ways that were 'truly responsive to their needs as well as to the global character of its industry'. Ohmae (1990) shaped this into his view of companies being global but acting locally; this was translated into the term 'glocal'.

Since Ohmae developed this line of thinking the world has become 'borderless' through the proliferation of the Internet. The Internet has provided, along with expansive air transportation, the ability to operate on a global platform. Today, both B2C and B2B transactions can be equally as global as local in their execution.

In this chapter we consider the reasons companies have sought an international and global dimension, and some of the issues they must consider in attempting to achieve their cross-border ambitions.

Learning objectives

On completion of this chapter you will be able to:

▌ examine the opportunities and constraints facing companies as they seek international customers;

▌ explain the trends that have led to a more global business environment;

▌ debate the reasons companies expand their markets overseas, and the difficulties in building international markets;

▌ evaluate marketing mix strategies and tactics within an international context;

▌ examine the reasons marketing internationally sometimes fails.

Definitions

It is useful at this early stage to consider some definitions. Terminology is often used out of exact context, and thus some clarification is useful.

Domestic marketing

As the phrase suggests, this is where the company or organization markets within its own domestic or home country environment. A company may decide to market both domestically and internationally. The UK supermarket chain Tesco, for example, has a solid base within its home market (where it is market leader, as of May 2003). However it has also ventured into Eastern Europe and the Far East, where it has built a strong market position.

International marketing

We can define international marketing as where a company or organization markets to two or more countries. This is sometimes referred to as transnational marketing.

Global marketing

Adcock (2000) describes global marketing as:

> marketing in an unbound geographic market. It is the most extreme development of international marketing and is applicable to products or services that have similarities stretching across national boundaries, and for which a unified strategy is feasible.

The scale on which a company undertakes such actions can range from the occasional indirect sale overseas to significant foreign direct investment (FDI). This range is illustrated throughout this chapter.

The global village and globalization

The term 'global village' was first postulated in the late 1960s by the Canadian writer and academic Marshall Herbert McLuhan (1911–1980). He used it to denote how the world was increasingly looked upon as a relatively small community. In his books *The Gutenberg Galaxy: The Making of Typographical Man* (1962), *Understanding Media: The Extensions of Man* (1964) and *The Medium is the Message* (with Fiore, 1967) he considered the impact of mass communication and modern technology on society. He predicted that the media through which information is transmitted would become more important than the information itself, and thus he coined the phrase, 'the medium is the message'. His view was that the role of the printed word would be significantly reduced in this world of instant awareness, where electronic communications technology would alter perceptions of space, time and personal identity.

Much of what McLuhan predicted has become a reality. Today we are very much, each and every one of us, wrapped up in the media that drive information dissemination.

That includes television and the Internet. We are now living in McLuhan's vision of a global village. Communication and transportation allow us to know what is happening in other regions of the world virtually instantaneously. This was plainly visible in the Iraqi conflict of 2003, where journalists embedded with coalition forces instantaneously broadcast live reports. Virtually the whole world could witness events as they unfolded.

The future development of the Internet will significantly increase the range of cross-border communication and transactions, by governments, businesses and ordinary citizens. Today virtually anyone can buy products or services via the Internet – there are no geographical boundaries.

In 1983 Levitt of the Harvard Business School outlined his view of the development of globalization in what can be considered a seminal article in the *Harvard Business Review*. He wrote:

A powerful force drives the world towards a converging commonality, and that force is technology. It has proletarianized communication, transport and travel. The result is a new commercial reality – the emergence of global markets for standardized consumer products on a previously unimagined scale of magnitude.

Gone are accustomed differences in national or regional preferences... The globalization of markets is at hand. With that, the multinational corporation operates in a number of countries and adjusts its products and practices to each – at high relative costs. The global corporation operates with resolute consistency – a low relative cost – as if the entire world were a single entity; it sells the same thing in the same way everywhere.

Commercially, nothing confirms this as much as the success of McDonald's from the Champs Elysees (Paris) to the Ginza (Tokyo), of Coca-Cola in Bahrain and Pepsi-Cola in Moscow, and of rock music, Greek salad, Hollywood movies, Revlon cosmetics, Sony television and Levi jeans everywhere.

Ancient differences in national tastes or modes of doing business disappear. The commonality of preferences leads inescapably to the standardization of products, manufacturing and the institutions of trade and commerce.

As you can probably imagine this was somewhat controversial when first stated in the early 1980s. To some extent today we might look upon it slightly differently. We can now point to truly global organizations and companies. However, was Levitt (1983) right to consider McDonald's or Coca-Cola as truly standardized products? Perhaps it depends increasingly on an individual's definition of 'standardization'. For instance, does a minor alteration to a product allow it still to be called a standard product? This is a point we want you to reflect on. We will return to this debate in the section on the marketing mix.

The differences between domestic and international marketing

Table 14.1 outlines the various differences between the domestic and international marketing environment.

Why market internationally or globally?

Various factors can lead companies and organizations to market their products internationally, and even globally. The decision to engage in international marketing may be driven by a single factor or a combination of several factors. Table 14.2 sets out these factors.

Changes that have affected international marketing

Kotler (2000) amongst others has illustrated numerous factors that have influenced the

Table 14.1 Comparison between domestic and international environments

Key factor	Description
Politics	The company must consider not only domestic politics but those of all the countries in which it is engaged. Political regimes vary greatly, and thus the level of political risk involved in marketing across borders must be considered. Governments vary enormously in their composition. They may comprise democratically elected members or be led by power-hungry dictators who protect their personal power at virtually any cost. (You may want to consider potential leaders who fit this particular category.) Therefore they can have a very strong influence over product imports, exports and business operations within their country.
Economics	Again, as well as home-based economics companies must consider the dynamics of the international economic environment. These range from the level of interest rates through to levels of income (and thus purchasing power), exchange rates and inflationary/deflationary pressures. Currencies vary in their stability and value, thus there are increasing transaction risks. Equally, some governments limit the amount of national currency that can be transferred to banks in other countries. At the time of writing (May 2003) India is an example.
Level and reliability of data	The quality of information available to the international marketer varies. For example, British companies wanting to market in the United States will have access to a wealth of information made readily available to them (including Internet sites) from both the British and United States governments. However, the accuracy of information about markets in other countries (though not all) is severely limited. As we already know from earlier chapters, the quality of information available to the marketer is paramount: multi-billion dollar decisions often depend upon the accuracy of information supplied to decision makers. These decision makers must weigh up the levels of risk involved. Developments based on flawed information may severely damage the company in the short and medium terms. It may take significant investment and resources for it to recover from such a position. In the meantime, competitors might take advantage of the company's vulnerability in both domestic and international markets.
Accounting and finance practices	Accounting standards vary from country to country. While some countries adopt British standards, others use international standards, and still others have their own variants. Equally, financial systems vary as do the enforcement powers of various regulatory bodies. The quality of international accounting standards has become of major concern since the Enron and WorldCom scandals of 2002.
Culture	While there is convergence of certain cultural views, for example the Americanization of fast food on a global scale, there are also significant diversities in cultures. These vary in intensity from country to country.
Business operations	The range and type of business operations vary from region to region. While there is some harmony of regulations within the European Union, a British company operating in India or the Middle East will be subject to very different procedures and operations. The rules for business operations can be diverse and complex, often driven by cultural and political influences. Linked to operations is the level of perceived and real control a company has over its plant and subsidiaries in different business environments.
Management skills	These vary depending on the level of education and skills training in particular countries and regions. If a company is involved in foreign direct investment (FDI) it might bring in employees from its home base to assist in the development of local employees. Eventually it could hand over control and operations to the local employees. Cheaper air transport has seen more young people travel abroad to be educated, especially at university level. Many return to their own countries, thus helping to develop and deepen the knowledge and skills base.

Table 14.2 Potential factors for going global

Key factor	Description
Saturated domestic market	A company might discover it has few opportunities to expand sales within its domestic market. There could be a combination of reasons including changing consumer tastes, consumer preferences, economic conditions and aggressive competition. In order to increase sales revenues and profits the company might be forced to market its products or services internationally. It might initially seek marketing opportunities in neighbouring countries before broadening its horizons further. The market for Volvo cars within its domestic market became saturated, thus it needed to enter and develop international markets in order to generate increased revenues.
A declining market	There might be a declining market for the product within the domestic market. However, there could be significant growth opportunities in overseas markets. For example, some soap products are in their declining stage of the product life cycle within the UK market. However they are in the growth phase in the Pakistan and Indian markets. This is simply because the manufacturers found a new market opportunity within those countries.
Drive to increase overall profitability	As well as operating within a highly diversified and dynamic environment, companies must seek to maximize their profit potential. At the beginning of the 21st century we are seeing an increasing number of companies undertake international or global strategic alliances to build their businesses, thus maximizing their market potential. Additionally, stakeholders (mainly shareholders) and the market makers within the equally global financial markets want to see stock market listed companies make significant year-on-year profits. This may only be achieved by expanding into highly profitable overseas markets.
A small domestic market	A small domestic market might provide insufficient sales for the company to grow over the medium term, and survive in the longer term, especially if it faces strong domestic and inward international competition. Companies such as Volvo (mentioned above) and Nokia Telecommunications probably would not have survived if they had only serviced their domestic markets. They are too small for the range of products they market, especially in the light of the heavy R&D investment. They have to internationalize in order to survive. For Volvo and Nokia internationalization has helped them to become major international players within the automotive and telecommunications industries respectively. As seen in Chapter 8, Nokia was the sixth most valuable brand in 2002 worth an estimated US $30 billion turnover.
Recession in domestic market	A recession may hit a company's domestic market, resulting in significant impact on its ability to generate revenues and profits. Therefore in order to survive in this low-growth environment the company needs to seek marketing opportunities elsewhere. The severe recession in the UK economy during the early 1990s placed immense pressures on numerous domestic businesses. Many did not survive; however others sought positions in overseas markets, especially in the then stronger economies of Europe. These moves into the international arena ensured survival for some companies. Therefore when the recession ended they were in a financially significantly stronger position to reinforce their position in their domestic market.

Table 14.2 *continued*

Key factor	Description
Cost factors	Increased costs within the domestic market may force companies to seek cheaper manufacturing and operations overseas. They move therefore from an exporting operation to foreign direct investment (FDI). Since the mid-1990s several major clothing manufacturers have sought lower cost resources in other countries, especially within Eastern Europe and the Far East. As well as manufacturing in these countries, this also provides companies with a base from which to launch products into neighbouring countries and regions. Associated with such moves, though, have been the allegations that several companies have acted unethically by allowing child employment. These allegations have led to boycotts and resultant negative public relations. You may want to reflect back to Chapter 3 and consider the ethical and business implications.
Customer-driven focus	Customers may expect their suppliers to have an international presence, especially if they themselves are engaged in international business. Major globally oriented companies might seek, for example, to have an international advertising and media campaign. They will look for an advertising agency that operates internationally, and can provide that level of support for them. Another example is component suppliers and their ability to provide their customers with parts within an effective and reasonable time frame. Some companies operate a just in time (JIT) system, therefore reliability in delivery is crucial as it directly affects production capacity, and thus has financial implications for the customer.
Spreading the risk	A company marketing in more than one geographical location is more likely to be able to adjust effectively to dynamic changes within its markets. Decline in one market (perhaps through recession or conflict) can be offset by increases in other markets.
Economies of scale	By introducing longer production runs to meet overseas orders, companies can often reduce unit costs, thus increasing their profit potential. However, the products must not be held too long in storage at the manufacturer's as this can significantly add to the company's inventory and thus costs. If this situation arises then the economies of scale will be reduced or indeed eliminated.
Reputation	Some companies believe that by marketing internationally or globally they increase the value of their reputation, both domestically and internationally. This may be the case within highly competitive industries where companies need to maintain their growth rates, and show their customers that they can match the competition. This could however be a high-risk strategy, especially if it stretches resources.
Potential of the Internet	The Internet offers immense possibilities for marketing both products and services across borders. The real key to success of such marketing is the quality of logistics, in say moving books or CDs from the United States where they are relatively cheap to other countries. While the Internet is the marketing communications tool, for most online-purchased products there is a need for on-time delivery support. However, it is very clear that the Internet will revolutionize international marketing practices and operations.

move towards an international and global marketing environment. We have expanded the issues, based upon some of Kotler's initial statements. While these are obviously of importance individually, we suggest that you consider them collectively, and reflect on the power of these dynamic drivers of change.

- Since the 1960s there has been at first a steady, then a rapid move towards the globalization of the world's economy. This has been reflected in the rapid growth of world trade and investment. One issue that needs to be taken into account is the potential impact of the Internet on international trade. Of course, there is a caveat: trade might not grow year on year. A global market slump, for instance, will be followed by a slowdown in international trade.

- The growth of investments is particularly important as we now operate in a virtual 24 hour investment market. Company share movements in one country probably will impact on shares (for example, industry sector shares) in other markets.

- The rising economic power of Japan and several Far Eastern countries in world markets had a significant effect. However, the collapse of the Malaysian, Indonesian, Thai, South Korean and Japanese economies in the late 1990s significantly impacted on the region. The early 21st century saw a resurgence in the Malaysian economy, with increased internal and external investment into that country.

These countries will re-emerge; however, this time their economies will be constructed on solid economic and business principles.

- The rising economic and business power of China. We have separated China from the other countries mentioned above because of its enormous size, physically and potentially economically. China commenced its historic economic reforms in 1979 when the then leader of the Communist Party, Deng Xiaoping (old style Teng Hsiao-p'ing, 1904–1997) opened up the first free trade zones. Since then China has developed its southern regions into a more market-oriented economy. Hong Kong, under Chinese control since the handover by the UK government in 1997, has retained a market-focused economy. While a larger percentage of the population is engaged in agriculture, a significantly larger proportion of its Gross Domestic Product (GDP) emanates from industrial production. Table 14.3 lists China's principal exports (*Economist*, 1999) and Table 14.4 lists its principal export markets.

- There will be the potential for dramatic growth once China is a fully fledged member of the World Trade Organization. How it is realized will depend partly on its own actions and attitudes towards internal political liberalization, and partly on the reactions of other WTO members over time.

Table 14.3 China's principal exports by value

Export	Value US $ billion
Textiles and clothing Machinery and electrical equipment	45.6
Food and tobacco Chemicals	12.1

Source: Andrews (1998)

Table 14.4   China's principal export markets

Country	Percentage of China's export market
Hong Kong	24.0
United States	17.9
Japan	17.4
South Korea	5.0
Germany	3.6
Netherlands	2.4

Source: Andrews (1998)

▌ The expanding economic and political power of regional trading blocks (see Table 14.5) has increased the opportunity for cross-border marketing.

▌ The formation of the World Trade Organization (WTO) created the groundwork for trade liberalization.

▌ In 1989 the world witnessed the fall of the Berlin Wall. With this came the democratization of the former communist countries of Eastern Europe. Some countries such as Poland, the Czech Republic, Estonia, Hungary, Slovakia and Slovenia have been relatively proactive in their move towards developing market economies. Indeed, all these countries have applied for European Union membership. Russia, however, has suffered both economic and political turmoil. It might be some years before Russia emerges as a truly economic power. The potential is undoubtedly there, and many American and European companies are investing in Russia for the long-term opportunities.

▌ Increased mobility of people. This covers education, vacation and business/work travel. Since the 1960s we have witnessed a dramatic increase in both regional and international travel. The introduction of wide-bodied aircraft (such as the Boeing 747 and 777) significantly reduced the cost of air travel, thus opening up markets that did not exist in the 1960s, indeed the 1980s. Overall more young people travel today – for education and vacation – than ever before, and the trend is likely to continue. This means they are exposed to different environments, products, societies and levels of service. They are the business people of the future, and many seek international products, brands, service levels and lifestyles. (While there are issues of terrorism and SARS – see Chapter 2 – overall there is still significant people, as well as goods, movement between nations.)

▌ In 1956 the first container port was opened in the United States, at Elizabeth, New Jersey. Slowly the introduction of containerization of cargo radically changed the handling and turnaround time of cargo loading and unloading of ships. Containers came to dominate the transportation of goods across the world. International agreements regarding container dimensions made it possible to use any mode of transport, virtually anywhere in the world.

▌ The development of specialized containers and refrigeration units has greatly improved the transportation of perishable products such as fresh foodstuffs and flowers over greater distances. It is now possible to buy Dutch-grown tulips in San Francisco, or Caribbean fish in London supermarkets.

Table 14.5   Regional trading blocs

Trading bloc	Geographical coverage
European Union	Member states as of September 2002: Belgium, France, Germany, Italy, Luxemburg, the Netherlands, Denmark, Ireland, the United Kingdom, Greece, Portugal, Spain and Austria. In 2002 the majority of EU countries became members of the single currency and formed the euro zone. In October 2002 the European Commission approved a report judging 10 countries ready for membership: Cyprus, Czech Republic, Estonia, Hungary, Latvia, Lithuania, Malta, Poland, Slovakia and Slovenia. There must be a final ratification of the decision. If there are no problems these countries will join the EU in 2004. Bulgaria and Romania could be eligible to join in 2007. The GNP of the European Union is estimated at US $6.6 trillion. The population is approximately 373 million (2001 figures). The additional 10 countries would add 75 million people to the EU's total population but no more than 5% to the EU's GNP.
North American Free Trade Area (NAFTA)	This comprises the United States, Canada and Mexico. The GNP is estimated at US $8.6 trillion. The population is approximately 390 million.
Mercosur	This comprises Argentina, Brazil and Paraguay. The GNP is estimated at US $1.2 trillion. The population is approximately 204 million.
Association of South East Asian Nations (ASEAN Free Trade Area)	This comprises Brunei, Cambodia, Indonesia, Laos, Malaysia, Myanmar, Philippines, Singapore, Thailand and Vietnam. The GNP is estimated at US $632 billion. The population is approximately 481 billion.
Asia Pacific Economic Co-operation (APEC)	This comprises Australia, Brunei, Canada, Chile, China, Hong Kong, Indonesia, Japan, Malaysia, Mexico, New Zealand, Papua New Guinea, the Philippines, Singapore, South Korea, Thailand and the United States.
Central American Common Market	This comprises Costa Rica, El Salvador, Guatemala, Honduras, Nicaragua and Panama.
Caribbean Community and Common Market (CARICOM)	This comprises Antigua and Baruda, the Bahamas (which is not currently a member of the Common Market), Barbados, Belize, Dominica, Grenada, Guyana, Jamaica, Montserrat, St Christopher-Nevis, St Lucia, St Vincent and Grenadines, Suriname and Trinidad-Tobago. The British Virgin Islands and Caicos Islands are Associate Members.
Andean Common Market (ANCOM)	This comprises Bolivia, Colombia, Ecuador, Peru and Venezuela.
Economic Community of West Africa (ECOWAS)	This comprises Benin, Burkina Faso, Cape Verde, the Gambia, Ghana, Guinea, Guinea-Bissau, the Ivory Coast, Liberia, Mali, Mauritania, Niger, Nigeria, Senegal, Sierra Leone and Togo. The population is approximately 160 million.
Gulf Co-operation States (GCC)	This comprises Bahrain, Kuwait, Oman, Qatar, Saudi Arabia and the United Emirates.
European Free Trade Association (EFTA)	This comprises Iceland, Liechtenstein, Norway and Switzerland. It has expanded its relationship with non-European Union states, signing free trade agreements with Turkey (1991), Israel, Poland and Romania (1992), Bulgaria, Hungary, the Czech Republic and Slovakia (1993) and Estonia, Latvia, Lithuania and Slovenia (1995).
Commonwealth of Independent States (CIS)	This is the multilateral grouping of 11 sovereign states that were formerly constituent republics of the former USSR.
Arab Free Trade Zone	In 2001 Egypt, Jordan, Tunisia and Morocco started the process of developing an Arab Free Trade Zone. The aim is to expand the zone over the decade. Equally, it will seek to expand its trading relationship with the EU.

▌ The development of efficient transportation networks has resulted in the relative reduction of production and transportation costs. This has made it more attractive to move a variety of products across increasingly long distances.

▌ The development of global brands in cars, food, clothing, electronics and computer systems. These include such household names as Coca-Cola, Microsoft, IBM, Ford, Disney, Intel, McDonald's, Nescafé, Sony and Heinz.

▌ The movement in many countries towards the deregulation and privatization of state-owned companies in order to make them more efficient and competitive. The UK is a prime example with, for example, the privatization of the former state-owned airline, British Airways. In the former communist countries of Eastern Europe, the old state-owned companies are being sold to domestic and international investors. In many cases the government retains a shareholding, but the bulk of the shares and the control of the business are in private ownership. The injection of finance, technology and skills has transformed formerly ailing state-owned companies. For example, in 1991 the German car manufacturer Volkswagen bought a controlling stake in the Czech vehicle manufacturer, Škodă. Its production line was completely overhauled, as was its image. Once the brunt of jokes, especially in Britain, it is now a profitable company producing award-winning world-class cars. Now the company uses the 'jokes' to advertise the cars, such is its level of confidence that it has world-beating cars.

▌ Shifting industrial boundaries and competitive structures. These include increased development of strategic alliances, acquisitions and mergers between major international companies from different countries. Consider the multi-billion dollar mergers and acquisitions in the mid to late 1990s, especially in the pharmaceutical industry. An analysis of these mergers illustrates the vast financial and global resources and markets involved.

▌ Sourcing of supplies and manufacturing. This can be global as companies seek out the most competitive rates for the production of goods. For example, many textile products are manufactured in the Far East rather than in Europe or North America. Standards can be maintained, however labour costs are usually significantly lower. This has led to the charge of exploitation by anti-global campaigners and labour groups (see Chapter 3 on ethical and social responsibility issues).

▌ Substantial development and expansion of international transportation networks and digital telecommunication systems.

▌ The influence of movies and television. *Baywatch*™, the US drama series featuring a small group of lifeguards patrolling the shoreline of Southern California, became the most watched television series in the 1990s. A combined total of more than a billion viewers in more than 144 countries tuned in to watch the drama every week. Translated into 15 languages, it crossed virtually all cultures from Europe to Saudi Arabia, Iran and China (Czinkota *et al*, 1998). In terms of movies you just have to think of the phenomenal success of the James Bond brand that has lasted some 40 years, from *Dr No* (1962) to *Die Another Day* (2002). Then there's James Cameron's 1997 multi-Oscar™ winning drama of the fateful 1912 voyage of the passenger ship RMS *Titanic*. Reputed to have cost US $200 million, the movie has grossed an estimated US $1.9 billion worldwide! That is for box-office receipts only, and does not include the lucrative merchandising ventures such as posters, novelizations, exhibitions and composer James Horner's best-selling soundtrack album through Sony Classical.

- Combined with the above is the impact of satellite news agencies such as CNN, BBC Worldwide and CNBC. All have influenced their multi-million-people audience in one form or another.

- Developments of technology and technological transfer. Since the 1960s there has been an increase in both the development of technologies and technology transfer between companies and nations. This has aided the development of both countries and companies, although much more is needed with regards to relevant technological transfers between developed and developing nations. Technology has been important in the development of certain types of manufacturer – consider, for instance, Japanese car and electronics companies.

- Some companies learnt quickly to operate both effectively and efficiently across cultures, as well as across borders. This meant understanding and coping with different work practices, levels of expectations, varying skill levels, different business and legal environments, and competitive environments.

- A 'similarity' of consumer needs. While there are cultural influences within regions and countries, there is an increasing convergence towards similar types of products or services. For example, McDonald's has very much a global presence. It operates over 25,000 restaurants in some 115 countries. Thus while it is an in-demand global brand it also has to cater for different cultural needs, for example, chicken-based menus in India. However, the point here is that a growing number of consumers worldwide seek out McDonald's, as they do Disney, Microsoft and Nike.

- The development of e-commerce and associated e-marketing will develop global opportunities in the 21st century.

Market entry strategies

There are various methods a company or organization can use to enter the international marketplace. These are briefly discussed below and in Tables 14.6 and 14.7. It is worth remembering that some companies may move from one stage through to another, while others go from a zero base directly to an overseas subsidiary. Companies need to consider what will work for them, rather than what has necessarily worked for others.

Where possible we have provided alternative names for the various strategies. As is often the case in business terminology, the meanings become distorted or blurred. What is quoted in one source as the meaning of a particular term might be different in another. This is especially true with indirect and direct exporting. Therefore, it is always important to cross-reference these terms where possible.

Indirect exporting: home base

With indirect exporting the company has generally little inclination, or few resources, to embark on widespread international marketing projects. Therefore it seeks the simplest, most cost-efficient and low-risk solutions. Table 14.6 details the potential indirect marketing routes a company can take.

Table 14.7 lists the possible direct exporting routes a company can embark on. This may be either as a follow-on from indirect operations or a straight embarkation on direct exporting as a means of exploiting possible overseas markets.

Forming alliances

A company could enter into some form of alliance where it 'shares' activities with a local company. Table 14.8 sets out the different types of alliance that companies can undertake as a strategic means of entering new markets.

Table 14.6   Indirect exporting

Mode of indirect exporting	Description
Domestic-based exporters (also known as domestic purchasing)	An individual or a company buys a product direct from the manufacturer. It then takes on the responsibility to export, market and distribute that product within an overseas marketplace(s). While the original manufacturer is not directly involved in international marketing once it has sold on their product, it nonetheless places that product within the international market (Doole and Lowe, 1999). Additionally, by selling on the product (even within their own domestic environment) it provides them with a 'flavour' of the international marketing (Doole and Lowe, 1999). However, as Doole and Lowe point out, while the SME finds this the easiest method of 'entry' it is probably unaware of the dynamic characteristics of consumer and competitor behaviour.
Domestic-based export agents	Here an agent seeks and negotiates international sales of products on behalf of the manufacturer. The agent receives commission for its services. The manufacturer is usually responsible for credit risk, shipping and insurance costs. However, it retains greater control as the product is marketed in its name.
Piggybacking (also known as piggyback marketing, complementary marketing and 'Mother Hen' marketing)	Piggybacking is where one manufacturer (the carrier) carries the products of another (the rider), and markets them through its distribution network. Therefore the 'piggybacking' manufacturer is able to gain from the reputation of the first manufacturer. Doole and Lowe (1999) suggest that SMEs can gain advantages when the two products are interdependent, or if the piggybacking product provides a service for the first. As Keegan and Green (1997) suggest, the manufacturer (or rider) using the piggyback arrangement benefits from reduced costs. An example of piggybacking is when a publishing company markets books internationally on behalf of other domestic publishers.
Cooperative organizations	These are organizations that carry on the exporting activities on behalf of several producers. Farmers, for instance, may use the cooperative system to market and sell their produce within international markets.
Export management companies (EMCs) or export houses	Keegan and Green (1997) describe these as a domestic independent export companies that act as export departments for more than one company. They can assist SMEs to initiate, develop and maintain their international sales by providing a number of services (Keegan and Green, 1997). These include marketing research, channel selection, arranging financing and shipping, and the appropriate documentation.
Trading companies (also known as export trading companies – ETCs)	The trading companies of today are based upon the historic legacies of the past, for instance the East India trading company of the 18th and 19th centuries. In Japan Sogo Shoshas (sometimes written as sogoshosha) have played an important role in the development of international business since the 17th century. The conglomerate Mitsubishi is one of the largest Sogo Shoshas. The historical development of US trading companies has been somewhat more recent. Such companies have only been permitted since 1982, and thus they have been slow at developing. The legislation was designed to help the export potential of SMEs (Doole and Lowe, 1997). As Doole and Lowe (1997) explain, one of the major benefits of trading companies is that their extensive operations and contacts provide them with the opportunities to trade in difficult areas.

Table 14.7 Direct exporting: overseas based

Mode of direct exporting	Description
Internet marketing	Internet marketing is now widely discussed in most marketing texts, indeed you will find various references to the use of the Internet in this book. We have placed it here because we feel this is a rapidly developing sector. An example is Amazon.com, the Internet retailer of books, CDs, DVDs, household electrical appliances and equipment. However, it is currently perhaps best known as an online book retailer. Through the Internet it markets directly to the world's book-buying public. From the acceptance of the order/payment, the parcelling and despatch of the book becomes a pure logistic operation using standard delivery methods. However, the Internet does, and will, allow direct interaction with the buying public.
Foreign-based sales agents/distributors	Here sales agents and/or distributors market and sell the products on behalf of the manufacturing company. As part of the contract the sales agent might be allowed exclusive rights to represent that manufacturer within a particular country or region.
Domestic-based sales representatives (also known as travelling export sales representatives, international sales representatives/managers)	These are the company's own sales representatives who are based at Head Office, but travel overseas on a regular basis. They will be highly knowledgeable not only about the company's products or services, but also about the overseas business environments in which they operate. In other words they are culturally sensitive.
Overseas marketing/sales office/branch office/subsidiary	A marketing, sales or branch office is an extension of the company's head office located in another country. Such offices vary in size and level of operational capability. However, they can help the company to generate a greater presence within the host country. They can, for example, provide opportunities for a better understanding of the market (consumers and competitors), and handle warehousing, distribution and promotion. Of course, the establishment of any branch or marketing office must comply with local legislation (taxation, employment and documentation), and this may be a convoluted and time-consuming procedure. In this regard, a subsidiary will most likely have to be legally incorporated as a local company.

The impact of macro factors

In Chapter 2 we considered the key concepts of the macro environment. We urge students to reread Chapter 2, adding your knowledge to the issues raised in this section. Marketers must reflect upon the likely impact of the macro factors, within their domestic environment and within each of their overseas markets. The macro factors of one country might be totally different from those of another. For example, compare the PESTEL factors of China with those of the United States. (See Chapter 2.) Are there any commonalities, or are there wide gulfs in approach and understanding?

For the international marketer it is not simply the macro factors applicable to their home country that are important. The PESTEL factors of every other country can, in one way or another, impact on their business. For companies that operate on a global scale, such

Table 14.8 Types of alliance

Type of alliance	Description
Joint venture	This is where the home country manufacturer joins forces with host country investors/company to create a new company. In this new company there is joint ownership and operational control. When more than two companies are involved in forming the joint venture it is often referred to as a consortium or consortia. There are, of course, numerous variations on the joint venture model. Daniels and Radebaugh (1992) quote various examples, and we have briefly listed them below: ▮ A foreign company joining a local company, the standard quoted model. ▮ Companies from two or more countries may establish a joint venture in a third country. ▮ A joint venture may be formed between a foreign private company and the host government. This is also known as a mixed venture. ▮ A government-controlled company may be part of a joint venture with a private company within the host country. Additionally, there may be further variations in shareholding. For example, one company might have controlling interest (say, 51%). Alternatively, there could be a host government regulation that stipulates that the host country party has either equal shareholding, or the controlling interest.
Strategic alliances	There are various phrases used in relation to strategic alliances including strategic international alliances, collaborative agreements and global strategic partnerships. Strategic alliances have grown in popularity since the 1980s. The term can be used to cover contractual relationships that are beneficial to all parties, but cannot be clearly defined as licensing or joint ventures. Bronder and Pritzl (1992) define a strategic alliance as where two companies combine value chain activities to gain competitive advantage. The cooperation could be between two companies who, under normal circumstances, are competitors within other markets. Competitors may form strategic alliances to work together on high-end technologies, thus having mutual competitive advantages, rather than potentially depleting both marketing and technological resources by competing. Since the mid-1990s the global airline industry has witnessed an increasing number of strategic alliances, as carriers attempt to maximize route potential. Additionally, airlines are increasingly developing alliances with hotel chains within particular regions of the world. The horrific events of 11 September 2001, subsequent terrorist attacks and the Iraqi conflict and the resultant effect upon the airline industry have forced more carriers to consider the possibility of long-term survival through strategic alliances.
Licensing (also known as technology licensing)	With a licensing agreement the company (the licensor) grants rights on intangible property to another company or individual (the licensee) for a specified time frame. Additionally, it is normal for the licensee to pay a compensation royalty to the licensor in exchange for the licence. This compensation may be a lump sum royalty, an ongoing or running royalty (a royalty based on volume of production) or a combination of both.

Table 14.8   *continued*

Type of alliance	Description
Licensing (also known as technology licensing)	Intangibles include patents, inventions, formulas, designs, patterns, copyrights, literary, musical or artistic compositions, trade marks, trade names, brand names, contracts, methods, programmes, procedures and systems. An example of licensing is the French fashion house Pierre Cardin. The label is used by some 800 licensees in 93 countries to produce a range of items from clothing, luggage and watches to brief cases, toiletries and pens (Czinkota *et al*, 1998). Some of the world's best-known beers are brewed under licence in various countries, and are only on sale within those countries/regions.
Concessions	In terms of retailing, concessions can be described as the next stage on from exporting or licensing (Alexander, 1997). A concession is a shop within a shop, usually a department store, operated by a separate retailer. The incoming retailer brings into the store the product, while the host store creates the environment for the effective flow of customers. As Alexander (1997) notes, concessions are ideal for retailers that have distinct product ranges and operating formats that can be contained within restricted spaces. Concessions can provide companies with the opportunity to access geographically and culturally distant markets to fulfil a niche strategy.
Franchising	Czinkota *et al* (1998) describe franchising as: 'the granting of the right by a parent company (the franchisor/franchiser) to another, independent entity (the franchisee) to do business in a prescribed manner'. Generally franchising is a combination of the right to market and sell the franchiser's products or services. Generally, the franchiser provides assistance, training, sourcing of components and promotion, while exercising significant control over the methods of operation. Czinkota *et al* (1998) suggest the reasons for the dramatic growth of franchise operations internationally are market potential, financial gain and saturated domestic markets.
Foreign direct investment (FDI)	As a company gains experience within the international marketplace, it may decide to invest in its own overseas manufacturing facilities. Of course, the company must be sure that there is market potential for such a high level of investment. Such levels of investment must be seen as a long-term commitment. Companies that have developed to an advanced stage of international business usually employ a foreign direct investment strategy. The highest level, and one reached by few companies, is the multinational enterprise or corporation (MNE/MNC). As Robbins (1998) states, it is hard to overstate their size and global influence. He quotes Exxon's sales as a case in point: they exceed the GNPs of countries such as Indonesia, Nigeria, Argentina and Denmark. For such companies both domestic and international operations are integrated. Companies that can be viewed as multinationals include Nestlé, the Ford Motor Company and Exxon Oil. In 1997 China received direct investments valued at some US $45.2 billion, making it the second largest recipient of FDI after the United States (*Economist*, 1998). Approximately 80 per cent of that investment came from other Asian countries including Hong Kong (part of China from 1997), Singapore, South Korea and Japan, with the balance emanating from the United States and Western Europe (*Economist*, 1998). From the 1970s to the late 1990s this inflow of funding resulted in some 145,000 enterprises in China, possibly providing some 20 to 30 per cent of China's economic growth in the late 1980s and 1990s (*Economist*, 1998).

interactions are both diverse and highly complex.

Political environments

When it comes to the internationalization of markets, we need to think of how both domestic and international politics affect business. While we may live in an increasingly global village, there are sadly an increasing number of conflicts engulfing regions. Since the early 1990s these have included wars in Iraq, the former Yugoslavia, Kosovo, Rwanda and East Timor.

Then there were the horrific events of 11 September 2001 and subsequent acts of terrorism. The effect of these human tragedies will be felt for many years to come. The resultant 'war on terrorism' has caused many people to reappraise the political landscape. This has impacted on both individuals and companies. For example, the increasing reluctance of many to travel by air had an effect on major airlines which are struggling for survival. Within a year of 11 September 2001, several major airlines were either bankrupt or seeking bankruptcy protection.

Countries that were once peaceful neighbours and involved in effective trade can later find themselves in conflict. If a company was solely dependent on that particular market, the onslaught of political conflict will probably lead to its closure. For example, companies that had built profitable markets with Iraq in the 1980s (sanctioned by both governments) found their markets closed virtually overnight by the imposition of embargoes and sanctions. Those that could not quickly develop new markets for their products faced financial ruin.

Although governments can and do exercise power, as we discussed in Chapter 2, both individuals and corporations have the potential to influence government action. For example, consider the fact that some of the world's richest business people have more personal financial power than the GDPs of many countries. Thus, as anti-globalization campaigners argue, unelected individuals can wield power and influence over governments and countries. This could be considered as a new form of imperialism. However, as yet there appears to be little evidence that individuals have wielded such negative power and influence. In some cases their philanthropic actions have benefited the sick and the needy of several countries. However, such financial power and potential political influence will remain an area of active debate.

Economics

Here again we need to consider two perspectives, what happens within both the domestic or home market and the host market. We now consider a selection of issues.

Exchange rates

Countries within the European Union that signed up to Monetary Union now have a single currency, the euro. This means that there are no exchange rate transactions across the borders of the countries that comprise the euro zone. However the UK has not joined the euro zone, so British-based companies exporting into the euro zone have exchange rate transactions to consider. This can result in their products being more expensive than products manufactured and sold within the euro zone.

Income levels and disposable incomes

The level of personal income varies enormously from country to country, region to region. Therefore the international marketer needs to understand different income levels, and whether a product can be marketed into a region or country. It is necessary to realize that a product that has a mass market appeal within one country may have only a niche market within another. This is very much a reflection of income levels.

Indirect taxation

Companies marketing internationally must also consider the levels of indirect taxation that are added to the cost of their product throughout the supply chain. Additionally governments often change indirect taxation rates, therefore companies need to be prepared for such changes. In some cases companies choose to absorb the cost of indirect taxation increases to reduce the risk of a fall in sales.

Societal

Linton (1945) defined culture as 'the configuration of learned behaviour and results of behaviour whose component elements are shared and transmitted by members of a particular society'. Doole and Lowe (1997) refine this for the international marketer, stating that culture is 'The sum total of learned beliefs, values and customs that serve to direct consumer behaviour in a particular country market'.

A global economy presents challenges to managers that they never had to confront when their operations were constrained within national borders. They face different legal, political and economic policies. But they must also deal with varying national cultures – the primary values and practices that characterize particular countries – many of which are nothing like those in which they have spent their entire lives (Robbins, 1998). Such differences can be highlighted by the behaviour and attitudes displayed by managers operating outside their own national culture. Table 14.9 outlines different types of attitude or cultural orientation.

Legal

Companies marketing internationally need to consider any legal issues relating to their

Table 14.9   Cultural orientations

Cultural orientation	Description
Parochialism	This can be described as having a very narrow view of the world. There is often an inability to recognize differences between the people of different cultures.
Ethnocentrism	This is the belief that one's own cultural values and customs are superior to all others. People who are ethnocentric in their orientation believe that others should fit in with their views of the world and business. For example, the same competitive and product–market strategies are applied to all markets. As a result any cultural differences are ignored. This can also be considered as total standardization.
Polycentrism	Here the focus is on the local environment and tends to be culturally sensitive. Generally the various country subsidiaries of a multinational are free to formulate their own objectives and plans to meet local market conditions. This can be considered as total adaptation.
Regiocentrism	This is the synthesis of ethnocentrism and polycentrism, and focuses on a region. It is based on the assumption that there are both similarities and differences across cultures that can be merged into regional transnational strategies. As many cultures converge, companies may well seek to adopt this strategic orientation.
Geocentrism	This is a further development of regiocentrism but considers it on a global scale. Here subsidiaries of a global business see themselves as an integral part of that business.

product or service within each country. Certain legal practices have international recognition, such as letters of credit for payment and Incoterms, a set of agreed terms of trade. Equally, there are international agreements that cover the treaties developed by organizations such as the International Monetary Fund (IMF) and the World Trade Organization (WTO). Table 14.10 sets out some of the legal issues marketers need to consider when operating internationally.

Environmental

In the international context, as with the domestic, environmental issues are often linked closely with legal aspects. Companies must follow environmental codes of practice. Equally, companies must be aware of changing external environmental conditions. Some countries are susceptible to dramatic environmental conditions ranging from extreme cold to heat. Such external factors

Table 14.10 Potential international legal issues

Potential legal issue	Description
Contract status	The legal status of any contract has to be determined. For example, if there was a dispute over advertising, under which country's legal system would it be resolved?
Local consumer protection laws	These generally vary from one country to another. In certain countries there are strict laws that impact, for example, on the marketing mix. The marketer must be mindful of the variants. Again, what is an acceptable practice in one country may not be in another.
Status of imports/exports	This involves knowing what can legally be exported or imported. Restrictions might be the result of multilateral or unilateral embargoes or sanctions, or they could be imposed by domestic laws. For example, during the European Union ban on British beef (after the outbreak of BSE) it was illegal to import British beef into other member states of the Union. Books and movies might be perfectly legal in one country but be banned for numerous reasons in another country. Indian-born novelist Salman Rushdie's controversial book *The Satanic Verses* (published 1988) was readily available in the UK and other European countries, but banned as blasphemous in Islamic countries. Food products containing alcohol, gelatine or certain E numbers are banned in the Middle East on religious grounds.
Protection of trademarks and patents	Mühlbacher, Dahringer and Leihs (1999) estimated that nearly 200 million illegal CDs are produced each year globally, with about 60 per cent emanating from China. While the majority of countries that have signed up to the various conventions rigorously police infringements, it is clear that not all countries are as vigilant. Companies that want to take action against the counterfeiters can often discover that the country's legal system is unsupportive, slow and bureaucratic. Therefore companies need to judge the level of risk in marketing their products into such countries.
Legal ownership of subsidiaries	Under 'entry strategies' we considered foreign direct investment. This too has several legal implications for a company. While some countries permit 100 per cent ownership, others will only grant a minority stakeholding through a form of strategic alliance. In most cases the company wishing to operate in another country through FDI needs to find a local partner(s) and form an alliance in order to operate. This might be the case whether it is supplying a product or services, such as educational courses. Equally, some governments have additional restrictions on the types of business in which a foreign company can have involvement. These restrictions usually relate to media and defence equipment suppliers.

Table 14.10   *continued*

Potential legal issue	Description
Technical standards	Through their regulatory authorities countries impose various levels of technical standards on products marketed within their country. In the UK the British Standards Institute (BSI) provides manufacturers seeking entry into the UK market with advice on technical and other requirements. This includes national laws, particularly in relation to safety and environmental protection, general technical standards and certification processes. To provide an idea of the complexity of technical standards, the BSI has a library with over 500,000 standards and regulations for over 100 countries, together with 10,000 English translations (see www.bsi.org.uk).
Labelling	Governments may impose strict labelling regulations for products ranging from food to textiles. In 1997 the Russian government passed a resolution requiring all foreign food products coming into Russia to feature Russian language labels or packaging for nutritional information, manufacturing date and ingredients. The regulation had been adopted because people had become ill by eating products (labelled in English) that were past their use-by date (Wendlandt, 1997).

impinge on what can be marketed in that particular region.

Trade control: tariff and non-tariff barriers

Although the WTO seeks to reduce and eventually eliminate tariff barriers and non-tariff barriers, they still exist within the global marketplace. In this section we explore some of the barriers used by nations to control the flow of products and services.

Tariffs

This is the most common form of trade control, and can be described as a government tax levied on products transported internationally. For some, most especially less developed nations (LDNs), this can be a valuable form of revenue generation. However, some countries have been criticized for the type of products on which they impose tariffs. For example, in the United States some luxury items carry no tariff at all, while products bought by those on much lower incomes are subject to tariff duties. Tariffs

can be segmented into three main areas which are outlined in Table 14.11.

Non-tariff barriers

Import licences

Some governments require companies to obtain special licences before they can ship products to that country. In the UK import licences are required for such products as guns, ammunition and radioactive materials.

Quotas

This is a numerical limit placed on the quantity of a particular product or range of products that can be imported into a country or economic region (such as the European Union). It is often used as a means of protecting domestic industry from lower cost imports. The European Union, for example, impose quotas on textiles imported from India.

Subsidies

These are generally used to help domestic industries that operate within international

Table 14.11 Types of tariff barrier

Tariff barrier	Description
Export tariff	This is where the government of the exporting country imposes and collects a tax.
Transit tariff	This is where the government of the country through which the products are trans-shipped collects a tax. For example, if products are being transported from Germany through Switzerland to Italy, Switzerland might impose a transit tariff.
Import tariff	This is where the government of the importing country levies a tax. This is currently the most common form of tariff barrier. The aim of such tax or duty is to raise the price of imported products so that domestically produced goods have a greater opportunity of competing successfully within the marketplace. Often this is used to protect inefficient industries against lower-priced high-quality products. Additionally, governments may increase import tariffs as a means to restrict consumer expenditure. This will be the case where there are severe balance of payments problems.

markets. The government pays a grant to the suppliers of the product or service. Subsidies can be classified into two groups. Service subsidies are those where the government provides potential exporters with an array of support services to help them market their product overseas. These services can include provision of exhibition sponsorship, export/import information, country information, market research and assistance with establishing contacts. For example, in the UK the Foreign and Commonwealth Office (FCO) and the Department of Trade and Industry (DTI) through their joint Overseas Trade Services operation provide a range of export services.

Economic subsidies are more controversial. These may be designed to keep prices lower (compared with imported produce), to maintain reasonable incomes for producers, or to maintain employment within a particular business sector or industry. Within the European Union, for example, government subsidies to either publicly owned or private companies are normally banned if they distort or threaten to distort competition. However, some types of subsidy are exempt from such controls. These include assistance to economically depressed regions and the promotion of new economic activities.

Buy local legislation or promotions

This can vary enormously in scope. Governments, who are often the largest purchasers within a country, may require departments to buy a proportion of locally produced goods and services. They might also, through public relations campaigns, attempt to persuade consumers to buy locally produced goods. For example, the British government led campaigns to buy British beef after the BSE scare.

Finally, governments may require companies to use a proportion of locally produced components within a finished product. This may range from automotive parts to electronic components.

Administrative barriers (also known as bureaucratic red tape)

As Czinkota et al (1998) state, administrative barriers are a complex of laws, regulations, documentation, rulings, health and safety standards, labelling and testing certification. It is important to state here that some of these regulations and procedures are absolutely necessary, for instance health and safety regulations. However, the issue is not necessarily the regulation itself but how it is administered or applied, which can lead to delays. These administrative procedures can be applied in such a way that it is difficult, expensive or virtually impossible to export products to a foreign country.

Even if these procedures can be complied with, the amount of time involved often adds further financial burdens, thus making the product more expensive. Table 14.12, based on World Bank statistics, illustrates the time taken and cost of registering a business within specific countries. Such time and costs impact on companies either setting up a local office or at the early stages of foreign direct investment. We have included extremes to convey the wide disparity between nations. We suggest that you compare and contrast the time and legal costs involved. Also consider the costs involved in the staff time dedicated to completing all necessary paperwork.

Sanctions

These are specific trade measures that can include the cancellation of trade financing or the prohibition of high-technology trade. For example, the US government prevents certain high-level technologies being exported to other countries, most especially those that could gain a military advantage within a particular volatile region of the world.

Embargoes

These tend to be broader in nature than sanctions in that they prohibit trade entirely. They may be imposed on imports or exports, or whole categories of products regardless of destination, or specific products to specific countries (for instance weapon systems to potentially 'hostile' countries.

Table 14.12   Cost of entry regulations

Country	Number of procedures	Duration (days)	Estimated costs of legal fees (US $)
Azerbaijan	15	104	113.02
Bolivia	19	104	1,483.95
Canada	2	2	125.62
Dominican Republic	20	117	853.04
Germany	9	45	1,461.39
Ghana	10	164	331.47
India	10	95	221.21
Indonesia	11	158	159.58
Mozambique	16	302	147.09
Norway	4	24	1,265.03
Russian Federation	19	50	114.25
Singapore	7	8	1,628.64
Spain	11	110	2,338.11
United Arab Emirates	10	29	4,982.64
United Kingdom	5	5	372.07
Venezuela	14	201	711.62

Embargoes are usually enforced for political reasons, for example diplomatic disputes between nations. However they generally have an economic impact on local producers, manufacturers and civilians. In 1990 when Iraq invaded Kuwait virtually all members of the United Nations condemned the invasion. At the end of the Gulf War, the United Nations imposed a multilateral trade embargo against Iraq. This was rescinded in 2003 after US and UK military action against Iraq.

The marketing mix

In this section we turn to the marketing mix and seek to explain how it relates to an international environment. At this stage you may want to refresh your memory of the marketing mix by referring back to the relevant chapters.

Products and branding

In Chapter 8 we listed the world's most valuable brands. It was clear from the list that American brands dominate. Here we need to reconsider the issues raised by Levitt. While some products can be standardized (to a greater or lesser extent) for an international marketplace, it is clear that others cannot. Let us first take music. We could say that British bands like The Beatles and The Rolling Stones produced standardized products in that their music was not changed for different markets. Contemporary pop culture and music is building upon the global success of such bands, as the young in many countries strive for UK and US sounds.

The same could be said of classical composers. The music of Beethoven and Tchaikovsky, for instance, can be heard in concert halls throughout Europe, America, South America and the Far East. The quality of the performances may vary, but the music is the same.

Earlier we mentioned the impact of movies. The cinema can have a global impact. You just have to consider the worldwide box-office figures for the James Bond movies or James Cameron's epic movie *Titanic*. However, some adaptations may be necessary. These vary from editing certain scenes by the local censor (this usually relates to the level and/or type of sex and/or violence portrayed, or on religious grounds) to dubbing or subtitling in the national language.

As Keegan and Green (1997) point out, Coca-Cola is positioned and marketed the same in all countries. The basic strategic principles that guide brand management are the same globally. However, the product may be varied slightly to accommodate local tastes. The adaptation focuses on sweetness and the level of carbonization (Keegan and Green, 1997). For instance, in India Cola-Cola is slightly sweeter than in the UK, and in Eastern Europe the level of carbonization tends to be lower.

Equally, McDonald's is a global brand. However, it modifies its menu in various countries to cater for local tastes. These tastes may be driven by a cultural imperative. The big breakfast served at a McDonald's in London is different from that served in New York, Paris or Mumbai.

Doole and Lowe (1997) suggest that product standardization is both encouraging and being encouraged by global trends. They suggest that this is due to the following three factors:

- Markets are becoming *increasingly* homogeneous.

- There are, *in many areas* more identifiable international consumer segments.

- There is an increasing number of organizations moving towards globalization.

(We need to add a word of caution here. It is easy to see a country as an homogeneous environment. However, such a perspective can be far from the truth. India is a good example. It is a diverse geographical region, with diverse cultures and a population of over 1 billion people. In the large cities of New Delhi and Mumbai, or the education centre of Pune, there are significant Western influences and a Western orientation. That, of course, does not mean that 'West is best'. In outlying towns and villages, in particular, there is likely to be a more deeply rooted traditional Indian society. The same is of course applicable to many other countries.)

Reasons for product adaptation

Technical factors

Electrical equipment ranging from computers to televisions and VCRs may have to be adapted to meet different voltage and transmission standards. This is one of the reasons that videos from the United States cannot be played on UK-manufactured VCRs. The colour television standard in the United States is NTSC (National Systems Television Committee), while parts of Europe, Africa and Australia/New Zealand use PAL (Phase Alternation by Line) and in France, parts of Africa and Eastern Europe it is SECAM (Sequential And Memory). As you can see the move towards different standards can only be confusing for many consumers. Since 1991, there has been greater harmonization with the European Union, and in theory the advent of advanced digital technologies should, in the future, overcome these technical problems.

Automotive manufacturers need to consider whether the vehicle requires left or right-hand steering and the modification of heating and cooling systems for different climates.

Cultural perspectives

Attitudes and cultural perspectives can vary enormously within regions and countries. We

have mentioned the risks of considering countries as strictly homogeneous environments. Let us take this further as a way of understanding cultural perspectives. Many people perceive the United States as one homogeneous environment. However, it is a vast country comprising not only diverse geographical landscapes but beliefs as well. These beliefs not only cover the vast political spectrum but extend to personal attitudes and behaviours. What we are saying here is that students should consider the rich diversity within their own as well as other environments.

The Barbie™ doll was first introduced into the United States in 1959. For years the American version – tall, slender and blonde-haired – was the only cultural version available. Today, this toy has undergone cultural adaptation for certain regions. For example, in Malaysia Barbie™ is known as Kebaya Barbie™, has long black hair, dark brown eyes and wears traditional Malay clothes (known as *sarong kebaya*). The Malaysian Barbie is available in three variations, wearing a white, dark green or pink kebaya.

Food

As Doole and Lowe (1997) state, 'food is a particularly difficult area for standardization, as the preparation and eating of food are often embedded in the history, religion and/or culture of the country'. As we have seen, companies such as McDonald's vary their menus to meet local tastes. Additionally we need to be aware of the impact of religion, for example the need for kosher or Halal food products.

Chinese consumers generally do not like the taste of cheese. This is because it has never been part of their food tradition, unlike in Britain and France which have traditions of cheese making.

Perception of numbers

The intrinsic value placed on numbers is extremely important within certain cultures. In the West we tend to consider the number 13 as unlucky. However in Japan the number 4 is considered bad luck, whereas the numbers 3 and 5 are considered lucky. Therefore packaging items in containers of four may not be received favourably in Japan. While in many countries the number 7 is considered lucky, in Ghana, Kenya and Singapore it is considered unlucky.

Perception of colours

Colour can have many meanings, most especially among the older generations. Kotler (2000) cites the example of the Ronnie McDonald character being used to promote the brand in Japan. The white-faced clown promotion failed because in Japan, as with many other Far Eastern nations, a painted white face means death or mourning. In Brazil mourning is represented by the colour purple, in Mexico it is yellow, and dark red within Africa's Ivory Coast (Kotler, 2000).

Language

As well as the dubbing or subtitling of movies, we need to consider the meaning of words and phrases and their translation. This impacts on brand names and slogans. A successful brand name in one country could be a household joke or obscenity in another. For example, in Japan there is a popular drink called Sweat, clearly not an inviting name from an English-speaking perspective.

When the Sunbeam Corporation introduced its Mist Stick – a mist-producing curling tong system – in Germany the promotional campaign failed. *Mist* in German means, in slang, excrement!

Of course such grammatical devices as apostrophes or spaces can significantly change meanings. The *Oxford English Reference Dictionary* describes 'nova' as 'a star showing sudden large increase in brightness and then slowly returning to its original state over a few months'. For General Motors it was an ideal name for a range of cars for both the US and UK markets. Indeed the model range sold well. Then it decided to sell it into Spain. In Spanish too 'nova' means 'star'. However, the Spanish phrase 'no'va' loosely translated means 'does not go'. The potential risk for GM was too great and the name was changed.

Legal issues

Products may have to be adapted for legal reasons to meet certain regulatory standards.

Safety

For example, various European Union directives regulate for safety reasons such products as cosmetics, pharmaceuticals, textiles (where the main concern is to prevent the use of flammable materials), toys and fireworks.

Food

Under European Union regulations food may contain E numbered ingredients (European numbers). This is a code number used as a standard way of identifying approved food additives when listing ingredients on food or drink labels. These additives, which may either occur naturally or be chemically produced, include colours, preservatives, antioxidants, emulsifiers, stabilizers, flavour enhancers and glazing agents. While these are acceptable under European Union regulations, the US Food and Drug Administration has banned certain E numbers from food and drinks because of the concern, suggested by some research, that they are carcinogenic.

Environment

The United States, for example, has strict regulations governing the permitted levels of exhaust emissions from vehicles. All vehicles imported into the United States must meet these legally enforced standards. For the manufacturer this can mean product (engine and exhaust system) modification.

Marketing insight: The game *Monopoly*

In 1933, at the height of the US depression, Charles Darrow developed the board game *Monopoly*. He marketed the game into a Philadelphia department store, and demand for it grew beyond his ability to meet it. Parker Brothers, who had originally rejected his idea, agreed a deal with Darrow to manufacture and market the game. In the first year of distribution, 1935, it became America's best-selling game. Not only has the game become a part of American popular culture, but so too for many other cultures. Today it remains the best-selling game in the world, and by October 2002 it had been sold into 80 countries and produced in 26 languages. In each case, through licensing arrangements, the board game represents local landmarks as well as the national language.

Hasbro, the American copyright owners of the game, believe that over 200 million games have been sold worldwide, and since 1935 some 500 million people have played the game.

Sources: www.monopoly.com and www.hasbro.com

Price

Generally speaking, price is the only element within the marketing mix that is revenue generating. The others are initially cost centres, although they can significantly assist in selling the product or service, thus generating sales and revenue. As we saw in Chapter 9, pricing strategies can be somewhat complex to determine. However pricing within the international or global context is more complicated than within the domestic environment. Numerous internal and external factors can influence international pricing. Terpestra and Sarathy (1997) identified these factors. We have adapted and expanded their original list.

Company and product factors

These are:

▌ corporate and marketing objectives;

▌ company and product positioning;

▌ the product range, life cycles (including rejuvenation of products through new markets), substitutes, production differentiation and unique selling proposition (USP);

▌ cost structures, manufacturing, experience effect and economies of scale;

▌ marketing and product development;

▌ availability and quality of resources;

▌ inventory;

▌ packaging and freight costs.

Market factors

These are:

▌ the consumer's perceptions and expectations of the product and/or service;

▌ the consumer's ability to purchase the products and/or services on offer;

▌ the level of product adaptation required;

▌ the level of product servicing required at launch, and over time (for example, for motorized equipment or vehicles);

▌ the structure of the market, including the range of distribution channels available and current and potential competitive pressures (for example, the pressure to discount);

▌ the requirement for credit facilities;

▌ the current and potential future competitors – their objectives, strengths, weaknesses and likely strategies for maintaining/gaining market share.

External factors

▌ The level and type of government influences, restrictions and constraints. (For example, the imposition of tariff charges or local subsidies. Here we have to take into consideration not only the actions of the host government, but also home governments and other unilateral and multilateral 'governmental' actions. These could include action taken by the United Nations or the World Trade Organization.)

▌ The potential for, and the degree of currency fluctuations within the global market. We can no longer just consider this in terms of the currency fluctuations between two countries. Severe fluctuations within a major currency will normally have repercussions for all currencies.

▌ The normality of business and economic cycles. These cycles fluctuate, and any severe changes in the cycles can have equally adverse effects on markets.

▌ The level of inflation and interest rates.

▌ The level of the use of non-money payments and leasing arrangements.

Types of pricing strategy

Unfortunately there is no one simple straightforward pricing mechanism. Marketers tackle this subject from so many different angles and perspectives that it can often be overwhelming and confusing. As an introduction to international pricing strategies, we have taken a simplistic overview. As such, we have divided the topic into three main components outlined in Table 14.13.

Table 14.13   International pricing

Pricing structure	Description
Standard worldwide pricing	This is a pricing strategy that covers all international markets. It is determined by averaging the unit costs that comprise fixed, variable and export-related costs (including special packaging, insurance, warehousing and tariff charges). Generally, this has been considered a theoretical model. However, with the development of European Monetary Union (the euro zone countries), it may be possible for companies operating within this zone to create standard pricing for some products.
Dual pricing	In dual pricing domestic and international prices are differentiated. Two approaches or methods can be used to calculate the international price: the cost-plus method and the marginal cost method. Cost-plus: this is full allocation of both domestic and international costs and includes a profit margin. There are two key problems with this method. First, it can make the product too expensive for the intended market. To overcome this obstacle, companies often build in a degree of flexibility. This usually comes in the form of discounts to meet local market conditions. Second, the company could underprice the product or service. In addition to the potential loss of revenues, buyers may perceive the product or service as 'poor quality' because of its low price. Marginal cost: here the company considers the direct costs of producing, marketing and selling the product for export. The fixed costs of plant, equipment, research and development, domestic overheads and domestic marketing costs are not included. As a result, the company can lower prices if it believes it needs to be more competitive (on price) within the market.
Market pricing (also known as the market-base pricing model)	Companies price their products and services appropriately for the individual markets. Such price discrimination, within the different markets, involves charging a price that the market will accept. The determinants are reflected within the company and products, market and external factors stated earlier in this chapter. These factors vary, to a greater or lesser extent, from one country to another. Therefore the pricing policies of multinationals often reflect these dynamic factors.

Marketing insight: McDonald's

Vignali (2001) states that fast-food producer 'McDonald's has realized that, despite the cost savings inherent in standardization, success can often be attributed to being able to adapt to a specific environment'. In his research paper Vignali illustrates the comparative price of a Big Mac from around the world. What can be deducted from Vignali's research is that McDonald's has developed a different pricing strategy for different countries, and thus markets. As Vignali contends, 'More importantly, rather than just having a different pricing policy for the Big Mac in these limited countries, McDonald's has had to select the right price for the right market.'

Vignali (2001) suggests that for each country there is a rigorous pricing process that is used to determine the price for that particular market. The process, as described by Vignali, Vrontis and Dana (1999) is as follows:

1. Selecting the price objective.
2. Determining the demand.
3. Estimating costs.
4. Analysing competitors' costs, process and offers.
5. Selecting a pricing method.
6. Selecting a final price.

This process provides the basic framework that allows McDonald's to set localized prices. What is key is that McDonald's overall pricing objective is to increase overall market share.

Table 14.14 is a comparative analysis of McDonald's pricing of a Big Mac in several regions of the world. As you can see from this table there is a marginal difference between some countries, while there is a comparatively significant difference between others. This issue links back to the ability of an individual, within the target group, to be able to afford a Big Mac in the first place.

Table 14.14 Comparative McDonald's 'Big Mac' Prices

Country	Cost in UK £ (All currencies have been converted to UK £ in order to benchmark the comparative prices)
Australia	0.87
South Africa	0.92
USA	1.13
South Korea	1.13
India	1.19
New Zealand	1.20
Turkey	1.25
Japan	1.27
Spain	1.44
Brazil	1.52
Ireland	1.52
Switzerland	1.58
Germany	1.58
Italy	1.59
Austria	1.61
Belgium	1.66
Denmark	1.80
UK	1.81

It is interesting, and is brought out in Vignali's article, that while McDonald's is a global brand, it takes the approach of thinking 'locally'. That is, it attempts to discover what works in terms of both food products and pricing in each local area or region.

Source: Vignali (2001).

Promotion

It is vital that a company builds an effective promotional campaign. However, it is necessary to appreciate the country-specific issues before embarking upon a potentially expensive campaign. Many otherwise successful brand name companies have undertaken costly campaigns, only to discover that they either did not apply the appropriate communications technique or offended the cultural sensitivities of the country.

Media availability

In some countries there are strict regulations on how media can be used. Additionally, some media are not available to advertisers: for example there might be no commercial television networks. However this to some extent, depending upon audience numbers, can be overcome by advertising on satellite channels such as CNN.

There may be very limited distribution of the 'national' newspaper, with it restricted to certain cities. Additionally, literacy levels may restrict communication via newspapers and magazines.

Cyberspace has enormous potential, and some companies are already actively marketing their products and services via the Web. There are, of course, currently limitations. The greatest concentration of Internet users is in the United States and Europe. However, as education levels improve and the distribution of computers widens, e-marketing and e-promotion opportunities will increase. Of course, the big question is, will everyone in the world have the opportunity to benefit from such developments and expansions?

Language and translations

As we witnessed earlier, not every language translates well into another. What is innocent in one language can be far from innocent in another. Sometimes advertising slogans do not translate particularly well into another language. For example, when Gillette introduced its Sensor Shaving System™ it launched a highly coordinated and successful marketing campaign in 19 countries. The slogan of the campaign was 'Gillette, the best a man can get'. Unfortunately this does not translate too well into French, so a local variant was created, 'La perfection au masculin'. Translated this means – 'Perfection, male style' (Levine, 1990).

Restrictions and taboos

In various countries the promotion of some products is banned, completely or partially – that is, regulated in some way. These include cigarette and tobacco products, alcoholic beverages, movies, books and pharmaceutical products.

Some countries are considered quite liberal in what can be shown on television. For many years condoms have been advertised on television, often humorously. However it was not until the late 1990s that condom manufacturers were allowed to advertise their products on British television networks. In many countries such advertisements are still prohibited.

When the French company Guy Laroche advertised its perfume for men Drakkar Noir in

Saudi Arabia it had to be very different from their advertisement in France. The French advertisement had a woman seizing the wrist of a bare-armed man as he held the perfume bottle. In the Saudi Arabian version the man is still clutching the perfume bottle, but he is wearing a shirt and a dark suit, and the woman's hand is merely stroking or brushing the edge of his hand with her fingers (Czinkota *et al*, 1998). Although this demonstrates the need to understand the social mores of a particular region or country, both advertisements demonstrate sexuality. In the French advertisement, for example, it can be argued that this is a very passionate response to the man wearing the perfume. It is overt. The Saudi advertisement could be considered much more sensual. In a sense it is much more subtle, but it still communicates the sexuality of the perfume without offending the Saudi culture.

Some countries, such as the United Kingdom and the United States, allow comparison advertising (as long as it meets the regulatory criteria). Comparison advertising is where one company compares its product's performance against a named competitor brand. However, in countries such as the Philippines this is prohibited (Czinkota *et al*, 1998).

There is now increasing regulation on what (and when) products can be advertised to children within certain age groups. In Sweden, for instance, no toy products can be advertised on television aimed at children under the age of 12. Various countries, the United States included, have considered specific legislation to protect children from being specifically targeted for a range of products including food, designer clothing and toys.

Marketing insight: Umbro© and Bosch Siemens

Naming a product, as we have already seen within the main body of text, can be fraught with difficulties. This 'Marketing insight' reflects on the ordinary German word *Zyklon*, which means 'cyclone'. Yet what appears to be an ordinary and innocent word unfortunately has connotations with a terrifying and brutal period in 20th century history.

In the 1930s the German chemical company I G Farben created an insecticide that it named Zyklon B. The word 'Zyklon' was presumably used because it would act as a 'cyclone' against the insects. However during the Second World War Nazi scientists realized that when Zyklon B crystals were exposed to air they formed a deadly gas. Thus Zyklon B became the killing agent that was used by the Nazis to gas millions of Jews and others deemed by the Nazi state to be undesirable (academics, communists, intellectuals, gypsies and anyone else who opposed the regime) in the concentration camps. An innocent normal word became associated with horrific death and a murderous regime.

In 1999 the sportswear manufacturer Umbro© launched a new trainer called Zyklon. The name appeared on the side of the box but not on the sports shoe itself. In 2002 the name of the trainer became public knowledge, and was subsequently received with outrage. Umbro© issued a public apology stating that it was purely coincidental that such a name had been chosen. The name was changed both in the UK and internationally.

In 2001 the German engineering company Siemens through its consumer product joint venture company Bosch Siemens Hausgeräte (BSH) filed two patent applications in the United States for the Zyklon name to be used across a range of home products. On this becoming public knowledge there was outrage among various groups in the United States. Subsequently the company decided against using the name in the United States and withdrew its trademark application.

A search of the Internet reveals that other companies use the word Zyklon to market products and activities, including rollercoaster rides.

Questions and activities

Clearly the use of the word Zyklon has become an emotive subject. What is your opinion of this issue? You may want to discuss this with your fellow students. Do you think companies need to be more sensitive to such issues, or do you believe they should ignore these concerns and market the product or service anyway? Why?

Sources: CNN.Com (2002), BBC (2002d, 2002e).

Marketing insight: Temptations and Cadbury India

In 2002 the political and military tensions between India and Pakistan, over the territory of Kashmir, escalated significantly. Both countries threatened each other with a potential nuclear conflict. Diplomatic efforts by the United Nations and various world leaders calmed the inflamed situation, although it remains a line of tension.

Cadbury India sought to 'capitalize' on the Kashmir situation, but it drew the company into deep controversy. Newspaper advertisements for the Temptation brand showed a map of Kashmir, alongside which were the words 'I'm good. I'm tempting. I'm too good to share. What am I? Cadbury's Temptations or Kashmir?' The release of the advertisement coincided with Indian Independence Day, which only sought to increase the degree of controversy.

Vinod Tawde, leader of the BJP Party in Bombay commented:

Kashmir is a very sensitive issue and thousands of *jawans* [soldiers] have sacrificed their lives for it. Such ads just trivialize the issue and lack basic sensitivity. How can an ad campaign, in the name of creativity, even imply that Kashmir is a state to be shared? ... Why use an emotive issue like Kashmir to promote products?

In a statement Cadbury India said, 'We offer our sincere apologies to any section of the public that may have been offended by the advert.' A spokesperson for Cadbury Schweppes, the parent company of Cadbury India, stated, 'From time to time local management make mistakes. This was clearly one.'

What this example illustrates is that even with local knowledge serious errors of judgement can be made. The damage to the Cadbury name in India may only be short-lived, since over some 50 years Cadbury has been able to forge a strong reputation in India. However, if it had been a new company entering the marketplace, the damage could have been irretrievable.

Questions

1. Can you think of any other examples of international promotions that particular groups found offensive? Consider why the groups found them offensive. Do you agree with them and why?
2. Why do you think companies deliberately take such risks, or is it an error of judgement? If the latter, how can companies minimize such risks internationally? Bear in mind that the Temptation advertisements were actually created by the company's subsidiary in India and not the parent company in England.

Source: Dodd (2002).

Placement (distribution, logistics/ channel management)

In Chapter 13 we discussed how products and services reach the marketplace through various channels of activity. In this section we focus on the international dimension of that part of the marketing operation. As Jobber (1998) states, companies need to realize that international distribution channels do not usually resemble their own domestic ones.

The objectives of channel management and distribution are fourfold, as described in Table 14.15. Taking Jobber's point made earlier, companies need to consider how these four objectives can be successfully met within the international context (Jobber, 1998).

A key factor that a company must consider

Table 14.15 Objectives of channel management

Objectives	Description
Place	This is making the product or service available to the customer at a particular location. It should be a location of the customer's choosing.
Time	This is the availability of the product or service when required by the customer. This issue has been highlighted increasingly by the development of e-commerce. The customer places an order at midnight via the company's Internet site. The question is, when can the customer expect delivery of that product or service?
Form	The availability of the product in its final form and usable condition. For example, consider a student who lives in Hong Kong and orders a textbook via an Internet site based in the United States. The company instructs its shipper to send the book to the student in Hong Kong. However, if it were poorly packaged the book might be damaged in transit, and be unusable. Consider further the form of delivery for something much more fragile than a textbook.
Information	The customer needs access to details regarding (1) the product or service's features and benefits, (2) helpline support and (3) tracking. Tracking is particularly important for B2B customers. However, there is an increasing need for B2C buyers to be able to track the delivery of their purchase. This links to the use of the Internet. The student in Hong Kong mentioned above should be able to gain information on the status of the delivery of the textbook via the Internet bookshop site: for example despatch date, mode of delivery, delivery date and time. Communication networks can provide such detailed information.

is its level of involvement in channel management. This, of course, may be predetermined by the type of market entry strategy originally chosen by the organization. The company has two main choices. First there is direct involvement with its own sales force and/or stores (owned or franchised). Second, there is indirect involvement where the company contracts to independent agents, distributors and wholesalers. In the latter case, there is usually the need to create incentives to encourage channel members to invest time promoting the company's products or services over those of a competitor's. In both cases it is vital that the sales force and agents understand not only the cultural differences but also the legal environment in which they operate.

Retail systems

The type and nature of retail outlets varies significantly, from highly concentrated to fragmented. Within a concentrated environment there are a few retailers supplying the majority of the market, whereas in a fragmented market there are many retailers and no one retailer has a significant market share. However, it should be stressed that markets tend to be highly dynamic and thus the situation can be subject to unpredictability and change.

Hill (2001) suggests that there is a tendency for greater retail concentration in developed nations. He cites three key factors: increased car ownership, the number of households with freezers/refrigerators, and the increasing number of households with two incomes.

Fragmented retail systems tend to have long or extended distribution channels, whereas concentrated retail systems tend to have short, focused channels. With a more fragmented retail system, the cost to the manufacturing company to make contact with each retailer is greater. The result could be either heavy investment in a large sales force to visit the individual retailers (with low returns per

visit), or a focus on one or two regions at the exclusion of others.

An alternative action is to focus on wholesalers who in turn contact the individual retailers. The wholesalers will most likely be handling a wider and more diverse range of products, so for them each visit will probably result in a reasonable level of product sales. Thus it is more profitable for the wholesaler to visit the independent retailers. However, where the channel is shorter and much more focused, manufacturers will seek direct contact with retailers. This is often more efficient and cost-effective for the manufacturer, even within an international context.

Physical evidence

We can link this, for instance, to the distribution systems stated above by considering retail outlets. The physicality of store layouts as seen, for example, in the UK or the United States is not necessarily replicated in other countries. As stated earlier, some countries have highly concentrated systems (for instance supermarkets and hypermarkets), while the fragmented systems of others consist of numerous smaller outlets.

People

Here you need to refer back to earlier discussions on cultural perspectives. For example, the level and quality of customer service may vary significantly from one region to another. Indeed you might discover the quality of service in certain Far Eastern countries, such as Singapore, is far higher than in some European nations.

Additionally how customers buy can be very different, depending on cultural implications. For instance there is a view that in developing nations purchases tend to be on an individual basis, whereas in India, for instance, purchases tend to be much more family or collective in form.

Hill (2001) cites the example of the differences between pharmaceutical sales to doctors in the United States, the UK and Japan. Whilst some companies use high-pressure sales tactics on doctors (you may want to consider the ethical implications of such actions separately) in the United States, such tactics cannot be used in the UK and Japan. As a result, companies have adopted different marketing strategies.

Equally for salespeople from the home country visiting host countries there is the issue of spatial zoning. Generally within Western societies there is a series of circles or zones around an individual. In physical terms only close friends tend to be allowed close up. This is not the case in some other societies where space is at a premium and people have become used to being physically close to each other. Additionally, in some cultures it is normal to stand close to the person you are talking to. Thus it is important for an international salesperson to understand the cultural norms in relation to spatial zoning. While it might be uncomfortable for someone from the West to have a businessperson (not a close friend or colleague) stand closer to them than normal, it could be rude to stand further away. Understanding such cultural perspectives helps secure the business, and build long-term partnerships.

Processes

In Chapter 12 we described 'processes' as the means of placing an order, conducting a transaction, dealing with a query or a method of payment. In most developed nations we tend to take for granted the use of credit cards as a natural daily process of buying products or services (perhaps increasingly so with online purchasing facilities). It is rare, although not impossible, to find a restaurant in the European Union, for instance, that does not take credit cards.

However, this is not always the case in other countries, even though the number of outlets that take credit cards is continually increasing. People in developed nations may consider that as visitors to certain countries they would be able to use their credit cards without restriction. This might not be the case for the local population, even though they are creditworthy. For example, in India strict financial controls have, in essence, limited credit card usage. Such restrictions are slowly being relaxed, however there is still government concern at the potential outflow of funds from the economy.

For example a university might market its courses in India. However, if the process of transferring funds to pay course fees and provide living expenses is too complex, a potential student might decide to study in India rather than say the UK or the United States.

International marketing failures

In this section we consider why international marketing strategies fail. Perlmutter (1995) has examined the various reasons some companies have failed to manage their international marketing effectively. He identified nine cross-border and cross-cultural management incompetencies. His research included Swedish and German companies in the United States, Korean companies in Mexico, Canadian companies in Venezuela, French companies in Korea and Japanese companies in the UK. In Table 14.16 we have adapted Perlmutter's findings and added a tenth issue for consideration, a failure to appreciate the impact of emotive issues.

Table 14.16 illustrates the problems that can beset a company or organization as it attempts to market its products or services across national boundaries. It is clear from the table that some of these problems can be avoided if management are able to consider the potential implications of their proposed actions. Of course, this is easier said than done. However, even though there is a greater convergence between nations and the cultures of those nations, managers and

Table 14.16 Reasons for international marketing failures

Reason	Description
Inability to find the right niche market	Companies must find the right market for their product or service. Equally, it must be right for them as a company. They must consider all aspects of the competitive environment. Perlmutter (1995) is clear that attacking the market held by a strong company operating within its domestic environment can lead to failure.
An unwillingness to adapt or update	Companies must be able to respond to changing local trends and the competitive environment. They need to be agile, most especially if the market(s) in which they operate is particularly volatile. Companies that are unable to adapt to changing local and international conditions risk failure within that marketplace. As a result companies may need to seek suitable exit strategies in order to minimize the costs associated with withdrawal from the market.
Not having unique products or services	Customers need to view the product or service as providing added value for them. This is especially the case if the product or service is more expensive than locally available substitutes.
Vacillating commitment	Patience is important in international marketing and business. It may take anything from five years onwards realistically to learn all the nuances of a particular market. As instant success in an international market is often rare, companies must be committed to the long-term development of the market.
Assigning the wrong people	The problem here is choosing an individual or team (sales team, operations or management) from the home country that does not understand or appreciate the issues within the host country. The people might be chosen because the head office team in the home country trusts them, but this might only further an ethnocentric view of the world. It can be argued that Euro Disney (now Disneyland Paris) had the wrong people overseeing it, in that as an all-American team they did not take into consideration European, especially French, cultural aspects. Equally, a company might choose people from the host country, only to discover that they too are the wrong people for the job or project.
Selecting the wrong strategic partners	Expansion regionally, internationally or globally may mean forming strategic alliances with local partners in the host country. This could be for several reasons, ranging from host government regulations on ownership to finding the best route to a regional market. The key, however, is to find the partner that has the right combination of skills and capabilities. Together the companies must share the same vision, and construct a business relationship based upon each other's strengths within an environment of mutual trust. Strategic alliances between two companies in a domestic environment can be fraught with difficulties. When this is translated to alliances between companies from different countries, the cultural differences, for instance, can become insurmountable. If this is the case the alliance will suffer, as will the marketing of the product or service.
An inability to manage local stakeholders	This includes the inability to manage and develop effective relationships with local government officials and other regulators, influencers or opinion formers such as environmentalists, the local community and the media.
Lack of mutual trust	Mutual trust between the head office and the internationally based affiliate offices is essential. When this breaks down, it is often followed by a lack of faith in the regional/international managers. Of course, this lack of trust could be generated through an ethnocentric view at head office. The end result however is often a 'them and us' mentality that does not benefit either group or the organization itself. Such infighting can often mean that both parties take their eyes off the ball, allowing competitors more manoeuvrability within the marketplace. This could prove exceedingly detrimental in the longer term.
Impact of emotive issues	This can relate to social morality and ethical decision making. A case in point was Toscani's death row advertisements for the Italian apparel company Benetton in the United States (See Chapter 10). This was a particularly emotive issue for those families who saw the convicted murderers of their relatives. The resulting anti-Benetton campaign significantly damaged the brand in the US market.

companies must seek to be sensitive to the needs of their intended audience. If they are not, then as well as the risk of reputational damage, competitors may be able to gain and sustain an advantage within the marketplace.

Chapter summary

As this chapter demonstrates, a number of issues arise as a company moves from a domestic marketing environment into an international one. Although societies are increasingly converging in their political, economic, legal and societal structures, 'going international' can be a complex and risky venture. There are no guarantees of success, as market forces and external factors impact on the marketing operation. It is increasingly clear, though, that as domestic markets become competitively saturated companies must seek cross-border markets. For such companies to sustain any form of competitive advantage they must seek viable international and global markets for their products and services.

While there is an increased globalization of ideas, media and products there remains an active debate as to whether there exist truly standardized products and services. There may be global brand names, for instance McDonald's and Coca-Cola; however there appears to be some form of market adaptation, no matter how minor. As Ohmae postulates, companies can be global but they have to think 'local'.

The Internet and the proliferation of media 'events' have made all of us think beyond our own local environment. Through the media we witness dramatic incidents live from anywhere in the world. We can converse with people across the globe and purchase goods from virtually anywhere. It has certainly revolutionized both our social and purchasing habits. There is little doubt that the Internet will significantly develop further and have even greater impact on our lives.

Since the late 1990s the term 'globalization' has been a topic of heated debate. While international trade is far from a recent occurrence (it can be traced back to the Greek and Roman empires), the contemporary implications of globalization are vast. Both sides of the argument for and against globalization have raised valid issues. However, they are far from clear cut. Globalization has clear values and equally clear concerns. Thus active all-inclusive debate is important if international marketing and globalization are to bring real benefits to all communities.

Exercises and questions for review and critical thinking

1. Explain the differences between indirect and direct exporting. Why would a company choose one method of exporting rather than another?

2. Outline why understanding a country's cultural background could be important to a company marketing into it.

3. Detail the potential risks to a company embarking upon a foreign direct investment programme.

4. 'It is possible to have a standardized global promotional policy.' Discuss the merits of this statement.

5. Explain why domestic competition can influence a company to seek cross-border markets.

6. In your opinion how could international marketers use the Internet in the future to secure markets? What are the potential advantages and disadvantages of using the Internet as an international marketing tool?

7. Individual governments or groups of governments may impose embargoes and sanctions. Consider how such actions can affect companies marketing internationally.

8. Do you consider that trade controls, such as tariff and non-tariff barriers, remain important in today's converging global business environment? Why?

9. Explain how the economic factors in both the home market and international markets can impact on the marketing operations of a business.

10. Some companies are successful in marketing their products and services across borders, while others are not. Critically evaluate why this is so.

Application: bringing the elements together

Introduction

Throughout this text we have introduced you to various models and theories, everything from the product life cycle to the elements that comprise the marketing mix. In this chapter we seek to provide you with an overview of the application of some of these models and theories. We have used the product life cycle (introduced in Chapter 7) as the base point. As we work through a 'standardized' product life cycle we consider what elements of the marketing mix a company might use to maximize its position (and that of its product or service) within the marketplace.

Of course, as with so much in marketing, this comes with a health warning! These are possible applications. The actions suggested may not be applicable in all situations. This is basically one scenario. However, it is nonetheless valuable in that it will help you to consolidate your critical thinking of the subject area.

Learning objectives

On completion of this chapter you should be able to:

▌ identify and analyse the different stages within the product life cycle, and the strategies and tactics that companies could use to develop and maintain products within this framework;

▌ debate why companies cull or terminate brands;

▌ explain the relationship between the marketing mix and the product life cycle.

The product life cycle

As discussed in Chapter 7, the product life cycle highlights the stages in the life or history of a product or indeed a service. We can parallel a product life cycle with that of the human life cycle. With humans there is birth, growth, maturity, decline and eventually death. Our life span might be short or long. Through this period we might undergo life-threatening illnesses that we survive. The same can be applicable to a product, although a product life span can be significantly longer than that of a human being! Just consider for a moment the age of products like Coca-Cola or Kellogg's cornflakes.

It is important to realize that the product life cycle can be modified. Think of product modification: changes in design, ingredients, size, packaging, rebranding and positioning, for instance. All these can contribute to extending the life cycle of a product. However, we must remember that a product or service will only survive if it meets customers' real needs or desires.

Understanding which stage the product has entered has a significant impact on the effectiveness of the marketing strategy undertaken. Astute marketing managers use the life cycle concept to make sure the introduction, alteration and termination of a product are timed and executed properly. By understanding the typical life cycle pattern, marketers are better able to maintain profitable products and terminate unprofitable ones (Dibb *et al*, 1997).

A product life cycle is generally described as a side-on S-shaped curve or perhaps more accurately the mathematical sine wave curve (~). This cycle is then generally divided into several differing stages or lives. While some authors suggest four stages – introduction, growth, maturity and death – we suggest, like others, that there can be several additional stages. This allows marketers to increase their level of precision when analysing their product life cycles:

▌ research and development;

▌ introduction;

▌ growth;

▌ maturity;

▌ decline;

▌ restaging/rejuvenation/ revitalization;

▌ death/extinction/termination.

The point at which these stages begin and end tends to be arbitrary, but an indicator can be the percentage changes in real sales year on year.

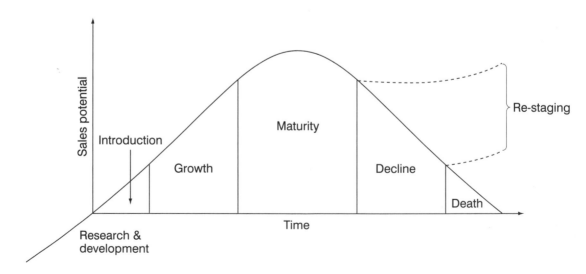

Figure 15.1   The product life cycle

Research and development phase

Prior to the introduction of the product or brand significant human, material and financial resources have generally been invested in research and development. This might take place over several years. While it is unlikely that there will be immediate returns on investment, the company will generally seek to manage product potential, and hence revenues. For example:

▌ Various high-tech companies are working on developing 'intelligent' refrigerators. These have inbuilt barcode readers and digital displays, which alert the householder to chilled products that have reached their use-by date, prompting him or her to decide to use the products or not. The refrigerator can also order fresh groceries via the Internet, based upon customer pre-set data. Then the supermarket delivers at a time to suit the customer (as already generally happens within online supermarket purchases). Early models of these refrigerators are available, but they retail at high prices. As more functions are added and they become more widely available and accepted by consumers (as a concept), they will most likely reduce in price.

▌ The research being undertaken by the University of Surrey in the UK to improve the power capacity of microchips. The aim is to use light as the energy source rather than micro-wires. If successful, this should greatly increase the power of computers.

▌ BMW is working on hydrogen fuel-cell powered cars where the only waste product is water.

However, not all R&D projects see the light of day. Equally, as we saw in Chapter 8, not all products are successful on launch.

Introduction phase

This is where the product/brand is introduced to the market, which might be local, national, transnational or global. Of course, introducing the product transnationally or globally has a high level of risk attached. A company would

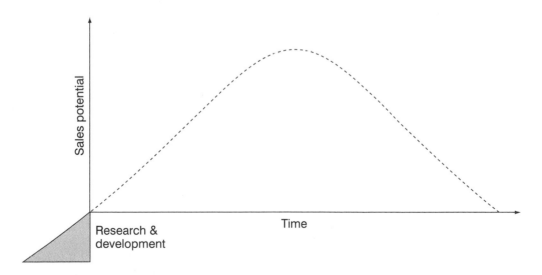

Figure 15.2   The product life cycle: research and development

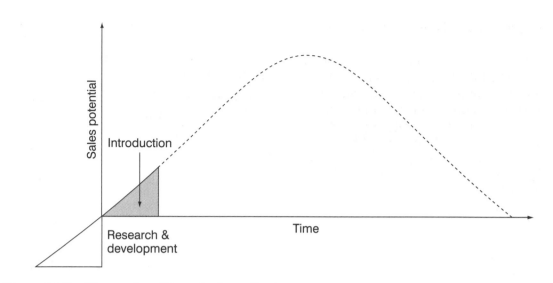

Figure 15.3 The product life cycle: introduction

have to be confident that it had accounted for the various micro and macro issues that could impinge on its overall success. (You may want to reflect on this in light of what you read in Chapter 14 on international marketing.)

Examples of recent new products are:

▌ digital flat-screen televisions;

▌ advanced speech recognition systems for the consumer computer market;

▌ 2 Ghz computer system;

▌ advanced photographic film for digital cameras;

▌ Microsoft Office 2000 software and Windows XP platform;

▌ 3G and picture-messaging mobile phones.

As we saw in Chapter 8, there are risks involved in developing and launching a new product (or service), or even a variant on an existing product. Market conditions and technical difficulties can lead to delays and thus impact on revenue generation. If revenue generation is severely restricted this could cause cash-flow difficulties for the business. If

the product is part of a successful product portfolio, the revenue generated by other products can be used to support the delayed product. This will, of course, depend on the length of the delay, and the potential financial impact upon the other products within the portfolio. Additionally, brand managers may be reluctant to support a product that is not under their direct control, as it will not contribute to their individual revenues. So it becomes more than a financial issue, it becomes one of managerial conflict.

Table 15.1 lists a selection of the key features of the introductory stage. Not all these features will impact on all products. However, you need to be aware of the strategic issues that can face companies at this often vulnerable point in the life of a product.

A company can seek to take various actions, using elements of the marketing mix, to stimulate demand for the new product. In Table 15.2 we consider the possible pricing initiatives that could be utilized, then in Table 15.3 the promotional strategies that can be considered.

Table 15.4 illustrates the distribution tactics that a company can employ to move its new product effectively and efficiently into the marketplace.

Table 15.1   Introductory stage: key features

Key feature	Description
Competition	Two general points can be considered here. First, if the product is new and designated for a new niche area there will be no initial competition. At a later stage other companies might enter the marketplace, depending on the strength of any barrier to entry. They might or might not initially pose any viable and effective competition. Second, a new product might be introduced into an already existing market, thus there will be established competition. The company introducing the new product might be seeking to challenge the market leaders, or will perhaps choose to take the safer option of initially being a market follower, thus not risking a strategic attack from the market leaders.
Sales	Generally these tend to be low at the point of introduction, especially if we focus on the 'traditional' life cycle curve. However, this is not always the case. Specific fashion items that have a short life span may gain high volume sales on introduction. Equally, a product that has aroused both media and consumer interest may experience high volume sales and maintain a long life span. An example here is the *Harry Potter* books written by J K Rowling. When *Harry Potter and the Philosopher's Stone* went on sale in the UK many bookshops (even with extra supplies) were sold out within hours of its release.
Profits	Because of the level of investment and associated costs, and slow sales, profits tend to be negative or low during this phase. Again, there are exceptions to the rule. The release of Rowling's *Harry Potter and the Philosopher's Stone* had an immediate positive impact to the bottom line for publisher Bloomsbury.
Flexibility	Companies may need to be flexible in terms of their launch date in order to maximize response from the marketplace. They also need to seek customer feedback in case product modifications need to be considered.
Production delays	Delays in meeting production targets in order to meet potential customer demand might be caused simply because demand for the product was underestimated. Market research can provide some indicators regarding the level of demand, however there is no such thing as 100 per cent accuracy or perfection. Over-demand can lead to production delays as companies seek to gear up production to meet the demand. Additionally, the company might need to outsource production to meet such demand, which could lead to short-term delays.
Technical problems	Technical problems that could lead to severe delays in production and thus distribution and purchasing levels. The company might need to make modifications that in turn lead to delays. Such delays could lead to negative public relations that focus on the technical difficulties, rather than the solutions being undertaken by the company. This could have a domino effect on the purchasing of the product.
Distribution delays	Delays caused by poor distribution networks, especially within international markets where there could be several obstacles. For example, non-tariff barriers (mainly bureaucracy) and transport difficulties (poor road and rail services) can cause problems in distributing the product to the intermediary and in turn the end-customers.
Customer behaviour	There might be customer reluctance to change to a new product, even though it has improved benefits and/or is more cost-effective: for example, mobile phone technology or new, faster and lighter portable computers. Consider this in relation to Roger's diffusion curve.

Table 15.1 *continued*

Key feature	Description
Pricing	Prices might have been set either too high or too low, thus requiring adjustment for local and regional market conditions. Normally only a relatively small number of people can afford premium priced (high ticket or high priced) items such as expensive sports cars, designer clothing, jewellery and luxury vacation resorts.
Raw material delays	Raw material delays, shortages and problems with quality. These could be caused, in the case of food ingredients, by poor harvests as a result of extreme weather conditions. These can include safety standards imposed by governments.
Quality control	Quality control: higher rejection level because the product does not achieve specified quality standards. These might include specific safety standards imposed by a government department or company.
Promotional costs	Heavy promotional costs. In a highly competitive environment a company might have to invest heavily in promotion to communicate the product's features and benefits to the potential customer base.
Negative public relations	A company might face negative PR on the launch of its product. In the 1980s the UK consumer company Amstrad faced criticism over the introduction of their 1512 Hard Drive computer because it was not fan cooled. Critics believed the system would overheat and fail if it was not fan cooled. Amstrad stated that the system was designed not to be fan cooled and would not overheat. However, the adverse publicity damaged sales of the 1512HD, and with mounting inventory Amstrad decided to retro-fit fans to the computers. However, sales had been damaged and with other companies entering the IBM clone market, Amstrad did not achieve the market position it sought. Eventually it divested itself of its own-brand computer, relying instead on the acquisition of the Viglen computer company. Another example is a movie that has experienced poor reviews and audience attendance. It might be re-cut and later reissued.

It is important that these tactics are considered as part of a longer-term life cycle. They should not be considered as purely instruments for short-term market share gain. If they are considered as short-term measures, the business could encounter severe operational and financial difficulties over the medium term. In the longer term the product and/or or the company could actually fail and exit the marketplace.

Growth phase

Examples of products that are arguably in a growth phase at present are:

▊ mobile phones;

▊ home computer systems and software products;

▊ the Internet and e-mail software products.

Table 15.5 lists the key features of this phase within the product life cycle. You will see that competition becomes an increasingly important factor within this phase. Rival companies see potential opportunities of moving rapidly into the market, especially if they can imitate the product at a reduced cost from the original. To combat such actions the company may seek to add further features and benefits to the product, thus staying one step ahead of the competition.

Table 15.2   Pricing strategies

Pricing strategy	Descriptions/actions
Rapid skimming	Skimming is a pricing strategy often used when a new product is introduced to the marketplace. New products tend, though not always, to be price inelastic (that is, the demand for them is relatively insensitive to the price). A high price for the product in the early stages of its life cycle may attract a customer group that values the prestige of owning something that has newly arrived into the marketplace. As the product matures and sales begin to slow down, the price can be lowered in order to attract new buyers into that market. **Possible actions** The company could launch a new product at a high price and support the product with high levels of promotional expenditure. Diverse media could be used to communicate its message, and accelerate market penetration. The aim here is to recover as much gross profit per unit as possible, as soon as possible.
Slow skimming	**Possible actions** The company could launch the product with a high price and low levels of promotional expenditure. The company's aim here is to recover as much gross profit per unit as soon as possible; however it needs to control marketing expenditure. A too great spend will impact on the objective, leaving a possible deficit. These strategies can be used when: ▌ The marketplace is limited in size: for example, a niche market. ▌ The marketplace is already aware of the product, especially its particular features and benefits. ▌ The current and potential buyers are willing to pay a higher price for the new product. ▌ There is no immediate competition. The product might be enjoying a monopolistic environment, for example a utility company providing telecommunications.
Rapid market penetration	**Possible actions** The company could launch the product at a low price but supported with relatively high levels of promotional expenditure. Here it aims to achieve rapid penetration of the market in order to gain an initial large market share. This strategy is used when: ▌ The market is organized on a large scale, for example, the washing powder/liquid market. ▌ The market is unaware of the introduction of the product, especially its particular features and benefits. ▌ The majority of buyers are particularly price-sensitive. ▌ There is strong potential (and actual) competition. This can also include additional new entrants to the marketplace. These new entrants may actively seek to challenge both market leaders and immediate followers. ▌ Economies of scale can be achieved through efficiencies within both the production process and distribution system. Thus companies will seek best production practices and channel effectiveness.

Table 15.2 *continued*

Pricing strategy	Descriptions/actions
Slow market penetration	**Possible actions** The company could launch the product at a low price and with low levels of promotional expenditure, aiming to encourage rapid product acceptance within the marketplace. Such action could allow the company to keep marketing expenses to a minimum. This strategy is used when: ▌ The marketplace is large and active (that is, there is potential for brand switching). ▌ The marketplace is aware of the product, especially its particular features and benefits. ▌ There is high price elasticity (that is, the customers are particularly price-sensitive, thus a minor price reduction should increase sales. Conversely a minor price increase could reduce immediate sales). ▌ There is a potential competitor(s) entering or about to enter the marketplace. Of course a new entrant into the market could feasibly reduce its prices even further, thus increasing pressure on existing companies within the market. The other companies may react by also reducing their prices, resulting in a price war that is unlikely to benefit the companies in the longer term, although consumers benefit from such action. If individual companies cannot sustain a price war (and maintain some margin for profitability) they may need to seek withdrawal from the market (this also results in cost) or increase their prices and mount a promotional campaign based on their quality product. However, if the consumer remains price-sensitive that might not help a company trying to recover its position in the market. Aggressive price wars could feasibly result in several players disappearing from the market.

Table 15.3 Promotion

Promotional tactics	Description
Advertising	In the introductory stage a company must create and maintain awareness for the product. The company may decide to invest heavily in an advertising campaign carefully aimed at its target audience. Earlier, we considered the impact of the *Harry Potter* books. There was a significant amount of advertising for *Harry Potter and the Philosopher's Stone* to announce its forthcoming availability. This built awareness and indeed expectation within the market. In turn this fuelled the need to buy the product, further enhancing its value within the market.
Publicity	The use of press releases, feature articles and demonstrations can build awareness. For example, motoring journalists test drive a new car model and report on its handling ability and particular features.
Word of mouth – viral marketing	In Chapter 11 we considered the impact viral marketing can have on a product or service. Of course, there can be negative as well as positive outcomes. Positive word of mouth can have a significant impact on sales. This was the case with the launch of Dava Sobel's book *Longitude*, the story of how John Harrison struggled over 40 years to find a solution to the problem of how to measure longitude. There was no advertising for the book. The marketing department at the publishers Fourth Estate sent out copies to reviewers. From their reviews and private conversations the word spread, and *Longitude* became a bestseller.
Direct marketing	If the company has an established product portfolio and customer base, it can use direct marketing techniques, including e-mails, to develop awareness of the new product. The company could also include trial packs (for example, small sachets of shampoo) to herald the launch of the product.

Table 15.4 Placement and distribution tactics

Placement or distribution tactics	Description
Selective	The company may decide to distribute the product to selective outlets. This could be because the product itself demands selective outlets (for example, high-priced fashion items), because of cost or as a strategy – slow penetration of the market.
Mass market	The product might be such that the company decides to mass distribute it. An example is the introduction of a new chocolate bar.

The objective within this phase is to sustain growth over a longer period. Table 15.6 lists some of the actions a company can take to improve or maintain its growth position within the life cycle. The company may use any or all of these tactics, with the aim of strengthening its position within a potentially highly competitive environment.

These tactics will increase costs associated with product improvement, increased promotion and the expansion of distribution channels. Thus profits will not be totally maximized. However, there is the opportunity to maintain reasonable levels of profit growth over the longer period.

Maturity phase

This phase can present several marketing challenges for the organization. In Table 15.7 we review the key features of a mature market (Kotler, 2000).

A slow down in the rate of growth in sales could create an over-capacity within that particular industry sector. The result is normally intensified competition, which could lead a company to consider the possible actions detailed in Table 15.8 to maintain an economically efficient and effective position within the marketplace.

A company could choose to modify the product, improving its quality, features and

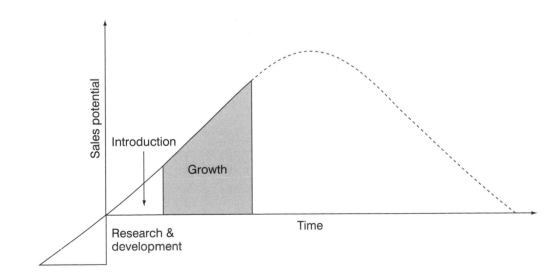

Figure 15.4 The product life cycle: growth

Table 15.5   Key features: growth phase

Key features	Description
Competition	New competitors may enter the market at this stage. They are attracted by possible opportunities, within the expanding market sector, for large-scale production and potential profit. There may be few real barriers to entry. However, it is important for companies to be aware that there is a cost in entering a market, as there is a cost in exiting a market. (You may want to refer back to the work of Porter and his five forces model in Chapter 7.) As more imitators enter the market, competitive turbulence will increase (often dramatically) as companies battle for some form of advantage.
New features and benefits	There is the opportunity for the company to introduce additional new product features and benefits. These can include both tangible and intangible benefits. For example, tangible benefits could include air conditioning as standard on a car model at no extra cost. Intangibles could include special credit/payment terms/facilities, extended free service arrangements, a period of free insurance (for example, two years) and extended warranties providing high-value after-sales support at no extra cost to the customer.
Expanding market	The company may move to expand the market, and thus their share of it. The total market demand can be increased through the company developing new users and encouraging present users to use the product more often. (See the section later in this chapter on new uses).
Increased distribution outlets	An influx of new competitors can lead to an increase in distribution, and in the diversity of outlets. Again this serves to open up and develop the market further.
Pricing	Within this environment prices may tend to remain static, although as competition increases there is risk of aggressive price reductions to gain some advantage. However, this advantage may be short lived, as not all companies will compete on price alone. They may seek some additional form of differentiation that helps to maintain their competitive stance. Indeed, a too severe price reduction might cause customers to become concerned at a potential decrease in product quality. It could only be a psychological perception rather than a reality, but nonetheless it will have impact upon sales, as customers potentially brand switch, thus leading to at least a short decline in revenue generation until the company decides to increase prices again on a par with competitors.
Promotional expenditure	The level of promotional expenditure is maintained or increased to combat competition as is necessary.
Increased profits	Profits increase during this phase as potential expenditure is spread over a larger volume. Additionally, the investment cost of the research and development may be written off in the accounts over several years (as through depreciation).
Decreasing unit costs	Unit production costs fall as the company becomes more experienced and efficient in manufacturing and distributing the product (thus achieving economies of scale).

Table 15.6   Potential actions: growth phase

Possible actions	Description
Improve product quality	A company may seek to improve product quality as part of an ongoing marketing/ business strategy. An example is detergent manufacturers that promote a recent extension to their product portfolio as 'new and improved' or 'now better than ever before'. The improvement could be either minor or major. However, it is how it is communicated to the consumer that is important for the company and its market position.
New features and benefits	A company may seek to add new features and benefits (including services). As stated in Table 15.5: Key features, a company may add a range of both tangible and intangible features and benefits.
Improve product styling	This includes not only the design of the product itself, but also the packaging, which can provide added value and benefits to the product. An example is the introduction of the Tetrapack™ which revolutionized milk cartons in the UK, making them easier to open and pour from. They greatly reduced spillage and thus wastage, and that of course has a cost implication, especially for the consumer.
Develop new market segments	A company can seek to enter new market segments. Increasingly we are seeing products expand outside their traditional market segments. An example is Johnson & Johnson's shampoo for babies. This is now marketed to adults on the basis that if it is 'kind and gentle to your baby, then it is kind and gentle to you'. Johnson & Johnson were also very successful in marketing their talcum powder for babies to an adult market.
Develop distribution channels	A company can seek to develop or enter new distribution channels, for example the use of the Internet for booking holidays direct, or consumers ordering grocery deliveries from the local supermarket direct to their homes. Early examples here were the European low-cost airline easyJet and the international (UK-based) grocery chain Tesco.
Re-directing promotional spend	A company may divert or redirect a portion of the advertising and promotional spend from building product awareness to reinforcing product conviction (the customer's belief in the product), and subsequent purchase. This could be achieved through personalized e-mails and other direct marketing tactics.

Pricing	Price reductions, permanent or for a specific limited time frame.
	    Special discounts, which might be limited to certain groups of customers, for example, department store card holders being eligible to an additional 10 per cent discount on sale prices on specific sale days. Some retailers in the UK call these 'blue cross' days, symbolized throughout the store with a blue cross. It is a means of persuading loyalty card holders to increase their expenditure.
	    Special offers, available to all customers for a limited time period.
	    Flexible payment/credit terms. The ability of companies to offer customers flexible payment terms is seen by many as a significant weapon in a company's arsenal in the highly competitive shopping market. For example, a UK-based computer company advertises computers on the basis: 'order now, no deposit, no payments for 9 months and no interest if cash price paid in full in 9 months'. Furniture companies have adopted similar payment structures. However, if the payment is not met by the due date, the company usually starts to charge interest at a very high APR.
	    Price rises. Companies may increase prices to differentiate their product from the competition. The objective here is to suggest to customers that they are buying an 'added value' quality product. Thus in order to achieve that quality a higher price needs to be charged.

Table 15.6 *continued*

Possible actions	Description
Placement	The company may be able to increase product support through existing outlets. Here the company has to build a strong relationship with the outlets, which can be achieved through the sales force. An example is a publisher's sales force developing and reinforcing its links with retail book chains, such as Waterstones in the UK or Borders in the United States.

Expansion of point of sale/point of purchase (POS/POP) material in existing outlets. Staying with the book trade example, the publisher might introduce dump bins to give a book a larger exposure within the bookstore.

Diversification into new distribution outlets. For example, publishers traditionally have focused their marketing activities on bookstores in town and city centres. Today, the outlets for books are significantly wider. They range from newspaper and magazine vendors at airports to supermarkets, petrol stations, specialist stores (cinema memorabilia and health food shops), multi-product department stores and the Internet. Books are now widely available through Internet providers, providing a global reach for publishers. |
| Promotion | The company may increase its overall advertising expenditure, or range of advertising, for example to include magazine and television advertising.

There could be a need to review the advertising campaign. This could result in a change of advertising agency. A new agency might have a fresh approach to increasing market share.

An alternative is to alter the frequency of advertising, for example making it regular rather than ad hoc, helping to reinforce the brand identity in the minds of customers.

The company may reconsider the size, shape and position placement of its press advertisements. Their current size and placement might not provide the required level of exposure to the marketplace.

The company might need to expand its range of advertising media, perhaps broadening from newspapers and magazines to the Internet.

The advertising message may need to be modified or radically changed to reach the appropriate target audience, and to stand out against competitors' advertising messages.

Analysis of sales promotion activities, for example, the use of special incentives for distributors. This could include special discounts.

The company might introduce customer incentive schemes. These can include free gifts (for example, make two purchases and receive a free gift) and coupons available through newspapers, magazines and on-pack promotions. These can be used for brand discount, a free gift, an item at a reduced price (for example a set of soup bowls with a soup manufacturer's logo on the side), or a prize draw competition.

If there are poor sales the company may need to consider the quality of the sales effort, and the facilities that support the sales operation. The issues here cover the quality of the training the sales force has received, the need for regular staff development, the possible need to expand the size of the sales force, restructuring of sales territories and the adequacy of support facilities. The level of motivation may be a critical factor here, thus it is the responsibility of management to create the appropriately positive motivational environment. |

Table 15.6   *continued*

Possible actions	Description
Process–customer orientation	The marketing team may need to consider the following questions and issues:
	▌ Can delivery times be improved to both our distributors and our end customers? If so, how can this be achieved? For example, Viking Direct™, the direct sales stationery supplier, provides a guaranteed same-day delivery within Central London if it receives the order by 11 am that morning. Several global parcel delivery services, such as UPS™, now guarantee next-day deliveries.
	▌ Should credit and payment terms be extended and developed? Customers within both consumer and business markets are becoming used to a range of payment options. Companies may need to consider if they have explored all the payment options, especially in the light of growing competition in a market segment.
	▌ Does the level of customer paperwork need to be reduced? If the process is kept simple, customers might react better to new offers, for example, upgrading a credit card from Gold to Platinum by requiring only the customer's signature rather than details of his or her financial income and home life status.
	▌ Does the company make it easy for the customer to purchase the product? For example, can the customer purchase by post, telemarketing and online?
	▌ Should warranties be extended? The extension of warranties could provide the intangible that leads to the sale. This links to the customer feeling 'protected' if something goes wrong with the product. Linked to this is the type of action behind the warranty. This affects both B2B and B2C environments. For instance companies cannot afford to have malfunctioning photocopiers, so they need to know how long it will take for a service engineer to reach their office and repair the fault, and if it cannot be repaired whether a replacement can be provided.
Physical evidence	The company could work with retail outlets to improve the positioning of the product within that outlet. We have already mentioned the use of POS/POP material. However, the company could take a larger space within the store to show/demonstrate its products. The layout of this section might reflect the particular characteristics of the company's product through colours, the use of particular wood finishes, sofas to make customers feel at home and signage. For example, a fashion house that rents space from a major department store can use physical evidence to say something about itself, such as 'up market and trendy' or 'traditional'.
People	People obviously play an important role in marketing any product as they provide the service component. The product, for example, could be supported by more vigorous pre-sales and after sales/customer care support.

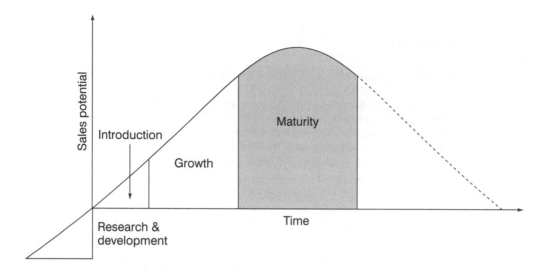

Figure 15.5 The product life cycle: maturity

Table 15.7 Features of the mature phase of the product life cycle

Key features	Indicator
Growth maturity	Sales growth starts to slow down. This may eventually lead to decline. The rate of decline will be determined by many factors, including both micro and macro environmental factors.
Stable maturity	Sales begin to flatten because of market saturation.
Decaying maturity	Sales decline and consumers decide to switch to other products/brands.

styling. Table 15.9 lists some of the quality improvements that could be undertaken.

In addition to these quality improvements a company might try to introduce feature and functional improvements. These are outlined in Table 15.10.

Table 15.11 outlines some style improvements a company could make to maintain position in a particularly difficult marketplace.

Product modifications: advantages and disadvantages

Modifications can create several marketing advantages for a product. Equally, there is the risk that modifications might alienate a proportion of the company's existing customers. Table 15.12 gives a brief overview of the potential advantages and disadvantages.

Both existing and new competitors can challenge the issues outlined in all these marketing mix modifications, and they could all reduce profit, usually for all within the market.

Decline phase

Table 15.13 lists the key features of this phase of the product life cycle. Sales fall at different rates and for a variety of different reasons, as we consider in a later section.

Table 15.8   Potential actions: maturity phase

Potential strategies, tactics or actions	Description
Pricing	The company might decide to reduce prices marginally or significantly. Alternatively, the company might attempt to increase sales through special pricing deals. This could, for example, include sales promotions such as bundling with other products within the company's portfolio, or longer-term payment plans. Examples are the UK computer market and the UK car market during the late 1990s. In the computer market companies bundled with the latest specification machine such items as additional software (from games to educational products), printers and scanners. In the car industry, features that had been previously considered as 'extras' were provided as standard.
Promotion	Increasing marketing communication expenditure in an attempt to maintain overall sales and market position. The company might decide to use one or two particular forms of marketing communication. Alternatively it could apply an integrated marketing communications strategy. Of course, it depends on a mixture of the budget available and the creativity of the marketing team in order to maximize the value of that budget.
Product	The company could change the product over to in-store own-label brands (for example, chocolate manufacturers seek to increase the manufacture of chocolate products for supermarket own brands, in addition to their mainstream brands). Another option is to withdraw the product from the market as it weakens in the face of overwhelming competitive forces. This allows the company, if it has a brand portfolio, to concentrate on more profitable brands. An example here is how Unilever in the late 1990s sought to reduce its large brand portfolio to focus on more profitable and developing brands. Of course, there is a cost in withdrawing from any market. Such cost has to be factored into the company's overall strategic objectives.
Attract new users	Here the company attempts to attract potential new users who are either unaware that the product exists, or have not been informed of the range of features and benefits the products has to offer them. Through a range of marketing communication activities the company seeks to demonstrate the product's various features and benefits. If the company discovers that the public are unaware of the product's existence, it needs to re-examine its promotional activities. This could result in changing its marketing communication agencies and/or increasing marketing spend to raise the profile of the product.
Enter new market segments	These segments can be geographical, demographic or socioeconomic. The product might in general be widely used, but not that particular brand. For example, there are numerous fast-food outlets. However, how does a company entice more people to try its particular variety of fast food? One way might be to open more stores in areas that have few, if any, fast-food outlets. McDonald's opening a fast-food restaurant in Moscow is one example. On opening day, the queues stretched far down the road, resulting in extensive media coverage not only in Russia but worldwide.

Table 15.8 *continued*

Potential strategies, tactics or actions	Description
Attract competitors' customers	The aim is to entice competitors' customers to at least try the company's product in the hope that they will switch. Various fast-food outlets, detergent and washing powder manufacturers have taken this type of action, as have major soft drink companies. In the UK even banks and financial institutions have applied this tactic. Both in the US and the UK, the credit card market has since the late 1990s become highly dynamic and competitive. To win customers from rivals, many banks are offering potential customers a range of additional benefits. These include: █ Lower interest rates on balance transfers from their existing credit card to the new one. This interest rate can exist for the life of the balance transferred. Thus the greater the debt transferred, the greater the saving to the customer who has transferred it. █ Overall lower annual percentage rates (APRs). █ Holiday insurance benefits. █ Reduction on holidays if the card is used to purchase the holiday from specified companies. █ Reduction on other purchases from specified providers. █ A potential one month where no payment is required (although interest on the balance is still accrued). █ No annual fee payments. There are, however, potentially significant risks attached to this strategy. One fast-food chain dramatically reduced its prices in an attempt to win customers away from its major competitor. The rival did not reduce its prices, and was adamant that it had no intention of entering a price war. In its view customers purchased its hamburgers not just on price but because of the method of cooking – flame grilled rather than fried. The price reduction failed to attract a sufficient number of customers. The result was that the fast-food chain that had reduced its prices had to hold those prices for a significant period of time before raising them, thus reducing revenue generation. This ultimately impacted on the company's profitability.

Table 15.8   *continued*

Potential strategies, tactics or actions	Description
New uses	This is a tactic within the strategy to increase the volume of purchases made by existing customers. Eckles (1990) gives several examples in an industrial context. DuPont's multi-purpose Nylon™ was first introduced as a synthetic fibre for parachutes. Since then it has been incorporated in a range of products ranging from women's stockings, car tyres, carpets and men's socks to medical sutures. In consumer marketing the pharmaceutical giant Johnson & Johnson, producers of talcum powder and shampoo for babies, developed a marketing strategy to widen the usage for these products. They successfully marketed the products to adults, reminding them of when they were 'Johnson's babies' and that if the products were so good for babies, why shouldn't adults use them too? The use of certain food products can also be widened. Tomato ketchup is a prime example. This is used as a complement to a range of 'host foods' such as the traditional British breakfast of eggs, bacon, sausage and tomato. There is the opportunity to increase the size of the tomato ketchup market by suggesting new food combinations for the product. In Sweden, ketchup is widely used as a pasta sauce. Today it is even used as a dip for potato crisps. Traditionally cornflakes have been considered as purely a breakfast cereal. However, in the late 1990s there were advertising campaigns promoting cornflakes as an all-round snack food that could be consumed at any time day or night. They focused on the nutritional value of the ingredients and the ease of preparation, just adding milk and sugar or sweetener, as preferred by the consumer. Again traditionally, soup was consumed either at lunchtime or as part of an evening meal. Companies have promoted soup, especially certain packet soups, as snack food to be consumed at any time.
Increase usage per occasion	The aim here is to persuade users to increase the number of times they actually use the product. For example, shampoo manufacturers usually recommend washing hair twice in succession, thus customers use two amounts of shampoo where one might have been sufficient. Credit card companies have used incentives to encourage customers to use their credit card to make purchases in a given month. The incentives range from travel bags and eligibility to be entered in a luxury holiday competition to reduced interest rates or interest rate holidays (a period where the interest is frozen even if the bank base rate is increased). During an advertising campaign in the late 1990s one cereal manufacturer in the UK suggested its product was so tasty that one bowl was never enough, thus promoting the idea of increased usage per occasion.

Table 15.9 Potential quality improvements or developments: maturity phase

Areas for improvement	Description
Durability	A company might seek to improve the overall durability of the product. This could lead to a competitive advantage over other similar products. For example Prestige, a UK manufacturer of stainless steel cookware, offers customers a 10-year guarantee on its product range.
Reliability	Companies can use quality improvements to build a reputation for designing and manufacturing reliable products. For example, certain electronics manufacturers have a powerful reputation for producing extremely reliable televisions and DVDs. The luxury car manufacturer Aston Martin (part of the Ford Motor Company) has, over the years, developed a reputation for reliability within all its quality processes.
Ingredients	Companies, especially within the food industry, seek to improve their ingredients. For example, the manufacturer might source a higher quality coffee bean from another supplier or another country. A retailer of convenience or ready foods might ask the manufacturer to include a wider selection of ingredients (for example, vegetables), more ingredients or a higher quality of ingredients. Supermarkets market such products as 'new and improved' in order to persuade customers to purchase the product line.
Taste	For example, a new improved recipe for an Italian pasta sauce or ready prepared microwaveable meals. Companies such as the UK's Marks & Spencer are continually seeking ways of improving the taste and ingredients of their meals. The prepared food market is both significant in value terms and highly competitive. In the UK alone, all the major supermarkets market own-label ready or convenience meals.
Speed of performance	Companies battle with their competitors to show their customers which product has a better performance. This can be seen in the marketing communications for computer processors and sports cars.
Improved performance	A classic example here is detergent manufacturers. They often improve the quality of their products, then market them as 'improved – now better than ever before'. Consider the development in consumer laundry detergents from powders through to liquids and now capsules. Hi-fi manufacturers seek to improve the reproduction quality of CDs through enhancements to their systems. Car manufacturers also make modifications to particular models to improve overall performance. These can include better operation in hazardous weather conditions, more efficient fuel consumption and computer systems that aid parking.

Table 15.10   New feature or functional improvements: maturity phase

Feature or functional improvement	Description

Size	For example, the miniaturization of components has allowed finished goods manufacturers to consider reducing the size of their products. Hi-fi micro systems and picture messaging/video mobile phones are examples.
	
	    The introduction by detergent manufacturers of concentrated powders in tablet/capsule form, and integrated fabric conditioners, has reduced the size of packaging.
	
	    Size, in this context, does not always mean making the product smaller. For example, televisions vary in size and shape. The development of flat-screen technology has led to televisions with larger screens. While the width of these televisions is greater than standard televisions, the depth has significantly narrowed.
	
	    In terms of B2B, the Boeing 747 and the Airbus A380 were designed as larger aircraft in order to increase passenger loads. This size increase was made possible by new design and manufacturing technologies.

Weight	The introduction of lightweight materials and fabrics can assist in reducing the weight of the finished product. For example, vacuum cleaner manufacturers have improved the performance of their products and reduced their weight. Both are heavily marketed as benefits to the consumer.
Safety	Improved safety may be a statutory requirement and/or a means of adding value to the product. For example, within the European Union it is now a statutory requirement that electrical appliances are fitted with a moulded plug. This was introduced to prevent accidental miswiring with resultant risk of fire or electrocution. Several manufacturers pre-empted the statutory requirements by fitting plugs at the factory and advertising 'with fitted plug' as an added benefit of the purchase. When air bags were first introduced by car manufacturers they tended to be for the driver only, a means of reducing serious injury if the driver impacted with the steering wheel. Car manufacturers later introduced air bags as standard for front-seat passengers. They continually develop new safety features, and such innovations can help companies gain a technical advantage over competitors. Consider electronic scanners that warn drivers they are too close either to the car in front or to the side. In the future computer systems will be able to take evasive action on behalf of the driver to prevent an accident. This is because computers react faster than human beings. Drivers can go into a temporary state of shock as they attempt to prevent an accident. A computer just takes the necessary action.
Environmental	Increasingly consumers are seeking energy-efficient appliances, because they cost less to run and are less damaging to the environment. Washing machine manufacturers, for instance, have invested heavily in developing systems that use less water and energy, but still fulfil their operational requirements.
Ease of use	Consumers often seek products that are easy to use, and additionally save time, such as a laundry detergent capsule that contains the required amount of detergent for a normal wash. It saves time and is easy to use.

Table 15.11 Potential style improvements: maturity phase

Potential actions	Description
Visual improvements and restyling	As is discussed in the text, packaging continues to make a significant contribution to the marketing of a product. Style improvements can cover every type and range of product from cars through to food items. For example, particular models of car might undergo a restyling. In the UK the Ford Escort is an example. Even the classic, much loved Volkswagen Beetle has been partially restyled to appeal to the style trends of the 21st century. As a result a car originally launched with its unusual shape in the 1930s has won the hearts and minds of 21st century drivers.
Restyling for a new generation of users	By restyling the product, the company may be able to appeal to a new generation of consumers. Henry John Heinz first introduced his tomato ketchup in 1876. In 1999 it held over 50 per cent of the US ketchup market, being used in 47 million US households (Heinz, 2000). During 1999 in order to reinforce its appeal to a younger generation, it launched a major advertising campaign. In addition, it restyled its squeezable plastic container to mimic a fluted glass bottle (Tomkins, 1999).
Futuristic styling	In the computer hardware market companies such as Apple have redesigned their monitors to create a more futuristic look. Additionally they are available in a range of different colours, other than the traditional white. Keypads and the ubiquitous computer mouse have undergone various redesigns and restylings. Cordless computer mice now use infra-red technology. Equally, consider the major car manufacturers and how their vehicles are not only functional but often futuristic in their styling.

Table 15.14 highlights the potential reasons for the decline in sales and the possible death of a product.

First the company needs to analyse market trends, return on investment, prices, indirect costs, direct costs, cash flow and profit forecasts. Trends must be assessed over several years to provide an accurate picture of sales performance. The company can undertake a range of strategies to ease the rate of decline of the product. See Table 15.15.

Restaging, product rejuvenation and revitalization

Some companies will undertake a restaging of a brand, perhaps through repackaging, repositioning or technical re-engineering (see Figure 15.7). Table 15.16 lists the possible actions a company could take to rejuvenate a product.

Death, extinction or termination of a product

Some products die, in essence, a natural death. They hold an extremely weak position in the marketplace, and there is no method of reviving their strength (see Figure 15.8).

In other situations a company might need to terminate a product for sound commercial reasons before it reaches the decline phase. However, as Jobber (1998) illustrates, there is a danger that the company's management will become emotionally attached to the product. For example, the company might have been founded on a particular product or portfolio of products, so they become 'part of the family' so to speak. In this situation emotional ties might transcend normal business considerations, so the declining sales continue. The company that maintains this course of action might find itself with a

Table 15.12 Product modification advantages and disadvantages

Advantages	Description
Innovative image	Can create an image of the company/product as being innovative, dynamic and futuristic.
Customer focused	Can create an image of the company being customer-focused or customer-driven. This might increase customer loyalty to the product/brand, as customers perceive the company as reactive to their needs and wants.
Help the sales force	Can be an aid to the sales force as they discuss the product's features, benefits and value with current and potential customers.
Reinforce customer loyalty	Enhancing an existing design style and packaging may reinforce customer loyalty by creating a unique identity for the product (think of the unique shape of the traditional Coca-Cola bottle, for instance), increase brand awareness, show a progressive approach by the manufacturer and create a feeling of 'added value' for the customer (for example, easy pour containers).
Disadvantages	**Description**
Costs	The company needs to continually seek feature improvements. This can place a burden on human, material and financial resources. Research and development costs are usually high, and do not always result in successful feature improvements.
Competitor imitations	Rival companies can usually modify the original idea and introduce similar improvements themselves. The initial competitive advantage might be relatively short-lived as both mainstream brands and own-label brands adopt the modifications. An example is the development of two-blade wet shaving systems. Rivals large and small were soon offering similar systems.
Affect established customer preferences	Customers who preferred the old style might cease to use the 'new' product. Any style change that could cause such action must be able to encourage a significant number of new customers if the product is to remain viable.
Unpredictability	If a new style is adopted it is difficult to predict accurately who will like the new style, and who will not. This is applicable in both product and service environments (for example, changes to the layout of a restaurant, theatre, a café, or even an airline's colours and motif). In 1997 British Airways announced it planned to remove the Union Flag from its aircraft's tail fins and replace it with colourful new designs. The designs by artists from South Africa, China and Canada were to symbolize that British Airways was a global carrier. This transformed British Airways' image outside the UK, where the majority of its customers lived. Rather than seeing the airline as conservative, the international customers saw BA as progressive and respectful of other cultures (Skapinker, 1999a, 1999b). However, it emerged that the older British male customers (mainly business class customers) disapproved of the new livery. While the majority of British Airways' customers are international travellers, the UK remains its single largest market. This includes the high-spending business and first-class markets, major profit generators for the airline. As a result, in 1999 the airline announced that approximately 50 per cent of the fleet would in future carry the Union Flag. However, the reintroduction of the Union Flag could alienate the growing youth and foreign markets. Only time will tell (Skapinker, 1999b).

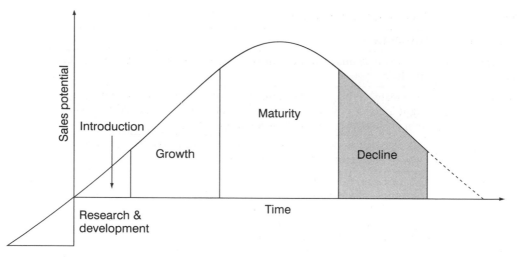

Figure 15.6   The product life cycle: decline

portfolio of products in decline and nothing to replace them (Jobber, 1998).

Companies might decide to terminate or cull the life of a range of products simultaneously because they believe their product portfolio is too large, and decide to focus on a core product range in order to maximize returns. In Chapter 8 we looked at brand culling, and in particular Unilever's decision to streamline its portfolio of brands. However, it should be borne in mind that there are usually costs, and indeed risks, associated with exiting a market(s) or terminating a product or range.

Table 15.13   Decline phase key features

Key features	Description
Slow decline	The sales of a product can decline slowly over a long period of time. Initially, the decline might only be considered a short-term difficulty. The view might be taken that sales will recover as there is still a market for the product. However, in this scenario the sales continue to fall. As the decline is slow there are still reasonable revenues being generated by the product, and if economies of scale are still viable the company might decide to take no action, but allow the product to decline and die out. This could be the case if there are other products within the portfolio in the introduction and growth phases.
Medium decline	Of course the decline of a product can be hastened by changing micro and macro factors. Again, the company might or might not see the change in the decline. Equally, it might not prove a difficulty for the company, especially if it is planning to let the product die out. There will be charges associated with the decline of the product, but judicious planning should provide for them on the balance sheet.
Rapid decline	This may be a natural progression from the previous two rates of decline, but that is not always so. A product can spiral out of control and enter a rapid decline for a variety of reasons. Probably the key reason is bad publicity that results in consumers immediately deserting the product. This can have a disastrous impact on not only product revenues but overall company performance.

Table 15.14   Possible reasons for a decline in product sales

Reasons	Description
Technological advances	As previously discussed, technology has, and will continue to have a significant impact on life expectancy of products, and to some extent companies themselves. Some examples are given below. The electronic typewriter superseded the manual typewriter. The computer in turn superseded the electronic typewriter. Companies that failed to make the technological leap suffered closure, acquisition or significantly reduced operations. The mechanical cash register, although still seen in small shops especially in less developed countries, has been replaced by barcode reading computerized systems. Advances in photographic films and cameras have seen a decline in the 110 format in favour of 35 mm and advanced film technology by companies such as Kodak. Analogue telephone systems being replaced by fibre optic, microwave and digital systems, not only in developed nations but also in developing nations.
Changes in consumer behaviour and tastes	Examples include changes in fashion. Who now remembers the flared trousers of the 1970s or the punk music period? Could denim jeans, for example, be in decline in favour of other styles of trouser? The rejection of cigarette smoking for reasons of health and as a socially unacceptable habit within certain groups. The rejection of fur coats in certain markets on both environmental and ethical grounds.
Increased domestic and international competition	Global competition is now a reality. Once companies considered the potential and real impact of their local competitors; now their competition could be almost anywhere. Consider, for instance, the impact of the Internet on the competitive environment. Increased competition can lead to over-capacity and price cutting. These in turn can lead to failure to rejuvenate brands and profit erosion.
Economic circumstances	A strong domestic currency could significantly affect the overseas sales for a product. Combine this with an intensely competitive market and changing tastes or demands and the product may face a swift decline.
Product side effects	This applies particularly to pharmaceutical products. Thalidomide (in the UK it was marketed as Distaval, Contergan and Valgraine) was introduced in the 1950s as a sedative, a sleeping pill, something that could calm nerves and help with morning sickness. The product was marketed as non-toxic. However by 1961 it was found to cause foetal malformations when taken by a mother in the early stages of pregnancy. There were over 10,000 recognized cases in the UK. The drug was withdrawn and legal action sought against the drug companies. At the time of writing (June 2003) the drug has been reintroduced under 50 different trade names and is being manufactured in Germany, United States, Canada, Brazil and the UK. Today it is closely controlled and is not used as a sedative. Various new uses have been found, such as combating leprosy and helping HIV and AIDS patients. Trials are also taking place to see if it can help cancer patients.
Damaging publicity	A product might receive damaging publicity as a result of a fault or imperfection. Consumers are then often reluctant to purchase the product. Additionally, a government might step in and ban a product, hastening its withdrawal from the marketplace. If the company does not opt to withdraw a product in this situation, supporting the weakened brand involves heavy direct and indirect costs.

Table 15.15 Possible actions when a product is in decline

Possible actions	Description
Increase spending	Increase the company's level of investment in the product/brand to dominate or strengthen its competitive position in the marketplace. This includes possible marketing communication spend.
Monitor spending	Monitor the company's investment level until any uncertainties in the market or industry are resolved.
Focus on profitable segments/ customers	The company could realign its focus on particular customer segments. By decreasing its level of investment in selective areas it could reduce the number of unprofitable customers. At the same time, it could channel its resources into strengthening investment in growing niche (narrow and specialist) markets.
Divest assets	Divest business assets to improve/enhance the company's cash flow position. This normally means focusing on profitable growth areas. However, as stated earlier there is normally a cost in exiting a market. If the company decides to sell the business asset it might not recover some of the costs incurred during this declining phase. It will also depend on overall market conditions at the time of the proposed asset sale.
Reduce prices	The company could consider price reductions to improve cash flow and help maintain market position. However, severe price cutting might affect customers' perception of brand quality, thus resulting in further degradation of market share.
Reduce distribution channels	The company could phase out unprofitable distribution channels and outlets, focusing on further development of the efficient ones.
Reduce promotion	The company could reduce promotional expenditure to a basic level necessary only to retain loyal customers.
Reduce sales promotion	The company could reduce sales promotion to a minimal operational level, again as a means of retaining loyal customers.
Improve promotional efficiencies	The company might maintain the promotional budget but seek ways of making it 'work harder'; in other words, be more efficient and effective.
Remove the product from the market	In the case of a faulty product or extremely negative publicity the company might have no choice but to remove the product from distribution. It is not just a question of the product being faulty; there are severe ethical and social responsibility issues to consider. If the company behaves unethically, there is not only a moral issue, but consumers might boycott all the company's products and services. This could drive the company into bankruptcy, with resultant impact on the workforce and the local community.

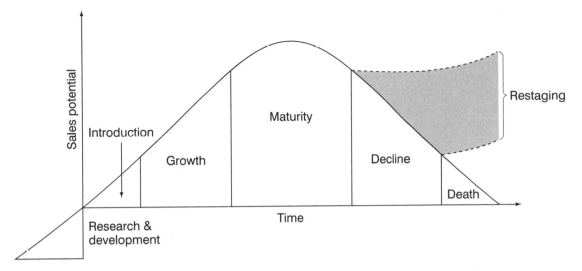

Figure 15.7   The product life cycle: restaging, product rejuvenation and revitalization

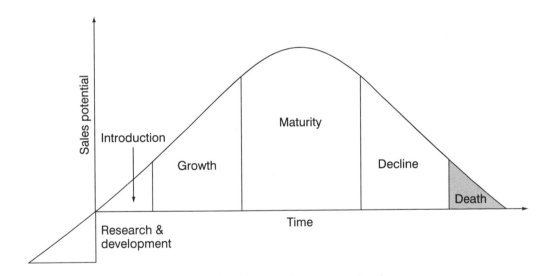

Figure 15.8   The product life cycle: death, extinction or termination

Table 15.16   Product rejuvenation

Product rejuvenation actions	Description
Create new users	This could be a new age group, for example, who believe the product or service has a particular value. Products may be classed as 'retro', a style or fashion that revives past styles. For example, in the UK there is a retro view of the 1970s in fashion items, music and food. Blue Nun, a German sweet white wine, was popular in the 1970s but declined thereafter as more French, Italian and New World wines entered the market and people's tastes changed. In 2000 it witnessed a revival in the UK as trendsetters harked back to the 1970s.
Create new uses	It might be possible to find a new use for a product, opening up a whole new potential market for it. Earlier we outlined how the drug Thalidomide had been reintroduced into the marketplace, but not as a sedative. Under strict control it has been found to be beneficial to patients suffering from leprosy, HIV and AIDS. It is currently (2002) being tested as a possible anti-cancer drug.
Create new more efficient distribution	The company might be able to develop new more efficient distribution outlets. For example where a product had only been sold through small grocery retailers, it could be sold at filling stations.
Develop new markets and territories	A product in decline in one market might present growth opportunities in other markets. For example, a soap product might be in decline in the UK but have growth potential in Pakistan.
Psychological repositioning	The company might be able to reposition the perception of the product in the minds of existing and new consumers.
Major product improvements	For example, new formulations of well-established toothpastes and detergents. A detergent might be changed from a powder to a liquid, or to soluble tablets and capsules. An example in the UK is the Elida Fabergé product Lux beauty soap. This has been revitalized using a range of new ingredients such as honey and almond milk. The packaging also reflects this change of direction and revitalization of the brand.
Restyling the packaging and design of the product	Repackaging of a product may help its appeal to a younger target market. Brylcreem was created in 1929 and mass marketed as the first male hair care product. In the 1960s changing fashions and the introduction of hair gels and sprays for men reduced Brylcreem's appeal. Since the 1990s a mixture of rockabilly retro-cultures and the introduction of brand extensions and packaging redesign have revitalized the brand.
Celebrity endorsement or sponsorship deals	A brand can be revitalized through celebrity endorsement. In 2001 England and Manchester United footballer David Beckham became the new face of the hair care product Brylcreem.

Marketing insight: Lucozade

In the 1970s the drink Lucozade was positioned in the health care market as a drink to help 'sick children to recover'. In the mid-1980s, when it was reaching the declining stage in its life cycle, it was repositioned as a refreshing high-energy drink. This has been further enhanced for the sports and youth markets, thus gaining the product, over time, a new lease of life. Sales grew fivefold from 1985 to 1995.

Since then the company has redesigned the packaging. The new bottle has a uniquely styled design which makes it stand out on the supermarket shelves, in very much the same way as the classic Coca-Cola bottle shape. Additionally, the colours of the packaging now reflect 'energy' and 'youth'. The company also increased the range of flavours available.

Since March 1995, tying the brand to Lara Croft™, the digital celebrity of Eido's *Tomb Raider* game, has further reinforced the brand's appeal to the youth market. The company supported its push into the youth market with a range of stylish, imaginative and dramatic television and poster advertisements featuring Lara Croft™ drinking Lucozade. In 2001 the release of the live action movie *Tomb Raiders* helped to reinforce the brand.

Questions/activities

1. By undertaking secondary research analyse Lucozade's sales growth since 1995. How does it now position itself within the marketplace and compete with the range of new energy drinks that have been introduced over the past five years?
2. Take a product that you believe is in the declining phase of its life cycle. Outline possible actions the company could take to rejuvenate that product. In each case provide evidential support as to why you would take such actions.
3. What are the potential risks for a company in aligning its products with a highly visible character (either live or fictitious)? Could it harm the brand in the longer term?

Chapter summary

In this chapter we have considered the application of the stereotypical product life cycle (as introduced in Chapter 7). The chapter has examined how various actions can be taken to maximize returns at each stage of the product life cycle. Of course, as stated above, this is a stereotypical product life cycle. As we discussed in Chapter 7, not all life cycles follow this precise route. However, by examining the stereotypical product life cycle we have been able to consider the strategies and tactics an organization needs to consider to maximize its return on investment.

Notes

Chapter 1

1 This is the current definition from the UK's Chartered Institute of Marketing. For more information visit the CIM Web site, www.cim.co.uk

2 There have been various definitions for marketing since the formation of the American Marketing Association in the early 1930s. The AMA's current definition first appeared in its publication Marketing News on 1 March 1985.

3 In Oliver Stone's 1980s movie *Wall Street*, Michael Douglas plays the role of megalomaniac arbitrageur Gordon Gekko. In one scene Gekko faces a hostile group of shareholders representing a company that is the heart of a small local community. They are concerned for the future of their community if his potential takeover bid is successful. He allays their fears, solemnly proclaiming to them that 'greed is good'. Unbeknown to the ordinary shareholders he intends to asset strip the business and lay off the employees. We can only guess at the consequences to the local community. In both the United States and the UK, the 1980s was portrayed as a decade of greed and selfishness. The 1990s witnessed a rejection of these beliefs in favour of a more ethical and socially responsible orientation. However, the turn of the 21st century has seen, most especially within North America, several high-profile business scandals. The most notable examples are the energy giant Enron (the largest collapse in US corporate history) and the communication group WorldCom. The history of these two companies has yet to be fully written.

Chapter 2

1 In 2002 there were some 35 ships under construction, on order or on option, for delivery between late 2002 and 2006. These ships range from 60,000 gross tonnage to over 100,000. While the Caribbean market is highly developed, there are significant future opportunities in the Far East, East African and Mediterranean markets. Source: Jonathan Groucutt's unpublished research.

Chapter 3

1 *An Inquiry into the Nature and Causes of the Wealth of Nations, I & II*. This work, often abbreviated to *Wealth of Nations*, was written between 1767 and 1775, and published on 9 March 1776.
2 Further details can be found at the US Department of Justice's Web site: www.usdoj.gov/criminal/fraud/fcpa/fcpa.html
3 Further information is available from two Nestlé company Web sites: www.nestle.com/html/responsibility/infantformula.asp and www.babymilk.nestle.com. The main company Web site provides an overview of the Infant Formula Charter.
4 This documentary was shown as part of the BBC 2's *Blood on the Carpet* series. Aired in January 2001, it examined the Death Row advertisements and the working relationship between Benetton and Toscani.
5 Further information on can be obtained from www.ilo.org
6 Levi Strauss's company Web site (www.levistrauss.com) has several pages devoted to social responsibility, which cover Values and Vision, Social Responsibility Commitment, Issues that the company supports, Employee involvement, Socially responsible worldwide sourcing: Global Sourcing and Operating Guidelines. There is also a link to the Ethical Trading Initiative (www.ethicaltrade.org).

Chapter 4

1 L L Bean Inc. The company's Web site provides background to the development of the business and their operating values. www.llbean.com
2 This is often attributed to the Swiss hotelier César Ritz (1850–1918), who said, 'Le client n'a jamais tort', translated as 'the customer is never wrong'. However, other sources suggest that the American Gordon Selfridge (1856–1947), who built (in 1909) the Selfridge department store on London's Oxford Street actually coined the phrase.
3 Details of prices of current civilian production aircraft are available on Boeing's Web site: www.boeing.com/commercial/prices/

Chapter 7

1 Information provided by Airbus Industries Web site on orders and deliveries: www.airbus.com

Chapter 8

1 Evergreen International Aviation Inc is a privately owned global aviation company headquartered in Oregon, USA. EIA operates through several Evergreen branded subsidiaries. One subsidiary is the Evergreen Aviation Museum in which the Spruce Goose and other historic aircraft are maintained and exhibited. The museum has its own Web site (www.sprucegoose.org) which details the history of this particular aircraft.
2 Refer to www.pillsburybaking.com. This site provides a background history of the Pillsbury brand and highlights the popularity of the Pillsbury Dough Boy as a brand icon. In 2001 Multifoods Brands Inc. acquired the Pillsbury dessert and baking businesses.
3 In a special edition of the regular BBC 2 TV business series *The Money Programme*, Richard Branson discussed various issues regarding his Virgin empire with an audience of UK business executives.

Chapter 10

1 Dugan and Dugan (2000) is based on *The Day The World Took Off*, a Channel 4 Television series broadcast in June 2000.

This critically acclaimed four-part series examined the development of the industrial revolution and why it started in the UK rather than in any other nation.

2 In 1992 a promotion marketing division was added to form Wunderman Cato Johnson. During a brief period in 2000 the agency was called Impiric and was part of the WPP Group plc. In 2001 it returned to the Wunderman name.

Chapter 12

1 National Cash Registers – now NCR (www.ncr.com) developed the barcode scanner. NCR remains a global market leader in retail point-of-sale stationary barcode scanning systems.

References

Aaker, D (1991) *Managing Brand Equity*, Free Press, New York

Abell, D (1980) *Defining the Business: The starting point of strategic planning*, Prentice Hall, Harlow

Adcock, D (2000) *Marketing Strategies for Competitive Advantage*, John Wiley, Chichester

Advertising Age (2000) Unilever's goal: power brands, *Advertising Age*, **71** (1) (3 January), p 1

Alexander, N (1997) *International Retailing*, Blackwell, Oxford

American Marketing Association (AMA) (1985) Definition of marketing, *Marketing News* (1 March)

Anderson, C H and Vincze, J W (2000) *Strategic Marketing Management: Meeting the global marketing challenge*, Houghton Mifflin, Boston, MA

Andrews, J (1998) *Pocket Asia*, 4th edn, Profile Books/Economist, London

Ansoff, H I (1987) *Corporate Strategy*, rev edn, Penguin, Harmondsworth

Apter, J (2000) European aircraft restructuring challenges Boeing monopoly, *Strategy* (September), pp 6–7

Baker, M (1997) People: the fifth P of marketing, in J Yudelson, Adapting McCarthy's four P's for the twenty-first century, *Journal of Marketing Education*, **21** (1) (April 1999), pp 60–67

Baker, M J (2000) *Marketing Strategy and Management*, 3rd edn, Macmillan, Basingstoke

Ballantyne, C and Payne, A (1995) Improving the quality of service marketing: service (RE) design is the critical link, *Journal of Marketing Management* **11**

Bangladesh Observer (1995) BGMEA, UNICEF, ILO sign MOU: elimination of child labour by October 31, *Bangladesh Observer* (5 July)

Barksdale, C and Harris, C E (1982) Portfolio analysis and product lifecycle, *Long Range Planning*, **15** (December), pp 74–83

Bartram, P (1998) Competitive intelligence: the spying game, *Director* (April), pp 46–50

Bateson, J (1989) *Managing Services Marketing*, Dryden Press, New York

BBC (1999) *Money Programme Special* featuring Richard Branson, BBC 2 Television UK.

BBC (2001a) *Benetton and Toscani*, documentary

BBC (2001b) Bond: nobody sells it better, BBC Online [Online] www.bbc.co.uk

BBC (2002a) US steelworkers rally import tariffs, BBC News Online [Online] www.bbc.co.uk (accessed 1 March)

BBC (2002b) Q&A: World steel dispute, BBC News Online [Online] www.bbc.co.uk (accessed 5 March)

BBC (2002c) Japan strikes back at US Steel tariff, BBC News Online [Online] www.bbc.co.uk (accessed 17 May)

BBC (2002d) Fury over Nazi gas sports shoe name, BBC News Online [Online] www.bbc.co.uk (accessed 29 August)

BBC (2002e) Siemens retreats over Nazi name, BBC News Online [Online] www.bbc.co.uk (accessed 5 September)

BBC (2002f) Labour strife disrupts Pacific trade, BBC News Online [Online] www.bbc.co.uk (accessed 1 October)

BBC (2002g) US port dispute hits Asian car firms, BBC News Online [Online] www.bbc.co.uk (accessed 4 October)

BBC (2002h) Bush intervenes in ports row, BBC News Online [Online] www.bbc.co.uk (accessed 7 October)

BBC (2002j) Asia counts cost of US port lockout, BBC News Online [Online] www.bbc.co.uk (accessed 8 October)

BBC (2002k) Q&A: The US port workers' dispute, BBC News Online [Online] www.bbc.co.uk (accessed 9 October)

BBC (2002l) US industry counts cost of port dispute, BBC News Online [Online] www.bbc.co.uk (accessed 9 October)

BBC (2002m) US ports reopen, BBC News Online [Online] www.bbc.co.uk (accessed 9 October)

BBC (2003a) 'Fast' goods for hectic lifestyles, BBC News Online [Online] www.bbc.co.uk (accessed 29 January)

BBC (2003b) Canada's grip on Sars weakens, BBC News online [Online] www.bbc.co.uk (accessed 19 April)

Bennett, P D (ed) (1988) *Glossary of Marketing Terms*, American Marketing Association, Chicago

Bennett, R (1999) *Corporate Strategy*, Financial Times/Pitman, Harlow

Benson, D and Whitehead, G (1975) *Transport and Distribution*, W H Allen, London

Berry, L L (1983) Relationship marketing, in *Emerging Perspectives on Service Marketing*, ed LL Berry, L Shostack and G Upah, American Marketing Association, Chicago

Bidlake, S (2000) Unilever's new direction, *Advertising Age International* (June), p 3

Bittar, C (2000) A new day For Dove, *Brandweek*, **41** (34) (4 September), p 1

Blackshaw, P (2001) Viral consumers, *Executive Excellence*, **18** (7) (July), pp 20–23

Blomqvist, R, Dahl, J, and Haeger, T (1993) *Relation-Smarknadsforing Stategi och Metod for Servicekonkurren* (Relationship Marketing Strategy and Methods for Service Operations), IHM, Gothenburg, Sweden

Bloomberg (accessed 4 June 1998) FTC seeks tough laws to protect children's privacy on the Internet, Bloomberg Newswire [Online]

Booms, B H and Bitner, M J (1981) Marketing strategies and organization structures for service firms, in *Marketing of Services*, ed J H Donnelly and W R George, American Marketing Association, Chicago

Borden, N H (1964) The concept of the marketing mix, *Journal of Advertising Research* (June), pp 2–7 (also in *Science in Marketing* ed G Schwartz, Wiley, New York (1965) and McCarthy *et al, Readings in Basic Marketing*, Irwin, New York (1975))

Borden, N H and Marshall, M V (1959) *Advertising Management: Text and cases*, Irwin, Illinois

Briggs, A (1999) *England in the Age of Improvement 1783–1867*, The Folio Society, London

Britannica (2002) various entries, *Encyclopedia Britannica*

Bronder, C and Pritzl, R (1992) Developing strategic alliances: a conceptual framework for successful competition, *European Management Journal*, **10** (4)

Burns, A, and Bush, R (2000) *Marketing Research*, 2nd edn, Prentice Hall, New Jersey

Buttell, F (1986) *Hotel and Food Service Markets*, Holt, Rinehart and Winston

Buzzell, R D and Gale, B T (1987) *The PIMS Principles: Linking strategy to performance*, Collier Macmillan, London

Cannon, T J (1968) *Business Strategy and Policy*, Harcourt, Brace and World, New York

Channel 4 (2001) *Building the Biggest Plane,* UK: Channel 4 documentary (February)

Chee, H and Harris, R (1993) *Marketing: A global perspective*, Pitman, London

Chartered Institute of Marketing (CIM) (1996) *CIM Marketing Dictionary*, CIM

Churchill, G A Jr and Peter, J P (1998) *Marketing: Creating value for customers*, 2nd edn, Irwin McGraw-Hill, New York

Clancy, K and Shulman, R S (1991) *The Marketing Revolution: A radical manifesto for dominating the marketplace*, Harper, New York

Clark, E (accessed 12 February 2002) Sports sponsors to weather the gloom? BBC News Online [Online] www.bbc.co.uk

CNN (accessed 28 August 2002) Umbro regrets Holocaust blunder, CNN.Com [Online]

Cooper, A (2002) No thaw in sight for UK's fridge mountain, *Reuters News* (30 January)

Cooper, R G and Kleinschmidt, E J (1991) New product processes at leading industrial firms, *Industrial Marketing Management* (May), pp 137 – 137

Council of Logistics Management (CLM) (2003) Definition of logistics, CLM, Illinois [Online] www.clm.org

Coupon Council (2003) All about coupons, Coupon Council [Online] www.coupon-month.com/pages/allabout.htm

Cowell, D (1984) *The Marketing of Services*, Butterworth-Heinemann, Oxford

Cravens, D (1982) *Strategic Marketing*, Irwin, Boston, MA

Croft, J (2001) Insurer bites the bullet and moves to phase out 'Man from the Pru', *Financial Times* (17/18 February), p 18

Culliton, J W (1948) *The Management of Marketing Costs*, Division of Research, Graduate School of Business Administration, Harvard University, Cambridge, MA

Czinkota, M R and Ronkainen, I A (1995) *International Marketing*, 4th edn, Dryden Press, Fort Worth

Czinkota, M B, Ronkainen, I A, Moffet, M H and Moynihan, E O (1998) *Global Business*, Dryden Press, Fort Worth

Daniels, J D and Radebaugh, L H (1998) *International Business: Environments and operations*, 8th edn, Addison Wesley, Reading, MA

Davidson, H (1997) *Even More Offensive Marketing: An exhilarating action guide to winning in business*, Penguin, London

Davidson, K (1998) Like marketers, consumers have responsibilities, *Marketing News*, **32** (6) (16 March), p 14

Davies, J M (1992) *The Essential Guide to Database Marketing*, McGraw-Hill, Maidenhead

Day, G S and Wensley, R (1983) Marketing theory with a strategic orientation, *Journal of Marketing* **47** (4) pp 79–830

Decker, C L (1999) *P&G 99*, HarperCollins, London

De George, R T (1993) *Competing with Integrity in International Business,* Oxford University Press, Oxford

Dept of Justice (DOJ) (1999) *Foreign Corrupt Practices Act: Antibribery provisions*, DOJ-DOC brochure, US DOJ and US Dept of Commerce [Online] www.usdoj.gov/criminal/fraud/fcpa/fcpa.html

Dibb, S (1995) Developing a decision tool for identifying operational and attractive segments, *Journal of Strategic Marketing*, **3**, pp 189–203

Dibb, S (1998) Market segmentation: strategies for success, *Marketing Intelligence and Planning*, **16** (7), pp 394–406

Dibb, S, Simkin, L, Pride, W M and Ferrell, O C (1997) *Marketing Concepts and Strategies*, 3rd edn, Houghton Mifflin, Boston, MA

Dobbing, J (ed) (1988) *Infant Feeding: Anatomy of a controversy 1973–1984*, Springer-Verlag

Dodd, W (2002) I'm good, I'm tempting, but I leave a bad taste in the mouth, *Guardian* (21 August)

Doole, I and Lowe, R (1999) *International Marketing Strategy: Analysis, development and implementation*, International Thomson Business Press, London

Doyle, P (1998) *Marketing Management and Strategy*, 2nd edn, Harlow: Prentice Hall

Drucker, P F (1994) *The Practice of Management*, Butterworth-Heinemann, London

Dugan, S and Dugan, D (2000) *The Day the World Took Off: The roots of the industrial revolution*, Channel 4/Macmillan, London

Dye, R (2000) The buzz on buzz, *Harvard Business Review*, **78** (6) (November/December), pp 139–48

Eckles, R (1990) *Business Marketing Management: Marketing of business products and services*, Prentice Hall, New Jersey

Economist (1999) *Pocket World in Figures*, 2000 edn, Profile/Economist, London

Economist (2000) Shrinking to grow, *Economist*, **354** (8159) (26 February), p 72

Ellinger, A E, Daugherty, P J and Keller, S B (2000) The relationship between marketing/ logistics interdepartmental integration and performance in US manufacturing forms: an empirical study, *Journal of Business Logistics*, **21** (1)

Emery Worldwide (1995) Emery Worldwide's priority fresh express service for perishable goods, press release (14 November)

Engel, J F, Blackwell, R D and Miniard, P W (1990) *Consumer Behavior*, Dryden Press

Enis, B M and Roering, K J (1981) Services marketing: different products similar strategy, in *Marketing of Services*, ed J H Donnely, and W R George, American Marketing Association, Chicago

Ethical Consumer (2003) Popular boycotts, *Ethical Consumer* [Online] www.ethicalconsumer.org

Evans, M (1999) Food retailing loyalty schemes – and the Orwellian millennium, *British Food Journal*, **101** (2), pp 132–47

Farhi, S (2000) Renault targets 15-day delivery time in Europe, *Automotive News Europe*, **4** (4) (14 February), p 16

Federal Trade Commission (FTC) (1998) *Privacy online: a report to Congress*, FTC, USA (June) [Online] www.ftc.gov

Felton, J W (1991) Consumer affairs and consumerism, in *Lesley's Handbook of Public Relations and Communication, 4th edn*, ed P Lesley, AMACOM, New York

Ferrell, J F and Ferrell, L (2000) *Business Ethics: Ethical decision making and cases*, Houghton Mifflin, Boston, MA

Fisk, R Y, Grove, S J and John, J (2000) *Interactive Service Marketing*, Houghton Mifflin, Boston, MA

Ford, H (1922) *My Life and Work*, Heinemann, London

Ford (2001) *Statistics from the Ford Motor Company* [Online] www.ford.com

Forsyth, P (1998) *One Stop Marketing*, ICSA Publishing/Prentice Hall, London

Foster, S (1998) Unravelling the mysteries of direct response TV, in *The Direct Marketing Guide*, Vol 1, Institute of Direct Marketing, London

Fox Market Wire, Top court upholds Bermuda's anti-fast food law [Online] www.foxmarketwire.com

Freudberg, D (1984) *The Corporate Conscience: Innovations in responsible business*, American Management Association

Frey, A W (1961) *Advertising*, 3rd edn, Ronald Press, New York

Gaschott, N (1986) Babies at risk: Infant formula still takes its toll, *Multinational Monitor* (October), pp 11–16

Gilbert, M (1999) *A History of the Twentieth Century, Vol 3: 1952–1999*, HarperCollins, London

Godin, S (1999) *Permission Marketing*, Simon & Schuster, New York

Grant, R M (2002) *Contemporary Strategy Analysis: Concepts, techniques, applications*, 4th edn, Blackwell, Oxford

Green, P S (1999) *Reputation Risk Management*, Financial Times/Pitman, London

Griffin, V (1999) US students to campaign on sweatshops, *Financial Times* (19 October), p 12

Griseri, P and Groucutt, J (1997) *In Search of Business Ethics*, Financial Times/Pitman, London

Grönroos, C (1990) *Service Management and Marketing*, Lexington, New York

Grönroos, C (1997) From marketing mix to relationship marketing: towards a paradigm shift in marketing, *Management Decision*, **35** (3–4), pp 322–40

Groucutt, J (2001) Own-label brands now coming of age, *CompuServe Business Online* (February)

Guptara, P (1990) *The Basic Arts of Marketing*, Hutchinson, London

Gwartney, J D and Stroup, R L (1987) *Macroeconomics: Private and public choice*, 4th edn, Harcourt Brace Jovanovich, New York

Hague, P and Jackson, P (1996) *Marketing Research*, Kogan Page, London

Handy, C (1995) quoted in P Sappal, Enjoying a state of virtuous reality, *Consult* (November/December)

Heinz (2002) *About Heinz: Relishing the past* [Online] www.heinz.com

Hertz, N (2001a) *The Silent Takeover*, Heinemann, London

Hertz, N (2001b) Why we stay silent no longer, *Observer* (8 April), p 22

Hill, C W L (2001) *International Business*, International edn, Irwin McGraw-Hill, Boston

Hillman, D and Gibbs, D (1998) *Century Makers*, Weidenfeld & Nicholson, London

Hindle, T (2000) *Pocket MBA*, Profile/Economist, London

Hoffman, K D and Bateson, J (1997) *Essentials of Service Marketing*, Dryden, New York

Houlton, S (2000) Brands for the future, *Manufacturing Chemist*, **71** (3) (March), p 3

Howe, W S (1992) *Retailing Management*, Macmillan, Basingstoke

Hoyer, W D and MacInnes, D J (1997) *Consumer Behaviour*, Houghton Mifflin, Boston

Hunt, S and Morgan, R (1994) The commitment–trust theory of relationship marketing, *Journal of Marketing*, **58**, pp 20–38

Institute of Grocery Distribution (IGD) (2002a) Ageing population: impact on the food and grocery industry, fact sheet, IGD

IGD (2002b) The changing consumer and consumption trends, fact sheet, IGD

ILO (1996) *Stop! Child Labour*, Press kit ILO. Includes Labour today: facts & figures; Child labour: action required at the national level; International action: standards need reinforcing

ILO (1999) ILO concludes 87th Conference adopts new instruments against child labour and resolution on Myanmar, press release (17 June), ILO/99/23

ILO (2002) IPEC action against child labour: highlights, *2002 Report*, ILO

Inwood, D and Hammond, J (1993) *Product Development: An integrated approach*, Kogan Page, London

James, B G (1985) *Business Wargames*, Penguin, Harmondsworth

Jefferson News Tribune (accessed 22 July 1999) Anti-fast food law upheld by Bermuda Court, *Jefferson News Tribune* [Online] www.newstribune.com

Jenkinson, A (1998) Retaining customers through genuine loyalty, in *The Direct Marketing Guide*, Vol 1, Institute of Direct Marketing, London

Jeremy, D J (1998) *A Business History of Britain: 1900s–1990s*, Oxford University Press, Oxford

Jobber, D (1998) *Principles and Practice of Marketing*, 2nd edn, McGraw-Hill, Maidenhead

Johnson & Johnson (1992) *The Johnson & Johnson Credo: Background information*, Johnson & Johnson External Relations Department, New Jersey

Johnson, G and Scholes, K (1999) *Exploring Corporate Strategy*, 3rd edn, Prentice Hall Europe, Hemel Hempstead

Judd, V C (1987) Differentiate with the 5th P: people, *Industrial Marketing Management*, 16, pp 241–47

Kapferer, J-N (1998) *Strategic Brand Management: Creating and sustaining brand equity*, 2nd edn, Kogan Page, London

Kaplan, R S and Norton, P (1992) The balanced scorecard: measures that drive performance, *Harvard Business Review* (January–February), pp 71–79

Kaplan, R S and Norton, D P (1996a) Linking the balanced scorecard to strategy, *California Management Review*, **39** (1) (Fall), pp 53–79

Kaplan, R S and Norton, P (1996b) Using the balanced scorecard as a strategic management system, *Harvard Business Review* (January–February), pp 75–85

Kashani, K (1999) A new future for brands, in *Mastering Marketing*, Financial Times, Harlow

Keegan, W J and Green, M C (1997) *Principles of Global Marketing*, Prentice Hall, New Jersey

Keith, R J (1960) The marketing revolution, *Journal of Marketing* (January)

Khermouch, G and Gree, J (2001) Buzz-z marketing, *Business Week*, 3743 (30 July)

Kotler, P (1986) Megamarketing, *Harvard Business Review*, **64** (March–April), pp 117–24

Kotler, P (2000) *Marketing Management: The millennium edition*, Prentice Hall, New Jersey

Kotler, P, Gregor, W and Rogers, W (1977) The MA comes of age, *Sloan Management Review*, **18** (1) (Winter)

Laczniak, G R and Murphy, P E (1991) Fostering ethical marketing decisions, *Journal of Business Ethics*, **10** (4), pp 259–71

Lamb, C, Hair, J and McDaniel, C (1998) *Marketing*, 4th edn, South Western

Laurent, G, and Kapferer, J N (1985) Measuring consumer involvement profiles, *Journal of Marketing Research*, **12** (February), pp 41–53

Lazo, H and Corbin, A (1961) *Management in Marketing*, McGraw-Hill, New York

Leadley, P (1992) *Leisure Marketing*, Longman/ILAM, London

Leadley, P and Hutchings, A (1994) *Marketing*, University of Humberside, Hull

LeDoux, L (1991) Is preservation the fifth 'P' or just another macroenvironmental factor? in *Challenges in a New Decade in Marketing*, ed C F McKinnon and C A Kelley, Western Marketing Educators' Association

Leonard, D (1998) *Guide to the European Union*, 6th edn, Economist/Profile, London

Lerer, L (2002) Pharmaceutical marketing segmentation in the age of the Internet, *International Journal of Medical Marketing*, **2** (2), pp 169–81

Levine, J (1990) Global lather, *Forbes*, **145** (3), pp 146–47

Levitt, T (1960) Marketing myopia, *Harvard Business Review* (July/August), pp 45–56

Levitt, T (1972) Production line approach to service, *Harvard Business Review* (September–October), pp 41–52

Levitt, T (1983) The globalization of markets, *Harvard Business Review* (May–June), pp 92–102

Levitt, T (1986) *The Marketing Imagination*, 2nd edn, Free Press, New York

Linton, R (1945) *The Cultural Background of Personality*, Appleton, Century

Lynch, R (2000) *Corporate Strategy*, 2nd edn, Financial Times/Prentice Hall, Harlow

Maciver, K (2001) Efficiency drive, *Information Age Business Briefing*, 16, pp B17–B19

Macrae, C (1990) *World Class Brands*, Addison-Wesley, Harlow

Magrath, A J (1986) When marketing services 4Ps are not enough, *Business Horizons* (May–June), pp 44–50

Makens, J C (1989) *The 12-day Marketing Plan*, Thorsons, Wellingborough

Marshall, N (1998) Why product placement? *Brandweek* (9 February)

Masood, S (2001) Model options, *Information Age Business Briefing*, 16, pp B10–B12

McCarthy, J (1981) *Basic Marketing: A managerial approach*, Irwin, New York

McCorkell, G (1997) *Direct Marketing and Database Marketing*, Institute of Direct Marketing/Kogan Page, London

McDonald, M (1996) *Strategic Marketing Planning*, 2nd edn, Cranfield University School of Management/Kogan Page, London

McDonald, M (2002) CRM: Faster, smarter, bigger – but is it working? Presentation at Oxford Brookes University, Oxford (17 November)

McDonald, M and Dunbar, I (1995) *Market Segmentation: A step by step approach to creating profitable market segments*, Macmillan, Basingstoke

McKenna, R (1991) *Relationship Marketing*, Addison-Wesley, London

McKitterick, J B (1957) What is the marketing management concept? in *The Frontiers of Marketing Thought in Action*, ed F Bass, American Marketing Association, Chicago

McLean, F (1995) A marketing revolution in museums, *Journal of Marketing Management*, **11** (6) (August)

McSmith, A (1999) UK launches bid to end child labour, *Observer* (7 November)

Michell, R and O' Neal, M (1994) Managing by values: is Levi Strauss' approach visionary or flaky? *Business Week International* (12 September)

Miles, R E and Snow, C C (1978) *Organizational Strategy, Structure and Process*, McGraw-Hill, New York

Miller, V (1999) *Sales Planning: Study guides 1–8*, University of Lincolnshire and Humberside, Hull

Mindak, W A and Fine, S (1981) A fifth 'p': public relations, in *Marketing of Services*, ed J H Donnely and W R George, pp 71–73, American Marketing Association, Chicago

Mintel (2001) *Pizza Market Report*, Mintel International

Mintzberg, H, Lampel, J, Quinn, J B and Ghoshal, S (2003) *The Strategy Process: Concepts, contexts, cases*, 4th edn, Prentice Hall, Harlow

Mitchell, A (1998) Why intimacy is vital to customer relationships, *Marketing Week*, **21** (37) (November)

Moore, J I (2001) *Writers on Strategy and Strategic Management*, 2nd edn, Penguin, London

Moorman, Zaltman, C and Deshpande, R (1993) Relationships between providers and users of market research: the dynamics of trust within and between organisations, *Journal of Marketing Research*, **29** (3), pp 81–101

Morris, D S, Barnes, B R and Lynch, J E (1999) Relationship marketing needs total quality management, *Total Quality Management*, **10** (4/5) (July), pp 659–66

Mühlbacher, H, Dahringer, L and Leihs, H (1999) *International Marketing: A global perspective*, International Thomson Business Press, London

Murphy, P R and Poist, R F (1994) The logistics-market interface: marketers' views on improving cooperation, *Journal of Marketing Theory and Practice*, **2** (2), pp 1–13

Nader, R (1965) *Unsafe at Any Speed*, Grossman, New York (reprinted by Bantam, 1973)

Nash, L L (1998) *Corporate Ethics: A prime business asset*, New York

Naylor, J (1999) *Management*, Financial Times/ Prentice Hall, Harlow

Nestlé (1985) *The Dilemma of Third World Nutrition: Nestlé and the Role of Infant Formula*, report prepared for Nestlé

Nickels, W G and Jolson, M A (1976) Packaging: the fifth 'p' in the marketing mix? *SAM Advanced Management Journal* (Winter), pp 13–21

Office of National Statistics (ONS) (2002) *Social Trends 2002*, ONS, London

Ohmae, K (1990) *The Borderless World: Power and strategy in the interlinked economy*, Collins, London

O'Malley, L, Patterson, M and Evans, M (1999) *Exploring Direct Marketing*, International Thomson Business Press, London

O'Reilly, B (1994) J & J is on a roll, *Fortune International* (26 December), pp 122–28

Ottman, J A (1994) *Green Marketing: Challenges and opportunities for the new marketing age*, NTC Business, New York

Oxenfeldt, A R (1960) Multistage approach to pricing, *Harvard Business Review*

Palmer, A (2000) *Principles of Marketing*, Oxford University Press, Oxford

Palmer, A and Hartley, B (1999) *The Business and Marketing Environment*, 3rd edn, McGraw-Hill, Maidenhead

Patty, T (1997) Mastering the new five P's of marketing, in Yudelson, J (1999) Adapting McCarthy's four P's for the twenty-first century, *Journal of Marketing Education*, **21** (1) (April), pp 60–67

Payne, C M A and Ballantyne, D (1991) *Relationship Marketing: Bringing quality, customer service and marketing together*, Butterworth-Heinemann, Oxford

Pelton, L E, Strutton, D and Lumpkin, J R (1997) *Marketing Channels: A relationship management approach*, Irwin

Peppers, D and Rogers, M (1997) *Enterprise One-To-One: Tools for building unbreakable customer relationships in the interactive age*, Piatkus, London

Perlmutter, M V (1995) Becoming globally civilised, managing across cultures: mastering management part 6, *Financial Times* (1 December)

Perreault, W D, McCarthy, E J, Parkinson, S and Stewart, K (2000) *Basic Marketing*, McGraw-Hill, London

Petrof, J V (1997) Relationship marketing: the wheel reinvented, *Business Horizons*, **40** (6) (November–December), pp 26–32

Piercy, N (1992) *Market-Led Strategic Change*, Butterworth-Heinemann, Oxford

Polanyi, K (1957) *The Great Transformation*, Beacon Press, Boston, MA

Porter, M E (1980) *Competitive Strategy*, Free Press, New York

Porter, M E (1985) *Competitive Advantage*, Free Press, New York

Proctor, T (2000) *Essentials of Marketing Research*, 2nd edn, Financial Times/Prentice Hall, Harlow

Prudential (2001) Prudential announces restructuring of direct sales force and customer service channels in the UK, Prudential Media Department, press release (13 February)

Quee, W T (1999) *Marketing Research*, Butterworth-Heinemann/Marketing Institute of Singapore, Singapore

Rafiq, M and Ahmed, P K (1995) Using the 7Ps as a generic marketing mix: an exploratory survey of UK and European marketing academics, *Marketing Intelligence and Planning*, **13** (9), pp 4–16

Rapp, S and Collins, T (1990) *The Great Marketing Turnaround*, Prentice Hall, New Jersey

Reichheld, F E (1993) Loyalty-based management, *Harvard Business Review*, **71** (March–April), pp 64–73

Rich, M K (2000) The direction of marketing relationships, *Journal of Business and Industrial Marketing*, **15** (2/3), pp 170–79

Ries, A and Trout, J (1986) *Positioning: The battle for your mind*, McGraw-Hill, New York

Robbins, S (1998) *Organizational Behavior*, Prentice Hall, New Jersey

Robbins, S P and Coulter, M (1996) *Management*, 5th edn, Prentice Hall, New Jersey

Rogers, E M (1983) *Diffusion of Innovations*, 3rd edn, Free Press, New York

Royal, W F (1995) Scapegoat: the mess at Met Life, *Sales and Marketing Management (US)* (January), pp 62–69

Schramm, W (1955) *The Process and Effects of Mass Communications*, University of Illinois Press, Urbana, IL

Shaw, R (1998) *Improving Marketing Effectiveness*, Economist /Profile, London

Sheth, J N and Gross, B (1988) Parallel development of marketing and consumer behavior, in *Historical Perspectives in Marketing: Essays in Honor of Stanley C Hollander*, ed T Nevett and R A Fullerton, Lexington Books, Lexington

Sheth, J N and Parvatiyar, A (1995) Relationship marketing in consumer markets: antecedents and consequences, *Journal of the Academy of Marketing Sciences*, **23** (4), pp 255–71

Shostack, G L (1977) Breaking free from product marketing, *Journal of Marketing*, **41** (April)

Sidhva, S (1995) Child labour: sweated labour of little hands, special report, *India Financial Times* (17 November)

Skapinker, M (1999a) BA opts to fly the flag in retreat from ethic look, *Financial Times* (7 June), p 1

Skapinker, M (1999b) Passengers force about-turn on BA's flight of fancy, *Financial Times* (7 June), p 8

Smith, A (1776) *An Inquiry into the Nature and Causes of the Wealth of Nations, Vols I and II*, Everyman's Library (1910); with intro by D Campbell (1991)

Smith, P (1993) *Marketing Communications: An integrated approach*, Kogan Page, London

Sorrell, T (1994) The customer is not always right, *Journal of Business Ethics*, **13**, pp 913–18

Stanton, W J, Etzel, M J and Walker, B J (1994) *Fundamentals of Marketing*, 4th edn, McGraw-Hill, New York

Stanton, W J, Etzel, M J and Walker, B J (1998) *Fundamentals of Marketing*, 10th edn, McGraw-Hill, New York

Steiner, G A and Steiner, J F (1994) *Business, Government and Society: A managerial perspective text and cases*, 7th edn, McGraw-Hill, New York

Sternberg, E (1994) *Just Business: Business ethics in action*, London, Little Brown

Stewart-Allen, A L (1999) Product placement helps sell brands, *Marketing News* (15 February)

Stock, J R (1990) Logistics thought and practice: a perspective, *International Journal of Physical Distribution and Logistics Management*, **20** (1), pp 3–6

Stock, J R and Lambert, D M (1983) Physical distribution management in international marketing, *International Marketing Review* (Autumn)

Stokes, D (1994) *Discovering Marketing: An action learning approach*, DP Publications, London

Swann, J E and Rink, D R (1982) Fitting marketing strategy to varying product life cycles, *Business Horizons* (January–February), pp 72–76

Tapp, A (1998) *Principles of Direct and Database Marketing*, Financial Times/Pitman, Harlow

Taylor Nelson Sofres (1999) Research cited in *The Marketing Pocket Book 2000*, NTC, New York

Tellis, G J and Crawford, C M (1981) An evolutionary approach to product growth theory, *Journal of Marketing* (Fall), pp 125–34

Terpestra, V and Sarathy, R (1997) *International Marketing*, Dryden Press, New York

Thompson, J L (1990) *Strategic Management: Awareness and change*, Chapman and Hall, London

Tibballs, G (1999) *Business Blunders*, Robinson, London

Tomkins, R (1999) Shaking out the last dollop of growth, *Financial Times* (12/13 June)

Tomkins, R (2001) Co-op's capsules launches another soap war, *Financial Times* (21 February), p 15

Traynor, K (1985) Research deserves status as marketing's fifth 'P', *Marketing News* (8 November), p 12

Trevino, T and Nelson, K (1995) *Managing Business Ethics*, Wiley, New York

Underhill, P (1999) *Why We Buy: The science of shopping*, Orion Business Books, London

Unilever (1999) *Annual Review 1999*, Unilever

Unilever (2000) Unilever plans faster growth, press release (22 February)

Unilever (2001) *Annual Report 2001*, Unilever

Unilever (2003) Unilever fact sheet 2003: Path to Growth summary and update, second quarter half year 2003, Unilever

Urban, G L and Starr, S H (1991) *Advanced Marketing Strategy: Phenomena, analysis and decisions*, Prentice Hall, New Jersey

Varey, R J (1995) A model of internal marketing for building and sustaining a competitive service advantage, *Journal of Marketing Management*, **11** (1–3) (January)

Vignali, C (2001) McDonald's: 'think global, act local' – the marketing mix, *British Journal of Food*, **103** (2), pp 97–111

Vignali, C, Vrontis, D and Dana, L (1999) *An International Marketing Reader*, Manchester Metropolitan University, Manchester

Wall Street (1987) movie directed by Oliver Stone

Walters, G and Bergiel, B J (1982) *Marketing Channels*, 2nd edn, Scott Foresman, Illinois

Walton, S and Huey, J (1992) *Made in America*, Doubleday

Webster, F E Jr (1994) Executing the new marketing concept, *Marketing Management*, **3** (1), pp 9–18

Welsh, R and Heyworth, T (1996) *Rapid Data Warehouse Methodologies: A business approach to data warehousing*, Technical White Paper Series, Business Objects (UK), London

Wendlandt, A (1997) Importers unfazed by Russian label rule, *Moscow Times* (10 January)

Wheeler, B (1999) Image guardians, *Marketing Week* (30 September), pp 29–31

Wheeler, S and Hirsh, E (1999) *Channel Champions: How leading companies build new strategies to serve customers*, Jossey Bass, New York

Wilkie, W L and More, E S (1999) Marketing's contributions to society, *Journal of Marketing*, **63** (special issue), pp 198–218

Wilson, R M and Gilligan, C (1997) *Strategic Marketing Management*, 2nd edn, Butterworth-Heinemann, Oxford

Wind, J (1997) *Big Questions for the 21st Century in Mastering Management*, Pitman, Harlow

Wing, R L (1989) *The Art of Strategy: A new translation of Sun Tzu's classic* The Art of War, The Aquarian Press, London

Witthaus, M (1998) Viking invasion, *dm Business*, 4 (June/July), pp 42–44

Worcester, R E (1999) Get trust up, *Profile*, 2 (December), p 16

Wright, M (1996) The dubious assumptions of segmentation and targeting, *Management Decisions*, **34** (1), pp 18–24

Yudelson, J (1999) Adapting McCarthy's four Ps for the twenty-first century, *Journal of Marketing Education*, **21** (1) (April), pp 60–67

Zikmund, W G (1994) *Business Research Methods*, 4th edn, Dryden Press, Fort Worth

Zikmund, W G and D'Amico, M (1999) *Marketing*, 6th edn, South-Western Publishing, Mason

Index